Canadian Politics

Canadian

Politics

SIXTH EDITION

Edited by
James Bickerton and
Alain-G. Gagnon

UNIVERSITY OF TORONTO PRESS

Higher Education Division

www.utppublishing.com

LIBRARY AND ARCHIVES CANADA CATALOGUING IN PUBLICATION

Canadian politics / edited by James P. Bickerton and Alain-G. Gagnon.—Sixth edition.

Includes index.

Issued in print and electronic formats.

ISBN 978-1-4426-0703-3 (pbk.).—ISBN 978-1-4426-0808-5 (bound).— ISBN 978-1-4426-0704-0 (pdf).—ISBN 978-1-4426-0705-7 (epub)

1. Canada—Politics and government—Textbooks.   I. Bickerton, James, editor of compilation   II. Gagnon, Alain-G. (Alain-Gustave), 1954–, editor of compilation

JL65.C35 2014   320.971   C2013-906786-8   C2013-906787-6

We welcome comments and suggestions regarding any aspect of our publications—please feel free to contact us at news@utphighereducation.com or visit our Internet site at www.utppublishing.com.

North America
5201 Dufferin Street
North York, Ontario, Canada, M3H 5T8

2250 Military Road
Tonawanda, New York, USA, 14150

ORDERS PHONE: 1–800–565–9523
ORDERS FAX: 1–800–221–9985
ORDERS E-MAIL: utpbooks@utpress.utoronto.ca

UK, Ireland, and continental Europe
NBN International
Estover Road, Plymouth, PL6 7PY, UK
ORDERS PHONE: 44 (0) 1752 202301
ORDERS FAX: 44 (0) 1752 202333
ORDERS E-MAIL: enquiries@nbninternational.com

Every effort has been made to contact copyright holders; in the event of an error or omission, please notify the publisher.

The University of Toronto Press acknowledges the financial support for its publishing activities of the Government of Canada through the Canada Book Fund.

Printed in the United States of America

The editors would like to dedicate this sixth edition of *Canadian Politics* to Richard Simeon, who passed away in 2013. One of Canada's eminent political scientists, and English-speaking Canada's foremost expert in the study of federalism, Richard was a mentor, inspiration, and valued collaborator to generations of students, scholars, and academic colleagues in both Canada and the international federalism community. His enduring presence, sage insights, and boundless curiosity and enthusiasm for his chosen field of study will be greatly missed by all those who had the good fortune to work with him and learn from him.

JB & AGG

Contents

Preface

The sixth edition of *Canadian Politics* continues the work of earlier editions in offering a comprehensive introduction to Canadian government and politics by a highly respected group of political scientists, writing on subjects on which they are recognized experts. For this edition, the editors have organized the book into six parts. Part I examines Canadian citizenship and political identities, while Parts II and III deal with Canadian political institutions, including Aboriginal governments, and contain new chapters on the public service and Quebec. Parts IV and V shift the focus to the political process, discussing issues pertaining to culture and values, parties and elections, media, groups, movements, gender, and diversity. The chapters on Parliament, bureaucracy, political culture, political communications, social movements, and media are authored by new contributors to this edition. Finally, three chapters in the last part of the book will analyze components of Canadian politics that have been gaining prominence during the last decade: the effects of globalization, the shifting ground of Canadian-American relations, and the place of Canada in the changing world order. Of the 21 chapters in this sixth edition of *Canadian Politics,* those retained from earlier editions have been revised and updated. The book also includes nine new chapters, with eight new contributing authors and coverage of five new topics.

Contributors

About the Editors

James Bickerton is Professor of Political Science at St. Francis Xavier University. He is the author of *Nova Scotia, Ottawa and the Politics of Regional Development* (University of Toronto Press), the co-author of *Ties That Bind: Parties and Voters in Canada* (Oxford University Press) and *Freedom, Equality, Community: The Political Philosophy of Six Influential Canadians* (McGill-Queen's University Press), and most recently the co-editor of *Governing: Essays in Honour of Donald J. Savoie* (McGill-Queen's University Press).

Alain-G. Gagnon holds the Canada Research Chair in Québec and Canadian Studies and is Professor in the Department of Political Science at the Université du Québec à Montréal. His publications include *The Case for Multinational Federalism* (Routledge), *Federal Democracies* with Michael Burgess (Routledge), *Political Autonomy and Divided Societies* with Michael Keating (Palgrave Macmillan), and *Multinational Federalism* with Michel Seymour (Palgrave Macmillan). He is also the author of *L'Âge des incertitudes: essais sur le fédéralisme et la diversité nationale* (Les Presses de l'Université Laval).

About the Contributors

Yasmeen Abu-Laban is Professor in the Department of Political Science at the University of Alberta. She has published widely on issues relating to the Canadian and comparative dimensions of gender, ethnicity, and racialization processes; border and migration policies; and citizenship theory. She is the co-editor of *Surveillance and Control in Israel/Palestine: Population, Territory, and Power* (2011); co-editor of *Politics in North America: Redefining Continental Relations* (2008); and editor of *Gendering the Nation-State* (2008).

Raymond Bazowski teaches in the Department of Political Science at York University. His research interests include the philosophy of law, comparative constitutionalism, and the effect of law on public policy. Among his recent publications is *The Charter at Twenty* (with Charles Smith).

Mark R. Brawley specializes in international political economy, with interests that stretch into international security. His most recent book, *Political Economy and Grand Strategy: A Neoclassical Realist View* (Routledge, 2010), explores the economic underpinnings of international power. His recent works include "A Post-American World? Perils, Possibilities, and Preparations," in *Debating a Post-American World: What Lies Ahead?* (Routledge, 2011), and "New Rulers of the World? Brazil, Russia, India and China," in *The Sage Handbook of Globalization*.

Stephen Brooks is Professor of Political Science at the University of Windsor and Director of the Ottawa Internship Program at the University of Michigan. His most recent books include *Understanding American Politics*, 2nd edition (University of Toronto Press, 2013) and *American Exceptionalism in the Age of Obama* (Routledge, 2013).

Andrew F. Cooper is Professor at the Balsillie School of International Affairs and the Department of Political Science, and Director of the Centre for the Study on Rapid Global Change, University of Waterloo. His recent books include as co-editor *The Oxford Handbook of Modern Diplomacy* (Oxford University Press, 2013), as co-author *The Group of Twenty* (Routledge, 2012), and as author *Internet Gambling Offshore: Caribbean Struggles over Casino Capitalism* (Palgrave Macmillan, 2011).

Lyne Deschâtelets received her Master's degree in Political Science from the Université du Québec à Montréal in 2013. Her research focuses on media and politics. More specifically, her master's thesis provided an in-depth case study of how gender rights discourses were used in the press during the reasonable accommodation debates in Quebec.

David C. Docherty is President of Mount Royal University in Calgary, Alberta. A political scientist by training, David has written extensively on the Parliament of Canada, provincial legislatures, and political careers. He is the author of *Mr. Smith Goes to Ottawa: Life in the House of Commons* and *Legislatures*. Prior to moving into university administration, David was a frequent commentator on national and provincial politics on CBC radio and other media outlets. As president of an undergraduate university that focuses on teaching, David is proud to work with political science and policy studies students and enjoys teaching a course on the Canadian democratic deficit.

Roger Gibbins served as President and CEO of the Canada West Foundation from 1998 to 2012. Since retiring in 2012, Roger splits his time between Vancouver and Calgary. He has authored, co-authored, and edited over twenty books, most dealing with Western Canadian themes and issues and constitutional politics.

Allison Harell is Assistant Professor at the Université du Québec à Montréal. She is a member of the Canadian Election Study team and the Centre for the Study of Democratic Citizenship. Her research focuses on public opinion and political behaviour in Canada and other advanced industrialized democracies. Her current work focuses on how race and gender influence policy support for the welfare state.

Will Kymlicka holds the Canada Research Chair in Political Philosophy at Queen's University. His books include *Finding Our Way: Rethinking Ethnocultural Relations in Canada* (Oxford) and, most recently, *Zoopolis: A Political Theory of Animal Rights* (Oxford), co-authored with Sue Donaldson.

Samuel V. LaSelva is Professor of Political Science at the University of British Columbia. He is the author of *The Moral Foundations of Canadian Federalism: Paradoxes, Achievements and Tragedies of Nationhood*. He has widely published, notably in the *Canadian Journal of Political Science*, *Review of Constitutional Studies*, and *BC Studies*. He is currently at work on the ethics of constitutionalism.

Alex Marland is Associate Professor of Political Science at Memorial University of Newfoundland. He researches the practice of communication, marketing, and electioneering in Canadian politics and government. He was the lead editor of *Political Marketing in Canada* (University of British Columbia Press) and *Political Communication in Canada*.

Éric Montpetit is Professor and Chair of the Department of Political Science at the Université de Montréal. His work has been published in numerous journals including the *Canadian Journal of Political Science*, *Political Studies*, *West European Politics*, and the *Policy Studies Journal*. In a forthcoming book, *Magnified Disagreement,* he argues that the media unfairly depict interest groups as parties in counterproductive quarrels over policy choices.

Michael Orsini is Associate Professor in the School of Political Studies at the University of Ottawa, and is currently Chair of the Institute of Women's Studies. His work has appeared in *Policy and Society*, *Social Policy and Administration*, the *Canadian Journal of Political Science*, and *Social and Legal Studies*, among others. He co-edited *Critical Policy Studies* with Miriam Smith

(University of British Columbia Press), and is co-editor of *Worlds of Autism: Across the Spectrum of Neurological Difference* (University of Minnesota Press).

Martin Papillon is Associate Professor at the School of Political Studies, University of Ottawa. His recent work focuses on emerging practices of Aboriginal multilevel governance as well as Aboriginal consultation practices in natural resources development in Canada. He is the author of a number of journal articles and book chapters on Aboriginal governance and is the co-editor of two recent volumes: *Federalism and Aboriginal Governance* (Presses de l'Université Laval) and *Les Autochtones et le Québec: des premiers contacts au Plan Nord* (Presses de l'Université de Montréal).

Ian Robinson teaches international and comparative political economy in the Department of Sociology and Residential College's interdisciplinary Social Science program at the University of Michigan-Ann Arbor. Between 2001 and 2008 he was co-director of the Institute of Labor and Industrial Relations' Labor and Global Change program. His research and publishing has focused on how the neoliberal model of economic globalization reshapes our lives and societies, and how workers, unions, and other social movement organizations are attempting to reshape globalization.

Donald J. Savoie holds the Canada Research Chair in Public Administration and Governance at the Université de Moncton. He has published numerous books on public policy, public administration, and federalism. His latest publication is *Whatever Happened to the Music Teacher? How Government Decides and Why.*

Richard Simeon was Professor Emeritus of Political Science and Law at the University of Toronto and a Fellow of the Royal Society of Canada. His works include *Federal-Provincial Diplomacy: The Making of Recent Policy in Canada,* re-printed in 2006; *State, Society and the Development of Canadian Federalism* (with Ian Robinson); and *Imperfect Democracies: The Democratic Deficit in Canada and the United States* (with Patti Lenard).

A. Brian Tanguay is Professor of Political Science and a member of the North American Studies Program at Wilfrid Laurier University. His main research interests are Quebec and Ontario politics, political parties, and electoral reform. In 2003–04, he drafted the Law Commission of Canada's report, *Voting Counts: Electoral Reform for Canada.* He is the co-editor, with Alain-G. Gagnon, of *Canadian Parties in Transition* (3rd edition). Among his recent publications (co-authored with L.B. Stephenson) is "Ontario's Referendum on Proportional Representation" in *IRPP Choices* 15:10.

Melanee Thomas is Assistant Professor of Political Science at the University of Calgary. Her research focuses on the causes and consequences of gender-based political inequality in Canada and other post-industrial democracies. She has published research in journals such as *Politics & Gender*, *Electoral Studies*, and the *Canadian Journal of Political Science*.

Paul G. Thomas is Professor Emeritus in Political Studies at the University of Manitoba where he taught for 40 years, receiving both a university and a national teaching award. He is the co-editor and the contributor of three chapters in *Manitoba Politics and Government: Issues, Institutions and Traditions* (2010). He has authored over 150 other book chapters and journal articles. He has served as chair or member of, and advisor to, numerous public boards and commissions of inquiry. Among the numerous awards he has received in recognition of his contributions to public life are the Order of Manitoba and the Vanier Medal for excellence in public administration.

Jennifer Wallner is Assistant Professor at the University of Ottawa. She is the author of *Learning To School: Federalism and Public Schooling in Canada* (University of Toronto Press). She is also the co-editor of two volumes with the UBC Press: *The Comparative Turn* and *Canada Compared*. Her work on federalism and public policy has been published in *Comparative Politics*, *Publius*, *Policy Studies Journal*, *The Peabody Journal of Education*, and the *Canadian Journal of Political Science*.

Lisa Young is Professor of Political Science at the University of Calgary. Her research interests include Canadian political parties, women's participation in politics, interest groups and social movements, and the regulation of electoral finance. Her publications include *Feminists and Party Politics* and *Advocacy Groups* (with Joanna Everitt).

PART I
Citizenship and Identities

one

Understanding Canada's Origins: Federalism, Multiculturalism, and the Will to Live Together

SAMUEL V. LASELVA

> More than most other countries, Canada is a creation of human will. It has been called a "geographical absurdity," an "appendage of the United States," a "4,000-mile main street" with many bare stretches. Nevertheless this country has existed for a long time, because its people have never stopped willing that there be a Canada.
> —*Preliminary Report of the Royal Commission on Bilingualism and Biculturalism*: 144

Introduction: The Canadian Enigma

Canada has existed for a long time, but Canada is a difficult country to understand and also a difficult country to govern, both in times of constitutional crisis and in periods of constitutional stability. Even if Canadians "have never stopped willing that there be a Canada," the near-successful sovereignty referendum in Quebec and the Supreme Court secession reference suggest that Canada's continued existence cannot be taken for granted. The sovereignty referendum and the secession reference focused on Quebec and revealed its complex relationship to the rest of Canada, a relationship that is not fully or easily encapsulated within Parliament's recent, ambiguous, and aspirational declaration that the Québécois form a nation within a united Canada. The difficulties that confront Canadians are by no means confined to the French-English question. Aboriginal nationalism, with its demand for Aboriginal sovereignty and social justice, raises equally difficult questions, as the "Idle No More" Movement illustrates. There are also multicultural groups. These groups—together with women, gays, lesbians, the handicapped—do not threaten the unity of Canada, but they seek to shape its identity and their demands can conflict with those of other political actors. The failed Meech Lake and Charlottetown Constitutional Accords demonstrate that the very pluralism of Canada can sometimes result in "mosaic madness" and may yet compel Canadians to "look into the abyss" (Bibby, 1990; Cairns, 1997).

When the focus is shifted away from mega-constitutional matters to issues like health care or the Canadian Social Union or the federal spending power, problems of disunity and fragmentation are just as evident, and Canada continues to be both a difficult country to understand and a difficult country to govern (Adam, 2007: 32–34; Petter, 1989: 463–68).

Consequently, Canada is often regarded as a "geographical absurdity" or even an "impossible country." Canada, it has been argued, "preserves nothing of value. It is literally nothing. It is the *absence* of a sense of identity, the *absence* of a common life" (Horowitz, 1985: 363). When such a view is taken, Canada is regarded as a country without a future and Canadians are urged to begin the process of deconfederation. But not everyone favours or believes inevitable the fragmentation of Canada, or the creation of regional and ethnic solitudes, or absorption into the United States. Many Canadians believe that Canada does preserve something of value and that the Canadian experiment differs from the American union. But why is Canada worth preserving? Historically, one of the most evocative expressions of Canadian distinctiveness has been the motto "true north, strong and free." As a northern country, Canada was held to differ from the United States and to express unique character values. Canada's cold climate was also used to explain its adherence to British liberty and its rejection of American-style democracy (Berger, 1966: 15). Just as evocative is the celebration of Canadian multiculturalism that often occupies pride of place in contemporary accounts of Canada's uniqueness. In his *Conversation with Canadians* (1972), Pierre Trudeau contrasted Canada with the American melting pot and insisted that a vigorous policy of multiculturalism formed the basis of fair play for all Canadians. Of course, Trudeau attached even greater significance to the Canadian Charter of Rights and Freedoms. In his *Memoirs,* he emphasized that his search for the Canadian identity "had led [him] to insist on the charter" (Trudeau, 1993: 323).

However, the adoption of the Charter has not settled the most difficult questions about the Canadian identity. If anything, Canadians are more divided than before on the most fundamental questions. Charter patriotism has come into conflict with the other particularisms that define Canada, with the result that Canada has become an even more difficult country to govern and a more difficult country to understand. Trudeau believed that the Charter would provide Canadians with a new beginning and a strong foundation for the future. Yet Canada existed for a long time before the Charter was adopted in 1982, and Trudeau took too little account of this fact. The Canadian nation, a distinguished historian has written, "is fragile indeed, and one reason ... might well be the lack of a history that binds Canadians together. It is not that we do not have such a history. It is simply that we have chosen not to remember it." He goes on to say: "If we have no past,

4

then surely ... we have no future" (Granatstein, 1998: xvii, xviii). Others, like Janet Ajzenstat, are more specific. They warn that "we have lost the Fathers' insight"; they pray that Canada will not "be wracked by the terrible passions that have inflicted such damage on European nations in the twentieth century"; and they hope "that our shortsightedness never catches up with us" (Ajzenstat, 2007: xii, 109).

Indeed, not only do Canadians have a past, but their past has demonstrated their will to live together. If they assume, as Trudeau often did, that "the past is another country," they lose the opportunity to reflect more deeply on the distinctiveness of their country, the values it has come to represent, and the challenges that bedevil it. Canada may never become an easy country to govern, but it can become a less difficult country to understand.

Confederation and Canadian Federalist Theory

Unlike Canadians, Americans do not need to be told about the importance of their history; they revere their past and draw sustenance from it even in times of crisis. In the Gettysburg Address, delivered during the American Civil War, Abraham Lincoln prayed for a "new birth" of freedom so that government by the people would not perish (Current, 1967: 284–85). But Lincoln began his address by invoking the Declaration of Independence and by remembering that the American founders had brought forth a new nation conceived in liberty and dedicated to equality. The paradox of Lincoln is that he was able to utter "the words that remade America" by appealing to the spirit of its most important founding document (Wills, 1992: 120).

In contrast, no theme of Canadian history seems better established or more often retold than the failure of the original Macdonald constitution. In textbook accounts, the Confederation Settlement of 1867 is identified almost exclusively with John A. Macdonald and his failed dream of creating a highly centralized state that reduced the provinces to little more than administrative units and that conferred almost imperial powers on Ottawa. Where constitutional scholars have diverged is with respect to the reasons for the failure. Some blame the Judicial Committee of the Privy Council (JCPC), and believe that its decentralizing judicial decisions undermined the original understanding of Confederation. Others insist that Macdonald's vision was flawed from the outset because it underestimated the pluralism of Canada, a pluralism that initially manifested itself though a strong provincial rights movement, though eventually incorporating Quebec's Quiet Revolution as well as the demands of new Canadians. If such accounts of Confederation are sound, then Canada's constitutional past is little more than a lesson in failure and, unlike American history, hardly worth remembering.

But there is more to the Constitutional Settlement of 1867 than Macdonald's understanding of it (Gwyn, 2007: 5, 322–33). Nor is the failure of his vision tantamount to the defeat of Confederation. In the debates of 1865, Macdonald announced that he favoured a strong unitary state for Canada because "it would be the best, the cheapest, the most vigorous, and the strongest system of government we could adopt" (Canada, 1865: 29). Macdonald was, after all, a Tory and he had a Tory vision of Canada. As a Tory, he celebrated the British connection, admired the unlimited sovereignty of the British Parliament, and exalted the nation. "The nation," Donald Creighton wrote in his account of Macdonald's idea of union, "transcends the group, the class, or section" (Creighton, 1972: 217). Macdonald dreamed of Canada as "a great nationality, commanding the respect of the world, able to hold our own against all opponents" (Canada, 1865: 41). But even Macdonald had to admit that his dream of a Tory union was "impracticable." It was impractical, he said in the debates of 1865, because it did not meet with the assent of Quebec, which feared that its nationality, language, religion, and code of law might be assailed in a legislative union. And even the Maritime provinces rejected the idea of a unitary state. As a result, Macdonald modified his views and accepted the project of a federal union. However, Macdonald still claimed victory: Canada would be a federal union, but the Parliament of Canada would have all the great powers of legislation as well as the residual power covering matters not enumerated in the 1867 Act. By so strengthening the central government, he insisted, "we make ... the Confederation one people and one government" (Canada, 1865: 41).

For Macdonald, the important contrast was with the United States and its federal experiment. Federalism is often regarded as an American invention. It is just as often praised for guaranteeing freedom. But in 1865, many Canadians viewed federalism with suspicion, partly because it was regarded as inconsistent with parliamentary institutions and partly because of its association with the American Civil War. In response, Macdonald's bold tactic was both to praise the United States Constitution and to insist that its framers "had commenced at the wrong end." They had made each state "a sovereignty in itself" and had conferred too limited powers on the general government. By so doing, they made "states' rights" the defining feature of their federation, and prepared the way for the Civil War. Moreover, the American President, Macdonald added, was merely a party leader and incapable of representing the whole of the American people. In contrast, Canadian Confederation accepted the monarchical principle and elevated the sovereign above the rivalry of political parties. Confederation would also confer the criminal law power on the central government, thereby correcting the American mistake of allowing every state to enact its own criminal code.

It would establish lieutenant-governors for the provinces and create a unified judicial system controlled primarily by the central government. Macdonald even boasted that Canadian Confederation so successfully arranged the powers of government that, unlike the American union, it would eliminate "all conflict of jurisdiction and authority." By centralizing power rather than dispersing it, Confederation would create a new dominion of the North, one demonstrably superior to its southern neighbour because it solved the difficult problems of federalism (Canada, 1865: 33).

Such, in outline, was Macdonald's understanding of Confederation. Its importance is difficult to exaggerate. Canada's first century was, in constitutional terms, little more than an engagement with his vision. Moreover, its eventual failure made a second constitutional beginning almost inevitable. But why did the Macdonald constitution fail? Macdonald himself provided one answer. Less than two years after Confederation, he complained: "It is difficult to make the local Legislatures understand that their powers are not so great as they were before the Union." He then added: "In fact, the question that convulsed the United States and ended in Civil War, commonly know as the 'States' Rights' question, has already made its appearance in Canada" (Rogers, 1933: 17–18). For Macdonald, it was the refusal of the provinces to accept the subordinate position assigned to them that shattered the original understanding of Confederation and, if pressed still further, would spell the failure of the Constitution.

Not only did the provinces press their demands, but the JCPC was often sympathetic to them, so much so that in 1937 it struck down much of Prime Minister Bennett's "New Deal" legislation. Critics of the JCPC believe that its decentralizing decisions were largely responsible for the failure of the Macdonald constitution, a failure that had severe economic and social consequences during the Great Depression of the 1930s. Its decisions also facilitated "province-building," which countered Macdonald's project of nation-building. Writing in 1979, Alan Cairns believed that province-building had produced "big governments" in Canada capable of embarking on policies usually reserved for sovereign nations. Province-building, he insisted, had turned the Canadian Constitution into "a lame-duck constitution." It had made Canadian federalism into a game similar to "eleven elephants in a maze" and just as self-defeating (Cairns, 1988 [1979]: 183, 188).

The defeat of the Macdonald constitution can also be explained in a way that does not privilege Macdonald's understanding of Confederation. In the debates of 1865, Macdonald's vision of Canada met with skepticism and even derision from critics of Confederation. Christopher Dunkin rejected Macdonald's boast that there would be no conflicts of jurisdiction and authority under Confederation. He not only accused Macdonald of failing to respect the distinction between a legislative and a federal union, but he also predicted the early demise of Confederation. The allocation of powers under the proposed constitution, he said, would fuel quarrels rather than quell them. The Senate would not perform the functions assigned to it, and lieutenant-governors, if they acted to control provincial legislatures, would provoke open resistance. Nor would judges appointed by the central government earn the confidence of the local legislatures. The provinces, he added, "cannot possibly work harmoniously together long; and so soon as they come into collision ... the fabric is at an end" (Canada, 1865: 530).

Dunkin was not alone in refusing to "prophecy smooth things" (Canada, 1865: 487, 508, 530). Joseph Perrault warned that although the French and English had come to a new world, they had brought their old hostilities with them. He recalled Lord Durham's assimilation proposals and complained that the real object of Confederation was, like Durham's, the obliteration of the French-Canadian nationality. He warned that French-Canadian patriots would defend their cultural heritage and predicted that racial tensions would disrupt Confederation (Canada, 1865: 596, 600, 612). For the critics of Confederation, it was the very pluralism of Canada that rendered Macdonald's constitutional vision untenable. For them, the Macdonaldian constitution had failed even before it was adopted.

The story of Canada is a story of failure so long as Confederation is understood as Macdonald's attempt to find a remedy for "states' rights" and other errors of American federalism by creating a highly centralized Canadian state. But there is more to Confederation. Confederation was also intended as a solution to Canadian problems, and it was hardly achieved by Macdonald alone. "Canadians," wrote Carl J. Friedrich, "... had a very special problem to deal with which found no parallel in the American experience: that was how to arrange a federal system that would satisfy their French-speaking citizens" (Friedrich, 1967: 60–61). In the debates of 1865, Dunkin surmised that "the two differences of language and faith ... were the real reasons" for the supposed federal union, whose purpose it was to meet a "probable clashing of races and creeds" (Canada, 1865: 509). If French Canadians provided the "real" reason, the Maritime provinces were the "other" reason, for they too rejected Macdonald's initial plea for a unitary state based on their concern to preserve their local identities and distinct destinies. Not the spectre of the American Civil War but the deep pluralism of Canada was the problem that most engaged Canadians in 1867. Moreover, when Confederation is understood as a response to the pluralism of Canada, pride of place belongs not to Macdonald but to his political co-equal, George Étienne Cartier. It was Cartier who, despite Macdonald's misgivings, insisted on significant autonomy for Quebec, and thereby guaranteed that Quebec and the other provinces would have exclusive and substantial powers of their own. Without him, Confederation would have remained nothing more than a political dream.

In Cartier's understanding of it, Confederation represented a novel engagement with the pluralism of Canada, one that rejected both assimilation and cultural solitudes and instead envisaged the creation of a new political nationality (LaSelva, 1996: 39–41, 156–60; Ajzenstat, 2007: 88–109). In response to Lord Durham and other advocates of assimilation, Cartier insisted that the project of racial unity was not only utopian but impossible, because diversity was "the order of the physical world and of the moral world." He also rejected the creation of cultural solitudes and the belief that cultural peace was impossible without them. On the contrary, he insisted that the racial, cultural, and religious diversity of Canada was a benefit rather than otherwise. "We were of different races," he observed, "not for the purpose of warring against each other, but in order to emulate for the general welfare." Moreover, unlike Macdonald, Cartier was an unequivocal federalist; he believed that federalism, when responsive to cultural and local differences and combined with a suitable scheme of minority rights, made Canada possible. In his view, Canadian federalism did not presuppose the Canadian nation but created it. Confederation, he said, would bring into existence a new Canada and a new nationality, "a political nationality with which neither the national origin, nor the religion of any individual, would interfere" (Canada, 1865: 60). While Macdonald worried about "states rights" and the American Civil War, Cartier reflected on the pluralism of Canada and imagined a new kind of nationality. But Cartier died in 1873, and his understanding of Confederation was nearly forgotten. Macdonald lived until 1891 and struggled to realize his vision of Canada, only to witness the emergence of a strong provincial rights movement as well as the compact theory of Confederation, both of which countered his view of the constitution and worked to defeat it.

A Second Beginning: Charter Canadians, Multicultural Citizenship, and Trudeau's Canada

In contemporary Canada, almost no one worries much about the fate of the Macdonald constitution. The past—and certainly Macdonald's idea of Tory union—almost does seem a different country, and the Canadian model is now increasingly identified with multiculturalism and the Charter of Rights (Igartua, 2006: 1, 164–92). That such a change has occurred is due in no small measure to Pierre Elliott Trudeau. For more than a century, Canadians struggled with Macdonald's vision of Confederation. But since the adoption of the Charter of Rights and the other constitutional changes of 1982, they increasingly live in a world reshaped by the liberal universalism of Pierre Trudeau.

Trudeau's constitutional world is not Macdonald's. Philosophically, Macdonald was a Tory; Trudeau, a Liberal. Macdonald cherished the past and valued the British connection; Trudeau looked to the future, and admired the American constitutional system. For Macdonald, sovereignty clearly resided in Parliament; for Trudeau, in the individual citizen. Macdonald feared federalism and attempted to fetter it; Trudeau celebrated the pluralism that federalism enables and accommodates. Moreover, Trudeau also embraced multiculturalism, and multiculturalism bears no resemblance at all to Macdonald's idea of Tory union. If Canadians increasingly neglect their past, only part of the reason is the failure of the Macdonald constitution. Just as important is the extent to which Trudeau's vision of the future has captured the public imagination of Canadians. In Trudeau's constitutional vision, the past *is* another country and the future is a liberal utopia (LaSelva, 2007: 11–18). But Trudeau's constitutional vision has not been embraced by all Canadians and it has not produced a more harmonious country. His vision has replaced Macdonald's, but Canadians struggle with it just as much.

Trudeau is an enigmatic figure, and revelations after his death about his youthful political activities have made him even more so (Nemni and Nemni, 2006: 173–74, 266–73). A philosopher turned politician, he initially warned against fundamental constitutional change, but then, as prime minister, introduced the most important innovations since Confederation. His motto was "reason over passion," yet he had passionate commitments to a reconstructed federalism, to a charter of human rights, and to Canada itself. In his earlier years, he rejected patriotism only to embrace it when he felt in his bones the vastness of his country. He regarded the Canadian mosaic as superior to the American melting pot and insisted that no such thing as a model citizen or ideal Canadian existed. For him, multiculturalism made Canada "a very special place" because it offered every Canadian "the opportunity to fulfil his own cultural instincts and to share those from other sources" (Trudeau, 1972: 32). Moreover, he regarded Canadian federalism as a profound experiment of major proportions. If French and English cooperated to create a truly multinational state, Canada could serve as an example for the world on "how to govern their polyethnic populations with ... justice and liberty." Such a Canada, he insisted, would have the best possible reason for rejecting "the lure of annexation to the United States" (Trudeau, 1968a: 178–79). Trudeau's commitment was to a Canada that differed fundamentally from the United States, yet Trudeau also believed that Canada required a constitutionally entrenched Charter of Rights and Freedoms that, like the American Bill of Rights, secured the "primacy of the individual" and the "sovereignty of the people." For Trudeau, such a Charter would secure "inalienable rights" and be an expression of the "purest liberalism." It would provide "a new beginning for the Canadian nation" and bring into existence a Canada with which all Canadians could identify (Trudeau, 1990: 363).

Trudeau attached the utmost importance to his proposed Charter and pinned virtually all his hopes for Canada on it. Even before he entered politics, he strongly favoured the adoption of a Charter of Rights while warning Canadians that other constitutional changes, such as modification of the division of powers or a reformed Senate, were either not pressing or too perilous to undertake. When he became minister of justice, he called on both Ottawa and the provinces to restrict their powers in favour of the basic human values of all Canadians—political, legal, egalitarian, and linguistic. With such a constitutional innovation, he said, "we will be testing—and, hopefully establishing—the unity of Canada" (Trudeau, 1968a: 54). Shortly after becoming prime minister, he renewed his call for an entrenched Charter and insisted that constitutional reform should take as its starting point the rights of the people rather than the prerogatives of government. The principal objective of constitutional reform, he said, should be to "construct a Canada in which the prime strength is ... in the people; a country which is knit [together] by persons confident of their individual rights wherever they might live; a Canada with which the people may identify" (Trudeau, 1972: 91, 94).

After the Charter was adopted, but well before such incidents as the Maher Arar terrorism case exposed additional concerns about the protection of human rights in Canada, Trudeau reminded Canadians of its crucial importance: it embodied a set of common values and ensured that all Canadians had the same rights. "All Canadians," he wrote, "are equal, and that equality flows from the Charter" (Johnston, 1990: 34). In his *Memoirs* (1993), Trudeau even surmised that the adoption of the Charter had solved the long-standing problem of the Canadian identity.

In Trudeau's conception of it, the Charter embodies common values and guarantees the equality of Canadians, thereby expressing the identity of Canada and securing its unity. But the fundamental fact about Canada is its many-sided pluralism, and Trudeau knew as much. Why else did he sponsor official bilingualism and multiculturalism or, in a speech on Louis Riel, remind Canadians that a democracy is ultimately judged by the way the majority treats the minority? Trudeau went further still. "Canada's population distribution," he noted as early as 1971, "has now become so balanced as to deny any one racial or linguistic component an absolute majority. Every single person in Canada is now a member of a minority group" (Trudeau, 1972: 32).

What, then, is to be done about minority rights? And how are minority rights to be reconciled with the fundamental equality of all Canadians? Trudeau provided an answer to these questions, and his answer is rooted in his commitment to liberalism. Trudeau said that because Canada was a mosaic rather than a melting pot, the Charter protected both individual rights and minority rights. In protecting the rights of minorities, however, the Charter sought, whenever possible and even in the case of the official languages, "to define rights exclusively as belonging to a person rather than a collectivity." Trudeau went on to say: "the spirit and substance of the Charter is to protect the individual against tyranny—not only that of the state but also any other to which the individual may be subjected by virtue of his belonging to a minority group" (Trudeau, 1990: 365). Put another way, the Charter treats all Canadians equally because it does not privilege minority rights but treats them as derived from individual rights. Had Trudeau's liberalism solved the problem of minority rights and created a Canada with which all Canadians could identify?

This is a difficult question. The answer can be partly gleaned from Trudeau's opposition to the 1987 Meech Lake Constitutional Accord, which had as its basic purpose the recognition of Quebec as a distinct society within Canada. Such recognition was deemed necessary partly because the government of Quebec regarded the Charter as unduly restrictive of its autonomy. The Accord was almost ratified, but eventually failed. In rejecting it, Trudeau both defended the Charter and reformulated his long-standing opposition to special status for Quebec. According to Trudeau, the Meech Lake Accord would require Canadians to "Say Goodbye to the Dream of One Canada." He wrote: "For Canadians who dreamed of the Charter as a new beginning for Canada ... where citizenship [is based on] commonly shared values, there is to be nothing left but tears" (Johnston, 1990: 10). He felt that the spirit of the Meech Lake Accord conflicted with the spirit of the Charter and that special status *of any kind* for Quebec destroyed the dream of one Canada (Cook, 2006: 151–62). But such a position encounters a host of difficulties, not the least of which is the fact that the Confederation Settlement of 1867 accommodated Quebec and even used Quebec's distinctiveness to shape the Canadian federation. If Trudeau's vision of the Charter cannot accommodate a distinct Quebec, then his conception of minority rights is problematic: Trudeau's Canada is not a Canada with which all Canadians can identify.

Trudeau's vision of Canada contains several unsettling ironies. His most basic objective was to delegitimate Québécois separatism by creating a truly pluralistic Canada with which all Quebecers and other Canadians could identify. The formula he initially embraced was "multiculturalism within a bilingual framework" (Trudeau, 1985 [1971]: 350). What his Charter adds to the formula is the theme of equality: Canadians are equal citizens in a multicultural society that exists within a bilingual framework. If the revised formula captures Trudeau's vision of Canada, then the first irony is that it does nothing at all to satisfy the historic demand of Quebec—namely, the recognition of Quebec's distinctiveness so that the French-Canadian homeland can flourish within Canada (Laforest, 2001: 304–05).

And even if Canada were to be conceived without Quebec, the formula remains untenable because it does not adequately accommodate Aboriginal Canadians. In its 1969 *Statement on Indian Policy,* the Trudeau government had asked Aboriginals to move off their reserves and become full members of Canada's multicultural society. They were told that different status for Aboriginal peoples was "a blind alley" (Government of Canada, 1969: 5, 9; Trudeau, 1972: 13–15). But Aboriginal peoples rejected this proposal. As Canada's First Nations with historic entitlements to self-government, they struggled to have their rights recognized first by the courts and then again in Sections 25 and 35 of the Constitution Act, 1982. Later, the Government of Canada apologized to Aboriginals for the treatment they had received in residential schools and sponsored a Truth and Reconciliation Commission. Taken together, these facts created the second irony for Trudeau's vision of Canada. The process of accommodating Aboriginal peoples within Canada began only when their claim to special status was recognized; but if their claim was (as I agree it should have been) recognized, then Quebec's claim to distinct status is and should be no less imperative and no less capable of explicit recognition and accommodation in the text of the constitution.

Trudeau said that the Charter protects minority rights; it would be more accurate to say that it brings minorities into conflict and thereby challenges the dream of one Canada (Cairns, 1991: 108). The Charter does not protect the right of French Canadians to a homeland within Canada or the explicit right of Aboriginal Canadians to self-government. But it does protect the rights of "Charter Canadians" (women, gays, lesbians, the disabled) and multicultural citizens (new immigrants). In *The Charter Revolution and the Court Party,* Fred Morton and Rainer Knopff argue that the Charter has transformed the Canadian constitutional system by transferring power from legislatures to courts. Moreover, although Trudeau often portrayed the Charter as a victory for minority rights over majority tyranny, they insist that the Charter revolution is not about tyranny at all. Canada, they write, would remain a liberal democracy "regardless of the outcome of such Charter issues as whether Sikhs in the RCMP are allowed to wear turbans or the legal definition of spouse is read to include homosexuals" (Morton and Knopff, 2000: 36). For them, the most sinister aspect of Charter litigation is that it enables special interest groups to advance their agendas under the guise of inalienable rights and at the expense of democratic politics.

Will Kymlicka takes a more benign view than Morton and Knopff. In *Multicultural Citizenship*, he argues that the recognition of multicultural or polyethnic rights is nothing less than a requirement of liberal justice. Such minority rights deserve recognition, he insists, partly because individual choices are made in a cultural context and partly because to deny them is to unfairly privilege the dominant culture. But Kymlicka stops short of saying that the recognition of multicultural or polyethnic rights has made Canada an easier country to understand or govern. In fact, he believes that Canadians lack a theory of what holds their country together (Kymlicka, 1995: 76, 109, 192). In a later essay, Kymlicka reflected again on Canada and insisted that the Canadian model of pluralism should be judged a success, at least when compared to European nations where ethnic and cultural pluralism has frequently resulted in reactionary policies, secession, and even civil war (Kymlicka, 2007: 69, 79–81).

As for Trudeau, with time he became less sanguine about Canada's future, as can be seen from his reflections on the Charlottetown Constitutional Accord of 1992, which provided him with a final opportunity to discuss minority rights and to explain his vision of Canada (English, 2009: 624–27). If the Charter is, as he called it, the "people's package," then the Charlottetown Accord was the "Canada round." Its purpose was to recognize the rights of Charter Canadians and multicultural citizens alongside the right of Aboriginal peoples to self-government and Quebec's status as a distinct society. The Accord also contained provisions for the reform of central institutions such as an elected Senate, outlined a comprehensive social and economic union for Canada, and modified aspects of the division of powers as well as the amending formula. When Canadians voted on the Accord, they rejected it, and Trudeau believed that they made the only choice possible. In a speech delivered before its defeat, Trudeau described the Accord as "A Mess That Deserves A Big 'NO'." He insisted that the Accord was nothing less than a recipe for dictatorship and a prelude to civil war because it undermined equality, established a hierarchy among citizens, and privileged collective rights over individual rights. Moreover, he reminded Canadians that his own constitutional vision was based on inalienable rights, and he reiterated his admiration for the American constitution. He urged Canadians to read Madison's *Federalist Paper* No. 10, informed them that the American Supreme Court had been established to defend individual rights, and reminded them that the American system had "worked out well" (Trudeau, 1992: 57–58, 44, 47–48). Trudeau regarded the Charlottetown Accord as such a mess that it almost drove him to abandon his conception of the Canadian mosaic and embrace the American model.

The Will to Live Together: Pluralism and the Canadian Constitution

What followed the defeat of the Charlottetown Accord was a near-successful sovereignty referendum in Quebec and then a landmark reference case in the Supreme Court on the secession question and the breakup of Canada. The Secession Reference is now part of Canadian constitutional history, but it also has an enduring and practical relevance because of the fundamental constitutional principles that the Supreme Court enounced in it. In the Secession Reference, the most immediate and pressing question was whether or not Quebec had a unilateral right of secession under the Canadian constitution. The Supreme Court ruled that Quebec had no such right, but it also insisted on the duty of all concerned parties to negotiate constitutional change, including the possible dissolution of Canada. The federalism principle, together with the democratic principle, the Court held, "dictates that the clear repudiation of the existing constitutional order ... would give rise to a reciprocal obligation on all parties to Confederation to negotiate constitutional changes" (Supreme Court of Canada, 1998: 424).

The Court's ruling is important, partly because it denies that secession is purely a political matter and brings it within the pale of the Constitution. It is also important for a different reason. To arrive at its decision, the Court had to analyze the Canadian Constitution, but instead of adopting a narrow or legalistic approach, it attempted to uncover nothing less than the Constitution's "internal architecture" and its fundamental principles. In fact, the Court identified four such principles: federalism, democracy, constitutionalism and the rule of law, and respect for minorities. The Court insisted that these four principles of Canadian constitutionalism were as new as the Charter and as old as Confederation (Supreme Court of Canada, 1998: 424, 410, 403). The Court's opinion is much more than a discussion of the secession question. It is also an innovative exploration of the Canadian constitution and the pluralism of Canada.

In the Secession Reference, the Court quietly corrected several widespread fallacies of Canadian constitutionalism and attempted to replace them with sounder positions. The first fallacy did not originate with Trudeau but is best exemplified by him. Trudeau never tired of insisting that the Charter provided a new beginning for the Canadian people. Others have described Canada before the advent of the Charter as a "lost constitutional world" (Cairns, 1995: 97). The Court did not deny the importance of the Charter or underestimate the changes that had come with it. The Court recognized that the Charter significantly restricted Parliament and the provincial legislatures while considerably enhancing the authority of the judicial branch. But it also insisted that, with respect to minority rights, the Charter represented a continuance of Canada's constitutional past rather than a break with it. "Although Canada's record of upholding the rights of minorities is not a spotless one," the Court wrote, "that goal is one towards which Canadians have been striving since Confederation, and the process has not been without successes." The Court insisted that even the "recent and arduous" achievement of Aboriginal rights was "consistent with this long tradition of respect for minorities, which is at least as old as Canada itself" (Supreme Court of Canada, 1998: 422). In the opinion of the Court, the goal of protecting minority rights did not suddenly emerge with the adoption of the Charter but was an integral part of the Confederation Settlement of 1867 and a defining feature of the Canadian identity.

The second fallacy corrected by the Court also relates to Confederation and, in particular, the interpretation of it in the Macdonald constitution. When the focus is on Macdonald, the emphasis is on the unitary features of the Canadian Constitution and the dream of a Tory union. What is remembered is the desire of the Fathers of Confederation to create a constitution similar in principle to that of the United Kingdom, and it is almost forgotten that, in the very same preamble to the Constitution, they first expressed their desire to be federally united. Canada becomes lost in the British connection, and the Canadian identity becomes almost impossible to comprehend. Such has been the influence of Macdonald. The Court did not so much deny Macdonald's influence as largely ignore it and drew attention instead to the importance of Cartier and his goal of creating a Canadian federal state that solved Canadian problems. The Court quoted at length Cartier's belief that Canadians had come together to contribute to the common welfare and to create a new political nationality with which neither the national origins nor the religion of any individual would interfere. Far from regarding federalism as an aberrant or incidental feature of the Canadian Constitution, the Court insisted that "the significance of the adoption of a federal form of government cannot be exaggerated." Federalism was the "lodestar" of the Constitution. The federal-provincial division of powers was "a legal recognition of the diversity that existed among the initial members of Confederation, and manifested a concern to accommodate that diversity within a single nation" (Supreme Court of Canada, 1998: 405, 412, 407).

By thus focusing on Cartier's vision of federalism and Canada, the Court reinterpreted Confederation and revealed its significance as the foundational event of Canadian constitutionalism and the defining moment in the evolution of Canadian pluralism. When so interpreted, Confederation is not a lost constitutional world, nor is it part of a past that is another country.

Macdonald's idea of a Tory union may be a failed constitutional experiment, but Cartier's vision of Canada is one that has yet to be achieved or even fully understood. For Cartier, the existence of Canada represented the will of Canadians to live together under a common political nationality that presupposed mutual obligations and collective goals but did not require them to submerge their allegiances and identities in a monolithic and all-embracing nationalism. Canadian federalism, with its scheme of minority rights, allowed multiple loyalties and multiple identities to flourish; it thereby enabled Canadians both to live together and to live apart in one country.

Conclusion: Understanding Canada

To understand Canada it is necessary to comprehend both the challenges that confront Canadians and the values that have grounded the Canadian experiment at least since Confederation and possibly, though very tentatively, as early as the Royal Proclamation of 1763 or the Quebec Act of 1774. For Canadians, the most basic challenge is to come to terms with their own diversity. Writing in 1946, W.L. Morton insisted that "the Canadian state cannot be devoted to absolute nationalism [because] the two nationalities and the four sections [regions] of Canada forbid it" (Morton, 1967: 49). Canada is still composed of the two nationalities and the four (or more) regions described by Morton, but it now contains self-governing territories as well as provinces, multicultural citizens and Charter Canadians, French- and English-speaking Canadians as well as Aboriginal and Québécois nationalists.

For some Canadians, this explosion of pluralism has called the existence of Canada into question; at the very least, it has made Canada an even more difficult country to govern. Other Canadians seek to reimagine Canada. They imagine a three-nations Canada composed of English Canada, Québec, and Aboriginal peoples. Or, believing that strong fences make good neighbours, they have called for the creation of a more autonomous Quebec, as well as sovereign Aboriginal nations within a highly decentralized Canada. There are also those who concentrate on articulating a theory of multicultural justice and redesigning the Canadian state to meet its quite different requirements. Reflecting on this Canadian pluralism, Robert Fulford has called the country a postmodern dominion and has insisted that it can be best understood as a postmodern state. The key to postmodernism, he suggests, is the absence of a master narrative and the questioning of any notion of a coherent, stable, autonomous identity (Fulford, 1993: 118). "What," he asks, "could be more Canadian than that?"

But Canada is not merely an ever-changing association of particularisms. Its very existence presupposes values that are seldom made explicit or fully understood. In *Lament for a Nation,* George Grant insisted that Canada was a country without a future because its foundational values conflicted with modernity. "To be a Canadian," he said, "... was to build a more ordered and stable society than the liberal experiment in the United States." Grant identified Canada with the values of British conservatism; he also insisted that Canada could not survive the encounter with technological progress and the American dream. For Grant, modernity meant the disappearance of local cultures and the emergence of an homogeneous universal state centred on the American empire (Grant, 1970: 4, x, 54).

Five decades after Grant wrote his book, a world state has not appeared, local cultures flourish, and Canada has not been absorbed into the United States. Grant did not simply fail to predict the future; he also misunderstood Canada's past and its foundational values. Grant identified Canada with Macdonald's idea of a Tory union, yet it was Cartier's rejection of cultural assimilation and his faith in a new kind of political nationality that grounded the Canadian experiment (Smiley, 1967). Macdonald identified Canada with order and stability; Cartier viewed it in terms of mutual recognition, the co-operative virtues, and the many faces of amity or fraternity. Cartier's vision is deeply rooted in Canada's past, but it also speaks to the complex issue of mutual recognition that confronts Canadians as they attempt to come to terms with an Aboriginal Truth and Reconciliation Commission, new experiments in Aboriginal self-government, demands for even more provincial autonomy and decentralized federalism, and the multicultural anxiety that non-Western ways of life can create, not only for Québec but for all of Canada.

Canada may yet disappear if Canadians fail to come to terms with the limitations inherent in Pierre Trudeau's constitutional vision or if they experience a failure of political will to remain together in the face of new challenges of diversity. "Other people besides Canadians," Michael Ignatieff writes, "should be concerned if Canada dies. If federalism can't work in my Canada, it probably can't work anywhere" (Ignatieff, 1993: 147; Ignatieff, 2010: 142–50). In a postmodern world increasingly characterized by competing nationalisms and multicultural identities, the fate of Canada concerns more than just Canadians.

References and Suggested Readings

Adam, Marc-Antoine. 2007. "Federalism and the Spending Power: Section 94 to the Rescue." *Policy Options* (March): 30–34.

Ajzenstat, Janet. 2007. *The Canadian Founding: John Locke and Parliament.* Montreal, Kingston: McGill-Queen's University Press.

Bailyn, Bernard. 1967. *The Ideological Origins of the American Revolution.* Cambridge, MA: Harvard University Press.

Berger, Carl. 1966. "The True North Strong and Free." In *Nationalism in Canada*, ed. Peter Russell, 3–26. Toronto: McGraw-Hill.

Bibby, Reginald W. 1990. *Mosaic Madness*. Toronto: Stoddart.

Bissoondath, Neil. 1994. *Selling Illusions: The Cult of Multiculturalism in Canada*. Toronto: Penguin.

Cairns, Alan C. [1979] 1988. "The Other Crisis of Canadian Federalism." In *Constitution, Government and Society in Canada*, 171–91. Toronto: McClelland & Stewart.

Cairns, Alan C. 1991. "Citizens (Outsiders) and Governments (Insiders) in Constitution-Making: The Case of Meech Lake." In *Disruptions*, 108–38. Toronto: McClelland & Stewart.

Cairns, Alan C. 1995. "The Constitutional World we Have Lost." In *Reconfigurations*, 97–118. Toronto: McClelland & Stewart.

Cairns, Alan C. 1997. *Looking into the Abyss*. Ottawa: C.D. Howe Institute.

Canada. 1865. *Parliamentary Debates on the Subject of the Confederation of British North American Provinces. Quebec: Hunter, Rose. Photographically reproduced*. 1951. Ottawa: King's Printer.

Cook, Ramsay. 1969. *Provincial Autonomy, Minority Rights and the Compact Theory, 1867–1921*. Ottawa: Information Canada.

Cook, Ramsay. 2006. *The Teeth of Time: Remembering Pierre Elliott Trudeau*. Montreal, Kingston: McGill-Queen's University Press.

Cooper, John Irwin. 1942. "The Political Ideas of George Étienne Cartier." *Canadian Historical Review* 23 (3): 286–94. http://dx.doi.org/10.3138/CHR-023-03-05.

Creighton, Donald. 1972. *Towards the Discovery of Canada*. Toronto: Macmillan.

Current, Richard N., ed. 1967. *The Political Thought of Abraham Lincoln*. Indianapolis: Bobbs-Merrill.

English, John. 2009. *Just Watch Me: The Life of Pierre Elliott Trudeau 1968–2000*. Toronto: Knopf.

Friedrich, Carl J. 1967. *The Impact of American Constitutionalism Abroad*. Boston: Boston University Press.

Fulford, Robert. 1993. "A Post-Modern Dominion: The Changing Nature of Canadian Citizenship." In *Belonging*, ed. William A. Kaplan, 104–19. Montreal: McGill-Queen's University Press.

Government of Canada. 1969. *Statement on Indian Policy, 1969*. Ottawa: Queen's Printer.

Granatstein, J.L. 1998. *Who Killed Canadian History?* Toronto: Harper Collins.

Grant, George. 1970. *Lament for a Nation: The Defeat of Canadian Nationalism*. Toronto: McClelland & Stewart.

Gwyn, Richard. 2007. *John A.: The Man Who Made Us*. Vol. 1 of *The Life and Times of John A. Macdonald, 1815–1867*. Toronto: Random House Canada.

Horowitz, Gad. 1985. "Mosaics and Identity." In *Canadian Political Thought*, ed. H.D. Forbes, 359–64. Toronto: Oxford University Press.

Igartua, Jose E. 2006. *The Other Quiet Revolution: National Identities in English Canada, 1945–71*. Vancouver: University of British Columbia Press.

Ignatieff, Michael. 1993. *Blood and Belonging: Journeys into the New Nationalism*. Toronto: Penguin.

Ignatieff, Michael. 2000. *The Rights Revolution*. Toronto: Anansi.

Ignatieff, Michael. 2010. *True Patriot Love*. Toronto: Penguin.

Johnston, Donald, ed. 1990. *Pierre Trudeau Speaks Out on Meech Lake*. Toronto: General Paperbacks.

Kymlicka, Will. 1995. *Multicultural Citizenship*. Oxford: Clarendon Press.

Kymlicka, Will. 2007. "The Canadian Model of Multiculturalism in a Comparative Perspective." In *Multiculturalism and the Canadian Constitution*, ed. Stephen Tierney, 61–90. Vancouver: University of British Columbia Press.

Laforest, Guy. 1995. *Trudeau and the End of a Canadian Dream*. Montreal: McGill-Queen's University Press.

Laforest, Guy. 2001. "The True Nature of Sovereignty." In *Canadian Political Philosophy*, eds. Ronald Beiner and Wayne Norman, 298–310. Don Mills: Oxford University Press.

LaSelva, Samuel V. 1996. *The Moral Foundations of Canadian Federalism: Paradoxes, Achievements and Tragedies of Nationhood*. Montreal: McGill-Queen's University Press.

LaSelva, Samuel V. 1999. "Divided Houses: Secession and Constitutional Faith in Canada and the United States." Vermont Law Review 23: 771–92.

LaSelva, Samuel V. 2007. "To Begin the World Anew: Pierre Trudeau's Dream and George Grant's Canada." *Supreme Court Law Review* 36 (2D): 1–30.

Levinson, Sanford. 1988. *Constitutional Faith*. Princeton: Princeton University Press.

McPherson, James M. 1991. *Abraham Lincoln and the Second American Revolution*. New York: Oxford University Press.

Morton, Fred L., and Rainer Knopff. 2000. *The Charter Revolution and the Court Party*. Toronto: Broadview Press.

Morton, W.L. 1967. "Clio in Canada: The Interpretation of Canadian History." In *Approaches to Canadian History*, ed. Carl Berger, 42–49. Toronto: University of Toronto Press.

Nemni, Max, and Monique Nemni. 2006. *Young Trudeau: Son of Quebec, Father of Canada, 1919–1944*. Toronto: McClelland and Stewart.

Petter, Andrew. 1989. "Federalism and the Myth of the Spending Power." *Canadian Bar Review* 68: 448–79.

Rogers, Norman McL. 1933. "The Genesis of Provincial Rights." *Canadian Historical Review* 14: 9–23.

Royal Commission on Bilingualism and Biculturalism. 1965. *Preliminary Report of the Royal Commission on Bilingualism and Biculturalism*. Ottawa: Queen's Printer.

Smiley, Donald V. 1967. *The Canadian Political Nationality*. Toronto: Methuen.

Supreme Court of Canada. 1998. *Reference re Secession of Quebec* 161 DLR. (4th) 385.

Sweeney, Alastair. 1976. *George-Étienne Cartier*. Toronto: McClelland and Stewart.

Taylor, Charles. 1993. *Reconciling the Solitudes: Essays on Canadian Federalism and Nationalism*. Montreal: McGill-Queen's University Press.

Trudeau, Pierre Elliott. 1968a. *Federalism and the French Canadians*. Toronto: Macmillan.

Trudeau, Pierre Elliott. 1968b. *A Canadian Charter of Human Rights*. Ottawa: Queen's Printer.

Trudeau, Pierre Elliott. 1972. *Conversation with Canadians*. Toronto: University of Toronto Press.

Trudeau, Pierre Elliott. [1971] 1985. "Statement on Multiculturalism." In *Canadian Political Thought*, ed. Hugh Donald Forbes, 349–51. Toronto: Oxford University Press.

Trudeau, Pierre Elliott. 1990. "The Values of a Just Society." In *Towards a Just Society*, eds. Thomas S. Axworthy and Pierre Elliott Trudeau, 357–85. Markham: Penguin.

Trudeau, Pierre Elliott. 1992. *A Mess That Deserves a Big NO*. Toronto: Robert Davies.

Trudeau, Pierre Elliott. 1993. *Memoirs*. Toronto: McClelland and Stewart.

Waite, Peter. 1962. *The Life and Times of Confederation*. Toronto: University of Toronto Press.

Wills, Garry. 1992. *Lincoln at Gettysburg: The Words that Remade America*. New York: Simon & Schuster.

two

Citizenship, Communities, and Identity in Canada

WILL KYMLICKA

Much of the Canadian political system is founded on the premise that, in the words of the Supreme Court, the "accommodation of difference is the essence of true equality."[1] While Canadian history contains its share of intolerance, prejudice, and oppression, it also contains many attempts to find new and creative mechanisms for accommodating difference. As a result, Canada has developed a distinctive conception of the relationship between citizenship and identity.

As in all other liberal democracies, one of the major mechanisms for accommodating difference in Canada is the protection of the civil and political rights of individuals, such as those listed in Sections 2–15 of the Canadian Charter of Rights and Freedoms. Freedom of association, religion, speech, mobility, and political organization enable individuals to form and maintain the various groups and associations that constitute civil society, to adapt these groups to changing circumstances, and to promote their views and interests to the wider population. The protection afforded by these common rights of citizenship is sufficient for many of the legitimate forms of diversity in society.

However, it is widely accepted in Canada that some forms of difference can only be accommodated through special legal measures, above and beyond the common rights of citizenship. Some forms of group difference can only be accommodated if their members have what Iris Marion Young calls "differentiated citizenship" (Young, 1989). These special measures for accommodating difference are the most distinctive, and also the most controversial, aspect of the Canadian conception of citizenship identity.

Forms of Group Difference in Canada

Historically, the major challenge in Canada has been the accommodation of ethnocultural difference. There are three forms of ethnocultural pluralism in Canada that need to be distinguished.

First, Canada is a New World *settler* state—that is, it was constructed through the European colonization and settlement of territories historically occupied by indigenous peoples. In this respect, it is like the other

21

British settler states—Australia, New Zealand, and the United States—or the Spanish settler states of Latin America. Although the nature of European colonization and settlement varies enormously in these different countries, the rights of indigenous peoples (and their relationship to the settler society built on their traditional territories) remains an issue in all of them, including questions about their land rights, treaty rights, customary law, and rights to self-government.[2]

Canada differs from these other European settler states, however, in that it was colonized and settled by two different European powers—Britain and France—who fought for supremacy over the territory of what is now Canada. While the British eventually won this struggle, and thereby incorporated "New France" into "British North America," the reality was that there were two distinct settler societies within Canada—one French, located primarily in Quebec, and one British—each with their own languages, laws, and institutions. As a result, when Canada became an independent state in 1867, it recognized "the French fact" through official bilingualism and through provincial autonomy for Quebec. In this respect, unlike other New World settler states, Canada is sometimes said to be a "bi-national" settler state, constructed through the joining together of its "two founding peoples"—the French and British settler societies.

Of course, to say that the French and British were "founding peoples" ignores the role of indigenous peoples, on whose territory this new country was built, and whose activities and agreements were vital to the building of Canada. They clearly are the "first peoples" of the country. As a result, it is more common today, and more accurate, to say that Canada is a *multination* state rather than a bi-national state. Its historical development has involved the federation of three distinct peoples or nations (British, French, and Aboriginals).[3] These groups are "nations" in the sociological sense of being historical communities, institutionally complete, occupying a given territory or homeland, and sharing a distinct language and history. Because Canada contains more than one nation, it is not a nation-state but a multination state, and the Québécois[4] and Aboriginal communities form "substate nations" or "national minorities." The desire of these groups to be seen as "nations" is reflected in the names they have adopted. For example, the provincial legislature in Quebec is called the "National Assembly"; the major organization of Status Indians is known as the "Assembly of First Nations."[5]

The original incorporation of these national minorities into the Canadian political community was largely involuntary. Indian homelands were overrun by French settlers, who were then conquered by the English. If a different balance of power had existed, it is possible that Aboriginals and French-Canadians would have retained their original sovereignty, rather than being incorporated into the larger Canadian federation. And it is still possible that Quebec will leave the federation. However, the historical preference of these national minorities has not been to secede, but to renegotiate the terms of federation, so as to increase their autonomy within it.

Many of the pivotal moments in Canadian political history have centred on these attempts to renegotiate the terms of federation between English, French, and Aboriginals. One such effort at renegotiation ended in October 1992, when the Charlottetown Accord was defeated in both a pan-Canadian referendum and a separate Quebec referendum. This Accord (discussed below) would have entrenched an "inherent right of self-government" for Aboriginals, and would have accorded Quebec a special status as "the only society with a majority French language and culture in Canada and in North America."

In addition to being a multination state, Canada is also a *multi-ethnic* or *polyethnic* state. Canada, like the US, accepts large numbers of individuals and families from other cultures as immigrants. They are expected to integrate into the public institutions of either the francophone or anglophone societies— for example, they must learn either French or English (Canada's two official languages) to acquire citizenship. Prior to the 1960s, they were also expected to shed their distinctive heritage and assimilate almost entirely to the dominant cultural norms. The ideal was that immigrants would become, over time, generally indistinguishable from native-born Canadians in their speech, dress, and lifestyle. However, in the early 1970s, under pressure from immigrant groups, the Canadian government rejected this assimilationist model, and instead adopted a more tolerant policy (known as the policy of "multiculturalism"), which allows and supports immigrants to maintain various aspects of their ethnic heritage. Immigrants are free to maintain some of their old customs regarding food, dress, recreation, and religion, and to associate with each other to maintain these practices. This is no longer seen to be (as it once was) unpatriotic or "unCanadian."

But such groups are not "nations" and do not occupy homelands within Canada. Their ethnocultural distinctiveness is manifested primarily in their private and social lives, and does not preclude their institutional integration. They still participate within either anglophone or francophone public institutions, and speak one or the other of the official languages in public life. Because of extensive immigration of this sort, Canada has a large number of "ethnic groups" who form loosely aggregated subcultures within both the English- and French-speaking societies.

So Canada is both multinational (as a result of colonization, conquest, and confederation) and multiethnic (as a result of immigration). Those labels are less popular than the term "multicultural," which can be confusing, precisely because it is ambiguous between multinational and multiethnic. Indeed, this ambiguity has led to unwarranted criticism of Canada's "multiculturalism policy," the term the federal government uses for its post-1971 policy of promoting accommodation rather than assimilation for immigrants. Some Québécois have opposed the "multiculturalism" policy because they think it reduces their historic claims of nationhood to the level of immigrant ethnicity. Other people had the opposite fear: that the policy was intended to treat immigrant groups as nations within Canada, and hence support the development of institutionally complete cultures alongside the francophone and anglophone societies. In fact, neither fear was justified, since "multiculturalism" is best understood as a policy of supporting the recognition and accommodation of immigrant ethnicity within the national institutions of the anglophone and francophone societies. This is indeed explicit in the phrase "multiculturalism within a bilingual framework" that the government used when introducing the policy.

Three Forms of Group-Differentiated Citizenship

There are at least three forms of differentiated citizenship in Canada intended to accommodate these ethnic and national differences: (a) self-government rights; (b) accommodation rights; and (c) special representation rights.[6] I will say a few words about each.

(a) *Self-government rights:* As I noted, Aboriginal peoples and the Québécois view themselves as "peoples" or "nations," and, as such, as having the inherent right of self-determination. Both groups demand certain powers of self-government that they say were not relinquished by their (initially involuntary) incorporation into the larger Canadian state. They want to govern themselves in certain key matters, to ensure the full and free development of their cultures and the best interests of their people.

This quest for self-government is not unique to Canada. National minorities in many other Western democracies make similar demands. Consider Puerto Rico in the United States, Catalonia and the Basque Country in Spain, Scotland and Wales in Great Britain; Flanders in Belgium; Corsica in France. These are just a few of the many national minorities seeking greater self-government within Western democracies. Similarly, indigenous peoples around the world are seeking greater autonomy, including the American Indians, the Maori in New Zealand, the Inuit in Greenland, and the Sami in Scandinavia.

One mechanism for recognizing claims to self-government is federalism. Where national minorities are regionally concentrated, the boundaries of federal subunits can be drawn so that the national minority forms a majority in one of the subunits. Under these circumstances, federalism can provide extensive self-government for a national minority, guaranteeing its ability to make decisions in certain areas without being outvoted by the larger society.

Federalism was adopted in Canada precisely for this reason. Under the federal division of powers, the province of Quebec has extensive jurisdiction over issues that are crucial to the survival of the francophone society, including control over education, language, and culture, as well as significant input into immigration policy. The other nine provinces also have these powers, but the major impetus behind the existing division of powers, and indeed behind the entire federal system, is the need to accommodate the Québécois. When Canada was created in 1867, most English-Canadian leaders were in favour of a unitary state, like England, and agreed to a federal system primarily to accommodate French Canadians. Had Quebec not been guaranteed these substantial powers—and hence protected from the possibility of being outvoted on key issues by the larger anglophone population—it is certain that Quebec either would not have joined Canada in 1867 or would have seceded sometime thereafter.

While federalism has served to satisfy the desire for self-government to a certain extent, it is not a magic formula for resolving the claims of national minorities. Indeed, federalism has itself become a source of division in Canada. The problem is that French- and English-speaking Canadians have adopted two very different conceptions of federalism, which we can call "multination" federalism and "territorial" federalism (Resnick, 1994). Whereas the former conception emphasizes the link between federalism and self-government for national minorities, the latter ignores or downplays this link. The public debates over the Meech Lake and Charlottetown Accords revealed that many of our constitutional dilemmas stem from these competing conceptions of federalism.

Purely "territorial" forms of federalism are not designed or adopted to enable a national minority to exercise self-government; they are simply intended to diffuse power within a single nation on a regional basis. The original and best-known example of such a "territorial" federalism is the United States; other examples include Germany, Australia, and Brazil. None of these federations have any federal subunits dominated by a national minority. As a result, they have no reason to give any of their subunits distinctive rights of national self-government.

In "multination" federations, by contrast, one or more subunits have been designed with the specific intention of enabling a national minority to form a local majority, and to thereby exercise meaningful self-government. Historically, the most prominent examples of federalism being used in this way to accommodate national minorities are Canada and Switzerland. Since the Second World War, however, there has been a flood of new multination federations, including India, Belgium, Spain, Nigeria, Ethiopia, Iraq, Sudan, and Russia.[7]

The Canadian federation has many of the hallmarks of a genuinely multination federation. This is reflected in the fact that the 1867 Constitution not only united four separate provinces into one country, it also divided the largest province into two separate political units—English-speaking Ontario and French-speaking Quebec—to accommodate ethnocultural divisions. This decision to create (or, more accurately, to re-establish) a separate Quebec province within which the French formed a clear majority was the crucial first step toward accommodating national self-government within Canadian federalism.

However, many English-speaking Canadians have not fully accepted a multination model of federalism. Instead, they tend to view American-style territorial federalism as the appropriate model for Canada. This is reflected in demands for an American-style "Triple-E" Senate. It is also reflected in opposition to any form of "special status" for Quebec, whether in the form of an asymmetrical division of powers, or in the form of a "distinct society" clause. From the point of view of multination federalism, the special status of Quebec is undeniable. It is the only province that is a vehicle for a self-governing national minority, while the nine other provinces reflect regional divisions within English-speaking Canada. Quebec, in other words, is a "nationality-based unit"—it embodies the desire of a national minority to remain a culturally distinct and politically self-governing society—while the other provinces are "region-based units," which reflect the decision and desire of a single national community to diffuse some of the powers of government on a regional basis.

In a multination conception of federalism, because nation-based units and region-based units serve different functions, there is no reason to assume that they should have the same powers or forms of recognition. Indeed, there is good reason to think that they will require some degree of differential treatment. Nation-based units are likely to seek different and more extensive powers than region-based units, both because they may need greater powers to protect a vulnerable national language and culture, and as a symbolic affirmation that they (unlike regional subdivisions within the majority) are "distinct nations." We see demands for asymmetry in most multination federations, including Spain, the United Kingdom, India, and Russia, as well as in Canada.

How we evaluate these demands for asymmetrical powers will depend on our conception of the nature and aims of political federation. For national minorities like the Québécois, federalism is, first and foremost, a federation of *peoples,* and decisions regarding the powers of federal subunits should recognize and affirm the equal status of the founding peoples. On this view, to grant the same powers to region-based units and nation-based units is in fact to deny equality to the minority nation, by reducing its status to that of a regional division within the majority nation. By contrast, for most English-speaking Canadians, federalism is, first and foremost, a federation of *territorial units,* and decisions regarding the division of powers should affirm and reflect the equality of the constituent units. On this view, to grant unequal powers to nation-based units is to treat some of the federated units as less important than others.

One of the fundamental questions facing Canada is whether we can reconcile these two competing conceptions of federalism. In the past, there was a sort of implicit compromise: English-speaking Canadians accepted a significant degree of *de facto* asymmetry in powers for Quebec, but rejected attempts to formally recognize asymmetry in the Constitution (Gagnon and Garcea, 1988). For much of the 1980s and 1990s, this compromise position seemed to be coming unstuck: the Québécois were becoming more insistent on explicit recognition, and English-speaking Canadians were becoming more hostile to even informal forms of *de facto* asymmetry. The Charlottetown Accord was an attempt to paper over the differences between these two conceptions. It contained some provisions that seemed to endorse the multination model (e.g., the "distinct society" clause) while other provisions seemed to endorse the territorial model (e.g., the equality of provinces clause). The failure of the Accord in the 1992 referendum suggests that there is no easy way to reconcile these two conceptions.

When the failure of the Accord was followed by the near-success of the 1995 referendum on secession in Quebec, many commentators argued that the opposing dynamics of public opinion within Quebec and the rest of Canada were inevitably pulling the country apart. Since 1995, however, there has been a noticeable pulling back from the precipice. One could argue, indeed, that the old historic compromise of *de facto* asymmetry without formal constitutional recognition has been successfully revived. This is reflected, for example, in House of Commons resolutions recognizing Quebec as a "distinct society" (1995) and as a "nation" (2006), in new intergovernmental agreements to expand Quebec's autonomy (e.g., the 2004 health care agreement), and in the Supreme Court's 1998 ruling that Quebec's distinctness must be taken into account when interpreting the constitution.[8] Many people on both sides have come to recognize that this historic compromise was actually quite an accomplishment. It enabled both sides to work together to create a peaceful and prosperous country, without insisting that either side renounce its fundamental beliefs about the nature of nationhood and statehood. The historic compromise allows the Québécois to think and act like a nation, while allowing English-speaking Canadians to think and act as if they live in a territorial rather than a multination federation. The result may seem unsatisfactory for those who believe that states require a single, unifying ideology or mythology, and of course the persistence of these opposing views makes federal-provincial relations an ongoing source of tension. But experience shows that these tensions can be managed, and potential conflicts sidestepped, so long as people put pragmatism over ideological purity.

The demands of Aboriginal peoples for recognition of their inherent right of self-government raise some of the same issues as Quebec's demand for asymmetry. In both cases, there is an insistence on national recognition, collective autonomy, distinctive rights and powers, and the equality of peoples. However, unlike the Québécois, Aboriginal peoples find traditional forms of federalism to be unsuitable, as there is no way to redraw provincial boundaries to create a province with an Aboriginal majority.[9]

Instead, Aboriginal self-government has been primarily tied to the system of Indian reserves and the devolution of power from the federal government to the band councils that govern each reserve. Aboriginal bands have been acquiring increasing control over health, education, policing, criminal justice, and resource development. In some provinces, they have also negotiated self-government agreements with the provinces (e.g., James Bay and Northern Agreement as well as Nunavik in Quebec). In the future, it is widely expected that they will become a constitutionally recognized third order of government within or alongside the federal system, with a collection of powers that is carved out of both federal and provincial jurisdictions, as was proposed in the Charlottetown Accord (RCAP, 1996; Cairns, 2000). However, the administrative difficulties are forbidding—Indian bands differ enormously in the sorts of powers they desire and are capable of exercising. Moreover, they are territorially located within the provinces, and must therefore coordinate their self-government with provincial agencies. And just as many Canadians reject "special status" for Quebec, so too are they reluctant to provide any explicit recognition of national rights for Aboriginals. In short, as with the Québécois, there is considerable *de facto* self-government for Aboriginal peoples, yet no explicit constitutional recognition of rights of self-government.

(b) *Accommodation rights*: Many immigrant groups and religious minorities have demanded various forms of public support and legal recognition of their cultural practices. These demands take a variety of forms, including recognition of Jewish religious holidays in school schedules; exemptions from official dress codes so that Sikh men can wear turbans; revisions to the history and literature curricula in public schools to give greater recognition to the historical and cultural contribution of immigrant groups; greater representation of immigrant groups in the police; CRTC guidelines to avoid ethnic stereotyping in the media; anti-racism educational campaigns; cultural diversity training for police, social workers, and health-care professionals; workplace and school harassment codes prohibiting racist comments; funding of ethnic festivals and ethnic studies programs; and so on.

Most of these demands have been accepted as part of the policy of "multiculturalism," and a general commitment to such measures is reflected in Section 27 of the Canadian Charter of Rights and Freedoms, which says that "This Charter shall be interpreted in a manner consistent with the preservation and enhancement of the multicultural heritage of Canadians."

Unlike self-government rights, these accommodation rights are usually intended to promote integration into the larger society, not self-government.[10] None of the demands mentioned above involves the desire to establish a separate and self-governing society. On the contrary, they typically aim to reform *mainstream* institutions so as to make immigrant groups feel more at home within them. These measures are consistent with, and intended to promote, the integration of immigrants into the public institutions of the mainstream society. They seek to help ethnic groups and religious minorities express their cultural particularity and pride without it hampering their success in the economic and political institutions of the dominant society.

Here again, Canada is not unique. We find similar developments in the other major immigration countries. While Canada was the first country to explicitly adopt an official "multiculturalism" policy, other countries quickly followed, including Australia, New Zealand, Britain, the Netherlands, and Sweden. We see many of the same developments occurring informally in the United States, even though the US does not have any official multiculturalism policy.

To be sure, these ideas are controversial, and some countries firmly resist any talk of multiculturalism (e.g., France). As well some countries that initially embraced multiculturalism have since witnessed a clear backlash and retreat (e.g., the Netherlands). Other countries such as Britain appear to have abandoned the word "multiculturalism" even as they maintain the policies that used to be justified in the name of multiculturalism, preferring now to use some other term such as "interculturalism" or "community cohesion" policies. The extent to which there has been a genuine (as opposed to merely rhetorical) retreat from multiculturalism in Europe is a matter of ongoing debate (Vertovec and Wessendorf, 2010; Banting and Kymlicka, 2013; Joppke, 2013).[11]

In Canada, however, popular and elite support for multiculturalism remains high, in part because of evidence that it has indeed facilitated the integration of immigrants (Adams, 2007; Bloemraad, 2006; Kymlicka, 2012). There was a lively debate in Quebec in 2007 about whether the "reasonable accommodation" of immigrants and religious minorities had "gone too far," and some people viewed this debate as a first sign that Canada might witness the sort of backlash against multiculturalism found in Western Europe. However, a provincial government commission, co-chaired by Charles Taylor and Gérard Bouchard, found that the existing policy of accommodation was in fact working well and that there was no basis for a U-turn in policy, although the issue remains contentious within Quebec.[12]

(c) Special representation rights: While the traditional concern of national minorities and immigrant ethnic groups has been with either self-government or accommodation rights, there has been interest by these groups, as well as other non-ethnic social groups, in the idea of special representation rights.

Many Canadians believe the political process is "unrepresentative," in the sense that it fails to reflect the diversity of the population. This was illustrated most vividly during the constitutional negotiations leading up to the Charlottetown Accord, in which the fundamental terms of Canadian political life were said to have been negotiated by 11 middle-class, able-bodied white men in suits (the prime minister and the premiers of the 10 provinces). A more representative process, it was said, would have included women, members of ethnic and racial minorities, and people who are poor or disabled.

This has led to increasing interest in the idea that a certain number of seats in the Senate should be reserved for the members of disadvantaged or marginalized groups. During the debate over the Charlottetown Accord, for example, the National Action Committee on the Status of Women recommended that 50 per cent of Senate seats should be reserved for women, and that proportionate representation of ethnic minorities also be guaranteed; others recommended that seats be reserved for the members of official language minorities or for Aboriginals.

The recent demands for special representation by women and other disadvantaged groups are largely an extension of long-standing demands for effective Senate representation by smaller provinces. Canada currently has an unelected Senate, which is widely viewed as illegitimate and ineffective. Many Canadians would like to simply abolish the Senate. But the less populated regions of English-speaking Canada—that is, the Atlantic provinces and the Western provinces—want to reform the Senate and use it as a forum for increased regional representation within the federal Parliament. Some have demanded an American-style Senate, in which each province would elect an equal number of senators regardless of its population. This is intended to ensure "effective representation" for smaller provinces that hold little sway in the House of Commons, where the majority of members of Parliament come from the two most populated provinces (Ontario and Quebec).

Some Canadians have begun to believe that if small, disadvantaged, or marginalized regions need special representation, then so surely do disadvantaged or marginalized groups, such as women or the poor. Historical evidence suggests that these groups, even more than smaller provinces, are likely to be underrepresented in Parliament and ignored in political decision-making. Here again, demands for group representation are not unique to Canada. We find very similar debates occurring in Great Britain, Scandinavia, France, and the United States (Phillips, 1995; Mansbridge, 2000; Williams, 1998; Htun, 2004; Rubio, 2012).

In the end, the Charlottetown Accord rejected most proposals for the guaranteed representation of social groups, and instead focused on increased regional representation. The one exception was a proposal for guaranteed Aboriginal seats. However, the Accord allowed each province to decide how its senators would be elected, and three of the 10 provincial premiers said that they would pass provincial legislation requiring that 50 per cent of the Senate seats from their province be reserved for women (Ontario, British Columbia, and Nova Scotia). While the Accord was defeated, it is possible that any future proposal for Senate reform will have to address the issue of group representation as well as regional representation.

Group representation rights are often defended as a response to some systemic barrier in the political process that makes it impossible for the group's views and interests to be effectively represented. For example, Iris Young, writing in the American context, argues that special representation rights should be extended to "oppressed groups" because they are at a disadvantage in the political process, and "the solution lies at least in part in providing institutionalized means for the explicit recognition and representation of oppressed groups" (Young, 1989: 259).

Insofar as these rights are seen as a response to oppression or systemic disadvantage, they are most plausibly seen as a temporary measure on the way to a society where the need for special representation no longer exists—a form of political "affirmative action." Over time, society should remove the oppression and disadvantage, thereby eliminating the need for these rights.

However, the issue of special representation rights is complicated in Canada, because special representation is sometimes defended, not on grounds of oppression, but as a corollary of self-government for national minorities. The right to self-government in certain areas seems to entail the right to guaranteed representation on any bodies that can intrude on those areas. Hence, it is argued, a corollary of self-government is that the national minority be guaranteed representation on any body that can interpret or modify its powers of self-government (e.g., the Supreme Court),[13] or that can make decisions in areas of concurrent or conflicting jurisdiction.

On the other hand, insofar as self-government reduces the jurisdiction of the federal government over the national minority, self-government may imply that the group should have *reduced* influence (at least on certain issues) at the federal level. For example, if self-government for the Québécois leads to the asymmetrical transfer of powers from Ottawa to Quebec so that the federal government would be passing laws that would not apply to Quebec, some commentators argue that Quebecers should not have a vote on such legislation (particularly if they could cast the deciding vote).[14] In this context, it is worth noting that although Quebec has its own pension plan, separate from the Canada Pension Plan, federal ministers from Quebec have often been in charge of the latter.

***

These are the three major forms of differentiated citizenship in Canada. As we've seen, they are not unique to Canada, but are found in most Western democracies. Insofar as differentiated citizenship involves the adoption of one or more of these group-differentiated rights, then virtually every modern democracy recognizes some form of it.

While these forms of differentiated citizenship are common, they remain controversial. Many liberals have opposed these policies as inconsistent with liberal democratic principles of freedom and equality. I will discuss two standard liberal objections—the conflict between group rights and individual rights, and the bases of social unity.

Individual and Group Rights

Recognizing groups in the constitution is often perceived as an issue of "collective rights," and many liberals fear that collective rights are, by definition, inimical to individual rights. This view was popularized in Canada by former Prime Minister Pierre Trudeau, who explained his rejection of collective rights for Quebec by saying that he believed in "the primacy of the individual" (Trudeau, 1990).

However, we need to distinguish two kinds of collective rights that a group might claim. The first involves the right of a group against its own members; the second involves the right of a group against the larger society. Both kinds of collective rights can be seen as protecting the stability of national, ethnic, or religious groups, but they respond to different sources of instability. The first kind is intended to protect the group from the destabilizing impact of *internal* dissent (e.g., the decision of individual members not to follow traditional practices or customs), whereas the second protects the group from the impact of *external* pressures (e.g., the economic or political decisions of the larger society). To distinguish these two kinds of collective rights, I will call the first "internal restrictions" and the second "external protections." Internal restrictions involve *intra*-group relations; external protections regulate *inter*-group relations.

Internal restrictions are arguably inconsistent with liberal-democratic values. Such collective rights are found in many parts of the world where groups seek the right to legally restrict the freedom of their own members in the name of group solidarity or cultural purity; this is especially common in theocratic and patriarchal cultures where women are oppressed and religious orthodoxy enforced. This type of collective right, then, raises the danger of individual oppression.[15]

External protections, by contrast, do not raise problems of individual oppression. Here the aim is to protect a group's distinct identity not by restricting the freedom of individual members, but by limiting the group's vulnerability to the political decisions and economic power of the larger society. For example, guaranteeing representation for a minority on advisory or legislative bodies can reduce the chance that the group will be outvoted on decisions that affect the community; financial subsidies can help provide goods and services to a minority that they could not afford in a market dominated by majority preferences; and revising dress codes and work schedules can help ensure that decisions originally made by and for the dominant group are sufficiently flexible to accommodate new ethnic groups.

These sorts of external protections are not inconsistent with liberal democratic principles, and may indeed promote justice. They may help put the different groups in a society on a more equal footing, by reducing the extent to which minorities are vulnerable to the larger society.

Do the three kinds of differentiated citizenship in Canada involve internal restrictions or external protections? Primarily the latter. The Québécois, Aboriginal peoples, and ethnic minorities are primarily concerned with ensuring that the larger society does not deprive them of the conditions necessary for their survival. They are less concerned with controlling the extent to which their own members engage in untraditional or unorthodox practices. Special representation within the political institutions of the larger society, the devolution of self-government powers from the federal government to the minority, and the protection of cultural practices through accommodation rights all reduce the vulnerability of minority communities to the economic and political decisions of the larger society.

These various forms of external protections are, I believe, compatible with liberal values. One can imagine cases where external protections go too far in protecting a minority from a majority, to the point where the minority in fact is able to rule over the majority—apartheid in South Africa is a clear example where "minority rights" for whites were invoked to dispossess the majority. However, this does not seem to be a real danger for the particular external protections currently being claimed in Canada. The special veto powers demanded by the Québécois, or the land rights demanded by Aboriginals, or the heritage language funding demanded by ethnic minorities will hardly put them in a position to dominate English Canadians. On the contrary, they can be seen as putting the various groups on a more equal footing, in terms of their relative power vis-à-vis each other.

Moreover, none of these external protections need conflict with individual rights, since they do not, by themselves, tell us anything about whether or how the ethnic or national group exercises power over its own members.

There are also some internal restrictions in Canada, although their scope is less clear. Both self-government rights and accommodation rights can, under some circumstances, be used to oppress certain members of the minority group. For example, some Québécois and Aboriginal leaders have sought qualification of, or exemption from, the Canadian Charter of Rights and Freedoms in the name of self-government. These limits on the Charter create the possibility that individuals or groups within Quebec or Aboriginal communities could be oppressed in the name of group solidarity or cultural authenticity.

Whether there is a real danger of intra-group oppression in Canada is a matter of debate. The most commonly discussed example concerns the potential for sexual discrimination in minority cultures.[16] Some women's groups (mostly from outside Quebec) worried that the Quebec government might use the "distinct society" clause to impose oppressive family policies on women (e.g., restricting access to birth control or abortion to maintain a high birth rate). Whether this was a realistic worry is dubious. Women's groups within Quebec were quick to reject the idea that enhanced or asymmetric autonomy for Quebec was a threat to their equality, and indeed Quebec has some of the most progressive policies on gender equality in the country.

The concern has also been expressed that Aboriginal women might be discriminated against under certain systems of Aboriginal self-government, if these are exempt from the Charter. This concern has been expressed by women's organizations both inside and outside Aboriginal communities. Indeed, the Native Women's Association of Canada has demanded that the decisions of Aboriginal governments be subject to the Canadian Charter (or a future Aboriginal Charter, if it also effectively protects sexual equality).

34

On the other hand, many Aboriginal leaders insist that this fear of sexual oppression reflects misinformed or prejudiced stereotypes about Aboriginal cultures. They argue that Aboriginal self-government needs to be exempt from the Charter of Rights—not to restrict the liberty of women within Aboriginal communities, but to defend the *external* protections of Aboriginals vis-à-vis the larger society. Their special rights to land, or to guaranteed representation, which help reduce their vulnerability to the economic and political pressure of the larger society, could be struck down as discriminatory under the Charter (e.g., guaranteed representation for Aboriginals could be seen as violating the equality rights of the Charter, as could restrictions on the mobility of non-Aboriginals on Indian lands). Also, Aboriginal leaders fear that white judges may interpret certain rights (e.g., democratic rights) in ways that are culturally biased. Hence many Aboriginal leaders seek exemption from the Charter, but affirm their commitment to the basic human rights and freedoms that underlie the Charter.

Similar debates have occurred over accommodation rights. There are fears that some immigrant groups and religious minorities may use "multiculturalism" as a pretext for imposing traditional patriarchal practices on women and children. There are fears that some groups will demand the right to stop their children (particularly girls) from receiving a proper education, so as to reduce the chances that the child will leave the community, or the right to continue traditional customs such as clitoridectomy or forced arranged marriages. Such fears were often expressed in Quebec's recent debate about whether reasonable accommodation had gone too far.

Such internal restrictions clearly do have the potential to deny individual freedom. But Canada's current multiculturalism policy does not endorse such practices, and there is little public support for allowing them, even within minority communities. Instead, most collective rights for ethnic and national groups are defended in terms of, and take the form of, external protections against the larger community. To be sure, there are always some conservative members within any given ethnic or religious group who try to encourage or pressure other members to follow what they believe to be the "authentic" practices of the community, and who oppose reformers who wish to revise or adapt these practices. But such internal debates existed long before the adoption of multiculturalism policies, and exist in countries that have rejected multiculturalism. Some commentators have worried that multiculturalism policies strengthen the hand of conservative members of groups, giving them greater power to impose particular "scripts" on other members about what it means to be a Jew, say, or to be Chinese. But here again, there is no evidence that multiculturalism favours conservatives over reformers within ethnic and religious groups, and indeed some evidence suggests that multiculturalism policies have helped to ensure the greater representation of women and youth within such communities, in part because norms of gender equality and human rights are themselves explicitly built into the goals of the federal multiculturalism policy.[17]

More generally, there is no enthusiasm for the idea that ethnic or national groups should be able to protect their historical customs by limiting the basic civil liberties of their members. For example, there is no public support for restricting freedom of religion in the name of protecting the religious customs of a community.

Social Unity and Differentiated Citizenship

Liberals are also concerned that differentiated citizenship will be a source of disunity and will inhibit the development of a sense of shared Canadian identity. They believe it could lead to the dissolution of the country, or, less drastically, to a reduced willingness to make the mutual sacrifices and accommodations necessary for a functioning democracy and effective welfare state. If groups are encouraged by the very terms of citizenship to turn inward and focus on their "difference" (whether racial, ethnic, religious, sexual, etc.), then citizenship cannot perform its vital integrative function. Nothing will bind the various groups in society together or prevent the spread of mutual mistrust or conflict.

This is a serious concern, reinforced by evidence from other countries that there may be a negative correlation between diversity and solidarity.[18] Indeed, this is now sometimes called the new "progressive's dilemma": progressives today want to be more open to diversity, yet this may erode the traditional progressive goal of a robust welfare state (Pearce, 2004).

In evaluating this concern, however, we need to keep in mind the distinction between the three forms of differentiated citizenship. Generally speaking, demands for both representation rights and accommodation rights are demands for *inclusion*. Groups that feel excluded want to be included in the larger society, and the recognition and accommodation of their "difference" is intended to facilitate this.

As I noted, the right to special representation can be seen as an extension of the familiar idea of guaranteeing special representation for underrepresented regions (e.g., an equal number of Senate seats for all states or provinces, whatever their population). This practice is widely seen as promoting both participation and fairness, and hence integration. Proponents of special representation simply extend this logic to non-territorial groups, who may equally be in need of better representation (e.g., ethnic and racial minorities, women, the disabled). There are practical obstacles to such a proposal

(Phillips 1995). For example, how do we decide which groups are entitled to such representation, and how do we ensure that their "representatives" are in fact accountable to the group? Nevertheless, the basic impulse underlying representation rights is integration, not separation.

Similarly, most demands for accommodation rights reflect a desire by members of ethnic minority groups to participate within the mainstream of society. Consider the case of Sikhs who wanted to join the Royal Canadian Mounted Police, but, because of their religious requirement to wear a turban, could not do so unless they were exempted from the usual requirements regarding ceremonial headgear. Such an exemption was opposed by many Canadians, who viewed it as a sign of disrespect for one of Canada's "national symbols." But the fact that these men wanted to be a part of the RCMP, and participate in one of Canada's national institutions, is evidence of their desire to participate in and contribute to the larger community.

Indeed, the evidence suggests that the adoption of the multiculturalism policy in 1971 has helped, rather than hindered, the integration process in Canada. Immigrants today are more likely to take out Canadian citizenship than immigrants who arrived before 1971. They are also more likely to vote, more likely to learn an official language, more likely to have friends (or spouses) from another ethnic group, more likely to participate in mainstream social organizations, and so on. On all of these criteria, ethnic groups in Canada are more integrated today than they were before the multiculturalism policy was adopted in 1971. Moreover, Canada does a better job of integrating immigrants on these criteria than countries that have rejected the idea of multiculturalism, like the United States or France.[19] Multiculturalism has been criticized for promoting ethnic segregation in Canada (Bissoondath, 1994), but in fact there is no evidence to suggest that multiculturalism has decreased the rate of integration of immigrants, or increased the separatism or mutual hostility of ethnic groups. On the contrary, it seems that multiculturalism has succeeded in its basic aim: making immigrants and their children feel more at home within mainstream Canadian institutions.

Self-government rights, however, do raise problems for the integrative function of citizenship. While both representation and accommodation rights take the larger political community for granted and seek greater inclusion in it, demands for self-government may reflect a desire to weaken the bonds with the larger community, and may indeed question its very nature, authority, and permanence. If democracy is the rule of the people, group self-government raises the question of who "the people" really are. National minorities claim that they are distinct peoples, with inherent rights of self-determination that were not relinquished by their (often involuntary) inclusion within a larger country. Indeed, the retention of certain powers is often explicitly spelled out in the treaties or federal agreements that specified the terms of their inclusion. Self-government rights, therefore, are the most complete case of differentiated citizenship, since they divide the people into separate "peoples," each with its own historic rights, territories, and powers of self-government, and each, therefore, with its own political community.

Can differentiated citizenship serve an integrative function in this context? If citizenship is primarily membership in a political community, then self-government rights seem to give rise to a sort of dual citizenship, and to conflicts about which community citizens identify with most deeply. Moreover, there seems to be no natural stopping point to the demands for increasing self-government. If limited autonomy is granted, this may simply fuel the ambitions of nationalist leaders who will be satisfied with nothing short of their own nation-state. Indeed, one of the defining features of nationalism, historically, has been the quest for an independent state. Even if not explicitly secessionist, nationalists typically insist that the nation is the primary locus of political loyalty and allegiance, so that participation in any supra-national political community is conditional, assessed on the basis of how well such participation serves the interest of the primary national community. Once the Québécois or Crees define themselves as a nation, therefore, it seems that their allegiance to Canada can only be derivative and conditional. Democratic multination states are, it would seem, inherently unstable for this reason.

It might seem tempting, therefore, to ignore the demands of national minorities, avoid any reference to such groups in the constitution, and insist that citizenship is a common identity shared by all individuals, without regard to group membership. This is often described as the American strategy for dealing with cultural pluralism. But with a few small-in-number exceptions—such as the Indian, Inuit, Puerto Rican, and Native Hawaiian populations—the United States is not a multination state. It has faced the problem of assimilating voluntary immigrants and involuntary slaves, who arrived in America as individuals or families, rather than incorporating historically self-governing communities whose homeland has become part of the larger community. And where the "ethnicity-blind" strategy was applied to national minorities (e.g., American Indians), it has often been a spectacular failure. Hence many of these national groups are now accorded self-government rights within the United States. Indeed, there are very few democratic multination states that follow the strict "common citizenship" strategy. This is not surprising, because refusing demands for self-government rights may simply aggravate alienation among these groups, and increase the desire for secession.[20]

It might seem that we are caught between Scylla and Charybdis: granting self-government rights seems to encourage a nationalist project whose end-point is independence; denying self-government seems to encourage alien-ation and withdrawal. It is not surprising, therefore, that many commentators have concluded that multination states are unlikely to be successful or stable.

And yet many multination federations have survived, and indeed flour-ished. Countries such as Switzerland, Belgium, Great Britain, and Canada have not only managed these conflicts in a peaceful and democratic way, but also have secured prosperity and individual freedom for their citizens. Indeed, it is a striking fact that no multination federation in the West has yet fallen apart. This is truly remarkable when one considers the immense power that nationalism has shown in this century. Nationalism has torn apart colonial empires and Communist dictatorships, and redefined boundaries all over the world. Yet democratic multination federations have succeeded in taming the force of nationalism. No other form of political structure can make this claim.

This suggests that multination federations combine a rather weak sense of unity with surprising levels of resilience and stability. Weak bonds of social unity may nonetheless be enduring, and conditional allegiances may none-theless be powerful. What "glue" provides this sort of resilience remains a matter of debate (Webber, 1994; Tully, 1995; Norman, 2006; Taylor, 1993; Gagnon and Tully, 2001; Gagnon, Rocher, and Guibernau, 2003). But the ideal of a stable and prosperous multination state—which recognizes the self-government rights of its national minorities while simultaneously promoting a common identity among all citizens—is neither a conceptual contradiction nor a practical impossibility. We do not yet have a theory about how such states are possible: we have no clear account of the basis of social unity in such a multination state. But we shouldn't let the lack of a theory blind us to the reality that such states exist and prosper in the modern world.

Conclusion

Canada has a long history of accommodating group difference, particularly national and ethnic difference. It is difficult to say whether this history is a successful one. On the one hand, the continued existence of the country has often been in question, and remains so today. On the other hand, Canada has enjoyed 140 years of peaceful coexistence between three national groups and innumerable ethnic groups, with an almost total absence of political vio-lence. While many groups continue to feel excluded, the political system has proven flexible enough to accommodate many demands for self-government, multicultural accommodations, and special representation. It is difficult to find a scale that allows us to add up these successes and disappointments to arrive at some overall judgements of the Canadian experiment in accommodating group difference. Indeed, perhaps the major lesson to be drawn from the Canadian experience is the sheer heterogeneity of group differences, and of the mechanisms for accommodating them. The sorts of demands made by national, ethnic, and social groups differ greatly in their content and in their relation to traditional liberal democratic principles of equality, freedom, and democracy.

Notes

1 Andrews v Law Society of British Columbia (1989) 10 C.H.R.R. D/5719 (S.C.C.).
2 For Canada in comparative perspective with other settler states, see Pearson (2001) and Havemann (1999).
3 It is misleading to describe Aboriginal peoples as a single nation, since the term "Aboriginal" covers three categories of Aboriginals (Indian, Inuit, and Métis), and the term "Indian" itself is a legal fiction, behind which there are numerous distinct aboriginal nations with their own histories and separate community identities.
4 Throughout this paper, I use "Québécois" to refer to the French-speaking majority in the province of Quebec. There are francophones outside Quebec, and the French nation in Canada was not always identified so closely with the province of Quebec. For the change in self-identity from *la nation canadienne-française* to *québécois*, see McRoberts (1997).
5 On the adoption of the language of nationhood by Aboriginal groups, see Jenson (1993) and Cairns (2000).
6 For a more elaborate typology of forms of differentiated citizenship, see Levy (1997).
7 For a discussion of this trend, see Gagnon and Tully (2001) and Kymlicka (2007).
8 For the Supreme Court discussion, see Reference re Secession of Quebec, [1998] 2 S.C.R. 217. For the *de facto* asymmetry in the 2004 health-care agreement, see the special series on asymmetric federalism commissioned by the Institute for Intergovernmental Relations). (http://www.queensu.ca/iigr/WorkingPapers/asymmetricfederalism.html). A new area of informal asymmetry concerns the role of provinces in international relations. Quebec has been much more active than other provinces in seeking representation and participation in international organizations and in engaging in "substate diplomacy."

9 There is one exception in the North, where the division of the Northwest Territories into two parts has created a territory (Nunavut) with an Inuit-majority population.

10 Some groups' demands take the form of withdrawal from the larger society. However, this is primarily true of ethnoreligious sects than of immigrant communities per se. For example, the Hutterites and Mennonites are allowed to pull their children out of school before the legal age of 16, and put restrictions on the ability of group members to leave their community. This is not the result of Canada's multiculturalism policy, as the legal exemptions accorded these Christian sects long predate the multiculturalism policy.

11 For a systematic attempt to track the adoption of multiculturalism policies across the Western democracies, see the Multiculturalism Policy Index project available at www.queensu.ca/mcp. The Index measures these policies at three points in time: 1980, 2000, and 2010.

12 For the Bouchard-Taylor report, see http://www.ukrainianstudies.uottawa.ca/pdf/Bouchard-Taylor-en.pdf. The report has generated a massive secondary literature: see, for example, Adelman and Anctil (2011).

13 Quebec, with a civil law tradition that differs from the rest of Canada, is in fact guaranteed three seats (out of nine) on the Supreme Court, and the 1996 Royal Commission on Aboriginal Peoples recommended guaranteed Aboriginal representation on the Court (an idea endorsed by both the Assembly of First Nations and the Canadian Association of Law Teachers in 2004).

14 This is one obstacle to asymmetrical federalism. There is no accepted model for determining the status of Quebec's MPs under a system of asymmetrical powers: How many MPs should Quebec have? What issues should they vote on? An analogous situation concerns the representation of Puerto Rico in the American federal government. Because Puerto Rico is generally self-governing, they have reduced representation in Congress compared to other American citizens.

15 For a recent defence of the legitimacy of some internal restrictions in the Canadian context, see Newman (2011).

16 The potential conflict between multiculturalism and gender equality has been an issue, not just in Canada, but internationally (Okin, 1999; Deveaux, 2006; Eisenberg and Spinner-Halev, 2005; Shachar, 2001).

17 There is now a vast literature on the extent to which multiculturalism runs the risk of imposing "essentialist" conceptions of group identity on members, freezing their cultural practices. For recent discussions, see Dick (2012), Eisenberg (2009), and Kymlicka (2013).

18 For two influential empirical studies of this apparent negative correlation, see Putnam (2007) for the American case and Alesina, Baqir, and Easterly (2001) for a global study. Within political theory, this is sometimes called the "recognition versus redistribution" debate: an identity-based politics focused on the recognition of cultural diversity is said to conflict with a class-based politics focused on the politics of redistribution (e.g., Fraser, 1997). For an overview of both the empirical and normative strands of this debate, see Banting and Kymlicka (2006).

19 For the evidence, see Kymlicka (2012), Adams (2007), and Bloemraad (2006).

20 In any event, the state cannot avoid giving public recognition to particular group identities. It must decide which language(s) will serve as the official language(s) of the schools, courts, and legislatures. This shows that the "strict separation of state and ethnicity" view proclaimed by many American liberals is incoherent. See Kymlicka (1995, chap. 6).

References and Suggested Readings

Adams, Michael. 2007. *Unlikely Utopia: The Surprising Triumph of Canadian Pluralism.* Toronto: Viking.

Adelman, Howard, and Pierre Anctil, eds. 2011. *Religion, Culture, and the State: Reflections on the Bouchard-Taylor Report.* Toronto: University of Toronto Press.

Alesina, Alberto, Reza Baqir, and William Easterly. 2001. *Public Goods and Ethnic Diversity.* NBER Working Paper No. 6069. Cambridge: National Bureau of Economic Research.

Banting, Keith, and Will Kymlicka, eds. 2006. *Multiculturalism and the Welfare State: Recognition and Redistribution in Contemporary Democracies.* Oxford: Oxford University Press. http://dx.doi.org/10.1093/acprof:oso/9780199289172.001.0001.

Banting, Keith, and Will Kymlicka. 2013. "Is There Really a Retreat from Multiculturalism Policies? New Evidence from the Multiculturalism Policy Index." *Comparative European Politics* 11 (5): 577–98. http://dx.doi.org/10.1057/cep.2013.12.

Bissoondath, Neil. 1994. *Selling Illusions: The Cult of Multiculturalism in Canada.* Toronto: Penguin.

Bloemraad, Irene. 2006. *Becoming a Citizen: Incorporating Immigrants and Refugees in the United States and Canada.* Berkeley: University of California Press.

Cairns, Alan. 2000. *Citizens Plus: Aboriginal Peoples and the Canadian State.* Vancouver: University of British Columbia Press.

Deveaux, Monique. 2006. *Gender and Justice in Multicultural Liberal States.* New York: Oxford University Press. http://dx.doi.org/10.1093/acprof:oso/9780199289790.001.0001.

Dick, Caroline. 2012. *The Perils of Identity: Group Rights and the Politics of Intragroup Difference.* Vancouver: University of British Columbia Press.

Eisenberg, Avigail. 2009. *Reasons of Identity: A Normative Guide to the Political and Legal Assessment of Identity Claims.* Oxford: Oxford University Press.

Eisenberg, Avigail, and Jeff Spinner-Halev, eds. 2005. *Minorities within Minorities.* Cambridge: Cambridge University Press. http://dx.doi.org/10.1017/CBO9780511490224.

Fraser, Nancy. 1997. "From Redistribution to Recognition? Dilemmas of Justice in a 'Postsocialist' Age." In *Justice Interruptus: Critical Reflections on the 'Postsocialist' Condition*, 11–40. New York: Routledge.

Gagnon, Alain-G., and Joseph Garcea. 1988. "Quebec and the Pursuit of Special Status." In *Perspectives on Canadian Federalism*, eds. R.D. Olling and M. Westmacott, 304–25. Scarborough: Prentice-Hall.

Gagnon, Alain-G., and James Tully, eds. 2001. *Multinational Democracies*. Cambridge: Cambridge University Press. http://dx.doi.org/10.1017/CBO9780511521577.

Gagnon, Alain-G., François Rocher, and M. Montserrat Guibernau, eds. 2003. *The Conditions of Diversity in Multinational Democracies*. Montreal: Institute for Research on Public Policy.

Havemann, Paul, ed. 1999. *Indigenous Peoples' Rights in Australia, Canada and New Zealand*. Oxford: Oxford University Press.

Htun, Mala. 2004. "Is Gender like Ethnicity? The Political Representation of Identity Groups." *Perspectives on Politics* 2/3: 439–58.

Jenson, Jane. 1993. "Naming Nations: Making Nationalist Claims in Canadian Public Discourse." *Canadian Review of Sociology and Anthropology. La Revue Canadienne de Sociologie et d'Anthropologie* 30 (3): 337–58.

Joppke, Christian. Forthcoming. "The Retreat is Real—But What is the Alternative? Multiculturalism, Islam, and the Limits of 'Muscular Liberalism'." *Constellations: An International Journal of Critical and Social Theory.*

Kymlicka, Will. 1995. *Multicultural Citizenship*. Oxford: Oxford University Press.

Kymlicka, Will. 2007. *Multicultural Odysseys: Navigating the New International Politics of Diversity*. Oxford: Oxford University Press.

Kymlicka, Will. 2012. "Multiculturalism: Success, Failure, and the Future." In *Rethinking National Identity in the Age of Migration*, ed. Migration Policy Institute, 33–78. Berlin: Verlag Bertelsmann Stiftung.

Kymlicka, Will. Forthcoming. "The Essentialist Critique of Multiculturalism: Theory, Policies and Ethos." In *The Political Theory of Multiculturalism: Essays in Honour of Bhikhu Parekh*, eds. Tariq Modood, Varun Uberoi, and Raymond Plant. Basingstoke: Palgrave.

Levy, Jacob. 1997. "Classifying Cultural Rights." In *Ethnicity and Group Rights*, eds. Ian Shapiro and Will Kymlicka, 22–66. New York: New York University Press.

Mansbridge, Jane. 2000. "What Does a Representative Do?" In *Citizenship in Diverse Societies*, eds. Will Kymlicka and Wayne Norman, 99–123. Oxford: Oxford University Press. http://dx.doi.org/10.1093/019829770X.003.0004.

McRoberts, Kenneth. 1997. *Misconceiving Canada: The Struggle for National Unity*. Toronto: Oxford University Press.

Newman, Dwight. 2011. *Community and Collective Rights: A Theoretical Framework for Rights Held by Groups*. Oxford: Hart.

Norman, Wayne. 2006. *Negotiating Nationalism: Nation-Building, Federalism and Secession in the Multinational State*. Oxford: Oxford University Press. http://dx.doi.org/10.1093/0198293356.001.0001.

Okin, Susan. 1999. *Is Multiculturalism Bad for Women?* Princeton: Princeton University Press.

Pearce, Nick. 2004. "Diversity versus Solidarity: A New Progressive Dilemma." *Renewal: A Journal of Labour Politics* 12 (3): 79–87.

Pearson, David. 2001. *The Politics of Ethnicity in Settler Societies: States of Unease*. London: Macmillan. http://dx.doi.org/10.1057/9780333977903.

Phillips, Anne. 1995. *The Politics of Presence*. Oxford: Oxford University Press.

Putnam, Robert. 2007. "E Pluribus Unum? Diversity and Community in the 21st Century." *Scandinavian Political Studies* 30 (2): 137–74. http://dx.doi.org/10.1111/j.1467-9477.2007.00176.x.

Resnick, Philip. 1994. "Toward a Multination Federalism." In *Seeking a New Canadian Partnership: Asymmetrical and Confederal Options*, ed. Leslie Seidle, 71–90. Montreal: Institute for Research on Public Policy.

Royal Commission on Aboriginal Peoples (RCAP). 1996. *Report of the Royal Commission on Aboriginal Peoples*. Ottawa.

Rubio, Ruth. 2012. "A New European Parity-Democracy Sex Equality Model and Why It Won't Fly in the United States." *American Journal of Comparative Law* 60 (1): 99–126.

Shachar, Ayelet. 2001. *Multicultural Jurisdictions: Preserving Cultural Differences and Women's Rights in a Liberal State*. Cambridge: Cambridge University Press. http://dx.doi.org/10.1017/CBO9780511490330.

Taylor, Charles. 1993. *Reconciling the Solitudes: Essays on Canadian Federalism and Nationalism*. Montreal: McGill-Queen's University Press.

Trudeau, Pierre Elliott. 1990. "The Values of a Just Society." In *Towards a Just Society*, ed. Thomas Axworthy, 357–404. Toronto: Viking Press.

Tully, James. 1995. *Strange Multiplicity: Constitutionalism in an Age of Diversity*. Cambridge: Cambridge University Press. http://dx.doi.org/10.1017/CBO9781139170888.

Vertovec, Steven, and Susanne Wessendorf, eds. 2010. *The Multiculturalism Backlash: European Discourses, Policies and Practices*. London: Routledge.

Webber, Jeremy. 1994. *Reimagining Canada: Language, Culture, Community and the Canadian Constitution*. Montreal: McGill-Queen's University Press.

Williams, Melissa. 1998. *Voice, Trust and Memory: Marginalized Groups and the Failings of Liberal Representation*. Princeton: Princeton University Press.

Young, Iris Marion. 1989. "Polity and Group Difference: A Critique of the Ideal of Universal Citizenship." *Ethics* 99 (2): 250–74. http://dx.doi.org/10.1086/293065.

PART II

Institutions: The Constitution and Federalism

three
Constitutional Politics

ROGER GIBBINS

Given the regularity with which constitutional issues pop up in Canadian political discourse, it may come as a surprise that our political life has not always been wracked by constitutional debate. In fact, constitutional politics played little role in the first 100 years following Confederation in 1867. True, the political institutions put into place by the 1867 Constitution Act shaped political life, as did principles implicitly embedded in the Constitution, such as responsible government and party discipline. However, the constitutional order itself received little attention. The great clashes of Canadian politics were not fought on the constitutional plain, nor did the Constitution provide many of the rhetorical weapons of political combat. The constitutionalization of political life is a recent event, albeit one that taps political cleavages generations old.

The objective of this chapter is to map out the evolution of constitutional politics. The first section will examine the 1867 constitutional settlement, the second the relatively static constitutional landscape from 1867 to 1960, and the third the more turbulent period stretching from 1960 to the 1995 Quebec referendum on sovereignty association. The chapter will conclude with some brief commentary on the current constitutional landscape, and with some speculation on what might lie ahead.

This historical treatment provides the essential context within which contemporary constitutional politics must be viewed; as we will see, the constitutional politics of any one era largely reflect the unresolved constitutional issues of preceding eras. Throughout, the primary although not exclusive focus will be on the formal Constitution as embodied in such documents as the Constitution Act, 1867 (formerly known as the British North America Act, 1867) and the Constitution Act, 1982, which includes the Charter of Rights and Freedoms. Less attention will be paid to the constitutional conventions such as those structuring party discipline and ministerial responsibility, conventions rooted in the formal constitution but lacking textual status. They are the "rules of the game" that can only be broken or set aside at considerable risk. Although these latter elements are important components of the larger constitutional order, they have not had as high a profile in recent decades as has the formal text of the Constitution.

The Confederation Settlement of 1867

When our founding fathers met in Charlottetown, Quebec City, and London, England during the mid-1860s to draft a new constitution, they were not writing on a blank slate. Documents such as the 1763 Royal Proclamation and the Quebec Act of 1774 were part of the frame within which they worked, as was the long history of British constitutional evolution dating back to the Magna Carta in 1215. Nor, for that matter, was the political agenda all that new: fending off military threats from the United States, overcoming deadlock in the colonial legislatures, providing a financial foundation for western expansion, and bridging both linguistic and religious conflicts between English and French Canada were ongoing tasks. Nonetheless, the immediate constitutional problems the founding fathers faced were new: (1) how to design a national government encompassing the existing colonies of Canada, New Brunswick, and Nova Scotia while allowing for the future entry of new provinces; (2) how to forge a *federal* system linking this national government to new provincial governments; and (3) how to create a new imperial relationship between Canada and the British Crown.

All of these tasks were accomplished through the Constitution Act of 1867. A Canadian Parliament was created with two legislative chambers: the elected House of Commons and the appointed Senate. The governor general, whose consent was needed before any bill passed by the two chambers became law, provided a link to the British Crown and, for some time, to the British government. Legislative assemblies were created for the new provinces of Ontario and Quebec, the existing legislative assemblies in Nova Scotia and New Brunswick were incorporated, and all four were linked by their lieutenant-governors to the government of Canada. A national judiciary was created, and the legislative powers of the new Canadian state were divided between the federal and provincial orders of government. The federal government was assigned the principal economic and taxation powers of the day while the provincial jurisdiction encompassed matters of more local concern, including schools, hospitals, municipal institutions, the management of public lands, and property and civil rights.

The Act also declared that Canada should have a system of government "similar in principle to that of the United Kingdom." It was through this clause that we imported the British conventions of responsible government and party discipline, and consolidated existing Canadian practice in these respects. The conventions included the assumption that governments will tender their resignation if they are unable to command a majority vote in the House of Commons for major legislative initiatives, and thus established the dominating role that party discipline plays to this day in legislative politics in both Ottawa and the provincial capitals. Despite the lack of a more explicit constitutional definition than "similar in principle to," Canadians were to hold fast to these conventions long after they had come under creative reform in the home Parliament. Oddly enough, Canadians have been more faithful than the British to the strict application of party discipline even though it can be argued that our far-flung, regionally diverse federal system is not well served by rigid party discipline in the national legislature.

Much was accomplished by the Constitution Act of 1867. However, when Canadians think of the Act, it is the *federal elements* of the Act that come to the fore. Indeed, for most people the division of powers in Sections 91 and 92 between the national and provincial legislatures is about all that comes to mind. This perception captures an important feature of the 1867 Act—its almost unbroken silence with regard to a host of fundamental issues.

1. Apart from the establishment of both English and French as languages of record and debate in the federal Parliament and Quebec National Assembly, the 1867 Act is silent on the place of the francophone community in the new Canadian nation and state. Quebec is present, to be sure, but in most respects it is present as a province like the others; there is no hint of a special constitutional status as a *distinct society*. Nor does *French Canada* figure in the Act, even though it was one of the most important realities with which the founding fathers wrestled.

2. The 1867 Act says nothing about the position of Aboriginal peoples in the new federal state other than the sparse Section 91, clause 24 assignment of "Indians, and Lands reserved for Indians" to the jurisdictional domain of the national Parliament. Certainly there is nothing to suggest that Aboriginal peoples should be recognized as founding peoples or that they might have some special relationship with the settler communities to come. The nation-to-nation underpinnings of the 1763 Royal Proclamation were not explicitly imported into the 1867 Act, although it can be argued that the eventual Canadianization of the Crown had this effect. Thus, when references to the Crown gradually came to mean "the Crown in Canada" rather than "the Crown in Britain," Aboriginal peoples would be asserting a new nation-to-nation relationship with the Government of Canada.

3. There is no recognition of popular sovereignty; the American notion of "We the People" is completely absent. Popular consent for the Act was not sought and might not have been found had it been sought.

4. There are no references in the Act to the rights of citizens. Whereas the French Revolution produced the 1789 Declaration of the Rights of

Man and Citizen, and the 1776 American Declaration of Independence referred even earlier to universal rights—"We hold these truths to be self-evident that all men are created equal"—the 1867 Act refers only to the powers of the Crown and the distribution of legislative responsibilities between the national and provincial governments. As a consequence, the Act has never served as a vehicle for civic education; schoolchildren have been spared the task of memorizing its dry and often arcane passages.

5. There was no declaration of independence from Britain embedded in the Act, or even the suggestion that this might come. Moreover, because the Act was an act of the British Parliament, it could only be amended by that Parliament. Unlike the earlier American Constitution (1791) or the later Australian Constitution (1901), the Constitution Act did not contain an amending formula; it could not be amended directly by Canadian legislatures until 1982.

There is one additional silence that warrants more detailed comment, and that is the matter of intergovernmental relations. Although we can read a form of national control of provincial legislatures into the role of the lieutenant-governors, and into the authority of the federal Parliament to disallow acts of provincial legislation even when these are passed within the legislative domain of the provinces, there is no hint of the vast network of intergovernmental relations that has come to characterize the contemporary federal state. This omission is not surprising. Both the national and provincial governments were new, minute in comparison with their contemporary counterparts, and were neither prepared nor inclined to fully occupy their own policy spheres, much less encroach on one another. Nonetheless, it is important to note that the contemporary intergovernmental infrastructure is not anchored to the 1867 Constitution, although it is connected to the governments created by that constitution and to the concentration of power within those governments brought about by the conventions of responsible government.[1]

When the many silences or abeyances in the 1867 Constitution Act are considered, we might have expected that the decades following Confederation would have been chock-full of debate as Canadians sought to flesh out their skeletal constitutional blueprint. This is particularly the case given that the "national question"—the key relationship between English and French Canada—had scarcely been addressed, much less resolved. However, this expectation was not met. Although many political conflicts were to come, the Constitution itself was seldom the target or arena of debate. It would take almost 100 years before Canadians began to address the gaps in the 1867 Act.

The Next Hundred Years

It is difficult to reconstruct in a few short pages the nearly 100 years of rich and complex Canadian political history stretching from Confederation to Quebec's Quiet Revolution in the early 1960s. Nevertheless, it is possible to offer a few broad observations.

The first and perhaps most important observation, and certainly the most surprising, is that the lack of specification for the relationship between French and English Canada produced very little constitutional agitation in Quebec and *no* agitation outside Quebec. There was no sustained campaign to change the constitutional framework. Rather, the primary effort of Quebec politicians was to protect the framework put in place in 1867. Admittedly, there was unease and even dismay when the settlement of the Canadian West departed so radically from the bicultural and bilingual format of central Canada, and when the constitutional guarantees for linguistic minorities embedded in the frameworks of the new prairie provinces were ignored. However, when conflicts arose, Quebec opted not to risk its own autonomy by encouraging federal intervention in the internal affairs of other provinces. Quebec nationalism was defensive in character, seeking to maintain rather than to change the status quo.

This strategy was put to the test in the 15 years following the end of World War II when the federal government began to flex its spending power to encroach on provincial fields of jurisdiction. The creation of conditional grant programs and the consequent infusion of federal funds with respect to health care, social assistance, highways, and post-secondary education raised little concern outside Quebec, in large part because they came at a time of exploding demand that provincial tax revenues were simply unable to meet. However, they were challenged by the Quebec government as an assault on the original federal pact. Again, Quebec's strategy was defensive: to protect the existing constitutional division of powers from intrusions by the federal government even when those intrusions were programs that came with funds attached.

The *potential* for constitutional discontent also simmered in the Canadian West. The regional agricultural community railed against freight rates, tariffs, bottlenecks in the transportation of grain, and inequities in the marketing of grain. At times, this regional discontent verged on challenges to the constitutional status quo. However, and with the important exception of agitation leading to the 1930 Natural Resources Transfer Act, which put Crown lands in the West on an equal footing with Crown lands elsewhere in the country, regional discontent was channelled into partisan outlets and attacks on the party system. Western Canadians sought a reduction in partisan constraints on political representation and, when that failed, launched a series of new political parties and movements to take the region's case to Ottawa. What was absent was any serious questioning of federal institutions or the federal division of powers. What was sought was a more effective voice within the national Parliament rather than the devolution of powers from Ottawa to provincial legislatures. This Western strategy stemmed from a simple reality: the legislative powers that really counted for Western Canadians—tariffs, international trade, interprovincial transportation, bank rates, and so forth—belonged logically to the national government; they could not be devolved to the provinces without breaking the country apart, and this Western Canadians had no desire to do.[2] As the Reform Party was to frame the issue in the late 1980s, "The West wants in." Thus, in the decades leading up to Quebec's Quiet Revolution, regional discontent seldom found expression through *constitutional* politics.

Other potential drivers of constitutional politics in this period were not factors in the first six decades of the twentieth century. After the suffragists won a monumental victory by securing the vote for women in the second decade of the century, feminism waned as a public policy issue until the early 1960s; there was no concerted effort to address the social, economic, and political aspirations of women through constitutional channels or constitutional reform. Aboriginal peoples, who were not given an unconstrained right to vote until 1961, were very much at the margins of Canadian political discourse and lacked sufficient political voice to drive constitutional reform even had they been interested in doing so. The Maritime Rights Movement in the early 1920s had challenged the fairness of the Canadian federal state, but the grievances it articulated came to be addressed through federal programs rather than through proposals for constitutional reform. Those who sought a more powerful central government capable of delivering universal social programs found that any constitutional constraints wilted before Ottawa's expanding revenues and unbridled use of the spending power.

Therefore, for almost 100 years after Confederation it appeared that the 1867 constitutional agreement was holding fast—that the founding fathers had constructed a durable constitutional framework for a country marked by great regional, ethnic, and linguistic diversity. This belief was quickly dispelled when Quebec's Quiet Revolution began in the early 1960s.

Constitutional Politics on the Boil

Although the onset of the Quiet Revolution is identified with the 1960 election of the Quebec Liberal Party, it is best seen as an accumulation of social and economic change that began before 1960 and carried through into the following decades. Quebec was transformed from a society in which religious institutions and norms played a dominant role to one of the most secular provinces in Canada. Economic activity shifted from the rural countryside to the urban heartland, and the public philosophy of government changed from narrow conservatism, both social and economic, to expansive state intervention in the social and economic orders. The Quebec birth rate dropped from the highest in Canada to the lowest within a period of little more than two decades. The French language enjoyed a strong renaissance, becoming the language not only of culture in the province but also of business. In short, Quebec rapidly emerged as a very different kind of province.

The political effects of the Quiet Revolution were somewhat unexpected, for although Quebec moved closer to the Canadian social and economic mainstreams, increased similarity did not moderate political differences between Quebec and the rest of Canada. The differences, in fact, intensified as a strong nationalist movement developed in Quebec. Its slogan—"*Maîtres chez nous*," or "masters in our own house"—captured a fundamental challenge to the constitutional status quo as a series of Quebec governments demanded, at the very least, the rollback of federal intrusions into provincial fields of jurisdiction and the expansion of those fields. More broadly, the nationalist movement advanced the argument that Quebec was not a province like the others, that it alone was home to a national community. This meant, in turn, that Quebec should have a unique constitutional status as a distinct society. More extreme manifestations of the same argument, and they were many, maintained that Quebec should become a sovereign state with full control over its own destiny.

Given that Quebec voters made up more than 25 per cent of the national electorate, there is no question that the Quiet Revolution would cause waves within the federal system. However, those waves were greatly amplified by the threat of separation and the possible destruction of Canada as we had come to know it. It was the existence of sovereigntists intent upon the creation of an independent Quebec that gave a sense of urgency to reform of the federal system. Now that Quebec had dropped its defence of the constitutional status quo, the rest of the country did the same and embarked on an extensive search for reform proposals to counter the arguments of Quebec sovereigntists. This process was intensified and complicated by the emergence of other sources of political unrest. Economic prosperity in the West coupled with the lack of effective regional representation in the House of Commons, the radicalization of Aboriginal peoples, and the growing political clout of new social movements such as feminism and environmentalism all added to the constitutional ferment.

Constitutional politics came to a boil in 1976 when Quebec voters elected a Parti Québécois (PQ) government committed to holding a referendum on sovereignty (or sovereignty association) before the end of its term. From the election of the PQ through to the referendum in the spring of 1980, the country went through an intense period of constitutional debate, proposals, and counter-proposals. The tension rose after February 1980, when Pierre Trudeau and his Liberal government returned to power in Ottawa after the short-lived Progressive Conservative government of Joe Clark. The 1980 federal election placed Trudeau and Quebec Premier René Lévesque toe-to-toe in the Quebec referendum campaign as the respective champions of federalism and sovereignty. In that campaign, Trudeau promised the Québécois specifically and Canadians more generally a "renewed federalism" should Quebec reject the ballot proposal for sovereignty-association between Quebec and Canada. When it was defeated by a 40/60 margin, Canadian governments turned again to constitutional negotiations.

Reform, it seemed, was inescapable, for although the Quebec sovereigntists had lost the referendum battle they had not been driven from the field. Held at bay in the referendum by the promise of constitutional reform, the PQ nonetheless won the subsequent provincial election. It was assumed, therefore, that any reform would explicitly address the place of Quebec in Canada. The Québécois may have rejected sovereignty-association, but the separatist threat was still very much alive. Something had to give.

The Constitution Act of 1982

There is no question that the proclamation of the Constitution Act on April 17, 1982, by Her Majesty Queen Elizabeth II at a rainswept ceremony on Parliament Hill was a momentous event in Canada's constitutional history and evolution. The Act patriated Canada's founding constitutional document (the Constitution Act of 1867) and established a set of amending formulas that would require only the consent of Canadian legislative assemblies and not the British Parliament.[3] It provided the first explicit constitutional acknowledgement of Aboriginal rights; a limited form of provincial equality; and constitutional recognition of multiculturalism, gender equality, regional equalization, and intergovernmental relations (through its mention of First Ministers' Conferences). The Act incorporated the Canadian Charter of Rights and Freedoms, and thus, for the first time, the courts could strike down federal or provincial legislation on grounds other than a violation of the federal-provincial division of powers. The courts were thereby catapulted into the centre of Canadian political life, although their power was counterbalanced by Section 1 ("The Canadian Charter of Rights and Freedoms guarantees the rights and freedoms set out in it subject only to such reasonable limits prescribed by law as can be demonstrably justified in a free and democratic society") and, less effectively, by the notwithstanding provision in Section 33.[4] It is difficult, therefore, to overestimate the impact of the 1982 Act.

Like the 1867 Act before it, the 1982 Act is also notable for what it did *not* do. Apart from providing some additional protection for the provincial ownership of natural resources, it did not modify the existing federal division of powers despite its being the focus of 15 years of constitutional debate. The Act, like its predecessor, did not embody any expression of popular sovereignty; the assent of the Canadian people was required neither for its passage in 1982 nor for its subsequent amendment.[5] Although the amending formulas do require legislative consent and not just the signatures of the first ministers, direct popular consent is not needed. Parliamentary institutions, including the appointed and widely scorned Senate, were left untouched. The most outstanding omission, however, was the Act's silence on the national question or, more specifically, on the place of French Canada and Quebec in the national fabric. The Act did constitutionalize the co-equal status of the English and French languages, but it did not address Quebec's role as a founding partner in Confederation. It did not provide any special role for Quebec in the amending formulas, nor did it address long-standing Quebec aspirations for a larger share in the federal division of powers.

The Act's silence on these issues provided a critically important *implicit* statement. Silence implied that Quebec had no special role, that the terminology of "founding peoples" had been rejected, that the Constitution could be amended in many respects without Quebec's consent, that Quebec provincial legislation would be subject to the Charter and to interpretation by a Supreme Court that Quebec played no role in appointing, and that the Quebec National Assembly would exercise (at least formally) the same powers as other provincial legislatures. In short, *Quebec within the 1982 Act was a province like the others*. This message was driven home when the new Constitution took effect even though it had not been signed by Quebec Premier René Lévesque and had been rejected by an all-party resolution passed in the Quebec National Assembly.

Here was a fascinating paradox: nearly two decades of constitutional debate, driven largely by the nationalist movement in Quebec, finally gave birth to a new constitutional order that failed to address (except by silence) the central concerns of the nationalist movement and was rejected by Quebec.[6] Indeed, it can be argued that with the possible exception of the constitutionalization of official bilingualism, the 1982 Act could well have been written by the rest of Canada without any reference to Quebec. Thus, the new constitutional order initiated by the desire to quell the sovereigntist movement soon led to a reinvigorated national unity crisis. Donald Smiley's 1983 description of the Act as a "dangerous deed" was prophetic.

The Legacy of 1982

The proclamation of the Constitution Act in 1982 left Canada an awkward legacy: a constitutional process designed to assuage nationalist sentiment in Quebec had instead rendered the province a constitutional outsider, bitter and angry that a new constitution had been "imposed" without its consent. Although the 1982 Act, and particularly the Charter, had been well received in the rest of Canada, Quebec political elites proved an exception. (Quebec elites did not oppose the liberal values embedded in the Charter but rather the constraints of Canada-wide jurisprudence on Quebec legislation.) It was inevitable, therefore, that someone would try to address this legacy and bring Quebec back into the "constitutional family." The man who stepped into this breach was Prime Minister Brian Mulroney who, during his term of office stretching from 1984 to 1993, enjoyed strong electoral support in Quebec.

Mulroney made two attempts to bring constitutional peace to the land: the Meech Lake Accord, drafted by the 11 first ministers in the early spring of 1987, and the Charlottetown Accord, put together through a much more elaborate process extending from the summer of 1991 to the late fall of 1992. Although both ended in failure, leaving the formal constitutional text unchanged, they had a lasting impact on constitutional conventions and the process of constitutional reform. Both, moreover, encapsulated a particular vision of the Canadian federal state, and it is the defeat of this vision that forms our new constitutional legacy for the twenty-first century.

Although there is insufficient space here to describe in detail the content of the two accords or the political dynamics in which they became enmeshed, it should be stressed that both were built around the core principle that Quebec should be recognized as having a constitutional status in some way distinct from that of other provinces. The Meech Lake Accord, put together in a private meeting of the 11 first ministers and with virtually no public anticipation much less participation, embraced little more than this principle. Quebec was to be recognized as a distinct society, and in light of this recognition, additional constitutional amendments were proposed relating to Quebec's role in immigration, constitutional amendment, the appointment of Supreme Court judges, and opting out of national social programs without financial penalty. Meech Lake was conceived and described as the "Quebec round" in an ongoing process of constitutional reform; other issues were delayed until the hypothetical rounds to follow. Issues such as Senate reform or the constitutional recognition of Aboriginal self-government, it was argued, could only be addressed once Quebec's aspirations had been satisfied and the Quebec National Assembly had retroactively endorsed the 1982 Constitution Act.

The Meech Lake Accord, even though it came within a whisker of ratification, is now remembered as a major failure and serious miscalculation by the Mulroney government. Failure came not on the heels of public outcry but rather through a series of miscues in New Brunswick, Manitoba, and Newfoundland. True, public support had waned considerably when the Accord finally died in the late spring of 1990, but there was no reason to conclude that Canadians had rejected the Accord's principled core. However, there was a broad political consensus on two important conclusions. First, any future attempt at constitutional reform would have to entail a much broader process of public consultation; reform could no longer be entrusted to "11 white men" meeting behind closed doors. An inevitable consequence of broader consultation would be an expanded reform agenda, and hence the second conclusion: Quebec's constitutional aspirations could no longer be addressed first or in isolation. The "Quebec round" in 1987 therefore became the "Canada round" in 1992 when Quebec's concerns were addressed in conjunction with the constitutional aspirations of Senate reformers, Aboriginal peoples, social democrats, feminists, environmentalists, and whatever other group or interest was able to shoulder its way to the increasingly crowded constitutional table.

There is no doubt in my mind that both conclusions were sound and seemingly inescapable, yet they also led to a constitutional process in 1991–92 that was unworkable. Too many competing demands hatched too many compromises, and the diluted final product—the Charlottetown Accord—satisfied no one. Senate reform was proposed—but not in a form that appealed to true believers in the West. Quebec's specificity was addressed—but not to the satisfaction of even "soft nationalists" in that province. Perhaps the only ones whose concerns were fully, even exceptionally, addressed were Aboriginal peoples, whose interests were woven into virtually every clause of the Accord. (Even then, Aboriginal people in the end did not support the Accord.) When it became clear that Quebec, Alberta, and British Columbia would hold referendums before ratification, the federal government reluctantly agreed to hold a rest-of-Canada referendum in conjunction with the Quebec vote. Despite endorsement from all federal parties except the Reform Party of Canada, and from aboriginal leaders, all provincial governments, and the business community, the Canadian electorate was not impressed. On October 26, 1992, the Accord went down to national defeat. Only voters in Newfoundland, Prince Edward Island, New Brunswick, and, by the narrowest of margins, Ontario approved the Accord. Across the country, 45.7 per cent voted "yes" and 54.3 per cent "no," virtually identical to the 43.3/56.7 per cent split in Quebec alone.

The referendum defeat brought the reform process to a shuddering halt. Intergovernmental constitutional negotiations stopped, and public consultation was avoided like the plague. If countries can "burn out" politically, then Canada had. Thus, when the PQ government held a referendum on sovereignty (with an economic partnership) in October 1995, the rest of the country could do little more than hold its collective breath. When the referendum was defeated by a very narrow margin—approximately 50,000 votes province-wide—the federal Liberal government rushed legislation through Parliament recognizing Quebec as a distinct society within the operations of the federal government and "lending" Parliament's veto to Quebec, thereby ensuring that Parliament could not pursue constitutional amendments without the prior consent of the Quebec National Assembly. (In effect, Parliament unilaterally overrode the 1982 amending formula by granting Quebec a *de facto* veto.) Still, the formal text of the Constitution was left unchanged, and there is little evidence that electoral support for independence was significantly eroded by the jerry-rigged amending formula and parliamentary recognition of an established fact of Canadian political life: that Quebec's concerns were to be treated with special sensitivity within the federal government.

In the wake of the 1995 Quebec referendum, the nine premiers from outside Quebec met in Calgary to consider a non-constitutional offer to the people of Quebec, an offer couched for the most part in general principles that might be acceptable across the country. Quebec would be recognized as a distinct society, but within a framework of individual *and provincial* equality, in more limited terms than in either the 1987 or 1992 accords, and through acts of provincial legislatures rather than in the formal text of the Constitution. The Calgary Declaration escaped the assumed prohibition on another "Quebec-only" round by appealing to general principles and characteristics of Canada, and by sidestepping the formalities of constitutional reform altogether. The Declaration was presented as an alternative to constitutional reform, although it is hard to escape the suspicion that the drafters saw it as much as a precursor as they did an alternative. Certainly the federal government, which had served as the behind-the-scenes midwife for the Declaration, did little to promote it as a constitutional initiative once mixed reviews came in from the Quebec electorate. The assumed need for public consultation was met by post hoc public consultations that differed from province to province, but in all cases stopped short of referendums.

The Calgary Declaration may have provided a modicum of constitutional relief. However, when the PQ government went to the people in a 1998 provincial election, the Declaration did little to equip federalists within the province with a "new offer" from Canada and it was soon abandoned even outside Quebec as a useful initiative. Francophone support for the sovereigntists held firm, and the arrival of former federal Progressive Conservative leader Jean Charest to lead the provincial Liberals had little immediate effect. The PQ was re-elected and promised to hold another referendum as soon as the "winning conditions" could be ensured. Canada's uneasy perch on the knife-edge of uncertainty continued.

The federal government's response to this uncertainty was the 1999 Clarity Act, which gave the national Parliament the right to determine whether any future referendum question met the Supreme Court's reference case requirements for a "clear majority" on a "clear question." In the words of the Act, the House of Commons and not provincial governments would determine if a referendum question on secession provided "a clear expression of the will of the population of a province on whether the province should cease to be part of Canada and become an independent state." The Clarity Act, however, does not define a clear majority, although it is assumed that 50 per cent plus one would fall short. The Quebec National Assembly responded in turn with Bill 99, which rejected the application of either the Supreme Court reference case or the Clarity Act to Quebec, deeming both unacceptable limitations on the democratic will of the Quebec people. While there is no question that, through the Clarity Act, the federal government holds the upper hand in a legal sense, the political dynamics—should another sovereignty referendum be held—are by no means clear.

Constitutional Politics: Back to a Slow Simmer

What, then, can be said of constitutional politics in the second decade of the twenty-first century? Certainly there is an emphatic consensus among political elites that Canadians are both wary and weary of constitutional debate; the failure to ratify the 1992 Accord has been taken to heart, and it will take an extraordinary set of circumstances to embolden political leaders to embark again on formal constitutional change. At the very least, mega-constitutional packages of the type exemplified by the 1992 Charlottetown Accord are not on the horizon, and even more limited constitutional initiatives such as Senate reform (discussed in more detail below) are argued to be impossible because they would require "to open the Constitution." Canadians, it is assumed and asserted, would much prefer to make do with political institutions poorly designed for the nineteenth century rather than engage in constitutional reform. And, to be sure, the existing amending formula, coupled with the commitment to public ratification found in Alberta, British Columbia, and Quebec, has rendered formal change difficult in the extreme. When the 1996 parliamentary amendments to the formula are taken into account—those that require regional acceptance before parliamentary action can even be initiated—the task seems virtually impossible. The constitutional status quo, for better or for worse, is assumed to be the legacy for our children and their children. We are, in a constitutional sense, an extraordinarily conservative country.

But what about the past drivers of constitutional reform? Will their pressure for change cease? Here the major player is still Quebec and, as the 2012 election of a minority PQ government demonstrates, the sovereigntist threat will never disappear. However, a *constitutional* response by the rest of Canada to that threat looks increasingly unlikely. There is no constitutional middle ground beyond the status quo that will appease significant numbers of sovereigntists and at the same time be acceptable to the rest of the country. Three decades of effort have dispelled any illusion that a compromise can be found.[7] Instead, we may be locked into a perpetual, albeit low-keyed, game of "constitutional chicken" between the status quo and an independent Quebec, a game in which one side or the other (or both) swerves at the last second, but does so only to race headlong toward a political crisis again. It is also a game for which there is no discernible audience outside Quebec, and perhaps even a diminishing audience within Quebec. Mega-constitutional change is more likely to come in the wake of Quebec's departure than it is to occur as a way to prevent that departure. There is simply no appetite within the current federal or provincial governments, or within the Canadian electorate, for a return to devising proposals for *pre-emptive* constitutional change. The country has moved on, and for most Canadians, and for many in Quebec itself, traditional national unity concerns have simply fallen off the screen.

In terms of other drivers of constitutional change, there is little doubt that the political power of the Aboriginal community has increased quite dramatically since the debate over the proposed Charlottetown Accord, and continues to increase. Nor have we made much headway in terms of land claim settlements and, more broadly, in building a new relationship between Aboriginal communities and the Canadian state. Both might appear to beg for constitutional resolution. What is not clear, however, is whether there is any appetite among Aboriginal peoples for formal constitutional change, or indeed any perceived need for it. As recent court decisions dealing with the rights of non-status Indians, Metis land settlements, and the "duty to consult" on resource development have demonstrated so emphatically, the constitutional status quo and a sympathetic Supreme Court provide Aboriginal peoples with a great deal of leverage (Chartier, 2013). Thus the general thrust of Aboriginal legal arguments is that Aboriginal rights and entitlements already exist; all that is missing is their full recognition and implementation by Canadian governments. The constitutional strategy, therefore, is one of articulating a deeper understanding of the status quo, and there is no interest in engaging in the treacherous and quite possibly unsuccessful pursuit of formal constitutional change. Why bother when the courts have used the existing constitution to such dramatic effect?

Interest in constitutional change as a means to address regional discontent is also fading in western Canada, in large part because regional discontent itself is fading as the West takes on a more prominent and powerful economic and political role in the national community. Senate reform, long the flagship of western Canadian constitutional politics, now enjoys at best tepid support among western Canadian governments and their electorates, and it is unclear whether the Triple E reform model long championed in the West—equal, elected, and effective—would still serve regional interests, particularly in the case of Alberta and British Columbia.

Somewhat surprisingly, and in marked contrast to past federal governments of all partisan stripes, the Government of Canada is the primary, indeed almost the only, champion of Senate reform left standing. Since forming the government in 2006, Stephen Harper's Conservatives have initiated a series of legislative initiatives to impose term limits on senators and to give provincial governments a much larger role in the selection of senatorial nominees. The federal government has also adhered to Alberta's Senatorial selection process. Throughout, however, the constitutionality of the government's initiatives has been vigorously contested, and thus in early 2013 the government asked the Supreme Court, through a reference case, to rule on whether the federal government can enact its proposed reform measures without provincial consent. If the Supreme Court rules that it cannot, and that the constitution must be re-opened if the Senate is to be reformed in any substantial way, then reform will be dead in the water for at least another generation even as the Senate itself sinks more and more into public disrepute.

In summary, the former advocates of constitutional change have either left the building or appear to be on their way out. Quebec nationalists and federalists, Aboriginal Canadians, and western Canadians have all but abandoned constitutional change as a political strategy, as have most of the more peripheral constitutional players of past decades—feminists, environmentalists, economic nationalists, and proponents of electoral reform. Canadians and their governments have also come to the conclusion that the constitutional status quo imposes few if any insurmountable constraints. Quebec's place in Canada continues to evolve, the West has moved from "out" to "in," and Aboriginal communities have racked up victory after victory in the courts. Budgets have been balanced (or not), and the federal government has been able to substantially change the nature of Canadian federalism by pulling back from provincial areas of responsibility such as health care, devolving greater policy autonomy to the Northwest Territories, and simply refusing to participate in multi-player intergovernmental relations; the prime minister has not called a first ministers conference with his provincial counterparts since 2009.

All of this, of course, does not mean that the Constitution writ large will be static in the years to come. It means only that the formal text is unlikely to change, and the Canadian electorate is unlikely to become embroiled again in constitutional politics. In many other ways change to the constitutional status quo will still occur. As noted above, in 1996 the federal Parliament unilaterally altered the constitutional amending formula by "lending" its constitutional veto to Quebec, thus demonstrating that even the amending formula is not immune to unilateral amendment. In a 2006 resolution, the Québécois were formally recognized as a nation by Parliament and the federal government has granted Quebec the right to send its own representative to international meetings of the Francophonie and UNESCO. In other areas, the federal government under the Harper Conservatives has pulled back from provincial areas of social responsibility and devolved its control over northern resources to the territorial governments, bringing them closer to province-like status. The Nisga'a and Nunavut settlements of the late 1990s show that a constitutionally entrenched third order of government can be created without modifying the text of the Constitution Acts of 1867 and 1982, and smaller-scale *de facto* constitutional change can still be pursued through tripartite negotiations among the First Nations, provincial, and federal governments, and through amendments to the Indian Act. The interpretive role played by the courts through their decisions will continue to rewrite and expand existing constitutional provisions. Indeed, and as the American experience has shown, the political rigidity of the formal amending formula gives the courts greater rein to pursue constitutional change through judicial interpretation, and Canadian courts have shown little reticence in this respect. Finally, international agreements arguably have imposed and will continue to impose constraints on Canadian governments that will have constitutional force even though they may not be formally incorporated into Canada's constitutional order.

The future, then, will not be devoid of constitutional politics, broadly defined. Political action and energies, however, will not be directed to formal changes in the written text of the Constitution. (Court action, it should be noted, is always directed to constitutional interpretation, to "reading in" new meaning and not to changes in the written text.) The big issues of the day will be fought within the existing constitutional order rather than being about that order. Moreover, constitutional politics will take place well away from the arenas of public participation, ratification, or consent. It might be argued, therefore, that it was not an oversight in the 1860s when the founding fathers failed to incorporate any notion of popular consent or sovereignty into Canada's constitutional framework. They may have had greater foresight than we often realize.

Notes

1 Canadian governments are able to negotiate with one another because they are not faced with the uncertainty of legislative ratification for any deals that might be struck. Because governments dominate their own legislative processes, they can be confident that any deal brought before their legislatures will be ratified. The only exception to this rule, and it is a big exception, is on the constitutional front, where provincial governments can no longer be confident of their ability to control the legislative and public consultation dynamics of constitutional amendment.

2 These economic powers could, however, be devolved to the market. This happened through the Canada-US Free Trade Agreement and the North American Free Trade Agreement (NAFTA).

3 The amending formulas are set out in Sections 38–49 of the Constitution. The basic formula calls for the consent of Parliament plus the legislatures of at least two-thirds (seven) of the provinces, which, among them, contain at least 50 per cent of the Canadian population.

4 The "notwithstanding" clause allows legislatures to override Sections 2 or 7 through 15 of the Charter for a period of up to five years (renewable) provided that they explicitly do so by invoking the notwithstanding clause.

5 For a still insightful look at the very tentative fashion in which Canadian constitutional politics has embraced popular sovereignty and democratic principles, see Whitaker (1983).

6 Perceptions outside Quebec of Quebec's rejection were blunted by the close association between Pierre Trudeau and the Constitution Act. The fact that Trudeau's Liberals held 74 of the 75 seats in Quebec made it possible to argue that although the government of Quebec rejected the new Constitution, the people of Quebec did not. Whether the people of Quebec sided in this matter with their provincial or federal representatives was not put to the test.

7 It is pessimism in this regard that led Guy Laforest and me to propose a new Canada-Quebec partnership. See Gibbins and Laforest (1998).

References and Suggested Reading

Boyer, Patrick. 1998. "'Whose Constitution is it, Anyway?' Democratic Participation and the Canadian Constitution." In *Challenges to Canadian Federalism*, eds. Martin Westmacott and Hugh Mellon, 79–99. Scarborough: Prentice Hall.

Cairns, Alan C. 1995. "The Constitutional World We Have Lost." In *Reconfigurations: Canadian Citizenship and Constitutional Change*, ed. Douglas E. Williams, 97–118. Toronto: McClelland and Stewart.

Chartier, Clément. 2013. *Métis Land and Natural Resources Developments*. Report presented on behalf of the Métis National Council at the Aboriginal Lands and Natural Resources Forum, Ottawa, May 30–31.

Gibbins, Roger. 1997. "Quebec and the West." *Québec Studies* 24 (Fall): 34–45.

Gibbins, Roger, and Guy Laforest, eds. 1998. *Beyond the Impasse: Toward Reconciliation*. Montreal: Institute for Research on Public Policy.

LaSelva, Samuel V. 1996. *The Moral Foundations of Canadian Federalism: Paradoxes, Achievements, and Tragedies of Nationhood*. Montreal: McGill-Queen's University Press.

McRoberts, Kenneth, ed. 1995. *Beyond Quebec: Taking Stock of Canada*. Toronto: Oxford University Press.

McRoberts, Kenneth, and Patrick Monahan, eds. 1993. *The Charlottetown Accord, the Referendum, and the Future of Canada*. Toronto: University of Toronto Press.

Russell, Peter H. 1993. *Constitutional Odyssey: Can Canadians Become a Sovereign People?* 2nd ed. Toronto: University of Toronto Press.

Smiley, Donald. 1983. "A Dangerous Deed: The Constitution Act, 1982." In *And No One Cheered: Federalism, Democracy, and the Constitution Act*, eds. Keith Banting and Richard Simeon, 74–95. Toronto: Methuen.

Taylor, Charles. 1993. *Reconciling the Solitudes: Essays on Canadian Federalism and Nationalism*. Montreal: McGill-Queen's University Press.

Thomas, David M. 1997. *Whistling Past the Graveyard: Constitutional Abeyances, Quebec, and the Future of Canada*. Toronto: Oxford University Press.

Whitaker, Reg. 1983. "Democracy and the Canadian Constitution." In *And No One Cheered: Federalism, Democracy, and the Constitution Act*, eds. Keith Banting and Richard Simeon, 240–60. Toronto: Methuen.

four

The Dynamics of
Canadian Federalism

RICHARD SIMEON, IAN ROBINSON, AND JENNIFER WALLNER

Introduction

Federalism is perhaps the most visible and distinctive element in Canadian
political life. More than in most other advanced industrial countries, our
politics have been conducted in terms of the conflicts between regional and
language groups and the struggles between federal and provincial governments. Many of our most important political issues—from the building of
the postwar welfare state, to the energy wars in the 1970s, to the constitutional wars of the 1980s and 1990s, to more recent economic and fiscal
crises—have been fought in the arena of federal-provincial relations and
shaped by the institutions of the federal system. It is clear that the very
structure of Canadian federalism, with its ebb and flow of power between
federal and provincial governments, has been at the heart of our political
debates.

We can think of federalism in several ways. Federalism refers, first, to a
particular set of governing *institutions* (the classic definition comes from K.C.
Wheare, 1964). It is a system in which political authority is divided between
two or more constitutionally distinct orders or levels of government. Each
has a set of constitutional powers such that neither is subordinate to the
other; each has an independent base of political legitimacy in the electorate
and should thus deal directly with its respective citizens as each government exercises its powers (Watts, 2008). In Canada, we talk of federal and
provincial governments. Municipal governments are also important in the
lives of Canadians, but they do not have independent constitutional status.
Furthermore, some speculate that Aboriginal governments may one day
constitute a "third order of government," parallel to federal and provincial
governments (Royal Commission on Aboriginal Peoples, 1993). For the moment, however, Ottawa and provincial governments take centre stage in the
political theatre of the Canadian federation.

Several other elements are central to the design of federal institutions
(Watts, 2008). There is the *constitution*, which sets out the *division of powers* and the relationships among the governments. In the Canadian context, there has been increasing debate about whether it is necessary for all

provinces to have identical powers ("symmetrical federalism") or whether powers can either formally or informally vary according to the needs and characteristics of individual provinces, as in the case of Quebec ("asymmetrical federalism") (Smiley and Watts, 1985). Most federal constitutions also create a Supreme Court, one of whose central purposes is to act as umpire between the orders of government, and an *amending formula*, establishing procedures for altering the division of powers and other elements in the constitution. Since one of the central characteristics of all federal systems is the wide range of shared and overlapping responsibilities (*interdependence*), federal institutions also include a set of *mechanisms of intergovernmental relations* (first ministers' conferences and the like) through which the governments deal with each other. Associated with these mechanisms is a complicated set of *fiscal arrangements* dividing up the revenue pie, financing shared responsibilities, and assisting the poorer provinces through equalization payments. Almost unique among federal countries, Canada is largely lacking in one other institution—that is, a *second chamber* in the Canadian Parliament explicitly designed to represent the states or provinces within central decision-making. Unlike the American Senate or the German Bundesrat, the Canadian Senate has conspicuously failed to play this role, thus forcing struggles within our federal system to be worked out between governments whose relations sometimes take on the character of international negotiations, or "federal-provincial diplomacy" (Simeon, 2006).

Federalism, then, is at heart an *institutional structure*—joining parliamentary or Cabinet government and, since 1982, the Charter of Rights and Freedoms, as one of the three institutional pillars of Canadian government. Each of these pillars embodies a somewhat different conception of democracy; they coexist in a dynamic tension (Cairns, 1992).

Second, federalism can be seen as *a characteristic of the society*. We talk of Canada as a "federal society" (Livingston, 1956). By that we mean the salience of differences that are organized and expressed largely on the basis of region or territory. Such differences may be rooted in language, history, and culture or in differences of economic interest. They interact strongly with the institutional dimension of federalism: Canada has federal institutions largely because of the initial differences in interest and identity among the founding provinces. But federal institutions, in turn, perpetuate these regional differences and reinforce Canadians' tendency to see politics in regional terms. Beyond simple regional differences, Canada is also a multinational democracy with two predominant internal nations—Quebec and Aboriginal Peoples—that coexist with the rest of Canada (Gagnon and Tully, 2001). These features of the Canadian polity serve to reinforce and are in turn reinforced by the federal institutions.

Third, federalism is underpinned by *multiple identities*. Citizens can be members of both a national community, ideally embodied in the national government, and provincial communities reflected in their provincial governments (Black, 1975). If the balance falls too far to one side, there remains little to hold the system together in the face of demands for provincial independence; if it falls too far the other way, there is little to prevent the aggrandizement of federal power and movement toward a unitary state. Federalism is thus about the coexistence of multiple loyalties and identities; about divided and shared authority; "national standards" and provincial variation; "self-rule" and "shared rule"; "coming together" and "coming apart." Finding the right balance among these is the trick. Much survey evidence confirms that Canadians are, indeed, federalists in this sense, valuing both their national and their provincial identities (Graves et al., 1999; Cutler and Mendelsohn, 2001). However, while being "federalists," Canadians have never come to a universal agreement about what the balance of powers between the federal and provincial governments should be or even what it is in practice. It is these debates about the balance of powers—which order of government should have the ability and capacity to act in certain areas—and changes to them that lie at the heart of many of the conflicts in the Canadian federation.

What ideas underpin a federal union? Federalism is often justified as a means by which different regional/linguistic communities can live together in a single state. On the one hand, it helps preserve local communities by assuring them the opportunity to manage their own affairs through their provincial government without fear of domination by the majority; on the other hand, it allows them to pursue their common interests through the federal government. Federalism is thus said to combine "*shared rule* through common institutions and *regional self rule* for the governments of constituent units" (Watts, 2008: 1). In the American political tradition, federalism is seen, along with the Bill of Rights and the separation of powers between the president and executive, as a way to check and limit excesses of governmental power through the separation of powers and "checks and balances." And in democratic theory, federalism serves the interests of popular sovereignty by placing governments closer to the people and by allowing citizens to pursue their interests through several governments (Simeon, 1983).

The interpretation that political leaders and other members of society have about a federal union—its purpose, the appropriate balance between shared rule and self-rule, and the legitimate role of the state in society—often lie beneath the crafting and maintenance of federal institutions (Burgess, 2001; Rocher and Smith, 2003). Those who desire a strong nation embodied in the central government, for example, will seek to invest Ottawa with greater authority while those emphasizing the virtues of self-rule will call for the empowerment of the provinces. In the meantime, members of an internal nation may petition for powers comparable to the central government and distinct from the other provinces, in pursuit of self-determination. Others that wish to curb the power of the state, in the meantime, may opt to place firm boundaries on the respective powers of the orders of government, adhering to what is known as a "water-tight" model of federalism. Ideas about federalism and their salience at particular points in time inform political leaders as they make choices, thus influencing the shape and character of the federal union.

In this chapter, we will talk about all three dimensions of Canadian federalism and see how different ideas of federalism have appeared in Canada over time. Our focus is primarily on what drives the federal system and what accounts for the changes over time. In this sense, for the most part we treat federalism as a *dependent variable*. Tracing the evolution of the Canadian federation, we discover that the country has transformed from a highly centralized system, where Ottawa could easily override provincial decisions in pursuit of "national interests," into a federation where the provinces enjoy considerable political authority, powers, and financial resources. In fact, according to a recent study completed by the Forum of Federations that compared 11 federations, Canada ranks as one of the most decentralized (Majeed, Watts, and Brown, 2006). Despite this transformation, at times the provinces find themselves subordinated to the federal government, leading some scholars to examine a "federative deficit" that persists in Canada today (Caron et al., 2009). What explains the relative balance of power and influence between federal and provincial governments? What explains the nature and level of conflict or disagreement among them? What accounts for the ways in which they manage their interdependence?

We can also look at federalism as an *independent variable*. Here we focus on the consequences of federalism. Does federalism make a difference? What are its effects on public policy or the structure of identities? Do some groups or interests benefit by federalism; are others weakened? How does federalism structure our party system or the role and strategies of interest groups? Many answers to such questions have been given, and most assume that federalism does shape our political life in profound ways. The links between the politics and institutions of federalism and specific outcomes, however, are often very difficult to trace (Fletcher and Wallace, 1986; Bakvis and Skogstad, 2008).

Viewing federalism as an independent variable quickly shades into a third kind of question: evaluation or judgement. Does federalism contribute to the quality of Canadian democracy? To making public policy that is timely and effective? To the successful management of the diverse social groups that make up the Canadian population?

On all these dimensions, federalism seems to point in two directions. It offers the democratic virtues of governments closer to the people and to local needs, but the closed nature of much intergovernmental decision-making has led many to report a "democratic deficit" (Simeon and Cameron, 2002; Laforest and Montigny, 2009). Federalism suggests effective ways to balance national and regional concerns in public policy, but again it can be criticized for slowing policy responses in areas where the responsibilities of governments overlap. This is the so-called "joint decision trap" (Scharpf, 1988). Finally, federalism does provide valuable tools for accommodating differences, providing regional and linguistic minorities with provincial governments they can use to pursue their own interests and resist control by the national majority. But at the same time, federal institutions help institutionalize and perpetuate these same divisions (Cairns, 1977; Simeon and Conway, 2001).

Evaluation, of course, also depends on the perspective and criteria one brings to the task. And, like the ranging ideas and interpretations about federalism articulated by political leaders, academics are engaged in similar debates about the balance of powers in practice. An important distinction in assessments of federalism in Canada is that scholars in Quebec tend to see it as centralized and Ottawa-driven, subordinating Quebec's autonomy (see Gagnon, 2009). English-speaking scholars tend to stress how decentralized it is and how much autonomy provinces enjoy (Caron et al., 2009: 136). Thus, similar facts can produce quite different views.

No single theoretical approach can possibly account for the evolution of the federal system over more than a century. We bring together elements of both societal and state-centred approaches, and we focus on the *interaction* between them. The causal arrow points both ways. In particular we emphasize the impact of economic and social forces in setting the basic context within which federalism operates. But how these forces are channelled and expressed, and how successful they will be, is in turn greatly influenced by the federal structure and by the choices made by individual leaders.

We begin with the Confederation settlement, then trace the period from 1867 to the 1920s, showing how centralized federalism, based in part on the extension to Canada of the British colonial model, was replaced by a more province-centred and *classical* form of federalism. Then we look at the crises that faced Canadian federalism in the Depression and World War II, followed by the development of the Keynesian welfare state through *cooperative federalism*. The period from 1960 to 1982 saw the intensification of federal-provincial conflict, driven first by Quebec nationalism and later by the resurgence of provincialism, especially in the West. We call this *competitive federalism*. Following 1982, we trace the conflicting pressures on federalism engendered on the one hand by the continuing need to resolve regional and linguistic tensions and on the other by the need to respond to newly mobilized social forces, armed with the Charter of Rights and Freedoms, which challenged many aspects of federal politics. This was the period of *constitutional federalism*. Woven through these social divisions were profound economic changes, which also challenged many elements of contemporary federalism. By the late 1990s, after the failures of constitutional federalism, attention turned to alternative ways to adapt and modernize the federation and to develop new strategies for provincial and federal governments to work collaboratively on economic and social issues (Lazar, 1998). We call this pattern *collaborative federalism*. But this was also the era of globalization (which some saw as hollowing out central governments and relocating power upwards to international corporations and institutions and downwards to smaller governments); of debts, deficits, and fiscal restraint that generated new tensions in the federal system; and of neoliberal strategies for economic development and public management, which also had implications for federalism (Lazar, Telford, and Watts, 2003). By 2008–09, the global economic crisis, combined with the perceived failures of collaboration, had shifted the environment again. Today we see an effort to return to *classical federalism* inspired in part by neoliberalism and the discourse of austerity, with Ottawa pursuing an agenda of disentanglement to separate the actions and activities of the two orders of government. As we shall see, change is seldom moving in one direction, and the economic and social pressures are not always synchronized.

The Confederation Settlement

Three sets of concerns drove the fiercely independent clutch of British colonies in British North America to create the Canadian federation in 1867. The first was political. The attempt to join what is now Quebec and Ontario into the single united province of Canada in 1840 had resulted in political deadlock that frustrated both language groups. The second was economic. Britain was dismantling colonial preferences that had given Canadian exports a competitive edge in Britain; the small separate colonies, deep in debt, were increasingly unable to borrow the funds needed for their economic development. The solution appeared to be the creation of a new national market reaching from sea to sea. That would require the creation of a new national state. The third concern was security, as the weak Canadian colonies feared the dominance of their powerful and expansionist neighbour to the south and sought strength in greater numbers. But what form would this new country take?

Sir John A. Macdonald, his eye on nation-building, would have preferred a powerful unitary state built on the British parliamentary model. But this was unacceptable to Quebec, which feared the dominance of the English-speaking majority, and to the other colonies, fearful of losing their independence. If there was to be a new country, it would have to be a federal one, like the United States. Even then, the Atlantic colonies were reluctant brides, and Prince Edward Island and Newfoundland initially remained outside the union.

And what kind of federalism would it be? Would it be weighted to a dominant central government or to strong provinces? Would it share responsibilities across the governments or divide powers into exclusive areas of jurisdiction or "water-tight compartments"? Which level of government would control the financial levers? Would there be a strong Senate to represent provincial interests in Ottawa? How would federalism be reconciled with the parliamentary model inherited from Britain? Again, the colonial negotiators had different ideas and different models to choose from.

In the end, the British North America Act (the BNA Act, later renamed the Constitution Act, 1867) was a compromise, adopting elements from among the competing views. On its face, though, the new Constitution leaned toward the centralized model. The federal government was given the powers thought to be essential to creating the new economic union—jurisdiction over trade and commerce, interprovincial transportation, banking, currency, and the like. It was also given responsibility for Aboriginal peoples and for protecting some minority religious and language rights. It had the power to raise money by any mode of taxation. More generally, the BNA Act seemed to place the federal government in much the same relationship to the provinces as Britain had been to its former colonies. Section 91 gave Ottawa the broad general power to make laws for the "peace, order and good government of Canada," and it was not initially clear that the list of specific responsibilities following was any more than a set of examples. The federal government was to appoint the lieutenant-governors of the provinces, and they were to have the power to "reserve" provincial legislation for the pleasure of the governor general. Moreover, Ottawa had a broad "declaratory power," which would allow it to bring "works and undertakings" in the provinces under federal control. On top of that was an unlimited power to "disallow" or invalidate any or all provincial laws (Simeon and Papillon, 2006).

Despite the centralizing thrusts of the BNA Act, provinces were given wide responsibilities as well, especially in matters of local and provincial concern, such as education, health, and what later came to be described as social policy. Many of these provincial powers were later to gain vastly increased importance as the modern welfare state was created. The provinces also had a broad, imprecise, residual power in "property and civil rights," which again was to expand as the regulatory role of the state increased in social, economic, and environmental affairs. Thus, the Constitution reflected differing and potentially competing models and ideas of federation. It also left some notable gaps: the Senate was to provide equal representation to regions, but unlike the American Senate, members were to be appointed by the federal government, thus vitiating its role as a strong regional voice. Nor was there a method for future amendment of the Constitution: that was to remain in British hands, on the request of the federal government. Also missing was a judicial umpire to resolve intergovernmental disputes. The federal government was empowered to create a Supreme Court, but ultimate judicial authority was to remain with Britain's highest court, the Judicial Committee of the Privy Council, until 1949. All these omissions and ambiguities meant that different groups could interpret the federal bargain very differently, each drawing on those aspects of the Constitution that appeared to support their preferred vision and interests. They also meant that the federal system would be adaptable enough to respond to shifting visions and policy agendas.

Colonial Federalism

After 1867 the federal government vigorously pursued the nation-building project. Western settlement led first to the creation of the province of Manitoba, and later Saskatchewan and Alberta. British Columbia joined with the promise of a railway to link it to the East. The transcontinental railway became a cornerstone of the Conservative government's National Policy of 1878. Western producers were expected to consume tariff-protected Canadian farm implements and supplies, while selling their products largely in international markets, thus creating conditions of provincial subservience to a "national" agenda.

Initially, Sir John A. Macdonald's government vigorously asserted the extraordinary powers of disallowance and reservation. Favouring a more provincialist interpretation of the constitution, provincial governments started resisting this model of centralized federalism. Ontario and Quebec organized the first interprovincial conference in 1887 to coordinate their demands and strategize against the federal government. In contrast to the colonial model, with its implied subordination of the provinces, Ontario Premier Oliver Mowat argued that Confederation was a "compact" among the provinces, which implied that the federal government was a creature of the provinces. This debate has reverberated through much of the subsequent history of the federation.

Macdonald's aggressive assertions of federal authority rested on precarious foundations. First, looking at the economy, centralization was not accompanied by the anticipated prosperity that could have cemented federal dominance. Second, considering the Canadian society, growing Protestant-Catholic and French-English conflict further fuelled pressures for a more decentralized federalism.

Most profound was the growing alienation of French Canada. The federal government's decision to let Louis Riel hang following the Rebellion of 1885, along with its failure to use its constitutional power to protect the rights of Catholics and French speakers under attack by provincial legislatures, led many Québécois to believe that they were destined to become a diminishing minority in Canada outside Quebec.

The moral of the story seemed obvious to many French Canadians: only where they were a majority—which was to say, only in Quebec—would their religious and linguistic rights be secure. Even then, they would be safe only if the government of Quebec had the final say on these matters within that province. These conclusions led inexorably toward the identification of language and religion with the provincial rather than the national community and to a constitutional orientation bent on strengthening the powers of the provincial government rather than improving minority rights at the federal level. In other words, the "French Canadians" became *les Québécois*.

Classical Federalism

Thus—with the notable exception of emergency centralization during World War I—the pendulum swung to the provinces. Much of the new resource and industrial development took place largely under provincial jurisdiction. Provincial revenues swelled, reducing their dependence on federal subsidies. The federal government's powers of reservation and disallowance were rarely used (though they remained in the Constitution), and in the era of the minimal state, federal and provincial responsibilities seldom overlapped. With important exceptions, such as battles between Ontario and Ottawa over resources and timber exports, intergovernmental conflict was relatively muted.

All this ended with the Great Depression of the 1930s. The resulting crisis of the state was also a crisis for federalism. With unemployment above 20 per cent, there was enormous pressure for welfare and relief, which fell largely on the provinces; at the same time their revenues shrivelled. Several provincial governments, like Saskatchewan, were driven to the brink of bankruptcy. A variety of ad hoc federal relief programs were put together, and in 1937 the federal government established the Rowell-Sirois Commission to recommend reforms to the federal system. In the United States the primary legislative response to the crisis was Franklin Roosevelt's New Deal, which was eventually declared constitutional by the American Supreme Court. These landmark decisions, based on a broad interpretation of the American trade and commerce power, effectively established the predominance of the central government in the American federal system. In Canada the Conservative Prime Minister R.B. Bennett sought to emulate Roosevelt with his "Bennett New Deal." His successor, Mackenzie King, referred the package to the Judicial Committee of the Privy Council, which ruled its key provisions *ultra vires*—beyond the powers of the federal government. The courts also reinforced the classical and decentralized model of federalism in other cases, as in the *Labour Conventions* case (1937), where federal legislation implementing an international agreement on hours of work and other matters that fell within provincial jurisdiction was overruled.

This experience led many observers, especially on the left, to mount a fundamental critique of the federal system. For the British scholar Harold Laski, federalism was "obsolete," unable to deal with the problems of a complex industrial society or to manage fiscal crisis. To Canadian critics, such as F.R. Scott (1977), the "dead hand" of the federal Constitution was a fundamental barrier to progressive reform. World War II temporarily halted such debates, as Ottawa assumed virtually all the powers of a unitary government under the emergency powers of the War Measures Act. But what sort of federalism would peacetime bring?

Many commentators built on the critics of the 1930s. Modernization, in this view, would inexorably push toward centralization. The emergence of national—and international—economic actors meant that the regulatory reach of the state had to be similarly expanded. Industrialization and urbanization inevitably meant that "traditional" identities rooted in language, ethnicity, and region would decline in significance to be replaced by interests and identities defined in class terms. Moreover, the economic and social roles of the state were changing as governments began to play a greater role in the management of the economy and in building a redistributive welfare state. Only central governments, with a national perspective and control of the major fiscal, jurisdictional, and bureaucratic resources, it was felt, could effectively play these new roles. Thus, writers such as Alec Corry (1958) predicted a steady flow of influence to Ottawa, echoing John A. Macdonald's much earlier hope that the provinces would one day be reduced to the role of municipalities. Provincial governments, however, had no wish to concede powers to Ottawa, and they possessed important constitutional and institutional powers to resist massive centralization.

The result of the interplay of these forces was that the new roles for the state were adopted with remarkably few changes to the federal Constitution. The major elements of social security—unemployment insurance and pensions—were shifted to Ottawa through constitutional amendments. But the primary instrument of adaptation was the federal spending power—the largely un-challenged ability of the federal government to spend money even on matters that lay within provincial jurisdiction. Because the new roles of government cut across jurisdictional lines, interdependence, overlapping, and sharing of responsibilities became the hallmarks of modern federalism in Canada as in all other federations. Along with this increased interdependence came an increased need for fiscal and administrative arrangements to manage inter-governmental relations. Hence, there was a steady increase in the number and scope of intergovernmental meetings. By 1970 Donald Smiley was to identify "executive federalism"—negotiations among officials and ministers of the federal and provincial governments—as a central characteristic of the Canadian policy-making process (Smiley, 1974). Political and economic events of the early twentieth century had thus rendered the water-tight compartments model of classical federalism obsolete as federal and provincial activities became increasingly entangled, ushering in the new period of co-operation between the two orders of government.

Cooperative Federalism

In 1945 the federal government placed before the provinces a comprehensive set of proposals known as the Green Book proposals. Ottawa would assume responsibility for some areas, such as pensions and unemployment insurance (already achieved in a 1940 amendment), and achieve national programs in other aspects of health and welfare through the sharing of costs with the provinces. In return, Ottawa would retain control over major tax fields and would make compensating grants to the provinces. These centralizing pro-posals were flatly rejected by wealthy Ontario, as well as British Columbia and Quebec. But over the next few years, most of their elements were put into place.

Unemployment insurance, pensions, and family allowances gave Ottawa responsibility for the basic income security system. The rest of the welfare state programs came about through the use of the federal spending power in the form of shared cost, or conditional grant, programs. These included hospital insurance in 1955, expanded to full medical care in 1968; assistance to post-secondary education; provisions for aid to disadvantaged groups, consolidated in the Canada Assistance Plan of 1968; and a host of smaller programs. Thus, the "complexities of federalism" may have slowed, but did not prevent, the implementation of the postwar project common to most advanced industrial countries (Banting, 1987).

Many of these activities advanced without major federal-provincial conflict. The postwar agenda did not divide Canadians sharply on regional lines. Provinces in most cases accepted federal leadership and welcomed the financial assistance that enabled them to spend "50-cent dollars." Furthermore, the federal government also established the first formal equalization program in 1957, installing the country's commitment to revenue-sharing and perhaps assuaging regional tensions before they could fester. Provincial pressure was also able to ensure that, unlike American "grant-in-aid" programs, the conditions in most programs were relatively loose and accommodating to provincial priorities. Intergovernmental relations tended to be conducted among officials within the various program areas. Provinces often reported onerous federal conditions or the distortion of provincial priorities by the lure of federal spending, but fundamental constitutional issues were pushed aside: federalism was largely an administrative matter.

There was one major exception to this generally harmonious pattern. From the very outset of the modern period, Quebec governments were strongly opposed to the expansion of federal policy influence. Quebec governments of all political stripes favoured a decentralized form of classical federalism, a vision clearly articulated by the Tremblay Commission (Royal Commission of Inquiry on Constitutional Problems) in 1956. In the Duplessis years, the Quebec government was closely allied with both the conservative wing of the Catholic Church and business interests that strongly objected to the expansion of the postwar welfare state into areas previously left to the Church and voluntary organizations. Thus, Quebec rejected both the content of the postwar model and the means by which it was achieved. Throughout the 1940s and 1950s, therefore, its strategy was largely to resist federal encroachments rather than to expand provincial powers.

Competitive Federalism

Competitive federalism refers to several changes from the postwar cooperative model: the escalation of interregional and intergovernmental conflict, stronger pressures for decentralization, expansion by both levels of government into new policy fields in a form of "competitive expansionism" or "province-building versus nation-building," and increasing efforts by both levels of government to mobilize their populations around competing images of federalism and how it should work. The process was triggered by the Quiet Revolution in Quebec.

The election of Jean Lesage's Liberal government in 1960 swept away the conservative coalition that had dominated Quebec politics. The Quiet Revolution embraced the secular modern bureaucratic state and its policy agenda. But the Québécois were to become *maîtres chez nous* (masters in our own house)—Quebec, not Ottawa, was to be the instrument. Hence, Quebec governments went beyond the resistance exemplified by Duplessis to seek the powers and financial resources with which they could undertake the same kinds of policies on behalf of the Québécois nation that the federal government was undertaking on behalf of the English-Canadian nation, without constitutional interference or financial penalty.

At first, Quebec's demands focused on fiscal arrangements and specific programs. Quebec led successful renegotiations of federal-provincial fiscal arrangements to give provinces a greater share of tax revenues and to enrich the equalization program. It also was able to achieve a measure of *de facto* special status in several areas: the establishment of a separate Quebec Pension Plan and the "opting out" of several shared-cost programs in return for a greater share of taxes.

It was not long, however, before the debate escalated to the constitutional level. Lesage's successor, Daniel Johnson, sought more fundamental changes, expressed in the slogan "*égalité ou indépendance.*" The Constitution should recognize Canada as a partnership of two nations, one centred in Ottawa, the other in Quebec City. More important, in 1968 René Lévesque founded the Parti Québécois from disaffected Liberals and other nationalist groups and led the party to power in 1976. The PQ model was "sovereignty-association," an independent Quebec that would maintain ties with the rest of Canada in a binational framework. Federalism, Lévesque argued, frustrated both sides: English Canada could not have the strong central government it desired; Quebec could not have the freedom it sought. Thus, among Quebec leaders the debate was now between those who sought greater autonomy for Quebec within a federal structure and those who argued for independence.

The alternative model was expressed by Pierre Trudeau, who came to Ottawa in 1965 expressly to battle what he considered a retrograde Quebec nationalism. Quebec's future, he argued, lay in a bicultural, bilingual, united Canada, in which Quebecers were strong participants in the national government and enjoyed rights from sea to sea. Recognition of Quebec as the primary political expression of Quebec society was to him an anathema; even the modest steps toward *de facto* asymmetry, he believed, were leading down a slippery slope whose outcome could only be separation. Thus, Trudeau insisted both on a strong central government and on the equality of all the provinces. The politics of federalism became dominated by a much larger debate over the future of Quebec and the country. The process culminated in the 1980 Quebec referendum, in which the PQ lost by a significant margin its request for a "mandate" to negotiate sovereignty-association. The subsequent constitutional negotiations, resulting in the Constitution Act, 1982, gave Canada a Charter of Rights and an amending formula but rejected not only the sovereigntist position but also that of Quebec federalists.

By the 1970s other provinces, especially the larger wealthier ones, were also mounting a challenge to the Ottawa-dominated federalism of the post-war period. In part this reflected the growing resources, competence, and confidence of provincial governments and their bureaucracies, which, fuelled by federal transfers, had been growing much faster than the federal government. As issues such as the environment entered the public agenda, both levels of government competed to enter the field. Provincial governments were less willing to accept federal definitions of national priorities. More generally, the rapid economic growth of the postwar period had ended, and Canada, like other countries, entered a period of economic volatility and instability that exacerbated regional tensions and forced a rethinking of the Keynesian economic policies that had inspired the creation of the welfare state. Increasingly, provinces sought to control the policy levers to ensure their ability to manage the economy—a phenomenon that came to be known as "province-building."

Nowhere were these economic difficulties more evident than in the field of energy. The energy shocks of the 1970s provoked profound regional conflict, pitting energy-producing provinces, like Alberta—or those who were potential producers, like Newfoundland—against central Canada. The producers sought to move toward world energy prices, to retain the proceeds of their provincially owned resources, and to enhance their capacity to manage energy development. Consuming provinces looked to the federal government to keep prices down and to ensure that oil and gas revenues would be shared across the country. The escalating conflict culminated in the federal National Energy Program (NEP) of 1980, in which the federal government asserted sweeping control over the industry—provoking Alberta briefly to limit the flow of oil to the rest of the country. The battle also tapped deeply held grievances in the West and in the smaller provinces about their economic and political subordination to central Canada and the federal government.

Thus, a provincial reform agenda emerged alongside Quebec's: on one hand, the provinces sought to limit the federal spending power and its ability to intervene in areas of provincial jurisdiction; on the other, they wanted to strengthen their own financial resources and powers in areas important to them. Also expressed was the idea of "we want in": a greater role for the provinces at the centre, reflected in the demand for Senate reform and in the growth of the Reform Party in the West. Increasingly, debates within federalism took the form of rival conceptions of the very nature of the system—the province-centred view, which saw Canada as a "community of communities" and governing Canada as a partnership between Ottawa and the provinces, and the "Canada-centred" view, which saw Ottawa as the primary order of government. It all culminated in the drawn-out battle over the Constitution following the 1980 Quebec referendum.

Constitutional Federalism

By the early 1980s, Canadian federalism had come to be dominated by the "high politics" of the Constitution. The 1982 constitutional settlement, while excluding Quebec, was otherwise a compromise: the nation-centred view was reflected in the Charter of Rights and Freedoms, to be enforced by the Supreme Court; the province-centred view was reflected in the amending formula, which ensured a strong provincial role in future amendment. After 1982 there was a brief hiatus in the conflict; a more harmonious federal-provincial relationship seemed likely when the Progressive Conservatives under Brian Mulroney were elected in 1984. The Mulroney government had all the authority of a sweeping mandate, with the most seats in every province. Moreover, by winning over many Quebec nationalists while maintaining its Western base, the Mulroney coalition seemed to bridge the fundamental divide in Canada. In his election campaign, Mulroney promised to find a way to "bring Quebec back into the Constitution with honour," to kill the National Energy Program (NEP), and to govern Canada as a collaborative partnership between the two orders of government.

The Quebec goal was achieved in the Meech Lake Accord of 1987. However, public opinion turned against the Accord, and three newly elected provincial governments, which had not been party to the original agreement, sought fundamental changes. Three years later the Accord died in a welter of recriminations. In Quebec the demise of Meech Lake was seen as a rejection of even a minimal set of objectives, adding insult to the exclusion of 1982. But in English Canada the mood was very different. Meech Lake had revealed a profoundly different political climate in the rest of the country. The advent of the Charter had shifted the constitutional discourse: now it was less about governing the relations among governments than a vehicle for popular sovereignty, defining the relations between citizens and governments. It was a Constitution more for citizens than for governments. The constitutional agenda broadened vastly, and the legitimacy of making constitutional change in the closed-door setting of first ministers' conferences was fundamentally challenged. So was the idea that compromise carefully crafted by elites could not be allowed to unravel in the legislative ratification process.

The changed climate in English Canada threatened key elements of the Quebec agenda. Many groups rejected any form of asymmetry or special status for Quebec: the Constitution should reflect the equality of citizens and the equality of the provinces; there should be no hierarchy of rights in which the rights of language groups would be privileged over the rights of women, multicultural groups, or Aboriginal peoples; Ottawa's ability to establish and enforce national standards in areas of provincial jurisdiction should not be limited. Moreover, there were new items on the constitutional agenda, notably the call for a "Triple E Senate"—equal, elected, and effective—and the Aboriginal peoples' call for the right to self-government.

The federal-provincial process was renewed in 1991. Now the leaders of the Aboriginal peoples and of the two territories were at the table. The resulting Charlottetown Accord sought to respond to the diverse forces at play, but the divisions were too wide to bridge and the process had lost its legitimacy. The consequence was the defeat of the Accord in the referendum of October 1992.

Constitutional federalism had failed. It did not disappear—the 1995 Quebec referendum on "sovereignty-partnership" and the subsequent federal Clarity Act saw to that. But now the emphasis would be on "making the federation work better" through "non-constitutional renewal," including, for example, passage of a federal resolution recognizing Quebec as a distinct society within Canada and a federal commitment not to support any constitutional amendment without the consent of Quebec (Lazar, 1998).

Collaborative Federalism

Constitutional federalism focused primarily on the character of Canada as a political community—on Quebec and Canada, the role of national and provincial governments, and the ability of federalism to accommodate the emergence of new identities and interests. But throughout this period Canada was also undergoing a wrenching set of economic changes in the face of an integrating global and North American economy, competition from newly industrialized nations, increased integration of financial markets, and the like. In some sense the Canada-US Free Trade Agreement and its successor, the North American Free Trade Agreement, constitute an "economic constitution" that parallels Canada's political constitution, with profound implications for the future of the Canadian political economy (Robinson, 2003). The changed economic climate also raised questions about the relative responsibilities of the two orders of government.

Trade also raised the question of the economic links among Canadian provinces. Ontario's manufacturing economy was turned 90 degrees from a tariff-protected east-west orientation to an open-border north-south one. Canada's economic regions were becoming less linked to each other than they were to other parts of the world, with important implications for regional disparities, for the ability to generate national policies, and for the long-run commitment to equalization or interregional sharing. Some argued that this suggested the need for a stronger federal government; for others, it was provinces that were more capable of forging the links among business, government, and labour necessary for economic success (Courchene, 1992).

A second fundamental challenge to federalism arose from the escalation of government debt and deficits at both levels of government. In the 1990s we saw a "federalism of restraint" as governments competed to reduce their deficits and avoid political blame. Thus, the 1995 federal budget rolled transfers for health care, welfare, and post-secondary education into a single "block grant," the Canada Health and Social Transfer (CHST). While there were fewer federal controls over how the money would be spent, this was accompanied by a dramatic reduction of $6 billion, or 37 per cent, over two years. This in turn helped drive up provincial deficits and threatened to erode the federal government's ability to shape national priorities through its use of the spending power: with its share in the cost of major social programs plummeting, what right would it have to call the tune? Thus, the elaborate structure of intergovernmental transfers that had been a hallmark of Canadian federalism came under profound challenge.

These pressures—combined with constitutional fatigue—helped fuel calls for a focus on the need for Canadian governments to work together. The first manifestation of this collaborative, non-constitutional approach to improving the management of the Canadian federal system was the Agreement on Internal Trade (AIT) in 1994, which was intended to address long-standing concerns about the strength of the Canadian economic union through intergovernmental collaboration (Trebilcock and Schwanen, 1995). Attention then turned to the "social union," the complex set of intergovernmental agreements through which the major elements of social policy—health, post-secondary education, and welfare—are developed and delivered. Here the issue was whether and how Canadians across the country could enjoy national standards while also permitting the variations in policy necessary to meet the needs of different provinces.

A Provincial-Territorial Ministerial Council on Social Policy Reform and Renewal was formed. Its work eventually led to a meeting of first ministers in February 1999, at which the Social Union Framework Agreement (SUFA) was adopted. This agreement included such commitments as equality of treatment across the country, access by all Canadians to adequate social programs wherever they live, the reduction of barriers to mobility among provinces, and greater transparency and accountability. In addition, the governments committed themselves to "mutual respect" and to working "more closely together to meet the needs of Canadians" (SUFA, 1999), including an obligation to plan social policy together and to consult before introducing new programs. For its part, Ottawa agreed that when using conditional transfers, it would "proceed in a cooperative manner that is respectful of the provincial and territorial governments and their priorities" (SUFA, 1999). A year's notice would be given before any change in funding. Moreover, it would not introduce any new program without the prior agreement of most provinces. Provinces would be responsible for "detailed program design," and where they already had a program in place, they would still receive the new funds, which could be used in related areas. This went some way to meeting provincial concerns that federal funding could distort provincial priorities.

There were, however, significant shortcomings (Noël, 2003). Ottawa did not concede any limitations—except for a commitment to prior notice and consultation—on its power to make direct grants to individual Canadians in areas within provincial jurisdiction (e.g., direct grants to post-secondary students). Furthermore, while the agreement also included a commitment by the governments to develop "timely, efficient, effective, transparent, and non-adversarial" mechanisms for avoiding and resolving intergovernmental disputes, such institutions were never formally entrenched. Consequently, the intergovernmental machinery that emerged in this period, including the Council of the Federation created by the provinces in 2004, have remained largely ad hoc, with no constitutional or statutory base, taking no votes, and the agreements signed have no enforceable legal status. Each government remains accountable only to its own legislature. Finally, the SUFA did not explicitly provide for provinces to opt out of new shared-cost programs and still receive federal funding, as an earlier interprovincial draft had suggested. This has been a long-standing goal of successive Quebec governments. Its omission led Quebec Premier Lucien Bouchard to refuse to sign the agreement. The actual impact on Quebec's finances would probably be minimal, but symbolically the isolation of Quebec meant that the distinct society status that had proved so difficult to achieve in the constitutional forum was becoming a reality in the daily practice of Canadian federalism.

Assessments of collaborative federalism vary. Some question whether governments were ever fully committed to the mutual trust and cooperation that collaboration requires. Agreements remain vague, reflecting the lowest common denominator of what governments can agree to rather than hard choices and commitments. Activists in areas such as social and environmental policy worry that the focus on power and position, combined with a preoccupation with the flow of money between federal and provincial governments, diverts attention from the substance of issues. In fact, the past 10 years have demonstrated that many of the intergovernmental promises made through these collaborations have produced disappointing results. Despite powerful criticisms about meetings behind closed doors, little progress has been made in opening the process to the public. Indeed, it is striking that despite the massive economic and social changes in Canada, the institutions and processes for the conduct of federalism and the dynamic of intergovernmental relations seem to have changed very little in recent decades (Simeon, 2006).

A Return to Classical Federalism?

In the opening years of the twenty-first century, Canada experienced a renewed set of economic pressures due in part to dramatic escalation of energy prices and catastrophic events in the global economy. Provinces with petroleum and natural gas deposits grew rapidly while energy-importing provinces, such as Ontario and Quebec, lost jobs and experienced fiscal contractions, reinforcing interprovincial economic inequalities. Then, in 2007 and 2008, the worst financial crisis since the Great Depression swept the world. While Canada has weathered the crisis relatively well due to policies put in place by previous federal and provincial governments, the country nevertheless experienced its first major economic recession in two decades. In the meantime, a new government took office in Ottawa—the first prime minister from the West to win consecutive mandates since John Diefenbaker—with different views of both the federal system and the role of the state from that held by the previous administrations. Put together, these economic and social pressures have ushered in a new era of federalism in Canada, one that suggests a return to the classical model.

The drive to return to the classical model reflects the pervasive growth of neoliberal approaches to government and the state, held by federal and provincial governments alike. This neoliberal approach includes a profound distrust in the role of the state and its potential for achieving collective goals. It is also closely related to the discourse of austerity, reductions in public spending, tax cuts, deregulation and, overall, downsizing the size and scope of the state writ large. Although the Liberal government did impose massive budget cuts in the 1990s, meaning that evidence of austerity politics can be traced back to the previous era, it was nevertheless willing to gradually reinvest in the state while simultaneously working with the provincial governments to attempt to address key policy challenges of the day. Today, however, the discourse of austerity and the image of the state inspired by neoliberalism held by the Conservative government have generated some interesting changes to the way federalism is practised in the country.

If there is one clear change, it is the withdrawal of Ottawa from working directly to shape the operation of the federal system. Previous federal governments sought to actively mould the relations between the federal and provincial governments. Since 2006, however, a new approach has taken hold. A term coined by Prime Minister Stephen Harper, "open federalism" (Institute of Intergovernmental Relations, School of Policy Studies, 2006) includes a mix of policies that are oriented toward disentangling the two orders of government. In pursuit of this new approach, Ottawa has pulled back from directly intervening in many policy areas and says that it is up to the provinces to work things out. In December 2011, for example, the federal finance minister Jim Flaherty announced a major change to the funding formula for health care, simply informing the provincial and territorial ministers over lunch. Where the previous Liberal government insisted on attaching certain priorities to the funding agreement, the Conservatives focused exclusively on the money itself, leaving everything else up to the provinces to decide. Framed around this idea of "open federalism," Ottawa's new approach to managing the federation is thus centred on getting the central and provincial governments to operate independently within their assigned constitutional powers in an effort to re-establish the classical "water-tight" model of federalism.

The Conservative government has also distanced itself from the intergovernmental machinery that used to bring all federal and provincial representatives together. Since the election of the current government in 2006, only five meetings of first ministers have taken place. Four of these were held at the height of the economic crisis, and all have focused exclusively on the economy. In lieu of multilateral meetings, the federal government now deals with the provinces on a bilateral basis. It therefore seems that the period of collaborative federalism—at least between the federal and provincial governments—appears well and truly over.

Finally, while in office, the Harper Conservatives have introduced tax cuts (such as reducing the Goods and Services Tax from seven to six per cent) and budget cuts that have diminished Ottawa's research and policy capacity (Doern and Stoney, 2012). These cuts, framed around the discourse of austerity and designed to scale back the scope of government writ large, also have implications for the provinces, as those governments will no longer have access to valuable information to support their own policy development and evaluation. The elimination of the mandatory long-form census marked the end of a rich data source that was used by policy-makers to gauge trends and assess the effectiveness of public programs. Similarly, the federal government's decision to close the Experimental Lakes Area, whose research helped explain the causes of acid rain and identified such hazards as rising mercury contamination from coal-fired power plants (Paris, 2013), means that the funder and sponsor of scientific evidence that provides the foundation for environmental policies will no longer be the federal government.

Interestingly, there are signs that the provinces are continuing with the collaborative approach among themselves, attempting to fill the leadership vacuum created by federal withdrawal. Frustrated with the lack of progress on the AIT, some Western provinces have spearheaded a parallel process to strengthen the common market at the regional level through the New West Partnership. Ontario and Quebec have also signed a Trade and Cooperation Agreement designed to foster their respective economies and reduce inter-provincial barriers to trade, investment, and labour mobility. Ontario also decided to step in and provide operating support for the Experimental Lakes Area facility to keep the research going. Indeed, the Council of the Federation could prove to be a valuable tool, if the provinces decide to use it effectively. Although it is too early to say conclusively, a side effect of Ottawa's approach of open federalism may be increasing provincial leadership in a variety of policy areas.

These changes to federalism, driven in part by the politics of austerity, have nevertheless been accompanied by striking continuities. During the period of cooperative federalism, constructing the welfare state was a key priority for the federal government, and in pursuit of this policy agenda Ottawa intervened in many areas of provincial jurisdiction. The current federal government is focused on the common market and immigration and similarly intervenes in areas of provincial jurisdiction pertaining to those arenas. After taking office, the federal government sought to introduce a centralized system to manage securities and replace the existing regime that is managed by the provinces independently. Led by Quebec and Alberta, several provinces challenged the initiative in the Supreme Court, which ruled in favour of the provinces. Despite being rebuffed by the Court, the Minister of Finance recently announced that the federal government will establish a common regulator on its own (Canadian Press, 2013). More recently, Ottawa announced that it was reclaiming authority over labour market training, cancelling Employment Insurance training transfers to the provinces (Ivison, 2013). The federal government has also cancelled long-standing intergovernmental agreements for immigrant settlement programs in an effort to establish Ottawa as the sole authority in this area (CBC News, 2012). Like previous federal governments, the current government is thus clearly willing to unilaterally intervene in areas of provincial jurisdiction in pursuit of their preferred policy agenda.

When faced with the global financial crisis, moreover, Ottawa—albeit initially unwillingly—ended up spearheading Canada's response to recovery (Simeon et al., 2013). The plan, introduced in the federal budget of January 2009, included a two-year stimulus package executed primarily through federal-provincial cost-matching in infrastructure. Working together through expedited negotiation processes, federal and provincial officials used existing agreements to rapidly inject money into the Canadian economy. Similar to the federal leadership supported by provincial cooperation witnessed in response to previous crises—such as world wars and the Great Depression—the successful navigation of major events required the intervention of both orders of government in Canada collectively engaging the levers of the state, despite the discourse of austerity.

Finally, the influence of austerity has yet to impact the intergovernmental transfer system. The major federal transfers in health and social policy remain in place (Doern and Stoney, 2012). Designed to ensure that each province, rich or poor, can provide similar programs at a similar cost to taxpayers, equalization continues to be a cornerstone of Canada's fiscal architecture. The neoliberal emphasis on promoting efficiency has nevertheless sparked new debates about the value and effectiveness of equalization with some wondering if the idea of Canada as a "sharing community"—or as a former premier put it, "a giant mutual insurance company"—is now unsustainable (Simeon et al., 2013). In 2014, the Canada Health Transfer (CHT), the Canada Social Transfer (CST), and the equalization accord are all set to expire. Only time will tell if the politics of austerity will end up fundamentally reshaping the fiscal architecture of the Canadian federation.

It is too early to conclude what the long-term impact of the recent turn to austerity politics will be. Some may be concerned that Ottawa's disengagement may tilt the balance too much in favour of provincial independence. Quebec continues to pursue its own path, particularly in social policies, further distancing itself from the rest of Canada. Other provinces are also striking out in new ways in a variety of social and economic fields. The question then becomes: Will the Canadian federation be flexible enough to accommodate these alternative paths without shattering? In the meantime, however, Ottawa's efforts to disentangle the two orders of government and return to the classical model have been impeded by both the institutional realities of the federation and the multifaceted challenges that face Canadians today. Causal factors in Canadian federalism thus continue to interact in complex ways, and change will not be in one direction.

Conclusion

Federalism, it has been said, is a "process" rather than a steady state. This has been abundantly true of Canadian federalism throughout its history, as the governments and institutions that make it up have responded to changing circumstances and shifting policy agendas. In this chapter, we have focused on the interaction between the history, institutions, and practices of Canadian federalism and the broader socioeconomic and political environment in which they are embedded. Most broadly, we have seen how postwar federalism has shaped and been shaped by economic growth, by rival conceptions of nationhood, and by the growth of the welfare state. We conclude with a few of the current and future challenges that the system faces.

1. *Alleviating the "democratic deficit."* How can intergovernmental relations be rendered more open and transparent to citizens? This could involve opening the process to more citizen participation or strengthening the role that parliaments and legislatures play in debating and scrutinizing the conduct of intergovernmental relations.

2. *Alleviating the "policy deficit."* Here the concerns are how to shift federal-provincial debates from often sterile arguments over turf, money, and status to a greater concern for the substance of issues. Behind that is the question of how to find the right balance between "national standards" that will apply across the whole country and the variations in policy that federalism is designed to encourage. And there is the further question of whether effective policy is more likely to emerge from close collaboration between governments or through more vigorous and open competition and debate between them. Another continuing challenge is getting the roles and responsibilities—and the financial resources to pay for them—right. Provinces have recently reported a "fiscal imbalance," arguing that the chief areas of growing government spending lie largely in their jurisdiction while Ottawa has more access to revenues. The solution, they say, is not in greater use of the federal spending power to act in areas of provincial jurisdiction but to move more taxing powers to the provinces. Social policy advocates have often worried that a declining federal role may lead to the erosion of national standards and a "rush to the bottom" in provincial programs. To date there is little evidence of this, however (Harrison, 2005).

3. *Accommodating difference.* Many of the difficulties in reconciling East and West, French- and English-speakers in Canada lie not in federalism itself, but in larger elements of our institutional structure discussed elsewhere in this book—an ineffective Senate, an electoral system that exaggerates regional differences, a regionally fragmented party system, and a parliamentary system that is dominated by the executive, leaving little room for individual MPs to speak for their local interests. This analysis suggests that simply improving the institutions of intergovernmental relations is insufficient. With respect to Quebec, the continuing question is how much "symmetry"—whether formal or informal—is possible or desirable in the Canadian federation.

4. *From federalism to multilevel governance.* Local governments provide a vast array of services, yet are constitutionally subordinate to the provinces. Local governments—especially the large urban areas that are the centres of economic growth and multiculturalism—are now calling for greater recognition and authority, for greater financial resources, and for seats at the intergovernmental table. Whether, and how, they will be integrated into the Canadian pattern of multilevel governance is an important question for the future. The same is true for Aboriginal governments. The idea that they would constitute a "third order of government" in Canada was included in the 1993 Charlottetown Accord and was a central recommendation of the Royal Commission on Aboriginal Peoples, but it has not been enacted. Nevertheless, court decisions and political negotiations are moving toward self-government, and critical questions remain about how they will relate to both federal and provincial governments in the future.

5. *Reform at the centre.* The practice of Canadian federalism focuses on the interstate dimension—the relation between the orders of government. But another aspect of federalism has been labelled "intrastate federalism," which focuses on the representation of the federal characteristics within central institutions. One reason for the strength of Canadian provinces is the weakness of Canada's federal government in this regard: an electoral system that emphasizes and exaggerates regional differences, a Parliament where party discipline makes it difficult for members to speak for their regional and local interests, and a Senate that fails to represent either provincial governments or regional populations (Smith, 2004; Simeon and Nugent, 2008).

6. *Responding to crisis.* In earlier times of national crisis such as the Great Depression, Canadians have tended to look to the federal government for leadership. In 2009, as Canadians faced an economic crisis at once local, national, and global, the pattern of federal leadership repeated itself. Despite federal withdrawal from the intergovernmental machinery in a variety of policy areas, when faced with a major crisis the governments were able to collaborate on coordinated solutions and prevented competing interests from frustrating coordinated action.

References and Suggested Readings

Essential resources for all students of federalism and intergovernmental relations in Canada and elsewhere are: The Institute of Intergovernmental Relations, School of Policy Studies, Queen's University, Kingston (http://www.iigr.ca); the Forum of Federations (http://www.forumfed.org); L'Idée Fédérale (http://www.ideefederale.ca); and the Institute for Research on Public Policy (http://www.irpp.org).

Bakvis, Herman, Gerald Baier, and Douglas Brown. 2009. *Contested Federalism: Certainty and Ambiguity in the Canadian Federation*. Toronto: Oxford University Press.

Bakvis, Herman, and Grace Skogstad, eds. 2008. *Canadian Federalism: Performance, Effectiveness and Legitimacy*. 2nd ed. Don Mills: Oxford University Press.

Banting, Keith. 1987. *The Welfare State and Canadian Federalism*. 2nd ed. Montreal: McGill-Queen's University Press.

Black, Edwin. 1975. *Divided Loyalties: Canadian Concepts of Federalism*. Montreal: McGill-Queen's University Press.

Burgess, Michael. 2001. "Competing national visions: Canada-Quebec relations in a comparative perspective." In *Multinational Democracies*, eds. Alain-G. Gagnon and James Tully, 257–74. Cambridge: Cambridge University Press. http://dx.doi.org/10.1017/CBO9780511521577.019.

Cairns, Alan C. 1977. "The Governments and Societies of Canadian Federalism." *Canadian Journal of Political Science* 10 (04): 695–725. http://dx.doi.org/10.1017/S0008423900050861.

Cameron, David, and Richard Simeon. 2002. "Intergovernmental Relations in Canada: The Emergence of Collaborative Federalism." *Publius: The Journal of Federalism* 32 (2): 49–72. http://dx.doi.org/10.1093/oxfordjournals.pubjof.a004947.

Canadian Press. 2013. "Ottawa Prepared to Go It Alone on Securities Regulator." *Maclean's*, March 22. http://www2.macleans.ca/2013/03/22/ottawa-prepared-to-go-it-alone-on-securities-regulator/.

Caron, Jean-François, Guy LaForest, and Catherine Vallières-Roland. 2009. "'Canada's Federative Deficit." In *Contemporary Canadian Federalism: Foundations, Traditions, Institutions*, ed. Alain-G. Gagnon, 132–62. Toronto: University of Toronto Press.

CBC News. 2012. "Manitoba Angry about Federal Immigration Changes." *Canadian Broadcasting Corporation*, April 13. http://www.cbc.ca/news/canada/manitoba/story/2012/04/12/mb-immigration-services-changes-manitoba.html.

Corry, J.A. 1958. "Constitutional Trends and Federalism." In *Evolving Canadian Federalism*, ed. A.R.M. Lower, 51–64. Durham: Duke University Press.

Courchene, Thomas. 1992. *Rearrangements: The Courchene Papers*. Toronto: Mosaic Press.

Cutler, Fred, and Matthew Mendelsohn. 2001. "What Kind of Federalism do Canadians (Outside Quebec) Want?" *Policy Options* (October): 23–29.

Doern, G. Bruce, and Christopher Stoney. 2012. "The Harper Majority, Budget Cuts, and the New Opposition." In *How Ottawa Spends, 2012–2013*. Montreal: McGill-Queen's University Press, 3–31.

Fletcher, Frederick J., and Donald C. Wallace. 1986. "Federal-Provincial Relations and the Making of Public Policy in Canada." In *Division of Powers and Public Policy*, ed. Richard Simeon, 125–206. Toronto: University of Toronto Press.

Gagnon, Alain-G., ed. 2009. *Contemporary Canadian Federalism: Foundations, Traditions, Institutions*. Toronto: University of Toronto Press.

Gagnon, Alain-G., and James Tully, eds. 2001. *Multinational Democracies*. Cambridge: Cambridge University Press. http://dx.doi.org/10.1017/CBO9780511521577.019.

Graves, Frank L., et al. 1999. "Identity and National Attachments in Canada." In *How Canadians Connect. Canada: The State of the Federation, 1998/1999*, eds. Harvey Lazar and Tom McIntosh, 307–54. Kingston: Institute of Intergovernmental Relations.

Harrison, Kathryn, ed. 2005. *Racing to the Bottom? Provincial Interdependence in the Canadian Federation*. Vancouver: University of British Columbia Press.

Hueglin, Thomas, and Alan Fenna. 2006. *Comparative Federalism: A Systematic Enquiry.* Peterborough: Broadview Press.

Institute of Intergovernmental Relations, School of Policy Studies. 2006. *Open Federalism: Interpretations, Significance.* Kingston: Institute of Intergovernmental Relations.

Ivison, John. 2013. "Ottawa Set to Cancel $2-Billion in EI Training Transfers to the Provinces." *National Post,* March 13. http://fullcomment.nationalpost.com/2013/03/04/john-ivison-ottawa-set-to-cancel-2-billion-in-ei-training-transfers-to-the-provinces/.

Laforest, Guy, and Éric Montigny. 2009. "Le fédéralisme exécutif: problèmes et actualités." In *Le parlementarisme canadien,* eds. Réjean Pelletier and Manon Tremblay, 337–78. Quebec: Les Presses de l'Université de Laval.

Lazar, Harvey, ed. 1998. *Canada: The State of the Federation, 1997.* Kingston: Institute of Intergovernmental Relations.

Lazar, Harvey, Hamish Telford, and Ronald L. Watts, eds. 2003. *The Impact of Global and Regional Integration on Federal Political Systems.* Kingston: Institution of Intergovernmental Relations, in association with McGill-Queen's University Press.

Livingston, William. 1956. *Federalism and Constitutional Change.* New York: Oxford University Press.

Majeed, Akhtar, Ronald L. Watts, and Douglas M. Brown, eds. 2006. *Distribution of Powers and Responsibilities in Federal Countries.* Montreal: McGill-Queen's University Press.

Noël, Alain. 2003. "General Study of the Framework Agreement." In *The Canadian Social Union Without Quebec: 8 Critical Analyses,* ed. A.-G. Gagnon, 9–35. Montreal: McGill-Queen's University Press.

Paris, Max. 2013. "Experimental Lakes Area in Danger of Closing." Canadian Broadcasting Corporation, March 7. http://www.cbc.ca/news/canada/story/2013/03/07/pol-experimental-lakes-to-be-mothballed.html

Robinson, Ian. 2003. "Neo-Liberal Trade Policy and Canadian Federalism Revisited." In *New Trends in Canadian Federalism,* 2nd ed., eds. François Rocher and Miriam Smith, 197–242. Peterborough: Broadview Press.

Rocher, François, and Miriam Smith. 2003. "The Four Dimensions of Canadian Federalism." In *New Trends in Canadian Federalism,* 2nd ed., eds. François Rocher and Miriam Smith, 21–44. Peterborough: Broadview Press.

Royal Commission on Aboriginal Peoples. 1993. *Partners in Confederation: Aboriginal Peoples, Self-Government, and the Constitution.* Ottawa: Minister of Supply and Services.

Royal Commission of Inquiry on Constitutional Problems. 1956. *Report of the Royal Commission of Inquiry on Constitutional Problems.* Quebec: Royal Commission of Inquiry on Constitutional Problems.

Scharpf, Fritz. 1988. "The Joint Decision Trap: Lessons from German Federalism and European Integration." *Public Administration Review* 66 (3): 239–78. http://dx.doi.org/10.1111/j.1467-9299.1988.tb00694.x.

Scott, F.R. 1977. *Essays on the Constitution: Aspects of Canadian Law and Politics.* Toronto: University of Toronto Press.

Simeon, Richard. 1983. "Criteria for Choice in Federal Systems." *Queen's Law Journal* 8/3: 131–51.

Simeon, Richard. 2006. *Federal-Provincial Diplomacy: The Making of Recent Policy in Canada.* Toronto: University of Toronto Press. First published 1972.

Simeon, Richard, and David Cameron. 2002. "Intergovernmental Relations and Democracy: An Oxymoron If Ever There Was One?" In *Canadian Federalism: Performance, Effectiveness and Legitimacy,* 1st ed., eds. Herman Bakvis and Grace Skogstad, 278–95. Don Mills: Oxford University Press.

Simeon, Richard, and Daniel Patrick Conway. 2001. "Federalism and the Management of Conflict in Multinational Societies." In *Multinational Democracies*, eds. Alain-G. Gagnon and James Tully, 338–65. Cambridge: Cambridge University Press.

Simeon, Richard, and Amy Nugent. 2008. "Parliamentary Canada and Intergovernmental Canada: Exploring the Tensions." In *Canadian Federalism: Performance, Effectiveness and Legitimacy*, 2nd ed., eds. Herman Bakvis and Grace Skogstad, 89–111. Don Mills: Oxford University Press.

Simeon, Richard, James Pearce, and Amy Nugent. 2013. "The Resilience of Canadian Federalism." In *The Global Debt Crisis: Haunting U.S. and European Federalism*, eds. Daniel Nadler and Paul E. Peterson, 201–22. Washington, DC: Brookings Institution.

Simeon, Richard, and Martin Papillon. 2006. "Canada." In *Distribution of Powers and Responsibilities in Federal Countries. Global Dialogue on Federalism*, vol. 2, eds. Akhtar Majeed, Ronald L. Watts, and Douglas M. Brown, 91–122. Montreal: McGill-Queen's University Press.

Smiley, D.V. 1974. *Constitutional Adaptation and Canadian Federalism Since 1945. Document of the Royal Commission on Bilingualism and Biculturalism*. Ottawa: Information Canada.

Smiley, D.V., and R.L. Watts. 1985. *Intrastate Federalism in Canada*. Toronto: University of Toronto Press.

Smith, Jennifer. 2004. *Federalism. The Canadian Democratic Audit*. Vancouver: University of British Columbia Press.

SUFA. "A Framework to Improve the Social Union of Canadians." 1999. An agreement between the Government of Canada and the Governments of the Provinces and Territories. February 4. Ottawa: Treasury Board of Canada Secretariat. http://www.scics.gc.ca/english/conferences.asp?a=viewdocument&id=638.

Trebilcock, Michael, and D. Schwanen, eds. 1995. *Getting There: An Assessment of the Agreement on Internal Trade*. Toronto: C.D. Howe Institute.

Watts, Ronald. 2008. *Comparing Federal Systems*. 3rd ed. Kingston: Institute of Intergovernmental Relations.

Wheare, K.C. 1964. *Federal Government*. 4th ed. New York: Oxford University Press.

five

Five Faces of Quebec: Shifting Small Worlds and Evolving Political Dynamics[1]

ALAIN-G. GAGNON

Introduction

The choice of concepts and narratives in the world of politics is not a question of details but rather it is a way to establish a worldview, to order priorities, or—stated more simply—to advance a political posture. So it is not insignificant when political leaders in a federal system speak of levels of government rather than orders of government; or utilize the notion of sub-national units to discuss multinational states; or substitute region for founding member of a federation. Similarly, in the Canadian context it matters when scholars of federalism and politicians alike use the notions of federal government, central government, or the Government of Canada interchangeably. This confuses lines of authority and power relations in the mindset of citizens by subtly suggesting that it does not matter where, how, or by whom decisions are being made.[2]

Richard Simeon made an important point when he stated 35 years ago that the concept of "regions [and other concepts for this matter] are simply containers ... and how we draw the boundaries around them depends entirely on what our purposes are: it is an *a priori* question, determined by theoretical needs or political purposes" (Simeon, 1977: 293). Consequently, when discussing Quebec it is important to come to terms with the objectives being pursued by various individuals, groups, and communities as well as political parties and political entrepreneurs in positions of influence and authority.

Various uses of key concepts such as political nationality, nation, distinct society, province state, and multinational democracy have a significant impact on the way one imagines constituent units in federal states. My intention in this chapter is to introduce the main faces or images of Quebec and the political narratives that have surfaced and resurfaced since the beginning of the Quiet Revolution in Quebec (Gagnon and Montcalm, 1990), and to assess their impact on the mindset of Canadians and Quebecers. I want to make clear at the outset that I have chosen not to include the notion of *stateless nation* to depict Quebec, as this political community has developed for itself major state apparatuses; whether in paradiplomacy, education, culture, economy, or intergovernmental matters, Quebec's activity in these areas would make many existing countries envious of its accomplishments. Nor will I make use of the concepts of *minority nation* or *global society* to discuss Quebec-Canada dynamics, since Quebecers generally conceive of themselves as forming one of the two principal political communities in the country.

Accordingly, in this chapter I will focus on five political faces[3] of Quebec: Quebec as a key partner in the formation of a new political nationality; Quebec as a founding nation in a dualist (binational) Canada, supporting the principle of co-sovereignty; Quebec as a province state that has led the battle for provincial rights and provincial autonomy; Quebec as a distinct society within Canada; and, finally, Quebec as a multinational democracy in its own right.

Face 1: Political Nationality

In the construction of narratives, the place of history matters a great deal, as we will see with the first image of Quebec to be discussed. Canada's beginning is characterized by a series of political events that have had a major impact on how Canadians see themselves. For instance: were French Canadians conquered by the British or did France simply cede its territory north of the 49th parallel to its arch rival? Was Confederation a compact between the French and the English cohabitating on Canadian soil, or was it a political arrangement between the four original provinces and the British imperial government? Who was the depository of sovereignty in 1867, or, stated differently, who formed the constituent power(s)? Contradictory answers have been provided to these questions based on either people's vision of the original compact or the influence exercised by one's dominant identity. George-Étienne Cartier remains a key political figure for Canada throughout the last century and a half. Cartier wanted the new federation, of which he was one of the founding fathers, to be built on political allegiance and loyalty to the country as a whole. This loyalty was not to be based on linguistic or cultural belonging. Cartier promoted a unity respectful of diversity. His understanding of the Canadian experiment, to borrow from Donald Smiley, was that it was a "noble vision" (Smiley, 1967: 128) that repudiated parochialism, majority nationalism, and imperialism; that it did not seek to "impose a single way of life on its citizens" (LaSelva, 1996: 24). "Confederation would be unacceptable if French and English had come together merely to war with each other; it would be equally unacceptable if it created an all-inclusive Canadian nationalism. If Confederation was to succeed, it had to create a new kind of nationality, which Cartier called a political nationality" (LaSelva, 1996: 25). However, it should be pointed out that Cartier's vision arguably failed to provide the core values and claims that would give meaning to being Canadian, while at the same time being respectful of other territorialized and circumscribed identities.

Cartier made it clear that French Canadians would not renounce their culture and identity because of Confederation, although they would form a national community of their own, respectful of different value systems with which "neither the national origin, nor religion of any individual would interfere" (LaSelva, 1996: 25). That being stated, in the years after Confederation the advent of a political community such as the one imagined by Cartier never gained traction. The period preceding the Great Depression of the 1930s can be depicted as a political tug of war between competing images and political projects tied to the differing political interests and intentions of the central state in Ottawa and provincial governments such as Ontario under Mitchell Hepburn (1934–42) and Quebec under Maurice Duplessis (1936–39, 1944–59) (Gagnon and Iacovino, 2007). This is why authors such as J.M.S. Careless have depicted this condition as being the expression of "limited identities" and made clear that Canada was not reducible to a single identity under which all identities were to be subsumed (Careless, 1969).

A point worth mentioning is the role played by the Judicial Committee of the Privy Council (JCPC) as Canada's final court of appeal before the Supreme Court of Canada took on this role in 1949. The JCPC was instrumental in defending the rights and powers of member states of the federation and thereby protecting their "limited identities." This surely contributed to making Quebecers strong defenders of British parliamentary traditions and practices, while encouraging them to continue their support for the Canadian federation.

Another point worth mentioning is the capacity of the central government, along with the nine predominantly anglophone provinces, to repackage over the years Cartier's original notion of political nationality as nothing less than Canada as an all-encompassing nation (Gagnon, 2010). This reinterpretation of Cartier's vision has undoubtedly contributed to the alienation of many Quebecers from central political institutions, and from federalism more generally.

Face 2: The Two-Nations View

The second image of Quebec imagines it as one of two founding nations at the origin of Canada's federal pact. Again it was George-Étienne Cartier who best expressed this two-nations view, without contradicting his more subsuming concept of Canada as a new political nationality. In 1867, Cartier made a statement that would be repeated throughout the following decades: "Such is ... the significance that we must attach to this constitution, which recognizes the French-Canadian nationality. As a distinct, separate nationality, we form a State within a State with the full use of our rights and the formal recognition of our national independence."[4] For Quebec, what mattered most about the constitutional deal embodied in the 1867 BNA Act, as we shall see shortly, was that Quebec's civil law tradition was formally recognized, that provincial autonomy was in matters dealing with education and culture, and further that social policies and language would fall under the jurisdiction of Quebec. Those terms were central in the eyes of French Canadians who saw them as a guarantee of the principle of equality between two founding peoples.

The image of a dualist Canada has been used mostly by French Canadians to depict Quebec-Canada dynamics. It portrays Canada as the constitutional expression of a compact that brought together two nations or, stated differently, two equal peoples with minority linguistic and religious guarantees secured throughout the country as a matter of respect and as a matter of right.

Historian Ramsay Cook, at the time of the Laurendeau-Dunton commission on bilingualism and biculturalism in the 1960s, depicted this view in the following terms:

> In the attempt to protect and extend the rights of the religious and
> linguistic minorities, the theory of Confederation as a compact
> between cultures, an Anglo-French entente, was developed.
> According to this theory, Confederation was a partnership of equal
> cultures whose rights were guaranteed mutually throughout the
> whole Confederation. It can be said that by 1921 the doctrine
> of provincial rights and its compact underpinnings had gained
> the ascendant among Canadian politicians, and was at least partly
> accepted by legal scholars. (Cook, 1969: 65)

While the two-nation view gained some prominence from 1867 to the end of the 1920s, it remains that some prominent English-Canadian historians (Frank Underhill and, closer in time to us, Jack Granatstein and Michael Bliss) refer to Canada as a single nation, showing a lack of sensitivity toward the original constitutive components of the federation (Gagnon and Dionne, 2009: 10–50).

In contrast, the young Pierre Trudeau, in reference to Canada's early history, remarked in 1962 that "British Canadians gave themselves the illusion of it [equating the Canadian state with the British Canadian nation] by walling in, as far as possible, the French fact in the Quebec ghetto—whose powers

were often clipped by centralizing measures—and by fighting with aston-
ishing ferocity against all symbols which could have destroyed this illusion
outside Quebec" (Trudeau, 1962).

This two-nations interpretation gives credit to the view that "Canada"
came into being through the voluntary consent of the two main political
communities. However, there has been a fair amount of debate on this issue,
as central government representatives at different junctures have attempted
to reinterpret Canada's key formative moment and have tried to impose
the view that "Canada" predated the creation of the four original provinces
(Lower Canada, Upper Canada, Nova Scotia, and New Brunswick).

The two-nations view of Confederation argues that, upon entering the
Canadian federation in 1867, Quebec possessed its own political personality
and maintained some of its original powers and institutions that had been
formalized almost a century before in the Quebec Act of 1774, and that had
been bestowed upon it by the British Crown. With Confederation, Quebec
consented to share some of its powers while relinquishing others to the
newly formed federal government. James Tully has argued approvingly in
connection with this point that "[t]he acts of confederation did not discontinue the long-standing legal and political cultures of the former colonies
and impose a uniform legal and political culture, but, rather, recognized and
continued their constitutional cultures in a diverse federation in which the
consent of each province was given" (Tully, 1994: 84–85).

Tully's position has been profoundly influenced by the writing of members of a school of thought rooted in legal pluralism that was clearly influenced by legal experts such as Judge Thomas-Jean-Jacques Loranger and
Judge P.B. Mignault. Judge Loranger summarized his interpretation in his
famous 1883 Letters on the Constitution.[5] That interpretation was later consolidated and further developed by P.B. Mignault. Here is what Mignault had
to say on the notions of shared, divided, and common sovereignties:

> We said that the contracting parties [the federal and the provincial
> governments] divide their sovereignty and create through common
> and reciprocal concessions a new power which contains them
> without absorbing them. We must draw one essential result from this.
> Each state or province maintains its own existence and the powers
> it has not yielded to the central government. The province is not
> subordinate to the central government nor is the latter subordinate to
> the province. There is absolute equality and a common sovereignty;
> each government is supreme within its own jurisdiction and within
> the scope of its power. (P.-B. Mignault quoted in Ramsay Cook,
> 1969: 66).

Michael Burgess and I have updated some of those well-anchored federal ideals in *Federal Democracies* (Burgess and Gagnon, 2010), and Burgess has continued this task in a recent and powerful book titled *In Search of the Federal Spirit* (Burgess, 2012).

It should be noted that this understanding of legal pluralism has been frequently restated and updated by Quebec representatives at various commissions throughout the years. Some examples are provided by the Tremblay Commission (1953–56) and the Bélanger-Campeau Commission (1990–92) as well as during various constitutional negotiations between Ottawa and the provinces.

So the image of Canada as a compact between two founding peoples has continued to be used by representatives of the Quebec government in a consistent manner since Confederation. Over the years, though, and especially after the 1982 patriation of the Constitution Act from Britain, the two-nations view has lost ground in the rest of Canada (ROC). This is due in good part to the fact that the central government has sought to speak as the national government of all Canadians and to impose its political authority accordingly. The receding of the two-nations view is also due to the fact that starting in the late 1960s there has been a growing schism between francophone communities evolving in a minority context in ROC and the Quebec government and people.[6] This is a matter that political scientists and historians alike have for too long neglected to research.

To sum up this section, over time and especially between the beginning of the Quiet Revolution in 1960 and the patriation of the Constitution Act in 1982, Canadians and Quebecers alike have tended to use the notion of dualism to depict the Canadian experiment (Wade and Falardeau, 1960). However, in proceeding with the patriation of the Constitution from Britain and the adoption of the Charter of Rights, Ottawa imposed its view that Quebec ought to be considered as a province like any other. This constituted a major setback for defenders of the notion of Canada as a binational political community.

Let's now turn our attention to a third way of conceiving Quebec.

Face 3: Province State

For many decades, it has been acknowledged that Quebec is not a province like any other, as most students of Quebec politics and provincial politics quickly discover. This said, it remains clear that Quebec has been at the forefront of political battles to uphold provincial rights in the country since its very foundation. In fairness to other provinces, Quebec was never alone in doing so. It has been accompanied by various provincial partners at different historical junctures, though over the past several decades more often than not it has been Alberta and Newfoundland that have joined Quebec at the forefront in defending provincial rights and autonomy in the Canadian federation.

Keith Brownsey and Michael Howlett have introduced the notion of *provincial state* to depict provinces in Canada since "they qualify as states. Not only are they constitutionally empowered to make binding decisions on their residents, they are shaped and defined by the very constitutional arrangements that give them their authority as much as they are by their internal class structures and external economic relations" (Brownsey and Howlett, 2009: 14). These authors made the valuable point that Canadian provinces and territories share significant institutional features that amount to state power. However, they fail to recognize the fact that Quebec is the only member of the federation that can truly be depicted as a *province state* since the principal focus of statehood is international; unlike other provinces, Quebec aspires to play a central role within the Francophonie as well as being a leader among minority nations in the world seeking to obtain a larger political status for themselves.

There is an important stream of political science literature that insists on the central role of Quebec as a historic champion of provincial rights. While that story is generally well known by English-speaking Canadians, it needs to be underlined here considering its influence in the defence of provincial autonomy and the non-subordination of government powers—two central features of federalism.

The Confederation of 1867 embodies a strong defence of provincial rights since the constitution confirmed that powers were to be shared between a central state and provincial states, all of which were to be accountable for their own spheres of jurisdiction before their population. A convention developed that the British North America (BNA) Act provided both the central and provincial governments with exclusive jurisdictions in those domains that were essential to their particular interests. This interpretation emerges clearly from the Quebec resolutions (known also as the *Confederation proposal*). Quebecers cling to their own worldview on this interpretation of Confederation, and ever since then have asked that the spirit of 1867 be respected by their partners, translated into appropriate political institutions, and reflected in power relations.

The most refined depiction of Canada as a compact of provinces was provided by Judge Loranger, one of Quebec's most influential jurists, who published a series of constitutional texts in 1883 that have had a long-lasting effect on Canada's jurisprudence. The most recent echoes can be found in the 1993 and 1995 reports tabled by the Royal Commission on Aboriginal

Peoples. The basic premises of Loranger's account of provincial rights are threefold:

- The confederation made up of the British provinces was the result of a compact entered into by the provinces and the United Kingdom.
- The provinces entered into the federal union with their corporate identity, former constitutions, and all their legislative powers intact. A portion of these powers was ceded to the federal Parliament, to exercise in the common interest of the provinces. The powers not ceded were retained by the provinces' legislatures, which continued to act within their own sphere according to their former constitutions, under certain modifications or form established by the federal compact.
- Far from having been conferred upon them by the federal government, the powers of the provinces are the residue of their former colonial powers. The federal government is the creation of the provinces, the result of their association and of their compact (Canada, Royal Commission on Aboriginal Peoples, 1993: 22–23).

This interpretation laid the foundation for a school of thought supportive of provincial rights and provincial autonomy, exerting much influence within Quebec and some other provinces over the years. It is particularly noteworthy that Loranger's account has gone virtually unchallenged in Quebec. In contrast, many political leaders in ROC and centralizing federalists have usually rejected this view and argued instead that provinces are simply the creation of the central government and therefore subservient to it. At times, this fundamental disagreement created an uneasy relationship between certain provinces and the central government, as illustrated by intense conflicts between Ontario and Ottawa from the 1870s to the 1940s.

Before World War II, Liberal party leaders such as Wilfrid Laurier and Mackenzie King were inclined to support provincial rights as long as they did not weaken Ottawa's political leadership and authority. However, this defence of provincial rights at the federal level declined after World War II as a succession of prime ministers (mostly Liberal) sought to invest the central government in Ottawa with a domineering power position within the federation; this was especially the case under the leadership of Pierre Trudeau and Jean Chrétien.

The 1956 report of the Quebec Royal Commission of Inquiry on Constitutional Problems (the Tremblay Commission) was inspired by the Loranger doctrine. In that report, emphasis was given to the concepts of provincial autonomy and coordination between orders of government (Rocher, 2009: 81–131). Both autonomy and coordination were to operate in tandem;

otherwise the federal spirit would not be fully expressed. Based on this understanding, it was possible (and perhaps even a duty) for a member state of the federation to refuse central government assistance to fully exercise its responsibilities as agreed to in the original compact. Building on the principle of subsidiarity and influenced by the social doctrine of the Catholic Church, the Tremblay Report argued that higher levels of authority should not seek to exercise powers that can be employed more effectively at lower levels. The Report stated:

> Only federalism as a political system permits two cultures to live and develop side by side within a single state: that was the real reason for the Canadian state's federative form (...). So, therefore, there can be no federalism without autonomy of the state's constituent parts, and no sovereignty of the various governments without fiscal and financial autonomy. (cited in David Kwavnick, 1973: 209, 215)

The Tremblay Report provided additional philosophical support to Loranger's earlier arguments. It is this historical and philosophical grounding that has made Quebec's constitutional position so powerful and persistent, to the point that the First Nations have built their arguments upon it to advance their self-government claims, as have provinces such as Alberta and Newfoundland when seeking to defend provincial autonomy.

The Quiet Revolution pursued similar autonomist ambitions for Quebec and pushed them much further than at any time before (Gagnon and Montcalm, 1990). This approach, known as the Gérin-Lajoie doctrine, argued for the extension of provincial jurisdictions beyond the borders of Canada: that is, any provincial competence could be exercised vis-à-vis other provinces or nation-states as long as Quebec (or any provincial state) was willing to assume its sovereign powers in areas of exclusive provincial jurisdiction (Paquin, 2006).

The Gérin-Lajoie doctrine attempted to shore up the role of Quebec as a province state by giving substance and meaning to Quebec's special status within Confederation. This doctrine was elaborated toward the end of the second Lesage government in the mid-1960s and has been revamped at different critical moments under successive Quebec governments, whether liberal in orientation under Premiers Robert Bourassa and Jean Charest or inclined toward social democracy under René Lévesque and Pauline Marois.

The Gérin-Lajoie doctrine remains to this day a constitutional position universally agreed to by key provincial actors in Quebec, and it confirms Quebec's intention to play a central role in Confederation. Brian Mulroney's decision to grant Quebec the status of a participating government in the

Francophonie starting in 1985 was inspired by the respect he had for the Gérin-Lajoie doctrine. One can make a similar remark with respect to Stephen Harper's decision to allow Quebec to play a significant role within the Canadian delegation at UNESCO starting in 2006.

Quebec has been (and continues to be) at the forefront of battles to defend provincial rights, to prevent Ottawa from intruding into provincial domains of competence, and to roll back such intrusion where it has already occurred. The best example is provided by the leadership role played by Quebec in the establishment of the Council of the Federation in 2003, in large part due to the determination of Quebec's former minister of Intergovernmental Affairs, Benoît Pelletier. During his tenure, Pelletier continued to push for the notion of provincial autonomy and made it palatable to government leaders in many other provinces. He spoke at dozens of meetings across the country during the years that followed the election of the first Charest government in 2003, making an important statement at each:

> In its universal aspect, the federal formula implies the existence of two orders of government, each being sovereign in the exercise of their constitutional jurisdictions. However, certain conditions must be met in order for any federation to be able to function and evolve in a healthy manner:
>
> 1. There must be a balanced distribution of powers between the two orders of government.
> 2. Each order of government must have the capacity, in terms of tax resources, to fully and adequately assume its responsibilities. No order of government should find itself in a position of financial dependence vis-à-vis the other.
> 3. The provinces must have the possibility to express their views on the governance of the federation and have a certain influence on the federal legislative process. As an example, this could be accomplished through a truly effective second house of the Federal Parliament, or other equivalent body, where the provinces could assert their points of view and, in so doing, have a real and positive influence on the future of our federation.
> 4. Effective mechanisms must be put in place to foster intergovernmental dialogue in sectors where convergence is required between a priori divergent interests. (Pelletier, 2004)

Quebec has advanced the cause of provincial rights through different means since the end of World War II. Let's mention a few constitutional and political battles that have taken place since then: on the fiscal front, Quebec has fought to regain control over postwar tax-rental agreements and to expand its fiscal powers; on the constitutional front, Quebec has supported the idea of granting all provinces a right of veto over constitutional changes on different occasions (the 1966 Fulton/Favreau amending formula and again at the Patriation conference in November 1981); on the social union front, Quebec has insisted that each and every province could exercise its right to withdraw from a national program that fell within provincial jurisdiction, with full compensation.

Face 4: Distinct Society

In the early 1980s constitutionalist Gil Rémillard (who later became Quebec minister of Intergovernmental Affairs) portrayed the BNA Act as a "constitutional treaty that would permit [French Canadians] to assert themselves as a distinct people on an equal footing with the Anglophone majority" (Rémillard, 1980: 112; also cited in O'Neal, 1995: 3). Politicians and intellectuals alike have used the phrase "distinct society" (and "distinct people") to convey the idea that Quebec possesses a specific culture in North America: a culture that has been shaped by its French language, its Catholic heritage, its civilist tradition, and its British parliamentary institutions. Over the years, the notion of distinct society has been transformed to mean a deep commitment to public policies based on a pronounced social solidarity in the areas of education, culture, daycare, and the third sector or nonprofit segment of the economy, as well as regional development and a progressive fiscal policy.

Notions such as *special status* for Quebec or Quebec as forming a *distinct society* have often been viewed with suspicion as they could constitute a slippery slope pointing toward Quebec's secession. Pierre Trudeau was very keen to undermine the distinct society concept during his tenure as Canada's prime minister (1968–79, 1980–84). However, historian Ramsay Cook reminds us that the idea of Quebec as a distinct society has been present in Canada since the very beginning of Confederation, although we should stress that the use of the notion has been popularized only during the last half of the twentieth century. For example, Cook writes that:

> Section 94 recognized the civil law of Quebec as distinct and, if the intent expressed in that provision had been fulfilled ("uniformity of all and any laws relative to Property and Civil" in all provinces except Quebec), Quebec would have had a "special status" in that area. In addition the special character of Quebec was recognized in Section 133 which not only made French, for the first time, an official

language of Canada, but also made Quebec alone among the original provinces, bilingual. (Cook, 1989: 149–50)

In other words, Quebec's distinct identity was a central pillar of the BNA Act of 1867 and, as we are reminded by the author(s) of *Partners in Confederation* released by the Erasmus-Dussault Commission on Aboriginal Peoples, "The distinct character of the Quebec civil law system was reflected in a clause that allowed the Parliament of Canada to make provision for uniformity of laws in all federating provinces except for Quebec, thus recognizing an asymmetrical element in Confederation" (Canada, Royal Commission on Aboriginal Peoples, 1993: 25).

The notion of distinct society forcefully entered the political milieu in the late 1950s in the wake of the Tremblay Commission (discussed above), as Quebec's provincial political parties tried to identify the best ways to assert Quebec's place within the Canadian federation. Public intellectuals and politicians rallied together to make clear to other partners in the Canadian federation that Quebec needed special instruments to protect the institutions, values, and culture that made Quebec so unique in North America.

Over the years, the distinct society notion has been interpreted by competing political forces in several ways: as a dangerous concept that could lead to Canada's dismantling, as the way to an expanded set of privileges, or as a political trick that could only enable cosmetic changes that would in no way satisfy Quebec's political claims. In other words, the concept has been disqualified by both nationalist Canadians and nationalist Quebecers for opposite reasons, in the process largely discrediting the idea within the two main language communities.

Some efforts were made over the years to sensitize Canadians to the presence of Quebec as a distinct society. It is worth pointing at two of Ottawa's initiatives: the Special Joint Committee of the Senate and the House of Commons on the Constitution (especially through its 1972 minority report) and the Task Force on Canadian Unity, known as the Pepin-Robarts Commission.

When the report of the Royal Commission on Bilingualism and Biculturalism was tabled in 1968, Ottawa decided to convene a federal-provincial conference with the aim of revamping the Constitution. Ottawa also struck a Special Joint Committee of the Senate and of the House of Commons on the Constitution to appraise potential changes. That committee tabled its report in March 1972. What matters here is not so much its main report but the minority report signed by Martial Asselin and Pierre De Bané. Both opposed the main report because it did not mention that Quebec constitutes a distinct society in Canada. Here is what they wrote:

"Nevertheless (...) Quebec's society forms a distinct entity (...) which is gradually realizing that it cannot achieve its fullest development without a freedom for action and the presence of certain psychological conditions which it lacks at the present time" (De Bané and Asselin, 1972: 8).[7] The two authors also heavily criticized the main report (and the Canadian Constitution) for the reason that "nowhere does it recognize the existence of a distinct Quebec society, a shortcoming which has real consequences" (De Bané and Asselin, 1972: 10). (It is worth mentioning that this minority report was received coldly in Ottawa and that indeed most MPs chose to ignore it. Nevertheless, in hindsight, we can say that Asselin and De Bané had clearly identified a fundamental shortcoming of the Canadian constitution.)

Following the election of the Parti Québécois government in November 1976, the central government launched its Task Force on Canadian Unity that would bring to the fore the concepts of regionalism and dualism. Members of the Task Force wrote extensively on the fact that Quebec forms a distinct society, stressing that "Quebec is distinctive and should, within a viable Canada, have the powers necessary to protect and develop its distinctive character[;] any political solution short of this would lead to the rupture of Canada" (Task Force on Canadian Unity, 1979: 87). Language politics were specifically targeted by the Task Force, which gave its endorsement to the Quebec government's policies, namely Law 101, backing "efforts of the Quebec provincial government and the people of Quebec to ensure the predominance of the French language and culture in that province" (Task Force on Canadian Unity, 1979: 51). This position was in sharp opposition to the one adopted by the Liberal Party of Canada after Pierre Trudeau's election as party leader in 1968.

Members of the Task Force were concerned that their report might be viewed as encouragement for the development of asymmetrical federalism; to avoid this they recommended giving all provinces the chance to act within the same sphere of jurisdictions—to do otherwise would ensure opposition in other parts of Canada. They suggested granting "to all the provinces powers in the areas needed by Quebec to maintain its distinctive culture and heritage" (Task Force on Canadian Unity, 1979: 87). As a result, Quebec's status as a distinct society would be granted to all provinces (Gagnon, 2002: 105–20). None of those powers were ever stipulated so as to provide Ottawa with leeway in its negotiation with the provinces. This approach to Quebec's status as a distinct society—in effect, extending a similar status to all provinces—rendered it much less significant politically. The idea was for Ottawa to accept the notion that every province constituted a distinct society, thereby imposing a political framework of individual and provincial equality that might be broadly acceptable within ROC but conflicted with Quebec's own vision of its place within Canada.

Nonetheless, the distinct society notion gained prominence in Quebec within the federalist camp in particular, as it was viewed as a minimal stand to preserve Canadian unity and respond to Quebec's claim to self-determination. The concept is present throughout the *Beige Paper* written by provincial Liberal leader Claude Ryan (1980) to advance the federalist cause in Quebec at the time of the first referendum. Federal Liberals, though never at ease with the notion, strategically agreed not to air their disagreement with their Quebec political allies in view of that referendum scheduled to take place on May 20, 1980. Subsequently, "distinct society" became a rallying cry to convince Quebecers to support the Meech Lake Accord (1987–90) negotiated with the provinces by Prime Minister Brian Mulroney and designed to bring Quebec back into the federal fold following its rejection of the 1982 Constitution. The federal Liberals under leader John Turner were divided over the wisdom of the Accord, although, in the end, the caucus—and all the parties in Parliament—voted in favour of it. In addition, former Prime Minister Pierre Trudeau catalyzed opposition by arguing that recognition of Quebec as a distinct society would encourage secessionist aspirations and provide Quebec with special privileges that would undermine the principle of equality of the provinces.

Though the failure of the Meech Lake Accord ensured that the distinct society concept would never be entrenched in the constitution, it was used by the Mulroney government to revamp an intergovernmental accord on immigration between Quebec and Ottawa, and later, following the second referendum in Quebec in 1995, by Jean Chrétien's Liberals when passing a motion in the House of Commons stating that Quebec formed a distinct society within Canada.[8] Since then, the once hotly contested notion of distinct society has received surprisingly little attention, especially in Quebec where other ideas or visions have superseded it, including the political image of Quebec as a multinational democracy.

Face 5: Multinational Democracy

To complete our political sketches of Quebec, let's examine the image of Quebec as a multinational democracy. I believe this image is most in tune with Quebec citizenry at this historical moment. At least four elements give shape and substance to this emerging form of political association. (Here I am particularly influenced by the pioneering work that James Tully has done on the topic.[9]) First, a multinational democracy contains more than one nation.

Minimally, members of these nations have the right to exercise internal self-determination and to engage in continuous deliberations and negotiations with a view to developing relations between partners based on mutual trust. Representatives of these constituent nations are free to seek recognition in international forums. Michael Keating has noted that self-determination of this sort does not necessarily lead to political secession. For Keating, there is "no logical reason why self-determination should be linked to statehood, apart from the entrenched dogmas of sovereignty discourse (...). Another way of looking at self-determination is to see it as the right to negotiate one's position within the state and supranational order, without necessarily setting up a separate state" (Keating, 2001: 10). I will come back to this second point shortly.

We are very far from the classic Westphalian model that conceives of states as forming a single *demos* within which "internal, subnational 'minorities' seek group rights" rather than "societies of two or more, often overlapping nations that are more or less equal in status" (Tully, 2001: 3).

Second, multinational federal democracies are characterized by the fact that each nation within the federation forms a plural society. Such is the case in Quebec. A concrete expression of this was given in 1985 when the Quebec National Assembly adopted a resolution recognizing the existence of the Arenac, Algonquin, Atikamekw, Cree, Huron, Micmac, Mohawk, Montagnais, Naskapi, and Inuit nations.[10] (An eleventh nation, the Malecite, was recognized in 1989.) In connection with this interpretation of Quebec as constituting a plural society, Tully goes as far as saying that in such contexts "[t]he jurisdictions, modes of participation and representation, and the national and multinational identities of citizens overlap and are subject to negotiation" (Tully, 2001: 3).

Third, multinational democracies adopt the principles of constitutional democracy, which challenge the norm of a democratic setting founded on a single-nation. As such, this "multinational association rests on their [each nation's] adherence to the legal and political values, principles and rights of constitutional democracy and international law" (Tully, 2001: 3).

Fourth, multinational democracies need to develop institutions that bring members and representatives of the various nations into permanent contact while encouraging political exchanges. In the case of Quebec, one can view the policy and politics of interculturalism (the Quebec version of multiculturalism) as a clear expression of the desire to erect a polity founded on interconnectedness between societal partners.

So far, Quebec's main political parties have been slow to seek the further empowerment of the province's Inuit and Aboriginal nations. Arguably,

Quebec's National Assembly has been a leader in identifying avenues for the economic and social development of the North of Quebec, territory traditionally inhabited by many First Nations, but much more needs to be done to eradicate the colonial heritage that long dominated relations between Quebec and its original peoples. Denys Delâge aptly reminds us that "current Aboriginal leaders are more involved in fighting for their rights than in engaging in an overall questioning of the colonial system that constrains them. (...) The goal would be for aboriginal people to escape the colonial heritage of wardship and the denial of access to full citizenship" (Delâge, 2001: 135). The dedicated pursuit of such objectives would contribute, in my view, to bringing Quebecers of all origins and all walks of life together with the purpose of building a better and fairer world for all to share.

Finally, I want to point out that if at some time Quebec should secede from Canada, it would have yet another nation to recognize: anglophone Quebecers. For the time being, however, this community identifies strongly with the Canadian majority, and as such does not perceive itself—and is not being perceived by others—as constituting a minority nation within Quebec.

Conclusion

In this chapter, I have analyzed five faces used to depict Quebec: political nationality, founding nation, province state, distinct society, and multinational democracy. Each of these faces tends to propose and promote different characteristics and suggests a unique worldview with particular meaning systems.

These various portrayals of Quebec also suggest different takes on relations of power. The use of these images are not insignificant as we are reminded by E.E. Schattschneider, who argued that "the definition of alternatives [read 'faces'] is the supreme instrument of power; the antagonists can rarely agree on what the issues are because power is involved in the definition. He who determines what politics is about runs the country, because the definition of the alternatives is the choice of conflicts and the choice of conflicts allocates power" (Schattschneider, 1960). So, the prevailing face of politics—the shared vision of the political community—gives overall direction to policy preferences and appropriate arrangements for power sharing.

To return to the point made by Richard Simeon in the introduction, it is clear that defining key concepts has consequences that go to the very core of societal arrangements and that can suddenly tilt the political balance in ways that have long-term consequences, as we were reminded in 1982[11] at the time of the patriation and the establishment of a new constitutional order in Canada.

Notes

1 The first version of this text was discussed at the international workshop organized by Michael Burgess on the theme of *Small Worlds: The Character, Role and Significance of Constituent Units in Federations and Federal Political Systems* under the auspices of the Centre international de formation européenne and Canterbury Christ Church University, Canterbury, April 21–26, 2013. My thanks go to all participants for their input. Special thanks go to Dan Pfeffer, postdoctoral researcher with the Canada Research Chair in Quebec and Canadian Studies at the Université du Québec à Montréal, and to Jim Bickerton for their valuable suggestions.

2 This will remind the reader of the book published by Harold Dwight Lasswell in 1936, *Politics: Who Gets What, When and How?*

3 The idea of "faces" was suggested by an article published by James Mallory in 1965 in which the author referred to the "five faces of federalism" to depict various phases experienced by the country's federal system between 1867 and the early 1960s, namely quasi, classical, emergency, cooperative, and double-image federalism. Mallory's way of categorizing Canada's transformation was highly accurate at the time. See Mallory (1965: 3–15). It is Michael Burgess, though, who suggested that I set some time aside to write on the various images to depict Quebec as an evolving small universe/world.

4 Quoted in Gagnon and Iacovino (2007: 78–79). Originally published in the newspaper *La Minerve,* Montreal, July 1, 1867.

5 For a solid discussion of those letters authored by Loranger, refer to Canada, Royal Commission on Aboriginal Peoples (1993).

6 On the *rupture thesis,* see Marcel Martel (2003: 129–45) and Anne-Andrée Deneault (2013).

7 The House of Commons refused to accept the official tabling of the minority report.

8 Most political commentators and jurists felt that such recognition fell short, as it was not entrenched in the Constitution Act, 1982. For such an account, see Gérald Beaudoin (1996).

9 In addition, one can consult an important collection of essays edited by Michael C. van Walt van Praag and Onoo Seroo (1999). http://www.unpo.org/downloads/THE%20IMPLEMENTATION%20OF%20THE%20RIGHT%20TO%20SELF.pdf

10 For a solid discussion of Quebec's evolving policy in autochtonous matters, refer to Éric Gourdeau (1993: 349–71).

11 For a critical account of the patriation of the Constitution Act in 1982, see François Rocher and Benoît Pelletier (2013).

References and Suggested Readings

Beaudoin, Gérald. 1996. "Constitution: Ne travailler que sur un plan B serait admettre que la sécession est inévitable." *La Presse*, 16 February.

Bickerton, James, and Alain-G. Gagnon. 2011. "Regions." In *Comparative Politics*, 2nd ed., ed. Daniele Caramani, 275–91. Oxford: Oxford University Press.

Brownsey, Keith, and Michael Howlett. 2009. *The Provincial State in Canada: Politics in the Provinces and Territories.* Toronto: University of Toronto Press.

Burgess, Michael. 2006. *Comparative Federalism: Theory and Practice.* Abingdon: Routledge.

Burgess, Michael. 2012. *In Search of the Federal Spirit: New Theoretical and Empirical Perspectives in Comparative Federalism.* Oxford: Oxford University Press. http://dx.doi.org/10.1093/acprof:oso/9780199606238.001.0001.

Burgess, Michael, and Alain-G. Gagnon. 2010. *Federal Democracies.* London: Routledge.

Canada, Royal Commission on Aboriginal Peoples. 1993. *Partners in Confederation: Aboriginal Peoples, Self-Government, and the Constitution.* Ottawa: Canadian Government Publishing.

Careless, J.M.S. 1969. "'Limited Identities' in Canada." *Canadian Historical Review* 50, 1–10.

Cook, Ramsay. 1969. *Provincial Autonomy, Minority Rights and the Compact Theory, 1867–1921, Studies of the Royal Commission on Bilingualism and Biculturalism.* Ottawa: Queen's Printer for Canada.

Cook, Ramsay. 1989. "Alice in Meechland or the Concept of Quebec as a 'Distinct Society'." In *The Meech Lake Primer*, ed. Michael Behiels, 285–94. Ottawa: University of Ottawa Press.

De Bané, Pierre, and Martial Asselin. 1972. *Special Joint Committee of the Senate and of the House of Commons on the Constitution, A Minority Report.* Ottawa, March 7.

Delâge, Denys. 2001. "Quebec and the Aboriginal People." In *Vive Quebec: New Thinking and New Approaches to the Quebec Nation*, ed. Michel Venne, 127–36. Toronto: James Lorimer and Company.

Deneault, Anne-Andrée. 2013. *Divergences et solidarité: Une étude sociologique des rapports entre le Québec et les francophones d'Amérique.* Ph.D. dissertation, School of Political Studies, University of Ottawa.

Gagnon, Alain-G. 2002. "La condition canadienne et les montées du nationalisme et du régionalisme." In *Le débat qui n'a pas eu lieu. La Commission Pepin-Robarts quelque vingt ans après*, ed. Jean-Pierre Wallot, 105–20. Ottawa: Les Presses de l'Université d'Ottawa.

Gagnon, Alain-G. 2010. *The Case for Multinational Federalism: Beyond the All-Encompassing Nation.* Oxford: Routledge.

Gagnon, Alain-G., and Xavier Dionne. 2009. "Historiographie et fédéralisme au Canada." *Revista d'Estudis Autonòmics i Federals* 9 (October), 10–50.

Gagnon, Alain-G., and Raffaele Iacovino. 2007. *Federalism, Citizenship and Quebec: Debating Multinationalism.* Toronto: University of Toronto Press.

Gagnon, Alain-G., and Mary Beth Montcalm. 1990. *Quebec: Beyond the Quiet Revolution.* Scarborough: Nelson Canada.

Gourdeau, Éric. 1993. "Quebec and the Aboriginal Question." In *Quebec: State and Society*, ed. Alain-G. Gagnon, 349–71. Scarborough: Nelson Canada.

Guibernau, Montserrat. 1999. *Nations Without States. Political Communities in a Global Age.* Cambridge: Polity.

Keating, Michael. 1996. *Nations against the State: The New Politics of Nationalism in Quebec, Catalonia and Scotland.* London: Macmillan. http://dx.doi.org/10.1057/9780230374348.

Keating, Michael. 1998. *The New Regionalism in Western Europe: Territorial Restructuring and Political Change.* Cheltenham: Edward Elgar.

Keating, Michael. 2001. *Plurinational Democracy: Stateless Nations in a Post-Sovereignty Era.* Oxford: Oxford University Press. http://dx.doi.org/10.1093/0199240760.001.0001.

Kwavnick, David. 1973. *The Tremblay Report: Report of the Royal Commission of Inquiry on Constitutional Problems.* Toronto: McClelland and Stewart.

LaSelva, Samuel V. 1996. *The Moral Foundations of Canadian Federalism: Paradoxes, Achievements, and Tragedies.* Montreal: McGill-Queen's University Press.

Mallory, James. 1965. "Five Faces of Canadian Federalism." In *The Future of Canadian Federalism,* eds. P.-A. Crépeau and C.B. Macpherson, 3–15. Toronto: University of Toronto Press.

Martel, Marcel. 2003. "Le débat de l'existence et de la disparition du Canada français: état des lieux." In *Aspects de la nouvelle francophonie canadienne,* eds. Simon Langlois and Jocelyn Létourneau, 129–45. Québec: Les Presses de l'Université Laval.

O'Neal, Brian. 1995. *Distinct Society: Origins, Interpretations, Implications.* Ottawa: Library of Parliament, BP-408 E, December.

Paquin, Stéphane, ed. 2006. *Les relations internationales du Québec depuis la Doctrine Gérin-Lajoie (1965–2005). Le prolongement externe des compétences internes.* Québec: Les Presses de l'Université Laval.

Pelletier, Benoît. 2004. "The State of Our Federation. A Québec Perspective." Speech given by Mr. Benoît Pelletier, Minister for Canadian Intergovernmental Affairs and Aboriginal Affairs during a luncheon organized by the Canada West Foundation, March 24.

Rémillard, Gil. 1980. *Le fédéralisme canadien.* Montréal: Québec Amérique.

Rioux Ouimet, Hubert. 2012. *Le 'Lion celtique': néolibéralisme, régionalisme et nationalisme économique en Écosse, 1979–2012.* M.A. thesis, Department of Sociology, UQAM.

Rocher, François. 2009. "The Quebec-Canada Dynamic or the Negation of the Ideal of Federalism." In *Contemporary Canadian Federalism. Foundations, Traditions, Institutions,* ed. Alain-G. Gagnon, 81–131. Toronto: University of Toronto Press.

Rocher, François, and Benoît Pelletier, eds. 2013. *Le nouvel ordre constitutionnel canadien. Du rapatriement de 1982 à nos jours.* Québec: Les Presses de l'Université du Québec.

Ryan, Claude. 1980. "Une Nouvelle Fédération Canadienne." Report of the Constitutional Commission of the Quebec Liberal Party, Quebec City.

Schattschneider, E.E. 1960. *The Semisovereign People: A Realist's View of Democracy in America.* Chicago: Holt, Rinehart and Winston.

Simeon, Richard. 1977. "Regionalism and Canadian Political Institutions." In *Canadian Federalism: Myth or Reality?* ed. J. Peter Meekison, 292–303. Toronto: Methuen.

Smiley, Donald V. 1967. *The Canadian Political Community.* Toronto: Methuen.

Task Force on Canadian Unity. 1979. *A Future Together: Observations and Recommendations.* Ottawa: Government of Canada.

Trudeau, Pierre Elliott. 1962. "The Multi-National State in Canada: the Interaction of Nationalism in Canada." *Canadian Forum* 42, 52–54.

Tully, James. 1994. "The Crisis of Identification: the Case of Canada." *Political Studies* 42, 77–96.

Tully, James. 2001. "Introduction." In *Multinational Democracies*, eds. Alain-G. Gagnon and James Tully, 1–33. Cambridge: Cambridge University Press. http://dx.doi.org/10.1017/CBO9780511521577.003

Wade, Mason, in collaboration with Jean-Charles Falardeau. 1960. *La dualité canadienne: essais sur les relations entre Canadiens français et Canadiens anglais/Canadian Dualism: Studies of French-English Relations*. Laval/Toronto: Les Presses de l'Université Laval/University of Toronto Press.

Walt van Praag, Michael C. van, and Onoo Seroo. 1999. The Implementation of the Right to Self-Determination as a Contribution to Conflict Prevention. Barcelona: Unesco Catalunya.

six

The Rise (and Fall?) of Aboriginal Self-Government

MARTIN PAPILLON

In the early days of 2013, the Idle No More movement reminded all Canadians that Aboriginal peoples are still engaged in a struggle to redefine their relationships with the Canadian state.[1] Faced with unparalleled social and economic challenges that are compounded by governing structures inherited from Canada's colonial period, Aboriginal peoples seek to reassert their presence as distinct communities capable of freely deciding their own future. The notion that Aboriginal peoples have a right to self-determination is now broadly acknowledged in the international community. It is at the heart of the United Nations' Declaration on the Rights of Indigenous Peoples, which Canada finally endorsed in 2010.[2] The challenge, of course, is to translate this principle into concrete institutional arrangements.

In the Canadian context, self-determination is generally associated with one form or another of self-government. Thanks to successful Aboriginal political and legal activism, the principle of an Aboriginal right to self-government has progressively become an integral part of Canada's institutional landscape in the past 30 years. The emergence of sophisticated self-governing structures, notably in the Yukon, the Northwest Territories, Nunavut, Quebec, and British Columbia, further testifies to this shift. But not everyone agrees that existing models of self-government represent a significant break with Canada's colonial past. Relatively few self-government agreements have been successfully negotiated, and most of them are in less densely populated areas of northern Canada. The Aboriginal nations who have agreed to federally sanctioned self-government also face frustrating delays and ongoing administrative battles as they seek to transform the letter of their agreements into governance practices. Many nations and communities simply refuse to engage in the negotiation of self-government agreements under the existing federal policy framework, arguing that the conditions offered amount to a denial of their inherent right to govern themselves. For indigenous scholar Taiaiake Alfred, self-government, as it exists today, is little more than a new form of colonial domination (2005: 37).

Perhaps more puzzling, federal and provincial governments appear to have backed away from their commitment to self-government in recent years. The very word "self-government" has almost (but not quite) disappeared from the website of Aboriginal Affairs and Northern Development Canada, the main department engaged in promoting and negotiating self-government agreements. It has progressively been replaced by a broader focus on "Aboriginal governance." What does this shift mean for Aboriginal peoples and their struggle for self-determination? Is self-government yet another of these failed attempts at reforming Aboriginal-state relations in Canada?

The objectives of this chapter are first to explain what self-government is and how it came about in the Canadian context, and second to assess its contemporary forms in light of recent policy developments emphasizing governance over self-government. A careful examination of existing self-government agreements suggests a fundamental gap still exists between the ideal of self-government, as understood by Aboriginal peoples, and the reality on the ground. The shift in emphasis to governance, which displaces the negotiation of formal self-government agreements in favour of sector-specific agreements for the management of programs and services, further reinforces this gap between principle and practice.

To explain both the rise to prominence of Aboriginal self-government in Canadian politics and the current shift in emphasis toward less formal governance arrangements, this chapter locates these changes in their broader historical context. Politics matter here. The idea of an inherent Aboriginal right to self-government gained currency at a time of great institutional instability. The constitutional battles of the 1980s and successive Supreme Court decisions defining the scope and meaning of Aboriginal rights proved a fertile ground for Aboriginal peoples to have their governing rights recognized by Canadian governments. The context shifted drastically in the mid-1990s, as deficits and economic preoccupations came to the forefront of the political agenda. Autonomy for Aboriginal nations came to be equated with economic self-sufficiency rather than with an inherent political right. It is in this context—as Aboriginal rights claims encounter neoliberal governance—that the battle for self-government is now fought. Before discussing the consequences of these ongoing shifts, this chapter looks at the history of self-government and its potential for transforming Aboriginal-state relations.

Challenging the Colonial Legacy

There are over one million self-identifying Aboriginal people in what is now Canada, representing four per cent of the total population.[3] It is a highly diverse group, with more than 800 First Nations, Inuit, and Métis communities scattered across the country, some of them linked together through ancient or more recent political ties, forming, according to the Royal Commission on Aboriginal Peoples (1996), 60 to 80 self-defined nations. Indigenous peoples also vary considerably in their institutional relationship with the Canadian federation. While all were recognized as having the same rights under the Constitution Act, 1982, there are significant differences in the governance regime of each nation. Not all have a treaty-based relationship with the Canadian state and if most First Nations are, at least formally, governed under the regime of the federal Indian Act, Inuit and Métis are not. To further complicate the portrait, more than half of all Aboriginal people in Canada now live in urban centres, where issues of status, membership, and political authority become far more complex (Andersen and Peters, 2013). This diversity in conditions and history explains in part why any generalization about an "Aboriginal perspective" on self-government is a hazardous enterprise. Aboriginal peoples are unified, however, in their common struggle to move beyond the legacies of past colonial policies.

Aboriginal peoples were governing themselves long before the arrival of European settlers. The Royal Commission on Aboriginal Peoples (1996, vol. 1) explains some of the governing practices of the original inhabitants of the land. In the Haudenosaunee (Iroquois) and Mi'kmaq confederacies, for example, relations between communities and nations were governed through a complex set of rules, equivalent to constitutional conventions, transmitted through oral traditions from one generation to the next. French and British authorities recognized these governing structures and engaged in diplomatic-type relationships with Aboriginal peoples to secure military alliances or gain access to the fur trade routes at the centre of the early colonial economy (Dickason and McNab, 2008).

The expansion of the settlers' society led to growing pressure on Aboriginal lands and traditional forms of governance. From early land cession treaties in Ontario and the Prairie provinces to the absence of Aboriginal representatives during the negotiations leading to the creation of the Canadian federation in 1867, Aboriginal peoples were increasingly marginalized politically and geographically. The adoption of the consolidated Indian Act in 1876, the expansion of the reserve system, followed by the imposition of the band council governance regime in First Nations communities are all part of a long process of displacement of traditional Aboriginal governing structures and economic relationships to the land (Tobias, 1991).[4] Despite significant resistance in several communities, previously self-governing and culturally distinct societies were eventually subjugated politically and legally to the authority of the federal government and forced to adopt the norms and social practices of the dominant society.

Aboriginal Resistance

The contemporary rise to prominence of self-government as a political ideal can be traced to the resurgence of Aboriginal political activism in the postwar period, in particular in the aftermath of the federal government's White Paper on Indian Policy (Canada, 1969). The Canadian government proposed to do away with treaties and differentiated status as a solution to socio-economic disparities between First Nations communities and other Canadians. This proposal came at a time when the decolonization and civil rights movements were influencing the political thinking of marginalized indigenous populations around the globe. Newly formed pan-Canadian Aboriginal organizations, such as the National Indian Brotherhood (which later became the Assembly of First Nations), rejected the notion that their differentiated status was the source of their disastrous socio-economic conditions. To the contrary, Cree leader Harold Cardinal argued in his famous reply to the White Paper that this distinct status must be recognized to its full extent in order for Aboriginal peoples to regain their sense of dignity and political agency (Cardinal, 1969).

Aboriginal leaders used the language of human rights and self-determination to assert their claims for proper recognition of existing treaties, for control over their lands, and for greater recognition of their status as politically autonomous nations. The Dene declaration of 1975 is a classic example of this emerging discourse:

> We the Dene insist on the right to be regarded as a nation. (...)
> Our plea to the world is to help us in our struggle to find a place
> in the world community where we can exercise our right to self-
> determination as a distinct people and as a nation. What we seek
> then is independence and self-determination within Canada.[5]

By the mid-1970s, Aboriginal peoples were challenging not only existing colonial institutions, such as the Indian Act, but also the very legitimacy of federal and provincial authority over their lands and communities. Regaining some degree of political autonomy was seen as key to the protection of Aboriginal cultures and traditions, but it was also a way to regain control over the land, to establish the foundation of a better and healthier economy, and, most significantly, to establish the basis of a new, more equal relationship with the Canadian state. It is in this context that self-government rose to prominence, both as an ideal and as a concrete policy alternative to existing models of governance.

What Is Self-Government?

What exactly is self-government and how can it be implemented? There is no single answer to these questions. Given their diverse history, geographic situation, and status in relation to the Canadian state, not all Aboriginal nations conceive of self-government in the same way. As Belanger and Newhouse (2008) suggest, the idea of self-government has also evolved significantly in the past 30 years. At the risk of oversimplifying, we can identify at least three narratives that have informed political debate and policy development related to self-government in the past 30 years: self-government as self-administration, self-government as an inherent right, and self-government as coexisting sovereignties (see also Abele and Prince, 2006). These narratives are associated with different understandings of self-government and its place in relation to Canadian federalism. They are also grounded in specific historical contexts.

Self-Government as Delegated Authority

Self-government was first defined as a delegation of federal, provincial, or territorial authority to local Aboriginal governments. As early as the 1930s Ottawa was encouraging band councils to take charge of local services. The federal government also initiated a series of experiments with local management of education, community development, and social services in the 1960s to foster "local empowerment" in First Nations communities (Weaver, 1981: 27). However, it was only with the rise of self-government on the political agenda in the late 1970s that the federal government proposed a more comprehensive approach to the transfer of administrative authority to band councils. It offered First Nations the possibility to "opt out" of the closely regulated governance regime of the Indian Act and instead to exercise a form of delegated authority through federal legislation in several policy areas.

According to this perspective, self-government is first and foremost defined as self-administration. Aboriginal autonomy is achieved through a delegation of state authority at the local level, much like municipalities, rather than through the formal recognition of Aboriginal nations as autonomous political entities (Abele and Prince, 2006: 572). Not surprisingly, indigenous peoples largely rejected this initial conception of self-government. An alternative narrative, more closely tied to the principle of self-determination, rapidly gained currency in Aboriginal political and academic circles in the 1980s.

Self-Government as an Inherent Right

The inclusion of Aboriginal and Treaty rights in Section 35 of the Constitution Act, 1982 was a significant victory for the fledging Aboriginal movement. It provided Aboriginal peoples with an institutional platform to challenge federal and provincial authority to regulate traditional aboriginal lands and activities, notably fishing and hunting practices. It also provided a focus to redefine the debate over self-government. Political autonomy, the Aboriginal leadership argued, is a fundamental right that derives not from Parliament or the Canadian constitution, but from their status as distinct nations who were governing themselves long before the creation of the Canadian federation.

The principle of self-government as an inherent right of nations gained traction in public debates following a report of a special committee of the House of Commons on Indian Government (Canada, 1983). The Penner Committee not only recognized the inherent nature of self-government rights, it also endorsed the principle of a "third order" of Aboriginal governments in the Canadian federation. The inherent right to self-government therefore became a focal point of the constitutional battles of the 1980s and early 1990s, as Aboriginal organizations were engaged in negotiations with federal and provincial authorities to clarify the exact meaning of Aboriginal rights under the Constitution Act, 1982.

Despite the ultimate failure of constitutional negotiations following the demise of the Charlottetown Accord in 1992, the process clearly shaped debates over Aboriginal self-government. In 1995, the federal government released a policy statement in which it recognized the inherent right to self-government as a basis for negotiating new governance arrangements with Aboriginal peoples (Canada, 1995). The Royal Commission on Aboriginal Peoples also endorsed the principle as a cornerstone of a renewed nation-to-nation relationship between Aboriginal peoples and the Canadian federation in its 1996 report. While the Supreme Court of Canada has not explicitly recognized self-government as an Aboriginal right under Section 35(1) of the Constitution Act, 1982, some legal experts suggest its jurisprudence points in that direction (McNeil, 2007).

Behind this apparent unanimity over the notion of self-government as an inherent right, fundamental divergences remained when it came to translating what is a relatively abstract moral and legal principle into political practice. From the federal government's perspective, the inherent right to self-government exists within the framework of the Canadian federation. This is the position developed in the 1995 federal policy statement: Aboriginal peoples have a right to self-government, but the modalities of the exercise of this right still depend on federal and provincial legislative consent. The Royal Commission on Aboriginal Peoples (RCAP) insists instead on the principle of continuing Aboriginal sovereignty as the basis of a renewed nation-to-nation relationship between Aboriginal peoples and the Canadian state. As previously self-governing political communities, each Aboriginal nation is entitled to negotiate a new division of powers with the federal and provincial governments, thus forming a third order of government within the Canadian federation (RCAP, 1996, v01.2: 215).

Coexisting Sovereignties

The articulation of self-government as a fundamental right remains central to Aboriginal discourse today, but the RCAP model and the federal policy statement of 1995 have their limits. Aboriginal self-government is assumed to operate *within* the predetermined boundaries of the Canadian constitution. As such, even if Aboriginal governments are recognized as predating the Canadian federation, they are ultimately still operating within a constitutional structure defined without their consent or involvement.

As an alternative to incorporating Aboriginal governments *within* the existing federation as a third order, several indigenous and non-indigenous scholars and activists have argued for the reaffirmation of Aboriginal sovereignty *outside* the institutions of Canadian federalism (see for example Ladner, 2005). In this perspective, partly inspired by theories of legal pluralism, pre-existing Aboriginal governing practices and institutions should be fully recognized for what they are: the expression of distinctive constitutional orders that today continue to exist parallel to Canada's own constitution (Borrows, 2010; Ladner, 2005). Aboriginal governance regimes were recognized as such by European powers, who engaged in the negotiation of treaties and alliances as if they were diplomatic relations between sovereign entities. According to Indigenous scholar Sakej Henderson (1994), these early alliances and treaties effectively created a form of federal alliance between mutually consenting polities. It is, according to Henderson, this "treaty federalism" that should be revived as the basis of contemporary relationships between Aboriginal nations and the Canadian federation.

The revitalization of indigenous constitutional traditions is, of course, fraught with legal and political difficulties. Not only is this a direct challenge to orthodox conceptions of state sovereignty but it also raises several very concrete institutional challenges. For example, it is not clear how or even *if* Aboriginal peoples would be represented in the shared institutions of a two-tier federal system. Should all nations, no matter their size, have equal representation in what would become an extremely complex structure of executive federalism? Moreover, as Alan Cairns (2000: 191) argues in his critique of nation-to-nation conceptions of Aboriginal governance, it is not evident how one can reconcile a treaty-based association with a substantive conception of shared citizenship, a necessary condition, in his view, to fostering a sense of solidarity and cooperation across communities that are bound to live together on a common territory. More pragmatically, even with access to land-base revenues, most Aboriginal communities would remain dependent on fiscal transfers from the federal government.

These obstacles are not insurmountable, but they illustrate the challenges in moving from theoretical constructs to more concrete institutional reforms. They also show the distance between conceptions of self-government as a form of devolution of powers, under which the foundations of Canadian federalism remain largely intact, and alternative models for coexistence between nations, which call for a fundamental rethinking of Canada's constitutional framework.

From Principle to Practice: Negotiating Self-Government

Throughout the 1980s and 1990s, as debates focused on the exact meaning and organizing principles of self-government, several Aboriginal nations engaged in the negotiation of self-government agreements with the federal government, the provinces, and the territories.[6] The competing narratives discussed above influenced these negotiations, but other pragmatic considerations also shaped the processes and their outcomes. For one, most self-government agreements negotiated so far in Canada are the result of larger land claims settlement processes. In the Calder case of 1973, the Supreme Court of Canada acknowledged the possibility that an Aboriginal title to the land could have survived the assertion of Canadian sovereignty in areas where no treaties were signed. As the natural resource extraction economy expanded further north, the clarification of Aboriginal rights and titles in these areas became a driving force compelling federal and provincial authorities to negotiate alternative governance arrangements with Aboriginal peoples. Land claims settlements offered legal certainty for governments and resource extraction industries. In exchange, Aboriginal peoples faced with growing pressures on their traditional lands sought to regain a voice in the management of their communities and territories through one form or another of self-government.

A First Model: The James Bay and Northern Quebec Agreement

The first self-government experiences were limited in scope and consisted essentially of administrative decentralization. One such example is the governance model established pursuant to the James Bay and Northern Quebec Agreement (JBNQA) of 1975 for the Cree Nation of Eeyou Istchee (the James Bay Crees) and the Inuit of Nunavik in Northern Quebec. The JBNQA was negotiated in a few months, while the construction of the James Bay hydroelectric complex was already under way. Under time pressure, both groups negotiated the cession of any potential rights to most of their traditional territory in exchange for monetary compensations, specific hunting, trapping, and fishing rights, and a series of new administrative arrangements under which they were to manage most government programs in their communities. Regional boards under the legislative authority of the province were created to administer services such as education and health care in Cree and Inuit communities. At the local level, the Inuit chose a public form of government under Quebec's municipal regime while Cree communities opted to remain under federal jurisdiction.

With the adoption of the Cree-Naskapi (of Quebec) Act by the federal government in 1984, a new framework outside the Indian Act was established for the local governance of Cree communities and their neighbours, the Naskapi. While it was a significant development, this new governance regime did not constitute a major break from the underlying logic of the Indian Act. Cree bands were granted marginally greater bylaw powers and their administrative decisions were no longer subject to the ministerial veto. But otherwise, Cree bands were still considered creatures of the federal government, largely dependent on the latter for their funding and limited in their capacity to adopt policies outside of the framework established in Ottawa.

Both the Crees and the Inuit have sought to modernize their limited self-government structures in recent years. The Paix des Braves agreement with Quebec paved the way for greater Cree involvement in the management of forestry and other resource-extraction activities in their region. The Crees have also ratified agreements with the federal government and Quebec toward a more integrated model of regional governance. In 2010, the Inuit of Nunavik rejected a project of public government for the region, but discussions are ongoing toward greater consolidation of the various administrative entities created under the James Bay and Northern Quebec Agreement.

A Second Generation of Self-Government Agreements

The limits of the JBNQA model rapidly became apparent to other Aboriginal peoples contemplating self-government. Not only did it reproduce the top-down logic of the Indian Act, it also was inconsistent with conceptions of self-government based on the recognition of pre-existing Aboriginal sovereignty. As discussed earlier, by the late 1980s the focus had shifted away from devolution perspectives to a debate on the constitutional foundations of self-government. Future arrangements would have to recognize that Aboriginal governments are more than administrative arms of the Canadian state; self-government was now considered an inherent right of distinct nations.

It is once again via the land claims negotiation process that the second generation of self-government agreements have taken shape. The Yukon Umbrella Final Agreement of 1993, the Nisga'a Final Agreement of 1998, and the Tlicho Agreement signed in 2003 are broadly similar in this respect. While self-government arrangements were negotiated separately from land claims in the case of the Yukon First Nations, both Nisga'a and Tlicho self-government provisions are directly included in their treaty. The Nisga'a Final Agreement was signed after 25 years of negotiation. It is the first comprehensive self-government agreement that establishes a distinctive Aboriginal legislative authority within a province. It provides for self-governing control of approximately 2,000 km^2 of land in the Nass Valley in British Columbia, including surface and subsurface resources. The agreement establishes law-making authority for the Nisga'a Lisims Government and four Village Governments. These governments operate according to the Nisga'a Constitution and have primary jurisdiction over several areas, including the management of community lands, education, environmental regulation, citizenship, and local matters.

The Nisga'a, Tlicho, and Yukon First Nations agreements are quite significant. Federal, provincial, and territorial signatories did recognize the legislative authority of Aboriginal governments in key areas of jurisdiction. In this respect, they go much further than the Cree-Naskapi Act of 1984. There are nonetheless significant limits to these second-generation self-government agreements. First, their land base is limited and so are the possibilities of raising independent sources of revenues. Despite provisions for a tax base, they will therefore remain, at least for the foreseeable future, dependent on federal, provincial, and territorial financial support. Second, even in areas where their legislative power is recognized, Aboriginal governments remain subject to significant constraints. The law-making authority of the Nisga'a government, for example, only prevails in certain areas in case of conflict with federal and provincial laws, and only as long as the Nisga'a law is consistent with equivalent federal and provincial legislation. It is thus hard to define these governments as a "third order" of government on par with their federal and provincial counterparts (Scott, 2012).

Self-Government as Public Government

The Nisga'a, Tlicho, and Yukon land claims and self-government agreements were negotiated with First Nations previously under the Indian Act. Their structures and operations do bear, to a certain degree, the legacy of Canada's colonial legislation. For example, they chose to reproduce the Aboriginal-only model of political membership so central to the Indian Act logic. Only members of the Nisga'a Nation can vote in Nisga'a regional elections. The Inuit were not subjected to the Indian Act and do not share the same legacy of status-based politics. The demographic pressures on their communities are also clearly not the same, as they still form a substantial majority on their traditional lands. Self-government in the North thus takes a very different form.

The Inuit in Nunavut opted for public government when they negotiated their own land claim settlement, the Nunavut Land Claims Agreement, signed in 1992. The agreement led to the creation of the Nunavut territory in 1999 and to the establishment of a territorial government elected by all residents of the territory but effectively controlled by the Inuit majority. The Government of Nunavut is similar in structure to other territorial governments in the north, with the important exception that there are no political parties. As a result, members of the legislative assembly choose in a collegial manner the executive, including the Premier.

Like the other two territories, Nunavut does not have the constitutional status of a province. Its authority is delegated through federal legislation. In practice, however, its authority is equivalent to that of a province in most areas of provincial jurisdiction, with the important exception of natural resources on Crown lands, which remain under federal control. Although it is a public government, the Nunavut government promotes, as a matter of policy, the interests, language, culture, and traditions of the Inuit majority. It is thus arguably a form of *de facto* self-government (Henderson, 2008).

As with other self-government experiences developed as offshoots of land claims settlements, the Nunavut model has significant limits. Its funding structure, while far more stable and predictable than that of First Nations self-government agreements, remains ultimately in the hands of the federal Parliament. The territorial government struggles with limited budgets and significant social and economic challenges in Inuit communities. More significantly, while explicit attempts have been made to adopt a working philosophy that corresponds to Inuit values (under the principle of *Inuit Qaujimajatuqangit,* or Inuit knowledge), the relatively rigid operational logic and institutional culture associated with Canadian-style public government, most notably the focus on hierarchical authority and concerns over efficiency and accountability, have proven difficult to adapt (Tester and Irniq, 2008). The public government established in Nunavut thus largely reproduces in its structure and operating logic the rational-bureaucratic model of other Canadian governments, leaving some to question its success as a self-government experiment designed to promote the interests, perspectives, and values of the Inuit (Henderson, 2008: 236).

Self-Government in Neoliberal Times

Clearly, the negotiation of a formal self-government agreement is a complex affair. It is time-consuming—the Nisga'a negotiated for more than 25 years, the Anishnabek Nation of Ontario has been negotiating for more than 20 years—and draining for the leadership of small communities who also have to deal with very concrete social and economic challenges. By their very nature, the negotiations are often secretive and adversarial, making it difficult for the populations concerned to truly engage and develop an emotional connection to the outcome (Irlbacher-Fox, 2009). What begins as a process for reconciling the original inhabitants of the land with the Canadian state often ends up looking more like an exercise in collective bargaining where lawyers acting on behalf of Aboriginal communities seek to extract the best possible deal out of governments. Not surprisingly, the results are often disappointing. Communities under a self-government agreement are invariably frustrated by the lack of government commitment in the implementation phase and often see limited positive social and economic impacts, at least in the short to medium term (Papillon, 2008).

It is therefore tempting for First Nations and other Aboriginal peoples to seek alternatives in order to move forward in the face of pressing economic and social challenges. Not only do many disagree with the meaning ascribed to self-government under the current federal policy framework, they are also critical of the conditions imposed for the negotiation and implementation of agreements. On their part, the federal government, provinces, and territories are increasingly reluctant to put their jurisdictional authority on the line in what are costly and uncertain negotiations. The rapid expansion of natural resource extraction industries in northern Canada places additional pressure on governments to find expedient alternatives to guarantee a stable and predictable jurisdictional and regulatory environment. Pressures are also mounting on governments to find quick fixes to the dire living conditions in many Aboriginal communities. This is where self-government meets neoliberalism.

Self-government emerged on the political agenda at a time when the contemplation of big institutional reforms were part of "normal" politics in Canada. With the closing of the "constitutional window" and the rise of neoliberal ideas in the 1990s, the focus shifted in federal government circles from a rights-based view of self-government to a very different conception of Aboriginal political autonomy that focused on "good governance" (Canada: Indian and Northern Affairs, 2005). Self-reliance, accountability, and partnerships toward greater Aboriginal participation in the economic life of the country began to replace self-government in the priorities of the federal Department of Indian Affairs (since renamed Aboriginal Affairs). This entrepreneurial view of Aboriginal governance did resonate with some Aboriginal leaders, who increasingly saw the negotiation of comprehensive self-government agreements as unnecessarily cumbersome.[7] It also nicely corresponds to neoliberal views on the necessary rebalancing of the roles of governments, markets, and communities in supporting the well-being of Canadians.

In policy terms, this new focus means greater emphasis on the participation of Aboriginal communities in the market economy. In resource-rich regions, Aboriginal communities are invited to participate in and benefit from, rather than oppose, development. Rather than face legal challenges or wait interminably for the resolution of governance disputes, mining, forestry, and energy industries are encouraged to negotiate joint venture partnerships and employment and training agreements with Indigenous communities affected by development projects (Caine and Krogman, 2010). Provincial governments themselves increasingly engage in revenue-sharing development agreements with Aboriginal peoples, especially in areas where the Aboriginal title remains unsettled or contested.[8]

The negotiation of this type of partnership agreement is not limited to resource development. In fact, the most significant shift in approach to governance is arguably in the delivery of services such as education, training, or the administration of child-care services, to name a few. Sector-specific governance agreements, the logic goes, are a concrete way to engage Aboriginal peoples in the management of their own societies without the complex structure of self-government agreements. They also foster Aboriginal responsibility for the success or failure of their development model. It is in this spirit that Ottawa undertook a massive transfer of responsibilities for the management of programs and services to Aboriginal organizations and local authorities through negotiated partnerships. By 2005, close to 85 per cent of the Aboriginal Affairs department's budget was directly managed by band councils, Inuit local authorities, or Aboriginal community-based organizations under new governance arrangements (Canada: Indian and Northern Affairs, 2005). Numbers have remained stable since. Provinces have also been active participants in these agreements, as most see an interest in facilitating coordination between provincial and Aboriginal programs and services, especially in a context of growing mobility between reserves under federal jurisdiction and urban areas where First Nations and other Aboriginal peoples regularly access provincial services.

While these measures are reminiscent of early understandings of self-government as decentralization, new governance arrangements often go much further than mere administrative transfers. They suggest a more integrated form of Aboriginal, federal, and provincial partnership in the financing, development, and delivery of services, toward a common goal—that is, to "close the gap" between the social and economic conditions of Aboriginal peoples and other Canadians. In exchange for their increased role, Aboriginal authorities are therefore invited to bear more responsibility for outcomes. It is in this spirit that, for example, a province-wide education agreement was reached between First Nations and the province of British Columbia in 2005, with the explicit objective of "closing the education gap" in First Nations education outcomes in the province.[9] Under this tripartite agreement, First Nations can opt out of the Indian Act provisions regarding on-reserve education and assert their own education jurisdiction and develop their own programs, in partnership with federal and provincial education authorities. Similar partnerships have been negotiated, notably in British Columbia, in housing and health care (British Columbia, 2013). As a result of these multiple sector-specific partnerships, Aboriginal policy-making has evolved over the past two decades from a highly centralized and homogeneous system to what is now a largely decentralized, place-specific, and multilevel model of governance (Papillon, 2012).

To be sure, this is not self-government. We are not talking about the recognition of comprehensive governmental authorities with legislative and executive capacities. Nor are we talking about the exercise of an inherent right to self-government, let alone coexisting sovereignties. These sector-specific governance arrangements follow a very different logic. Federal and provincial governments are motivated at least as much by efficiency and cost-savings as they are by the ideal of Aboriginal autonomy and Aboriginal rights. Accounting and reporting mechanisms under these governance arrangements are more constraining than under more comprehensive self-government agreements, and budgets are highly vulnerable to shifts in federal or provincial priorities. Perhaps more significantly, the democratic input of the Aboriginal population is barely greater under these agreements than it was under the old model of direct federal control. Most of these agreements do not establish democratic accountability structures; instead they establish joint objectives and responsibilities for services, including for budgeting, program content, and, ultimately, results. Typical of neoliberal forms of governance, they constitute new mechanisms for integrating Aboriginal governments and organizations into a looser but nonetheless constraining regulatory regime that operates at arms' length from formal democratic institutions.

Many are critical of these new governance arrangements precisely because they shift the burden of responsibility to frontline Aboriginal organizations without fully transferring authority and accountability to the people most concerned (MacDonald, 2011). On the other hand, they do create, in practice, significant scope for Aboriginal authorities to develop their own policy expertise and capacity in key sectors such as education, heath care, or economic development. Those with the capacity and resources to engage in partnership-based governance may succeed in closing the gap and thence chart their own development course. However, smaller, isolated communities with a limited land base to produce economic opportunities, or who are reluctant to engage in market-based economic activities, are left with little to hope for. In a sense, the shift from self-government to "governance" presupposes a model of autonomy that has little to do with the rights-based model that first emerged in Canada over 30 years ago. It remains to be seen if these two conceptions of self-determination—one focused on concrete, incremental economic and social changes and the other on broad constitutional and political principles—can coexist.

Conclusion

With the displacement of rights-based politics for a more economic-focused agenda, the pressures on Aboriginal communities to embrace a different form of autonomy are very real. For better or for worse, the push for self-government is no longer what it used to be. While inherent rights and sovereignty are still part of the Aboriginal narrative, they don't hold the same sway in public discourse or government policy. Limited partnership-based governance arrangements have slowly replaced the negotiation of comprehensive self-government agreements as the cornerstone of federal Aboriginal policy in the past decade. This alternative model has its advantages. Governance agreements are more flexible, are less complex, and tend to focus on concrete results. All parties have a stake in their success, contrary to more formal self-government agreements. But these agreements are by no means comprehensive attempts at constructing a third order of Aboriginal government in the Canadian federation. They are also a far cry from the hopes and aspirations embedded in the discourse of self-determination that has motivated Aboriginal peoples to politically mobilize for change, from the protests in the wake of the 1969 White Paper to the more recent Idle No More movement.

Self-determination is ultimately about a community's capacity to decide on its future orientations and collective well-being. Doing so according to governance practices that correspond to one's culture and values is perhaps as important as the concrete outcomes of the process. So far, it has been a constant challenge for Aboriginal governments and organizations to make room for culturally relevant practices in the development of policies or negotiations with their federal and provincial counterparts. No matter their degree of institutional autonomy, existing Aboriginal governments and organizations tend to reproduce, in both their operating logic and policy outcomes, what non-Aboriginal governments do, and how they do it. Experiences so far suggest that this is just as true under comprehensive self-government arrangements as it is in more specific new governance arrangements.

In this respect, Taiaiake Alfred (2005) may well be right when he argues self-government and other types of negotiated governance arrangements are simply new forms of political containment that ultimately contribute to the assimilation of Aboriginal peoples through the penetration of Western values and ideas embedded in governance structures that have nothing to do with traditional Indigenous ways (see also Coulthard, 2007). Whether this can be avoided at all is debatable. After all, Aboriginal governments are modern governments operating in a complex policy environment, traversed by ideologies and economic dynamics that have little to do with the context under which traditional governance practices were developed. But the broader issue of whether or not self-government can actually contribute to the development of alternative, culturally relevant governance practices is certainly a pertinent question.

Ultimately, the transformation of Aboriginal-state relations is a slow and frustrating process. The resistance encountered along the way should not be surprising given the stakes. Federal, territorial, and provincial governments have little interest in jeopardizing their control over resource-rich areas of the country or in creating precedents that could lead to an unworkable patchwork of institutional arrangements. Given the profound power imbalance between the parties involved and the inherent resistance to change in what are, after all, deeply embedded conceptions of governance, radical breakthroughs are ultimately unlikely. Instead, incremental transformations, similar to the ones we have seen over the past 30 years, are likely to continue to reshape Aboriginal-state relations. In the long run, these cumulative changes could lead to a more significant redefinition of Canadian federalism.

Notes

1 Following the practice in Canada, the term "Aboriginal peoples" is used in this text interchangeably with the more internationally recognized

term "Indigenous peoples" to refer to the descendants of the original inhabitants of the continent. The Canadian constitution recognizes three groups of Aboriginal people: American Indians (now referred to as First Nations), Métis, and Inuit. Distinctions between these groups are made in this text when necessary.

2 The United Nations Declaration on the Rights of Indigenous Peoples defines the right to self-determination as the right of Indigenous peoples to "freely determine their political status and freely pursue their economic, social and cultural development" (Section 3). See http://www.unhcr.org/refworld/docid/471355a82.html. See also Canada's endorsement statement: http://www.aadnc-aandc.gc.ca/eng/1309374239861/1309374546142.

3 These numbers are based on Statistics Canada estimates from the 2006 census. It is important to note that a number of First Nations communities refuse to participate in the census and some individuals of Aboriginal ancestry may not identify as Aboriginal people.

4 Most dispositions of the Indian Act never applied to Métis and Inuit communities, who were largely ignored by governments until late in the twentieth century.

5 The *Dene Declaration of 1975* is available at http://www.denenation.com/dene_declaration.html.

6 For a more complete overview of the nature of the various agreements negotiated in the past 30 years, see Morse (2008).

7 Chief Clarence Louie of the Osoyoos Indian Band, an economically successful community in British Columbia's Okanagan Valley, is often used as an example to illustrate this shift in discourse. See Platt (2013) for a recent example.

8 Some of the most interesting developments in this respect are taking place in British Columbia and Quebec, while Alberta and other provinces covered by treaties are still resisting revenue-sharing. See British Columbia (2013) and Narine (2013) for an interesting contrast.

9 On the British Columbia First Nations Education Agreement, see http://www.fnesc.ca/jurisdiction/index.php.

References

Abele, Frances, and Michael Prince. 2006. "Four Pathways to Aboriginal Self-Government in Canada." *American Review of Canadian Studies* 36 (4): 568–95. http://dx.doi.org/10.1080/02722010609481408.

Alfred, Taiaiake. 2005. *Wasáse: Indigenous Pathways of Action and Freedom*. Peterborough: Broadview Press.

Andersen, Chris, and Evelyn Peters, eds. 2013. *Indigenous in the City: Contemporary Identities and Cultural Innovation.* Vancouver: University of British Columbia Press.

Belanger, Yale D., and David Newhouse. 2008. "Reconciling Solitudes: A Critical Analysis of the Self-Government Ideal." In *Aboriginal Self-Government in Canada: Current Trends and Issues,* 3rd ed., ed. Yale Belanger, 1–19. Saskatoon: Purich.

Borrows, John. 2010. *Canada's Indigenous Constitution.* Toronto: University of Toronto Press.

British Columbia. 2013. *New Relationships with Aboriginal People and Communities in British Columbia. Report on Progress, 2011–2012,* Ministry of Aboriginal Relations & Reconciliation. http://www.newrelationship.gov.bc.ca/shared/downloads/ARR_AnnualProgressReport2011–12_web_enabled.pdf.

Caine, K.J., and N. Krogman. 2010. "Powerful or Just Plain Power-full? A Powerful Analysis of Impact Benefit Agreements in Canada's North." *Organization & Environment* 23 (1): 76–98. http://dx.doi.org/10.1177/1086026609358969.

Cairns, Alan C. 2000. *Citizens Plus.* Vancouver: University of British Columbia Press.

Canada. 1969. *Statement of the Government of Canada on Indian Policy (The White Paper).* Ottawa: Department of Indian Affairs and Northern Development.

Canada. 1995. *Aboriginal Self-Government, Federal Policy Guide: The Government of Canada's Approach to the Implementation of the Inherent Right and Negotiation of Aboriginal Self-Government.* Ottawa: Public Works and Government Services.

Canada. House of Commons. 1983. *Report of the Special Committee on Indian Self-Government.* Ottawa: Supply and Services Canada.

Canada. Indian and Northern Affairs. 2005. *Performance Report for the Period Ending March 31, 2005.* Ottawa: Public Works and Government Services Canada.

Cardinal, Harold. 1969. *The Unjust Society.* Edmonton: M.G. Hurtig.

Coulthard, Glen. 2007. "Subjects of Empire: Indigenous Peoples and the Politics of Recognition in Canada." *Contemporary Political Theory* 6 (4): 437–60. http://dx.doi.org/10.1057/palgrave.cpt.9300307.

Dickason, Olive, and David McNab. 2008. *Canada's First Nations: A History of Founding Peoples from Earliest Times.* 4th ed. Don Mills: Oxford University Press.

Henderson, Ailsa. 2008. "Self-Government in Nunavut." In *Aboriginal Self-Government in Canada: Current Trends and Issues,* 3rd ed., ed. Yale Belanger, 222–39. Saskatoon: Purich.

Henderson, James Youngblood (Sakej). 1994. "Empowering Treaty Federalism." *Saskatchewan Law Review* 58 (2): 241–329.

Irlbacher-Fox, Stephanie. 2009. *Finding Dahshaa: Self-Government, Social Suffering and Aboriginal Policy in Canada.* Vancouver: University of British Columbia Press.

Ladner, Kiera L. 2005. "Up the Creek: Fishing for a New Constitutional Order." *Canadian Journal of Political Science* 38 (04): 923–53. http://dx.doi.org/10.1017/S0008423905040539.

MacDonald, Fiona. 2011. "Indigenous Peoples and Neoliberal "Privatization" in Canada: Opportunities, Cautions and Constraints." *Canadian Journal of Political Science* 44 (02): 257–73. http://dx.doi.org/10.1017/S000842391100014X.

McNeil, Kent. 2007. *The Jurisdiction of Inherent Right Aboriginal Governments,* Report prepared for the National Centre for First Nations Governance. http://fngovernance.org/ncfng_research/kent_mcneil.pdf.

Morse, Bradford. 2008. "Regaining Recognition of the Inherent Right of Aboriginal Governance." In *Aboriginal Self-Government in Canada: Current Trends and Issues,* 3rd ed., ed. Yale Belanger, 55–84. Saskatoon: Purich.

Narine, Shari. 2013. "No to Resource Revenue Sharing, Says Alberta Government." *Alberta Sweetgrass* 20:3. http://www.ammsa.com/publications/alberta-sweetgrass/no-resource-revenue-sharing-says-alberta-government.

Papillon, Martin. 2008. "Aboriginal Quality of Life under a Modern Treaty. Lessons from the Experience of the Cree Nation of Eeyou Istchee and the Inuit of Nunavik." *Choice* 14 (9): 1–33.

Papillon, Martin. 2012. "Adapting Federalism: Indigenous Multilevel Governance in Canada and the United States." *Publius: The Journal of Federalism* 42 (3): 312–26.

Platt, Michael. 2013. "Chief Clarence Louie Took His Band from Rags to Riches." *Calgary Sun*, January 15. http://www.calgarysun.com/2013/01/14/chief-clarence-louie-took-his-band-from-rags-to-riches.

Royal Commission on Aboriginal Peoples (RCAP). 1996. *Final Report.* 5 vols. Ottawa: Canada Communication Group Publishing.

Scott, Tracie Lea. 2012. *Postcolonial Sovereignty? The Nisga'a Final Agreement.* Saskatoon: Purich.

Tester, Frank James, and Peter Irniq. 2008. "*Inuit Qaujimajatuqangit:* Social History, Politics and the Practice of Resistance." *Arctic* 61 (suppl.1): 48–61.

Tobias, John L. 1991. "Protection, Civilization, Assimilation: An Outline History of Canada's Indian Policy." In *Sweet Promises: A Reader on Indian-White Relations,* ed. J.R. Miller, 128–44. Toronto: University of Toronto Press.

Weaver, Sally. 1981. *Making Canadian Indian Policy: The Hidden Agenda, 1968–1979.* Toronto: University of Toronto Press.

PART III

Institutions: Executive, Parliament, Bureaucracy, Courts

seven
Power at the Apex: Executive Dominance

DONALD J. SAVOIE

The executive has long held a dominant position in Westminster-style parliamentary governments. In formal constitutional terms, power is concentrated in the hands of the prime minister and Cabinet. Recent developments in Canada, however, suggest that the hand of the prime minister has been considerably strengthened. Indeed, when it comes to the political power inherent in their office, it remains that Canadian prime ministers have no equals in the West. If anything, Canadian prime ministers have been able to strengthen their power still further at the expense of other political, policy, and administrative actors over the past several years.

Gordon Robertson, former secretary to the Cabinet and once described as the gold standard for the position of clerk of the Privy Council, wrote 30 years ago that in our system "ministers are responsible. It is their government" (Robertson, 1971: 497). The Privy Council Office (PCO) argued in its 1993 publication on the machinery of government that "we operate under the theory of a confederal nature of decision-making where power flows from ministers" (Canada, 1993). I maintain, to the contrary, that power no longer flows from ministers, but from the prime minister, and unevenly at that.

The above speaks to the evolution of how policies are struck and decisions are made in Ottawa. J.S. Dupré argued that an "institutionalized" Cabinet replaced the "departmentalized" Cabinet in the late 1960s and early 1970s. Individual ministers and their departments lost a great deal of autonomy to full Cabinet as well as shared knowledge and collegial decision-making (Dupré, 1987: 238–39). But, I argue, this era did not last very long before court government started to take root. To be sure, information was gathered at the centre. However, it was gathered for the benefit of the prime minister and a handful of senior advisors operating in the Privy Council Office (PCO) and the Prime Minister's Office (PMO), not for collegial decision-making. Court government took root in Ottawa under Trudeau and, if anything, has grown stronger under Mulroney, Chrétien, Martin, and Harper. It will be recalled that Paul Martin said in his leadership campaign that under his predecessor, Jean Chrétien, the key to getting things done was the PMO. He made the point that "who you know in the PMO" has become what matters in Ottawa. However, according to observers, once in power his government was "more centralized than anything seen in the Chrétien era" (Simpson, 2005: A15).

Stephen Harper has continued in the tradition of centralizing power in his office. It will be recalled that he tabled a motion in Parliament in 2006 that read "This House recognizes that the Québécois form a nation within a united Canada" after consulting only a handful of his closest advisors. Cabinet was left outside the loop. Even the minister responsible for intergovernmental affairs was not informed, let alone consulted, before the decision was made and before full caucus was told (*Globe and Mail,* 2006: A1, A4).

There are other still more recent examples. Senator Lowell Murray, a highly respected minister in the Mulroney Cabinet, maintains that cabinet government is now dysfunctional. How could it not be, given that the key decisions regarding Canada's military deployments in Afghanistan (one by a Liberal government and another by a Conservative government) were made by the prime minister with the help of only a handful of political advisors and civilian and military officials? The two relevant ministers—of National Defence and Foreign Affairs—were not even in the room. They, like Cabinet, were informed after the fact (Murray, 2013).

This chapter reports on the forces that have strengthened the hand of the prime minister in government. It then reviews the levers of power available to the prime minister and new developments that have made his or her office and central agencies the dominant actors within the federal government—in short, the arrival of court government.

The Forces

An important development that gave rise to court government in Ottawa was the 1976 election to office of the Parti Québécois (PQ), a provincial party committed to taking Quebec out of Canada. The impact was felt in every government building in Ottawa, but nowhere was it more strongly felt than in the Langevin Building, home to both the PMO and the PCO.

One's place in history matters a great deal to prime ministers. No Canadian prime minister wants the country to break up under his or her watch. Thus, the main task at hand is keeping the country united. No other politician in Canada feels so directly responsible for Canadian unity as does the prime minister. Indeed, should Canada break up, the prime minister will be the first to be held to account.

The preoccupation with national unity tends to recast substantive policy is-sues into the question of their impact on Quebec and the likelihood of securing federal-provincial agreements. There are plenty of examples. Andrew Cooper, for example, in his comparative study of Canadian and Australian foreign affairs, writes, "a tell-tale sign of how Canada's economic and diplomatic strategy was subordinated to political tactics in agricultural trade was the routing of all important decisions in this area ... through the central agencies of the Prime Minister's Office and the Privy Council Office. The decisive impact of the constitutional issue in this matter inevitably stymied the government's ability to perform effectively in the concluding phase of the Uruguay Round" (Cooper, 1997: 217). The participants directly involved in recasting or rerouting the issues are for the most part political strategists or generalists operating at the centre and are not usually specialists in health care, social or economic development policy, and so on (Cameron and Simeon, 2000: 58–118). They are also often directly tied to the prime minister and his office in one fashion or another.

Provincial premiers have direct access to the prime minister and do not hesitate to pursue an issue with him. If the prime minister decides to support a premier, then the issue is brought to the centre of government in Ottawa for resolution. Commitments are made between two first ministers for whatever reasons, and the prime minister cannot take the risk of seeing the system or the process not producing the right decision. As a result, someone at the centre will monitor the decision until it is fully implemented. When that happens, ministers and their departments inevitably lose some of their power to the prime minister and his advisors.

The Program Review exercises of the mid-1990s and 2011–12 brought home the point that Cabinet is not able to make spending decisions and that the decision-making power had to be concentrated in the hands of a few individuals, notably the prime minister, the minister of finance, and the President of the Treasury Board. It is accepted wisdom in Ottawa that the reason the federal government lost control of its expenditure budget was that ministers in Cabinet were unwilling to say no to the proposed spending plans of colleagues, knowing full well that the time would come when they too would come forward with their own spending proposals (Savoie, 1990). One can hardly overstate the importance of the expenditure budget to public policy and government operations. It steals the stage. When the prime minister and his or her courtiers decide to bring both fiscal policy and key spending decisions to the centre of government, they are also bringing the key policy-making levers. The prime minister, with his minister of finance, has kept a tight control of all Program Review exercises since 1978. In brief, none have been Cabinet-driven exercises.

The Media

All important files have the potential to bring the centre of government into play. But what makes a file important is not at all clear. It depends on the circumstances. Media attention can, on very short notice, turn an issue, however trivial, into an important file. When this happens, there is no distinction made between policy and administration. A file that receives media attention becomes political, and at that point the prime minister and his advisors will want to oversee its development. Without putting too fine a point on it, the front page of the *Globe and Mail* or *Le Devoir* or a CBC or CTV news report can make a file important, no matter its scope or nature.

Today, the media, much like society itself, are far less deferential to political leaders and political institutions. Nothing is off-limits anymore, and political leaders and government officials must continually be cautious of letting their guard down when meeting the press. Twenty-four-hour news channels and the rise of social media have made controlling the message still more important than in years past. This too has strengthened the hand of the prime minister and his close advisors.

The media will also focus on party leaders at election time rather than on selected party candidates, even those enjoying a high profile. Journalists buy seats on the chartered aircraft of party leaders and follow them everywhere. In Canada, at least, the media and by extension the public focus on the clash of party leaders. For one thing, there are the leaders' debates on national television, in both English and French. How well a leader does in the debates can have an important impact, or at least be perceived to have an important impact, on the election campaign, if not the election itself (Johnston et al., 1992: 244). It is now widely accepted in the literature, however, that "debates are more about accidents and mistakes than about enlightenment on the capabilities of candidates to govern" (Polsby and Wildavsky, 1991: 246).

Increasingly, Canadian political leaders would appear to be the only substantial candidates in the election race. In the past, Canada had powerful Cabinet ministers with deep roots in the party or strong regional identification and support. One can think of Jimmy Gardiner, Chubby Power, Jack Pickersgill, Ernest Lapointe, Louis Saint-Laurent, Don Jamieson, and Allan MacEachen. We no longer seem to have powerful regional figures able to carry political candidates to victory on their coattails or speak to the prime minister from an independent power base in the party.

In Canada, winning candidates on the government side are aware that their party leader's performance in the election campaign explains in large measure why they themselves were successful. The objective of national political parties at election time is more to sell their leaders to the Canadian electorate than it is to sell their ideas or their policies. Canadian elections invariably turn on the question of who—which individual—will form the government (Savoie, 2013). It should come as no surprise, then, that if the leader is able to secure a majority mandate from voters, the party is in his debt, not the other way around.

National political parties, at least the Canadian variety, are not much more than election-day organizations, providing the fund-raising and poll workers needed to fight an election campaign. They are hardly effective vehicles for generating public policy debates, for staking out policy positions, or for providing the capacity to ensure their own party's competence once in office. Robert Young once argued that "the Pulp and Paper Association has more capacity to do strategic analytical work than the Liberal and [Progressive] Conservative parties combined" (quoted in Sutherland, 1996: 5). Regional cleavages in Canada, as is well known, dominate the national public policy agenda, and national political parties shy away from attacking regional issues head on for fear they will split the party along regional lines and hurt its chances at election time. The thinking goes, at least in the parties that have held power, that regional issues are so sensitive and politically explosive, that they are best left to party leaders and a handful of advisors.

The Centre of Government

The centre of government has remained largely intact, despite a management delayering exercise in the early 1990s, a massive government restructuring introduced in 1993, and the program review exercises in the mid-1990s and again in 2011–12. It has remained intact even though the workload of central agencies should have decreased substantially, given that the PCO has far fewer Cabinet committees to service than was the case in the 1970s and 1980s under Trudeau and Mulroney.

One might well ask, then, what do officials at the centre do? When Trudeau decided to enlarge the size and scope of the PMO in the late 1960s, his first principal secretary sought to reassure critics and Cabinet ministers that the office would remain essentially a service-oriented organization. He explained that it existed to "serve the prime minister personally, that its purpose is not primarily advisory but functional and the PMO is not a mini-Cabinet; it is not directly or indirectly a decision-making body and it is not, in fact, a body at all" (quoted in Sutherland, 1996: 520). It is, of course, not possible to distinguish between a service function and a policy advisory function in this context. Drafting a letter or preparing a speech for the Prime Minister can constitute policy-making, and many times it does. There is also no doubt that several senior officials in the PMO do provide policy advice to the prime minister, and if some in Trudeau's early PMO denied this, present-day advisors and assistants certainly do not (Savoie, 2013).

PMO staffers have the prime minister's ear on all issues they wish to raise, be it political, policy, administrative, or the appointment of a minister or deputy minister. They can also work hand in hand with a minister to initiate a proposal, and the minister will feel more secure, knowing that someone close to the prime minister is supportive of the proposal. They can also, however, quickly undercut a proposal when briefing the prime minister. In short, senior PMO staff members do not consider themselves simply a court of second opinion. They are in the thick of it and do not hesitate to offer policy advice or to challenge a Cabinet minister.

The role of the PCO has also changed in recent years. Arnold Heeney, the architect of the modern Cabinet office in Ottawa, wrote after his retirement that he had successfully resisted Mackenzie King's desire to make the secretary to the Cabinet "a kind of deputy minister to the Prime Minister" or "the personal staff officer to the Prime Minister" (Heeney, 1967: 367). It is interesting to note, however, that no secretaries to the Cabinet since Gordon Robertson have described their main job as secretary to the Cabinet. In 1997, the PCO produced a document on its role and structure whose very first page makes it clear that the secretary's first responsibility is to the prime minister. The document has not been revised to this day. It states that the "Clerk of the Privy Council and Secretary to the Cabinet" has three primary responsibilities:

1. As the Prime Minister's Deputy Minister, provides advice and support to the Prime Minister on a full range of responsibilities as head of government, including management of the federation.
2. As the Secretary to the Cabinet, provides support and advice to the Ministry as a whole and oversees the provision of policy and secretariat support to Cabinet and Cabinet committee.
3. As Head of the Public Service, is responsible for the quality of expert, professional and non-partisan advice and service provided by the Public Service to the Prime Minister, the Ministry and to all Canadians. (Canada, 1997: 1)

It is also important to recognize that the prime minister no longer needs to rely on regional ministers for an understanding of how government policies are being received. Public opinion surveys are more reliable, more objective, less regionally biased, more to the point, and easier to cope with than are ministers. Trudeau had Martin Goldfarb; Mulroney had Allan Gregg; Chrétien had Michael Marzolini; Paul Martin had David Herle; and Stephen Harper has relied on Ottawa-based Praxicus Public Strategies. Surveys can enable prime ministers and their advisors to challenge the views of ministers. After all, how can even the most senior ministers dispute what the polls say?

A pollster in court always at the ready with data can be particularly helpful in dealing with the problem of political overload. "Political overload" refers to a pervasive sense of urgency and an accompanying feeling of being overwhelmed both by events and the number of matters needing attention. A pollster can also advise the prime minister on "hot button" issues.

Prime ministers, at least since Trudeau, have decided that the best way to deal with the overload problem is to focus on a handful of policy issues and to rely on central agencies to manage the rest. All of the major policy initiatives in Trudeau's last mandate (1980–84), including the national energy program, the Constitution, and the "six and five" wage restraint initiative, were organized outside of the government's formal decision-making process (*Globe and Mail*, 1997: A1). Similarly, Mulroney sidestepped Cabinet in pursuing constitutional reform, the Canada-US Free Trade Agreement, and the establishment of regional economic development agencies. At a considerable cost to the Treasury, Chrétien paid no attention to the formal decision-making process when he decided to introduce the millennium scholarship fund for low- to moderate-income students. The Cabinet was not consulted before the fund was unveiled, even though Chrétien called it "the government's most significant millennium project" (Savoie, 1999: 297). Chrétien, like Mulroney and Trudeau before him, also did not consult Cabinet before striking several important bilateral deals with provincial premiers. Martin negotiated a costly health-care agreement with the provinces without consulting Cabinet, and Harper, as already noted, decided to recognize Quebec as a nation within Canada without consulting Cabinet and decided to deploy military personnel to Afghanistan without consulting the relevant minister, let alone Cabinet.

So, what actually goes on in Cabinet meetings? The first item is "General Discussion," which the Prime Minister opens and leads. He can raise any matter he chooses, ranging from a letter he may have received from a premier, to a purely partisan matter, to diplomacy. The PCO prepares a briefing note of possible talking points for the Prime Minister to speak from. But he can, of course, completely ignore it. However, the "General Discussion" can be particularly useful to prime ministers as a cover to make it appear that Cabinet has indeed considered an important issue that could, for example, be life-threatening or require military intervention. Mulroney, for instance, agreed to participate in the first Gulf War in a discussion with President George H.W. Bush, but raised the matter in Cabinet so that he could report that Cabinet had indeed reviewed the situation.

The second item on the Cabinet agenda is called "Presentations." Ministers, at times accompanied by their deputy ministers, are on occasions invited to give briefing sessions on various issues. The minister of finance and his deputy minister might present a "deck" on the government's fiscal position. Or the minister of industry and his deputy might make a presentation on Canada's productivity in relation to the United States. At the end of the presentation, ministers are free to raise any question or to ask for further clarification or explanation. But actual decisions rarely, if ever, flow out of these discussions. The purpose is to brief Cabinet, not to secure decisions.

The third item is "Nominations." Government appointments, ranging from Supreme Court judges, to senators, to deputy ministers, to members of the board of a Crown corporation, all require an order-in-council. There is always a list of appointments to be confirmed at every Cabinet meeting. However, the nominations have all been sorted out well in advance of the meeting. The PMO and the PCO manage the appointment process, and they consult with others only to the extent they want to.

To be sure, prime ministers do not seek Cabinet consensus when appointing Supreme Court judges or even senators. Suffice to note that the *Ottawa Citizen* had it right when it wrote that "Mulroney's Supreme Court may soon become Jean Chrétien's court" because of "an unusual confluence of expected retirements" (*Ottawa Citizen*, 1997: A7). The Supreme Court is now well on its way to becoming Harper's court. Nor do prime ministers seek Cabinet consensus when appointing deputy ministers or the administrative heads of government departments. Frequently, they do not even consult the relevant minister when appointing his or her deputy. I asked a former senior PCO official why it was that Jean Chrétien—when minister of, say, justice or energy in Trudeau's government—could not be trusted to appoint his own deputy minister, but that the moment he became prime minister he could be trusted to appoint all the deputy ministers? His response was simply: "Because he became king" (Savoie, 1999: 283).

The fourth item is "Cabinet committee decisions," presented as appendices on the agenda. In overhauling the Cabinet decision-making process, Trudeau made it clear that all decisions taken in Cabinet committee could be reopened for discussion in Cabinet. A former Trudeau minister reports that in his early years in office Trudeau was quite willing to let ministers reopen a Cabinet committee decision in full Cabinet. In time, however, he became annoyed with the practice and did not hesitate to show his displeasure whenever a minister sought to review an appendix item. Cabinet, he felt, simply did not have time available to discuss Cabinet committee decisions. In any event, by the late 1970s and the early 1980s, Trudeau automatically sent a Cabinet committee decision back to the committee for review whenever a minister raised questions about it in full Cabinet. Mulroney did much the same or relied on the operations committee of Cabinet, chaired by Don Mazankowski, to sort out problems with Cabinet committee decisions.

Chrétien did not react well when a Cabinet committee decision was challenged, and, like Trudeau in his later years, he automatically referred it back to the Cabinet committee without any discussion in full Cabinet. Harper is much like Chrétien. The result is that Cabinet committee decisions are now very rarely challenged in full Cabinet.

Mulroney, we now know, had little patience for the Cabinet process and at one point said that he "favoured any decision-making system that minimized the time he spent in cabinet" (Kroeger, 1998: 10). He preferred to deal with the big issues outside of Cabinet. The telephone and face-to-face conversation were his stock-in trade. Indeed, we are now informed that "under Mulroney, important matters such as energy mega-projects were often decided without benefit of any Cabinet documents at all" (Kroeger, 1998:10). The point is that Trudeau, Mulroney, Chrétien, Martin, and now Harper have all preferred to deal with major issues outside of the constraints imposed by the system. The result is that we now have policy-making by announcements. That is, the prime minister makes a major policy announcement, for example, as Chrétien did in the case of the Kyoto Accord, and the system scrambles to implement it.

On the heels of his 2008 re-election, Harper sent a directive to his minister of finance to scrap the $28 million in public subsidies that political parties receive for each vote they garner in a federal election. Word soon circulated around Ottawa and in the media that the decision was Harper's alone. His Cabinet was not consulted, nor obviously his caucus. He simply sent, at the last minute, a directive to the minister of finance to include it in his economic update statement "without ministers or deputy ministers knowing." This, in turn, the media argued, demonstrated that he was a "ferociously partisan leader" with a profound desire to centralize "everything in his own hands" (Simpson, 2008). We also know that Harper turns to Cabinet from time to time to prepare ministers for Question Period. It is part of Harper's desire and ability to control the government's agenda and message from the centre (Savoie, 2013).

To be sure, prime ministers do not always bypass their Cabinets or only consult them after the fact. They pick and choose issues they want to direct and in some circumstances may decide to let the Cabinet's collective decision-making process run its course. They may also even let the government caucus have its day from time to time and permit a government proposal or legislation to be pulled back and reworked to accommodate the views of caucus members. Mulroney, for example, attached a high priority to working with his caucus. These also are issues on which a prime minister may hold no firm view, and decide that it is best to keep one's political capital in reserve for another day and another issue.

Globalization

"Globalization" has also served to strengthen the hand of the prime minister. In hindsight, we may well have overstated the probability that globalization would spell gloom and doom for nation states (Savoie, 1995). Many national governments are discovering that the international environment can actually enhance their own power. The 2008 financial crisis, for example, forced the hand of national governments to intervene in financial markets and introduce new measures to stimulate economic growth.

In any event, Canadian prime ministers belong to a series of recently created international clubs of heads of government, from the G8 to Asia Pacific Economic Cooperation (APEC) and *la Francophonie*. Deals, even bilateral ones, between heads of governments are struck at these meetings. The globalization of the world economy means that many more issues or files are placed in the prime minister's in-basket. Everything in a government department now seems to connect to other departments and other governments, whether at the provincial level or internationally. In Canada, prime ministers and premiers sit at the centre of the public policy process, and when they decide to focus on a policy issue, they can very easily make it their own.

National governments, precisely because of global economic forces, now increasingly need to work with each other and with regional and international trade agreements. They also need a capacity to move quickly to strike new deals when the time is right or to change course because of emerging political and economic circumstances and opportunities. The focus will be on the heads of national governments. It is also they, not their ministers, who lead the discussions at G8, at Commonwealth meetings, at *la Francophonie,* and at the APEC conference, to name several of the international fora in which the prime minister participates.

That said, the global economy and the interconnected world of public policy issues have caused some power to move away from national governments, drifting up to international or regional trade agreements or organizations and down to local governments (Rose, 1984). Perhaps because there may now be somewhat less power to go around in the national government, the prime minister and his courtiers can rule with a heavy hand.

The Canadian prime minister, unlike the American president, who has to deal with Congress, or the Australian prime minister, who has to deal with a powerful and elected Senate, has a free hand to negotiate for his government and to make firm deals with foreign heads of government. The final hours of negotiations on NAFTA between Prime Minister-elect Chrétien and American President Bill Clinton, through his ambassador to Canada, are telling. At one point, the American ambassador wondered about Chrétien's political authority to agree to a final deal, given that he had yet to appoint his Cabinet. The ambassador put the question to Chrétien: "What happens if we work all this out and then your new trade minister doesn't agree?" Chrétien replied, "Then I will have a new trade minister the following morning" (Greenspon and Wilson-Smith, 1996: 48). It is hardly possible to overemphasize the fact that the Canadian prime minister has few limits defining his political authority within the government. The prime minister's power is limited only by the court of public opinion because his government has to seek a new mandate every four years, and by the scarcity of time because he cannot possibly attend every important meeting and deal with every issue.

The Working of Court Government

Canadian prime ministers have in their hands all the important levers of power. Indeed, one way or another all major national public policy roads lead to their doorstep. They are elected leader of their party by party members; they chair Cabinet meetings, establish Cabinet processes and procedures, set the Cabinet agenda, and establish the consensus for Cabinet decisions; they appoint and fire ministers and deputy ministers, establish Cabinet committees, and decide on their membership; they exercise virtually all the powers of patronage and act as personnel manager for thousands of government and patronage jobs; they articulate the government's strategic direction as outlined in the Speech from the Throne; they dictate the pace of change and are the main salespersons promoting the achievements of their government; they have a direct hand in establishing the government's fiscal framework; they represent Canada abroad; they establish the proper mandate of individual ministers and decide all machinery of government issues; and they are the final arbiter in interdepartmental conflicts. The prime minister is the only politician with a country-wide constituency, and unlike MPs and even Cabinet ministers, he does not need to search out publicity or national media attention, since attention is invariably focused on his office and his residence, 24 Sussex Drive. Each of these levers of power taken separately is a formidable instrument in its own right, but when you add them all up and place them in the hands of one individual, they constitute an unassailable advantage.

There is nothing new about this; Canadian prime ministers have enjoyed these avenues of power for some time. However, there have been other developments lately that have served to consolidate the position of the prime minister and his advisors even further. Indeed, this is now evident even before they and their party assume office. Transition planning has become a very important event, designed to prepare a new government to assume power.

Transition planning also strengthens the hand of court government, given that by definition it is designed to serve the prime minister. It is the PCO, however, that leads the process, and it is clear that "transition services are for the incoming prime minister" (Savoie, 1993: 8). Indeed, the focus of the PCO transition planning process is entirely on party leaders or would-be prime ministers. In any event, it would be difficult for it to be otherwise, since in the crucial days between the election victory and formally taking power, the only known member of the incoming Cabinet is the prime minister-elect. For other potential Cabinet ministers, it is a "moment of high anxiety," waiting to see if they will be invited to sit in Cabinet, and if so, in what portfolio (Savoie, 1993: 8).

The central purpose of transition planning is to equip the incoming prime minister to make his mark during the government's first few weeks in office. It is now widely recognized that these early weeks can be critical in setting the tone for how the new government will govern. It is also the period when the prime minister, as recent history shows, will make important decisions on the machinery of government and decide which major policy issues his government will tackle during its mandate. These and such key decisions as whether to try to amend the Constitution or fight the deficit are taken or set in motion during the transition period.

In the late 1970s, the PCO began the practice of preparing mandate letters for delivery to ministers on the day of their appointments. It has since become an integrated part of the Cabinet-making process. Mandate letters are also now handed to all ministers when they are assigned to a new portfolio. All ministers in the Chrétien government, for example, were given a mandate letter at the time he formed the government in 1993, again when his second mandate began in 1997, and yet again in his third mandate in 2000. The same was true for Paul Martin in 2003 and 2004 and Stephen Harper in 2006, 2008, and 2011.

What are the contents of these mandate letters? In most cases, they are brief, only about two to three pages in length. They are also tailored to the recipient. That is, a mandate letter to a newly appointed minister will be different from one to a veteran minister. In the first instance, it will outline basic information about becoming a Cabinet minister, including conflict-of-interest guidelines, and the need to respect the collective nature of Cabinet decisions. In all cases, the letters will delineate issues the minister should attend to and identify priority areas, if any, to be pursued. Here, again, there are two basic mandate letters. One states, in effect, "Don't call us, we'll call you." That is, the Prime Minister has decided that the department in question should not come up with a new policy agenda or legislative program. In these cases, the message is essentially: keep things going, do not cause any ripples, and keep out of trouble (Savoie, 1999: 138). In other instances, the letter will refer to particular policy objectives and major challenges. In these cases, they can be quite specific, singling out proposed legislation, a special concern that needs attending to, or a program that needs to be overhauled. Mandate letters are now also prepared for newly-appointed deputy ministers. Here again the purpose is to outline the main challenges the new deputy ministers will be confronting and the priorities they will be expected to follow.

Are mandate letters taken seriously? The answer is yes. Indeed, ministers consulted said that it is the very first thing that they read after leaving the swearing-in ceremony at Rideau Hall and that they take their contents quite seriously. They know, as one observed, that "the prime minister can always dig out his copy and ask about the status of a particular point" (personal communication). More importantly, the letters reveal what the prime minister expects from them during their stay in their departments. Both present and former PMO and PCO officials report that all prime ministers, from Trudeau to Harper, take the mandate letters seriously and that they spend the required time to ensure that each says what they wish it to say.

Ministers, leaving aside a few exceptions, no longer leave Cabinet over a policy disagreement. Much more often, ministers leave after receiving a patronage appointment from the prime minister—a Senate, judicial, or diplomatic appointment. Notable recent exceptions include Lucien Bouchard (1990) from the Mulroney Cabinet and Michael Chang (2006) from the Harper Cabinet. Both resigned over national unity questions.

The budget has become the government's major policy statement and defines in very specific terms what the government will do in the coming months and where it will be spending new money. Traditionally, the government's budget process pitted guardians (e.g., the prime minister and minister of finance) against spenders (ministers of line departments and regional ministers) (Savoie, 1990). Efforts were made under Trudeau and Mulroney to establish various systems to allocate the spending of "new" money, but they all fell far short of the mark.

The prime minister, the minister of finance, and their advisors have, for some time now, combined the guardian and spender roles. The budget exercise is no longer strictly concerned with the country's broad economic picture, projecting economic growth, establishing the fiscal framework, and deciding which taxes ought to be introduced, increased, or decreased. It now deals with both "big" and "small" decisions, "revenue" projections, and spending decisions (Good, 2007). For example, when senior military officials in Canada sought to replace their armoured vehicles, they bypassed Cabinet to appeal directly to the prime minister. Lieutenant-General Andrew Leslie told the media that he hoped "Stephen Harper will replace the old tanks," adding that he expected "the Prime Minister's decision within about a week" (*Globe and Mail*, 2007: A1). In addition, when the centre of government decides to sponsor new initiatives, it will much more often than not secure the required funding outside of the Cabinet process (Savoie, 2013).

The role of the Clerk of the Privy Council and secretary to the Cabinet has changed a great deal in recent years, and the clerk's influence in Ottawa is readily apparent to everyone inside the system. Outsiders, however, know very little about the clerk's role and responsibilities. One of the main challenges confronting a clerk is to establish a proper balance between representing the public service as an institution to the prime minister and Cabinet and representing the prime minister to the public service. The balance appears to have shifted to the latter with the appointment of 37-year-old Michael Pitfield as clerk-secretary in 1975 by Pierre Trudeau. The balance may well have shifted even further in favour of the prime minister when Paul Tellier decided, as clerk-secretary under Mulroney, to add the title of the prime minister's deputy minister to his job.

Tellier's decision, however, probably simply reflected the reality of his day-to-day work. Indeed, the clerk-secretary is accountable to the prime minister, not to Cabinet, and the great majority of his daily activities are now designed to support the prime minister, not Cabinet. The prime minister, not Cabinet, appoints the clerk; the prime minister, not Cabinet, evaluates his performance; and the prime minister, not Cabinet, will decide if he stays or if he should be replaced. All this is to say that not only does the secretary to Cabinet wear the hat of deputy minister to the prime minister, it is without doubt the hat that fits best and the one he wears nearly all the time. A former senior PCO official observed that "all clerks since Pitfield have done an excellent job at being deputy minister to the prime minister. As far as secretary to the Cabinet, the performance has been spotty."[1]

The way to govern in Ottawa—at least since Trudeau—is for prime ministers to focus on three or four priority issues, while also always keeping an eye on Quebec and national unity concerns. Tom Axworthy, former principal secretary to Pierre Trudeau, in his appropriately titled article, "Of Secretaries to Princes," wrote that "only with maximum prime ministerial involvement could the host of obstacles that stand in the way of reform be overcome ... the prime minister must choose relatively few central themes, not only because of the time demands on the prime minister, but also because it takes a herculean effort to coordinate the government machine" (Axworthy, 1988: 247). To perform a herculean effort, a prime minister needs carefully selected individuals in key positions to push his agenda. Cabinet, the public service as an institution, or even government departments are not always helpful.

The result is that important decisions are no longer made in Cabinet. They are now made in the PMO, in the PCO, in the Department of Finance, in international organizations, and at international summits. There is no indication that the one person who holds all the cards, the prime minister, and the central agencies that enable him to bring effective political authority to the centre, are about to change things. The Canadian prime minister has little in the way of internal institutional checks to inhibit his ability to have his way.

In Canada, national unity concerns, the nature of federal-provincial relations, and the role of the media tend, in a perverse fashion, to favour the centre of government in Ottawa. The prime minister's court dominates the policy agenda and permeates government decision-making to such an extent that it is only willing to trust itself to overseeing the management of important issues. In a sense, the centre of government has come to fear ministerial and line department independence more than it deplores line department paralysis. As a result, court government is probably better suited to managing the political agenda than is Cabinet government. The prime minister, like the European monarchs of yesterday, decides, at least within the federal government, who has standing at court. Prime Minister Chrétien left little doubt that Canada had made the transition to court government when he observed that "The Prime Minister is the Prime Minister and he has the cabinet to advise him. At the end of the day, it is the Prime Minister who says 'yes' or 'no'" (*Globe and Mail*, 2000: A4).

Advisors, much like courtiers of old, have influence, not power. Jean Chrétien made his view clear that ministers have influence, not power, in Cabinet when he wrote: "ministers may have great authority within his department, but within Cabinet he is merely part of a collectivity, just another advisor to the prime minister. He can be told what to do and on important matters his only choice is to do or resign" (Chrétien, 1985: 85). One of Chrétien's former senior policy advisors unwittingly described court government well when he wrote that "Everything a prime minister says is unfortunately taken by some as coming from the fount of all wisdom. Often the prime minister is just throwing out an idea or suggestion for debate and discussion—it is solemnly transcribed as if it were one of the Ten Commandments" (Goldenberg, 2006: 83). He was referring to both elected politicians and senior civil servants. Henry VIII and his ilk, the absolute monarchs of yore, would have expected nothing less from their courtiers.

Note

1 Consultation with a former senior PCO official, Ottawa, November 1997.

References and Suggested Readings

Axworthy, Thomas S. 1988. "Of Secretaries to Princes." *Canadian Public Administration* 31 (2): 247–64. http://dx.doi.org/10.1111/j.1754-7121.1988.tb01316.x.

Cameron, David, and Richard Simeon. 2000. "Intergovernmental Relations and Democratic Citizenship." In *Revitalizing the Public Service: A Governance Vision for the XXIst Century*, eds. B. Guy Peters and Donald J. Savoie, 58–118. Montreal: McGill-Queen's University Press.

Canada, Privy Council Office. 1993. *Responsibility in the Constitution*. Ottawa: Government of Canada.

Canada, Privy Council Office. 1997. *The Role and Structure of the Privy Council Office*. Ottawa: Government of Canada.

Chrétien, Jean. 1985. *Straight from the Heart*. Toronto: Key Porter Books.

Cooper, Andrew F. 1997. *Between Countries: Australia, Canada and the Search for Order in Agricultural Trade*. Montreal: McGill-Queen's University Press.

Dupré, J.S. 1987. "The Workability of Executive Federalism in Canada." In *Federalism and the Role of the State*, eds. H. Bakvis and W. Chandler, 236–58. Toronto: University of Toronto Press.

Globe and Mail. 1997. "Spending Limits Irk Cabinet," December 3: A1.

Globe and Mail. 2000. "Penalty Killer PM Plays Rough," December 1: A4.

Globe and Mail. 2006. "Inside Story," November 24: A1, A4.

Globe and Mail. 2007. "All LAV IIIs to Be Replaced Within a Year," April 3: A1.

Goldenberg, Eddie. 2006. *The Way It Works: Inside Ottawa*. Toronto: McClelland and Stewart.

Good, David A. 2007. *The Politics of Public Money: Spenders, Guardians, Priority Setters and Financial Watchdogs Inside the Canadian Government*. Toronto: IPAC and University of Toronto Press.

Greenspon, Edward, and Anthony Wilson-Smith. 1996. *Double Vision: The Inside Story of the Liberals in Power*. Toronto: Doubleday.

Heeney, A.D.P. 1967. "Mackenzie King and the Cabinet Secretariat." *Canadian Public Administration* 10 (3): 359–75.

Johnston, Richard, André Blais, Henry Brady, and Jean Crête. 1992. *Letting the People Decide: The Dynamics of a Canadian Election*. Stanford: Stanford University Press.

Kroeger, Arthur. 1998. "A Retrospective on Policy Development in Ottawa." Ottawa: Mimeo.

Murray, Lowell. 2013. "Power, Responsibility and Agency in Canadian Government." In *Governing: Essays in Honour of Donald J. Savoie*, eds. James Bickerton and B. Guy Peters, 25–31. Montreal: McGill-Queen's University Press.

The Ottawa Citizen. 1997. "Chrétien Set to Remake Top Court," December 14, A7.

Polsby, Nelson W., and Aaron Wildavsky. 1991. *Presidential Elections: Strategies of American Electoral Politics*. New York: Free Press.

Robertson, Gordon. 1971. "The Changing Role of the Privy Council Office" *Canadian Public Administration* 14 (4): 487–508. http://dx.doi.org/10.1111/j.1754-7121.1971.tb00295.x.

Rose, Richard. 1984. *Understanding Big Government*. London: Sage.

Savoie, Donald J. 1990. *The Politics of Public Spending in Canada*. Toronto: University of Toronto Press.

Savoie, Donald J. 1993. "Introduction." In *Taking Power: Managing Government Transitions*, ed. Donald J. Savoie, 1–15. Toronto: Institute of Public Administration of Canada.

Savoie, Donald J. 1995. "Globalization, Nation States, and the Civil Service." In *Governance in a Changing Environment*, eds. B. Guy Peters and Donald J. Savoie, 82–112. Montreal: McGill-Queen's University Press.

Savoie, Donald J. 1999. *Governing from the Centre: The Concentration of Power in Canadian Politics*. Toronto: University of Toronto Press.

Savoie, Donald J. 2013. *Whatever Happened to the Music Teacher: How Government Decides and Why*. Montreal: McGill-Queen's University Press.

Simpson, Jeffrey. 2005. "From Pariah to Messiah: Send in the Clerk." *Globe and Mail*, March 9: A15.

Simpson, Jeffrey. 2008. "After the Storm." *Globe and Mail*, December 5: A17.

Sutherland, Sharon. 1991. "Responsible Government and Ministerial Responsibility: Every Reform is Its Own Problem." *Canadian Journal of Political Science* 24 (01): 91–120.

Sutherland, Sharon L. 1996. "Does Westminster Government Have a Future?" Ottawa: Institute of Governance, Occasional Paper Series.

eight
Parliament:
Making the Case for Relevance[1]

DAVID C. DOCHERTY

Parliament Hill in Ottawa is the heart of democracy in Canada. Yet, for many Canadians, Parliament seems to have decreasing relevance to their lives. Politicians are seen as out of touch, and political parties, due to ineptitude or self-interest, as concerned more with their political survival than with the public good. Members of Parliament (MPs) are viewed as slaves to their party leadership. Trade agreements such as NAFTA and the Canada-European Union Trade Agreement, and international organizations such as the World Trade Organization (WTO), seem to place the management of the economy well beyond the control of parliamentarians and even government policy-makers. On many social and criminal issues the courts seem more progressive—or at least more proactive—than our elected officials do.

For these and other reasons, it is no wonder that many Canadians, particularly young Canadians, find Parliament a remote and irrelevant institution. This is unfortunate, as the business of Parliament is truly the people's business. If the people care little about it and give little attention to it, perhaps it should not be surprising if parliamentary actors respond in kind.

In this chapter, we will argue that legislatures in Canada do matter; to function properly, however, they require not only a strong prime minister and Cabinet, but also a strong opposition and a government caucus willing to keep government leaders in line. Legislatures remain relevant only to the extent that governments allow them to be; this is a fundamental requirement of good and accountable government in a parliamentary system. In order for Canadians to truly understand this, they must first understand Parliament's constitutional roles and functions.

Responsible Government in Canada

To some, the very term "responsible government" suggests an outdated system of representation. Some critics of our system suggest that this form of government is not acutely responsive to the day-to-day problems of Canadians. According to this critical view, a government that is responsive automatically answers the demands of the public. The past, however, has provided disastrous evidence of what can happen when this kind of populist form of government runs amok: in 2003, a California governor was recalled and then replaced on the same ballot, with 135 candidates seeking the position. When politicians are forced to continually run for office, there is little time left for them to devote to actually governing.

Canada's system is far from that responsive, but that is not to say it is immune to public demands, or that it lacks accountability to the electorate. Responsible government does not, by definition, mean unresponsive. Truly responsible government is responsive both directly to citizens and to their elected representatives in Parliament.

The principle of responsible government is remarkable for its simplicity and elegance.

- Members of Parliament are elected to sit in a legislature. Citizens hold these representatives responsible to be honest and straightforward in their spending of the public's money. If citizens are displeased with the performance of their MPs, they may remove them from office at the next election.
- Cabinet members are selected by the prime minister from the legislature. The Cabinet introduces legislation in Parliament that raises money (via taxes) and spends money (via programs), and is responsible to the legislature for the proper administration of the civil service and programs under their supervision.
- The professional public service is charged with implementing legislation, and is responsible to Cabinet for its conduct.

Governments are responsive in several different ways. First, governments must always have the confidence of the majority in the House of Commons to govern effectively. Typically, this has meant that the government is formed by the party with the most seats in the assembly, either with more than half the seats (majority government), or without a majority but more seats than any other party—a plurality (minority government). Soon after an election, the leader of the party with the most seats in the House of Commons visits the governor general to state his/her ability to form a government and maintain the confidence of the House. That person then becomes prime minister and governs for up to five years (the constitutional limit on governments), or as long as they enjoy that confidence, which is continually tested through votes in the legislature.

The threat that such confidence may not exist on a continuing basis makes the prime minister responsive to the concerns of his/her own government caucus and even the opposition parties. Should they lose the confidence of the House (as signified by defeat on a vote), the government would fall and an election would likely be forthcoming. This has led some political scientists to suggest that parliamentary democracy is the most sensitive (or responsive) of all forms of government (J. Smith, 2001). However, Canada's traditional emphasis on party discipline has meant that, in times of majority government, retaining the confidence of the House is a must. In circumstances where prime ministers attempt to govern with only a plurality of seats, the governments they lead become much more responsive to the opposition.

Of course, as we witnessed in 2008, the failure of a government to keep the confidence of the House does not necessarily trigger an election. Shortly after winning a minority Prime Minister Harper learned that he would lose a vote of confidence in the House of Commons and that the Liberals had an agreement with the New Democratic Party to form a coalition government to replace him. By proroguing (temporarily shutting down) Parliament, the prime minister bought time to take actions to prevent his defeat. However, with defeat in the House coming so soon after the election, it was clear that the constitution would permit a change of government without another election, something that had not happened for nearly 90 years.

A government needs to proceed with its agenda. A government is elected based on a specific platform, and it must be allowed to implement these election promises upon its victory. At the same time, it must be recognized that unplanned events or problems may thwart its plans (Atkinson and Docherty, 2004). Whatever its agenda, a government needs to know it has, at a minimum, the support of its own legislators in Parliament to govern effectively, or at least to have the opportunity of doing so.

At the same time, the legislature has many avenues available to keep the government accountable. These include but are not limited to Question Period, legislative committees, caucuses, and legislative debates. All of these mechanisms play a role in helping to ensure government is both responsible and accountable. The challenge for any Parliament is to strike a balance that allows the government to pursue the implementation of its plans and agenda, while also allowing those in Parliament who are outside cabinet (both government supporters and opponents) to hold the executive accountable by questioning its decisions and planned course of action and by ensuring that it governs in a transparent manner.

Though it may take some time, the public will lose patience with legislatures that move too far from this delicate balance. If the opposition and government backbench MPs do not perform their duties, citizens may feel they are living in a system of benign dictatorship, where the government can impose its will in an unimpeded fashion—getting away with anything between elections. Certainly, the governments presided over by Jean

Chrétien between 1993 and 2003 came close to fitting this description (Savoie 1999). A weak, inexperienced, and divided opposition—combined with a strictly disciplined government caucus—allowed successive Liberal majority governments to implement their policies with little impediment. Under Stephen Harper, strict party discipline has been supplemented by a tightly controlled message from his cabinet. Over his first seven years in office, the prime minister gained a deserved reputation for having his fingers on every government file. Only a select few cabinet ministers enjoyed the privilege of speaking openly without first having their comments cleared by the Prime Minister's Office (PMO). The era of strong regional ministers, once the hallmark of Canadian governments, has long since been replaced by a regime of authoritative communications officers and other non-elected advisors who report directly to the prime minister.

Citizens may also grow to fear a government that avoids the legislature and attempts to govern without having to bother with the accountability mechanisms built into the rules and procedures of Parliament. When the government limits the number of days for which an assembly sits, for example, there are fewer opportunities for opposition members to question the cabinet about its spending. If the government limits the number of days a bill may be debated, there is less chance for the public to have input on proposed legislation and for opposition members to propose constructive amendments or alternatives based on this input. Under these conditions, citizens may justifiably suspect that there is a democratic deficit. For Parliament to work, all elected members must be provided the opportunity to perform their responsibilities—whether or not they are in cabinet posts.

Of course, it is not just the government's own actions that can discredit Parliament in the eyes of Canadians. If the opposition is needlessly obstructive, the government may be hamstrung in the pursuit of its own reading of the public good. It is one thing for an opposition party to attempt to disrupt the government's legislative agenda through aggressive questioning; it is quite another to allow unsubstantiated allegations of impropriety to gridlock legislative proposals or budget measures. When parliamentary stalemate becomes the norm and the government is rendered unable to govern, the public interest is poorly served, and it conveys the sense that the system is dysfunctional: simply not working as it should.

It is hardly surprising, then, that Canadians may believe that Parliament has become irrelevant—there are so many opportunities for members on all sides of the House to make it so! Responsible government may deteriorate very quickly into either reckless or stagnant government. In such circumstances, Canadians are left to wonder whether the problems lay with the design of their political institutions or with the men and women elected to serve within them. All too often, they conclude it is both.

In many ways, this vague understanding is correct. In order for Parliament to function effectively and therefore to be relevant in a modern democracy, a combination of properly constructed and observed rules and good representatives is required. Legislators cannot effectively represent citizens if they are bound too tightly by the rules of the assembly. Similarly, if the legislature is peopled predominantly by individuals who are self-interested or incompetent, it might just as well stand empty. At the same time, the public and press often focus on one or two examples of bad behaviour and ignore the meritorious good works that Parliament and parliamentarians perform every day.

The remainder of this chapter provides an overview of Canada's parliament—both the institution itself and some of the primary rules governing its functions. The men and women elected to public office in Canada are generally well disposed to provide strong representation. However, the rules and conventions of Parliament place a great deal of authority in the hands of Cabinet and the prime minister. As a result, elected representatives not surprisingly place much emphasis on joining the ranks of Cabinet. New rules to reinforce the relevance of parliamentary careers outside of Cabinet would go a long way toward making a more effective and relevant legislature.

The House of Commons and the Senate

The Parliament of Canada is made up of three components: the Crown, the Senate, and the House of Commons. These positions are attained through hereditary title, appointment, and election, respectively. At first blush, this arrangement may appear undemocratic, particularly when one thinks of Parliament as the elected branch of the government, and then realizes that only one of its three parts is chosen via the expressed will of the public.

Many Canadians may forget that the Crown (in the person of the Queen or her representative, the governor general) is an integral part of Parliament. The governor general must sign legislation in order for it to become law. This is just as important as a bill being approved by both the House and Senate. This signature (referred to as Royal Assent) is a public declaration that the deliberative process to turn a bill into a law has been followed and that the law is therefore legitimate.

There are other ways, though, that the Crown remains an important part of the present legislative system, even if one believes—as many do—that the royal connection to Canada has lost its relevance. For example, the opening of every parliamentary session begins with the Speech from the Throne. Read by the governor general, this speech sets out the government's plans for the coming legislative session. The debate that takes place during the subsequent six days provides all members with an opportunity to share the concerns of their particular constituency or party with the rest of the country. Governments also use royal commissions to investigate matters of substantial public interest and importance. Commissions enjoy an independence from the government of the day and are thus able to bring an objective (or at least non-partisan) approach to their work. (Some examples of recent Crown commissions include the Royal Commission on the Future of Health Care in Canada, the Commission of Inquiry into the Sponsorship Program and Advertising Activities, and the Commission of Inquiry into the Investigation of the Bombing of Air India Flight 182.)

The Crown is also responsible for ensuring that Parliament can function by asking a party leader to form a government. Had Stephen Harper faced and lost that planned vote of non-confidence in 2008, he would have visited the governor general to indicate that he could no longer lead the government. The governor general would have then decided whether an election was necessary or whether someone else (in the case in question, then Liberal leader Stéphane Dion) should become prime minister. As previously noted, Mr. Harper was able to avoid the vote when the governor general allowed him to prorogue Parliament.

The Canadian Senate is one of the few non-elected upper chambers in democratic states (another being the British House of Lords). Because the Senate was created to represent Canadian regional interests, it is not surprising that it was constituted along regional lines rather than provincial boundaries. The four regional divisions in the Senate that exist to this day are defined as the West, Ontario, Quebec, and the Maritimes, each with 24 Senate seats. Upon its entry into Confederation, Newfoundland and Labrador was allocated six senators and the three northern territories have one each, for a total Senate complement of 105.

The single largest criticism of the Senate is that this is an unelected—and therefore, in the minds of most Canadians, undemocratic—body. It is true that to become a senator all one needs is a small plot of land, a Senate vacancy and a prime minister who owes you for your hard partisan work.[2] Once appointed, and provided you follow proper expense reimbursement procedures, you are not accountable for your actions in that you enjoy job security until age 75. As long as the prime minister follows the regional constraints, they have unlimited power to select whomever they wish. With the exception of Paul Martin, recent prime ministers have been loath to appoint senators who represent opposition parties, or to take advice from premiers on who to appoint, in the interests of rebalancing the partisan affiliations after a shift in power.

As a result, the Senate has a difficult time establishing itself as a relevant legislative body. This is further hampered by the fact that it does not do a great job of representing regional interests. While these are not the same as provincial interests, the fact is that premiers are seen as a far more legitimate voice for local interests than senators. Canadians seem far more comfortable with our present system of interstate federalism than with intrastate models where regions are represented inside the federal government. Further, voters see a unicameral legislature in their own province and legitimately wonder why two chambers, one of which is appointed, are necessary at the federal level.

Critics of the Senate sometimes argue that it is obstructionist and slows down the work of the democratically elected House. Supporters of the Senate might agree but would quickly and correctly add that this is one of its primary functions. Like all upper chambers, the Canadian Senate was designed specifically to act as a check on the lower House. However, it must do so in a responsible manner. That is, its role is to slow the process of governing in a manner that allows the government to reflect carefully on the policies and legislation it is pursuing. This is the essence of the Senate function of "sober second thought."

In this regard, the Canadian Senate's record is mixed, though it fares better than most Canadians imagine. Unfortunately, much of the good work of the Senate is marred by occasional incidents of poor performance, such as lack of attendance on the part of some, or holding up legislation that has been passed with the majority of elected MPs supporting it. Personal gaffes and indiscretions are also increasingly visible due to the proliferation of social media streams such as Twitter. In 2013 the Senate came under scrutiny for the behaviour of some of its members. Senators are supposed to live in the region they represent and receive an Ottawa living allowance if that residence is more than 100 kilometres away from the capital. Three senators were found to have their primary residence in Ottawa, thereby being subsidized for the wrong residence. An additional Senator has been under investigation for her rather extravagant travel expenses. The fact that three of the appointees were Conservative members has placed the prime minister—no fan of the Senate—in an awkward situation. He has benefited from public anger at the existing Senate but now is seen as being unable to do much to fix the structure of the Senate. Such actions from less than three per cent of the Senate membership make it difficult for others to paint the Senate in a better light.

Less heralded by the media and parliamentary observers is the amount of hard work and effort exerted by most senators in the governing process. For example, the Senate is often able to examine important national issues free of overtly partisan content and free from the pressure of government time restraints. During debate on the Clarity Act,[3] for example, the Senate did not break down along party lines: several Liberal senators were unafraid to oppose the wishes of their government (Franks, 2003, 168). In addition, witnesses who appeared before the Senate on this bill were accorded far more time to discuss their views than were those who presented their views in front of the Commons committee (Joyal, 2000: 15; see also D. Smith, 2003: 133–35).

The Senate also provides an invaluable investigative service. As Franks points out, Senate committees have produced thoughtful and detailed reports on everything from euthanasia to the financial services sector (Franks, 1987: 177–80). The Senate is able to draw on the experience of its members (and the fact that it often works beneath the radar) to draft reports that are relatively free of the dissent and division that may characterize reports written by House of Commons committees.

Finally, it is worth noting that one benefit to an appointed body is that it can actually be more representative of the general population. The Senate has a better record on the representation of women and aboriginal Canadians than most elected legislatures. It may not be democratically elected, but it can be representative. Critics of this argument correctly point out that such representation is dependent upon a prime minister who sees diversity as important and the Senate could just as easily be less diverse than elected legislatures.

There have been many attempts at Senate reform, but most have met with failure. Major Senate reform requires some constitutional amendments, and the political price of engaging in constitutional discussions is higher than most politicians are willing to pay.[4] As a result, most observers are reduced to considering non-constitutional reforms that could make the Senate more satisfactory to the Canadian public. Stephen Harper has appointed senators who have pledged self-imposed term limits. In addition, Alberta holds elections for Senate nominees during provincial votes. Prime Minister Harper has been honouring this list and may well establish a practice that might become constitutional custom. At the same time, the prime minister's own attempts at Senate reform have not been very successful, and in turning to the courts to weigh on the constitutionality of his proposals the prime minister may be indicating that this is a battle that cannot be easily won.

The House of Commons would have a harder time than the Senate does in blaming selection rules for its lack of support. It is true that the Canadian electoral system tends to distort the relationship between the number of votes a party receives and its share of seats. For this reason, it is difficult for any government to lay claim to a countrywide mandate. Often, large Canadian regions are underrepresented in the governing party and cabinet. But, having conceded this, one can agree that it is the Commons that

Canadians acknowledge as the democratically selected branch of Parliament. Therefore, if there is a perception of the irrelevance of Parliament, it is the Commons that should be the focus of attention. If one cannot argue that the elected branch is relevant, one might as well forgo any discussion of the other two components and concentrate instead on building a completely new institution. Of course, that is not likely to happen any time soon. Thus, the remainder of this chapter examines the House of Commons, its primary accountability mechanisms and functions, and the problems it faces. The chapter concludes with a discussion of recommendations for making the Commons more relevant.

Cabinet versus Private Members

The House of Commons is an executive-centred institution. The executive is composed of some members of the governing caucus. With the typical exception of the government leader in the Senate, most cabinet ministers are members of the Commons. Despite the fact that Cabinet is accountable to all members, there are three factors that give Cabinet ministers added influence and authority in the lower house.

First, only Cabinet ministers can introduce legislation that raises or spends public money. Members of the executive are "ministers of the Crown" and seek parliamentary approval for the raising and spending of money. This historic fact effectively institutionalizes two classes of MP. Once introduced in the house, money bills are almost automatically considered matters of confidence.[5] Should a government introduce such a piece of legislation and have it defeated, it must then call an election. Typically, money bills are only brought forward for a vote when the government knows it will be successful. Governments can also fall if opposition parties can garner majority support for votes of non-confidence in the government. Recently the previous two minority governments of Paul Martin and Stephen Harper were brought down due to opposition votes of non-confidence.

The second factor, closely related to the first, is that Cabinet ministers have far greater influence in the policy process. While all MPs enjoy some degree of influence, there is little argument that an executive-centred Parliament provides the most authority to Cabinet ministers (Docherty, 1997: 95–7). Having the ability to introduce legislation is perhaps the greatest (but far from only) perk of being in Cabinet. Policies and plans of the government are vetted by the Cabinet and its various committees. Spending priorities and the direction of social and fiscal policy are ultimately determined by the prime minister and the minister of finance. The closer one is to these power brokers, the more influence one holds.

Finally, although large electoral swings can make any member vulnerable, cabinet ministers tend to enjoy longer and more electorally secure political careers than private members or even former cabinet ministers (Atkinson and Docherty, 1992). Part of this security is derived from the greater national profile enjoyed by members of Cabinet, and from the apparent local rewards they are provided.

Even beyond the higher pay and the provision of a car and driver, the combination of formal and informal power makes Cabinet a most desirable career option. It is not surprising, therefore, that most MPs hope to one day "make it" into Cabinet. Surveys of MPs have consistently found that over three quarters of them think that getting into Cabinet is at least somewhat important to having a successful political career (Docherty, 1997: 98–100). Since fewer than 20 per cent of all legislators make it to Cabinet, this career objective is rooted more in optimism than reality.

But the primacy of Cabinet also places great control in the hands of the prime minister. As with Senate appointments, it is the head of the government who chooses who will be at the cabinet table. In the process of cabinet formation, a prime minister must balance many considerations. In an ideal world, the brightest and most able members of the governing party would be equitably distributed among the provinces and also reflect perfectly the mix of gender, religion, and ethnic diversity of the country. Not surprisingly, this has yet to happen. This means the prime minister must balance the requirement of talent and expertise with the political goal of having at least one cabinet minister from every province, while balancing the risks of either excluding or including former rivals for their job. Close rivals often find their way into Cabinet, while the supporters of failed leadership contenders may be marginalized. Consequently, possessing a fortuitous combination of demography and loyalty is often a quicker route to the Cabinet table than the possession of skill and talent.

Private members, elected members who are not appointed to Cabinet, have a less glamorous, but nonetheless important role in the governance process. Among the myriad responsibilities of private members, five stand out in particular.

1. One of their primary functions is to keep Cabinet ministers accountable. They do this in the full knowledge that ministers spend much of their day trying to avoid answering questions, so this duty can often been seen as an uphill battle. Opposition parties arrange their caucuses in a manner that tries to facilitate this role: for each Cabinet minister there is at least one "shadow Cabinet" member or opposition critic. Critics are expected to become experts on the department they are

shadowing. In smaller parties, where the caucus is smaller than the Cabinet, critic portfolios are often doubled up, and one member shadows more than one minister.

2. Private members also try to influence and shape public policies. Members are expected to be the voice in Ottawa of their constituency. This means they must push policies that reflect the public sentiment in their riding, knowing that on many issues the public sentiment is at best split. Whether through committee work, private members' business, questions in the House, or meetings with cabinet ministers and government officials, individual members can sometimes influence which public policies are implemented—and how.

3. They are also expected to examine government legislation in detail. Franks correctly argues that MPs do not initiate legislation, they pass or defeat it (1987: 5–8). In the process of passing legislation, however, there is much work to be done, and bills may be altered significantly. Committees provide backbenchers a great opportunity to strengthen and modify government initiatives, to the point that they become the unsung heroes of the House of Commons. They excel when examining bills and overseeing activities of the government, despite the many challenges they face. One of the biggest barriers for committees is workload. The central government is so large that using the committee system as an accountability mechanism is very labour-intensive. For committees engaged in looking at government policies and programs, there is no end in sight.

4. Bills are amended in committees, where the nitty-gritty of legislation is considered. It is during the committee stage that MPs may receive public input on the merits or drawbacks of legislation. Unfortunately, most legislation goes to committee only after its second reading, when a vote on the principles of the bill is taken. Thus, it is more difficult for committees to make major changes to the legislation, as the House has already publicly registered its decision on the key elements of the matter in question. Committees also hear from the public (in the form of witnesses) when examining broader public policy areas. Between legislation and policy examination, hundreds of Canadians appear before parliamentary committees each year; thus, committees provide a critical link between the public and the all-too-faceless machinery of government.

5. Finally, MPs spend a great deal of time helping constituents. This constituency work is often overlooked by the public, but it is a valuable service. Some constituency service is very simple, such as expediting a passport or bringing greetings on behalf of the prime minister

to someone celebrating an 80th birthday. Other issues may be easy to solve but are critical to the individual, such as helping someone receive their employment insurance or a pension entitlement. In still other cases, such as immigration and refugee situations or large-scale projects for the district, the work of the local MP is not only helpful but often critical. Members of Parliament from large urban centres have informally correlated the rise of immigration cases in their riding offices with the decrease in staffing in the Department of Citizenship and Immigration (Government of Canada, 2009).

Members enjoy this one-on-one work and indicate that it gives them tremendous personal satisfaction (Docherty, 1997). Most studies have found that there is little electoral reward for members who dedicate long hours to constituency work (Ferejohn and Gaines, 1991: 292–94; Docherty, 1997: 190–92). Conversely, however, there may be severe electoral penalties for those who neglect their district. The level of satisfaction with Parliament is far higher among Canadian citizens who have made personal contact with their member of Parliament (Docherty, 2002: 182–83). This certainly makes sense on an intuitive level. Canadians who have availed themselves of the help of their MP are more likely to have positive views of representation. But the reality is that most citizens do not rely on their member of Parliament for day-to-day assistance; their interaction with Parliament is fleeting and largely passive, at most consisting of watching the highlights (or lowlights) of Question Period on the television news or following the antics of the parties in the newspaper. Convincing these Canadians of the relevance of Parliament is a more daunting task.

Question Period

Question Period represents all that is the best and all that is the worst of the Westminster system. It is often unruly, it is rarely congenial, and it provokes the type of behaviour that would make a schoolteacher shudder and draw unsportsmanlike conduct penalties in professional sport. The frequent heckling, yelling, and insults lend a sense of the surreal to Question Period that would appear to justify the accusation of many Canadians that Parliament does not work. Ministers try to avoid questions, and those posing them seem less interested in an honest response than they are in embarrassing the minister.

But, behind the boxing ring atmosphere—if Canadians listen closely—one can hear the sound of Cabinet ministers being held to account, and being forced, in public, to address or obfuscate questions about their own behaviour and that of the government. While the resignation due to personal misconduct of a minister of the Crown is never something for the government to be proud of, such misconduct uncovered in Question Period is a signal of parliamentary success. This dual nature has caused many parliamentary observers to wonder if it would in fact be possible to keep the scrutiny while doing away with the political grandstanding.

The Canadian version of Question Period is distinct from the practice in the House of Commons at Westminster upon which it is modelled. In the United Kingdom Parliament at Westminster, ministers have the benefit of receiving a written question earlier in the day (or the evening before). This practice allows the minister and his staff to research the question thoroughly and provide a detailed response; it also allows the minister to be fully prepared and rehearsed. In the Canadian House, no such prior notice is required. Ministers must hope that their daily briefing books are complete and that they are personally familiar with the issues being raised; either that or they must bluff their way through a response and in doing so not provide a detailed or even coherent answer.

The routine of Question Period is straightforward. The Speaker first recognizes the leader of the official opposition (or a designate) who is allowed to ask one question with two additional supplementary questions. Each other recognized party then takes it in turn, usually with the party leader asking the first question. Private members on the government side of the Speaker are also allowed to ask questions, though they are often accused of throwing "puff balls" at cabinet ministers who are fully prepared with responses calculated to extol the virtues of the government in general and their own departments in particular. When government private members use this opportunity to ask a serious question on a topical issue, opposition parties are likely to paint a portrait of a divided government. On the other hand, when the questions from government backbenchers are set-ups, the government is accused of wasting valuable time. Question Period could become more relevant if all parties more fully embraced accountability principles.

Question Period may act to encourage collective action among opposition parties having little in common ideologically, but they understand that there are benefits that can be realized from working together when it comes to holding the government accountable. Bev Oda was pressured to step down from her position as minister responsible for Canada's International Development Agency, a job she was otherwise doing competently, when repeated incidents of wild spending were brought to light (Fitzpatrick, 2012). Without Question Period, the government might have hoped to keep the issue off the front page of the newspapers or, at the very least, to hunker down and let it run its course. But opposition parties on this occasion and others have used Question Period effectively to badger the government into ethical behaviour. By doing so, they may also prevent the government from pursuing its legislative agenda and in the face of an otherwise unstoppable government majority this may be one of the best forms of opposition possible.

One informal portion of Question Period that is uniquely Canadian is the press scrum that follows. The term "scrum" refers to the rough-and-tumble part of a rugby match in which all players lock arms and scramble for the ball. In the Canadian parliamentary context, journalists are given the opportunity to scrum cabinet ministers and private members as they leave the chamber. In many ways, the scrum provides a great opportunity for private members. While the press tends to congregate around leaders and cabinet ministers, a media-savvy private member may quickly land a spot on the evening news and develop a national profile. Conversely, media scrums can magnify the ill-preparedness or incompetence of ministers if they are unable to handle the questions thrown at them by the press. Occasionally party leaders try to forgo the scrum and opt for a more dignified press briefing. These experiments rarely last, as the media prefers spontaneity over scripted statements following Question Period.

As prime minister, Stephen Harper has taken another tack on the scrum, opting to avoid entering the foyer at all if possible by using a carefully arranged escape route. In 2009, EKOS Polling's Frank Graves opined that Harper's "tight media strategy and disciplined control over his caucus" was apparently working in his favour to ensure that there were no unanticipated or unprepared remarks carelessly let fly in the presence of the press. While this strategy appears to have had the desired effect by generally keeping the statements of caucus members "on message" and unwanted press coverage subdued, it has not won favours with the press and supports portrayals of the prime minister as distant and controlling (Naumetz, 2012).

Ministers who do their job well, stay on top of their files, and keep their hands clean survive the gruelling process of Question Period with their reputations intact, if not enhanced. Canadians should take some comfort from the knowledge that most cabinet ministers meet this tough standard, most of the time; for those that do not, their tenure at the Cabinet table will be less secure. But Canadians should recognize that this rough-and-tumble part of the parliamentary calendar provides the opportunity for weaknesses to be exposed. Despite its sometimes rancorous atmosphere, Question Period forces the government to face its fiercest critics on a daily basis when Parliament is in session.

Caucus Meetings

While Question Period—along with other activities in the actual legislative chamber—garners most of the attention, what is happening in party caucus meetings remains far less visible. The government caucus plays a far greater role in the accountability process than do the regular meetings of opposition parties. Opposition caucus meetings are important, but are driven more by strategy than by process. Opposition parties hold their caucus meetings to discuss Question Period strategy, their policy stance on various pieces of legislation, and the direction in which they should take their opposition to the government. Opposition party leaders can use these meetings to rally the support of their caucus and to hear what constituents are telling their members; thus, they must be sensitive to the needs and goals of their caucus to maintain confidence. Though it rarely happens in Canada, leaders can lose this confidence, as Canadian Alliance party leader Stockwell Day learned to his chagrin in 2001 (Malloy, 2003: 68).

For the government party, the Wednesday morning caucus is a critical meeting that provides an additional avenue of accountability. Ideally, government caucus meetings allow backbench members of the governing party to inform the Cabinet and prime minister of the views of their constituents. Caucus secrecy permits these individuals to openly criticize the Cabinet and its leader for unpopular policy stances, unwise spending of tax dollars, and other instances of poor leadership. In theory, caucus meetings are the time for Cabinet ministers to unveil proposed legislation, obtain feedback from their colleagues, and revise their plans accordingly. Caucus provides the opportunity for private members to tell the prime minister and Cabinet how their plans will (or why they won't) sell in Moose Jaw, Brandon, Rimouski, Sackville, and Corner Brook. It also allows cabinet ministers to make their case to private members, explaining how an unattractive policy might actually be in the country's best interest and why—and how—they should sell it back home in their constituencies.

Some government caucuses have worked more effectively than others. Former Prime Minister Brian Mulroney was widely regarded for his ability both to listen to his caucus and to rally members behind important policies.[6] His Progressive Conservative government was very sensitive to the concerns of some of its private members on issues like gun control. At the same time, Mulroney convinced his colleagues of the need to stick together on issues like the Goods and Services Tax, arguing that it was in Canada's best interest to introduce some tough but necessary medicine. Mulroney is given credit for balancing the often widely divergent views in his large caucus (Crosbie, 1997: 270–74). Since 1993, Canada has not had a prime minister who both understood and managed his caucus as well as Mulroney. Thus, more recent portrayals of domineering prime ministers continue to create a sense of dysfunction on Parliament Hill.

The problem with caucus may be one of unrealistic expectations on the part of some private members. This is particularly true after a new government takes office and private members are expecting to become fully engaged in the policy process. However, in the quest to demonstrate leadership, governments are loath to back down on campaign or budgetary commitments, even if their caucus is pushing them in a different direction. Success for a caucus backbencher is usually found at the margins, as much as members might hope for larger victories.

Party Discipline

If there were one aspect of Westminster government that Canadians might point to as the single largest cause of their discontent, it would be party discipline. The unwritten but closely observed convention of parties voting as a single unit has become the whipping boy of parliamentary democracy in Canada. The House of Commons may be executive-centred, but it is also dominated by political parties. This is not something that sits well with many voters.

The understanding that members of Parliament are bound to a party vote strikes many Canadians as contrary to their own view of representative democracy: elected officials are supposed to represent the interests of voters, or at the very least their own judgement or conscience, and not those of the party leaders. It is difficult not to feel sympathy for voters who think they have elected a strong voice only to find that, on most issues, their elected voice is merely a faint echo of the party leader's. The success of the Reform Party of Canada in the 1990s was in large part a populist reaction to the dominance of party over local interests (Carty, Cross, and Young, 2000: 8–9).

Often, expressions of discontent by MPs are manifested over issues of conscience. Conservative MP Brian Trost sparked a flare-up in the long-running debate about strict party discipline when he decided to voice his frustrations to a radio station after being denied his ability to vote against his party's position on the question of abortion. However, to suggest that party discipline should simply be eliminated would betray a naïve understanding of parliamentary democracy. The first priority for a prime minister is to ensure that they maintain the confidence of the House. A prime minister who goes into a vote without foreknowledge of the outcome is recklessly tempting fate. This means that most government MPs will vote with the government on money bills, campaign pledges, and matters raised in the Speech from the Throne. The easiest way to do this is simply to treat all legislation introduced by members of Cabinet as a matter of confidence in the government, as has been common Canadian practice (J. Smith, 2003: 151). Government back-benchers may dislike being out of cabinet, but they prefer that to being out of a job, or their party out of power. Minimizing political risk to all members by avoiding unnecessary elections tends to rally a government caucus behind a prime minister.

In addition, there is a tendency among both opposition members and the Canadian public to be too hasty in their association of a unified government with ironclad party discipline. In many cases, government backbenchers actually prefer to shelter behind party discipline, whether their intentions in doing so are honourable or not. Difficult economic times might require unpleasant fiscal medicine that could prove unpopular with local voters. It is far easier for a backbencher to sell tough budget measures back home knowing that all members of the party are in the same boat. If government members can simply jump ship on such occasions, it would become impossible to ensure adequate backing for government policies on an ongoing basis.

In addition, knowing the preferences of most constituents is easier to achieve in theory than it is in reality. While members of Parliament attempt to maintain contact with constituents on a regular basis, measuring the exact pulse of the riding on all but a few large issues is next to impossible. In many cases, MPs hear strong opinions from voters on either extreme of an issue, and generally not at all from the majority of constituents. Rare is the citizen who contacts their MP to indicate they are ambivalent, torn, undecided, or simply unaware on the matter of tax changes or same-sex marriages! In the absence of scientific polling on every issue, or clearly formulated majority opinions within their riding, MPs can take comfort in a thoughtful caucus debate and cast their vote with their peers.

Finally, it is often too convenient for opposition parties to blithely criticize the government for relying on party discipline. Broadly speaking, successful governments in Canada have brought together diverse individuals and opinions under one party banner. The Mulroney Progressive Conservative government of 1984–93 formed a federal government that held together a diverse caucus of economic liberals, social conservatives, moderate "red Tories," and Quebec nationalists (Cross, 2002: 117). Likewise, Stephen Harper's government has been faced with internal division on issues such as abortion (mentioned above) and the multibillion-dollar purchase of Nexen Oil by Chinese-owned CNOOC (Harris, 2013). Party discipline under these circumstances is a necessary tool. The more broad-based and inclusive a governing party, the higher its potential for internal divisions, and the more important its need to enforce unity if it is to continue to govern. In fact, a study of voting between 2011 and 2013 found that Conservatives broke ranks from their caucus more often than opposition MPs (Cross and Thomson, 2013).

Having acknowledged the problems facing the government party, it is important to understand that retaining the confidence of the legislature does not by definition require strict party discipline in the government ranks (J. Smith, 2003: 151). Certainly the British example is instructive in this regard. At Westminster, the government employs what is known as a "three-line whip" whereby legislative matters are ranked by importance. There are no recriminations for backbench members voting independently on one- or two-line whips. In other words, a bill can be defeated (and government members may vote against it), and the Cabinet and prime minister will continue to govern as if nothing had occurred. However, all government members must support their Cabinet and prime minister on such bills and motions that have been deemed a three-line whip. Failure on these bills or motions—which the government defines as votes of confidence—would require an election.

Historically, Canadian governments have tended to avoid this model, instead encouraging their members to treat almost all matters as if they were votes of confidence. This is not surprising. After all, it perfectly suits the prime minister's purpose to have unwavering backbench support on all matters. While this certainly makes governing more efficient, it can cause many Canadians to question the quality of their parliamentary democracy between elections.

Tackling the Democratic Deficit and Making Parliament Relevant

This chapter began by recognizing that the Parliament of Canada, like many modern political institutions, suffers from a lack of public confidence. At the same time it is understood that, of all our national institutions, Parliament is the one that holds a democratically elected group of individuals who must debate and pass laws. One could make the case that if Parliament in general, and the House of Commons in particular, is not relevant, then Canada's democracy is in trouble. After all, why bother to vote if you are sending a representative to a body that is neither functional nor relevant to governing?

The Crown, as personified by the Queen and governor general, is a formal institution with little noticeable impact on Canadian government. The unelected Senate is generally seen as a retirement villa for the cronies of prime ministers. The House of Commons is an arena of partisan conflict, far removed from solving complex problems of public policy. Yet, in each of these three political bodies may be found critically important elements of parliamentary democracy. Commissions (appointed in the name of the Crown) allow for open and detailed studies on wide-ranging issues and inquiries in specific matters. The Senate provides a forum for interest groups across the country to state their case in Parliament. And, most critically, the House of Commons actually works—despite the occasional similarity to a staged wrestling match. Amid the name-calling, heckling, and political shenanigans, elected parliamentarians debate the public business, refine legislation in committees, keep cabinet ministers on their toes. and pass (or occasionally defeat) legislative bills that enact important public policies that are relevant to the day-to-day life of Canadians. The courts may define and defend the highest constitutional principles when rendering decisions on issues such as same-sex marriage or the legality of prostitution, but it is within Parliament that the public interest is debated and the laws of the land are eventually constructed.

Of course, Parliament can always improve, and Canadians should not be deterred from exploring better ways to ensure that their political institutions serve the public good. Much of what ails Parliament lies in those areas that encourage opportunistic career building and unquestioned party loyalty over proper democratic rule. In seeking to make Parliament more relevant, it is important to focus on improving the everyday practice of democracy within the legislature, not just at election time.

There are several possible reforms that members of Parliament and prime ministers should consider, starting with the Senate. The failure of past attempts at Senate reform can be partially blamed on their grandeur. All too often, proposals for Senate reform have been bound together with other constitutional changes, sharply circumscribing the possibility of a successful outcome. As a result, politicians have more recently avoided Senate reform that is in any way tied to a broader constitutional agenda. But that is not to say that changes cannot take place away from the constitutional minefield. Indeed, given the recent transgressions by a few, changes may be inevitable.

To begin, the power enjoyed by the prime minister to appoint senators could be used more judiciously and might alleviate some public concern over the Senate. For example, the prime minister could appoint more opposition or independent senators or agree to appoint individuals recommended by premiers. If premiers chose to hold elections and submit the names of the victors to the prime minister, this informal election process could begin to build legitimacy for this oft-maligned institution. It would be difficult to dismantle such a model once it had received strong public approval.

Within the Commons one critical, if somewhat counterintuitive, change that should take place is in the promotion of parliamentary careers. In an age of cynicism, it is easy to criticize politicians as self-interested robbers of the public purse. Indeed, many people have contested elections by running against the very political office they seek! "Vote for me—I'm not a politician" is not an unfamiliar refrain. In the past decade, six provinces have actually decreased the size of their provincial assembly. (In one case, Ontario proudly boasted that their "Fewer Politicians Act" was bound to save taxpayers millions of dollars as "politicians only spend money," Docherty, 2005).

Such a cultivation of public ill-will toward elected officials betrays a naive understanding of parliamentary democracies. No legislature that has decreased its size has had a similar reduction in the size of its cabinet. As a result, the number of politicians who spend money does not decrease, since it is politicians who hold Cabinet positions who are the designated "spenders" of public money.

In any event, it is not the size of legislatures and the number of politicians that matters. Of greater importance is improving the attractiveness of a parliamentary career. As long as members of Parliament see Cabinet as the goal of a political career, and loyalty to their leader as the primary means of climbing into its ranks, government backbenchers will meekly let prime ministers dictate how they vote on virtually all issues.

One method of making a parliamentary career as a private member more attractive is to increase the power of House of Commons committees. Far from the glare of the cameras in the main chamber, much important work is done in these committees. But, too often overworked and ignored, the members of committees may just as easily be frustrated as satisfied by their work. There are several changes to the committee system that could both substantially improve their work and highlight their relevance.

First, committees could make more use of what is known as pre-legislative hearings on bills. Currently, committees study legislation only after parties have voted on the bill in principle, at the second reading stage. If more bills were sent to committee immediately after first reading, parties would not have staked a position on the issue. As a result, committee members would be freer to develop their own public positions on legislation, which might serve to inform the government. This power exists but is rarely used.

As an extension to this type of proposal, committees could be charged with developing draft legislation on particular issues. Under this scenario, a cabinet minister would ask a committee to examine a particular policy question. The committee report would take the form of draft legislation which the minister would then present in the House.

Committees could also be used more effectively in the appointment of senior officials. At present, the prime minister enjoys unilateral authority in appointing senators, Supreme Court of Canada justices, ambassadors, and senior government officials. Even when qualified people are appointed to these positions (most often the case), the closed nature of the process and the personal exercise of power involved can sully the image of both the position and the appointee. The use of Commons committees could provide candidates with the opportunity to demonstrate their suitability for the position in question. The current practice of having Supreme Court nominees appear before a parliamentary committee for information purposes is a case in point. Thankfully the committee does not have the veto authority that has politicized US court appointments. One of the strengths of the parliamentary system is that it does not overtly politicize positions (such as judges) that should remain neutral. Any move to reform the appointment process would have to ensure that unilateral decision-making is not replaced with rancorous partisan debate over the merits of the candidates.

Finally, committees could be effective overseers of government policies, but only when committee members work together. All-party consensus is both more easily obtained and more desirable in committees than it is on the floor of the Commons. In the 2012 report on the state of the Veterans Review and Appeal Board, a House committee consisting of government and opposition members came to a unanimous decision on the potential reforms. The strength of this committee was its unanimity, which provided its recommendations with greater legitimacy in the eyes of government, opposition, and the affected constituency, increasing the likelihood of its implementation (Kerr, 2012).

Unlike in the House of Commons, where the parties have strict and enforced party lines, committees can provide a reprieve from partisan politics. The secret election of committee chairs for standing, joint, and special committees, thereby allowing members on these committees to elect the individuals they determine to be the most qualified, has eased the sense of partisan division and unmitigated adversarial relations that is typical of the House of Commons (Compendium of Procedure, 2006). It should be noted that none of the changes proposed here require large-scale institutional redesign. A complete overhaul of Canada's legislative branch may be desirable, but it is far from practicable. Instead, Canadians should focus their attention on making the present system work better. Parliament is relevant, but it can be made more so. All too often, legislators are hamstrung in their attempts to perform their duties. Changes aimed at giving legislators a larger role in crafting legislation would go a long way to convincing the Canadian public that their only nationally elected legislature does perform its crucial democratic oversight and accountability function, and that the institution is deserving of both the attention and the respect of the citizens that it serves.

Notes

1 The author wishes to thank Mount Royal undergraduates Miranda Anderson and Cameron Kenny for their assistance with this chapter.

2 The Canadian Constitution requires that prospective senators be at least 30 years old and own $4,000 of real estate.
3 The Clarity Act was introduced on December 13, 1999, during the 36th Parliament to spell out the federal conditions that would have to be met for Quebec to secede from Canada.
4 The 1987 Meech Lake Accord proposals included a selection process for senators; changes to the regional composition were included in the 1992 Charlottetown Accord proposal. When these failed, both the federal and provincial appetite for constitutional change was lost.
5 This is particularly the case with bills that are part of the annual budget. All budget bills and the motion on the tabling of the budget are considered questions of confidence in the government.
6 This experience of the Progressive Conservative party might be considered an anomaly due to leadership skills and personality. Prior to Mulroney, the Progressive Conservative caucus had developed a reputation for turning against its leaders.

References and Suggested Readings

Atkinson, Michael, and David Docherty. 1992. "Moving Right Along: The Roots of Amateurism in the Canadian House of Commons." *Canadian Journal of Political Science* 25 (2): 295–318. http://dx.doi.org/10.1017/S0008423900003991.

Atkinson, Michael, and David Docherty. 2004. "Parliament and Political Success in Canada." In *Canadian Politics in the 21st Century*, eds. M. Whittington and G. Williams, 5–29. Toronto: Thomson Nelson.

Carty, R. Kenneth, William Cross, and Lisa Young. 2000. *Rebuilding Canadian Party Politics*. Vancouver: University of British Columbia Press.

Compendium of Procedure. 2006. House of Commons. Modified May 2006. http://www.parl.gc.ca/About/House/Compendium/Web-Content/c_a_index-e.htm.

Crosbie, John. 1997. *No Holds Barred: My Life in Politics*. Toronto: McClelland and Stewart.

Cross, William. 2002. "The Increasing Importance of Region to Canadian Election Campaigns." In *Regionalism and Party Politics in Canada*, eds. L. Young and K. Archer, 116–28. Toronto: Oxford University Press.

Curry, Bill, and Stuart A. Thompson. 2013. "Conservative MPs Break Ranks More Often than Opposition," *Globe and Mail*, February 3. http://www.theglobeandmail.com/news/politics/conservative-mps-break-ranks-more-often-than-opposition/article8156279/.

Docherty, David C. 1997. *Mr. Smith Goes to Ottawa: Life in the House of Commons*. Vancouver: University of British Columbia Press.

Docherty, David C. 1998. "It's Awfully Crowded Here: Adjusting to the Five Party House of Commons." *Parliamentary Perspectives* 2 (October): 1–18. http://www.studyparliament.ca/English/pdf/ongoing/David_Docherty_Paper_Eng.pdf.

Docherty, David C. 2002. "Our Changing Understanding of Representation in Canada." In *Value Change and Governance in Canada*, ed. Neil Nevitte, 165–206. Toronto: University of Toronto Press.

Docherty, David C. 2005. *Legislatures: A Democratic Audit.* Vancouver: University of British Columbia Press.

Ferejohn, John, and Brian Gaines. 1991. "The Personal Vote in Canada." In *Representation, Integration and Political Parties in Canada. Royal Commission on Electoral Reform and Party Financing 14*, ed. H. Bakvis, 275–302. Toronto: Dundurn Press.

Fitzpatrick, Megan. 2012. "Oda's travel expenses causes dissent in Tory caucus." CBC online. http://www.cbc.ca/news/politics/oda-s-travel-expenses-cause-dissent-in-tory-caucus-1.1256585.

Franks, S. 1987. *The Parliament of Canada.* Toronto: University of Toronto Press.

Franks, S. 2003. "The Canadian Senate in Modern Times." In *Protecting Canadian Democracy: The Senate you Never Knew*, ed. S. Joyal, 158–88. Montreal: McGill-Queen's University Press.

Government of Canada. 2009. "The Governments of Canada and Ontario Partner with the City of Guelph to Help Newcomers." Department of Citizenship and Immigration Canada. Modified 2009. www.cic.gc.ca/english/department/media/releases/2009/2009-09-22a.asp.

Harris, Kathleen. 2013. "3 Conservative MPs Raised Concerns about CNOOC-Nexen Deal." *CBC News*, January 23.

Joyal, Serge. 2000. "The Senate You Thought You Knew." Paper presented at the annual meeting of Canadian Political Science Association, Quebec, July.

Kerr, Greg. 2012. "Restoring Confidence in the Veterans Review and Appeal Board." Report of the Standing Committee on Veterans Affairs. Ottawa: Government of Canada.

Malloy, Jonathan. 2003. "The House of Commons Under the Chrétien Government." In *How Ottawa Spends*, ed. B. Doern, 59–71. Don Mills: Oxford University Press.

Naumetz, Tim. 2012. "PM Harper's Iron Message Control Working." *The Hill Times.* http://www.hilltimes.com/news/2009/11/16/pm-harpers-iron-message-control-working/22800.

Savoie, Donald. 1999. *Governing from the Centre: The Concentration of Power in Canadian Politics.* Toronto: University of Toronto Press.

Simpson, Jeffrey. 2002. *The Friendly Dictatorship.* Toronto: McClelland and Stewart.

Smith, David E. 2003. *The Canadian Senate in Bicameral Perspective.* Montreal: McGill-Queen's University Press.

Smith, Jennifer. 1999. "Responsible Government and Democracy." In *Taking Stock of 150 Years of Responsible Government in Canada*, eds. F.L. Seidle and L. Massicotte, 19–50. Ottawa: Canadian Study of Parliament Group.

Smith, Jennifer. 2003. "Debating the Reform of Canada's Paliament." In *Reforming Parliament Democracy*, eds. L. Seidle and D. Docherty, 150–68. Montreal: McGill-Queen's University Press.

nine

Two Cheers for Bureaucracy: Canada's Public Service

PAUL G. THOMAS

Introduction

This chapter examines the role, structure, and influence of the public service of the Government of Canada in the national policy-making process of the twenty-first century. It starts from the premise that the public service performs numerous tasks that contribute significantly to economic and social progress in Canadian society. The public service also supports Canada's role in the world. It even helps to strengthen democracy in Canada and the world.

These positive assumptions do not reflect a naïve view that the public service is a perfect institution. Clearly, as the chapter title implies (two cheers rather than three), Canada's public service has significant shortcomings, including a poor public image, and it faces serious challenges for the future. Many of these problems arise from the political context in which the public service operates; some are inherent in the operation of any large complicated institution; and some arise from leadership and management weaknesses inside the public service itself.

In popular discourse the public service is often called "the bureaucracy," which has become a term of opprobrium meant to disparage the institution. Negativity toward the public service is not new. There have always been vocal critics prepared to find fault with the institution on different, not always consistent, grounds. However, the stereotype of the public service that exists today involves a more extensive critique and is more entrenched in the political culture than ever in the past.

On a regular basis the media report opinion surveys indicating that public trust and confidence in government as an institution has been eroding (Ibbitson, 2012; Ipsos Reid, 2007; Thomas, 2009). However, other academic surveys reveal that many citizens have limited knowledge of government and pay scant attention to developments within the governing process (Gidengil, 2004; Milner, 2001).

Opinion surveys seldom ask citizens whether their poor impressions of government arise mainly from the actions of politicians or of public servants. However, when asked to rank the trustworthiness of various occupations, politicians are usually ranked lowest and public servants fall in the middle of such rankings. Almost 60 per cent of Canadians in a survey in 2006 thought that public service ethical standards had slipped over the previous decade, and they rated the public service poorly on accountability (Ipsos Reid, 2007; Green, 2008). Inside government there is also a trust deficit, but one that is not easily documented. Levels of trust between governments and the public service have fluctuated over time. Since 2006, however, the rhetoric and the actions of the government led by Prime Minister Stephen Harper appear to have widened the trust gap and reduced morale in the public service (Delacourt, 2008; Jeffrey, 2011). There are also problems of low trust between the senior leadership of the public service and employees in the middle and front-line ranks.

The existence of external and internal "trust deficits" is made more serious by the fact that the public service is operating in a globalized, turbulent, external environment that requires continuous policy innovation. It is also dealing with budgetary restraint and downsizing at a time when a generational turnover in its ranks is taking place. In combination these circumstances have created a stressed, defensive, risk-averse public service that is uncertain about its future (Savoie, 2013: 19; Zussman, 2010).

In elaborating upon these themes, this chapter provides a brief introduction to the concept of bureaucracy. This is followed by an overview of the composition and organization of the public service and an examination of the role of the public service based on the constitutional order and the dynamics of power within our political system. The main criticisms of public bureaucracies will then be presented, along with a more positive countervailing perspective. Attention then shifts to various aspects of the prevailing relationship between the government of Prime Minister Stephen Harper and the public service. The chapter concludes with a brief analysis of the confluence of forces that have left the public service in a precarious state with few determined defenders.

The Concept of Bureaucracy

The academic use of the concept of bureaucracy to analyze the key features of large organizations began with the work of German sociologist Max Weber writing in the late nineteenth and early twentieth centuries. The phrase "Weberian bureaucracy" is still used to refer to the essential attributes of large specialized organizations.

According to Weber, bureaucracies are designed and organized on the principle of hierarchy and specialization of activities and occupations. Each office within an organization has a defined sphere of authority and competence. Personnel are appointed to particular positions on the basis of merit consisting of background education, knowledge, skills, and experience. Policy direction comes from the top of the organization, with authority and resources being delegated to different divisions and levels of the organization. Controlling by commands and rules allows decisions made at higher levels to be executed consistently by lower-level officials, and accountability for actions and results flows back to leaders at the top of the organization. Anonymity and relative security of employment supports the notion that a position in the public service means a career for life (Wilson, 1989).

For government, the Weberian model offered a clear delineation of responsibilities and accountabilities between politicians and public servants. Public servants would be appointed on the basis of merit rather than political patronage. Based on their expertise they would contribute to the formulation of policy, but they would remain subordinate to their elected political masters. Once policy was determined, the bureaucracy would implement it in an efficient and effective manner. In interpreting and applying the law, public servants would act in a professional and objective manner that did not show favouritism toward particular individuals and organizations. In short, the ideal Weberian bureaucracy represented a controllable and reliable instrument by which politicians could see their policy decisions carried out by a professional, impartial public service (Doern and Sutherland, 1985).

The Organization and Size of the National Public Sector

The Government of Canada website describes the national public sector as consisting of over 350 organizations performing a bewildering array of tasks and operating under several different institutional formats. These basic organizational facts contradict the popular image of the bureaucracy as a homogeneous, monolithic institution performing routine, mundane operational tasks. Only a small number of the 350 organizations are high profile and continuously entangled in the political process; most operate out of public view and far from the political spotlight.

Three basic types of organizations compose the public sector: (1) the core public service, which consists of departments under the direction of a cabinet minister; (2) crown agencies, which enjoy some freedom from direct political control and are widely varied in their purposes and structures; and (3) a range of advisory bodies, which also take on various tasks and organizational formats intended to make them semi-independent of political control. Also within the core public service is the subcategory of "central agencies," which are meant to push the policy goals of the prime minister and Cabinet down into the bureaucracy and to ensure coordination of activity across the vast sweep of departmental and non-departmental bodies. The list of central agencies usually includes the Prime Minister's Office (PMO), the Privy Council Office (PCO), the Treasury Board Secretariat (TBS), and the Department of Finance.

The scope of the national public sector leads to many debates, including over how many people work for the Government of Canada. On this issue, it does not help that total employment is reported by three different organizations in three different ways (TBS, 2012). The Public Service Commission (PSC) defines public sector employment according to the Public Service Employment Act (PSEA), which covers mainly federal departments and excludes 30 other institutions such as the numerous crown corporations and the non-civilian members of the Canadian Armed Forces. In March 2011 there were 216,709 people working in the PSC universe of employees. A second, overlapping universe of employment is defined by the TBS as composed of all departmental employees plus employees who work in non-departmental bodies such as crown corporations and regulatory commissions. In 2011 the TBS reported 282,352 employees in this category. The final and most inclusive inventory of public sector employment is produced by Statistics Canada. It defines the public sector as all institutions controlled by government. In 2011 Statistics Canada reported that 427,093 people worked in the national public sector broadly defined.

These statistics on employment do not speak for themselves and they say different things to different observers. They are really just a starting point for perennial debates over whether the bureaucracy has become too large and uncontrollable. A 2012 report from the TBS put the employment numbers in a recent historical perspective. From 1983 to 2011, Canada's population grew by 34 per cent whereas the public service increased from 250,882 to 282,352 people, an increase of only 12.5 per cent. As of 2011 the public service composed 0.82 per cent of the Canadian population compared to approximately 1 per cent during the 1980s and 1990s (TBS, 2012). Further analysis reveals that, based on government budgetary priorities, both selective expansion and contraction has taken place during this time period. Contrary to the popular myth, runaway growth has not been the pattern.

The Public Service in the Constitutional Order

The Canadian constitutional order is based on a blend of laws and politics (Heard, 1991). Vitally important aspects of government are shaped by unwritten conventions that have arisen from long-standing political practices. These constitutional conventions vary in the extent to which they are seen as morally binding by prime ministers, ministers, parliamentarians, public servants, and others in public life. The broad, unwritten nature of the conventions means that different actors can play "fast and loose" with the informal rules, a tendency that has become more common in recent years.

One of the foundational principles of Canada's constitutional order are the doctrines of collective and individual ministerial responsibility. The two halves of the doctrine are based mainly on convention and have only a limited expression in public law. The conventions provide a theoretical and practical basis for the distribution of authority and the use of power throughout the political system. The main concern here is the connection between ministerial responsibility as practised under modern conditions and the related notion of a professional, anonymous, neutral, career public service ready to serve successive governments equally loyally and effectively (Good, 2008; Thomas, 1997, 2008).

According to the principle of collective responsibility, governments are granted the authority to make collective cabinet decisions on proposed legislation, spending, and administrative changes to existing programs. In practice, the prime minister is the single most powerful figure in the governing process, controlling, among many other matters, the size, shape, and role of the public service (Savoie, 2008). It is the prime minister who appoints most senior public servants and they serve at pleasure, which means they can be removed from office at any time. This concentration of power creates problems and concerns, but it also focuses accountability on the prime minister, who must explain and defend government actions before Parliament and wider audiences. In principle, governments can be defeated by votes of no confidence in the House of Commons but this rarely happens because of party loyalty and strict discipline enforced by party leaders on their MPs.

In addition to collective ministerial responsibility, individual cabinet ministers are legally responsible for their departments and politically answerable for all departmental actions. In theory, ministers are obliged to resign for major policy mistakes or serious administrative errors. However, there has never been a strong Canadian tradition of ministers resigning for either of these reasons. Serious damage to the reputation of the minister and perhaps to the reputation of the government has become the real sanction behind individual ministerial responsibility.

In the nineteenth and early twentieth century, when the scope of government was limited, it was conceivable that strong ministers could actually set the agenda and direct the activities of their departments. Today, many departments are sprawling entities with many specialized activities, making it extremely difficult for ministers to be aware of, let alone be involved in, all actions that legally are done in their name. The major policy challenges faced by government, such as climate change, health, and justice, require cross-departmental actions that prevent ministers from acting alone. Moreover, beyond departments there is a wide array of entities such as Crown corporations, regulatory agencies, special operating agencies, and various types of partnership arrangements that operate at arm's length from the immediate pressures of the political process. Ministers are not directly involved in the daily operations of such organizations, leading to questions about the extent to which they are willing and capable of answering for their performance (Aucoin, 2006).

Debating Bureaucracy

Over the past three decades, hostility, skepticism, frustration, and disappointment with government as an institution have become prominent themes of Canadian political life. With respect to the public service, three broad complaints have been expressed: (1) the excessive power of the bureaucracy in the policy process, (2) the threat that delegated administrative decision-making represents to individual freedom, and (3) the overall problem that government performs poorly and wastes public money (Goodsell, 2004). Only a brief discussion and assessment of each of these concerns is possible in the space available here.

As governments intervened more extensively in the economy and society, politicians came to rely heavily on public servants who understood more fully the technical, administrative, and financial feasibility of policy options. The key public servants involved with the provision of policy advice are deputy ministers in departments and the administrative heads of non-departmental bodies. Most such senior public servants spend their careers working full-time on policy and administration. As part of the process of providing policy advice, they keep in touch with developments in their field, including through interactions with interest groups and the representatives of other governments. Such contacts add to the validity and persuasiveness of the advice they provide.

Two features of the Canadian political system added to bureaucratic influence during the twentieth century. The first was the relatively non-ideological nature of the party system. The two main parties, the Liberals and the Progressive Conservatives, were pragmatic and opportunistic, basing their electoral appeals more on leadership personality than on elaborate policy platforms. This created a policy vacuum that the bureaucracy filled.

A related factor was a close working relationship between the Liberal Party, which held power for most of the twentieth century, and the public service. So close was the relationship that the senior ranks of the public service became an important source of ministerial talent for Liberal governments. The partnership between the Liberals and the senior public service probably contributed to a "managerial" style of governing that was based on accommodation and compromise among private and public elites concerning what policies were feasible in political, financial, and administrative terms.

It is generally accepted that public servants are highly influential in formulating public policy (although this appears to be less true under the recent Harper governments). More contentious is the charge that they effectively decide policy and can block the policy ideas of ministers. Support for the charge comes mainly from anecdotal evidence or from abstract theories (like the principal-agent theory), which claim that an information advantage gives public servants the upper hand in the relationship. However, when interviewed, many former ministers state that public servants generally respect the right of the minister to have the final word on policy matters and are responsive to policy directions set by the minister. Inexperienced and weak ministers are most susceptible to being "captured" by their bureaucrats. However, most public servants prefer strong ministers who can, in collaboration with the prime minister and Cabinet, set the policy agenda of the department and have the political skills to move that agenda forward.

The second fear is that public servants have too much discretionary authority to make and apply rules that affect individuals and organizations. For various reasons, such as a lack of knowledge and the need for flexibility in policy-making, Parliament has found it necessary to pass vague general laws and to grant bureaucrats the authority to fill in the details through thousands of regulations passed annually (Thomas, 2009). Public servants must then interpret and apply the rules on a daily basis in complicated factual, legal, and ethical circumstances. In quantitative terms at least, public servants can be said to have become the real lawmakers. The fear is that bureaucrats can deprive people of their rights incrementally, one ruling at a time.

However, there are controls over administrative decision-making. Ministers must sign regulations that are binding on individuals and organizations. There is a Committee of Parliament that provides scrutiny of the exercise of rule-making authority granted to ministers and public servants. To support Parliament in this scrutiny role and to assist citizens in achieving fairness in their dealings with the bureaucracy, there are several "watchdog" bodies, such as the information, integrity, and privacy commissioners. Finally, citizens have recourse to appeal certain administrative actions through the courts.

Given the volume and technicality of administrative decision-making, there is no possibility that these review mechanisms can achieve anything close to comprehensive coverage of the exercise of bureaucratic discretion. Therefore, it is an internalized, subjective sense of restraint and fairness on the part of public servants that is most important to ensuring legal and fair administrative decision-making. And there is compelling evidence that public organizations develop their own procedures and precedents to produce what has been called "bureaucratic justice" (Mashaw, 1985, 2010).

The third complaint about the public service is its alleged poor performance. In recent decades, unfortunate events such as the tainted blood tragedy, the so-called billion-dollar HRDC boondoggle, and the sponsorship scandal have provided fodder for expensive public inquiries, theatrical parliamentary debates, and sensational media coverage. Such episodes reinforce a pervasive and wide-ranging critique of government, including the public service. The criticisms of this type that are levelled against government are too numerous, and often highly ideological, to be fully evaluated here. However, some countervailing positive arguments and evidence need to be presented to achieve a more balanced perspective.

In recent decades, an influential source of anti-government and anti-bureaucratic thinking was "public choice" theory (Niskanen, 1994). The theory was based on an assumption of self-interested behaviour by politicians and public servants. For politicians the bottom line is to win power. To this end they "bribe" voters with their own money and target the benefits and costs of government where it will contribute to their re-election. This leads to short-term decision-making in government. For public servants the bottom line is to increase (or in hard times to defend) their authority, budgets, and staffing levels. The combined motivations of politicians and public servants produce a dynamic that favours government growth and avoids the termination of outdated or ineffective programs.

There is a more positive, less deterministic view of the motivations of both politicians and public servants. If politicians believe in the value of their policy ideas, their preoccupation with winning elections makes perfect sense because only in office can they put those ideas into practice. The same preoccupation also encourages politicians to keep their election promises and stay in touch with public opinion, two things we presumably want to happen in a democracy. Furthermore, not all politicians, all the time, are motivated solely by re-election calculations; at least a minority of them are prepared to challenge prevailing public opinion and to think beyond the horizons of the four-year election cycle.

As for public servants, there is recent theoretical and empirical research on public service motivation (PSM) that examines how public employees develop a strong sense of public service and how that sense influences their behaviour (Moynihan and Pandey, 2007; Perry, 2000; Taylor, 2010). Research suggests that public servants develop a sense of "stewardship" that leads them to subordinate their personal interests to serve the values embedded in the mandate and culture of the organization (Hernandez, 2012).

Other critics point to the monopolistic role of government in producing certain goods and services within society. Without the pressure of competition and the risk of failure, there is no strong incentive to eliminate outdated and effective programs. Politicians accuse the public service of resisting cuts and the public service insists there is a lack of political will to eliminate programs for which there are vocal supporters within society.

A response to this critique might begin with the observation that the tasks of government are set through the political process. Often those tasks involve an attempt to deal with the most intractable problems within a society. Different parts of government are often given contradictory tasks. If governments have overreached in terms of trying to do too many things, it is not the job of the public service to decide which tasks should be retained or discarded.

The nature of the tasks assumed by government means that public organizations must cope with more complicated environments than private firms. Government decision-making must accommodate a much wider range of interests and values than any corporation confronts. There is competition in government, but it is more political than economic in content, with ministers and public servants striving to advance the department's interests on the government agenda.

Reflecting the requirement to accommodate competing perspectives, the goals of programs tend to be multiple, vague, and shifting, making it difficult to define and measure what qualifies as success. Compared to the private sector, government operates in a fishbowl created by access-to-information laws and public reporting requirements. Also, in the private sector there is nothing like a parliamentary opposition and an aggressive 24–7 media system, who provide continuous, usually critical, scrutiny of government performance.

For many reformers the solution to the deficiencies of government is to force the public service to become more "business-like" in its operations. There are many ways that this goal could be approached. Insistence that private management approaches be adopted is one way. Adopting the language and practices of "customer service" is another. During the past three decades, under the influence of "New Public Management" thinking, Canada's public service did, in fact, borrow many fashionable tools of management from the private sector (Aucoin, 1995). For several reasons, the outcome was a mixture of many new processes and reports, only a limited number of tangible accomplishments, a residual legacy of some new knowledge and skills, and lots of unfulfilled promises.

For more than a decade a citizen-centred service delivery initiative has been coordinated by the TBS, and all departments/agencies have introduced service improvement strategies. Surveys indicate that on key dimensions of service delivery, satisfaction with public organizations now compares favourably with many private firms. Furthermore, recent research suggests that the perceptions of the public service tend to improve when people have direct contact with it; as well, there is a presumed positive link between engaged employees, quality service delivery, and public trust in government (Heintzman and Marson, 2006).

Leading and managing in the public sector is more complicated than in private firms (see Rainey, 2003, for an extended analysis). Public managers have numerous bottom lines, including serving their political masters. Ideally they strike the right balance between responsiveness and loyalty to the government combined with an appropriate measure of independence and professionalism that allows them to offer frank advice on policy and to apply laws on an impartial basis. The worry among experts on the public service over the past few decades is that an increasingly narrow preoccupation with pleasing the prime minister and other ministers has become too strong a motivation among senior public servants.

The Harper Philosophy and the Bureaucracy

There was reason for some trepidation in the public service when Stephen Harper and the Conservative Party of Canada won the 2006 election. In his former roles as an opposition MP and as the head of a conservative interest group, Harper was known for his strong opposition to "big government" (Flanagan, 2007; Martin, 2010). He was also suspicious of senior public servants whom he described as "Liberal hacks" (Jeffrey, 2011: 1).

Like prime ministers before him, Stephen Harper has spoken all the right words about the value of the public service, has recognized individual public servants for outstanding achievements, and has maintained a blue ribbon advisory committee on how to improve the institution. However, the Harper government has also taken several actions that, to many informed observers, indicate a lack of respect and confidence in the public service.

Four aspects of the Harper record will be examined: (1) control over the size of the public service, (2) use of the public service for policy advice, (3) respect for the anonymity and neutrality of public servants, and (4) separating partisan political and professional administrative communications activities.

Shrinking the Bureaucracy?

On the size of government, the expectation was a drastic downsizing of the public sector. In fact, the record is mixed, with some selective expansion under the first two minority Harper governments (2006–08 and 2008–11) followed by what critics described as a transformative budget after majority status had been achieved in the 2011 election.

When the Conservatives took office in 2006, the economy was in relatively good shape and the new government inherited a budgetary surplus. Given its minority status, political survival was an overriding preoccupation of the first two Harper governments. Radical downsizing and service cuts that might antagonize voters were too risky. Instead, strategic reviews were launched to identify long-term potential savings. There was also some selective expansion of the public sector in priority areas such as the RCMP and the military.

After the global economic downturn hit in 2008, the government introduced an Economic Action Plan (EAP) that involved stimulus spending through the provinces and the private sector on infrastructure projects. This required some new hiring to distribute and monitor the spending, as well to support an elaborate communications strategy intended to gain political credit for the Harper government (Thomas, 2010).

The first budget produced after achieving majority government status in the 2011 election was seen to be a truer reflection of Conservative thinking on the role of government and the bureaucracy. The budget of March 2012 announced expenditure reductions of $5.5 billion annually for the following five years. Several organizations were eliminated and many programs were reduced in their scope.

On the staffing front, over the next three years an estimated 19,200 public service jobs would be eliminated. Where those job cuts would fall within the public service was not made clear. The government blamed the lack of transparency on the requirement to respect convoluted workforce adjustment policies adopted by previous Liberal governments.

The government presented several defences of its downsizing decisions. First, reducing the number of employees and the total compensation benefits paid to those who remained was needed to deal with the deficit and debt. Personnel expenses (salaries and benefits) represented 70 per cent of the operating expenses of the Government of Canada. During the period from 1999 to 2012 the total compensation per employee had increased by an average 5.1% annually, more than twice the inflation rate. Of the 19,000 layoffs, 7,200 would occur through attrition. Finally, the actual job losses were described as modest compared to the drastic downsizing (45,000 employees) of the Program Review exercise in the mid-1990s under a Liberal government.

By the time the 2013 budget was released, internal reports obtained under the access-to-information law indicated that the job losses would actually total 28,700 by 2016, not the 19,000 originally announced (May and Spalding, 2013). Opposition parties, public service unions, and some left-of-centre advocacy groups charged that the cuts would reduce services to Canadians. They also criticized the indignity of the lengthy layoff process of sending notices to "affected employees," forcing them to compete for remaining positions and waiting months to learn their fate. Survivors of the process would face higher volumes of work and experience more workplace stress. Morale in the public service, already poor, would decline further. A decade-long campaign to make the federal public service "the employer of choice" for Canada's top talent would be harmed.

Reliance on the Policy Advice of the Public Service?

This section contrasts the actions of previous Liberal governments, which eroded the "policy capacity" of the public service, with the neglect of public service advice by the Harper government. Policy capacity is a loose notion that refers to the resources and procedures devoted to intelligence gathering, policy formulation, the provision of policy advice, the evaluation of past policies, and the quality of the policy products that result from these processes.

The Program Review exercise, launched in the mid-1990s to address deficit and debt problems, produced the most drastic downsizing of the public service in Canadian history. In many departments, policy planning and evaluation units were seen as the most expendable. In 1996 a bureaucratic task force appointed by the Clerk of the Privy Council, Canada's most senior public servant, presented a report, "Strengthening Our Policy Capacity," which diagnosed the problem and prescribed some solutions (Felligi, 1996).

After 1997, when the government returned to a surplus position, efforts were made to renew policy capacity, including through networking with outside institutions (Bakvis, 2000; Lindquist, 2009; Lindquist and Desveaux, 2007). To this day, however, many informed observers argue that the public service lacks the deep analytical capabilities of earlier eras when highly creative policy work was a source of pride for public servants. There is definitely some nostalgia involved with this view because many of the commentators claiming policy advice was better in the past were the public servants providing the advice back then (Drummond, 2011; Sheikh, 2011).

If the problem in the 1990s was a lack of supply of policy advice, the problem in the Harper government is said to be a lack of demand for such advice. While nothing like a full study of the policy process under Stephen Harper's leadership exists, the available evidence suggests that the prime minister has neglected policy advice from the public service and outside experts on major issues.

Stephen Harper is a politician with strong ideological convictions derived from lifetime of involvement in public affairs (Johnson, 2005: 68). As a neoconservative thinker he has confidence in the correctness of his beliefs about the dangers of government intervention. Graduate training in economics reinforced his pro-market orientation and provided him with the analytical skills to analyze complex policy problems. Rather than trust policy specialists who lacked political intelligence, he preferred to rely on his own judgement of issues. He once observed: "Grand blueprints that have been done on the blackboard, and endorsed by experts with no practical experience in the economy and society, are disastrous" (Geddes, 2010).

Harper entered government with the suspicion that the permanent bureaucracy had a Liberal bias resulting from years of partisan appointments to strategic locations across the public sector. Having spent time in opposition criticizing the policies of Liberal governments, he believed that the public service either was too submissive to its political masters or lacked the policy creativity to bring forth truly innovative ideas. What Harper expected from the public service was not the traditional idea of neutral, professional competence but rather an enthusiastic embrace of and commitment to the government's agenda.

A trend toward centralizing policy-making in the PMO had been under way for more than four decades, but Stephen Harper sought to exert tighter control than any previous prime minister. As the head of a precarious minority government, Harper initially relied more on political staff serving in the PMO than on the career bureaucrats serving in the PCO. Once he was in a majority position and had greater trust in the professionalism of the PCO, there was more balance in the reliance upon the two offices.

The practice of appointing chiefs of staffs to ministers to support them in pushing government policy goals into the bureaucracy began under the Conservative government of Brian Mulroney in the 1980s. The chiefs of staff were given status and pay equivalent to an assistant deputy minister. No longer was the deputy guaranteed the last word of advice to the minister. Harper took this approach one step further by having all chiefs of staff appointed through his office. This meant that they owed their position to the prime minister and were expected to ensure that the government's priorities were reflected in the actions of departments.

Based on the public record, the Harper government appears to have rejected the advice of the public service and outside experts on some major issues:

- The cancellation of the mandatory long-form census that provided valuable data to support decision-making by all three orders of government and many private organizations;

- The launch of an aggressive law and order agenda that disregarded the data which showed declining crime rates, the ineffectiveness of harsh penalties as a deterrent, and the rising costs of incarceration;
- The reduction of the Goods and Services Tax rather than cuts to income taxes, which the majority of mainstream economists recommended;
- The firing of the President of the Canadian Nuclear Safety Commission after she defied a minister by shutting down on the grounds of safety the production of nuclear isotopes at a government facility;
- The disregard of the scientific evidence on climate change, the closing of the internationally renowned experimental lakes project, and the imposition of restrictions on the freedom of government scientists to talk about their research;
- The elimination in the 2012 budget of funding (in total the modest sum of $7.5 million was saved) for three advocacy organizations—the National Council on Welfare, the First Nations Statistical Agency, and the National Round Table on the Environment and the Economy—which were seen to be critical of government policy.

The purpose here is not to examine these controversies but rather to suggest there is a pattern of neglecting the advice of experts, especially those critical of government plans.

Naming, Blaming, and Shaming Public Servants?

Another disturbing pattern under the Harper government has been the practice of identifying and ridiculing public servants who found themselves in the spotlight for some reason. Such incidents had taken place under previous Liberal governments; for example, Prime Minister Chrétien blamed the sponsorship scandal on "rogue bureaucrats" who became the focus of a public inquiry and intense media scrutiny. However, the naming, blaming, and shaming of individual public servants became more frequent and mean-spirited under the Harper government:

- When Linda Keen was dismissed as President of the Nuclear Safety Commission, she was described by the prime minister as a partisan Liberal appointee, implying not too subtly that she lacked the qualifications to head the agency;
- When Richard Colvin, a career public servant in Foreign Affairs, raised questions about the too-rosy picture being presented by the

government regarding the role of Canada's military in Afghanistan, he was ridiculed by the defence minister as not being credible;

- When the government cancelled the mandatory long-form census, Munir Sheikh, the Chief Statistician, felt compelled to resign because of the erroneous claim by the government that Statistics Canada believed the substitution of a voluntary survey would not pose serious problems in terms of the reliability and validity of the data collected.

These are just three among several cases in which damage was done to the reputations and careers of public service professionals, as well as to the tradition of an anonymous, neutral public service.

Controlling the Message?

Soon after taking office, Prime Minister Harper became known for practising tight control over the flow of information and for an aggressive approach to news management. Promoting a positive image of the government and preventing bad news from emerging were the aims of several new practices that went beyond the efforts of previous governments to "spin" the news. Three practices will be highlighted (Thomas, 2013). The use of government advertising to claim political credit for initiatives has long been the practice of governments. The Harper government carried it further and made the message more personal in terms of enhancing the reputation of the prime minister. After the economic downturn, the government launched its Economic Action Plan (EAP) with an ad blitz that involved $89 million in spending across 10 departments in 2009–10. It was not so much the amount of spending (a Liberal government had spent $111 million in 2003–04) as the content of the advertising that led to criticisms. Initially the advertising campaign was riddled with images of the prime minister and links to his website. Government MPs across the country staged photo ops with oversized cheques bearing the logo of the Conservative Party of Canada rather than the Government of Canada. When the criticism arose that this amounted to political propaganda, the more blatant political content was removed. Subsequently, however, departmental emails were disclosed that required all news releases to refer to the national government as "the Stephen Harper government." To this day there is a dispute over whether "branding" the government in personal terms is still a requirement.

In 2006 the government put in place a communications tool called Message Event Proposals (MEP). These are documents prepared by departments and agencies and submitted to the PMO and PCO for approval. MEP documents employ such headings as event type, key messages, strategic objectives, media lines, desired headlines, and ideal speaking backdrop. The clear purpose of the MEP process was to provide the governing party with message control by carefully scripting external communications (Martin, 2010: 58; Thomas, 2013). It covers everything from major announcements about the acquisition of fighter jets to minor grants to community organizations. Originally the PMO ran the MEP process, but by 2008 there was a huge backlog of proposals and the PCO (comprising career public servants) was conscripted to coordinate the vetting process. For many observers this arrangement crossed an important line, because neutral public servants were now being asked to support "partisan political" communications activity rather than restrict themselves to the communication of factual background information.

A related development was allegations of political interference in the application of the Access to Information Act (ATIA), which established the right of Canadians, subject to a limited number of exemptions, to gain access to government documents. The ATIA had been in place since 1983, and over the years there had been criticism, particularly from information commissioners (the parliamentary watchdogs established to promote and enforce the law), that successive governments and the bureaucracy had adopted several defensive strategies to block the release of sensitive, potentially embarrassing information.

The Harper government took these strategies to a new level by adopting an elaborate colour-coded rating system for handling access to information requests. Based on the source of the request (requests from opposition MPs and the media were treated as highly sensitive) and the potential for controversy, access requests were routinely sent to ministers' offices and even to the PMO for clearance rather than being resolved by professional access coordinators in departments and agencies (Thomas, 2010). When these practices were revealed, the information commissioner undertook an inquiry that prompted the prime minister to order political staff to stay out of the access process (Legault, 2011).

In summary, in comparison to previous governments, the Harper government has practised tighter control over the flow of information along with more systematic attempts at news management. In doing so, it has violated the spirit (if not the letter) of the official communications policy of the Government of Canada, which declares that the public service must communicate openly, honestly, and objectively with Canadians.

The Precarious State of the Public Service

Back in 1996 the clerk of the Privy Council and head of the public service reported to Liberal Prime Minister Jean Chrétien that the public service was suffering from a "quiet crisis" of identity and purpose (Johnson and Molloy, 2009; Zussman, 2010). Years of budgetary restraint, downsizing, and pay freezes had taken their toll on morale in the public service. Public servants reported that their talents were not being used effectively. The boomer generation of public servants was about to retire, and surveys indicated that young Canadians would not consider a public service career if other options were available. The government agreed to a public service renewal initiative (called *la Relève* or the Reawakening), which brought to the forefront long-neglected human resource management issues such as succession planning, recruitment and retention, and organizational learning.

Whether there was a genuine crisis and whether *la Relève* effectively addressed the problems remain matters for debate (Johnson and Molloy, 2009). In 2013 the public service was facing a confluence of challenges that seem to exceed those of a decade ago.

In addition to the actions of the Harper government described above, several other trends and specific developments produced an anxious public service that exists in a precarious state:

- Under the influence of anti-government thinking, budgetary scarcity, and the impacts of information technology, new, networked approaches to governance have emerged. These new arrangements do not fit with conventional understandings of bureaucracy and create tensions between the internal and external roles of public servants;

- Exempt political staffs in the PMO and in ministers' offices have gained greater influence in the governing process. It is unrealistic to deny the prime minister and other ministers the advisors and support staff needed to perform their political roles. However, there must be appropriate limits on the actions of political staff (Australia and the United Kingdom have codes of ethics for political staff), and they must respect the role of an impartial public service;

- In 2006 the Harper government had Parliament pass the Federal Accountability Act (FedAA), which created several new oversight bodies to monitor and report on the behaviour of public officials. These new accountability mechanisms were in addition to a thick web of rules and a powerful internal audit function introduced by the previous Liberal government. In combination, these measures sent a powerful negative message about the motives, behaviours, and competence of public servants.

- When there is an insistence on error-free government and an elaborate accountability apparatus exists, the public service becomes risk averse, candid conversations are stifled, blaming trumps learning, and the

innovation demanded by governments does not happen to the extent
that it should;

- A new generation of middle managers recruited during the
  expansionary years of the *la Relève* initiative moved ahead quickly, and
  the worry is that these future top leaders are too willing to tell the
  government what it wants to hear;
- Employee surveys done every three years reveal growing levels of
  skepticism that the senior leadership of the public service will act on
  employee concerns;
- In the aftermath of the layoffs announced in the 2012 budget the
  demand for counselling services has increased dramatically (May, 2012);
- Public ignorance and suspicion of the public service leads to
  indifference and complacency about the health of the institution.

In public statements Prime Minister Harper declares his belief in a capable, vibrant public service. But there are many critics who say his actions
contradict his rhetoric.

Conclusions

Once, there was widespread acceptance of the Weberian model of bureaucracy because it delineated a clear division of labour between politicians and
public servants. Today, there is no longer the same confidence in the public
service as a reliable instrument to carry out the wishes of the politicians.

There has been much loose talk about "banishing bureaucracy," but that
will not happen. In complex policy environments, governments will continue
to rely on public service advice to formulate policies and on administrative
discretion to implement policies. In general the public service will continue
to perform a wide array of tasks effectively and efficiently. There will continue to be isolated cases of policy mistakes, mismanagement, waste, excessive
rules, abuse of authority, and secrecy. A parliamentary and media culture of
scandal will amplify, distort, and sensationalize these problems. We should not
ignore the shortcomings of the federal public service, but those shortcomings need to be understood in terms of their origins mainly in the political
context and the complexity of the institution.

In an era when many policy problems transcend jurisdictional and organizational boundaries, influential public servants rely less on in-depth policy
expertise and more on the skills of navigating in a series of horizontal relationships with other actors inside and outside of government. In this way the
roles and the skills of politicians and public servants have become blurred.
A constructive working partnership between politicians and public servants

based on mutual respect, trust, and honest communication is crucial for the future.

International studies indicate that strong, professional public services are essential to good governance. The pride that Canadians once took in the high quality of their public service has declined. It is time to take the actions necessary to restore the capacity and reputation of the public service as a vital national institution.

References and Suggested Readings

Aucoin, Peter. 1995. *The New Public Management: Canada in a Comparative Perspective.* Montreal: Institute for Research on Public Policy.

Aucoin, Peter. 2006. "Improving Government Accountability." *Canadian Parliamentary Review* Autumn: 20–27.

Bakvis, H. 2000. "Refunding Policy Capacity in the Era of the Fiscal Dividends: A Report from Canada." *Governance: An International Journal of Policy, Administration and Institutions* 13 (1): 71–103. http://dx.doi.org/10.1111/0952-1895.00124.

Delacourt, Susan. 2008. "Tory Government Takes Aim at Bureaucracy." *Toronto Star*, January 17.

Doern, G. Bruce, and Sharon L. Sutherland. 1985. *Bureaucracy in Canada: Control and Reform.* Toronto: University of Toronto Press.

Drummond, Don. 2011. "Personal Reflections on the State of Public Policy Analysis in Canada." In *New Directions for Intelligent Government in Canada: Papers in Honour of Ian Stewart*, eds. Fred Gorbet and Andrew Sharpe, 337–52. Ottawa: Centre for the Study of Living Standards.

Dunn, Christopher, ed. 2010. *The Handbook of Canadian Public Administration.* Don Mills: Oxford University Press.

Felligi, I. 1996. *Strengthening Our Policy Capacity.* Report of the Deputy Ministers' Task Force. Ottawa: Canadian Centre for Management Development. http://publications. gc.ca/site/eng/100120/publication.html.

Flanagan, Tom. 2007. *Harper's Team: Behind the Scenes in the Conservative Rise to Power.* Montreal: McGill-Queen's University Press.

Geddes, John. 2010. "Why Stephen Harper Thinks He's Smarter than Experts." *Maclean's* (August): 9.

Gidengil, Elizabeth. 2004. *Citizens.* Vancouver: University of British Columbia Press.

Good, David A. 2008. "An Ideal Model in a Practical World: The Continuous Revisiting of Political Neutrality and Ministerial Responsibility." In *Professionalism and Public Service: Essays in Honour of Kenneth Kernaghan*, eds. David Siegel and Ken Rasmussen, 63–83. Toronto: University of Toronto Press.

Goodsell, Charles T. 2004. *The Case for Bureaucracy: A Public Administration Polemic.* 4th ed. Washington: CQ Press.

Green, Ian. 2008. "The Public Service and Trust." In *5 Trends That Are Transforming Government*, 18–26. Ottawa: Public Policy Forum.

Heard, Andrew. 1991. *Canadian Constitutional Conventions: The Marriage of Law and Politics.* Toronto: University of Toronto Press.

Heintzman, Ralph, and Brian Marson. 2006. "People, Service and Trust: Is There a Public Sector Service Value Chain?" *International Review of Administrative Sciences* 71 (4): 549–75. http://dx.doi.org/10.1177/0020852305059599.

Hernandez, Morela. 2012. "Toward an Understanding of the Psychology of Steward-ship." *Academy of Management Review* 27 (2): 17–193. http://dx.doi.org/10.5465/amr.2010.0363.

Ibbitson, John. 2012. "Canadians Have Little Confidence in Governments to Solve Is-sues That Matter Most: Study." *Globe and Mail*, July 25.

Ipsos Reid. 2007. Poll of Most Trusted Professions. http://www.ipsos-na.com/news-polls.

Jeffrey, Brooke. 2011. "Strained Relationships: The Conflict Between the Harper Conser-vatives and the Federal Bureaucracy." Paper presented to the annual conference of the Canadian Political Science Association, May 17, Waterloo, ON.

Johnson, David, and A. Molloy. 2009. "The Quiet Crisis and the Emergence of *La relève*: A Study of Crisis Perception and Executive Leadership Within the Canadian Federal Public Service, 1997–2002." *Canadian Public Administration* 52 (2): 203–23. http://dx.doi.org/10.1111/j.1754-7121.2009.00072.x.

Johnson, William. 2005. *Stephen Harper and the Future of Canada*. Toronto: McClelland and Stewart.

Legault, Suzanne. 2011. *Interference with Access to Information*. A special Report to Parlia-ment by the Information Commission of Canada. Ottawa: March.

Lindquist, Evert. 2009. *There's More to Policy Than Alignment*. Ottawa: Canadian Policy Research Networks.

Lindquist, Evert, and James Desveaux. 2007. "Policy Analysis and Bureaucratic Capacity: Context, Competencies, and Strategies." In *Policy Analysis in Canada: The State of the Art*, eds. L. Dobuzenkis, M. Howlett, and D. Laycock, 116–42. Toronto: University of Toronto Press.

Martin, Lawrence. 2010. *Harperland: The Politics of Control*. Toronto: Viking.

Mashaw, Jerry L. 1985. *Bureaucratic Justice*. New Haven: Yale University Press.

Mashaw, Jerry L. 2010. "Federal Administration and Administrative Law in the Gilded Age." *Yale Law School, Faculty Scholarship Series.* Paper 3867.

May, Kathryn. 2012. "PS Downsizing Creates a Big Rise in Requests for Counseling," *Ottawa Citizen*, September 20.

May, Kathryn, and Derek Spalding. 2013. "More Federal Front-line Positions to Be Cut Than Once Anticipated, Report Says," *Ottawa Citizen*, April 1.

Milner, Henry. 2001. "Civic Literacy in a Comparative Context: Why Canadians Should Be Concerned." *Policy Matters* 2 (2): 1–32.

Moynihan, Donald P., and Sanjay K. Pandey. 2007. "The Role of Organizations in Fos-tering Public Service Motivation." *Public Administration Review* 67 (1): 40–46. http://dx.doi.org/10.1111/j.1540-6210.2006.00695.x.

Niskanen, William A. 1994. *Bureaucracy and Representative Government*. Chicago: Aldine-Atherton.

Perry, James L. 2000. "Bringing Society In: Toward a Theory of Public-Service Moti-vation." *Journal of Public Administration: Research and Theory* 10 (2): 471–88. http://dx.doi.org/10.1093/oxfordjournals.jpart.a024277.

Rainey, Hal G. 2003. *Understanding and Managing Public Organizations*. San Francisco: Jossey-Bass.

Savoie, Donald J. 2008. *Court Government and the Collapse of Accountability in Canada and United Kingdom*. Toronto: University of Toronto Press.

Savoie, Donald J. 2013. *Whatever Happened to the Music Teacher? How Government Decides and Why*. Montreal: McGill-Queens University Press.

Sheikh, Munir A. 2011. "Good Data and Intelligent Government." In *New Directions for Intelligent Government in Canada: Papers in Honour of Ian Stewart*, eds. Fred Gorbet and Andrew Sharpe, 305–36. Ottawa: Centre for the Study of Living Standards.

Taylor, Jeannette. 2010. "Public Service Motivation, Civic Attitudes and Actions of Public, Nonprofit and Private Sector Employees." *Public Administration* 88 (4): 1083–98. http://dx.doi.org/10.1111/j.1467-9299.2010.01870.x.

Thomas, Paul G. 1997. "Ministerial Responsibility and Administrative Accountability." In *New Public Management and Public Administration in Canada*, eds. M. Charih and Arthur Daniels, 141–64. Toronto: Institute of Public Administration of Canada.

Thomas, Paul G. 2007. "Parliamentary Scrutiny and Redress of Grievances." *Canadian Parliamentary Review* Spring: 6–11.

Thomas, Paul G. 2008. "The Swirling Meanings and Practices of Accountability in Canadian Government." In *Professionalism and Public Service: Essays in Honour of Kenneth Kernaghan*, eds. David Siegel and Ken Rasmussen, 34–62. Toronto: University of Toronto Press.

Thomas, Paul G. 2009. "Trust, Leadership and Accountability in Canada's Public Sector." In *Evolving Physiology of Government: Canadian Public Administration in Transition*, eds. O.P. Dwivedi, T. Mau, and B. Sheldrick, 215–48. Ottawa: University of Ottawa Press.

Thomas, Paul G. 2010. *Advancing Access to Information Principles Through Performance Management Mechanisms: The Case of Canada.* Washington: World Bank Institute.

Thomas, Paul G. 2013. "Communications and Prime Ministerial Power." In *Governing: Essays in Honour of Donald J. Savoie*, eds. James Bickerton and B. Guy Peters, 53–84. Montreal: McGill-Queen's University Press.

Treasury Board of Canada Secretariat. 2012. *Population of the Federal Public Service.* Ottawa. http://www.tbs-sct.gc.ca/res/stats/ssen-ane-eng.asp.

Wilson, James Q. 1989. *Bureaucracy: What Government Agencies Do and Why They Do It.* New York: Basic Books.

Zussman, David. 2010. "The Precarious State of the Public Service." In *How Ottawa Spends, 2010–2011: Recession, Realignment, and the New Deficit Era*, eds. G. Bruce Doern and Christopher Stoney, 219–42. Montreal: McGill-Queens University Press.

ten

Judicial Politics in the Age of the Charter

RAYMOND BAZOWSKI

The distinguished American legal theorist Ronald Dworkin created an estimable body of work based on the proposition that a distinction can be drawn between matters of policy and those of principle.[1] Matters of policy are the stuff of politics. In their legislative role, governments frame their policy objectives based on deliberations about what programs might advance the general welfare of the nation or of a particular constituency and at what cost, on estimates about the relative availability of public resources and, of course, on calculations about electoral advantage. Matters of principle, by contrast, involve a different order of decision-making and are said to be the special province of courts. Matters of principle refer to the rights and obligations that individuals are said to possess in a settled legal system. In Dworkin's view, to determine the particular extent of such rights and obligations a judge must be prepared to undertake an interpretative exercise that aims at supplying a principled construction of the law. Such a principled interpretation is meant to weave together legal facts (legislation, procedural law, and precedents) and a compelling moral theory that can be shown to underlie those same facts. What Dworkin tries to convey in his portrayal of "law as integrity" is the rather conventional idea that judges are (or should be) moved by higher ideals of fairness and justice and, for this reason, occupy a somewhat different moral-political universe than politicians, who tend to make a virtue out of utilitarian arithmetic and the arts of compromise and expediency.

If opinion polls are any indication, Dworkin's positive valuation of adjudication is broadly shared by the Canadian public.[2] Yet curiously, a significant number of political scientists in this country have been more skeptical about the capacity of judges to rise above the vicissitudes of ordinary politics. Indeed, a recurring theme in the literature in political science on the judiciary is that there has been an ill-fated judicialization of politics that supposedly has materialized following the adoption of the Charter of Rights and Freedoms in 1982. The obverse of this observation is that courts have become increasingly politicized as they engage their Charter-enhanced adjudicative role. Both points require some elaboration.

The term "judicialization of politics" has at least two interrelated meanings. Most directly it implies that courts have intruded into the policy-making arena to an extent not contemplated by the classic doctrine of the separation of powers. That doctrine holds that well-ordered government consists of distinct functional branches best kept within their own spheres of competence. Elegant in its simplicity, the idea that governmental powers should be housed in separate institutions is beset by some elementary problems: precisely what are those separate powers that need to be sequestered into different branches, and what assurances can one have that these branches will restrict themselves to their official remit? One solution to this problem is modern constitutionalism, that is, defining the scope and limits of governmental authorities by way of a higher law that is binding on those authorities. But this solution raises more questions. For instance, who gets to devise this constitution and under what circumstances? And equally significant, who gets to decide if the terms of the constitution have been breached by office-holders? In Canada we have become accustomed to answering this latter question by saying that courts must play this crucial role of supervising the constitution by exercising their power of judicial review. But it pays to remember that there are several possible solutions to the boundary problem contained in the doctrine of the separation of powers. Britain, for example, has a constitutional court with only a limited power of judicial review. Observing the principle of parliamentary sovereignty (the idea that Parliament is the supreme law-making body), Britain's version of constitutionalism presently accords its constitutional court the power only to invalidate secondary legislation (i.e., regulations made by subordinate bodies), and to make a declaration of incompatibility in those instances where it believes a law passed by Parliament breaches one of the rights contained in the European Convention on Human Rights. Such a declaration of incompatibility does not, however, nullify the offending law, for in Britain parliamentary sovereignty trumps judicial review, which means that only Parliament can decide whether to alter or rescind a law of its own making.

Given Canada's political heritage, it should come as no surprise that devotion to the principle of parliamentary supremacy has long been a commonplace in this country's democratic discourse. Reconciling that principle with the power of judicial review was relatively uncontroversial in the pre-Charter era because constitutional jurisprudence before 1982 was confined largely to questions of which level of government, federal or provincial, was entitled under the 1867 BNA Act to legislate on some contested subject matter. A metaphor frequently used to describe the Court's unassuming constitutional role was that of an umpire impartially administering the rules defining the Canadian game of federalism. While umpires might be essential to the successful conduct of any game, they are hardly expected to displace the players themselves, but instead are intended to remain in the background, rulebook always at the ready. This benign image of the unbiased referee has not carried over into the age of the Charter. Rather, armed with the newly minted capacity to review and invalidate a law not only on the basis of whether it rightly belongs to the jurisdiction of the enacting government, but also on the basis of whether its substance infringes one of the enumerated rights in the Charter, courts have acquired a much more contentious image in some quarters as self-appointed and self-important oracles of the constitution with their own legislative ambitions.

In addition to concerns about an imperial judiciary exceeding its traditional adjudicative responsibilities, critics of the judicialization of politics often raise a second related objection by claiming that conflicts which are, at root, political are increasingly being transformed into legal issues to be resolved through a categorical judicial language in an impenetrable institutional setting by an appointed and largely unaccountable body. In this alternate depiction of the phenomenon of the judicialization of politics, what is presented as particularly worrisome is the notion that the vocabulary by which we come to identify issues requiring public action has become infected by a rights-based language that prioritizes the individual over the collective. Not only does this mean that efforts to imagine a public good have been made more difficult, but also that the arena in which contested claims about individual rights and public goods takes place has for all intents and purposes become the courts. As a well-known authority on the courts had warned at the onset of the Charter era, this development could only accelerate the flight from politics by contributing to a "deepening disillusionment with the procedures of representative government and government by discussion as a means of resolving fundamental questions of political justice" (Russell, 1982: 32).

While reproaches offered by critics such as Russell focus on the effects of judicialized politics on parliamentary democracy, an opposite case can be made that the Charter has contributed to the politicization of a judiciary that normally has been averse to mixing politics with legal analysis. On this view, an illicit boundary crossing has been forced on judges by parliamentarians who are only too willing to shun their own legislative responsibilities and thrust onto courts politically sensitive issues they would prefer to avoid. Retired Justice Marie Deschamps is only the latest Supreme Court judge to have reported just this tendency when she spoke of the avoidance behaviour of politicians who pass on "hot potato" issues to the courts to resolve: "The clear message is: Let the judges do it ... We are caught in these situations. We see those cases coming and we cannot say no" (quoted in Makin, 2013c).

Are the critics right in deploring a trend toward the judicialization of politics or, alternatively, of the politicization of the judiciary in Canada? In this chapter, it will be argued that misgivings about the political role of the modern judiciary are in part overstated, and otherwise are offered up in a way that usually is too decontextualized to afford us a truly useful perspective on the relationship between law and politics. To this end it will be necessary to briefly recount the history of courts and constitutional jurisprudence, if only to show that a conception of courts as a non-political institution supplying narrow technical interpretations of the law has always been problematic.

The Courts and the Constitution Before the Charter

It must be conceded that the image of the Court as an umpire in constitutional affairs alluded to in the introduction to this chapter does on the face of it have a certain compelling force. After all, when the Canadian Constitution consisted primarily of the BNA Act, virtually the only constitutional disputes that ever arose centred on the division of powers. In the circumstances, it makes eminent sense to assume that some institution—and who better than the courts?—must be able to settle authoritatively any arguments over which level of government is empowered to regulate particular activities. Created in 1875 through a simple act of Parliament and staffed by judges appointed solely on the discretion of the prime minister, the Supreme Court was devised with this role of constitutional adjudication especially in mind. But from the very beginning there were suspicions, particularly among provincial governments such as that of Quebec, that the court's responsibility for deciding constitutional matters might be more than a little adulterated by politics. Provincial wariness concerning a federally appointed Supreme Court was not ill-founded. After all, when he first introduced legislation to create a general appellate court, Prime Minister John A. Macdonald did not conceal its intended political objective, proposing that its jurisdiction in constitutional law be restricted to examining only provincial legislation. Established eventually not by Macdonald's Conservatives but by the Liberal government of Alexander Mackenzie, the Court's constitutional purview was expanded to include federal legislation, though many parliamentarians still anticipated it would act to invalidate primarily provincial legislation, thereby accomplishing more circumspectly the same nationalizing results that hitherto had been produced through the heavy-handed federal power of disallowance (J. Smith, 1983: 125–26; Snell and Vaughn, 1985: 5–10).

If the Supreme Court was initially thought to be a tool of Ottawa to fashion the still young federal state according to its own centralist design, it proved not to be particularly adept at the task. There were several reasons for this. To begin with, the judges of the early court disappointed many of their provincial counterparts with the legal quality of their rulings, thus failing to inspire the kind of confidence that is indispensable for a national appellate court in a unified legal system. Its authority undermined by its own unimpressive legal performance, the Supreme Court also faced the embarrassing fact that it was only nominally supreme because, somewhat controversially, the legislation that created it allowed for a continuation of appeals to the imperial tribunal for the British colonies, the Judicial Committee of the Privy Council (JCPC).[3] Even more confounding was the fact that decisions from provincial courts of appeal could be appealed directly to the JCPC, a measure that could only intensify skepticism about the capability of the Supreme Court. Not surprisingly, such *per saltum* appeals became a common feature of Canadian jurisprudence in the first few decades following the establishment of the Supreme Court, in no small measure because provincial governments expected the imperial tribunal to be more dispassionate in resolving disputes over the division of powers.[4] An obliging JCPC repaid the trust that provincial governments reposed in it with a series of inventive rulings in cases such as *Attorney General of Ontario v. Attorney General of Canada [1896], re Board of Commerce Act and Combines and Fair Prices Act [1919, 1922]*, and *Toronto Electric Commissioners v. Snider [1925]*. With these judgements the JCPC, it is generally conceded, altered the Canadian constitution by diluting the federal government's authority over trade and commerce and its general power to legislate in the interests of peace, order, and good government, while at the same time enhancing provincial powers over property and civil rights, and matters of a local and private nature.

This reordering of the relative powers of the federal and provincial governments by a distant imperial body, whose experience of federalism was entirely academic, did attract its share of criticism, principally from English-Canadian nationalists and other partisans of a strong central government (Cairns, 1971). But the JCPC also had its defenders, including the political essayist Pierre Elliott Trudeau, who once remarked that the British tribunal had helped keep Quebec in Confederation by fashioning a more accommodating division of powers than that envisaged by the designers of the BNA Act (Trudeau, 1968: 198). Yet even defenders of the JCPC have been hard-pressed to say its disputed judgements were legally correct because it is only too evident that they were intrinsically political judgements, not simply in their consequences, but also in their source. Indeed it is almost impossible to imagine any court giving substance to the letter of constitutional law without drawing upon conceptions of justice, political ideals, theories of government, administrative assumptions, and a host of other considerations that can only be characterized as political. Whatever the exact reasons behind its provincialist inclinations, the JCPC, particularly in the interwar years, was anything but an impartial umpire, and the political landscape of Canada became different as a result.

Political too were the circumstances that led the Canadian government finally to abandon appeals to the JCPC in 1949. A series of detested rulings on the so-called Bennett New Deal legislation that hampered the federal government's efforts to respond boldly to the economic hardships brought on by the Great Depression,[5] together with sentiments of an increasingly self-confident nationalism, drew together federal politicians of all parties to support a motion to abolish appeals to the JCPC. Unsaid but certainly wished for in many quarters was that the Supreme Court, unshackled from its judicial superior, would reverse the decentralizing momentum that the JCPC had facilitated. Initially these hopes were indulged by the Supreme Court, as in *Johannesson v. West St. Paul [1952]*, where it offered an interpretation of the "peace, order, and good government" clause of the constitution more commodious to the federal government. But for the most part, the Supreme Court did not disturb to any great extent the precedents established by the JCPC, and at least for the first two decades of its newly acquired supremacy, it moved cautiously and often inconsistently in constitutional cases. This was true not only of its federalism cases, but also of its incipient civil rights cases, for which a potential constitutional justification had emerged in the form of the "Duff doctrine." Enunciated by Chief Justice Duff in what amounted to a judicial conjecture in *Reference re Alberta Statutes [1938]*, this doctrine suggested that the preamble to the BNA Act implicitly contains a guarantee of those freedoms, such as freedom of speech, that are essential to the functioning of democratic government. Although occasionally cited by subsequent judges, notably in a series of civil rights cases in Quebec in the 1950s, the Duff doctrine failed to reach the level of a binding precedent and the prospect of an activist court spiritedly safeguarding civil liberties was never realized during this period. Not even when the federal government passed a Bill of Rights in 1960 did the courts eagerly take up the assignment it seemed to offer. An ordinary piece of legislation, and only applicable to actions of the federal government, the Bill of Rights had so uncertain a constitutional status that, in the main, the courts ignored its provisions.[6]

Commentators have frequently remarked on the conservatism of the Supreme Court in constitutional and civil rights matters during the 1950s and 1960s, and its almost slavish adherence to common law precedents established by British judicial authorities, even after it had become the final appellate court in Canada (Bushnell, 1992). No doubt this is true as a description of the Court's jurisprudence, but there is a political context to this judicial diffidence. By the time the Supreme Court had become the court of last resort in division-of-powers cases, federal and provincial governments were embarking on concerted efforts in taxation and social policy in what came to be called the era of cooperative federalism. The relative political harmony that ensued made the Court's constitutional role less momentous if only because fewer federalism disputes were litigated. Significantly, once this cooperative era began to languish in the 1970s, and as private corporations fought to escape unwanted regulations, the number of division-of-powers cases multiplied and the Court assumed a much larger role in the political affairs of Canada. And while such cases have again generally declined in significance in recent years, the Court still periodically makes a jurisdictional decision that has a notable impact on federalism, as arguably happened in *Reference re Securities Act, [2011]*, where the Supreme Court advised that a proposed scheme for the creation of a single national securities regulator fell outside the authority of the federal government.

As for the Court's reluctance to use its legal resources to vigorously defend civil rights before the introduction of the Charter, there again is a political background that needs to be taken into account. In his comparative study of judicial activism, Charles Epp has suggested that courts are much more likely to be emphatic champions of civil liberties if there already exist within society institutional and cultural support structures that can reinforce an emboldened judiciary (Epp, 1998). The relative absence in Canada in the early postwar years of such a foundation for judicial activism goes some way in explaining the Supreme Court's disappointingly intermittent concern for protecting civil liberties. By the same token, the subsequent decades-long campaign for a constitutionally entrenched charter of rights, the multiplication of public interest groups prepared to include legal action in their repertoire of political tactics (helped in some instances by government programs designed for just such a purpose), the demonstration effect of successful civil rights undertakings in the United States under the Warren Court,[7] changes in professional legal education as well as assorted efforts to make legal knowledge more widely available to the general public all acted to produce an environment more conducive to judicial activism.

Alongside the influence of these various political and social forces, there were some important transformations occurring in the Supreme Court itself that prepared it for a more activist role. Introduced during the tenure of Pierre Trudeau as Justice Minister and, later, as prime minister, these changes included reforming the appeal process to give the Court virtually complete control over which cases it would hear, and therefore the capacity to determine which areas of the law it would influence through its judgements.[8] One very visible result of this revised appeal process was the heightened prominence the Court began to give to *public* as opposed to *private* law cases. Another less formal but equally consequential change involved judicial appointments. In an effort to enhance its legitimacy, the Trudeau government inaugurated a pattern of appointments to the Supreme Court, imitated by subsequent prime ministers, in which partisan connections and political experience were downplayed in favour of academic reputation and judicial experience. As one judicial scholar has observed, this "revolution by appointment," which began in earnest with the pre-Charter Laskin court, "delivered on the hopes of those who wanted a powerful court playing a strong public role" (McCormick, 2000: 103).

One rather clear sign of the metamorphosis taking place in the Supreme Court occurred in a 1976 reference case, re Anti-Inflation Act [1976]. Reference cases, it must be pointed out, are a peculiarity of the Canadian judicial system and illustrate just how tenuous the distinction between judicial and political functions can be.[9] The reference procedure allows the federal government to refer legal issues to the Supreme Court for an advisory opinion. Usually though not exclusively constitutional questions related to a federal law or proposed policy (occasionally the federal government refers provincial laws), reference questions, strictly speaking, have no legal consequences because they do not involve an actual legal dispute. Because the Court's opinion in these circumstances is only advisory, it is conceptually more in the nature of political counsel than legal ruling, though governments have always treated the Court's response to a reference question as authoritative (Hogg, 2002: 8.6d). The reference procedure calls into question the separation of powers doctrine, not simply because the Court is called upon to provide what amounts to political advice, but because the process lends itself to political exploitation. It is only too easy for a government that wishes to delay the introduction of a law for political reasons,[10] or stake out a claim in a federalism dispute,[11] or squarely avoid confronting a controversial issue,[12] to hand over to the Court responsibility for the problem with hopes that a judicial pronouncement will facilitate a desired political outcome. Although the Anti-Inflation Act reference was not devised for any such blatant political purpose, it did nonetheless exhibit features that would become commonplace in the subsequent Charter era, including granting standing to groups with a valid public interest in the outcome of the case and, perhaps more notably, deciding to admit social scientific evidence relevant to the issue at dispute. What bears comment about these practices is that, by engaging in them, the Court places itself in a position of judging not simply the legal qualifications but also the substantive merits of a disputed government measure. By so inquiring into the policy justifications of a law, it can be argued that courts are straying illicitly into the legislative domain, a charge that becomes familiar in the era of the Charter although the exercise is already prefigured in re Anti-Inflation Act.

Judicial Activism in the Era of the Charter

Changes in types of judicial appointments, changes in the way the Court chooses and administers its caseload, and changes in its evidentiary rules all signalled a Court ready to become more actively engaged in the policy domain. But without doubt it was the introduction of the Charter of Rights and Freedoms that did most to augment the Court's power of judicial review. This power to evaluate the constitutionality of government actions, and to strike down those found to be unconstitutional, could not but be magnified after 1982 for the simple reason that the Charter explicitly proscribes certain kinds of state conduct. Considering its reluctance to seize upon a civil rights agenda when provided the opportunity with the earlier Bill of Rights, it remained to be seen whether the Court would be more favourably disposed to wield its enhanced power under the Charter. As it turned out, the Supreme Court initially proved a Charter enthusiast, awarding victories in decisions that were almost always unanimous to more than half of the claimants who had invoked its constitutional guarantees in the period 1982–84. Thereafter, however, the success rate for Charter challenges has declined, ranging from a third to as little as a fifth, as was the case in 2012. At the same time disagreements in the Court have become more commonplace. While the latter might be taken as a sign that ideological camps are solidifying in a manner comparable to what has occurred in the United States, students of the attitudinal characteristics of Canadian Supreme Court Justices have concluded that for the most part simple liberal/conservative ideological distinctions are inadequate in accounting for the incidence of concurrences and dissents in the Court (Alarie and Green, 2009; Ostberg and Wetstein, 2007; McCormick, 2004). If anything, as Patrick Monahan suggests, the emergence of different voting blocs in recent years might best be explained by the degree of deference different groups of judges are prepared to show to elected governments, particularly in disputes that have fiscal consequences (Monahan cited in Makin, 2008).

Success rates for Charter challenges and the frequency of dissents do not, however, tell us all that much about the impact of Charter jurisprudence on public policy. More revealing are the patterns discernable among the hundreds of Charter cases heard by the Supreme Court in the Charter's first 30 years, and the interpretative strategies the Court has developed over this period. The Charter, it should be recalled, has some unique features that were meant to guide courts in their interpretation of its enumerated rights. For example, the general legal right contained in Section 7 guaranteeing the right to life, liberty, and security of person is qualified by the phrase "in accordance with the principles of fundamental justice" to indicate broadly the circumstances where governments may be justified in depriving citizens of this right. Or again, Section 15, guaranteeing equal treatment before and under the law, and equal protection and benefit of the laws, has an additional phrase implying that its purpose is to protect against specific types of discrimination, for instance that based on race or religion or sex. Moreover, Section 15 is followed by a clause exempting from Charter challenge affirmative action programs, thereby reinforcing the notion that it should be seen primarily as a remedial right aimed at those historically disadvantaged by prejudices and intolerance.

The internal limitations and interpretative clues contained in these and other rights in the Charter are further qualified by three pivotal application clauses: Sections 1, 24, and 33. Section 1 instructs courts to treat the rights and freedoms of the Charter as only conditionally guaranteed, as they are subject to "such reasonable limits prescribed by law as can be demonstrably justified in a free and democratic society." This latter phrase permits governments to defend a *prima facie* Charter breach by arguing that it is a reasonable limitation on the infringed right. Should a Charter violation be found to exist and not be justified under Section 1, courts are charged under Section 24 with devising a remedy they consider "appropriate and just in the circumstances." This enforcement section confers on the courts discretionary power in deciding just how to respond to a Charter violation, which means that when totalling up Charter victories one should always pay heed to the remedy ordered because a Charter "win" does not automatically mean that the victor obtains the sought-after result. Finally, Section 33 acts to bracket almost all the fundamental rights of the Charter by allowing the federal parliament or provincial legislatures to override Sections 2 and 7 through 15 through simple statutory declarations for repeatable periods of five years. This controversial "notwithstanding" clause was a concession that the federal government made during constitutional negotiations leading up to the Charter to those provincial premiers who were hesitant to relinquish the principle of parliamentary supremacy, though it should be noted that this same provision had also been a part of the 1960 Bill of Rights.[13] While Section 33 seems to impose a considerable restriction on the Charter, and hence on the Court's power of judicial review, in practice this has not been the case. Except for a period in the 1980s when the government of Saskatchewan used the notwithstanding clause to try to pre-empt a constitutional challenge to back-to-work legislation, and governments in Quebec for symbolic political reasons used it to insulate as much of that province's legislation as possible from Charter challenge and later to override an adverse court ruling on its language laws, Section 33 has become increasingly a less credible option for governments as its public legitimacy declined in the intervening years.

Alongside these assorted cues and directives, the Supreme Court has developed several of its own interpretative strategies to give substance to Charter rights. One such strategy has been to interpret the purpose of the rights contained in the Charter, that is, the values they are designed to protect or advance, by canvassing their historical, political, or philosophical sources. This "purposive approach" to Charter interpretation, first articulated by Chief Justice Dickson in his ruling in *Hunter v. Southam [1984]*, ensured that the Court would not confine itself to legally narrow representations of the newly entrenched constitutional rights. Another interpretative approach favoured by the Court has been called "contextualism." The contextual approach, first elaborated by Justice Wilson in *Edmonton Journal v. A.G. Alta [1989]*, invites courts to be more sensitive to the complexities of individual rights claims by acknowledging that "a particular right or freedom might have a different value depending on the context" (1355–56). By endorsing a contextual approach, the Court has signified that it is indisposed to rely on a simple formula to decide upon the validity of a rights claim, preferring instead to examine the underlying circumstances and competing values that might clarify what actually is at stake in the claim.

Understandably, there are those uncomfortable with the interpretative latitude the Court seemingly enjoys when it uses a purposive approach to define the meaning of Charter rights and a contextual approach to decide upon their relative weight in concrete legal disputes. Likewise there are those who are disconcerted by how the courts have come to interpret the limitations clause of Section 1. In an early Charter case, *The Queen v. Oakes [1986]*, Chief Justice Dickson outlined a four-part analysis to determine when a government might be justified in infringing a Charter right. The so-called Oakes test, originally devised to be quite rigorous but subsequently relaxed in practice, requires governments found in violation of a Charter right to satisfy the Court that a pressing and substantial public purpose is being served by the controverted measure, that it is rationally connected to that purpose, that the affected right has been impaired in a minimal fashion, and that the public benefits of the measure outweigh the costs of this impairment. Significantly, the way the Oakes test has been construed invariably involves the Court in policy assessments, for there is no other practical way for it to conclude whether a disputed law or government action is rationally connected to the public purpose it is meant to serve, or, even more acutely, whether a right has been minimally impaired, except to compare policy alternatives. Predictably it is at the Section 1 stage of a Charter hearing that courts are most vulnerable to the charge of subverting the democratic process by substituting their own policy preferences for those of elected legislatures.

Whether an unelected judiciary has indeed used its heightened power of judicial review to illicitly inject its values into the field of democratic policy-making is something that can best be determined by first trying to get a sense of the kinds of Charter-based nullifications the courts have dispensed. Before embarking on such an historical review, however, it is worthwhile observing in some detail the way in which a court contends with a Charter challenge, for it is in these details that a sense of the Court's so-called policy-making role can be more clearly discerned.

In a decision handed down in early 2013, a divided Supreme Court offered a complex ruling in a family law dispute that vividly illustrates the embedded politics of Charter cases. *Quebec (Attorney General) v. A* involved the rights of common-law spouses under the Quebec Civil Code. Unlike most other provinces, which have made varying statutory provisions for support and property division following the break-up of a common-law relationship, the Quebec government chose not to extend to such couples any of the financial protections it accords to married couples or those who have entered into a legally binding civil union. This absence of financial protection was challenged by "Lola," who had been in a seven-year common-law relationship with "Éric," during which time they had three children together. She argued that her exclusion from the legal entitlements the Quebec Civil Code provided for married individuals amounted to discrimination on grounds of marital status and hence was a breach of her equality rights as guaranteed under Section 15 of the Charter. The Quebec government responded that its decision not to make these legal entitlements available to common-law spouses reflected its commitment to personal autonomy. Specifically, its legal regime was said to enable couples to freely choose whether they wished to commit to the financial obligations of support and property division that came with marriage or civil union, or embark upon whatever personal arrangements they considered appropriate to their circumstances. As has been commonplace in cases with such potentially far-reaching consequences, interveners appeared in support of both sides to the dispute. Backing "Lola's" claim were Legal Education and Action Fund (LEAF), a frequent Supreme Court intervener which promotes women's equality rights, and *Fédération des associations de familles monoparentales et recomposées du Québec,* a provincial association representing the interests of single-parent and blended families. Intervening on behalf of the position of the Government of Quebec were the Attorneys General of New Brunswick and Alberta.

While "Lola" enjoyed a partial victory in the Quebec Court of Appeal, the Supreme Court reversed that decision in a ruling that included four separate judgements. A minority of four judges decided that there was no Charter breach because, while the Civil Code does treat common-law spouses differently from married couples or those in civil unions, this differential treatment is not motivated by, nor does it reinforce, prejudices against or stereotypes about such relationships. Five judges, however, decided that the differential treatment of common-law spouses was an infringement of Section 15. Writing for this majority, Justice Abella noted that the purpose of the equality clause in the Charter is to protect those who belong to groups suffering from historical patterns of discrimination, a goal she felt surely should extend to vulnerable and economically dependent common-law spouses. This majority finding of a Charter breach was not, however, the end of this legal drama, for there were still Section 1 arguments to contend with. In this particular case the Oakes test highlighted a political divide that is an enduring feature of the modern political landscape, a divide that is likewise inscribed in the Charter itself. The four minority judges, who saw no violation of the Charter in the first instance, did not of course require the government to supply a Section 1 justification of its policy toward common-law couples. As for the five majority judges who had detected a Charter violation, they parted ways when it came to the Oakes test. Justice Abella concluded that there was no way to justify any of the exclusionary policies of the Quebec Civil Code because the equality rights of common-law couples were wholly, not minimally, impaired. Three other judges found only a single unjustifiable provision in the Quebec Civil Code after Section 1 arguments. In the circumstances, the opinion of the fifth judge, Chief Justice Beverley McLachlin, became decisive in disposing of this case. Despite her agreement with Justice Abella that there was a breach of equality rights, the Chief Justice ruled that all of the Code's provisions for support and property division were nonetheless constitutionally permissible according to the norms of Section 1. By having the option of a common-law relationship bereft of legal protections, Chief Justice McLachlin stated, Quebec couples enjoy a rather unique state-sanctioned ability to give personal meaning to their relationship, a value consistent with the Charter's promotion of autonomy. When this ruling was added to that of the four judges who had held there was no Charter violation in the first place, a final majority of five was formed with a judgement in favour of the Quebec government.

What makes *Quebec (Attorney General) v. A* so instructive a case is that one can witness in its details virtually all the elements associated with the continuing controversy over the judicialization of politics. First, the case arose because of the reluctance of the Quebec government to deal with the politically contentious issue of common-law spousal protections, something that most other provinces have done in the past few decades. In effect, legislative inaction shifted the issue to the courts. Second, in raising the conflicting values of equality and liberty, the case throws into sharp relief a rather basic feature of Charter jurisprudence: more often than not Charter disputes require judges to make choices about preferred political values, something that is as much a political as a judicial assignment. Third, by obliging courts to weigh the relative merits of Section 1 policy arguments, judges to some degree or other have to engage the legislative perspective. Ronald Dworkin's distinction between policies and principles seems quite implausible at this stage of a court hearing. Fourth, when judges find themselves divided on principles and policy preferences in a specific case, they are encouraged by the very nature of their own decision-making process to form voting blocs—in short, they demonstrate a propensity for the same kind of strategic and tactical behaviour that is a feature of all political organizations. Finally, as this case involved a challenge to a provincial law, its resolution had implications for federalism. Had the Court, for instance, found the provisions of the Quebec Civil Code relating to common-law couples unconstitutional, it would have supported the contention that the Charter was, by design or by jurisprudential tendency, a nationalizing instrument.

The various structural features of judicial decision-making noted in *Quebec (Attorney General) v. A* have shown up again and again in cases throughout the Charter's history. But that history also shows patterns in the decision-making that tell a more fulsome story about the temper and tempo of judicialized politics in Canada. For example, in the period between 1982 and 2012 the Supreme Court ruled that 91 federal or provincial statutes or regulations contravened the Charter or Section 35 of the *Constitution Act, 1982*, the latter containing guarantees of Aboriginal and treaty rights that are not a part of the Charter, but that have been approached by the Court in a manner analogous to its Charter jurisprudence.[14] Of these 91 constitutional invalidations, 50 involved federal and 41 provincial statutes or regulations. The majority of federal laws or regulations found to be unconstitutional (30 out of 50) were faulted for procedural rather than substantive matters, which has meant in principle that Parliament could with relative ease remedy the problem with amended legislation or new regulations. In the case of impugned provincial statutes and regulations, the majority (32 out of 41) have been judged unconstitutional on substantive grounds, which means that it has been comparatively harder, though again not impossible, for these governments to repair the legislation or regulation.

The contrast between federal and provincial experiences with the Charter on the face of it seems to support the view that implicit in the Charter's design was a nationalizing mission to harmonize provincial legislation and regulatory practices (Russell, 1983; Cairns, 1992; Laforest, 1992). Yet closer analysis of the actual disposition of Charter cases suggests that such a national alignment among provincial laws has not taken place to any significant degree. For instance, in the area of language rights, which many thought had the greatest potential to produce federal homogenization, it turned out that after interpreting these provisions relatively strictly during first few years of the Charter, the Supreme Court has lately been much more willing to approve provincial variations in language and cultural policies.[15] These and other trends in Charter jurisprudence have led the constitutional scholar, James Kelly, to conclude that the Charter has had "a minimal impact on federal diversity" (1999: 685).[16]

If the Supreme Court has not used the Charter to further the nationalizing project often attributed to it, there are nonetheless some general motifs evident among its Charter rulings that suggest it is appreciative of both the perils and possibilities of its enhanced political role. The most conspicuous of these patterns has been the extent to which legal rights dominate Charter jurisprudence. Most frequently invoked in Charter litigation (Section 7 arguments in particular outnumber all others), legal rights claims also have tended to be the most successful. Not surprisingly, the Supreme Court, just as it had done in a much more modest fashion with the Bill of Rights, has proved most receptive to Charter arguments in a realm of the law—the criminal justice system—for which it feels it possesses a special competence. This relative concern for the rights of the accused that the Court has hitherto exhibited does not mean that it will always be firmly wedded to a due process model of law enforcement, and indeed recent trends point to a Court more willing to side with the state in legal rights cases (Makin, 2013b). Whether this comparatively more deferential judicial attitude will continue to prevail at a time when the federal government has embarked on a more forceful law and order political agenda, as evinced in the passage in 2013 of the *Safe Streets and Communities Act*, with its provisions for mandatory minimum sentences, is uncertain. But if some of the latest appointments to the Court are taken as evidence, this is an area of Charter jurisprudence that the current federal government almost certainly hopes to influence.

As for fundamental freedoms—freedom of expression, religion, association, and assembly—the Court has in the past tried to establish a balanced approach, though in the process has also laid itself open to the charge of constitutional capriciousness. For instance, in *The Queen v. Big M Drug Mart Ltd [1985]*, the Court struck down the federal Lord's Day Act on grounds that it infringed the guarantee of freedom of religion, but subsequently upheld the validity of Ontario's Retail Holiday Act in *Edwards Book and Art Ltd v. the Queen [1986]*, ruling that the latter was a justifiable limitation on the same right. Freedom of expression cases have also come in for some rather variable treatment. In *R. v Keegstra [1990]*, for example, the Court upheld a federal law on hate speech under Section 1, but in *R. v. Zundel [1992]* declared another federal hate speech law unconstitutional because it was deemed to be overly broad and for this reason an objectionable encroachment on freedom of speech. In pornography cases, the Supreme Court has upheld the federal obscenity law in *R. v. Butler [1992]*, although it also effectively read that law down to narrow its application. Likewise, in *R. v. Sharpe [2001]* the Supreme Court upheld the federal law on the possession of child pornography, but at the same time read in exceptions to that law to cover situations it believed posed no risk of harm to children. The Court has thus far been willing to countenance abridgements to free speech in the realm of erotica so long as they can be justified under a notoriously vague "community standards test."

The Court's equality jurisprudence has been especially notable for its doctrinal difficulties, and as in other Charter cases, has entailed contrasting rulings.[17] For example, the Court refused arguments that various provisions in the Income Tax Act discriminated against women in *Symes v. Canada [1993]* and *re Thibaudeau and the Queen [1995]*, but allowed the argument that failure to provide translation services for deaf patients in BC hospitals constituted a violation of Section 15 in *Eldridge v. BC [1997]*. If the *Eldridge* ruling signalled the advent of a substantive interpretation of the equality section of the Charter, it was a short-lived episode as evidenced by the ruling in *Auton v. British Columbia [2004]*, where the Court decided not to order the provincial government to fund costly, specialized treatment of autistic children.

One of the most demonstrable instances of the Court's shifting constitutional position on equality rights has been its response to claims of discrimination brought forward by gays and lesbians. A bare majority of the Court, for example, found that the federal government's refusal to extend spousal allowance benefits under the Old Age Security Act to gay and lesbian partners in long-term relationships was an acceptable departure from the Charter's equality guarantee in *Egan et al. v. the Queen [1995]*. But within a few years the Court altered its approach and in *Vriend v. Alberta [1998]* found the Alberta government contravened Section 15 by failing to provide gays and lesbians protection from discrimination in its provincial human rights act. In the same vein, the Court ruled in *M. v H. [1999]* that by excluding same-sex couples from provisions in its Family Services Act that allow domestic partners to sue for support in the event of a marital breakdown, the Ontario government had violated their equality rights. And in *Attorney General v. Hislop [2007]* the Court repudiated entirely the approach it had taken in *Egan* by ruling that the federal government's attempt to limit the time period in which a surviving partner of a same-sex union could claim survivor benefits under the Canada Pension Plan breached the equality guarantee of Section 15.

The vacillations exhibited in these and other rulings seem to illustrate not so much a court seized with Charter hubris but one that has been rather gingerly muddling through with its enhanced power of judicial review, usually choosing to nullify laws for procedural defects or for being overly broad rather than reproving of them in their entirety. This is not to say that courts have not produced controversial Charter judgements. Whether extending to corporations the same legal rights available to individuals in *Hunter v. Southam [1984]*, or invalidating the federal abortion law in *R. v. Morgentaler [1988]*, or nullifying Quebec's sign law in *Ford v. Quebec [1988]*, or declaring the common-law definition of marriage unconstitutional thereby opening the door to gay marriage in *Halpern et al. v. Attorney-General of Canada et al. [2003]*, courts have periodically handed down highly contentious decisions that arguably have encroached upon the policy prerogative of legislatures. Significantly, when the Court has produced politically divisive rulings, it has done so in the manner of an equal opportunity antagonist by alternately incensing left- and right-wing constituencies.

Two cases illustrate this propensity of the Court to attract censure from opposing ideological camps. In *Sauvé v. Canada (Chief Electoral Officer) [2002]* (otherwise known as *Sauvé 2*), a bare majority of the Supreme Court ruled that the federal government's amendment to the Canada Elections Act found in Section 51(e) that denied to prisoners serving sentences of two years or more the right to vote—an amendment prompted by an earlier successful court challenge by the same litigant—was a violation of the Charter's basic democratic guarantee in Section 3. This ruling was decried by many a conservative commentator as an altogether inappropriate judicial repudiation of Parliament's role in defining the scope of Charter rights, especially considering that the disputed amendment to the Canada Elections Act represented Parliament's calculated response to the Court's previous ruling on what was entailed by the Charter's guarantee of the right to vote (see, for example, Manfredi, 2007). A few years later another deeply divided Court ruled in *Chaoulli v. Quebec (Attorney General), [2005]*, that the provision in Quebec's Health Insurance Act and Hospital Insurance Act prohibiting citizens of that province from obtaining private insurance to cover health care services already available under the provincial public health care plan was a violation of the guarantee to life and security of person found both in the Quebec Charter of Human Rights and Freedoms and the Canadian Charter of Rights and Freedoms. This was a ruling that invited an equally harsh share of criticism from liberal or left-wing commentators because of the way the majority of the Court found a constitutional violation by drawing its own conclusion about the efficacy of a publicly funded medicare plan in supplying reasonably prompt medical services, in the process laying open all other provincial medicare plans to constitutional challenge on similar grounds (see, for example, Flood, 2006).

How can one possibly justify permitting unrepresentative and unaccountable judges to replace the policy preferences of elected officials with their own, as they arguably did in these two cases? It is instructive to observe that both left- and right-wing analysts of the Court refer to this counter-majoritarian dilemma when sounding the alarm about the judicialization of politics.[18] But there are significant differences between left and right appraisals of judicial politics that are worth recounting. Left critics have generally been concerned that judges, by virtue of their class background and training, will invariably tend to be conservative in outlook. A principal fear is that this conservative judiciary will use the Charter—in particular, its ostensibly libertarian components such as Section 7—to reinforce the already powerful position business interests possess at common law.[19] A related concern is that the Charter conveys a beguiling message to progressives by suggesting that genuine social reform is possible through courtroom forensics, something that not only is unlikely but also debilitating for truly effective political action (Petter, 1987; Mandel, 1994; Hutchinson, 1995; Bakan, 1997).

While some of the force of this left critique had dissipated over the years as the Supreme Court repeatedly refused to employ Section 7 to fortify economic rights (but by the same token also declined to use this section to help those who sought a constitutional guarantee for welfare and other social rights), the *Chaoulli* decision has certainly revived left-wing apprehensions about rights-based jurisprudence. But in the event, it has been the right-wing critics of the Court who have become more influential in the debate about the judicialization of politics, a fact that perhaps should be unsurprising given the contemporary growth of political conservatism (Morton and Knopff, 2000; Manfredi, 2001; Leishman, 2006). For the right, the overriding trepidation is that the Court will exploit the egalitarian sections of the Charter, principally Section 15, to advance a radical redistributive agenda.[20] Given the prominence that the writings of F.L. Morton and Rainer Knopff have gained in both academic and political circles, their arguments on this score repay close attention. Morton and Knopff's (2002) main contention is that self-serving special interest groups such as feminists, gays and lesbians, and ethnic and other identity-based groups, which they deem the Court Party, have allied themselves with the jurocracy (a shorthand for legal professionals and advocates within law schools, the bureaucracy, and the judiciary who are Charter enthusiasts) to get through the courts what they haven't been able to secure through the ordinary legislative process. This Court Party, they protest, typically inflates its claims when employing the vocabulary of rights in a way that is inhospitable to the spirit of compromise and conciliation supposedly characteristic of the legislative arena. Morton and Knopff have frequently been criticized for assimilating a deliberately selective cast of characters into what amount to ideological categories of Court Party and jurocracy, and for using a disingenuous conception of democracy as a normative foundation for their critique of the courts (M.C. Smith, 2002). But the impression of a furtive style of politics conducted in courtrooms remains powerful enough to have summoned a variety of justificatory arguments for the power of judicial review.

The most straightforward defence of the Court's constitutionally enhanced role under the Charter is that the capacity to strike down legislation to protect vulnerable minorities from the depredations of legislative majorities is precisely what is intended by a bill of rights in the first place (Bayefsky, 1987). A more refined version of this proposition relies on a process-based conception of democracy. According to this argument, judicial review based on a bill of rights actually promotes democracy by giving the courts the power to ensure that the mechanisms of political representation operate fairly, with special consideration given to the plight of minorities who might otherwise be effectively excluded from the political process (Monahan, 1987). On either view an activist court is ordinarily regarded as a success rather than a problem. Needless to say, judicial adversaries are hardly persuaded by such arguments, countering that the very fact that courts are unaccountable hardly qualifies them for presuming to act as guardians of democracy.

Because courts are forever susceptible to this latter charge, their supporters have lately fastened on another justificatory strategy in which it is asserted that judges do not have the final word on the disposition of individual rights and freedoms but rather are engaged in a dialogue with elected legislatures over their interpretation. Proponents of the judicial dialogue thesis contend that so long as a judicial decision is capable of being reversed, modified, or avoided by ordinary legislative means, the relationship between courts and legislatures should be regarded as a colloquy rather than one of subordination and super-ordination (Hogg and Bushell, 1997; Roach, 2001). The Charter supposedly facilitates this dialogue because it features such clauses as Sections 1 and 33, which offer legislatures room to contribute their own interpretations of contested constitutional values and in some instances ignore entirely their judicial explication. In one of the more compelling versions of this argument, Peter Hogg and Allison Bushell have ventured proof of a dialogue by surveying the laws invalidated by the Court on Charter grounds, finding that in two-thirds of the cases the relevant legislative body responded with amended laws, most of which incorporated minor refinements that did not compromise the objectives of the original legislation (Hogg and Bushell, 1997).[21]

Hogg and Bushell's evidence of dialogue, it should be pointed out, has been disputed,[22] and even proponents of the thesis disagree over whether courts, legislatures, or executives guide the process (Hiebert, 2002; Kelly, 2005). These reservations notwithstanding, courts are for obvious reasons attracted to the dialogue thesis because it makes judicial review appear a benign exercise in value discovery. It is not surprising, therefore, that shortly after the Hogg and Bushell article was published Justice Iacobucci, writing for the majority of the Supreme Court, cited it approvingly in the *Vriend* case, remarking that "dynamic interaction among branches of government ... has aptly been described as a 'dialogue'" (para 139). Even more telling, Chief Justice McLachlin and Justice Iacobucci, again writing for the majority in *R. v. Mills [1999]*, referred to the dialogue thesis in support of their decision not to overrule the federal government's amended "rape-shield" law, even though that law departed from what the Court had previously announced would be constitutionally acceptable (para 57). Governments have also gravitated to this portrayal of judicial power. For instance, after courts in British Columbia, Ontario, and Quebec ruled separately that marriage must be open to same-sex couples, the federal government decided not to appeal, electing instead to recruit the Supreme Court as a political advisor by submitting to it a set of reference questions related to the constitutionality of same-sex marriage. Significantly, the Department of Justice declared that in "taking this course of action, the Government of Canada is ensuring, through a dynamic dialogue between the Courts and Parliament, that our laws reflect the fundamental values of the Charter" (Canada, Department of Justice, 2003).

This manifest concern for public acceptance on the part of both the Supreme Court and the federal government, in the first instance for the power of judicial review, in the second for a potentially unpopular law, suggests that there is a much more fundamental process underlying the judicialization of politics than its critics are prepared to grant. This more fundamental process is nothing less than the recurrent legitimation crises experienced by executive-centred governments in the postwar period. "Legitimation crisis" is routinely described in social scientific literature as a situation where government fails to elicit sufficient allegiance to its authority. The roots of these crises are typically complex and multi-faceted. In Canada, for example, legitimacy crises of varying intensity emerged as the postwar pattern of elite accommodation, predicated on the creation of a regulatory and welfare state, began to decompose in the face of accelerated social change. Among these changes was a breakdown in the political compromise between French and English Canada at a time when other identities demanded acknowledgement in something other than a narrowly construed binational/bicultural state. This period also witnessed a growing economic enfranchisement of women with accompanying demands for equal treatment. At the same time the ideal of the nuclear family increasingly became contested and the presumptive norms of heterosexuality more openly defied. Added to these various bids for recognition and equitable treatment, struggles between capital and labour, never entirely displaced during the formation of the welfare state, gained a new salience as neoliberalism emerged as a dominant economic and political paradigm. And that paradigm itself, no less than its welfarist predecessor, encountered escalated attacks by opponents of immoderate economic growth and a consumerist culture.

While these diverse political currents presented challenges to settled democratic norms and practices, they were also more-or-less vigorously opposed by the very interests and institutions most closely associated with the postwar regulatory and welfare state. In these circumstances, where many of the new movements found their claims marginalized and their political ventures effectively organized out of established democratic pathways, it is not surprising that some would seek to influence public policy through the courts. Nor should it be surprising that the judiciary might sometimes be solicitous of these otherwise powerless groups. After all, one of the by-products of the postwar political settlement was the relative decline of the Supreme Court's constitutional purpose as witnessed in its dwindling number of federalism cases. The Charter made it possible for the Court to redefine its constitutional role as defender of so-called "discrete and insular" minorities[23] just at the time that the legitimacy of existing democratic practices, and the distribution of goods and services they have underwritten, increasingly came to be assailed, and politics-as-usual more difficult to pursue.[24]

It is in the confluence of these events that the judicialization of politics gains its significance, both as an emerging political reality and as an object of normative critique. While this phenomenon has provoked a great deal of concern and demands for reform ranging from a more transparent appointments procedure to an outright curbing of the courts, rather less attention has been paid to the underlying circumstances that have sustained the judiciary's growing political prominence and the counter-tendencies that have worked to moderate it. Of the latter, suffice it to say that as courts become more of a focal point in public policy debates that polarize Canadians, they too risk having their legitimacy undermined, particularly when they are involved in fundamental questions about entitlements, both public and private. Perhaps it has been a recognition of just such a risk that has led to the marked decrease in Charter cases reaching the Supreme Court. While the Court averaged over 25 Charter cases a year in its first two decades, that number has declined notably this last decade and a half, reaching a low of around a dozen cases annually between 2005 and 2012 (the exception being 2010 when the Court heard 26 Charter cases out of a docket of 67). This waning of Charter jurisprudence is matched by another noteworthy develop-ment—the growing inclination of the Court to construe Charter violations more narrowly either as instances of misconduct on the part of state officials (e.g., police officers) or procedural defects in impugned legislation, thereby averting direct quarrels with legislatures over substantive issues in law. It may well be, as Kelly suggests, that this latter tendency has coincided with the cultivation by the federal executive of a bureaucratic apparatus more compe-tent in the ways of drafting legislation that would survive Charter challenges, thereby signalling that the cabinet and its officials are becoming as important in defining Charter values as the Court (Kelly, 2005).[25] Either way, whether it is a Court becoming more deferential in response to legitimacy concerns, or a federal executive becoming more aggressive in asserting the Charter credentials of its own laws, a full-scale judicialization of Canadian politics against which so many critics have sounded dire warnings seems not to have taken place.

But this is not to say that the Court has been entirely absent from politics as its recently disputed ruling in *Canada (Attorney General) v. PHS Community Services Society [2011]* so amply demonstrates. Ruling in this case that the federal government's attempt to close down the drug treatment facility in Vancouver known as Insite was a violation of its patients' Section 7 rights, a unanimous court seemed to create a new and potentially wide-ranging constitutional test for what constitutes arbitrary and disproportionate govern-ment action as measured against the norms of credible scientific evidence of harm reduction. What is striking about the Insite ruling is how excep-tional it seems in a time noted for judicial quiescence, a fact that leads at least some to question its precedential value for any kind of robust positive rights (MacFarlane, 2013). Regardless of its future impact on Canadian ju-risprudence, the Insite ruling points out a simple truth about constitutional adjudication. And that is that given the way the Charter has come to inspire litigation strategies involving public law, the Court will never be able to withdraw from politically charged cases. Nor can its members, as divided as the rest of the population over fundamental political values, convincingly maintain that they are unmoved by political considerations in their judge-ments. Opponents of judicial politics too often imagine a judiciary somehow limited to a world of legal principles safely distanced from the contests over power that obtain in democratic arena. If, however, political power and legal principles are not so easily separable, as has been argued throughout this

Judicial Politics in the Age of the Charter

chapter, then the vision of a sequestered court may not only be illusory, but may distract us from more fruitful lines of empirical inquiry concerning the process of democratic demand-setting and the periodic eruption of judicial policy-making.

Notes

1 While Dworkin had over the years created a formidable body of work, the central proposition that animates his jurisprudential thinking can be fairly easily discerned in his seminal article, "The Forum of Principle" (1981).

2 A point confirmed by Joseph F. Fletcher and Paul Howe in their pioneering study of public opinion and the Canadian judiciary (Fletcher and Howe, 2001, 255–96).

3 The Supreme Court Act of 1875 contained a backbencher's amendment, clause 47, which was supposed to make judgements of the Canadian court "final and conclusive" except for those appeals granted by royal prerogative. Persuaded by imperial authorities that this clause left intact the established appeal process, the Canadian government ignored the letter of its own law and did not foreclose constitutional appeals to the JCPC for the next 75 years (Russell, 1987: 336).

4 Figures cited by Peter Russell indicate that almost half (77 out of 159) of all appeals to the JCPC prior to its withdrawal from Canadian judicial affairs were *per saltum,* the majority of which came in the early post-Confederation years (Russell, 1987: 336).

5 The rulings in question were *Attorney General of Canada v. Attorney General of Ontario (Employment and Social Insurance Act Reference) [1937]; Attorney General of British Columbia v. Attorney General of Canada (Natural Products Marketing Act Reference) [1937];* and *Attorney General of Canada v. Attorney General of Ontario (Labour Conventions Case) [1937].*

6 The Supreme Court upheld rights claims under the Bill of Rights only five times, four of which involved reading into federal criminal law due process requirements. The lone federal law that the Court invalidated under the Bill of Rights was a provision of the Indian Act in *The Queen v. Drybones [1970]* (Morton, 1986: 5).

7 The Warren Court is named after Earl Warren, who presided as Chief Justice of the United States Supreme Court from 1953 to 1969. During this period the Court made a series of notable liberal (and in some quarters controversial) decisions, starting with the seminal desegregation ruling in *Brown v Board of Education.*

8 Prior to amendments to the Supreme Court Act made in 1975, anyone had a right to appeal a civil law case to the highest court if it involved a monetary matter in excess of $10,000, and any criminal law case involving a capital crime. Such appeals by right occupied a disproportionate amount of the Supreme Court's time. After 1975 appeals by right (aside from reference questions, which constitute a different order of pleading) are available only in criminal law cases where there is at least one dissenting judge at the level of the provincial court of appeal (McCormick, 2000: 86).

9 Just how unique the Canadian reference procedure is can be seen by comparing the experiences of other common-law countries with constitutional courts. For example, both the United States Supreme Court and the Australian High Court have refused to supply advisory opinions on grounds that it would offend the principle of the separation of powers (Hogg, 2002: 7.3.a).

10 As arguably happened in the Bennett New Deal reference cases. See Note 5.

11 As was the case in *re Secession of Quebec [1998]*.

12 As in the reference on same-sex marriage consequent on the ruling in *Halpern et al. v. Attorney-General of Canada et al. [2003]*.

13 For opposing views on the wisdom of including Section 33 in the Charter, see Whyte (1990) and Russell (1991).

14 These data are taken from Kelly (1999), Monahan (2002), and from a statistical analysis of Supreme Court cases between 2002 and 2012 undertaken by the author.

15 It should be noted that language cases have not disappeared entirely from the purview of the Court. Thus in both *Société des Acadiens et Acadiennes du Nouveau-Brunswick Inc. v. Canada, 2008*, and *Doucet-Boudreau v. Nova Scotia (Minister of Education), 2003*, the Supreme Court was compelled to return to some of the constitutional language issues with which it had been preoccupied in the 1990s.

16 It should be added that this is a conclusion that is not necessarily shared by all Quebec scholars. See for instance, Andrée Lajoie (2009), who argues that rulings on the division of powers by the Supreme Court of Canada have favoured a centralized federalism in recent years, a tendency its Charter decisions have reinforced because they recognize only those minority rights claims least threatening to the federal status quo.

17 Chief Justice Beverley McLachlin, for instance, has protested that the Charter right to equality is the "most difficult right" (McLachlin, 2001). The Supreme Court's jurisprudence certainly bears out this observation as evidenced by the often sharp disagreements amongst the justices over

how to understand this constitutional guarantee. See, for instance, the disputes among several justices in *Quebec (Attorney General) v. A [2013]*.

18 The term "counter-majoritarian" was coined by the American legal scholar Alexander Bickel (1986) when writing about the civil rights jurisprudence of the Warren Court.

19 The cautionary tale left-wing critics of the Court most frequently invoke when warning of the reactionary potential of a bill of rights is the regrettable Lochner era in US constitutional history. For most of the first three decades of the twentieth century a very conservative US Supreme Court elevated the reference to property rights in the 14th Amendment into nothing short of a constitutional warrant for laissez-faire capitalism, in the process continually striking down progressive legislation passed by state and federal governments.

20 For right-wing critics it is also a US judicial episode—the vigorous civil rights program of the Warren Court—that stands as the embodiment of all that can go wrong with an unbridled judiciary.

21 Just how influential the Hogg/Bushell argument has been can be gathered from the fact that the *Osgoode Hall Law Journal* produced a special issue debating the merits of the dialogue thesis on the 10th anniversary of their original article. See *Osgoode Hall Law Journal Special Issue: Charter Dialogue Ten Years Later* 45: 1 (Spring 2007).

22 See Manfredi and Kelly (1999) and the reply furnished by Hogg and Thornton (1999). See also Sujit Choudhry and Claire Hunter (2003), whose study of judicial activism casts doubt on the claim that the Supreme Court frequently strikes down majoritarian legislation.

23 The phrase "discrete and insular minorities" was introduced by Justice Stone of the United States Supreme Court in his oft-cited footnote in *United States v. Carolene Products Co. [1938]* where he proposes that the Court defer to the legislatures in economic policy but subject to "more exacting judicial scrutiny" legislation that relies on prejudices against minorities. The same phrase appeared in Canadian jurisprudence as the Court attempted to devise a credible test for applying the Section 15 equality right (Hogg, 2002: 52.7.g).

24 Doubtless it was this sense of political paralysis that led a chagrined Chief Justice Lamer to complain that the reason the Supreme Court has become involved in policy issues in the era of the Charter is because "too often timid politicians have been afraid to confront them directly" Lamer cited in Greene et al. (1998: 194).

25 Though there is contrary evidence that the reputed care with which Justice officials vet legislation for potential Charter breaches is overstated. In fact, a senior lawyer working in the Justice Department has

launched a lawsuit against his own employer claiming that the Department has in the past 20 years violated its duty to ensure that proposed laws comply with the Charter. See Makin (2013b).

References and Suggested Readings

Alarie, Benjamin, and Andrew Green. 2009. "Charter Decisions in the McLachlin Era: Consensus and Ideology at the Supreme Court of Canada." *Supreme Court Law Review* 47 (2d): 475–511.

Bakan, Joel. 1997. *Just Words: Constitutional Rights and Social Wrongs.* Toronto: University of Toronto Press.

Bayefsky, Ann. 1987. "The Judicial Function under the Canadian *Charter of Rights and Freedoms.*" *McGill Law Journal. Revue de Droit de McGill* 32: 791–833.

Bickel, Alexander. 1986. *The Least Dangerous Branch: The Supreme Court at the Bar of Politics.* 2nd ed. New Haven: Yale University Press.

Bushnell, Ian. 1992. *The Captive Court: A Study of the Supreme Court of Canada.* Montreal: McGill-Queen's University Press.

Cairns, Alan C. 1971. "The Judicial Committee and Its Critics." *Canadian Journal of Political Science* 4 (03): 301–45. http://dx.doi.org/10.1017/S0008423900026809.

Cairns, Alan C. 1992. *Charter versus Federalism.* Montreal: McGill-Queen's University Press.

Canada, Department of Justice. 2003. *Backgrounder: Reference to the Supreme Court.* http://canada.justice.gc.ca/en/news/nr/2003/doc30946.html.

Choudhry, Sujit, and Claire E. Hunter. 2003. "Measuring Judicial Activism on the Supreme Court of Canada: A Comment on Newfoundland (Treasury Board) v. NAPE." *McGill Law Journal. Revue de Droit de McGill* 48: 525–62.

Dworkin, Ronald. 1981. "The Forum of Principle." *New York University Law Review* 56: 469–518.

Epp, Charles R. 1998. *The Rights Revolution: Lawyers, Activists, and Supreme Courts in Comparative Perspective.* Chicago: University of Chicago Press.

Fletcher, Joseph, and Paul Howe. 2001. "Public Opinion and the Courts." In *Judicial Power and Canadian Democracy.* Eds. Paul Howe and Peter H. Russell. Montreal: McGill-Queen's University Press.

Flood, Colleen M. 2006. "Chaoulli's Legacy for the Future of Canadian Health Care Policy." *Osgoode Hall Law Journal* 44: 273–310.

Greene, Ian, Carl Baar, Peter McCormick, George Szablowski, and Martin Thomas. 1998. *Final Appeal: Decision-Making in Canadian Courts of Appeal.* Toronto: James Lorimer & Company Ltd.

Hein, Gregory. 2000. "Interest Group Litigation and Canadian Democracy." *Choices (New York)* 6: 3–30.

Hiebert, Janet L. 2002. *Charter Conflicts: What is Parliament's Role?* Montreal: McGill-Queen's University Press.

Hogg, Peter W. 2002. *Constitutional Law in Canada. Student Edition.* Toronto: Carswell.

Hogg, Peter W., and Allison Bushell. 1997. "The Charter Dialogue between Courts and Legislatures (Or Perhaps the Charter of Rights Isn't Such a Bad Thing After All)." *Osgoode Hall Law Journal,* 35: 75–124.

Hogg, Peter W., and Allison Thornton. 1999. "Reply to 'Six Degrees of Dialogue'." *Osgoode Hall Law Journal* 37: 529–36.

Hutchinson, Alan C. 1995. *Waiting For CORAF: A Critique of Law and Rights.* Toronto: University of Toronto Press.

Kelly, James B. 1999. "The Charter of Rights and Freedoms and the Rebalancing of Liberal Constitutionalism in Canada, 1982–1997." *Osgoode Hall Law Journal* 37: 625–95.

Kelly, James B. 2005. *Governing with the Charter: Legislative and Judicial Activism and Framers' Intent.* Vancouver: University of British Columbia Press.

Laforest, Guy. 1992. "La Charte canadienne des droits et liberté au Québec: nationalisme, injuste et illégitimate." In *Bilan québécois du fédéralisme canadien*, ed. François Rocher, 213–24. Montreal: VLB.

Lajoie, Andrée. 2009. "Federalism in Canada: Provinces and Minorities—Same Fight." In *Contemporary Canadian Federalism: Foundations, Traditions, Institutions*, ed. Alain-G. Gagnon, 184–90. Toronto: University of Toronto Press.

Leishman, Rory. 2006. *Against Judicial Activism: The Decline of Freedom and Democracy in Canada.* Montreal: McGill-Queen's Press.

MacFarlane, Emmett. 2013. "Supreme Court—Supreme Confusion." *Policy Options* (March): 45–48. http://www.irpp.org/en/po/living-with-slower-growth/supreme-court-supreme-confusion/

Makin, Kirk. 2008. "Top Court Takes More Time on Fewer Decisions," *Globe and Mail,* April 18: A4.

Makin, Kirk. 2013a. "Justice Department Whistleblower on a Crusade to Sustain the Rule of Law," *Globe and Mail,* February 23. http://www.theglobeandmail.com/news/national/justice-department-whistleblower-on-a-crusade-to-sustain-the-rule-of-law/article9001991/.

Makin, Kirk. 2013b. "Supreme Court Becoming 'Charter-Averse,' Expert Says," *Globe and Mail,* April 12. http://www.theglobeandmail.com/news/national/supreme-court-becoming-charter-averse-expert-says/article11177678/.

Makin, Kirk. 2013c. "Supreme Court Needs More Women, Departing Judge Says," *Globe and Mail,* February 2. http://www.theglobeandmail.com/news/national/supreme-court-needs-more-women-departing-judge-says/article8149711/.

Mandel, Michael. 1994. *The Charter of Rights and the Legalization of Politics in Canada.* Rev. ed. Toronto: Thompson Educational Publishing.

Manfredi, Christopher P. 2001. *Judicial Power and the Charter: Canada and the Paradox of Liberal Constitutionalism.* 2nd ed. Don Mills: Oxford University Press.

Manfredi, Christopher P. 2007. "The Day the Dialogue Died: A Comment on Sauvé v. Canada." *Osgoode Hall Law Journal* 45: 105–23.

Manfredi, Christopher P., and James Kelly. 1999. "Six Degrees of Dialogue: A Response to Hogg and Bushell." *Osgoode Hall Law Journal* 37: 513–27.

Martin, Robert I. 2003. *The Most Dangerous Branch: How the Supreme Court Has Undermined Our Law and Our Democracy.* Montreal: McGill-Queen's University Press.

McCormick, Peter. 2000. *Supreme At Last: The Evolution of the Supreme Court of Canada.* Toronto: James Lorimer & Company.

McCormick, Peter. 2004. "Blocs, Swarms and Outliers: Conceptualizing Disagreement on the Modern Supreme Court." *Osgoode Hall Law Journal* 42: 99–138.

McLachlin, Beverley. 2001. "Equality: The Most Difficult Right." *Supreme Court Law Review* 14: 17–26.

Monahan, Patrick. 1987. *Politics and the Constitution: The Charter, Federalism and the Supreme Court of Canada.* Toronto: Carswell/Methuen.

Monahan, Patrick. 2002. "The Charter at Twenty." Paper delivered at *The Charter at Twenty* Conference. Professional Development Programme Centre (Osgoode Hall), Toronto. April 13.

Morton, F.L. 1986. "The Political Impact of the Charter of Rights." In *Occasional Papers Series, Research Study 2.2.* Calgary: Research Unit for Socio-Legal Studies, University of Calgary.

Morton, F.L., and Rainer Knopff. 2000. *The Charter Revolution and the Court Party*. Peter-borough: Broadview Press.

Morton, F.L., Peter H. Russell, and Troy Riddell. 1994. "The Canadian Charter of Rights and Freedoms; A Descriptive Analysis of the First Decade, 1982–1992." *National Journal of Constitutional Law* 5: 1–69.

Ostberg, C.L., and Matthew E. Wetstein. 2007. *Attitudinal Decision-Making in the Supreme Court of Canada*. Vancouver: University of British Columbia Press.

Petter, Andrew. 1987. "The Immaculate Deception: The Charter's Hidden Agenda." *The Advocate,* 45, 857–66.

Roach, Kent. 2001. *The Supreme Court on Trial: Judicial Activism or Democratic Dialogue*. Toronto: Irwin Law.

Russell, Peter H. 1982. "The Effect of a Charter of Rights on the Policy-Making Role of Canadian Courts." *Canadian Public Administration* 25 (1): 1–33. http://dx.doi.org/10.1111/j.1754-7121.1982.tb02063.x.

Russell, Peter H. 1983. "The Political Purposes of the Canadian Charter of Rights and Freedoms." *Canadian Bar Review* 61: 30–54.

Russell, Peter H. 1987. *The Judiciary in Canada: The Third Branch of Government*. Toronto: McGraw-Hill Ryerson Ltd.

Russell, Peter H. 1991. "Standing Up for Notwithstanding." *Alberta Law Review* 29: 293–309.

Smith, Jennifer. 1983. "The Origins of Judicial Review in Canada." *Canadian Journal of Political Science* 16 (01): 115–34. http://dx.doi.org/10.1017/S0008423900028031.

Smith, Miriam C. 2002. "Ghosts of the JCPC: Group Politics and Charter Litigation in Canadian Political Science." *Canadian Journal of Political Science* 35: 13–29.

Snell, James G., and Frederick Vaughn. 1985. *The Supreme Court of Canada: History of the Institution*. Toronto: University of Toronto Press.

Trudeau, Pierre Elliott. 1968. *Federalism and the French-Canadians*. Toronto: Macmillan of Canada.

Whyte, John D. 1990. "On Not Standing for Notwithstanding." *Alberta Law Review* 28: 347–57.

PART IV

Culture, Parties, Elections, Media

Political Culture(s) in Canada: Orientations to Politics in a Pluralist, Multicultural Federation

ALLISON HARELL AND LYNE DESCHÂTELETS

Political culture is a powerful and often-used concept to describe key characteristics of Canadian politics. It usually refers to the shared values, orientations, and attitudes that define various social groups (such as nations, regions, and groups of people that share ethnic or religious backgrounds). Political culture has been used to both describe and explain how and why Canadian society differs from that of other countries, as well as what differences exist across regions in Canada. Yet, despite its long-standing allure to social scientists, defining and measuring political culture presents some conceptual and empirical challenges. In this chapter, we explore what we mean by political culture, how it has been used to study Canadian politics, and what we know about the defining characteristics of Canadian political culture today.

Defining Political Culture

Since it was first described by Almond (1956: 396) as a "particular pattern of orientations to political action," the concept of political culture has come to be understood as a set of collective assumptions about the political world. These assumptions can either be on a cognitive level—the way people *think* about politics—or on an affective level—the way people *feel* about politics (Stewart, 1990: 89). They cover a broad range of political orientations, from perceptions of how society is organized, to the goals of political life and to what is considered "political." They also shape the boundaries of a political community, identifying its members and how others should be perceived (Elkins and Simeon, 1979: 133). In this regard, political culture is not limited to voting patterns, political behaviour, public opinion, or culture more generally (Stewart, 2001: 24). Nor is it to be seen only as a set of political values shared by a community. As Berns-McGown (2005: 342–43) notes:

> Political culture is the crucible of forces in which that set of attitudes, beliefs, and sentiments—those individually held values, if you will— combine with historical and current events, as well as with myth and

symbol, to produce a collective response that is then translated into policy and practice, and that itself comes to be seen as a shared value. Political culture is both the space in which, and the process by which, context and events translate into individual and collective political behaviour.

Bell (1992) specifies that both historical development and current social arrangements keep political culture alive and give it its meanings. In other words, collectivities both define and are defined by political culture.

A few characteristics help circumscribe what political culture is. First, a given political culture tends to "focus attention on certain features of events, institutions, and behavior, define the realm of the possible, identify the problems deemed pertinent, and set the range of alternatives among which members of the population make decisions" (Elkins and Simeon, 1979: 128). At an individual level, it determines whether one should be seen as a legitimate political actor, since a legitimate political actor would act within a given range of alternatives. However, every member of a community does not necessarily embrace the prevailing political culture, although it is widely shared and generally taken for granted. In this sense, assumptions and beliefs that are held by only a small group of individuals within a society should not be seen as a political culture, unless this group constitutes a consequential elite (one whose decisions affect society as a whole) or an identifiable and/ or concentrated minority.

This suggests another fundamental aspect of political culture: it is interpersonal and is bound to a collectivity, such as a nation, region, class, ethnic community, formal organization, or political party. As Elkins and Simeon (1979) point out, individuals may have beliefs, values, or attitudes, but they do not have cultures. In this respect, political culture should be seen as a holistic concept, rather than the aggregation of individual beliefs in a community (see also Stewart, 2001). It is also best understood as a complement to psychological, structural, and institutional explanations of society.

Political culture scholars generally identify two major approaches in this field: a descriptive one and an explanatory one. On the one hand, political culture as a descriptive category focuses on political values and attitudes with respect to political institutions, actors, or policies in a given community, such as election turnout, public support for a particular policy, or trust in government. Here, the content of a particular political culture is the outcome of interest in the analysis.

On the other hand, the use of political culture as an explanation usually focuses on the consequences for current policies and practices of a given political culture, or it is employed as a means to understand

Des: Values

ex: actions/

Consequences

the differences between communities (usually along with other forms of social science explanation). Elkins and Simeon (1979) suggest that the procedure, scope, and content of state policy-making are affected by political culture. For instance, procedures may be influenced by what behaviours and which people are perceived by decision-makers as legitimate. The content of policy-making, in contrast, may depend on assumptions within the political culture about the role of the state or about the appropriate realm for collective versus individual decisions. These in turn can be influenced over time by institutions and policies (Fowke, 1952; Brodie, 1989, 1990).

Yet, paradoxically, Elkins and Simeon note that political culture is less useful in explaining politics in a community where there is a wide spectrum of political assumptions, because fewer cultural constraints will exist (1979: 140). Hence, they argue that institutional and structural explanations—like differences in income levels and demographic factors such as ethnicity, age, gender, urbanization, and so on—are more likely to explain differences between two communities. As a matter of fact, Elkins and Simeon suggest that those explanations should first be applied and found wanting before turning to political culture. In other words, political culture becomes a residual explanation, resorted to only when other explanations fail to fully explain the differences between communities that we observe.

This is because political culture often is used as both an independent (causal or explanatory) variable as well as the dependent variable (the result *Casual / result* or outcome of interest). Elkins and Simeon (1979: 130) warn us that "eventually we can reformulate most differences in structural terms, and eventually we will be tempted or forced to explain structural features in cultural terms. In this sense, it may be a matter of semantics whether explanations are called cultural or something else." In other words, one must avoid the trap of using circular logic: explaining political structures and institutions by political culture while at the same time explaining political culture by political structures and institutions.

The Study of Canadian Political Culture(s)

The study of political culture in Canada has been marked by two comparative tendencies: comparisons of regional and group political cultures within Canada, and comparisons between Canada and other countries, notably the United States (Brooks, 2009: 45). These comparisons often occur simultaneously because one of the reasons that Canada's political culture is perceived to differ from American political culture is precisely because of the extent of internal diversity within Canada.

So what defines Canadian culture and distinguishes it from its US counterpart? One of the recurring findings in the literature is that Canadian society is less individualistic than American society and more deferential toward state institutions and intervention in society (Lipset, 1986, 1990). Canadians tend to believe that the state can and should play an active role and in turn they are more willing to support egalitarian public policies such as public health care and state-owned enterprises such as public broadcasting (Brooks, 2009). One of the classic arguments explaining this difference comes from Lipset (1986, 1990) and his theory of *formative events*. For Lipset, the driving differences between these two societies stems from how they experienced the American Revolution. In the US, Lipset argues the revolution led to the endorsement of liberal individualism and a rejection of hierarchical and centralized state power. Canada, in contrast, remained tied to Britain, which bred a more conservative liberalism that was reinforced by an influx of loyalists fleeing the United States. As a result, Canadians became more deferential to authority, more willing for the state to intervene in society in terms of both economic development and social policy, and more concerned about maintaining social order than maximizing individual freedom.

There is some empirical support that Canadians and Americans do differ, on average, with respect to these fundamental values. In Lipset's 1990 study, he argues that there are durable differences along these dimensions, and others have found (some) supporting evidence (e.g., Perlin, 1997; Cole, Kincaid, and Rodriguez, 2004; Brooks, 2009). One of the conclusions is that collective equality (including equality of outcomes) is a more important value for Canadians than for Americans, who tend to rate individual equality (and equality of opportunity) more highly. This can be seen in the ways in which rights conflicts emerge in Canada, where individual claims are often discussed in collective, group rights terms.[1] This may be in part because Canadian political culture itself is far from homogeneous and includes distinct collectivities that interact within the federal state. Yet, we should be careful not to overstate the differences. On many dimensions, the similarities between Canadians and Americans stand out more than their differences (Perlin, 1997; Brooks, 2009; although see Adams, 2003, for a counter-argument). Indeed, within certain sectors of the population, there is more ideological similarity between Canadians and Americans than among Canadians (Farney, 2012).

One of the key characteristics of Canadian society that distinguishes it from the US is its multinational nature, where Aboriginal nations exist simultaneously with two "founding" societies defined in ethnolinguistic terms (Gagnon and Tully, 2001). Attempts to describe and explain this internal diversity has been a dominant theme in political culture research in Canada (Hartz, 1964; Horowitz, 1966; McRae, 1978; Elkins and Simeon, 1979, 1980;

Bell, 1992; Henderson, 2004; Wiseman, 2007). While First Nations, Inuit, and Métis communities are often ignored when discussing Canadian political culture (although see Henderson, 2007), the difference between English Canada and French Canada is of enduring interest.

Perhaps the most well-known approach to Canadian political culture is *fragment theory*. American historian Louis Hartz (1964) argued that New World colonies were settled by groups representing only ideological fragments of the European societies from whence they came. That is to say, whereas European societies tended to contain the full spectrum of political and social thought (including feudal/conservative, liberal, and socialist ideologies), immigrant waves from these societies were not fully representative of this diversity. Settler societies, shaped by who was emigrating and at what point in history, tended to be biased toward a specific ideological orientation, creating in the New World what Hartz viewed as homogeneous societies in cultural terms. Kenneth McRae (1964, 1978) and others[2] applied this approach to Canada and argued that English Canada's political culture congealed around a liberal fragment, while French Canada (New France and Acadia) was settled by a feudal—or conservative—fragment.

Like the United States, liberalism in English Canada was imported by British immigrants—not only from England, but also from loyalists fleeing the American Revolution south of the border (see especially Horowitz, 1966). Unlike in the United States, then, some fragment theorists claimed that English Canada's liberalism was "tory-touched." In other words, whereas American liberalism was defined heavily in terms of individualism and personal freedom, the more conservative elements in Canada resulted in more acceptance of social hierarchy (society as comprising interdependent social classes) and recognition of the key role of the state in the pursuit of the public good. The result was a dialectic between the dominant liberalism and more conservative elements in Canadian society, allowing for greater recognition and acceptance of collective concerns, expressed through a variant of mild socialism.

French Canada, in contrast, was settled (according to fragment theorists) by a purely pre-revolutionary fragment from France. These conservative elements "congealed" before French Canada could be affected by the liberalizing effects of the French Revolution, and were further reinforced by the dominance of conservative institutions, such as the Church, following the ceding of French Canada to Britain. Characterized as an anti-liberal and collectivist ideology, this quasi-feudal conservatism, often referred to as the idea of *la Survivance* in French Canada (and especially in Quebec), was the dominant form of political culture until the Quiet Revolution. Unlike in English Canada where a dominant liberalism was only "touched" by conservative toryism, in Quebec the opposite was true: the dominant conservative culture was "touched" by liberal elements, creating a dialectic that allowed for the creation of Quebec's own version of socialism, which combines active state intervention and liberal elements with collective concerns about national identity. As Wiseman (1988: 804) notes:

> Nationalism and its different manifestations in Quebec came full circle as Hartz suggested it could: a feudal past when combined with a sudden influx of liberal ideas in the mid-twentieth century produced the environment where the seeds of socialism sprouted. Quebec socialists since the 1960s have drawn on both the collectivist and organic principles of French Canada's feudal past and the egalitarian and rationalist components of its liberal Quiet Revolution.

Today, then, Quebec is no more traditional or socially conservative than English Canada, but it does have a distinct political culture that continues to be more collectivist, more pacifistic, and more open to non-traditional lifestyles than other Canadians (Brooks, 2009).

While the distinction between English and French Canada's political cultures is clearly a key component of understanding political culture more generally in Canada, many authors argue that this view is too simplistic, especially with respect to English Canada (Horowitz, 1966; Wiseman, 2007). Canadian politics has long been characterized by its regional nature (Meisel, 1964; Blake, 1972; Elkins and Simeon, 1974; Schwartz, 1974; Young and Archer, 2002). Indeed, some authors have gone so far as to argue that "Canadian politics is regional politics; regionalism is one of the pre-eminent facts of Canadian life" (Elkins and Simeon, 1974: 397).[3]

For fragment theorists, the causes of this regional variation in everything from values, party systems, and political behaviour stem from different waves of immigration as well as the shared social experiences (or formative events) that occurred in conjunction with them while provincial political cultures were in formation. For example, Wiseman (2007) argues that because immigration waves arrived at different times throughout history and are regionally concentrated in their settlement patterns, we see distinct regional political cultures rather than the development of a strong, unified Canadian political culture. For example, early Ontario was largely populated by United Empire Loyalists whose "tory-touched" liberalism produced a political culture that allowed for the development of liberal, conservative, and socialist currents within its boundaries. In contrast, the Prairies' greater affinity for social democracy (historically) is attributed to waves of European immigrants who arrived with a more collectivist orientation, combined (especially in Alberta) with an important wave of American immigrants whose ideological baggage included the anti-elite populism and laissez-faire individualism that have been more characteristic of Alberta's political culture.

Along with fragment theory's emphasis on history and immigration, other authors have pointed to the importance of geographic and structural characteristics in the formation of regional political cultures. This is perhaps most evident in the classic political economy approach known as the *staples theory* (Innis and Drache, 1995). Staples theory suggests that societal characteristics, including political culture, result from the social and political organization, and the techniques of exploitation, associated with Canada's vast geography and its varied natural resource economies (see also Bell, 1992: Ch. 5). The immigration and settlement patterns identified in fragment theory are viewed from the perspective of the staples approach as being the consequence of these underlying economic factors.

Political economy approaches also highlight the important role that institutions play in the development of regional political cultures (Brodie, 1989, 1990). Clearly, Canadian federalism is organized according to territorial principles. If political culture is about how people view and understand politics within their society, then the regional organization of political life means that "politics and political conflict revolve around the distribution of resources across geographic space ... Politics is judged to be about 'place' instead of 'people' prosperity" (Brodie, 1989: 140). Political economy scholars have focused specifically on how the requirements of economic development, and specifically how national policies since Confederation, have shaped the uneven development and varied political cultures of Canada's regions. The result has been political, social, and economic relations that have a highly regionalized dimension.

Fragment theorists and political economy approaches point to various factors (history and immigration patterns, resources and geography, institutions) that help us to understand how and why different political cultures have developed across the country. With the regional diversity that characterizes Canadian society, then, can we really talk about a single Canadian political culture?

While there are clearly internal differences across Canada, as well as similarities between Canada and other pluralist democracies on many cultural dimensions, if we view Canadian political culture as a general orientation toward politics (rather than a collection of specific attitudes), several features can be delineated, notably its federalist, pluralist, and multicultural components. Cole, Kincaid, and Rodriguez (2004) argue that federalism is a way of thinking as well as a particular constitutional and structural arrangement. For them, a federal political culture not only relates to how people feel about the decentralization of power, but also affects how people relate to each other and the extent to which they accept various ethnic, linguistic, and religious diversities. Canadians, they argue, have a particularly strong federal political culture compared to other federal countries, such as the United States and Mexico. This understanding of federal political culture is very much in line with Elkins and Simeon's (1974) view that the concept of political culture should not be limited to the aggregation of individual attitudes and values at the national or regional level, but rather as a general orientation to the political world that both shapes societal perceptions about who are considered as legitimate political actors and defines the scope of politics and the range of political alternatives that are available.

In the Canadian case, this federal political culture is combined with two other dimensions—a pluralist one as well as a multicultural one. The pluralist dimension relates to equality understood at the individual level and is clearly tied to Canadians' adherence to broadly liberal values as expressed in strong support for individual rights and non-discrimination. Yet, unlike its US counterpart (which has a similar pluralist dimension), the federal political culture in Canada could also be characterized as multicultural.[4] A multicultural political culture, in this respect, is more willing to view collectivities within society as legitimate actors in public debate, be they historic national minorities, social groups defined by race, ethnicity, or religion, or other culturally distinct collectivities that have played an important role in Canadian politics. This dimension of Canadian political culture not only recognizes the country's ethnocultural diversity, but defines this diversity as an essential component of contemporary Canada.

Canadian Political Culture Today

Political culture is not a static entity, despite the deterministic nature of many early accounts of political culture in Canada. Recall that the formative events approach and the fragment approach both place immense importance on historical events during key periods. From both these perspectives, once a political culture is in place (the process of *congealment* in fragment theory), it remains a relatively stable force in structuring political and social outcomes. Yet clearly political values and attitudes change, as do the general orientations to politics that structure these values and attitudes within a more coherent political outlook and dialogue.

Advanced industrialized democracies such as Canada have experienced some cultural change over the course of the past century. Attitudes have tended to become more secular, more liberal insofar as the focus has shifted to individual rights, and more supportive of equality in all its forms (gender, race and ethnicity, sexuality) (Brooks, 2009). While these trends vary across countries, they share a common direction. This suggests that the causes of changing values cross regional and national boundaries. The predominant approach to explaining this mega-cultural shift comes from *post-materialism* scholars (Nevitte, 1996; Inglehart, 1997; Achterberg, 2006). The post-materialism thesis is essentially that cultural change is driven by economic and social development. As countries move from industrialized economies to post-industrial economies, the underlying ideological cleavages in society shift as well: from older class-based conflicts on a left-right ideological dimension to a new cleavage based on emerging cultural and environmental concerns (Inglehart, 1997). This shift occurs largely through a process of generational change, growing in strength as newer generations replace older ones. Younger generations are socialized within a different socio-economic environment than their forebears, and as a result develop a cultural orientation toward politics that reflects this altered environment.

In Canada, Nevitte (1996) has applied the post-materialism thesis to demonstrate that Canadians have increasingly become less deferential to authority and are more likely to embrace post-materialist values associated with quality of life and personal identity concerns as compared to the primarily materialist (economic) concerns that structured the political agendas of past generations. This shift in values and outlook has also led to a shift in how citizens engage in politics, with a greater tendency to challenge authority through non-electoral forms of participation. To understand political culture in Canada today, post-materialists would argue, we need to understand both how political culture has developed historically and how it has transformed over time in conjunction with other socio-economic and technological changes.

So what does Canadian political culture look like today? In the remainder of this chapter, we consider the three dimensions (federalism, pluralism, and multiculturalism) that we suggest are essential to understanding Canadian political culture. Through the use of public opinion research, we will briefly examine the overall societal picture that emerges along these dimensions, as well as divergences along linguistic, regional, and generational lines.

We suggested that Canadian political culture can be described in a trifold manner: federal, pluralist, and multicultural. Yet, what does this mean when it comes to how we expect citizens to think about politics? When it comes to federalism, we expect that federalism and the regional organization of political life in Canada will result in a conflict between nation-building versus province-building. There should be an important cleavage between national/federal identities and regional/provincial identities. Both political identities should be present, and their presence and importance should vary by region.

If we examine responses to the 2011 Canadian Election Study (CES), it is clear that federalism in Canada is a source of political debate.[5] When asked

Table 11.1 Support for a Strong Federal State by Region

Region	Mean Support for Strong Federal (1) vs. More Provincial Power (0)
Canada	0.50
NFL	0.37
Maritimes	0.54
Quebec	0.30
Ontario	0.65
Prairies	0.50
Alberta	0.50
BC	0.59

Source: Canadian Election Study, 2011 (unweighted)

whether we should have a strong federal state (coded 1) or if more power should be given to the provinces (coded 0), Canadians are evenly split between these two alternatives. Table 11.1 shows, however, that this cleavage is not distributed equally across the country. If we consider support for a strong federal government, we would expect, based on past political culture research, that it would be strongest in Ontario and weakest in Quebec. This turns out to be largely true. In Ontario, about 65 per cent of respondents supported the strong federal state option, compared to only 30 per cent in Quebec. In other words, the question of federalism in Canada is clearly an important cleavage, and this cleavage is regionally distributed in a way consistent with more historical accounts of the development of political cultures across the regions.

Expectations for how this cleavage is changing over time, however, are less obvious from previous research. Given the strong federal nature of Canadian politics and the regional dynamics of the system that foster and reinforce regionalized thinking, we might expect that support for a more decentralized system should become stronger over time. If we look at how various generational groups address the question of federal versus provincial power, we can see (Figure 11.1) that there is a clear trend among younger age cohorts to support more power at the provincial level. Whereas over 60 per cent of those born before 1940 support a strong federal state, only a third of those born after 1980 endorse this option.

Regionalism in Canada is both a lens through which political alternatives are understood (concentration of power in federal institutions) and a cleavage along which these alternatives are distributed. It is also a dimension

Figure 11.1 Support for a Strong Federal State by Generation

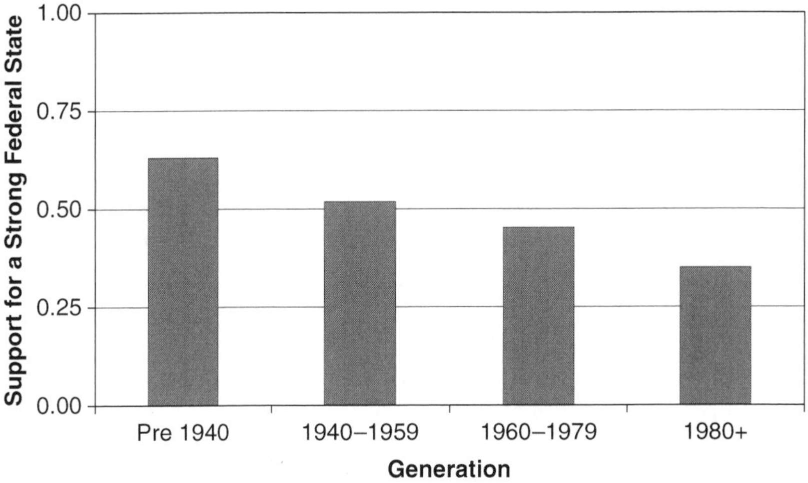

Source: Canadian Election Study, 2011 (unweighted)

along which we expect political identities to be framed. When Canadians were asked how much they identify with various geographic units, from their neighbourhood to the world at large, we expected provincial units and the Canadian state to dominate responses in a federal system. Table 11.2 shows that this is partly the case, although to a lesser extent than might be expected. On a scale from 0 to 1, where 0 means "not at all" and 1 means "a great deal," respondents tended to place at least some importance on each of these identities. Yet, the rank order is consistent with our federalism argument. Canada (.74) and Province (.69) tend to receive the highest level of importance, followed by Town (.67), Neighbourhood (.66), and then the World (.56). Also consistent with expectations, the difference in importance of provincial identification in contrast to Canadian identification is smallest in the two regions that most advocated increased provincial autonomy (Quebec, and Newfoundland and Labrador), with province ranked higher than Canada in importance only in Quebec. Canadian identification outweighs provincial identification the most in Ontario (a difference of .15), the same province in which a strong central state received the highest level of support.

If we consider the age distribution of these identifications in Figure 11.2, we see far fewer distinctions across age cohorts. Canada receives the highest mean importance, followed by Province in all age groups except the youngest cohort, where Town takes on slightly more importance. This is somewhat surprising given the previous distribution on the question of federal power,

Table 11.2 Importance of Geographic Identities by Region

	Neighbourhood	Town	Province	Canada	World
Canada	0.66	0.67	0.69	0.74	0.56
NFL	0.66	0.63	0.73	0.72	0.57
Maritimes	0.66	0.63	0.69	0.75	0.52
Quebec	0.64	0.70	0.75	0.64	0.55
Ontario	0.65	0.65	0.63	0.78	0.56
Prairies	0.70	0.70	0.72	0.79	0.56
Alberta	0.63	0.65	0.69	0.75	0.57
BC	0.67	0.68	0.71	0.81	0.63

Note: Responses varied from "not at all" (0) to a "a great deal" (1).
Source: Canadian Election Study, 2011 (unweighted)

but it is consistent with the argument among post-materialism scholars that younger generations are rejecting national politics in favour of the local. Yet, in general, Figure 11.2 suggests remarkable similarity across age cohorts when it comes to identification with geographic units.

There clearly is a federal cleavage that is fundamental to understanding Canadians' political orientations. We have suggested that two other dimensions—pluralism and multiculturalism—are also important for understanding Canadian political culture. As much past research has suggested, Canadians endorse, at least in principle, the liberal values associated with pluralism (Sniderman et al., 1989, 1996; Harell, 2008, 2010). Support for liberal principles is perhaps most evident if we examine support for the Charter of Rights and Freedoms, which enshrined liberal principles in the Canadian constitution. Fletcher and Howe (2001, 2000a, 2000b) have conducted one of the only studies that examines attitudes toward the Charter itself. They find that there is widespread support for the Charter among Canadians, even higher in 1999 (87 per cent) than in an earlier study conducted in 1987 (84 per cent). Moreover, they find a surprising amount of consistency in people's attitudes toward the Supreme Court at these two points, and little difference across salient social and demographic categories, reinforcing the view that this support for constitutionally entrenched rights is widespread. In short, since the adoption of a bill of rights, Canadians seem to feel very positive about it.

Part of this support for liberal values is expressed with increasing concern over equality and anti-discrimination of various groups in society. For example, individual attitudes toward gender equality (Brooks, 2009), support for same-sex marriage (Rayside, 2008), and support for pluralism more generally (Nevitte, 1996) have all increased over time. Of particular importance is

Figure 11.2 Importance of Geographic Identities by Generation

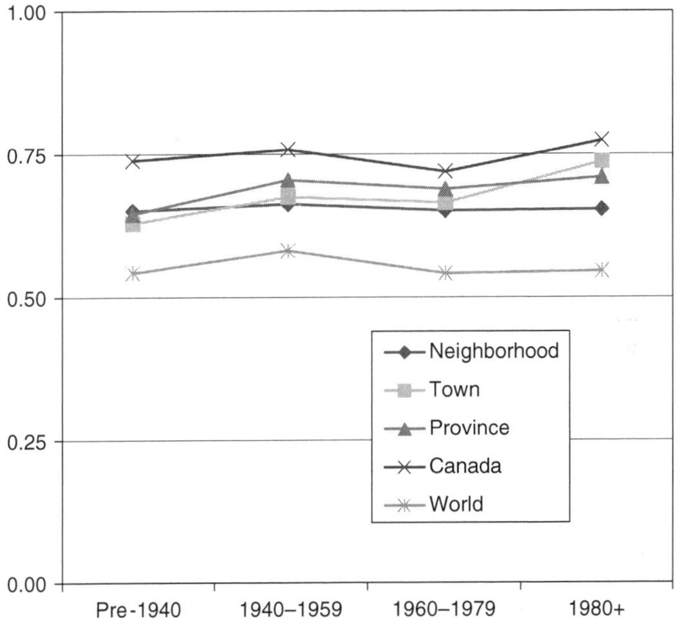

Source: Canadian Election Study, 2011 (unweighted)

evidence that Canadians have become increasingly supportive of pluralism, as measured by a variety of tolerance measures, and that this is especially true for younger generations (Lambert and Curtis, 1984; Nevitte, 1996).

One of the key components of pluralism is respect for diversity. Figure 11.3 presents the trends in responses to eight different questions about immigration and racial minorities that were asked a minimum of three times between 1975 and 2006 by various polling firms in Canada and in various Canadian Election Studies. The lines represent a two-point moving average for responses that were considered positive toward diversity.

While there was some movement during the 1970s and 1980s, there appears to be a significant upswing in support across the board during the 1990s across all nine questions—which range from support for immigration to how much should be done for racial minorities. For example, whereas roughly one-third of Canadians disagreed with the statement that there was too much immigration in the early 1990s, this number doubled to nearly two-thirds of Canadians by the early 2000s.[6] These trends are particularly evident among younger Canadians beginning in the 1990s, and today the youngest generation is most likely to have higher pro-diversity scores across a

Figure 11.3 Attitudes toward Diversity over Time

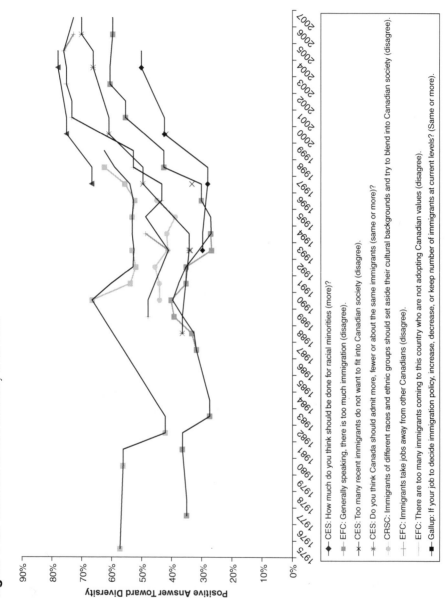

Positive Answer Toward Diversity

◆ CES: How much do you think should be done for racial minorities (more)?
■ EFC: Generally speaking, there is too much immigration (disagree).
✳ CES: Too many recent immigrants do not want to fit into Canadian society (disagree).
✶ CES: Do you think Canada should admit more, fewer or about the same immigrants (same or more)?
● CRSC: Immigrants of different races and ethnic groups should set aside their cultural backgrounds and try to blend into Canadian society (disagree).
+ EFC: Immigrants take jobs away from other Canadians (disagree).
  EFC: There are too many immigrants coming to this country who are not adopting Canadian values (disagree).
■ Gallup: If your job to decide immigration policy, increase, decrease, or keep number of immigrants at current levels? (Same or more).

*young are
more
open due
to ability
to expand
own ability
to learn
from
different
sources*

range of indicators. For example, if we combine six items about immigration in a 2006 Environics survey to create a pro-immigration scale (Cronbach's alpha = 0.74), those born after 1980 have a significantly higher score than previous age cohorts.

As we noted earlier, support for liberal values and increasing support for pluralism are hardly unique to Canada. Still, we would argue that there are unique components to how these discussions are framed on a national basis. One of these components is the role that groups play in this discourse. Canada has a long history of focusing not only on individual rights, but also on collective group rights. Religious and linguistic groups have been recognized in various ways since before Confederation, whereas Aboriginal peoples and ethnic groups have struggled to have their rights entrenched through the courts and the Charter. For example, the idea of a multicultural Canada is an important symbol in Canadian political culture, especially outside of Quebec.[7] As Berns-McGown (2005) argues, multiculturalism represents "the myth of the diversity-friendly Canadian" in contrast to the American model. The "mosaic versus melting-pot" metaphor clearly captures this distinction. Whereas the Canadian mosaic suggests that diversity remains a defining feature, the US melting-pot suggests national integration that eventually erases these differences.

In other words, Canadian political culture is much more likely to include group actors and to see group-based policies as legitimate alternatives. While this is hard to measure with traditional survey instruments, it is nonetheless true that groups play an important role in shaping how politics is discussed and understood. One of the most powerful symbols of group rights in Canada is the discourse around both bilingualism and multiculturalism. Clearly, debates over language rights and Quebec independence stem in part from Canada's history of federalism, but they also shape how politics is understood in Canada. The tension between a multinational and a multicultural vision of Canada has animated political life in Canada in the second half of the twentieth century. As with questions about federalism, we expect that citizens will have a diversity of opinions about how best to accommodate language and Aboriginal rights versus the rights and practices related to anti-discrimination and fair treatment of ethnoracial minorities. What makes Canadian political culture unique is both the set of legitimate alternatives available to address these complex issues and the ways in which these issues emerge so regularly on the political agenda.

Conclusions

Whether it is a comparison between regions and ethnolinguistic communities, or between Canada and the United States, political culture research tends to focus on political culture as a collective phenomenon, although it is often measured at the individual level through the use of survey research that captures the attitudes, beliefs, and orientations toward politics of various collectivities. It can be the focus of research (for instance, how can we describe a Canadian political culture and what caused it) as well as the main explanatory factor (what are the consequences of a specific political culture for public policies or political institutions).

In this chapter, we have argued that political culture should be thought of as the collective characteristics of society that relate to how people think about the political in their communities: who the legitimate actors are, what conflicts are of public concern, and what types of options are available to deal with these conflicts. We have argued that Canadian political culture can best be understood as a culture that is inherently diverse. In fact, we have argued that this diversity, and how it is debated and accommodated, is key to the study of political culture in Canada. We have argued that Canadian political culture is federal in nature, but also strongly pluralist and multicultural. This tri-dimensional orientation to politics can help us understand what issues Canadians are concerned about, but equally importantly, how these issues are framed in terms of actors and alternatives. In addition, any study of Canadian political culture(s) would be incomplete without a real focus on how political culture is changing over time. This requires a focus on how macro-level processes such as economic development and immigration patterns, as well as generational change, interact to shift political culture over time.

Notes

1 For theoretical work on group rights, see Kymlicka (1995). For an empirical study of attitudes toward group rights, see Sniderman et al. (1989, 1996).

2 Hartz's fragment theory was adopted and modified by a whole generation of scholars interested in explaining political culture. The difference between English Canada's "tory-touched" liberalism and French Canada's feudalism are present across these analyses. See, for example, Horowitz (1966), McRae (1964, 1978), Bell (1992), Leuprecht (2003), and Wiseman (2007).

3 It should be noted that there is no consensus on what the relevant category for region is. While some focus on provincial cultures (Elkins and Simeon, 1974; Simeon and Elkins 1980), others take a broader regional perspective that separates the country into several regions, such as the Maritimes, central Canada (Ontario), the Prairies, and so on. (Wiseman, 2007). Henderson (2004) provides a valuable empirical comparison of

these two analytic approaches and argues that regions in Canada do not simply conform to provincial boundaries.

4 Here we refer to Kymlicka's use of the concept of multicultural citizenship that recognizes both national minorities as well as ethnic and immigrant-driven minority groups.

5 Detailed information about the survey is available online at http://ces-eec. org/.

6 This level is particularly remarkable because the wording of the question is biased toward an anti-immigrant response. Acquiescence bias may in fact mean this level is muted.

7 In Quebec, multiculturalism is viewed as an ideology that in part denies the unique position of francophones as a nation. In Quebec in particular, a discourse of interculturalism is much more dominant (see, for example, Bouchard, 2011).

References and Suggested Readings

Achterberg, Peter. 2006. "Class Voting in the New Political Culture. Economic, Cultural and Environmental Voting in 20 Western Countries." *International Sociology* 21 (2): 237–61. http://dx.doi.org/10.1177/0268580906061378.

Adams, Michael. 2003. *Fire and Ice: The Myth of Converging Values in Canada and the United States.* Toronto: Penguin Press.

Almond, Gabriel. 1956. "Comparative Political Systems." *Journal of Politics* 18 (3): 391–409. http://dx.doi.org/10.2307/2127255.

Bell, David. 1992. *The Roots of Disunity: A Study of Canadian Culture.* Rev. ed. Toronto: Oxford University Press.

Berns-McGown, Rima. 2005. "Political Culture, Not Values." *International Journal (Toronto, Ont.)* 60 (2): 341–49. http://dx.doi.org/10.2307/40204292.

Blake, Donald E. 1972. "The Measurement of Regionalism in Canadian Voting Patterns." *Canadian Journal of Political Science* 5 (01): 55–79. http://dx.doi.org/10.1017/S0008423900027359.

Bouchard, Gérard. 2011. "What is Interculturalism?" *McGill Law Journal. Revue de Droit de McGill* 56 (2): 435–68.

Brodie, Janine. 1989. "The Political Economy of Regionalism." In *New Canadian Political Economy*, eds. Wallace Clement and Glen Williams, 138–59. Montreal: McGill-Queen's University Press.

Brodie, Janine. 1990. *The Political Economy of Canadian Regionalism.* Toronto: Harcourt Brace Jovanovich.

Brooks, Stephen. 2009. "Canadian Political Cultures." In *Canadian Politics*, 5th ed., eds. James Bickerton and Alain-G. Gagnon, 45–70. North York: University of Toronto Press.

Cole, Richard L., John Kincaid, and Alejandro Rodriguez. 2004. "Public Opinion on Federalism and Federal Political Culture in Canada, Mexico, and the United States." *Publius* 34 (3): 201–21. http://dx.doi.org/10.1093/oxfordjournals.pubjof.a005037.

Eckstein, Harry. 1966. *A Theory of Stable Democracy*. Princeton: Princeton University Press.

Elkins, David J., and Richard E.B. Simeon. 1979. "A Cause in Search of Its Effects, or What Does Political Culture Explain?" *Comparative Politics* 11 (2): 127–45. http://dx.doi.org/10.2307/421752.

Elkins, David J., and Richard Simeon, eds. 1980. *Small Worlds: Provinces and Parties in Canadian Political Life*. Toronto: Methuen.

Everitt, Joanna, and Brenda O'Neill. 2002. *Citizen Politics: Research and Theory in Canadian Political Behaviour*. Toronto: Oxford University Press.

Farney, James. 2012. *Social Conservatives and Party Politics, Canada and the United States*. Toronto: University of Toronto Press.

Fletcher, Joseph, and Paul Howe. 2000a. "Canadian Attitudes toward the Charter and the Courts in Comparative Perspective." *Choices (New York)* 6: 4–29.

Fletcher, Joseph, and Paul Howe. 2000b. "Supreme Court Cases and Court Support: The State of Canadian Public Opinion." *Choices (New York)* 6: 30–56.

Fletcher, Joseph, and Paul Howe. 2001. "Public Opinion and Canada's Courts." In *Judicial Power and Canadian Democracy*, eds. Paul Howe and Peter Russell, 255–96. Montreal: McGill-Queen's University Press.

Fowke, Vernon. 1952. "The National Policy: Old and New." *Canadian Journal of Economics and Political Science* 18 (3): 271–86. http://dx.doi.org/10.2307/138568.

Gagnon, Alain-G., and James Tully, eds. 2001. *Multinational Democracies*. Cambridge: Cambridge University Press. http://dx.doi.org/10.1017/CBO9780511521577.

Harell, Allison. 2008. *The Micro-Story of Multiculturalism: Diverse Social Networks and the Socialization of Tolerance*. Doctoral dissertation, McGill University.

Harell, Allison. 2010. "The Limits of Tolerance in Diverse Societies: Hate Speech and Political Tolerance Norms Among Youth." *Canadian Journal of Political Science* 43 (02): 407–32. http://dx.doi.org/10.1017/S0008423910000107.

Hartz, Louis, ed. 1964. *The Founding of New Societies: Studies in the History of the United States, Latin America, South Africa, Canada, and Australia*. New York: Harcourt, Brace and World.

Henderson, Ailsa. 2004. "Regional Political Cultures in Canada." *Canadian Journal of Political Science* 37 (03): 595–615. http://dx.doi.org/10.1017/S0008423904030707.

Henderson, Ailsa. 2007. *Nunavut: Rethinking Political Culture*. Vancouver: University of British Columbia Press.

Horowitz, Gad. 1966. "Conservatism, Liberalism, and Socialism in Canada: An Interpretation." *Canadian Journal of Economics and Political Science* 32 (2): 143–71. http://dx.doi.org/10.2307/139794.

Inglehart, Ronald. 1997. *Modernization and Postmodernization: Cultural, Economic, and Political Change in 43 Countries*. Princeton: Princeton University Press.

Innis, Harold A., and Daniel Drache. 1995. *Staples, Markets, and Cultural Change: Selected Essays*. Montreal: McGill-Queen's University Press.

Kymlicka, Will. 1995. *Multicultural Citizenship: A Liberal Theory of Minority Rights*. New York, Oxford: Clarendon Press.

Lambert, Ronald, and James Curtis. 1984. "Québécois and English Canadian Opposition to Racial and Religious Intermarriage, 1968–1983." *Canadian Ethnic Studies* 16 (2): 30–46.

Leuprecht, Christian. 2003. "The Tory Fragment in Canada: Endangered Species?" *Canadian Journal of Political Science* 36 (02): 401–16. http://dx.doi.org/10.1017/S000842390377869X.

Lipset, Seymour Martin. 1986. "Historical Traditions and National Characteristics: A Comparative Analysis of Canada and the United States." *Canadian Journal of Sociology* 11 (2): 113–55. http://dx.doi.org/10.2307/3340795.

Lipset, Seymour Martin. 1990. *Continental Divide: The Values and Institutions of the United States and Canada.* New York: Routledge.

McRae, Kenneth D. 1964. "The Structure of Canadian History." In *The Founding of New Societies: Studies in the History of the United States, Latin America, South Africa, Canada, and Australia,* ed. Louis Hartz, 219–74. New York: Harcourt, Brace and World.

McRae, Kenneth. 1978. "Louis Hartz's Concept of the Fragment Society and Its Application to Canada." *Études canadiennes* 5: 17–30.

Meisel, John. 1964. "Conclusion: An Analysis of the National (?) Results." In *Papers on the 1962 Election: Fifteen Papers on the Canadian General Election of 1962,* ed. John Meisel, 272–88. Toronto: University of Toronto Press.

Nevitte, Neil. 1996. *The Decline of Deference: Canadian Value Change in Cross-National Perspective.* Peterborough: Broadview Press.

Perlin, George. 1997. "The Constraints of Public Opinion: Diverging and Converging Paths." In *Degrees of Freedom: Canada and the United States in a Changing World,* eds. Keith Banting and George Hoberg, 71–149. Montreal: McGill-Queen's University Press.

Rayside, David. 2008. *Queer Inclusions, Continental Divisions: Recognition of Sexual Diversity in Canada and the United States.* Toronto: University of Toronto Press.

Schwartz, Mildred A. 1974. *Politics and Territory.* Montreal: McGill-Queen's University Press.

Simeon, Richard E.B., and David J. Elkins. 1974. "Regional Political Cultures in Canada." *Canadian Journal of Political Science* 7 (03): 397–437. http://dx.doi.org/10.1017/S0008423900040713.

Simeon, Richard, and David Elkins. 1980. "Provincial Political Cultures in Canada." In *Small Worlds: Provinces and Parties in Canadian Political Life,* eds. David Elkins and Richard Simeon, 31–76. Toronto: Methuen.

Sniderman, Paul, Joseph F. Fletcher, Peter Russell, and Philip E. Tetlock. 1989. "Political Culture and The Problem of Double Standards: Mass and Elite Attitudes Toward Language Rights in the Canadian Charter of Rights and Freedoms." *Canadian Journal of Political Science* 22 (02): 259–84. http://dx.doi.org/10.1017/S000842390000130X.

Sniderman, Paul, Joseph F. Fletcher, Peter Russell, and Philip E. Tetlock. 1996. *The Clash of Rights: Liberty, Equality, and Legitimacy in Pluralist Democracy.* New Haven, CT: Yale University Press.

Stewart, Ian. 1990. "The Study of Canadian Political Culture." In *Canadian Politics: An Introduction to the Discipline,* eds. Alain-G. Gagnon and James P. Bickerton, 89–105. Peterborough: Broadview Press.

Stewart, Ian. 2001. "Vanishing Points: Three Paradoxes of Political Culture Research." In *Citizen Politics: Research and Theory in Canadian Political Behaviour,* eds. Joanna Everitt and Brenda O'Neill, 21–39. Toronto: Oxford University Press.

Wiseman, Nelson. 1988. "A Note on 'Hartz-Horowitz at Twenty': The Case of French Canada." *Canadian Journal of Political Science* 21 (04): 795–806. http://dx.doi.org/10.1017/S0008423900057450.

Wiseman, Nelson. 2007. *In Search of Canadian Political Culture.* Vancouver: University of British Columbia Press.

Young, Lisa, and Keith Archer, eds. 2002. *Regionalism and Party Politics.* Don Mills, ON: Oxford University Press.

twelve
Competing for Power:
Parties and Elections in Canada

JAMES BICKERTON

Introduction

This chapter will divide its discussion of parties, voters, and elections into four parts. The first section provides an overview of Canada's first three party systems, noting the distinctive characteristics of each as well as certain persistent features of party and electoral politics. Historically, several reorderings of the party system were occasioned by high-volatility elections with marked realignments of the electorate. While major social and cultural changes played a role in these dramatic disruptions of "politics as usual," so too did other institutional features of the political system that have had a shaping effect on the party system, such as federalism, an executive-dominated parliamentary system, and the first-past-the-post electoral system. An analysis of the contribution of these institutional factors to the rise of third parties and the regionalization of the party system constitutes the second section of the chapter.

The third section deals with political parties as organizations: how they operate and how they have reformed themselves, within limits, to adapt to changing political dynamics and cultural shifts, on the one hand, and to the steady advance of state regulation on the other. Some of these reforms have been triggered by the need to match the innovations of competitors in the political marketplace, while others were imposed by changes to the regulatory environment within which parties must operate. Lastly, our attention will be turned to various theories of vote choice and their application to recent elections by political scientists who attempt to make sense of electoral outcomes and the voting behaviour of Canadians. Consideration in this final section will be given to the perennial balancing act that parties must perform: to sustain themselves they must build and maintain a stable foundation of voter support within a changing electorate; but to be truly successful they must find ways to reach beyond their core supporters to gather sufficient votes to contest for power.

Brokerage Politics and Party System Change

Of first importance in Canada's party system is that it has not always been as it is today in terms of the number of political parties, the kind of appeals they make to voters, and their bases of support in the electorate. At the same time, there are certain constants that continue to structure and shape Canadian party politics. If a party system is defined as the pattern of competition and cooperation among all political parties within a given political system, then Canada can be said to have had several party systems (Carty, 1993; Carty, Cross, and Young, 2000). This section will provide a brief overview of the first two, before moving on to a closer examination of the modern era of Canadian party politics that began in the 1960s.

The First and Second Party Systems

The first period of Canadian party politics spanned the half-century from the country's origins in 1867 until 1921, the year of the first general election following World War I. Party competition during these early decades of Confederation took the form of a classic two-party system, which political scientists consider to be a normal feature of political systems that use the simple plurality or "first-past-the-post" electoral system. The Liberal and Conservative parties operated as broad-based national parties, alternating in power and building electoral coalitions comprised of different regions, classes, religions, and language groups. As noted in 1907 by André Siegfried in *The Race Question in Canada* (1966), politics at that time was primarily a battle over the spoils of power between the "Ins" and "Outs," unsullied by ideological principle and focused mainly on parochial concerns at the local level. For Siegfried, the one defining characteristic of Canadian politics was the smoldering antagonism between the English-speaking majority and the French-speaking minority—"two nations warring within the bosom of a single state." Not that there weren't some basic policy differences between the parties, in particular surrounding the type of commercial relations there should be with the United States and the related question of retaining imperial ties with Britain. These differences certainly helped to structure the vote during this period by defining the core support base for each party and occasionally to realign the partisan loyalties of the electorate—such as the key election of 1896, which brought Laurier's Liberals to power, and 1911, which turfed them out (Blake, 1979; Johnston, 1992).

This combination of classic two-party competition and highly personalized politics, with its focus on the use of patronage, policy, and patriotic appeals to build and maintain national party organizations and winning electoral coalitions, had the additional effect over time of integrating a diverse polity and constructing the political sinews of a viable nation-state. The first party system, however, did not survive the nationalist-imperialist cross-pressures generated by Canada's participation in World War I. The issue that proved particularly vexing was wartime conscription, the need for which was strongly supported by British Canadians and strongly opposed by French Canadians. This deep political division along ethnolinguistic lines reduced the Liberal Party to a largely French-speaking rump of parliamentarians facing a cobbled-together bipartisan coalition (the "Unionist" Party) with Conservative Robert Borden as leader and prime minister. The political effects and aftermath of this wartime experience were both profound and long lasting (English, 1977).

The system-changing election of 1921 did more than simply unseat the Conservatives (who had re-emerged out of the rapid postwar dissolution of the Unionist Party) and bring the Liberals back to power, in the pattern of previous elections. It also unveiled a new party that won more seats than the Conservatives, disrupting the cozy two-party affair that had defined pre-war party politics. This new entrant into the competition for power, the Progressive Party, was backed by a populist, agrarian movement that opposed the whole idea of party politics and argued instead for a new form of cooperative politics and government. In a stunning electoral debut, it succeeded in capturing an outright majority of the seats in western Canada (Wood, 1975; Morton, 1991). There were also several independent labour candidates elected across the country, emblematic of the growing strength and militancy of the industrial working class. The appearance of these new political actors marked the increasing salience of class and regional cleavages in a rapidly urbanizing and industrializing Canada; their electoral success in 1921 marked the failure of the traditional parties to contain rising political tensions and conflicts within the country (Brodie and Jenson, 1980).

This change in the number and character of political parties was effectively the beginning of Canada's second party system. Though the old-line parties were able to stave off the challenge of the Progressives and for a brief time re-established the familiar pattern of bipolar competition, this return to "politics as normal" proved illusory. Soon the social and political strains that accompanied the 1930s Depression altered once and for all the old pattern of party allegiances. Two new versions of "prairie populism"—the socialist Cooperative Commonwealth Federation (CCF) and the conservative Social Credit Party—contested the election of 1935 and quickly established durable voter bases, permanently altering the political landscape and the dynamics of electoral politics federally and in several provinces.[1]

Canada's original two-party system had buckled under the diversity of demands and interests that were welling up in the interwar period, rooted in growing regional, rural-urban, and class antagonisms. Yet despite these political shocks, the traditional parties were able to adapt, with the Liberals becoming the dominant party based on their continuing hold over Quebec's parliamentary seats (which had begun with Laurier and was reinforced by the conscription crisis) and their superior ability to accommodate the interests of different regions, classes, and language groups in classic brokerage style. Liberal leader Mackenzie King, who succeeded Laurier and became Canada's longest serving prime minister, was particularly adept at this process. In the words of poet and professor of constitutional law Frank Scott, King retained power by "doing nothing by halves that could be done by quarters ... and never taking sides, because he never allowed sides to take shape" (Scott, 1967: 36). This cautious, accommodative approach was a recipe for managing social tensions and maintaining political stability, but it did not produce inspiring leadership or frame the task of governance in terms of lofty ideals and goals. As the unbroken string of Liberal governments under King and his successor Louis St. Laurent stretched into the 1950s, some critics raised concerns about the increasingly close (and closed) relationship among political, bureaucratic, and corporate elites (Whitaker, 1977); others remarked on the absence of a creative and progressive politics in a country that seemed obsessed with stability and national unity (Porter, 1965); while Canadian nationalists were critical of policies that produced economic growth by encouraging (or not opposing) the gradual economic and cultural integration of Canada with the United States. The latter trend, documented by several government-commissioned reports, produced growing unease about the future of Canadian sovereignty and identity, as well as the country's long-term development prospects (Bashevkin, 1991; Russell, 1966; Grant, 1970).

The Diefenbaker Interlude and the Third Party System

Canadians were always both repelled and attracted by their neighbour's aggressive growth and dynamism, its growing appetite for Canadian resources, the economic opportunities presented by its huge consumer market, and its postwar rise to global hegemon (Berger, 1976). So the drift toward continental integration was bound to create stresses within the national fabric and psyche. The deepening relationship with the United States and the corporate, managerial style of Liberal government in the postwar years became key issues in the latter's eventual political defeat. This occurred when the Progressive Conservative Party, under their new leader John Diefenbaker, scored an unexpected minority victory in 1957, to be quickly followed by a massive majority in 1958—the largest (in proportional terms) in Canadian history.

"Dief the Chief," as he came to be known, was an impressive speech-maker and political campaigner, an ardent defender of Canada's traditional British ties, and wary of the ever-closer embrace of the United States driven by Cold War politics and continental economic integration. His lasting contribution to Canadian party politics was to turn the Progressive Conservatives (the party had changed its name in 1942) into a nationally competitive party by adding western Canada to their traditional Ontario base. Diefenbaker is generally acknowledged to have been a better leader of the opposition than prime minister, and it did not take long for his governing style to alienate many voters in Canada's large urban centres, as well as French Canadians at odds with his views on Canadian national identity (summed up as "One Canada, One Nation"). Although he remained the popular choice in the west, and more generally throughout rural and small-town English-speaking Canada, Diefenbaker's government was reduced to minority status in 1962 and then defeated in 1963. This sequence of elections effectively ushered in Canada's third party system (Newman, 1963).

In the third party system, the Liberals would once again assume their traditional role as Canada's dominant party, returning to power under the leadership of Lester B. Pearson, a former senior civil servant and Nobel Peace Prize winner. They would retain control of the government until 1984 (absent a short stint in opposition in 1979). The prime minister for most of this period was Pierre Trudeau, a prominent Quebec intellectual recruited by Pearson (who retired from politics in 1968) to help the federal government meet the rising challenge of Quebec nationalism and separatism (English, 2009). The third party system was primarily a three-party affair, with the Liberals and Progressive Conservatives locked in a contest for power and the smaller New Democratic Party (NDP), founded in 1961 as a successor to the CCF, occasionally acting as the spoiler or gaining political leverage during periods of minority government (Johnston, 1992).

The profound changes taking place in Canadian society during this period—progressive urbanization, expansion of a well-educated and relatively affluent middle class, the increasingly multicultural character of society (especially in the major cities), and the changing role and status of women as they made advances toward gender equality—profoundly affected the dynamics of party competition and placed new demands on all political parties. The Liberals renovated their organization, leadership, and electoral appeal, becoming more centre-left and urban-oriented in their policies and voter base. By moving to adopt the mantle of moderate social democracy that was the dominant leitmotiv of western industrialized societies at that time, they were able to stem the electoral gains of their NDP rivals on the left (Smith, 1973; Wearing, 1981). Even more crucial, by developing a national unity/national identity strategy under Trudeau based on the policies of bilingualism and multiculturalism, they were able to reinforce and expand upon the party's traditional support base among French Canadians, Catholics, and visible minorities. It was their strong positioning in this key *cultural* dimension of politics that kept the centrist Liberal Party from being squeezed out by parties to their right (Progressive Conservatives) and left (NDP), a fate that befell many centrist parties elsewhere in the western world (Johnston, 2010).

Continuing to enjoy a seemingly impregnable Quebec base but virtually shut out of western Canada after 1958, the Liberals were forced to pursue electoral majorities in urban Ontario, a strategy sometimes thwarted by the NDP's oscillating appeal to left-of-centre voters there. The Progressive Conservatives, whether under Diefenbaker or subsequent leaders Robert Stanfield and Joe Clark, were often successful in winning the most seats in English Canada, but were hugely disadvantaged by their chronically dismal performance in Quebec. As Table 12.1 illustrates, the overall result was the absence of any truly national party that was competitive in all regions of the country, and the ever-present possibility of minority governments (Johnston, Blais, Brady, and Crête, 1992).

Brian Mulroney and the Collapse of the Third Party System

Following Trudeau's departure from politics in 1984, Liberal political dominance was brought to an end by the Diefenbaker-style landslide victory won by the Progressive Conservatives, then under the leadership of Quebec native Brian Mulroney. The Tory tidal wave of 1984 included most of Quebec's federal seats, something promised by Mulroney if he was selected by his party's 1983 leadership convention. This turnabout of party fortunes altered the tenor of both party politics and the national unity debate, as Mulroney's appeal in Quebec was aimed primarily at francophones who constituted the "soft" nationalist vote there. His ability to win over this important segment of the Quebec electorate was aided by his fluency in French, his native Quebecer credentials, and his intimate knowledge of politics there; it was also helped by his openness to further constitutional negotiations that would satisfy Quebec's objections to the revised Canadian constitution, to which the province had refused their agreement in 1982. This was a political strategy that had its risks; it relied upon building a rather incoherent and unstable electoral alliance of francophones and francophobes, to be sealed by a constitutional deal that would somehow be acceptable to both the new Quebec wing of the Progressive Conservative party and its traditional bedrock voter base in western Canada. As awkward a political marriage as this appeared to be, Mulroney temporarily accomplished it with the signing of the Meech Lake constitutional accord in 1987 and the Canada-US Free Trade Agreement (favoured by both Quebec and Alberta) in 1988. This laid the foundation for a second Progressive Conservative majority (see Table 12.1

Table 12.1 Valid Votes Cast (%*) and Candidates Elected (N) by Political Party at Canadian General Elections, 1963–1988

Party	1963	1965	1968	1972	1974	1979	1980	1984	1988
Liberal	41.7% **128**	40.2% **131**	45.5% **155**	38.5% **109**	43.2% **141**	40.1% 114	44.3% **147**	28.0% 40	31.9% 83
PC	32.8% 95	32.4% 97	31.4% 72	34.9% 107	35.4% 95	35.9% **136**	32.5% 103	50.0% **211**	43.0% **169**
NDP	13.1% 17	17.9% 21	17.0% 22	17.7% 31	15.4% 16	17.9% 26	19.8% 32	18.8% 30	20.4% 43
Ralliement des créditistes	—	4.6% 9	4.4% 14	—	—	—	—	—	—
Social Credit	11.9% 24	3.7% 5	0.8% 0	7.6% 15	5.0% 11	4.6% 6	1.7% 0	0.1% 0	** 0
Reform	—	—	—	—	—	—	—	—	2.1%–
Others	0.4% 1	1.2% 2	0.9% 1	1.2% 2	0.9% 1	1.5% 0	1.7% 0	3.0% 1	2.6% 0
Total valid votes	7,894,076	7,713,316	8,125,996	9,667,489	9,505,908	11,455,702	10,947,914	12,548,721	13,175,599
Voter turnout	79.2%	74.8%	75.7%	76.7%	71.0%	75.7%	69.3%	75.3%	75.3%
Total seats	265	265	264	264	264	282	282	282	295

*Columns may not add up to 100% due to rounding
**Less than 0.1%
Source: T.J. Coulson, revised by S. Geobey (2007); Elections Canada, "Voter Turnouts" (www.elections.ca).

for details), thereby confirming the Quebec-West alliance that was at the core of Mulroney's political success (Johnston, Blais, Brady, and Crête, 1992).

Mulroney's dream of permanently displacing the Liberals as Canada's "natural governing party" was not to be, however; instead, the federal election of 1988 was its high water mark. His second mandate as prime minister was marked by sustained conflict, controversy, and ultimately a spectacular collapse of voter support for his party, by then under the leadership of his successor (Kim Campbell, the only woman ever to serve as prime minister). Contributing mightily to the demise of the Progressive Conservatives were two new regional parties—the Bloc Québécois and the Reform Party (later to become the Canadian Alliance)—which were spurred into creation by fundamental disagreement within the party base over key government policies. Each of these new parties, secure in their regional base of support, would serve a term as Canada's official opposition to the governing Liberals, who were comfortably returned to power in 1993 under the leadership of Jean Chrétien.

The issues that triggered this dramatic change in the party system were constitutional, cultural, and economic: two failed constitutional accords that polarized the debate between Quebec and English-speaking Canada, a hotly contested free trade agreement with the United States, and a deteriorating fiscal and economic situation. In the process, many Canadians became alienated not only from the governing Progressive Conservatives, but also more generally from the brokerage-style politics being practised by all the old-line parties (Tanguay, 1994; Bickerton, 1997). To some extent, the easy hegemony of the Chrétien Liberals (the election of 1993 was the first of three consecutive majority wins) was premised on being the last brokerage party left standing. However, the resumption of its familiar role as Canada's "natural governing party" concealed fragile foundations: a narrowed regional base (with the loss of Quebec and the West requiring near-total Liberal dominance in Ontario) and the fragmentation of right-of-centre votes between the Reform Party and the fatally weakened Progressive Conservatives (Bickerton, Gagnon, and Smith, 1999). The Liberals were helped to victory by the continued support of their traditional social base among Catholic voters—a much-queried but never adequately explained anomaly of Canadian politics (Blais, 2005)—and visible minority communities throughout Canada.

While the Liberals were somewhat restored by the election of 1993, it was the implosion of the Progressive Conservative coalition constructed by Mulroney in 1984 that ushered in a new era of party politics, one that was more fragmented, regionalized, and ideologically polarized. The Reform Party led by Preston Manning, which undid Diefenbaker's legacy of a large base of PC seats in western Canada, pushed the party system's ideological spectrum in a more radically right-wing and populist direction. The national-ist Bloc Québécois (BQ), vowing to defend Quebec's interests in Ottawa while supporting the push for sovereignty by the Parti Québécois (PQ) at the provincial level, took over Mulroney's coveted base of moderate nationalists in francophone Quebec (save for a lone seat belonging to Jean Charest, who quickly became the PC party's new leader). The election outcome reduced the NDP and Progressive Conservatives to unprecedented lows of eight and two seats respectively, pushing both to the edge of political oblivion (Bickerton, Gagnon, and Smith, 1999).

Clearly, as indicated by these election returns, many Canadians at that time were alienated from and angry with the mainstream political parties, though apparently not with political parties *per se*, since two new political parties were able to attract significant organizational, financial, and electoral support in those regions of the country most disaffected with "politics as usual." While this represented a crisis for particular parties and radically trans-formed the party system, it also seemed to confirm that party politics was the primary means of registering political protest and that change, renewal, and renovation of parties and the party system were still possible. New parties could form and succeed; older ones could decline and even disappear if they failed to adapt to their changing environment or respond adequately to voter concerns, demands, and preferences.

II. Third Parties and Regionalization of the Party System

Canada has long been something of an exception among comparable politi-cal systems in terms of its propensity to support "third parties" (Lipset, 1990; Gagnon and Tanguay, 1996; Belanger, 2007). Although only two parties have ever formed the government in Canada (Liberal and Conservative, or some variant thereof), the party system since 1921 has included three to five par-ties with elected members of Parliament. Most of the smaller parties have had distinct regional bases of support, even those presenting themselves as national alternatives with candidates in all regions. Others have had no such pretensions beyond their narrow regional appeal.[2]

Various explanations have been offered for this characteristic of the Canadian party system. Some have been case- or situation-specific, such as C.B. Macpherson's interpretation of Alberta's unusual "quasi-party" tradition, the origins of which, he argued in the 1950s, lay in its neocolonial rela-tionship with eastern Canada and its homogeneous agrarian class structure (Macpherson, 1962). Other perspectives on third-party formation have been more generally applicable, such as Maurice Pinard's theory of minor party formation that identifies two factors structurally conducive to third-party formation: sustained one-party dominance joined with conditions of societal strain that discredits both the long-governing party as well as the traditional alternative (Pinard, 1975). For their part, Gagnon and Tanguay (1996) cite a more general composite factor at work in third-party formation and success: the "non-responsiveness" of the national party system to particular regional interests and concerns.

The concept of "non-responsiveness" in this context suggests a kind of systemic failure of the brokerage role played by Canada's national parties. At least one scholar has directly faulted the parties themselves for this shortcoming (Smith, 1985), but others have targeted the interaction of the party system with other institutions in the political system: the executive dominance and strict party discipline typical of Westminster-style parliamentary democracy, the inadequacies of the Canadian Senate as a forum for regional representation, the perverse workings of the first-past-the-post electoral system, and finally Canada's highly decentralized form of federalism.

Canada's parliamentary system has been widely criticized for its democratic failings. The biggest knock against it is the dominant position assumed by the political executive, and more particularly the prime minister. To some critics, the concentration of power in the hands of the prime minister, the doctrine of cabinet and caucus secrecy, and the strict enforcement of party discipline effectively turns elected members of the House of Commons into "trained seals" rather than true representatives of their constituents (Simpson, 2001). Relatively powerless and rigidly bound by party discipline, MPs are ill-suited to the task of effective regional representation. Further, the federal cabinet—once a primary venue for regional accommodation, and still constructed to give every region an appropriate share of ministerial posts—is a shadow of its former self, as ministerial autonomy and power has faded relative to the prime minister and the central agencies that provide him or her with information and advice (Bakvis, 2000–01; Savoie, 1999).

The poor design of the House of Commons for regional representation is not balanced by Canada's other chamber of Parliament. Almost alone among comparable federal states—witness the substantive role of senates in the USA, Australia, and Germany—the Canadian Senate has never been an effective forum for regional representation within the national Parliament (Sayers, 2002). As prime ministerial appointees, its members have neither the legitimacy nor the inclination to act as articulators and defenders of regional interests within the legislative process, contributing to popular and scholarly opinion that the institution is largely dysfunctional or irrelevant. This imposes the full burden of ensuring regions are appropriately represented within the national legislature on the ill-suited House of Commons (Smiley and Watts, 1986; Sayers, 2002; Bickerton, 2007).

A similarly long-standing vein of criticism has been levelled at the electoral system, which distorts regional interests and identities by frequently misrepresenting regional voter preferences within Parliament. It does this by overrepresenting the strongest parties in regions (the "winners") and underrepresenting weaker ones (the "losers"), often out of all proportion to the actual levels of voter support enjoyed by each party. Minor parties with regional bases of support are rewarded, while minor parties with diffuse national support are punished. Parties find themselves bereft of seats in some regions and oversupplied in others. Regions that are poorly represented within the caucuses of particular parties are more likely to become alienated from those parties and therefore less likely to vote for them in future, creating a self-perpetuating cycle of regionalized party politics (Cairns, 1968; Gibbins, 2005). The high degree of regionalization encouraged by the electoral system is also a relevant factor in the sustained downturn in voter participation. Regionalization—whereby particular parties dominate whole regions—reduces political competitiveness in many electoral districts, which over time suppresses voter turnout (see Tanguay, Chapter 13 of this book, for further discussion of this topic).

Finally, Canada's form of federalism is a constitutional and institutional arrangement that turns provinces into powerful subnational governments and the dominant "voice of region" in Canadian politics. As autonomous political arenas with their own discrete party systems, provinces can become platforms capable of sustaining regional parties at the federal level, especially if those parties (or affiliated versions thereof) are successful in capturing power at the provincial level (Simeon, 1975; Cairns, 1977). There can be no question that the impact of federalism on party organization and behaviour has been far-reaching. Several parties have existed primarily or exclusively at either the provincial or federal level, creating gaps and discontinuities between party systems (Johnston, 2010).[3] Federal and provincial parties have evolved to be separate and distinct, despite the coincidence of party labels, with parties of the same name sometimes quite hostile toward each other.[4] This lack of national integration reduces the capacity of the party system to secure political stability through the intra-party accommodation of diverse regional interests, a role performed by party systems in most other federations (Tanguay, 2003; Bakvis and Tanguay, 2012).

The Contributions of Minor Parties

Although the regionalized character of the party system can exacerbate regional conflict and widen regional divisions, regional and other minor parties of protest should be given their due. Indeed, it can be argued that their resilience and surprising success historically has been important for the vibrancy of Canadian democracy. For instance, they have been key sources of both policy and organizational innovation. The traditional mainstream parties have been poor performers, if not largely moribund, when it comes to policy development and innovation, traditionally relying on government-appointed royal commissions to advise them on new policy directions (Bradford, 1999). Third parties, on the other hand, have brought radical proposals for change to the electoral and parliamentary table, and when they gain power at the provincial level have often have been innovators of new policies and programs (Thorburn, 1991).[5]

Another way in which "third" parties have been of service is in the area of organizational reform, grassroots participation, and new member recruitment. Minor parties on both the left and the right have been innovators in terms of party organization, fund-raising techniques, and election campaign tactics in ways that have internally democratized parties or extended their popular reach. As observed long ago by French political sociologist Maurice Duverger, such changes have a "contagion effect" on others in the party system who attempt to emulate and counter the introduction of any successful innovation by a competitor (1951). The effective use of radio by the populist Social Credit; the class-based appeal of the socialist CCF; the union-affiliated membership, door-to-door campaigning techniques, and affirmative action initiatives of the NDP; the universal ballot leader-selection process introduced by the Bloc Québécois; the fund-raising techniques employed by the Reform Party: these are just some examples of innovations introduced by minor or protest parties in Canada (Gagnon and Tanguay, 1996; Cross, 2004).

Finally, new parties have acted as a safety valve for Canadian democracy. Their presence has given voters an institutional outlet for their frustration, anger, or disillusionment with government policies, with the mainstream parties, or more broadly with the political system. By channelling dissent into the electoral arena, new parties (unless they immediately sweep the older parties aside) can give the mainstream parties time to adapt to clear evidence of their failings and to craft policy or institutional remedies in response. As well, by becoming part of the "national conversation" in the electoral arena and within Parliament, new parties themselves gradually become institutionalized, containing and moderating the more radical or extreme elements within their own support base. In this way, the party and political system that is initially threatened by the rise of radical protest parties is stimulated to respond in ways that moderate and absorb political dissent (Gagnon and Tanguay, 1996).

This interactive cycle of third-party insurgency and systemic response provides part of the explanation for the findings of Richard Johnston, who argues that the latest rise of regional parties in 1993 is consistent with the unfolding of a recurring and long-term "cycle of protest" in Canadian electoral history. This happens when protest party success results in regional fragmentation, only to be followed by a period of reconsolidation and renationalization of the party system. However, Johnston notes that the cycle does not exhibit itself as an unchanging loop; reconsolidation appears to happen at a higher level of party system fragmentation than existed previously, suggesting that the Canadian party system may be suffering from a diminishing capacity over time to "shoulder the burden" of national political integration imposed by the country's regional, ethnic, and linguistic diversity (Johnston, 2005).

III. Parties as Organizations

As organizations, just how inclusive are political parties of different segments of Canadian society, and how responsive are they to the views of their activists? What role do grassroots members play in their parties, and how (if at all) has this changed over time as parties have moved to "democratize" their internal operations?

In general, Canadian political parties have had member organizations that are fairly dormant at the constituency level between elections, only to be activated and pumped up with new members during general elections and party leadership contests. When their key role in the electoral process (choosing candidates or delegates) recedes in the aftermath of an election or leadership contest, the organizations tend to shrink back to a dedicated core group dominated by local executives. During these times, it is estimated that somewhere between one and two per cent of Canadians may be members of a political party, a figure that compares unfavourably with other Western democracies (Cross, 2004: 15–19). This is the case even though parties in Canada are highly permeable, with relatively open membership; even noncitizens and those not yet of voting age are able to join. As well, those belonging to political parties do not tend to be representative of the population as a whole. In his research William Cross has found that about two-thirds are men, with an average age around 60, and most of these are of European ancestry. Younger and visible minority or "new Canadians," as well as those without a university education, tend to be left out (2004: 21–22). To their credit the parties have not been insensitive about these discrepancies and the criticisms they provoke. Efforts have been made to attract more women, youth, and ethnic minorities into party ranks. Internal party structures were created to effect the greater participation of these groups, with the New Democratic and Liberal parties going farthest to ensure a more representative membership base (Cross, 2004; MacIvor, 2003).

During the 1960s and 1970s, there were other positive developments regarding political parties and democracy. One of these concerned the regulatory context for parties and elections. The passage of the Election Expenses Act in 1974 placed limits on the amount of money parties could spend during election periods, imposed legal requirements on parties to disclose the names of donors, and used the tax system to encourage individuals to donate to parties, thereby broadening the financing of parties beyond corporations, unions, and wealthy private donors. All of this had the effect of making more transparent and placing limits on the role of money in party and electoral politics and began the process of moving parties away from their dependence on large (and presumably influential) contributors to party coffers (Paltiel, 1987).

The parties also experienced a dramatic expansion of their membership numbers during this period and actively recruited women and minorities to join their ranks. Party conventions became more open and participatory, with typically thousands of delegates congregating to choose new leaders and discuss policy resolutions. At the same time, progress in terms of getting more women and minorities elected to Parliament was painfully slow, and the parties were often criticized as a barrier to progress. Beyond selecting new leaders and periodically passing judgement on their performance, member participation tended to be shallow, sporadic, and largely meaningless in terms of deciding party policies. And, as previously noted, new member recruitment tended to occur only during leadership contests or elections, with a dramatic fall-off in membership numbers and participation between these episodes (Perlin, 1988; Goldfarb and Axworthy, 1988).

By contrast with this historical trend, there was a movement away from such affirmative action measures by the upstart Reform Party and its successor, the Canadian Alliance, both of which rejected special treatment or measures for women and minorities. This difference of approach has continued after the merger of parties on the right to form the new Conservative Party of Canada. Finally, language composition is another area of uneven representation, which became worse in the 1990s due to the collapse of the Progressive Conservatives and success of the nationalist Bloc Québécois. Following the latter's emergence, only the Liberals among the remaining parties were able to boast francophone membership numbers that were not risibly low (Cross, 2004: 22–23).

As for the relatively few Canadians who are party members, most are inactive most of the time; few spend any time in the average month on party activity, with a financial contribution or posting a lawn sign the most common contributions during election periods. They do express widespread dissatisfaction with this level of participation, with most being of the opinion that there should be more discussion of matters of public policy and a greater role in developing the party's election platform. This member interest in some form of policy study and development role touches on an area of weakness exhibited by Canadian political parties, which historically have committed few resources to ongoing policy study, eschewing formal policy institutes or foundations, or strong ties with independent policy groups. Instead they have been content to leave policy-making in the hands of party leaders and their personal entourages (Cross, 2004: chap. 3).

This long-standing tendency to operate as leader-centric parties, focused on short-term issues and paying little attention to long-term policy development, has been a persistent characteristic of political parties that has proven highly resistant to change. For party leaders and their advisors to craft electoral appeals that could produce a potentially winning coalition of voters has required flexibility in the realm of ideology, with policy consistency and ideological coherence sacrificed to strike the right policy balance to make the broadest possible electoral appeal. Whether this approach was imposed on parties by Canada's regional diversity, social pluralism, and national unity concerns, or was the result of the failings of new parties to reorient national political discourse toward a more ideologically coherent, class-based politics, the fact remains that clear and lasting distinctions in policy platforms—or the policies pursued while in power—have not been a hallmark of Canadian party politics (Brodie and Jenson, 1996; Bradford, 1999).

Clearly Canada's main political parties have not been participatory organizations when it comes to questions of policy. However, the same cannot be said about the selection of local candidates or party leaders. R.K. Carty argues that Canadian parties have been "franchise" operations, whereby local autonomy is granted to constituency organizations to choose their own candidates and delegates to party conventions, in return for leaving control over policies and election platforms to the leader and caucus—particularly the leader (Carty, 2002). Local nomination contests are relatively open affairs, generating significant recruitment drives that can bring in hundreds of new party members, often friends and associates of the candidates, but those recruited do not always remain active or even stay as party members, particularly if they were recruited to the losing side in a nomination contest. As well, many nomination contests—and almost always where there is an incumbent—remain uncontested (Wolinetz, 2007).

Although the nominees of local constituency organizations still face the hurdle of leadership approval before becoming candidates, imposing candidates on a local association (the prerogative of party leaders who must sign nomination papers) risks arousing resentment and, in some instances, defections to other parties. This does not mean that it never happens. Leaders have appointed local candidates because they are "stars" expected to improve the party's electoral prospects or to demonstrate they are open to members of target groups such as women or visible minorities who are still woefully underrepresented. This proclivity to interfere with the ability of local associations to nominate candidates of their own choice has been particularly prevalent in the Liberal Party (Cross, 2004: 68; Wolinetz, 2007: 184).

As for party leadership selection, its history "is one of continual pressure for an expanded electorate, with greater rank-and-file participation" (Cross, 2004: 76). This steady evolution toward more inclusive and participatory forms of leadership selection has not prevented parties from adopting a variety of selection methods that reflect their party's history and particular circumstances. The first leader selected by delegate convention, in 1919, was Mackenzie King. For decades thereafter the convention became the standard mechanism for choosing leaders, but these were usually small and managed affairs. The modern open convention with thousands of delegates arrived in the 1960s, forcing leadership candidates to engage in intensive recruitment drives and to pack local delegate selection meetings with their supporters. This placed a premium on money and organization as the keys to mounting a serious leadership bid. It also forced the opening up of what had been a relatively closed, elitist process to groups that were previously excluded, such as women, youth, and visible minorities, as parties sought to keep pace with broader societal demands for democratization, equality, and inclusiveness (Perlin, 1988; Preyra, 2001).

The crisis of the third-party system brought on by the rise of the Bloc Québécois and Reform Party was the occasion for the transition from delegate conventions to either direct election of the party leader through some sort of universal ballot or alternatively hybrid systems that combined features of direct election and delegate convention. With provincial parties, the Bloc Québécois, and the Reform Party all adopting direct election of the leader with a vote for all party members, the other federal parties felt compelled to follow suit simply to meet the expectations of party members and the broader public, who increasingly considered this to be the litmus test of a party's democratic character. It also was seen as a way to revitalize parties after a devastating electoral defeat or a period in the political wilderness of opposition. Some parties, notably the Liberals, adopted a hybrid system that was a compromise aimed at satisfying the demands of the grass roots for a direct say and their continuing preference as a brokerage party for a collective and deliberative decision-making process. Unique party histories and dynamics played a role in the decision made by other parties to water down the one-member, one-vote principle by adopting special weighting procedures, for instance to provide equality for constituencies (Conservatives and Liberals) or to guarantee a certain degree of influence for affiliated groups (the NDP). No party has yet to fully embrace a system based on the US presidential primary model, where participation rates—and the costs for leadership contestants—are dramatically higher (Preyra, 2001; Cross, 2004: chap. 5). However, this may be changing; in an attempt to broaden the party base, the 2013 Liberal leadership contest that selected Justin Trudeau used a more open selection process whereby a new category of non-member "supporters" were given the right to vote (Westwood, 2013).

Parties in Parliament

While political parties as organizations have changed appreciably, their role in Parliament has not. Successful candidates who win a seat in Parliament can expect to have their legislative role circumscribed by the strictures and requirements of responsible government, leader-determined strategy and tactics, and rampant partisanship. The tolerance of party leaders for internal dissent may vary, but members of party caucuses generally are punished if they stray from party lines, as enforced by party whips under the direction of the party leader. The resulting requirement to remain in lockstep with the party means that most backbenchers either turn to constituency work to sustain their motivation and original impulse to serve the public interest, or they stay on as members of Parliament for only one or two terms (see Docherty on Parliament, Chapter 8 in this volume).

The primary outlet for parliamentarians to express their own point of view is the weekly caucus meeting. Ideally, caucus will allow backbench members to voice the concerns of their constituents and, since meetings are conducted in secret, to criticize the performance, strategy, and tactics being employed by the party leadership. In other words, at least in theory it can be a venue for accountability, a vehicle for representation, and a forum for information exchange, discussion, and deliberation. However, there are several problems with realizing this potential role for the party caucus in parliamentary democracy. First, it is often left untapped by party leaders; second, backbenchers—particularly those recently elected—often have unrealistic expectations of their role in the policy process; and third, the whole exercise occurs behind closed doors, denying the visibility that politicians crave (and need) to convince constituents that their interests are being properly represented (Thomas, 1985; Docherty, 2004).

While party caucus influence within Parliament has declined, the party leader's entourage is a site of increased power. As described by Sid Noel, these entourages, mainly comprising political professionals, are essentially clientelistic formations, with "no purpose beyond providing loyalty, service, and acclaim to their leader," and each linked directly to the leader by bonds of mutual obligation (Noel, 2007: 197). Most of the enhanced party resources made available through party finance reforms have been diverted from party building at the grassroots level to larger and more sophisticated leader entourages "delegated the tasks of designing and running national, media-focused, leader-oriented election campaigns" (Noel, 2007: 206; see also Marland on political communication, chapter 14 in this volume). Entourages have also become useful for intraparty competition to help leadership aspirants to challenge incumbent leaders, or alternatively, to fend off such challenges (Martin, 2003).

There have been some suggestions offered for reforms to party organization and practices that would better equip political parties to meet the changing expectations of Canadians in the twenty-first century.[6] In his study of political parties and democracy, William Cross (2004) argues that parties should radically open up candidate nomination and leadership selection processes, including moving toward US-style primaries, as a means of enticing more Canadians to belong to parties and to choose to be participants on an ongoing basis. His second suggestion is to enhance the role of grassroots members in policy study and development as a way to make their participation in party activity more meaningful. In particular, parties could establish policy foundations that "would allow members to study policy issues, to debate alternatives, and to present their legislative caucuses with alternative policy approaches" (Cross, 2004: 179). Finally, Cross and others have argued that the system of campaign finance should be further reformed to make parties less dependent on the public purse and to remove any remaining financial barriers to potential political candidates. The idea is that this could have the effect of increasing communication with and responsiveness to party members, helping to avoid an even steeper decline in party membership due to the latter's growing sense of alienation from the remote, professional machinery of party organization (Cross, 2004: 180–82; Tanguay, 2009: 280). Whether reducing public support for parties has this salutary effect can now be tested since the Harper government, on its second attempt to do so, legislated an end to annual public subsidies to the parties shortly after attaining a majority of parliamentary seats in 2011 (see Tanguay, Chapter 13 in this volume).

IV. Parties and Voters: Ties That Tether but Do Not Bind?

It has been argued here that the role of political parties in both Parliament and government has diminished. As well, it seems that reforms to party structures and modes of operation have not altered in any fundamental way their basic organizational format and political purpose. Their role in the electoral process, however, remains both their *raison d'être* and essential for the functioning of Canadian democracy. Their competition gives form and meaning to elections by organizing alternatives from which citizens can choose, and it is this important role in "structuring the vote" that is their defining contribution to representative democracy. This turns our attention to the complex relationship between parties and voters.

As discussed above, the Canadian party system has been described in terms of periodic system-changing realignments, one-party dominance, and a propensity to third-party formation or "multipartism." There can be no clear explanation for these persistent features, however, without some understanding of party-voter relations. Broadly speaking, there are three general models that offer competing explanations for electoral outcomes in Canada over the past few decades. One model portrays voters as political consumers choosing between parties that offer them competing packages of benefits (often in the form of campaign promises), and making their vote choice strictly on the basis of their own narrow self-interest, unhindered by other factors or considerations.[7] While this *rational choice* model of voter behaviour undoubtedly captures an important dimension of electoral politics and voter behaviour, it greatly underestimates the non-rational, "non-calculating" considerations in people's evaluations and perceptions of the political realm. As a result, it has been widely critiqued and shown to be difficult to sustain in the face of contrary evidence.

The second model sees voting as primarily a response to psychological factors, with vote choice heavily dependent upon two short-term influences: voters' evaluations of the political candidates (and particularly the party leaders) and voters' issue attitudes. Both of these tend to be linked, however, to a third, long-term factor: voters' emotional attachment to a political party (partisanship).[8] Clarke et al. (1984) and others have applied a variation of this general approach to Canadian elections to argue that Canada can best be understood as a case of "stable dealignment". This describes a situation where *partisanship* (voter attachment to a particular party) is weak and growing weaker, increasing the potential for electoral volatility (defined as dramatic shifts in voter support for various parties). LeDuc has argued that a dealigned Canadian electorate means a high potential for sudden change, "whether or not such change actually takes place in any particular election" (LeDuc, 2007: 167–68). Using data from successive Canadian National Election Surveys (CNES), he suggests that the percentage of Canadians who are only weakly partisan or do not identify with any federal political party has risen steadily since 1993, eroding any solid basis of partisan support within the Canadian electorate. Indeed, his conclusion, one shared by at least some other election analysts, is that Canadians have the weakest political-party affinity in the Western world (Valpy, 2008).

It is further argued that declining levels of partisanship in the electorate have been accompanied by ideological weakness or confusion; LeDuc notes that 40 per cent of respondents to national surveys place themselves in the ideological centre and another 30 per cent either reject the notion of ideological placement entirely or fail to locate themselves appropriately on a simple left-right continuum (LeDuc, 2007: 170). In contrast to US voters, "who tenaciously hold on to their ideological orientations and are much more conservative, much more moral, with more religiosity and so forth," a huge shift of Canadian voters has occurred into an ideological no man's land (Valpy, 2008). It is argued that this combination of weak partisanship and lack of ideological orientation to politics, whatever its ultimate causes, creates a situation in which parties are discouraged from offering clearly distinguishable ideological appeals, and this pragmatism, in reciprocal fashion, reinforces the already prevailing tendencies and trends within the electorate. This can be seen to have consequences, both good and bad, for democracy, but one conclusion is that it makes centrist politics and ideological inconsistency the most likely winning electoral strategy for Canadian political parties. By default this places party leaders front and centre in terms of crafting an appeal to voters and defining the party in terms of both policy and personality, but particularly the latter.

There is not universal agreement with this well-established portrait of the Canadian voter. Another prominent perspective in the scholarly literature on voter behaviour rejects it for being too dismissive or simply incorrect concerning the continuing influence on vote choice of stable, long-term factors such as the social background characteristics of voters, their fundamental values and beliefs, and their party attachment (Gidengil et al., 2012). This reintroduces an older sociological approach that sees political parties as reliant in the first instance on a core bloc of voters that tend to be overrepresented within certain identifiable social groups.[9] It has also been argued that these core party supporters tend to hold certain basic values and beliefs that in broad terms are in accord with the philosophy or ideological orientation expounded by the party to which they become attached (Gidengil et al., 2012: 14–18). This third model is clearly at odds with the characterization of voters as increasingly "dealigned" from parties and ideologically adrift—not anchored in any particular set of values and beliefs that could be characterized as an ideological world view.

In support of this perspective, Gidengil et al., Blais, Nevitte, and others have reinterpreted the results of earlier voter surveys as well as more recent voter data to argue that it is difficult to make sense of voting behaviour in

Canada unless the effects of certain key social background characteristics are taken into account. Further, while Canadians typically do not have a clear grasp of concepts like "left" and "right," this does not mean they lack basic values and beliefs that underlie coherent views on topics like the appropriate balance between the state and the market, or moral questions and gender roles, topics that are central to the ideological dimension in politics. As for party identification or attachments, Gidengil et al. argue that this is influenced by both social background characteristics and basic values and beliefs, and that "this anchoring in social identities and in values and beliefs is what limits the flexibility of people's party ties" (Gidengil et al., 2012: 16). In short, even when voters who have a partisan tie defect to a rival party, they usually do not stray very far (in ideological terms) and they often later return to their original party of identification. In effect, though they may not be tightly bound to a particular party, they tend to be "tethered" by quite durable, if flexible, ties.

How do these models of voter behaviour, and particularly the third model cited above, help us to make sense of voter-party relations in Canada's fourth party system? In 2012, a group of researchers engaged with the Canadian Election Study (CES) published *Dominance and Decline: Making Sense of Recent Canadian Elections* (Gidengil et al., 2012), a book purporting to explain the interparty dynamics of voter support and the dramatic shift in the electoral fortunes of Canada's national political parties over the first decade of the twenty-first century.[10] The following overview of party-voter relations in the fourth party system, except where otherwise indicated, represents a selective synopsis of their findings and analysis.

In terms of the social bases of party support, the Liberals in the fourth party system continued to be heavily favoured by Catholics and visible minority voters, as well as anglophones within Quebec and francophones outside Quebec. Their lack of appeal in western Canada and with francophone Quebecers continued to act as a serious drag on their overall levels of support. Between 1993 and 2003, the Reform/Canadian Alliance (CA) Party attracted strong support from western and rural voters, as well as fundamentalist Christians. The party also fared better with married people and male voters. The 2003 merger of the Progressive Conservatives and the CA to form the Conservative Party transferred the CA's distinctive social base to the new party, though under Stephen Harper this base expanded to become less western and rural. The gender gap in the Conservative support base continued, but again less prominently (and damagingly) than with its Reform/CA predecessor. To the extent that the NDP had an identifiable social base, the party did better with voters from unionized households, as well as secular voters (no religion) and women. Unlike most other industrialized democracies, there has never been much evidence of class-based voting (when a person's material circumstances has a clear effect on party choice) in Canada, and this anomaly of non-class voting continued in the fourth party system. As for the BQ, language has clearly been the defining cleavage for its support base, with other sociodemographic factors exerting only a mild effect on vote choice in Quebec (Gidengil et al., 2012: chap. 2).

In the realm of basic values and beliefs, or what we might call ideological orientation, it is the Conservatives who have the most ideologically distinct and coherent voter base, rooted in support for market liberalism (pro-market, anti-state) and moral traditionalism (socially conservative views). They also have benefited from the political alienation felt by voters in the west. Liberals and New Democrats, on the other hand, compete for the same voters in terms of values and beliefs: socially liberal, with a more positive view of the role of government and more skeptical about the benefits of an unfettered free-market economy. This is also the ideological terrain that is worked by the BQ and the Green Party, creating severe electoral fragmentation on the centre-left in Canada. While moral traditionalism and religiosity have been declining in Canada, and the number of Canadians professing views consistent with support for market liberalism has been stagnant at best, the Conservative Party since 2004 has been greatly helped by vote-splitting on the centre-left, just as the Liberals had previously benefited from the same process on the centre-right (see Table 12.2). But importantly, there has been no growth over time in the Conservative core constituency in terms of Canadians' ideological orientation, suggesting a real constraint on the *potential* electorate for the Conservative Party (Gidengil et al., 2012: chap. 3). This finding, which confirms previous studies that shed a similar light on Canadian values and beliefs (Adams, 2009), casts doubt on recent assertions by some commentators that the national constituency for a more conservative Canada has grown significantly and will continue to do so in future (Bricker and Ibbitson, 2013).

Gidengil and her colleagues (2012) also find that partisanship remains meaningful in Canada, both in terms of the number of voters with an attachment to party and the relevance of this partisanship to vote choice. The Conservative Party benefits from partisans that are the most "hard-core" in terms of ideology and loyalty to their party of choice, and between 2004 and 2011 this partisan core grew while the Liberal core diminished in size. Another problem for the Liberals was the tendency for their supporters to vote for another party, while nonetheless continuing to identify as Liberals: fully one-third did this in the 2008 election. This suggests some room for growth in the Liberal vote share, though this partisan core is smaller than it used to be. As for the NDP, though progressively improving its performance under leader Jack Layton (2003–11), the party continued to have both the

Table 12.2 Valid Votes Cast (%) and Candidates Elected (N) by Political Party at Canadian General Elections, 1993–2011

Party	1993	1997	2000	2004	2006	2008	2011
Liberal	41.3% **177**	38.5% **155**	40.8% **172**	36.7% **135**	30.2% 103	26.2% 77	18.9% 34
PC	16.0% 2	18.8% 20	12.2% 12	—	—	—	—
Reform Party/ Canadian Alliance[1]	18.7% 52	19.4% 60	25.5% 66				
Conservative[2]	—	—	—	29.6% 99	36.3% **124**	37.6% **143**	39.6% **166**
NDP	6.9% 9	11.0% 21	8.5% 13	15.7% 19	17.5% 29	18.2% 37	30.6% 103
BQ	13.5% 54	10.7% 44	10.7% 38	12.4% 54	10.5% 51	10% 49	6.0% 4
Green	—	—	—	4.3% 0	4.5% 0	6.8% 0	3.9% 1
Others	3.6% 1	1.6% 1	2.3% 0	1.3% 1	1.0% 1	1.2% 2	0.9% 0
Total valid votes	13,863,135	13,174,698	12,997,185	13,683,570	14,908,703	13,929,093	14,823,408
Voter turnout*	69.6%	67.0%	64.1%**	60.9%	64.7%	58.8%	61.1%
Total seats	295	301	301	308	308	308	308

[1]The Canadian Reform Conservative Alliance replaced the Reform Party of Canada in the 2000 election.
[2]The Conservative Party of Canada was formed from the merger of the Progressive Conservatives and Canadian Alliance parties in December 2003.
*For earlier figures on voter turnout, see Elections Canada Voter Turnout, 1867–2008. www.sfu.ca/~aheard/elections/historical-turnout.html
**Official figure was 61.2% but Elections Canada later corrected this when they realized the voter's list was artificially inflated by almost a million duplicate names.
Source: T.J. Coulson, revised by S. Geobey (2007); Elections Canada, "Past Elections" (www.elections.ca).

smallest partisan core of the three national parties, as well as the least loyal (in terms of supporters' propensity to switch their vote to another party). This highlights a key task for the NDP: consolidating and maintaining their partisan base in the electorate to reduce potential volatility in the party's vote share (Gidengil et al., 2012: chap. 4). This undoubtedly was a factor in the choice of Quebecer Thomas Mulcair as the party's new leader in 2012, soon after that province's voters had awarded the majority of its seats to the NDP.

After three consecutive elections that returned minority parliaments (2004, 2006, 2008), with the Conservatives forming the government following Paul Martin's brief period as prime minister, Stephen Harper finally won a majority victory in 2011 (see Table 12.2). This sequence of four elections in seven years transformed the dynamics of party competition in Canada, first by progressively shaking loose Liberal voters to the benefit of the Conservatives, and secondly by transferring the votes of francophone Quebecers from the BQ to the NDP. This left a political landscape that would have been almost unimaginable a decade previously: a majority Conservative government, the NDP as official opposition on the strength of its popularity in Quebec, the Liberals struggling with their humiliating relegation to third place, and the BQ—the party of choice for francophone Quebecers for almost two decades—reduced to a mere handful of seats.

These dramatic changes in electoral outcomes cannot be explained solely by the gradual shifts taking place in the size and composition of each party's core support base, though this is certainly a relevant factor, especially the shrinking Liberal base and the apparent loss (finally) of its privileged position with Catholic voters (Gidengil et al., 2012: 175). Short-term factors played a role, too, particularly the issue of the sponsorship scandal in Quebec, which was a key factor in the decline of Liberal fortunes in the 2004 and 2006 elections and in changing the relative electoral position of Canadian parties (Gidengil et al., 2012: 94–96, 173–74). Leader evaluations were also a factor, though much less determinant than is often portrayed in media coverage (Gidengil et al., 2012: 114), while another media trope lacking evidence in voter surveys is the idea that Canadians gave a majority to the Conservatives in 2011 because of their growing aversion to minority governments (Gidengil et al., 2012: chap. 8).

Conclusion

Over the past several decades political parties in Canada have gone through a series of reforms to their organizational structures, financing, and leadership selection processes. This has created broadened and more diversified membership bases and party caucuses, extensive public regulation of the raising and spending of monies, and more democratic and participatory methods of leadership selection. Yet in some important ways the parties have not changed much in their mode of operation or their basic functions in Canadian democracy. They remain leader-dominated organizations (arguably more than ever) with centralized decision-making over policy and strategy. Member involvement is largely restricted to candidate recruitment and leader selection (though even the latter is beginning to escape the remit of party members, as shown by the 2013 Liberal leadership contest). Nonetheless, political parties remain crucial to the democratic process by structuring the vote, organizing government and opposition, and providing voters with alternative programs and leaders from which to choose.

Over time, both individual parties and the party system as a whole have experienced dramatic changes. The Mulroney interlude and the collapse of the third party system that followed revealed the rewards but also the perils for parties involved in brokerage politics and coalition-building across regions and language groups in Canada. Brian Mulroney's success in maintaining the Progressive Conservatives' western base of support while extending the party's appeal to French-speaking Quebecers provided his party with two consecutive majorities and seemed to herald an end to the perpetual dominance in federal politics of the Liberal Party of Canada. However, the regional and ideological fault lines created by such an ungainly coalition—with western conservatives and Quebec nationalists harbouring opposing views on the constitution, Canadian identity, and the level and scope of state spending on social programs—widened amidst unresolved fiscal, economic, and constitutional problems. In 1993 the grand coalition underlying the electoral success of the Mulroney PC Party split along regional, ideological, and linguistic lines, to be only partially reassembled a decade later with the merger creating the new Conservative Party.

The national patchwork of party support created by the 1993 election constituted the most regionalized and ideologically polarized party system in Canadian history. Atlantic Canada, Quebec, Ontario, and the West all became discrete regional arenas of electoral politics, with each exhibiting different patterns of party competition. Yet even before this, truly national party competition in Canada was sporadic at best, and there is little indication that the future will be any different. The Westminster system of one-party government inherited by Canada works reasonably well when there are two national parties: a governing party and an official opposition that has a reasonable prospect of replacing the government. For most of the time since the election of 1921, this was not the case, usually to the benefit of the Liberals (though more recently the Conservatives) as the only party in a position to govern. Exacerbation of the tendency to regional fragmentation has been accompanied by growing levels of voter dissatisfaction and alienation from the political system. It seems paradoxical, then, that several attempts to reform an electoral system that consistently fails to accurately reflect voter preferences have been rejected by citizens in provincial referenda (see Tanguay, Chapter 13 of this book).

Perhaps Canadian voters do exhibit a declining allegiance to political parties and a pervasive pragmatism that lacks any consistent ideological outlook, with the result that all parties are now exposed to more volatility and insecurity in the political marketplace. On the other hand, Canada may simply represent, in its own way, the characteristics of a European-style multiparty system, with each party cultivating its own relatively stable base of support within the electorate, reliant upon core supporters that are sociologically and ideologically predisposed to their programs and appeals. Electoral shifts, when they inevitably occur, will happen within broad "ideological families" of like-minded parties, rather than across the main ideological rift that separates the left from the right (Nevitte et al., 2000). As argued by Gidengil et al. (2012), while issues and leadership have from time to time made a significant difference in party fortunes, of greater continuous import has been the persistence of core electorates that are "tethered" to particular parties—or party types—as a function of their social and regional characteristics, fundamental values and beliefs (ideological orientation), and established partisan allegiances.

While this description of the Canadian party system would suggest a basic similarity with European-style multipartism, a key difference is that Canada's political institutions are not well designed to accommodate a large measure of cooperation and power sharing between two or more competing but like-minded parties. Yet given the embedded regional fragmentation and more recently the ideological polarization of Canada's electorate and party system, clinging to the traditional way of doing things is becoming an option increasingly harder to justify and defend.

Notes

1 Social Credit would hold power for the next 36 years in the province of Alberta and for the better part of four decades in British Columbia; the CCF would win power in the western province of Saskatchewan in 1944, the first socialist party to form a government in North America.

2 Examples of the former include the CCF-NDP and the Reform Party; of the latter, Social Credit and the Bloc Québécois.

3 The United Farmers, Social Credit, CCF, NDP, and Saskatchewan Party in western Canada; the NDP in Ontario; the Union Nationale and Parti Québécois in Quebec.

4   For example, this was the case for decades with the federal and provincial Liberal parties in Quebec, while in the 2008 federal election the provincial Conservative government in Newfoundland and Labrador ran an ABC (anyone but Conservative) campaign against their federal counterpart.

5   Such was the case, for instance, with regard to Canada's system of public health care, which was first instituted by an NDP government in the province of Saskatchewan. Family policy innovations were pioneered by the Parti Québécois. And the western-based Reform Party was the first to fully embrace the neoliberal critique of big government, prescribing lower taxes, spending cuts, deregulation, and decentralization as the cure for Canada's ills.

6   In this connection, see the work of Ronald Inglehart, Neil Nevitte, and others who have studied the changing values and attitudes of citizens in the advanced industrial countries, and on this basis developed their post-materialism thesis of value change (Nevitte, 1996; Inglehart, 1997).

7   The political economy work of Anthony Downs is usually credited with providing the intellectual foundations for this approach to party and voter behaviour (Downs, 1957).

8   This approach to voting studies is closely associated with the social-psychological model of voter behaviour developed by researchers at the University of Michigan, who were motivated to do so by perceived shortcomings of the established Columbia model, which relied heavily on the distribution of social background characteristics of voters to explain election outcomes (Gidengil et al., 2012: 8). Campbell et al. (1960) were pioneers of this social-psychological approach.

9   This sociological approach is often referred to as the Columbia school (see Note 8 above), and is associated in the first instance with the work of Paul Lazarsfeld et al. (1944).

10 Using data from a series of Canadian Election Studies, and employing a multistage model of statistical analysis, the researchers—Elizabeth Gidengil, Neil Nevitte, André Blais, Joanna Everitt, and Patrick Fournier—constructed a composite model of vote choice that seeks to incorporate all of the major explanatory factors associated with the three models introduced to the reader in the preceding paragraphs (Gidengil et al., 2012: chap. 1).

References and Suggested Readings

Adams, Michael. 2009. *Fire and Ice: The United States, Canada and the Myth of Converging Values*. Toronto: Penguin Canada.

Bakvis, Herman. 1991. *Regional Ministers: Power and Influence in the Canadian Cabinet.* Toronto: University of Toronto Press.

Bakvis, Herman. 2000–01. "Prime Minister and Cabinet in Canada: An Autocracy in Need of Reform?" *Journal of Canadian Studies* 35 (4): 60–79.

Bakvis, Herman, and A. Brian Tanguay. 2012. "Federalism, Political Parties, and the Burden of National Unity: Still Making Federalism Do the Heavy Lifting?" In *Canadian Federalism: Performance, Effectiveness, Legitimacy*, 3rd ed., eds. H. Bakvis and G. Skogstad, 112–33. Toronto: Oxford University Press.

Bashevkin, Sylvia. 1991. *True Patriot Love: The Politics of Canadian Nationalism.* Toronto: Oxford University Press.

Belanger, Éric. 2007. "Third Party Success in Canada." In *Canadian Parties in Transition*, 3rd ed., eds. A.B. Tanguay and A.-G. Gagnon, 83–109. Peterborough: Broadview Press.

Berger, Carl. 1976. *The Writing of Canadian History.* Toronto: Oxford University Press.

Bickerton, James. 1997. "Crime et Châtiment: Le Parti Progressiste-Conservateur du Canada entre 1984 et 1993." *Politique et Sociétés* 16 (2): 117–44. http://dx.doi.org/10.7202/040069ar.

Bickerton, James. 2007. "Between Integration and Fragmentation: Political Parties and the Representation of Regions." In *Canadian Parties in Transition*, 3rd ed., eds. A.B. Tanguay and A.-G. Gagnon, 411–35. Peterborough: Broadview Press.

Bickerton, James. 2010. "Political Parties and Democracy in Canada: Regional Fragmentation, Institutional Inertia, and Democratic Deficit." In *Political Parties and Democracy: Volume 1: The Americas*, eds. Kay Lawson and Jorge Lanzaro, 3–26. New York: Praeger.

Bickerton, James, Alain-G. Gagnon, and Patrick Smith. 1999. *Ties That Bind: Parties and Voters in Canada.* Toronto: Oxford University Press.

Blais, André. 2005. "Accounting for the Electoral Success of the Liberal Party in Canada." *Canadian Journal of Political Science* 38 (December): 821–40.

Blais, André, Elisabeth Gidengil, Richard Nadeau, and Neil Nevitte. 2002. *Anatomy of a Liberal Victory: Making Sense of the Vote in the 2000 Canadian Federal Election.* Peterborough: Broadview Press.

Blake, D. 1979. "1896 and All That: Critical Elections in Canada." *Canadian Journal of Political Science* 12 (2): 259–80. http://dx.doi.org/10.1017/S0008423900048113.

Bradford, Neil. 1999. "Innovation by Commission: Policy Paradigms and the Canadian Political System." In *Canadian Politics*, 3rd ed., ed. J. Bickerton and A.-G. Gagnon, 541–64. Peterborough: Broadview Press.

Bricker, Darrell, and John Ibbitson. 2013. *The Big Shift: The Seismic Change in Canadian Politics, Business and Culture and What it Means for our Future.* New York: Harper Collins.

Brodie, J., and J. Jenson. 1996. "Piercing the Smokescreen: Stability and Change in Brokerage Politics." In *Canadian Parties in Transition*, 2nd ed., eds. A.B. Tanguay and A.-G. Gagnon, 52–72. Toronto: Nelson.

Brodie, Janine, and Jane Jenson. 1980. *Crisis, Challenge and Change: Party and Class in Canada.* Toronto: Methuen.

Cairns, Alan C. 1968. "The Electoral System and the Party System in Canada, 1921–1965." *Canadian Journal of Political Science* 1 (1): 55–80. http://dx.doi.org/10.1017/S0008423900035228.

Cairns, Alan C. 1977. "The Governments and Societies of Canadian Federalism." *Canadian Journal of Political Science* 10 (4): 695–725. http://dx.doi.org/10.1017/S0008423900050861.

Campbell, Angus, Philip Converse, Warren Miller, and Donald Stokes. 1960. *The American Voter*. New York: John Wiley.

Carty, R.K. 1993. "Three Canadian Party Systems: An Interpretation of the Development of National Politics." In *Canadian Political Party Systems*, ed. R.K. Carty, 563–86. Peterborough: Broadview Press.

Carty, R.K. 2002. "The Politics of Tecumseh Corners: Canadian Political Parties as Franchise Operations." *Canadian Journal of Political Science* 35 (04): 723–45. http://dx.doi.org/10.1017/S0008423902778402.

Carty, R.K., and W. Cross. 2010. "Political Parties and the Practice of Brokerage Politics." In *The Oxford Handbook of Canadian Politics*, eds. J.C. Courtney and D.E. Smith, 191–207. New York: Oxford University Press. http://dx.doi.org/10.1093/oxfordhb/9780195335354.003.0011.

Carty, R.K., William Cross, and Lisa Young. 2000. *Rebuilding Canadian Party Politics*. Vancouver: University of British Columbia Press.

Carty, R. Kenneth, William Cross, and Lisa Young. 2000–01. "Canadian Party Politics in the New Century." *Journal of Canadian Studies* 35 (4): 23–39.

Clarke, H.D., J. Jenson, L. LeDuc, and J. Pammett. 1984. *Absent Mandate: The Politics of Discontent in Canada*. Toronto: Gage.

Coulson, T.J., revised by S. Geobey. 2007. "Statistical Appendices: Canadian Federal Election Results, 1925–2006." In *Canadian Parties in Transition*. 3rd ed., eds. A.-G. Gagnon and A.B. Tanguay, 518–48. Peterborough: Broadview Press.

Cross, William. 2004. *Political Parties*. Vancouver: University of British Columbia Press.

Docherty, David. 2004. "Parliament: Making the Case for Relevance." In *Canadian Politics*, 4th ed., eds. J. Bickerton and A.-G. Gagnon, 163–84. Peterborough: Broadview Press.

Downs, Anthony. 1957. *An Economic Theory of Democracy*. New York: Harper Collins.

Duverger, Maurice. 1951. *Les Partis Politiques*. Paris: Armand Colin.

English, John. 1977. *The Decline of Politics: The Conservatives and the Party System, 1901–1920*. Toronto: University of Toronto Press.

English, John. 2009. *Citizen of the World: The Life of Pierre Trudeau Volume One: 1919–1968*. Toronto: Vintage Canada.

Gagnon, A.-G., and A.B. Tanguay. 1996. "Minor Parties in the Canadian Political System: Origins, Functions, Impact." In *Canadian Parties in Transition*, 2nd ed., eds. A.-G. Gagnon and A.B. Tanguay, 106–35. Toronto: Nelson.

Gibbins, Roger. 2005. "Early Warning, No Response: Alan Cairns and Electoral Reform." In *Insiders and Outsiders: Alan Cairns and the Reshaping of Canadian Citizenship*, eds. Gerald Kernerman and Phillip Resnick, 39–50. Vancouver: University of British Columbia Press.

Gidengil, E., N. Nevitte, A. Blais, J. Everitt, and P. Fournier. 2012. *Dominance and Decline: Making Sense of Recent Canadian Elections*. Toronto: University of Toronto Press.

Goldfarb, M., and T. Axworthy. 1988. *Marching to a Different Drummer: An Essay on Liberals and Conservatives in Convention*. Toronto: Stoddart.

Grant, George. 1970. *Lament for a Nation*. Toronto: McClelland and Stewart.

Inglehart, Ronald. 1997. *Modernization and Postmodernization: Cultural, Economic and Political Change in 43 Societies*. Princeton: Princeton University Press.

Johnston, R., A. Blais, H.E. Brady, and J. Crête. 1992. *Letting the People Decide: Dynamics of a Canadian Election*. Montreal: McGill-Queen's University Press.

Johnston, Richard. 1992. "The Electoral Basis of Canadian Party Systems, 1878–1984." In *Canadian Political Party Systems*, ed. R. Kenneth Carty, 587–623. Peterborough: Broadview Press.

Johnston, Richard. 2005. "The Electoral System and the Party System Revisited." In *Insiders and Outsiders: Alan Cairns and the Reshaping of Canadian Citizenship*, eds. Gerald Kernerman and Phillip Resnick, 51–64. Vancouver: University of British Columbia Press.

Johnston, Richard. 2010. "Political Parties and the Electoral System." In *The Oxford Handbook of Canadian Politics*, eds. J.C. Courtney and D.E. Smith, 91–207. New York: Oxford University Press. http://dx.doi.org/10.1093/oxfordhb/9780195335354.003.0012.

Lazarsfeld, Paul, Bernard Berelson, and Hazel Gaudet. 1944. *The People's Choice: How the Voter Makes Up His Mind in a Presidential Campaign*. New York: Columbia University Press.

LeDuc, Lawrence. 2007. "Realignment and Dealignment in Canadian Federal Politics." In *Canadian Parties in Transition*, 3rd ed., eds. A-G. Gagnon and A.B. Tanguay, 163–78. Peterborough: Broadview Press.

Lipset, Seymour Martin. 1990. *Continental Divide: The Values and Institutions of the United States and Canada*. London: Routledge.

MacIvor, Heather. 2003. *Women and Politics in Canada*. Peterborough: Broadview Press.

Macpherson, C.B. 1962. *Democracy in Alberta*. 2nd ed. Toronto: University of Toronto Press.

Martin, Lawrence. 2003. *Iron Man: The Defiant Reign of Jean Chrétien*. Toronto: Viking.

Morton, William. 1991. "The Progressive Tradition in Canadian Politics." In *Party Politics in Canada*, 6th ed., ed. H. Thorburn, 318–23. Scarborough: Prentice Hall.

Nevitte, Neil. 1996. *The Decline of Deference: Canadian Value Change in Cross-National Perspective*. Peterborough: Broadview Press.

Nevitte, Neil, André Blais, Elisabeth Gidengil, and Richard Nadeau. 2000. *Unsteady State: The 1997 Canadian Federal Election*. Don Mills: Oxford University Press.

Newman, Peter C. 1963. *Renegade in Power: The Diefenbaker Years*. Toronto: McClelland and Stewart.

Noel, Sid. 2007. "Leaders Entourages, Parties, and Patronage." In *Canadian Parties in Transition*, 3rd ed., eds. A.-G. Gagnon and A.B. Tanguay, 197–214. Peterborough: Broadview Press.

Paltiel, Khayyam. 1987. "Canadian Election Expense Legislation 1963–1985: A Critical Appraisal or Was the Effort Worth It?" In *Contemporary Canadian Politics*, ed. R. Jackson, 228–47. Scarborough: Prentice Hall.

Perlin, George. 1988. *Party Democracy in Canada: The Politics of National Party Conventions*. Scarborough: Prentice Hall.

Pinard, Maurice. 1975. *The Rise of a Third Party*, enlarged ed. Montreal: McGill-Queen's University Press.

Porter, John. 1965. *The Vertical Mosaic: An Analysis of Social Class and Power in Canada*. Toronto: University of Toronto Press.

Preyra, Leonard. 2001. "From Conventions to Closed Primaries? New Politics and Recent Changes in National Party Leadership Selection in Canada." In *Party Politics in Canada*, eds. H. Thorburn and A. Whitehorn, 443–59. Toronto: Prentice Hall.

Russell, Peter. 1966. *Nationalism in Canada*. Toronto: McGraw Hill.

Savoie, Donald. 1999. *Governing from the Centre: The Concentration of Power in Canadian Politics*. Toronto: University of Toronto Press.

Sayers, Anthony. 2002. "Regionalism, Political Parties, and Parliamentary Politics in Canada and Australia." In *Regionalism and Party Politics in Canada*, eds. Lisa Young and Keith Archer, 209–21. Don Mills: Oxford University Press.

Scott, F.R. 1967. "WLMK." In *The Blasted Pine*, 36. Toronto: Macmillan.

Siegfried, André. [1907] 1966. *The Race Question in Canada.* Toronto: McClelland and Stewart.

Simeon, Richard. 1975. "Regionalism and Canadian Political Institutions." *Queen's Quarterly* 82 (4): 499–511.

Simpson, Jeffrey. 2001. *The Friendly Dictatorship.* Toronto: McClelland and Stewart.

Smiley, Donald, and Ronald L. Watts. 1986. *Intrastate Federalism in Canada, Research Studies: Royal Commission on the Economic Union and Development Prospects for Canada,* vol. 39. Toronto: University of Toronto Press.

Smith, David E. 1985. "Party Government, Representation and National Integration in Canada." In *Party Government and Representation in Canada, Peter Aucoin, research coordinator, Research Studies: Royal Commission on the Economic Union and Development Prospects for Canada,* vol. 36, 1–68. Toronto: University of Toronto Press.

Smith, Denis. 1973. *Gentle Patriot: A Political Biography of Walter Gordon.* Edmonton: Hurtig.

Tanguay, A.B. 1994. "The Transformation of Canada's Party System in the 1990s." In *Canadian Politics,* 2nd ed., eds. J. Bickerton and A.-G. Gagnon, 113–40. Peterborough: Broadview.

Tanguay, A.B. 2003. "Political Parties and Canadian Democracy: Making Federalism Do the Heavy Lifting." In *Canadian Federalism,* eds. Herman Bakvis and Grace Skogstad, 296–315. Don Mills: Oxford University Press.

Tanguay, A.B. 2009. "Reforming Representative Democracy." In *Canadian Politics,* 5th ed., eds. J. Bickerton and A.-G. Gagnon, 221–48. Toronto: University of Toronto Press.

Thomas, Paul. 1985. "The Role of National Party Caucuses." In *Party Government and Regional Representation in Canada, P. Aucoin, research coordinator, Research Studies: Royal Commission on the Economic Union and Development Prospects for Canada,* vol. 36, 69–136. Toronto: University of Toronto Press.

Thorburn, Hugh. 1991. "Interpretations of the Canadian Party System." In *Party Politics in Canada,* 6th ed., ed. H. Thorburn, 114–24. Scarborough: Prentice-Hall.

Valpy, Michael. 2008. "The Growing Ideological No Man's Land," *Globe and Mail,* September 21.

Wearing, Joseph. 1981. *The L-Shaped Party: The Liberal Party in Canada 1958–1980.* Toronto: McGraw-Hill Ryerson.

Westwood, Rosemary. 2013. "Explainer: What Comes Next in the Liberal Vote?" *Maclean's Magazine,* April 5. www2.macleans.ca/2013/04/05/the-liberal-leadership-vote-who-what-where-when-how-could-it-go-wrong/

Whitaker, Reginald. 1977. *The Government Party: Organizing and Financing the Liberal Party of Canada, 1930–1958.* Toronto: University of Toronto Press.

Wolinetz, Steven. 2007. "Cycles and Brokerage: Canadian Parties as Mobilizers of Interest." In *Canadian Parties in Transition,* 3rd ed., eds. A.-G. Gagnon and A.B. Tanguay, 179–96. Peterborough: Broadview Press.

Wood, L.A. 1975. *A History of Farmers' Movements in Canada: The Origins and Development of Agrarian Protest 1872–1924.* Toronto: University of Toronto Press.

thirteen

The Limits to Democratic Reform in Canada

A. BRIAN TANGUAY

Canadians, for the most part, appear to be quite happy with the way their political system in general is functioning. Ask them whether they are satisfied with the way democracy works in their country, and a solid majority will answer yes. This has been the case in a wide variety of public opinion surveys conducted since the late 1990s, although the size of the majority has fluctuated from the mid 50s to the low 70s over this period. Moreover, Canadians are inordinately proud of their polity and much more likely than their counterparts in the United States to believe that the basic rights of citizens are well protected by their political system. Many scholars share this exuberance about Canadian democracy: in his assessment of the work of the Democratic Audit project,[1] R. Kenneth Carty baldly declared that "most comparative measures suggest that Canada and Canadians have built one of the most successful societies and polities anywhere" (Carty, 2010: 244).

Despite this prevailing optimism, there are a few disquieting signs of what one group of researchers refers to as a "weakness in Canada's democratic fabric" (Gidengil, Nadeau, Nevitte, and Blais, 2010: 95) and others simply label a "democratic malaise" (Law Commission of Canada, 2004: 3) or a "democratic deficit" (Axworthy, 2003–04; Martin, 2002–03; Norris, 2012). Voter turnout in this country, at both the federal and provincial levels, is low by international standards and with very few exceptions seems to be declining with each successive election. Young voters in particular are often uninterested in or disengaged from the traditional mechanisms of representative democracy. And Canadians of all ages combine an immoderate pride in their democratic system with a deep, corrosive distrust of the institutional actors that work within it—political parties, most obviously, but also the media, Parliament, and the prime minister himself.

This cynicism about the political class has no doubt deepened since the Conservative Party and Stephen Harper came to power in January 2006. Over the course of the past seven years, Canadians have witnessed the prorogation of Parliament—not once but *twice*—essentially for partisan purposes: first in November 2008 to allow the ruling party to avoid certain defeat in the House of Commons and thwart the formation of a Liberal-NDP coalition government, and a second time a year later to hamstring opposition questioning about the Afghan detainees affair.[2] The "robocalls" scandal that came to light in the aftermath of the 2011 federal election (Canada, Chief Electoral Officer, 2013); unsavoury revelations in the spring of 2013 about questionable expenses made by several senators, including such high-profile Harper appointees as Mike Duffy, Pamela Wallin, and Patrick Brazeau (Collenette, 2013); and widespread concern over the hypercentralization of power in the PMO and obsessive attention to information control under Harper have also raised fundamental questions about the health and effectiveness of our democratic institutions (see Chapters 7, 8, and 9 by Savoie, Docherty, and Thomas in this volume).

These two seemingly contradictory elements of the same reality—voters' untrammelled faith in the democratic polity combined with their deep distrust of key political institutions, or more precisely, the actors operating within them—provide some insight into the limits to democratic reform in Canada. As the next section of the chapter shows, there are compelling reasons to be worried about the long-term health of our democratic polity. Subsequent sections of the chapter will demonstrate, however, that the majority of voters do not appear to believe that the democratic deficit, if it exists, can be remedied by substantive institutional reform, such as a more proportional electoral system, let alone by relatively minor tinkering such as the implementation of fixed election dates or new rules for financing parties and election campaigns. Moreover, on the issue of electoral reform, its advocates have not been able to convince voters that there is a link between a more proportional electoral system, on the one hand, and more transparent and responsive governance on the other. The prospects for major democratic reform in Canada, therefore, appear to be limited.

One caveat lector: the focus here will be on a limited number of possible democratic reforms of the middle range: fixed election dates, tightened rules regarding party and election finance, and a more proportional electoral system. So-called mega-constitutional reform, such as restructuring or abolishing the Senate, is beyond the scope of this chapter.

Democratic Malaise in Canada? Good News ... Bad News

In a 26-nation survey of attitudes toward democracy and governance in the Americas, conducted in 2012, Canadians rank among the most satisfied in the hemisphere with respect to the state of democracy in their country.[3] Seventy per cent of Canadians indicated that they were either satisfied or very satisfied with the way democracy works in their country, a figure exceeded only in Uruguay, with 79 per cent (see Table 13.1a). Canadians also exhibited a great deal of pride in their political system, as the data in Table 13.1b show. Again, the citizens of only one other country—in this case Nicaragua—had higher levels of pride in their political system. Finally, Canadians, by a substantial margin, were the most likely among the 26 countries surveyed to believe that their political system does a good job of protecting citizens' rights, although the authors of the AmericasBarometer report caution that "a majority (59%) do not have a clear opinion" on this question (Environics Institute, 2012a: 6).

Data from the Canadian National Election Studies (CNES) over the past decade reinforce the findings of the AmericasBarometer. Figure 13.1 shows that levels of satisfaction with democracy increased quite markedly between the 2004 and 2008 elections, from 56 per cent in 2004, to 62 per cent in 2006, and to 71 per cent in 2008. It dropped to 65 per cent in 2011,

Table 13.1 Attitudes toward Democracy in the Americas, 2012

A: In general, would you say that you are very satisfied, satisfied, dissatisfied, or very dissatisfied with the way democracy works in your country?[†]

	Canada	USA	Mexico	S. America[‡]	Caribbean[§]
%	70	50	46	62	50
N[*]	1501	746	726	10848	2927

[†]Figures in each cell represent the "net satisfied"—the percentage of respondents who are either "very satisfied" or "satisfied."

B: To what extent do you feel proud of living under the political system of [your country]?[**]

	Canada	USA	Mexico	S. America[‡]	Caribbean[§]
%	39	31	28	20	19
N[*]	1501	1499	1537	18983	5891

C: To what extent do you think that citizens' rights are well protected by the political system?[**]

	Canada	USA	Mexico	S. America[‡]	Caribbean[§]
%	29	14	21	14	11
N[**]	1501	1499	1510	18800	5852

[*]Ns are unweighted.
[**]For Tables 13.1b and 13.1c, responses are on a 7-point scale, where 1 = "not at all" and 7 = "a lot." Figures in each cell represent the percentage of respondents in each country or region in the two highest categories (6 and 7).
[‡]South America includes 12 countries (Venezuela, Guyana, Suriname, Colombia, Ecuador, Peru, Bolivia, Brazil, Paraguay, Chile, Uruguay, and Argentina). The figure in the cell represents the average for all 12 countries.
[§]Caribbean includes four countries (Jamaica, Dominican Republic, Haiti, and Trinidad and Tobago); the figure in the cell represents the average for all four countries.
Source: Environics Institute (2012b), Tables 29c, 29d, and 33.

Figure 13.1 Satisfaction with Democracy in Canada (Canadian Election Studies)

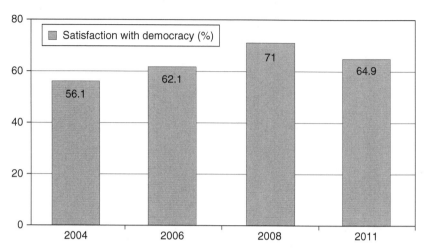

Source: Canadian Election Study (CES). 2004-2006-2008-2011 Merged File. http://www.queensu.ca/cora/ces.html

however, perhaps reflecting an elevation in voter fatigue caused by some of the shenanigans of the Harper governments—the prorogation crises, the muzzling of dissent within the ruling party, the seemingly paranoid and thin-skinned attitude toward criticism of any kind directed at the government.

It is also interesting to note that although a solid majority of Canadians in 2011 indicated that they were very satisfied or somewhat satisfied with the functioning of democracy in their country, there was a significant and politically relevant exception to this general rule: francophones in Quebec were much less satisfied than their anglophone or allophone counterparts in the province (see Table 13.2). Slightly less than half (49 per cent) of the francophones in Quebec expressed satisfaction with the way democracy works in Canada, almost 19 percentage points lower than the figure for the other linguistic groups in the province and 16 percentage points lower than the average for all 10 provinces. Whether the grievances of Quebec's francophones are primarily economic, political, or constitutional in nature—a subject beyond the scope of this chapter—these data point to a fundamental, still unresolved problem in the Canadian polity (see Gagnon, Chapter 5 in this volume).

In stark contrast to their generally positive evaluations of the overall health of their democratic system, Canadians reveal a deep distrust of specific political institutions in their country, as the data in Table 13.3, drawn from the AmericasBarometer, show. Political parties and the mass media are particularly

Table 13.2 Satisfaction with Democracy in Canada, 2011

Province	% net satisfied[*]
Alberta	77.8 (216)
Newfoundland	74.8 (151)
New Brunswick	73.9 (153)
Saskatchewan	73.5 (200)
Ontario	70.1 (1288)
Nova Scotia	68.5 (149)
British Columbia	68.1 (489)
Manitoba	68.0 (206)
Prince Edward Island	65.5 (145)
Quebec (total)	51.8 (1151)
Quebec (non-francophone)	67.3 (199)
Quebec (francophone)	48.7 (952)
Total	**65.1 (4148)**

[*]Ns are in brackets.
Source: Canadian Election Study, 2011. Investigators: Patrick Fournier, Fred Cutler, Stuart Soroka, Deitland Stolle. http://www.queensu.ca/cora/ces.html

distrusted, with only 6 and 10 per cent of Canadians respectively indicating that they have "a lot" of trust in them. This places Canadians down near the bottom of the 26 countries, along with the Americans, in terms of their distrust of these two important linkage institutions between citizens and the state. The prime minister in Canada does not elicit much more trust: 16 per cent of Canadians place themselves in the top two categories on this variable, a figure that is lower than all but three other countries in the survey—and significantly lower than the level of trust that Americans display in their president (27 per cent having "a lot" of trust in their head of government). Seventeen per cent of Canadians express a lot of trust in Parliament, a figure

Table 13.3 Political Trust in the Americas, 2012

To what extent do you trust:	Canada	USA	Mexico	S. America	Caribbean
Justice system	26	20	19	17	15
Armed forces	53	60	51	40	38
RCMP[†]	37	27	14	22	23
Parliament	17	6	24	16	15
Prime minister[**]	16	27	32	33	42
Supreme Court	34	20	23	21	16
Political parties	6	2	12	9	11
Mass media	10	4	29	37	36

[*]Responses are on a 7-point scale, where 1 = "not at all" and 7 = "a lot." Figures in each cell represent the percentage of respondents in each country or region in the two highest categories (6 and 7).
[†]Or national police force, depending on the country in question.
[**]Or president, depending on the country in question.
Source: Environics Institute (2012b): Tables 29f, 29g, 29h, 29i, 29j, 29k, 29l, and 29p.

that places them somewhere in the middle of the 26 countries surveyed. Only the Supreme Court (34 per cent) and the justice system in general (26 per cent) seem to garner the trust of a substantial portion of Canadians; in fact, Canada has the third-highest level of trust in its Supreme Court of the 26 countries included in the survey. The state institutions most trusted by Canadians are the armed forces (53 per cent) and the RCMP (37 per cent): these figures represent the second- and third-highest levels of trust respectively for these institutions among the countries surveyed.

Public mistrust of politicians and government has been growing stronger over the past three decades or so, not only in Canada but in most of the established democracies. An analysis of survey data from about 20 of the so-called Trilateral democracies[4] concluded that between the mid-1970s and the turn of the century there was a steady decline in public confidence in politicians in 12 out of 13 countries for which data were available. A similar decline in confidence in legislatures occurred in 11 out of the 14 countries. Over the same period, membership in political parties in most of these countries plummeted and the percentage of citizens expressing a partisan attachment (party identification) also declined significantly (Putnam, Pharr, and Dalton, 2000: 14, 17, 19). Membership in Canada's political parties continues to be extremely low even by these already low international standards (Carty, 2010: 227). Cross and Young (2004: 428) contend that "Canadian parties are generally in a less than healthy state. Few Canadians belong to political parties. Those who do belong are not representative of the general electorate, and for the most part their commitment to their parties—as demonstrated by contribution of volunteer labour—is relatively weak."

Politicians and political parties have become a lightning rod for voter discontent in Canada, as they have elsewhere in the industrialized democracies. Pammett and LeDuc (2003: 7), in their study of non-voters in the Canadian federal election of 2000, remark that there "is a widespread perception that politicians are untrustworthy, selfish, unaccountable, lack credibility, are not true to their word, etc." Or, to use the pithy formulation of the German essayist and social critic Hans Magnus Enzensberger, parties in the industrialized world "have degenerated into corrupt self-service stores"—at least in the view of large swathes of the electorates in these countries (1987: 81).

This deep-seated distrust of political parties and politicians is one factor among several contributing to rapidly declining voter turnout—the second major indicator of democratic malaise in Canada and most of the industrialized nations today. As Pammett and LeDuc (2003: 7) point out, an overwhelming majority of Canadians—almost 70 per cent—cite "negative public attitudes toward the performance of ... politicians and political institutions" as the principal factor underlying declining voter turnout in the country. Former Prime Minister Paul Martin, Jr., in a speech on parliamentary reform and public ethics that he delivered at Osgoode Hall in the fall of 2002, when he was still minister of finance in Jean Chrétien's government, noted that in the general elections of 1997 and 2000, non-voters outnumbered those who supported the winning party by a considerable margin. Martin acknowledged that particular circumstances in each election might account for some of the drop in political interest among voters, but he nonetheless argued that "at some stage we have to face up to the fact: *something is going wrong here, and in a fundamental way.* Casting a ballot is the most basic function of our democratic system. That so many Canadians choose not to do so is the political equivalent of the canary in the coal mine. ... far too many Canadians cannot be bothered to vote because they don't think their vote matters" (Martin, 2002–2003: 11; emphasis added).

Figure 13.2 displays data for turnout in federal elections in Canada from 1945 to 2011, expressed as a percentage of registered voters.[5] Through the first four decades of the postwar period, voter turnout averaged in the mid to high 70s; the sole exceptions were the elections of 1953 (68 per cent), 1974 (71 per cent), and 1980 (69 per cent). Pammett and LeDuc note that these three "exceptional" elections were held either at the height of summer (August 1953 and July 1974) or during the winter (February 1980). Each took place in an exceptional political situation as well: "The 1953 election came during a long period of one-party dominance. The 1974 and 1980

Figure 13.2 Turnout in Federal Elections, 1945–2011

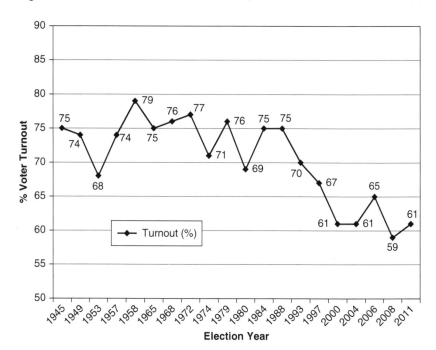

elections were occasioned by the fall of minority governments and held in a climate of relative public dissatisfaction with politics in general" (2003: 4).

Since 1988, however, turnout declined in each successive election until 2006: from 70 per cent in 1993, to 67 per cent in 1997, to 61 per cent in 2000 and 2004. The 2006 election, in which the Conservative Party under Stephen Harper succeeded in ousting the Liberals after a 13-year tenure in power, witnessed a small uptick in turnout, to 65 per cent. The competitiveness of this particular election, with the two major parties so evenly matched and the stakes of the outcome so high, was certainly a contributing factor in this increase. In 2008, however, several factors—confusing rules regarding voter identification, along with the existence of a contingent of demoralized Liberal supporters who could not bring themselves to vote for the distinctly uncharismatic Stéphane Dion and his Green Shift program (Heard, 2008)—contributed to a precipitous drop in turnout, to an historic low of 59 per cent. Turnout recovered modestly in the 2011 federal election, however, reaching 61 per cent in a contest that yielded Harper's long-sought majority government.

All 10 provinces have also experienced drops in voter turnout since 1990, as Table 13.4 illustrates. Most of these declines are quite substantial: a full 26

Table 13.4 Voter Turnout in Provincial Elections since 1990 (percentage of registered voters)

Province	First	Second	Third	Fourth	Fifth	Most Recent	Decline 1990–present
BC*	75 (1991)	72 (1996)	71 (2001)	62 (2005)	55 (2009)	52[†](2013)	−23
Alberta	60 (1993)	54 (1997)	53 (2001)	45 (2004)	41 (2008)	54 (2012)	−6
Sask.	83 (1991)	65 (1995)	66 (1999)	71 (2003)	76 (2007)	67 (2011)	−16
Manitoba	69 (1990)	69 (1995)	68 (1999)	54 (2003)	57 (2007)	56 (2011)	−13
Ontario	64 (1990)	63 (1995)	58 (1999)	57 (2003)	52 (2007)	48 (2011)	−16
Quebec	82 (1994)	78 (1998)	70 (2003)	71 (2007)	57 (2008)	75 (2012)	−7
NB	80 (1991)	75 (1995)	76 (1999)	69 (2003)	68 (2006)	70 (2010)	−10
NS	75 (1993)	69 (1998)	68 (1999)	66 (2003)	60 (2006)	58 (2009)	−17
PEI	81 (1993)	86 (1996)	85 (2000)	83 (2003)	84 (2007)	77 (2011)	−4
NL	84 (1993)	74 (1996)	70 (1999)	72 (2003)	61 (2007)	58 (2011)	−26

*Turnout in British Columbia is calculated both as the percentage of *eligible* voters who voted and the percentage of *registered* voters who cast a ballot. The figures in this row are based on registered voters, to keep the data comparable with the other provinces. The turnout figures most widely reported in the BC media are based on eligible voters, which depresses the rate considerably.
†Unofficial results. See Huffington Post Canada (2013).

Sources:

BC: http://www3.elections.bc.ca/index.php/resource-centre/statistics-and-surveys/
Alberta: http://www.elections.ab.ca/
Saskatchewan: http://www.elections.sk.ca/publications/reports
Manitoba: http://www.electionsmanitoba.ca/downloads/HistoricalSummary.pdf (1990–2007) and http://www.electionsmanitoba.ca/downloads/PDF_Summary_GE2011.pdf (2011)
Ontario: http://www.elections.on.ca/en-CA/Tools/PastResults.htm
Quebec: http://www.electionsquebec.qc.ca/francais/provincial/resultats-electoraux/elections-generales.php
New Brunswick: http://www.gnb.ca/elections/publications-e.asp#1
Nova Scotia: http://electionsnovascotia.ca/sites/default/files/Comparative%20Stats%202009.pdf
PEI: http://www.electionspei.ca/pdfs/statistics.pdf
Newfoundland and Labrador: http://www.elections.gov.nl.ca/elections/ElectionReports/index.html

percentage points in Newfoundland and Labrador and around 20 points in British Columbia, from 75 per cent in 1990 to the low 50s in 2013.[6] Nova Scotia (−17), Ontario (−16), and Saskatchewan (−16) have also witnessed dramatic drops in voter turnout since 1990. In 6 of the 10 provinces, turnout in the most recent elections has been less than 60 per cent of registered voters. Only PEI (−4) and Quebec (−7) have been able to resist this trend somewhat; in both provinces, turnout remains in the mid-70s, although it dipped down to 57 per cent in the 2008 election in Quebec. The drop in voter turnout in Alberta has been comparatively small, at six percentage points, but this province has always had historically low turnout rates in comparison with the other provinces.

Canada is not unique in experiencing a drop in voter turnout since the end of World War II. Wattenberg (2000: 71) has observed that declining turnout is a "nearly universal" trend in the OECD countries: of the 19 states included in his study, turnout figures during the 1990s were in most cases substantially lower than those of the early 1950s. In Switzerland, turnout in the two elections before 2000 was 24 percentage points lower than the figure for the first two elections of the 1950s. Comparable declines occurred in New Zealand (18 points), France (13 points), and Austria (12 points). Only Denmark and Sweden resisted this trend: in each, there has been an increase in turnout of four percentage points over this period. Wattenberg (2000: 71) remarks that "[i]t is rare within comparative politics to find a trend that is so widely generalizable." This trend was largely confirmed in a later study undertaken by the International Institute for Democracy and Electoral Assistance (Ellis, 2004: 8): "average turnout for elections to national parliaments in Western Europe has indeed declined since the early to mid-1990s."

Widespread disengagement of young voters constitutes the third indicator of democratic malaise in Canada. As Thomas Axworthy puts it, "turnout has not declined in the electorate as a whole but it has fallen like a stone among Canadians born after 1970" (2003–04: 16). Pammett and LeDuc's study of non-voters in the 2000 federal election demonstrates that Canadians born after 1975 were far less likely to vote than their elders. Only 22 per cent of voters between the ages of 18 and 20, and 28 per cent of those aged 21 to 24, bothered to vote. Voter turnout increased with each successive age cohort: 83 per cent of voters 68 years or older cast a ballot in 2000, as did 80 per cent of those aged 58 to 67. A more recent review of the empirical evidence suggests that Pammett and LeDuc may have underestimated turnout among young voters in the 2000 federal election. Nonetheless, the basic trend they identified holds true in subsequent elections: turnout among the group of voters most likely to go to the polls—those aged 65 to 74—"has been more or less double that of young adults under twenty-five in each of the ... three federal elections" held between 2004 and 2008 (Howe, 2010: 7).

Young voters are not necessarily more cynical about politics than their older counterparts—in fact they are slightly less so (Blais et al., 2002: 54)—but they are markedly less interested in or informed about politics than any previous generation. They are, in the words of Gidengil et al., a "tuned out" generation rather than a "turned off" one (2003: 11; cf. Blais et al., 2002: 57, 61). In addition to their lack of interest in politics generally and in the nuances of particular election campaigns, young voters (aged 18 to 25) are more likely to experience problems with the registration process (getting their names on the permanent voters' list) than any other group of voters, apart from those over 65 years of age. Young voters are also most likely to report that they were simply too busy with work or family or school to get out to the polling station (Pammett and LeDuc, 2003: Table 12). This suggests that a combination of administrative reasons and lack of interest in and knowledge about politics prevents young Canadians from voting in higher numbers. The former, at least, might be rectified through the use of new technologies—like the Internet—for registration and voting itself. The latter, however, constitutes a much more intractable problem: strategies for increasing young voters' awareness of and interest in politics include more intensive instruction of civics and government at the high school level, but there is no guarantee that this will make a dent in the turnout rates among youth (see the discussion in Pammett and LeDuc, 2003: 52–59).

Rampant distrust of the major political institutions in the country, declining voter turnout at both the federal and provincial levels, and high levels of political disengagement among the young in Canada: these three trends documented above were certainly evident in the early 2000s to political decision makers in the country. Growing concern over the democratic malaise in Canada prompted several provincial governments to investigate ways of improving the responsiveness of representative institutions in their jurisdictions. In March 2003, the Quebec government's Estates-General on the Reform of Democratic Institutions (better known as the Béland Commission) issued a report in which the democratic deficit was highlighted as a prominent theme. Over the course of its public consultations, the Béland Commission met numerous citizens who complained that existing democratic institutions seem to lack real power, that decision-making authority is centralized in the hands of the political executive, that excessive party discipline disempowers elected representatives, and that women, ethnic minorities, and Aboriginals continue to be underrepresented in the legislature and other government bodies (Québec, Comité directeur des États généraux sur la réforme des institutions démocratiques, 2003: 22–23). The Commission made several far-reaching recommendations to improve democratic performance in the province, among them the adoption of a new electoral system based on regional proportional representation, fixed dates for elections, a law permitting citizen initiatives, and direct election of the head of government.

Similar consultative initiatives were undertaken in several other provinces. In British Columbia, the Liberal government of Gordon Campbell adopted a law in 2001 setting a fixed date for future provincial elections. It also created an independent Citizens' Assembly consisting of individuals drawn randomly from the BC voters' list (two from each of the 79 constituencies) and charged it with reviewing the strengths and weaknesses of the existing first-past-the-post electoral system (Ruff, 2003). In Ontario, the government of Dalton McGuinty established a Democratic Renewal Secretariat and announced plans "to reach out to Ontarians and engage them in the most ambitious democratic renewal process in Ontario history, including fixed election dates, new ways to engage young people and innovative tools that could include Internet and telephone voting" (Ontario, Ministry of the Attorney General/ Democratic Renewal Secretariat, 2003). In New Brunswick, Premier Bernard Lord fulfilled one of his election promises by establishing a Commission on Legislative Democracy, whose mandate was to "examine and make recommendations on strengthening and modernizing New Brunswick's electoral system and democratic institutions and practices to make them more fair, open, accountable and accessible to New Brunswickers" (New Brunswick, 2003). Finally, the government of Pat Binns in Prince Edward Island set up a one-man Commission on Electoral Reform under the Honourable Norman Carruthers, which issued its final report in December 2003, recommending the adoption of a German-style mixed member proportional (MMP) electoral system in the province (Prince Edward Island, Commissioner of Electoral Reform, 2003: ch. 9).

What did this brief flurry of democratic reform initiatives yield in terms of concrete policies? Disappointingly little, as it turns out. In the next section we will examine two reforms that did emerge out of this period of introspection about the root causes of and possible solutions to our democratic malaise. We will then turn to a discussion of the still unreformed electoral system in the country and explore both the possible reasons for the apparent failure of electoral reform and what this might mean for the future health of our democratic polity.

Mostly Quiet on the Democratic Reform Front

One popular reform at both levels of government in the past decade has been the adoption of fixed election dates, in an effort to remove or minimize the presumed electoral advantage that redounds to the governing party when it can determine by itself the timing of an election. The federal government (2007) and nine provinces—British Columbia (2001), Newfoundland and Labrador (2004), Ontario (2005), New Brunswick (2007), Saskatchewan (2008), Prince Edward Island (2008), Manitoba (2008), Alberta (2011), and Quebec (2013)—along with the Northwest Territories (2006), have all adopted legislation establishing fixed election dates (Canada, Parliament, n.d.; Canadian Press, 2013). However, as several critics have pointed out, Stephen Harper was able to circumvent his own law when trying to manufacture a dissolution of Parliament in 2008—so that his party could profit from favourable public opinion at the time—a tactical manoeuvre that "makes it apparent that even such a limited reform may be of uncertain value" (White, 2010: 59).

A more significant reform, modelled on the pioneering legislation enacted by the Parti Québécois during its first mandate in 1977—and later adopted by the NDP government of Manitoba in 2000—was in the area of party finance. In this case, it was the Liberal government of Jean Chrétien that took the lead. During his 10 years as prime minister, Chrétien gave few indications that he thought the modernization and revitalization of the structures of representative democracy were urgent priorities. Chrétien was a reactive rather than an innovative leader, content to work within the institutions and mores of political life as he had found them when he assumed office. It was only when Paul Martin's accession to the leadership of the Liberal Party became inevitable that Chrétien began to think about his legacy as prime minister and focus on restoring public confidence in representative government. Chrétien's hand was also forced by Auditor General Sheila Fraser's report in the spring of 2002, which first raised concern about questionable spending under the sponsorship program, and by several other comparatively minor scandals at this time.

On June 11, 2002, Chrétien outlined an eight-point action plan on ethics in government in a speech in the House of Commons. A key item in this action plan was a proposed overhaul of the *Canada Elections Act* to ban contributions by corporations and trade unions to political parties. Chrétien's intention was to restore the public's faith in the democratic system, which was being eroded by the perception—rooted in ignorance, in the view of many Liberal MPs—that large contributions to political parties by their friends in the corporate sector were buying access to government decision makers and favourable policies.

Bill C-24, "An Act to Amend the Canada Elections Act and the Income Tax Act (Political Financing)," was tabled in the House of Commons on January 29, 2003 and received royal assent on June 19 of that year. At the time of its introduction, Don Boudria, House Leader, claimed that the proposed law would enhance "the fairness and transparency of our political system by ensuring that full disclosure of contributions and financial controls would apply to all political participants. ... Together these reforms [will] increase the confidence of Canadians in our electoral system" (Canada, Parliament, 2003: 2849). The bill represented the most significant reform of Canada's election finance laws since the 1974 *Election Expenses Act* established the existing regime of party finance, one based on spending limits for candidates and parties, disclosure of campaign expenses and contributions, and partial public reimbursement of election expenditures (Canada, Library of Parliament, Parliamentary Research Branch, 2003: 1–2).

In addition to severely restricting corporate and union contributions to parties and candidates, and establishing limits on individual donations (initially set at $5,000 annually, since reduced to $1,000), Bill C-24 provided for annual public subsidies of registered political parties, intended to compensate them for foregone revenue from the now drastically reduced corporate and trade union donations. The law initially set the subsidy at $1.75 (subsequently raised to $2) per vote received by the party in the previous election, for any registered party winning more than two per cent of the popular vote, or five per cent of the vote in those ridings where it ran candidates.

This provision of the legislation quickly became its most controversial feature. The Conservative Party, which emerged as the most successful fundraiser—by far—under the new dispensation, was unalterably opposed to any form of state "allowance," arguing that existing tax credits and other financial inducements were more than sufficient to subsidize party activities. Shortly after being returned to power with a second consecutive minority government in October 2008, the Harper administration unveiled a fiscal update that was supposedly intended to outline Canada's response to the quickly accelerating meltdown in the world economy. Not only did the update adopt a perplexingly complacent attitude toward the crisis—Finance Minister Jim Flaherty portrayed Canada as the lone western country capable of navigating the extremely perilous financial situation without implementing bailouts or other stimulus measures—but it included several nakedly partisan provisions. Among the latter was the elimination of the per-vote subsidy to qualifying registered political parties. Flaherty's fiscal update precipitated the parliamentary crisis that ultimately led to the nascent Liberal-NDP coalition and Harper's tactical prorogation of Parliament (Valpy, 2009: 8–17). In the midst of this crisis, the Conservative government backed away from its pledge to abolish the per-vote subsidy.

Once he had achieved his long coveted majority government in 2011, however, Stephen Harper homed in on the party allowance yet again. In the massive budget implementation bill introduced into the House in December 2011, the *Keeping Canada's Economy and Jobs Growing Act,* the Harper government announced that it would gradually phase out the subsidy over a period of four fiscal years, completely eliminating it by April 2015. Minister of State for Democratic Reform, Tim Uppal, announced that this measure would save taxpayers as much as $30 million a year. "Funding for political activities," he claimed, "should come from ordinary Canadians who choose to contribute—not from corporations, not from unions, and not from government" (Canada, Minister of State [Democratic Reform], 2012). Interestingly, this ban on party subsidies is one of the very few concrete measures highlighted on the website of the Minister of State for Democratic Reform, along with the government's continuing commitment to Senate reform and its legislation to redistribute seats in the House of Commons, the *Fair Representation Act,* which received royal assent in December 2011.

State funding of political parties can help to strengthen the quality of democracy, but it involves certain intrinsic risks as well. On the positive side of the ledger, state financing can, in theory, help divert some of a party's focus away from the accumulation of the money needed to harvest votes and direct it toward policy innovation and similar activities. In Canada, where the educational dimension of party life is particularly atrophied, this might improve the quality of democracy (see Cross, 2010a: 158–59). Clifford Lincoln, a Liberal MP from Quebec and former member of the provincial Liberal Cabinet of Robert Bourassa, articulated this idea in debates on the second reading of Bill C-24. Lincoln remarked that one of the positive features of Quebec's party finance law was that it

> made it possible to get additional funding directly to the political parties [and] allowed the parties to worry less about funding and focus more on policy, research, and groundwork with the voters. In fact, the party I belonged to had hundreds of thousands of members. It was always a lively and dynamic membership. There was no link between the legislation and decreased support in the party. On the contrary, it stimulated support within the party. (Canada, Parliament, 2003: 3485)

This was certainly true during the first 15 years or so in which the legislation was in effect. The need to solicit numerous small donations from individual voters to replace corporate and trade union funding forced both major parties to attend to their grassroots, and the Liberals eventually became something of a mass party, just like their competitor, the Parti Québécois. State funding served as a kind of emergency reserve for the parties, providing them with the necessary resources to fulfill their policy development and education functions between elections more successfully than many or even most other provincial political parties.

Over time, however, there has been growing concern that state funding is crowding out individual contributions as the principal source of party revenue: the major parties in Quebec, critics argue, have become addicted to state funds, limiting their ability to reach into and communicate with civil society. At the federal level, a 2007 study concludes that the presumed benefits of state funding of parties—augmenting their policy and educational functions—never did materialize: "there is little evidence to suggest state funding has liberated the parties to engage in more meaningful ways with the electorate. Parties have not taken on a more prominent role in policy development, mobilization of citizens, or public education with their new funds" (Young, Sayers, and Jansen, 2007: 352). Canada's parties continue in the main to be vote-harvesting machines.

There is one possible unintended consequence of Harper's abolition of the per-vote subsidy, however: as the Quebec case shows, eliminating corporate and union donations, while keeping individual contribution limits low, spurs parties to find illicit sources of the "mother's milk of politics." As we are learning in hair-raising detail from the revelations before Quebec's Charbonneau Commission of Inquiry into corruption in Montreal's construction industry, almost from the moment the PQ's new party financing regime was in place, major corporate donors and the parties themselves were crafting ingenious ways to circumvent its regulations. What is needed—not just in Quebec but in the other provinces and at the federal level as well—is much greater transparency on both the donation and spending sides of party finance. Perhaps a system of public accounts could be posted on the Internet, documenting not only whose money is going to which candidate and which political party, but also who is making policy decisions, whenever government at any level spends money.[7] For this to be more than a pipedream, the surveillance and investigation capabilities of the chief electoral officers in all jurisdictions would need to be beefed up considerably—an idea that the current Harper administration has given no indication of embracing (Wingrove, 2013).

Electoral Reform: Possible Solution to Canada's Democratic Malaise?

As noted above, five provincial governments in the early 2000s explored the possibility of replacing the existing single-member plurality (SMP) or first-past-the-post (FPTP) system with a more proportional alternative. Electoral reform also became the focal point for civil society organizations— groups such as Democracy Watch, Fair Vote Canada, and the *Mouvement pour une démocratie nouvelle* (MDN)—that sought to revitalize representative democracy in Canada. This despite the fact that Canada had long established itself as one of the advanced democratic countries most resistant to any discussion of electoral reform (Weaver, 2001: 542–44).

At the federal level, the Law Commission of Canada, an independent federal agency that used to advise Parliament on how to improve and modernize Canada's laws—it was abolished by the Harper government in 2006—submitted a report to the minister of justice in early 2004 urging the adoption of a mixed member proportional electoral system, modelled on the one in use for the Scottish Parliament, as a necessary step in promoting a more representative political system (Law Commission of Canada, 2004).[8] In its report, *Voting Counts*, the Law Commission acknowledged that FPTP has undeniable virtues, especially its simplicity (to the "average" voter), ease of administration, promotion of territorial representation (the link between the voter and "his/her" MP in a defined constituency), fostering of accountability (voters can identify the decision makers—parties—to either reward with re-election or punish after their term in office), and, finally, its ability (in theory, at least) to produce strong, stable majority governments (Law Commission of Canada, 2004: 12).

It has become increasingly obvious in recent years, however, not just to activists critical of the status quo but to many ordinary voters as well, that these virtues come at a very high price. The catalogue of defects in FPTP is well known and does not need a lengthy rehearsal here. But among them we might flag the following:

- It provides the first-place finisher with an electoral "bonus" and thereby translates a plurality of votes into an artificial legislative majority. This is one of the chief reasons that the federal Liberal Party was granted a seemingly permanent monopoly on power at the federal level from 1993 until the mid-2000s, and why the Conservatives under Stephen Harper appear poised to reap those same benefits with a still-divided opposition.
- It contributes to the regionalization of the country, and to the perception that the West, for example, is "Conservative" country, and that Ontario from 1993 to 2000 was a one-party (Liberal) bastion.
- It allows the governing party, with its artificially swollen legislative majority, to dominate the political agenda almost completely for a period of four or five years, thereby contributing to the marginalization of Parliament. By the mid-1970s political scientists were bemoaning the hypercentralization of power in the hands of the prime minister, who was acting more and more like an American-style president without any of the checks and balances built into the republican

system that is used south of the border. Few would deny that this process has accelerated since that time, first under Jean Chrétien and most recently under Harper, with his iron-fisted control over government messaging, his cabinet ministers, and the civil service (Martin, 2010; Coyne, 2013).

- It wastes a large number of votes: unless a voter supports the winning candidate in a given riding, there is effectively no connection between the voter's choice and the eventual make-up of the House of Commons.
- It excludes new voices—like those in the Green Party, for instance—from the legislature.
- It poses artificially high barriers to the election of female, minority, and aboriginal candidates. This was one of the arguments made by advocates of PR as long ago as the 1850s: that the FPTP system did not do a good job of electing minority candidates. John Stuart Mill attacked FPTP for its tendency to elect "mediocre party 'hacks'" (quoted in Carstairs, 1980: 193).

Two basic alternatives to the existing first-past-the-post system were recommended by the advocates of democratic reform in Canada in the early 2000s: some form of *hybrid* or *mixed member proportional* (MMP) system was the preferred option in Quebec, PEI, New Brunswick, and Ontario, while a variant of the *single transferable vote* (STV) was recommended by the Citizens' Assembly in British Columbia. Under STV, voters rank candidates on their ballots, from favourite to least preferred; elections are held in multi-member ridings (Law Commission of Canada, 2004: 22).[9] This electoral system, in use in the Republic of Ireland and Malta, produces reasonably proportional results and is, in the estimation of one study, "the most sophisticated of all electoral systems, allowing for choice between parties and between candidates within parties" (Reynolds and Reilly, 1997: 83).

In MMP systems, currently in use in Scotland, Wales, New Zealand, and Germany, among other jurisdictions, voters are normally given two votes on the ballot paper, one for a single candidate in their riding, and another for a party. Voters are free to "split their ticket"—to vote, for example, for the Green Party and the NDP candidate in their riding. A party's share of the party vote determines its share of the seats in the legislature; the number of constituency seats a party wins is subtracted from its proportional allotment, and the remaining seats are filled from party lists (Law Commission of Canada, 2004: 90). Depending on the ratio of constituency seats to list seats,[10] the results are usually highly proportional: that is, if a party wins 20 per cent of the party vote, it will gain very close to 20 per cent of the seats in Parliament. By combining increased proportionality with the territorial representation that is the hallmark of first-past-the-post, MMP systems are thought to "combine the best of both worlds" (Shugart and Wattenberg, 2001).

A more proportional electoral system could help to address the democratic malaise in several ways. First of all, it might help boost voter turnout. In a study done for the International Institute for Democracy and Electoral Assistance, Richard Rose (2004: 22) found that the existence of PR in a country was second in importance only to compulsory voting (as found in Belgium and Australia, among other countries) as factors that raised voter participation in elections. PR systems are also likely to lower the barriers to the representation of new voices—like those of the environmental movement, for example—in Parliament. The entry of new parties like the Greens into the legislature might serve to generate increased interest in politics among young voters, who are more likely than their older counterparts to support these non-mainstream parties. The party lists that are used in many PR systems might actually broaden the pool of potential candidates to include individuals who lack the wealth and extensive social networks that appear to be necessary to win a nomination in the existing system. Women and visible minority candidates will find it easier to win election to the legislature under PR than they do under the current system.

Most important of all, a more proportional electoral system would make majority governments a thing of the past; minority or coalition governments would become the norm, although a reasonable threshold (three to five per cent) could help weed out nuisance and extremist parties and ensure the election of only those organizations that enjoy substantial support among the voters. For its proponents, this feature of PR is one of its greatest strengths: coalition governments would force the parties to cooperate with one another, thereby reducing the mindless adversarialism that is endemic in the existing system. Moreover, the need to form coalition governments would, in theory at least, place limits on executive power. Of course, opponents of PR see this feature of the system in a darker light: instability and paralysis, according to the critics, are likely to become permanent features of the political landscape if a PR system were adopted.

As the data in Table 13.5 indicate, the electoral reform proposals, with one exception, were defeated decisively in provincial referendums, with support for an alternative to FPTP failing even to pass the 40 per cent threshold. Researchers have cited several different factors in trying to explain the referendum outcomes. Pilon (2010: 74) emphasizes elite manipulation of the referendum process: each time an electoral reform proposal was put to the citizens of a province, Pilon argues, political elites devised "numerous innovative ... barriers against change"—such as the unprecedented

Table 13.5 Electoral Reform Referendums in the Provinces, 2005–2009

Province	Date of Referendum	Turnout (%)	% in favour of new system	Majority in favour of new system in how many ridings?
British Columbia	17 May 2005	61.5	57.7	77 out of 79
British Columbia	12 May 2009	55.1	39.1	8 out of 85
Prince Edward Island	28 November 2005	33.2[*]	36.4	2 out of 27
Ontario	10 October 2007	50.2[†]	36.9	5 out of 107

[*]This is an estimate, since no separate enumeration was done for the plebiscite. Elections PEI, in its report on the plebiscite, indicates that this turnout figure is based on the enumeration for the preceding provincial election, held in 2003.
[†]Ontario, unlike BC, calculated separate turnout figures for the referendum and the provincial election, with which it was being held concurrently. 111,766 voters in Ontario who cast ballots for a candidate did not mark the referendum portion of their ballot, Hence this turnout figure is lower than the reported average for the provincial election (52.1%).
All four referendums/plebiscites (PEI was the only province to use the latter designation) established a "supermajority" or threshold that support for the new electoral system would have to break before the referendum could be considered binding:
BC 2005: 60% of valid votes cast in at least 60% of the ridings (48 out of 79).
BC 2009: 60% of valid votes cast in at least 60% of the ridings (51 out of 85).
PEI 2005: 60% of valid votes cast in at least 60% of the ridings (16 out of 27).
Ontario 2007: 60% of valid referendum votes cast in at least 60% of the ridings (64 out of 107).
Sources:
BC: http://www.elections.bc.ca/docs/rpt/SOV-2005-ReferendumOnElectoral Reform.pdf
http://www.elections.bc.ca/docs/rpt/2009Ref/2009-Ref-SOV.pdf
PEI: Chief Electoral Officer (2005)
Ontario: http://www.elections.on.ca/NR/rdonlyres/61A53BBE-4F27-41F7-AF0E-5D3D6F8D153D/0/ReferendumStatisticalResults.pdf

super-majorities required to make the results binding. According to Pilon, this partially accounts for the near success of the first referendum in BC: established elites were insufficiently prepared to counter the spasm of populist outrage that nearly led to the adoption of STV. The hostility of mainstream political parties to any deviation from the status quo, or in some cases, the confused signals sent out by party elites on the desirability of electoral reform, also militated against successful electoral reform (Stephenson and Tanguay, 2009: 20–21; Fournier et al., 2011: 139–41). In all four provinces where referendums were held, widespread ignorance among voters about the basic features of the proposed alternatives to the first-past-the-post system was a primary contributor to the outcome (McKenna, 2006: 58–59; Pilon, 2010: 82).

Despite the demoralizing defeats suffered by the advocates of PR in BC, Ontario, and Prince Edward Island between 2005 and 2009, the window for significant electoral reform in the country has not closed entirely. Civil society organizations such as Fair Vote continue to wage an energetic campaign to change the country's electoral system, and the federal Liberal Party, in the wake of its humiliating reduction to third-party status in the 2011 election, passed a resolution supporting the adoption of "preferential voting"—a non-proportional system also known as the alternative vote or instant runoff voting (Liberal Party of Canada, 2012). Prospects for substantive electoral reform in Canada are dim, however, for three reasons. First, the mainstream parties will continue to act overtly or covertly against meaningful reform, because they view their chances of winning power as being maximized under the existing rules of the game. The closer a party gets to power, as with the federal NDP, the more likely it is to backpedal on previous commitments to electoral reform. Second, if reform proposals are put to a referendum, the decision will ultimately be made by a majority of voters who lack sufficient knowledge of or interest in the niceties of electoral system design and who are therefore most likely to opt for the status quo. This is the pessimistic conclusion drawn by Fournier et al. (2011: ch. 9) in their examination of the work of the Citizen Assemblies in BC, Ontario, and the Netherlands. Third, as Johnston, Krahn, and Harrison (2006: 175, 178) have pointed out, electoral reform proposals seem to many voters to be too "formal and abstract"; for most ordinary citizens, "concerns over the health of democracy are much more immediately rooted in a widespread general distrust in government as being too powerful and secretive than in concerns about the inadequacy of political institutions."

Conclusion

This chapter has reviewed the evidence that Canada is in the grip of a democratic malaise, despite the fact that large numbers of voters continue to express their overall satisfaction with the way their polity works. Virulent distrust of key political institutions such as political parties, the media, and Parliament; sharply declining rates of voter turnout at both the federal and provincial level over the past 25 years; and the rise of a disengaged cohort of young voters—these are all indicators that former Prime Minister Paul Martin was not far off the mark when he claimed that there was something fundamentally wrong with our political system.

Political elites in the country were certainly not unaware of these indicators of democratic malaise, and in the early part of the twenty-first century concerted efforts were made at both the provincial and federal level to improve the quality of democratic governance. As we have seen, however, relatively minor reforms such as the adoption of fixed election dates by the federal government, nine provinces, and the Northwest Territories have not had much of an impact in lessening voter cynicism. Stephen Harper himself demonstrated in 2008 that this legislation could easily be circumvented if partisan interests dictate it—at least when a minority government is in power. A more substantive reform, such as the Chrétien government's ban on corporate and union donations to political parties, along with its implementation of state subsidies for registered parties—which were designed to increase popular confidence in the country's electoral system and the parties themselves—has also had limited beneficial effect on political trust among voters. Some of the putative benefits of the legislation, such as strengthening the educational function of political parties and bolstering the ties between party elites and the organizational grassroots, have simply not been realized. Now that the Harper government is phasing out the per-vote subsidy of registered parties, Canadians are left with a political financing regime that seems ripe for abuse, since it combines a prohibition on corporate and union donations with very low individual contribution limits. If the Quebec experience is at all instructive, parties are going to seek out new and possibly illicit sources of money to fund their vote-harvesting operations, with attendant increases in voter cynicism. Finally, efforts to replace the existing first-past-the-post electoral system have failed in the face of elite intransigence and voter ignorance. Established elites within the mainstream political parties are wedded to the existing system, and, as Dennis Pilon (2010) has argued, they have worked diligently in each referendum to throw up ingenious obstacles to reform. Moreover, most voters have tended to see electoral reform as an abstract issue, championed by intellectuals and other heretics. Advocates of PR have not been able to convince sufficient numbers of voters that a new electoral system would help make government more transparent and trustworthy.

Some will argue that the limited success of democratic reform efforts in the first decade of the twenty-first century is of little consequence. What does it matter if electoral reform or attempts to clean up the realm of party finance fail, when a solid majority of voters continue to express their satisfaction with the state of democracy in the country? On this view, distrust of political institutions and of the political class will always exist as the background noise of Canadian political life. Advocates of democratic reform counter that poorly designed institutions create perverse incentives and thus have a way of inducing even the best and the brightest public servants to behave in less than salutary ways. For this reason, democratic reform is not simply a concern for intellectuals or geeks; it ought to be at the core of political debates in the country.

Notes

1 The Democratic Audit project brought together a team of social scientists who were asked to evaluate various components of Canada's political system according to the criteria of inclusiveness, participation, and responsiveness. This resulted in the publication of nine monographs in 2004 and 2005 on such topics as legislatures, executives, federalism, the media, political parties, and advocacy groups. See Cross (2010a) for a summary of the Democratic Audit project.

2 See Martin (2010) for a discussion of these two episodes. Additional sources on the "crisis of parliamentary government" precipitated by Harper's manoeuvres include Aucoin, Jarvis, and Turnbull (2011), Docherty (2010), Valpy (2009), and Weinrib (2009).

3 In the spring of 2012, the Latin American Public Opinion Project (LAPOP), housed at Vanderbilt University in Nashville, Tennessee, conducted a 26-country survey of citizens' attitudes toward democracy and governance. The Environics Institute for Survey Research conducted the Canadian portion of the survey. Total sample size for the 26 countries was just under 42,000 citizens aged 18 and over; the Canadian sample was 1,501. Online surveys were utilized in Canada and the United States; in the remaining countries, questionnaires were administered in personal interviews in people's homes. These differences in survey methodologies dictate that the results be interpreted with some caution, especially when making cross-national comparisons. Details of the survey methodology, sample sizes, and countries surveyed are available at the Environics Institute (2012a). For brief summaries of the main findings of the survey, see Neuman (2012) and Leblanc (2012).

4 The Trilateral countries include those of North America, Western Europe, and Japan. The Trilateral Commission, an influential private think tank founded in 1973 to foster cooperation among the three major democratic industrialized areas of the world on common problems facing them, issued a report on "governability" entitled *The Crisis of Democracy* (Crozier, Huntington, and Watanuki, 1975). The volume of essays edited by Pharr and Putnam was published to commemorate the 25th anniversary of the publication of this earlier Trilateral Commission study.

5 Voter turnout can be calculated as a percentage of registered voters or of the voting-age population (all citizens above the legal voting age). The United States employs voting-age population to determine voter turnout, while most jurisdictions in Canada use registered voters. The two methods yield quite different results. According to the International Institute for Democracy and Electoral Assistance (International IDEA, 2003), the voting-age population figures tend to be more accurate in countries where large numbers of voters are, for whatever reason, left off the register. Blais, Massicotte, and Dobrzynska (2003: 3), however, note that both methods have their biases, as voting-age population figures often include people who are not eligible to vote (such as recent immigrants), thus depressing the actual voter turnout figure.

6 Official figures for the election held on May 14, 2013 are not yet available. It is also important to remember—as I note in Table 13.4—that BC records turnout figures in two separate ways: as a percentage of registered voters and as a percentage of eligible voters. It is the latter figure that seems to be most often cited in the popular media, and this tends to be a bit lower than turnout as a percentage of registered voters.

7 This idea was raised in a discussion the author had with Henry Milner, political scientist at the Université de Montréal and co-editor of the journal Inroads. See Tanguay (2013).

8 The author of the present chapter helped draft the Law Commission report. He would like to stress that the views contained in this chapter are his alone, and do not necessarily reflect the opinions of any of the LCC's former commissioners.

9 For detailed descriptions of how STV and MMP work, see Law Commission of Canada (2004) and Reynolds and Reilly (1997).

10 In Germany, this ratio is 50:50, while in New Zealand it is 58:42. "In the Scottish Parliament, which consists of 129 members, 73 (57 per cent) are elected in constituencies by means of first-past-the-post and the remaining 56 (43 per cent) are awarded to regional lists" (Law Commission of Canada, 2004: 90). The Law Commission proposed that two-thirds of the members of the House of Commons be elected in constituencies on the basis of simple plurality voting, with the remaining one-third selected from party lists (2004: 104).

References and Suggested Readings

Aucoin, Peter, Mark D. Jarvis, and Lori Turnbull. 2011. *Democratizing the Constitution: Reforming Responsible Government.* Toronto: Emond Montgomery Publications.

Axworthy, Thomas S. 2003–04. "The Democratic Deficit: Should This Be Paul Martin's Next Big Idea?" *Policy Options* 25 (1, December-January): 15–19.

Blais, André, Elisabeth Gidengil, Richard Nadeau, and Neil Nevitte. 2002. *Anatomy of a Liberal Victory: Making Sense of the Vote in the 2000 Canadian Federal Election.* Peterborough: Broadview Press.

Blais, André, Louis Massicotte, and Agnieszka Dobrzynska. 2003. "Why is Turnout Higher in Some Countries than in Others?" Elections Canada (March). www.elections.ca

Canada. Chief Electoral Officer. 2013. *Preventing Deceptive Communications with Electors. Recommendations from the Chief Electoral Officer of Canada Following the 41st General Election.* Ottawa: Elections Canada. http://www.elections.ca/content. aspx?section=res&dir=rep/off/comm&document=index&lang=e

Canada. Library of Parliament. Parliamentary Research Branch. 2003. "Bill C-24: An Act to Amend the Canada Elections Act and the Income Tax Act (Political Financing)—Legislative Summary." LS-448E (Feb. 5, revised Feb. 11).

Canada. Minister of State (Democratic Reform). 2012. "Harper Government Highlights Taxpayer Savings Through Diminished Subsidies for Political Parties." News Release, May 17. http://www.democraticreform.gc.ca/eng/content/harper-government-highlights-taxpayer-savings-through-diminished-subsidies-poltical-parties

Canada. Parliament. 2003. *Debates.* 37th Parliament, 2nd Session. January—June.

Canada. Parliament. n.d. Fixed-Date Elections in Canada. http://www.parl.gc.ca/Parl Info/Compilations/ProvinceTerritory/ProvincialFixedElections.aspx

Canadian Press. 2013. "Nine Provinces Now Have Fixed Election Dates, After Quebec Adopts Measure," *Victoria Times-Colonist,* June 14. http://www.timescolonist.com/ nine-provinces-now-have-fixed-election-dates-after-quebec-adopts-measure-1.322192

Carstairs, Andrew McLaren. 1980. *A Short History of Electoral Systems in Western Europe.* London: George Allen & Unwin.

Carty, R. Kenneth. 2010. "Canadian Democracy: An Assessment and an Agenda." In *Auditing Canadian Democracy,* ed. William Cross, 223–46. Vancouver: University of British Columbia Press.

Collenette, Penny. 2013. "Mike Duffy Scandal Finds the Tories in a Moral Maze Without a Compass," *Globe and Mail,* May 16. http://www.theglobeandmail.com/commentary/ mike-duffy-scandal-finds-the-tories-in-a-moral-maze-without-a-compass/ article11959426/#dashboard/follows/

Coyne, Andrew. 2013. "Tory Government has Alienated Just About Everybody," *Montreal Gazette,* May 10.

Cross, William. 2010a. "Political Parties." In *Auditing Canadian Democracy,* ed. William Cross, 143–67. Vancouver: University of British Columbia Press.

Cross, William. 2010b. "Constructing the Canadian Democratic Audit." In *Auditing Canadian Democracy,* ed. William Cross, 1–17. Vancouver: University of British Columbia Press.

Cross, William, and Lisa Young. 2004. "The Contours of Political Party Membership in Canada." *Party Politics* 10 (4): 427–44. http://dx.doi.org/10.1177/1354068804043907.

Crozier, Michel, Samuel P. Huntington, and Joji Watanuki. 1975. *The Crisis of Democracy. Report on the Governability of Democracies to the Trilateral Commission.* New York: New York University Press.

Docherty, David. 2010. "Legislatures." In *Auditing Canadian Democracy,* ed. William Cross, 65–92. Vancouver: University of British Columbia Press.

Ellis, Andrew. 2004. "Introduction." In *Voter Turnout in Western Europe Since 1945*, 8–9. Stockholm, Sweden: International Institute for Democracy and Electoral Assistance (IDEA). http://www.idea.int/publications/voter_turnout_weurope/

Environics Institute. 2012a. *AmericasBarometer: The Public Speaks on Democracy and Governance Across the Americas. Canada 2012. Final Report*. http://www.environicsinstitute. org/uploads/institute-projects/environicsinstitute%20-%20americasbarometer%20 canada%202012%20final%20report.pdf

Environics Institute. 2012b. *AmericasBarometer 2012: International Data Tables*. http:// www.environicsinstitute.org/uploads/institute-projects/environics%20-%20 americasbarometer%202012%20-%20international%20banner%20tables%20-%20 nov%2014-2012.pdf

Enzensberger, Hans Magnus. 1987. *Europe, Europe*. Trans. Martin Chalmers. New York: Pantheon Books.

Fournier, Patrick, Henk van der Kolk, R. Kenneth Carty, André Blais, and Jonathan Rose. 2011. *When Citizens Decide: Lessons from Citizen Assemblies on Electoral Reform*. Oxford: Oxford University Press.

Gidengil, Elisabeth, André Blais, Neil Nevitte, and Richard Nadeau. 2003. "Turned off or Tuned out? Youth Participation in Politics." *Electoral Insight* 5 (2): 9–14.

Gidengil, Elisabeth, Richard Nadeau, Neil Nevitte, and André Blais. 2010. "Citizens." In *Auditing Canadian Democracy*, ed. William Cross, 93–117. Vancouver: University of British Columbia Press.

Heard, Andrew. 2008. "Historical Voter Turnout in Canadian Federal Elections and Referenda, 1867–2008." http://www.sfu.ca/~aheard/elections/historical-turnout. html

Howe, Paul. 2010. *Citizens Adrift: The Democratic Disengagement of Young Canadians*. Vancouver: University of British Columbia Press.

Huffington Post Canada. 2013. "Voter Turnout: B.C. Election Results 2013 by Numbers," May 15. http://www.huffingtonpost.ca/2013/05/15/voter-turnout-bc-election-results_n_3282380.html

International IDEA [Institute for Democracy and Electoral Assistance]. 2003. "Voter Turnout—A Global Survey." http://www.idea.int/vt/survey/voter_turnout.cfm

Johnston, W.A., Harvey Krahn, and Trevor Harrison. 2006. "Democracy, Political Institutions and Trust: The Limits of Current Electoral Reform Proposals." *Canadian Journal of Sociology* 31 (2): 165–82.

Law Commission of Canada. 2004. *Voting Counts: Electoral Reform in Canada*. Report submitted to the Minister of Justice (March).

Leblanc, Daniel. 2012. "Harper Among Least Trusted Leaders, Poll Shows," *Globe and Mail*, November 12. http://www.theglobeandmail.com/news/politics/harper-among-least-trusted-leaders-poll-shows/article5187774/

Liberal Party of Canada. 2012. *Biennial Convention* (13–15 January). http://convention. liberal.ca/governance/21-electoral-reform/

Martin, Lawrence. 2010. *Harperland*. Toronto: Viking.

Martin, Paul. 2002–03. "The Democratic Deficit." *Policy Options* 24 (1): 10–12.

McKenna, Peter. 2006. "Opting Out of Electoral Reform—Why PEI Chose the Status Quo." *Policy Options* (June): 58–61.

Neuman, Keith. 2012. "Canadians Widely Concerned About Income Equality: Survey," *Embassy*, November 19. http://www.embassynews.ca/print_out_story/32849

New Brunswick. (2003). "Premier Bernard Lord Creates Commission on Legislative Democracy." *News Release* (December 19). Available on-line at http://www.gnb.ca/ cnb/news/ld/2003e1208ld.htm

Norris, Pippa. 2012. "The Democratic Deficit: Canada and the United States in Comparative Perspective." In *Imperfect Democracies: The Democratic Deficit in Canada and the United States*, eds. Patti Tamara Lenard and Richard Simeon, 23–50. Vancouver: University of British Columbia Press.

Ontario, Ministry of the Attorney General/Democratic Renewal Secretariat. 2003. "McGuinty Government to Strengthen Our Democracy and Improve the Way Government Serves People." News Release, December 8. http://www.attorneygeneral.jus. gov.on.ca/english/news/2003/20031208-dr1.asp.

Pammett, Jon H., and Lawrence LeDuc. 2003. "Explaining the Turnout Decline in Canadian Federal Elections: A New Survey of Non-Voters." Elections Canada (March). www.elections.ca

Pilon, Dennis. 2010. "The 2005 and 2009 Referenda on Voting System Change in British Columbia." *Canadian Political Science Review* 4 (2–3): 73–89.

Prince Edward Island: Chief Electoral Officer. 2005. *Report of the Chief Electoral Officer of Prince Edward Island Plebiscite for the Mixed Member Proportional System*. Prince Edward Island: Chief Electoral Officer.

Prince Edward Island, Commissioner of Electoral Reform. 2003. *Report* (December 18). http://www.gov.pe.ca/photos/original/er_premier2003.pdf

Putnam, Robert D., Susan J. Pharr, and Russell J. Dalton. 2000. "Introduction: What's Troubling the Trilateral Democracies?" In *Disaffected Democracies*, eds. Susan J. Pharr and Robert D. Putnam, 3–27. Princeton: Princeton University Press.

Québec, Comité directeur des États généraux sur la réforme des institutions démocratiques [Béland Commission]. 2003. *Prenez votre place! La participation citoyenne au coeur des institutions démocratiques québécoises.* Quebec.

Reynolds, Andrew, and Ben Reilly. 1997. *The International IDEA Handbook of Electoral System Design*. 2nd ed. Stockholm, Sweden: International Institute for Democracy and Electoral Assistance (IDEA).

Rose, Richard. 2004. "Voter Turnout in the European Union Member Countries." In *Voter Turnout in Western Europe Since 1945*, 17–24. Stockholm, Sweden: International Institute for Democracy and Electoral Assistance (IDEA). http://www.idea.int/publications/ voter_turnout_weurope/

Ruff, Norman. 2003. "BC Deliberative Democracy: The Citizens' Assembly and Electoral Reform 2003–2005." Paper presented at the annual conference of the Canadian Political Science Association, Halifax, NS (June 1).

Shugart, Matthew Soberg, and Martin P. Wattenberg, eds. 2001. *Mixed-Member Electoral Systems: The Best of Both Worlds?* Oxford: Oxford University Press.

Simpson, Jeffrey. 2013. "Conservatives Have Been Sailing Close to the Wind." *Globe and Mail*, May 29. http://www.theglobeandmail.com/commentary/conservatives-have-been-sailing-close-to-the-wind/article12205395/#dashboard/follows/

Stephenson, Laura, and A. Brian Tanguay. 2009. "Ontario's Referendum on Proportional Representation: Why Citizens Said No." *IRPP Choices* 15 (September).

Tanguay, A. Brian. 2013. "The Stench of Corruption: Is Montreal Different, and If So, Why?" *Inroads* 33 (Summer/Fall): 90–92.

Valpy, Michael. 2009. "The 'Crisis': A Narrative." In *Parliamentary Democracy in Crisis*, eds. Peter H. Russell and Lorne Sossin, 3–18. Toronto: University of Toronto Press.

Wattenberg, Martin P. 2000. "The Decline of Party Mobilization." In *Parties without Partisans: Political Change in Advanced Industrial Democracies*, eds. Russell J. Dalton and Martin P. Wattenberg, 64–76. Oxford: Oxford University Press.

Weaver, R. Kent. 2001. "Electoral Rules and Electoral Reform in Canada." In *Mixed-Member Electoral Systems: The Best of Both Worlds?*, eds. Matthew Soberg Shugart and Martin P. Wattenberg, 542–69. Oxford: Oxford University Press.

Weinrib, Lorraine E. 2009. "Prime Minister Harper's Parliamentary 'Time Out': A Constitutional Revolution in the Making?" In *Parliamentary Democracy in Crisis*, eds. Peter H. Russell and Lorne Sossin, 63–75. Toronto: University of Toronto Press.

White, Graham. 2010. "Cabinets and First Ministers." In *Auditing Canadian Democracy*, ed. William Cross, 40–64. Vancouver: University of British Columbia Press.

Wingrove, Josh. 2013. "Elections Canada Chief Says Tories Not Consulting Him on Electoral Changes," *Globe and Mail*, May 28. http://www.theglobeandmail.com/news/politics/elections-canada-chief-says-tories-not-consulting-him-on-electoral-changes/article12197491/

Young, Lisa, Anthony Sayers, and Harold Jansen. 2007. "Altering the Political Landscape: State Funding and Party Finance." In *Canadian Parties in Transition*, 3rd ed., eds. Alain-G. Gagnon and A. Brian Tanguay, 335–54. Peterborough: Broadview Press.

fourteen
Political Communication in Canada: Strategies and Tactics

ALEX MARLAND

Introduction

This chapter argues that the communication strategies and tactics employed by political actors in Canada are becoming more sophisticated in response to new opportunities and competitive pressures. It begins with a review of theoretical concepts that continue to be applicable amidst technological change. This is followed by a summary of key considerations for managing personal and mass political communication. It suggests that political actors are increasingly interested in pinpointing targeted messages to narrow segments of the electorate through media channels that bypass journalists. While this is a more efficient way of communicating with Canadians, it comes at a cost of reducing the objectivity of the political information that they receive.

Concepts

The "permanent campaign" has come to characterize Canadian politics. Its roots are in American politics where it initially meant that a governing party should unabashedly avail itself of government resources to gain public support for its agenda (Blumenthal, 1980; Ornstein and Mann, 2000). It has evolved to describe the persistence of partisan electioneering by political parties and elected officials, even during governance periods between elections. In election campaigns, resources are devoted to local politicking within electoral districts, known as the "ground war," as compared to the broader narrative communicated through broadcast media known as the "air war." As the speed of political communication has intensified, the need to connect the air and ground war has increased, and political actors are pressed to manage a growing variety of contact points with the electorate throughout the electoral cycle. Advertising, fundraising, grassroots mobilization activities, rapid response messaging, polling, and a communications "war room" mentality have become a normal component of everyday politicking, as has the media's interest in "horse race" coverage of who is up or down, winning or losing. Contemporary political communication thus continually operates

309

with an urgency, intensity, and centralization that used to be identified only with election periods.

In Canada, permanent campaigning was clearly evident throughout the years of minority government between 2004 and 2011, when political parties braced for the possibility of a snap election. This was most apparent in the Conservative Party of Canada's negative advertising blitz directed first at Stéphane Dion and then Michael Ignatieff, after each in turn had assumed leadership of the Liberal Party of Canada (in 2006 and 2009, respectively). The pattern continued, however, even after the Conservatives gained their coveted majority in the 2011 election, such as when they were linked to phone calls spreading the false rumour that a veteran Liberal MP in Montreal would be resigning, and hired the defeated Conservative candidate to represent the government in that riding (Payton, 2012). While this constant communication and melding of the air and ground wars reflect the unrelenting battle for the voting sentiments of Canadians, it is still unclear how successful this strategy is over the long term. Deemed necessary to deny partisan opponents the opportunity to frame the debate in their favour, party strategists will nonetheless often describe all political communication before the televised leaders' debates (typically midway through an election campaign) as a "phony war," since most people do not pay close attention to electoral politics between elections. Effective or not, the permanent campaign is the "new normal" in Canadian politics (Rose, 2012: 149).

Constant political communication seeks to shape how citizens feel and think about political issues and leaders. This gives rise to tactics such as the party headquarters attempting to "spin" a topic with their preferred slant, authorizing which of their members are allowed to communicate publicly and instructing these representatives in what to say. The news media's response to such centralized communication varies. Media "lapdogs" are prone to repeating these centralized political messages for any number of reasons: because they share the same point of view, lack the resources to support proper investigative journalism, face the time pressures of the 24-hour news cycle, or simply have no other way to obtain the information that is fed to them. Political communications personnel exploit such media weaknesses by providing "information subsidies" such as news releases, opinion pieces, written quotes instead of interviews, and other free content, including postings on social media (e.g., Berkowitz and Adams, 1990). They stage news conferences, speeches, protests, and photo-ops that are so obviously designed to attract and shape media publicity that these are collectively known as "pseudo events" (Boorstin, 1992). Canadian media that are the most resistant to such tactics are well-resourced organizations with large audiences such as the Canadian Broadcasting Corporation (CBC) / Société Radio-Canada,

The Globe and Mail, the Toronto Star, and *La Presse.* These and other members of the Canadian Parliamentary Press Gallery (CPPG) are defenders of the fourth estate's institutional role in Canadian democracy. They fancy themselves as watchdogs with the capacity to filter political messages, integrate a variety of perspectives, and report on matters that would otherwise not be disclosed or exposed. Nevertheless, as newsroom budgets continue to shrink, and as the availability of information generally expands, all media organizations are under competitive pressure to avail themselves of politically managed and manipulated information subsidies.

Independent observers of Canadian politics have been especially concerned by the communications strategy of the Harper Conservative government. In 2010 the Canadian Association of Journalists (CAJ) issued an open letter to express concerns that democracy is being undermined. In the past, journalists were able to interview public servants who had expertise about a policy area, and could mine government sources for information; now, only designated ministers are authorized to speak on behalf of the government on the premise that it is members of cabinet, not bureaucrats, who are accountable for policy. Other frustrations cited by the CAJ include limited access to cabinet ministers (which often leaves them with no spokesperson to include in their stories); the government's thwarting of access to information requests; restrictions placed by communications staff on which journalists are permitted to ask questions of the prime minister; and constraints on the media's presence at staged events. The association reasoned that when journalists are prevented from properly doing their job:

> Genuine transparency is replaced by slick propaganda and spin designed to manipulate public opinion. The result is a citizenry with limited insight into the workings of their government and a diminished ability to hold it accountable ... This breeds contempt and suspicion of government ... This is not about deteriorating working conditions for journalists. It's about the deterioration of democracy itself. (Canadian Association of Journalists, 2010)

Another Canadian-based organization, the Centre for Law and Democracy (2013), has judged Canada's access to information regime to be on a steady decline, ranking 55th out of the 93 countries being evaluated in 2012. Academics such as Kirsten Kozolanka have also listed a variety of concerns, ranging from the sponsorship scandal under the Liberal governments of Jean Chrétien and Paul Martin, to the "communication by stealth" approach of Stephen Harper's Conservative government (Kozolanka, 2009, 2012). That the Conservative Party was able to win the most seats in 2011 without acquiescing to the demands of journalists for greater transparency and accessibility, or the concerns of think tanks and academics, is indicative that communications control can be made to work to partisan advantage. Political parties have found other ways to communicate their message to Canadians—or, at least, with selected segments of the electorate.

The culture of distrust between journalists and politicians has been likened to a downward spiral, whereby subversive political tactics breed negative reporting about politics, which contributes to public cynicism and civic disengagement (Cappella and Jamieson, 1997). While many are sympathetic to the position that the media should have greater access to government information and spokespersons, and trust journalists to objectively interpret partisan messages, one must consider why information limitations may be warranted. When reporters have unfettered access to politicians they may develop close personal relationships that inhibit their ability to be objective; they risk becoming information conduits (lapdogs). Journalists are not impervious to their own political biases. They may have their own political agenda and their reporting does not always treat their interviewees fairly (e.g., Miljan and Cooper, 2003). Moreover, the notion that journalists must rely on interviews is somewhat outdated. Copious amounts of information about government that was previously hidden from public view can be located online. This includes policy documents and details of ministers' expenses; accountability reports that did not previously exist (such as public opinion research and government advertising); responses to access to information requests that used to be proprietary to the requester; and, via the Government of Canada's Open Data portal (data.gc.ca), thousands of government datasets.

Even as their exclusivity over information wanes, media and political elites remain locked in a perpetual struggle of public persuasion, jockeying for power to frame events and control the public agenda (Nesbitt-Larking, 2001; Scheufele and Tewksbury, 2007). "Framing" refers to the manner in which subject matter is presented to audiences. Political actors are motivated to shape how a leader, an issue, or an opponent is presented with the belief that this will in turn influence citizens' perceptions. For instance, when a government announces cutbacks, it may frame this as a responsible decision made by strong economic stewards, whereas the opposition and interest groups will attempt to frame it as having dire consequences for vulnerable populations. When journalists filter these conflicting positions they must choose what frame to apply, and in addition may introduce their own. This competition for controlling not only how political information is framed but what deserves the public's attention is known as "agenda setting." It assumes that the greater the prominence that the mass media gives a topic, the more importance audiences will attach to the matter. People involved in politics are thus in a constant state of attempting to ensure that the issues they want citizens to think about are receiving major media coverage. They simultaneously attempt to frame how topics are presented as well as aim to limit attention to what they deem from a partisan perspective to be undesirable issues. Reporters, editors, and producers must sift through information subsidies, through "spin," through their own investigative work, and through other sources of information as they decide what deserves to be on the public agenda and what does not.

It is within this context that political elites collect and analyze public opinion data to help them identify what people think and what they want. They use this intelligence to devise strategy and set priorities, and to communicate their preferred political message in the most efficient way. This has given rise to what is known as political marketing: in effect, treating electors as consumers (Lees-Marshment, 2001). An idealistic view of marketing in politics holds that democracy is enriched by the process of using opinion research to objectively and scientifically establish citizens' needs and desires. Survey data and other market intelligence theoretically can inform decisions about public policy and political communication in a manner that prioritizes the electorate's preferences. However, this benign view overlooks that political leadership must make unpopular decisions, and that the public almost always lacks sufficient information or expertise to appraise the implications of most policies. Moreover, the reality of politics is that strategists use marketing foremost for their own partisan purposes rather than for the benefit of electors, and for their own ideological reasons irrespective of democratic purposes or ideals.

Personal Communication

Canada is a "mediated democracy," meaning that most Canadians obtain information about their elected representatives through the media, rather than through personal interactions. The exception is that during an election campaign, vote-hungry candidates engage in one-on-one political communication by talking to electors on their doorsteps and shaking hands, though in a large jurisdiction they cannot meet everyone. In between elections, elected officials may have a private conversation with their constituents by telephone or by email, or delegate this to their assistants. However, all forms of personal communication are time-consuming, so the task often falls to party workers and local volunteers.

To communicate in person with a large number of people, a politician may address groups by delivering speeches, participating in debates, or attending rallies. Years ago, candidates would address crowds from tree stumps, overturned soap crates, and temporary election structures known as hustings. They attended campaign picnics, which were literally outdoor lunches where electors munched on cold meats while listening to candidates and a brass band, and which were John A. Macdonald's "major campaign innovation" (Nolan, 1981: 33). Leaders covered large distances by train so as to greet waiting supporters and local notables at stops along the way. These tactics of yesteryear have given rise to idioms used in news coverage of Canadian elections such as a politician who is "stumping" for votes, an activist expressing their views from a "political soapbox," and a travelling candidate who is "on the hustings" or on a "whistlestop" tour. More modern ways of mixing with groups of electors include visiting retirement homes, coffee shops, and hockey arenas. These and other sheltered locations such as shopping malls were especially popular during the Canadian winter election campaign of 2005–06.

An important evolution in personal communication was direct marketing, whose sophistication has grown in tandem with computing. Direct marketing uses technology to facilitate personal interactions with a large universe of citizens and attempts to cultivate a relationship with this audience. Direct mail gives the illusion of personalized correspondence if the recipient's name is inserted in the salutation of a form letter, while telemarketing follows the same principle but by telephone. Computers, photocopiers, facsimile machines, and dramatically cheaper long-distance rates have contributed to the popularity of direct marketing because the same script can be easily customized for thousands of electors, each of whom can be reached without the editorial filter applied by the mass media, and without the knowledge (or ability to respond) of political opponents.

The practice of direct marketing has been evolving and in Canadian politics dates to at least the Brian Mulroney era in the 1980s (Taras, 1990: 186).[1] Computerized phone-dialing programs have been used in Canada since at least 1993 (Whitehorn, 1994) and their diminishing cost, ready availability, and precision have made them increasingly popular; by the 2011 general election campaign, robocalls and telephone town halls were commonplace. Direct mail is less popular in Canada, ostensibly because telemarketing offers better value for money. Incumbents may therefore seek to avail themselves of franking privileges that accompany holding elected office. In 2010 there was controversy over the Conservative and Liberal parties' use of parliamentary flyers known as "10 percenters" to mail out negative partisan messages. The media pressure culminated in a parliamentary ruling to discontinue that aspect of the permanent campaign, and since then political direct mail appears to have waned.

Direct marketing must draw upon a data set of names and contact details. In Canada the advent of sophisticated database management coincided with the transition from door-to-door enumeration of electors to the creation of a permanent National Register of Electors in 1997. Contact data for the 93 per cent of Canadian electors who are captured by the register are provided to Elections Canada by the Canada Revenue Agency, Citizenship and Immigration Canada, National Defence, driver's licence agencies, vital statistics agencies, and other political jurisdictions' lists, as well as by electors themselves (Canada, 2013). For each registered elector, Elections Canada maintains the name, mailing address, and a unique code for record management. These data are available in an electronic file to election candidates to assist them with identifying the vote. More significantly, the list is provided annually to political parties and members of Parliament, thereby facilitating a permanent campaign that includes direct communication, fundraising appeals, and membership recruitment. Political actors supplement the list with additional data provided by electors, such as information supplied to a party website or provided at a political event; by scrutinizing public records that identify the names of people who donated over $200 to a party or candidate; and voter identification results from the last election. The cost efficiencies and speed of electronic media are incentives for parties to build lists of elector email addresses, Facebook accounts, and Twitter handles. Canada's political parties maintain databases known as Liberalist, NDP Vote, and the Conservative "constituent information management system" (CIMS) to issue robocalls and emails to potential supporters to advise them of a local party event, to invite them to participate in a live group phone or video discussion, to remind them to vote, or to encourage them to donate, volunteer, or post a sign.

Mass Communication

Mass communication uses technology to reach hundreds, thousands, or even millions of citizens. If personal communication is foremost about quality (i.e., optimal targeting), then the overriding feature of mass communication is quantity. However, advertising to citizens through newspapers, radio, or television is expensive, and using media relations tactics such as pseudo events to earn free news coverage is a gamble. The evolution of information and communication technologies (ICTs) that permit the rapid, inexpensive, and targeted transmission of text, audio, and video through computers has permanently altered how political elites, journalists, and electors communicate with large numbers of people.

Several works have explored the evolution of Canadian political news media (e.g., Levine, 1993; Nesbitt-Larking, 2001; Taras, 1990; Sauvageau, 2012). It is reasonably well known that Canadian newspapers were organs of political parties in the nineteenth century and were used to promote propaganda; that newspapers' biased interpretation of parliamentary proceedings provoked the commissioning of official Hansard transcriptions beginning in 1875; that by World War I the partisan press gave way to more independent operations which became viable due to the considerable revenues generated from commercial advertising; and that newspapers and news magazines offer more in-depth coverage and analysis than broadcast media tend to do. The emergence of radio in the 1920s ended the print media's monopoly on mass communication. Elites could use their own voices to connect with the masses and the later emergence of political talk radio gave a voice to the concerns of average Canadians. During this period, some citizens obtained information about public affairs through news reels that were presented at movie theatres and, beginning in 1939, through National Film Board of Canada features about government policy (Druick, 2007). But it was when Canadians began buying TV sets in the 1950s that mass communication experienced its most dramatic change. From that point forward the importance of images, emotion, personalities, soundbites, symbols, and "cues" in politics would increase because, as observed by David Taras, paying close attention to the political process "seems a particular anathema to television because it is time consuming, cumbersome, difficult to explain, and involves meticulous detail" (Taras, 1990: 111). Television coverage of politics has evolved with the introduction of cameras into the House of Commons in 1977; the emergence of all-news programming on the CBC News Network in 1989; and the broader political coverage and availability of raw footage provided by the Canadian Public Affairs Channel (CPAC) in 1992. Canadian television's most recent foray into political news programming is the Sun News Network. Launched in 2011, it puts a conservative and populist slant on news coverage, similar to Fox News in the United States.

Sun News is an example of a phenomenon known as media convergence. The network is owned by Québecor Media, a conglomerate that operates the Sun newspaper chain, Videotron cable services, TVA broadcasting and magazine publishing, the Canoe online news portal, as well as a book publishing business, a music chain, a video distributor, and a video game development studio (Québecor, 2013). As media outlets are acquired or merged, and as identical content is communicated through multiple mediums, there are rising concerns about the implications of this degree of ownership concentration. The Canadian Radio-Television and Telecommunications Commission (CRTC), which regulates Canadian communications systems, has signalled that the concentration of ownership of wireless and Internet networks is a potential problem because Canadians are increasingly receiving information on laptops, smartphones, and tablets (Theckedath and Thomas, 2012). This matters because a political bias is discernible in the content of the news coverage provided by these massive corporate organizations (Taras, 1990: 48). Women, the working class, the poor, youth, the elderly, homosexuals, and religious groups are among the groups who are depicted by the mainstream media in "erratic, shallow and tokenistic" manners (Fleras, 2011: 3).

While television remains Canadians' preferred source of news, increasingly they are getting political information online, including from Facebook news feeds (Canadian Media Research Consortium, 2011). The emergence of ICTs in the 1990s led to the growing importance of campaign websites, political blogs, email blasts, social networking, and tweeting. This "democratization" of media is having profound consequences for the public sphere. The print media is in severe crisis because a "freebie culture" of news consumption has exacerbated the industry's difficulty in adapting to technological innovations (Sauvageau, 2012: 33), and newspapers are struggling to compete for advertising revenues (see, for instance, Table 14.1). The speeding up of information transfer means that complex policy or political matters can be reduced to short, sometimes superficial, messages. ICTs make it easier to coordinate petitions, to organize political events, to mobilize protests, and to draw attention to a call for action. Political actors create websites with provocative images whose existence is rapidly disseminated (and thereby promoted) by individual viewers and the mainstream media (Rose, 2012: 153). People tend to huddle in online communities that act as echo chambers reinforcing a particular view, rather than exposing themselves to a pluralistic range of opinion. Of course, whether all this is good or bad for Canadian democracy is a matter of opinion.

Well-known distinguishing features of Canadian political communication include the prevalence of two official languages and the funding of a public broadcaster (CBC/Radio-Canada). Official bilingualism matters because it means that in federal politics all communication is expected, if not required, to be in both official languages. As well, the tone of media coverage varies depending on language; French political journalists are often interested in reporting on different topics than their English counterparts and they tend to be more analytical (Taras, 1990: 76). But it is the so-called ethnic media whose political clout is increasing. There are nearly as many allophones— Canadians whose mother tongue is neither English nor French—as there are francophones, and the population of the former is growing faster than the latter (Canada, 2012a). The Conservative Party of Canada (Flanagan, 2009) and the Conservative government (Table 14.1) have targeted the hundreds of small newspapers, more than 20 radio stations, and a cluster of TV stations

Table 14.1 Government of Canada Media Placements (Agency of Record data, 2010–11)

Type of Media Advertising	Expenditures ($, millions)	Expenditures (% of total)
Cinema (i.e., movie theatres)	3.72	5.79
Internet (e.g., banner ads, search engine results)	9.38	14.58
Out-of-home (e.g., billboards, transit ads)	4.96	7.71
Print dailies/national news	2.79	4.34
Print magazines	3.56	5.53
Print weeklies/community (e.g., local, ethnic, and Aboriginal newspapers)	4.28	6.65
Radio	4.87	7.58
Television	30.79	47.83
Total	$64.35M	100%

Source: Canada (2012b).

(such as OMNI) that serve ethnic minority groups.[2] These operations are well suited to adapt to the Internet regardless of the size or geographic concentration of the populations they serve, or their financial, human, or technological resources. What Karim (2012: 179) calls "diasporic cybercommunities" includes the multitude of online news sites, blogs, social media, and listservs accessed by ethnic minorities, including recent immigrants, which can be used to urge action on domestic issues and transnational political causes.

Several further themes are worthy of mention. First, the relationship between political and media elites is "like a chess game" where each player seeks to exploit their symbiotic relationship and never truly trusts the other's motives or agenda (Taras, 1990: 47). Opposition politicians tend to be on chummy terms with reporters, but government officials must always be on guard (Levine, 1993: 334). Those in power develop friendly relations with some reporters to whom they divulge government news with a *quid pro quo* understanding that they will receive positive coverage in return. Conversely, they freeze out journalists whom they believe are antagonistic and even scold the political watchdogs when they disapprove of their reports (Levine, 1993: 218; Taras, 1990: 44, 125).

Second, political elites exploit norms of communication if it is in their interest to do so, while journalists decry any changes that curtail their ability to gather information. Message control and the centralization of communications is a trend that makes many journalists, scholars, and research-ers uneasy because it appears to undermine the democratic system of govern-ment (Kozolanka, 2009: 2012). Yet controlling information can be necessary to implement a political agenda that is deemed to be for the greater good and for which the governing party can claim to have obtained a mandate in the previous election. A journalist's career benefits when she receives exclu-sive insider information, while the media industry as a whole profits from controversy, be it a spokesperson going "off message" or a full-blown political scandal. Leaks and damage control abruptly shift the public's attention, which has varying implications for politicians and the government. During election campaigns, making available evidence of an opposing candidate saying some-thing unpalatable is a common tactic that detracts from more meaningful policy discourse (Marland, 2011: 185–186); during periods of governance, po-litical insiders with their own agendas feed the media stories for reasons that include cultivating a relationship with a reporter, leaking details of a policy, destabilizing opponents, and correcting false information (Taras, 1990: 83). An example of a high-profile leak occurred during the media frenzy over the Idle No More movement and the protest of Theresa Spence, the Chief of the Attawapiskat First Nation, who in early 2013 went on a hunger strike to pressure Prime Minister Harper to discuss treaty matters. The media's tone changed when a leaked audit of federal funding for the Attawapiskat First Nation revealed that $104 million of expenditure did not have proper docu-mentation (CBC News, 2013). The tactic succeeded in shifting the media coverage and illustrates how the media gravitates toward "what is episodic and ephemeral rather than thematic and enduring" (Rose, 2012: 151).

Third, journalists want to set the terms of communication with politi-cians, but are frustrated when these demands are rebuffed. Furthermore they may lack perspective. For instance, in Ottawa it is common for a throng of impatient reporters to circle around a politician, rudely shouting questions as they thrust microphones in their subject's face. Prime Minister Harper has been widely panned for not deigning to participate in such media scrums, for refusing to disclose when his Cabinet meets (thereby denying the media the opportunity to pounce on ministers), and for restricting the CPPG's ability to set the terms for their questioning. Furthermore, during the leader's tour in the 2011 election campaign, the Conservative campaign required assembled journalists to stand 10 metres away from Harper, who accepted a maximum of five questions per day. While these terms of engagement are worrying, they are not extraordinary. At one point during his tenure as prime minister, Louis St. Laurent went eight months between press conferences and broadcast media were not permitted to record them, but this was because the CPPG denied membership to broadcast reporters until 1959 (Levine, 1993: 186, 214; Taras,

1990: 72)! As well, Pierre Trudeau developed his own ways of bypassing the CPPG (Taras, 1990: 140). For instance, during the 1974 election campaign, he answered a total of six questions during a four-day train tour. After he was returned to power with a majority government, he stopped participating in scrums in favour of press conferences where his staff selected which reporters could ask questions (Levine, 1993: 287–290). Heads of government, regardless of party stripe or era, over time develop tense relations with journalists and devise tactics for managing their relationship with the media.

Fourth, the media is interested in political personalities and infotainment, and in turn politicians are concerned about their image. There is considerable research that indicates that a leader's image is related to their popularity and their ability to control the agenda (Mayer, 2004). As well, politics and popular culture are converging in a media environment that is fascinated with celebrity (Street, 2004). This importance of image management grew with television. Diefenbaker defeated St. Laurent in the 1957 election in large part because of how both men appeared on TV; television coverage of Lester Pearson emphasized his lack of charisma even though he was charming in person; and reporters sometimes paid more attention to Trudeau's personal life than to his politics (Levine, 1993: 248, 278). Under Harper, government resources are used by the Prime Minister's Office (PMO) to issue photos and video, sometimes of the Harper family, to the media (Marland, 2012). Innovations such as the permanent campaign, information subsidies, message targeting, and pseudo events are all practised in the name of framing the prime minister's image and increasing his ability to implement a political agenda.

Strategic Communication

This brings us to the current communication strategies and tactics employed by political parties. There is little doubt that political strategists' recommendations to leaders are fuelled by the latest market research and data mining. This reflects the affordability of opinion polling that is supplemented with other sources of intelligence, including detailed election results and Statistics Canada data. The ability to understand these data has improved with computing software and skilled analytics; in the future more attention will be paid to using Internet cookies to profile voters based on their web viewing history and online purchasing behaviour (Trish, 2012). These insights into the electorate's mindset enable smarter, though not necessarily more palatable, use of finite communications resources in the following ways.

- Segmentation: Data analysts divide "heterogeneous markets into homogeneous groups" based on the groups' shared characteristics

(Baines et al., 2003: 225). The segmentation of electors into clusters, such as "hockey moms," identifies existing supporters who need reinforcement; potential supporters who need persuasion; and opponents who can be ignored. The Conservatives' segmentation of the electoral marketplace by examining socio- and geo-demographic data has been a competitive advantage (Flanagan, 2009).

- Policy targeting: A series of minor policy commitments that are tailored to narrow subsegments of the electorate can be promoted to potential supporters. The design of micro policies is dependent on what will appeal to targeted market segments in a manner that is consistent with the party's overall ideology. For instance, the Conservatives have introduced tax credits in an effort to appeal in particular to working parents with young children, which is a large group of potential Conservative supporters and fits with that party's overall message theme of reducing taxes. The 2013 federal budget's elimination of import tariffs on baby clothes and sporting equipment is another example.
- Seats triage: Just as medical emergency personnel make quick decisions to prioritize the allocation of resources (triage), political parties use data to identify which electoral districts to focus their attention on, and which ones to ignore. With the increasing precision of political communication, it is possible to prioritize resources for air and ground war activities that will reach narrow segments of the electorate who reside in key seats. For instance, the Conservative Party has communicated micro policies and prioritized community media in an effort to reach targeted electors residing in suburban ridings in the Greater Toronto Area (GTA), helping them to defeat several sitting Liberal MPs in the region.
- Narrowcasting: The fracturing of broadcast media allows strategists to reach narrow segments of the electorate through regional and specialist media. For instance, not only does the Conservative Party opt to advertise on The Sports Network (TSN) but it earns free coverage when Prime Minister Harper is depicted attending curling, hockey, and other sporting events that are viewed by targeted elector segments.
- Database marketing: The aforementioned party datasets are used by political parties to communicate directly with targeted electors who are normally their supporters. The clever integration of social media and the ground war with database marketing by the Barack Obama presidential campaigns (Masket, 2009) has provided a communication model for Canadian strategists. However, the federal election robocall scandal[3] drew negative attention to the potential misuse of party databases (Ivison, 2012).

- Branding: To achieve synergies between all types of communication, a consistent underlying message is needed. Political parties pay close attention to logos, colour schemes, visual backdrops, and the overall image of their leader as part of their effort to shape a political brand. The Government of Canada's branding is formalized through the Federal Identity Program, which outlines how public servants should attempt to communicate a clear corporate identity. As the permanent campaign intersects with the Canadian public service, there is conflict when the government's brand begins to assume partisan characteristics. For instance, it is common for the colour palettes of government advertising, websites, and communications products to be synchronized with the governing party's colours.
- De-branding: Political parties routinely use advertising to communicate factual statements about an opponent's policies or behaviour with the intent of damaging their political brand. Commentators and the public often express indignation, yet research indicates this tactic is effective and some academics maintain that truth-based advertising, even when it presents negative messages, is a net positive for democratic discourse (Rose, 2012). There is an added incentive of stretching resources because the news media often runs "adwatches" where the latest partisan advertising is discussed, especially if it features conflict. De-branding impedes attempts by political leaders to control their image and can influence how they are framed in the news media.

In addition to these and other forms of strategic communication, there are several tactical communications manoeuvres available to political actors. An excellent example is the Conservative government's introduction of the message event proposal (MEP). This communications policy tool synchronizes all communication by requiring any department that wants to coordinate a public event to first complete a MEP. It ensures that considerable thought is put into the communications aspects of the event by requiring information about the desired news headline, key messages, media lines, the desired sound bite, the preferred speaking backdrop, the ideal event photograph, participants' attire, and rollout materials (Blanchfield and Bronskill, 2010). A completed MEP must be reviewed by the non-partisan Privy Council Office (PCO) before being approved by the partisan PMO. Despite the considerable public consternation about the line-blurring between partisanship and the public service that was made apparent by revelations about the Liberal sponsorship scandal, the introduction of MEPs demonstrates to some observers that "the same mistake" is being repeated (Kozolanka, 2012: 112). Other political communication tactics that have been reported in recent years run the gamut: a PMO directive that all Government of Canada news releases refer to "Canada's New Government" and later "the Harper government"; the government's all-encompassing and seemingly never-ending Economic Action Plan advertising campaign (Kozolanka, 2012); a libel suit by the Conservative Party against the Liberal Party over defamatory statements posted online (CBC News, 2008); and the PMO tweeting photos of a "day in the life" of the prime minister.

Conclusion

This chapter has illustrated that many aspects of political communication in Canada are evolving with technology while others seem impervious to change. Certainly the emergence of social media and the interactivity of online communication are having profound implications for how political parties, interest groups, election candidates, and journalists engage with the attentive public. Less well known are the strategies and tactics that are employed by political actors who are embroiled in a contest to control the public agenda, to frame the debate, to shape their leader's image, to de-brand political opponents, and to covertly target particular elector segments for partisan political messaging.

This has several implications for Canadian democracy. On the one hand, computing and communications technology assists political parties with understanding what it is that citizens want, and improves their ability to respond to public preferences. New ways of communicating enable them to disseminate information in the most efficient and direct manner possible. The availability of email, websites, and social media allows political actors and electors to avoid the gatekeeping filters of the mainstream media. More information than ever before about government is available to anyone with Internet access. This democratization of media and information reduces the power, influence, and bias of news editors and members of the press gallery, and is a counterforce to the trend of many journalistic perspectives being absorbed into media conglomerates. As well, the relentless permanent campaigning by political parties has increased their outreach and accountability.

On the other hand, trends in political communication threaten the quality of Canadian democracy. Political parties can more easily communicate by stealth in an attempt to reach only selected narrow segments of the electorate, to avoid the scrutiny of media watchdogs, and to thwart critical reaction from detractors. They have more marketing tools to derail their critics' agenda and to damage an opponent's brand. Government officials risk becoming consumed with the short-term implications of policy decisions and what is released under access to information legislation. Public servants are prevented from answering journalists' questions while designated government spokespersons, if they can be reached, may insulate themselves from scrutiny by emailing a statement instead of having a conversation. Citizens' elected representatives are losing their independence as the need for message consistency increases the clout of the party centre and the strength of party discipline. Journalists, who are increasingly chasing what's new and trending, are unable to explore important matters that deserve scrutiny; moreover, they are susceptible to information subsidies and seem endlessly fascinated by the "horse race" aspect of party politics.

There is no definitive answer about whether all of this is a net positive or negative for Canadian democracy. It is clear, however, that as the techniques, tactics, and strategy of political communication evolves, there are several enduring themes and practices—such as framing, agenda setting, image management, pseudo events, spin, leaks, and infotainment—that will continue to shape this increasingly important aspect of Canadian government and politics.

Notes

1 There are different terms and conceptual nuances concerning direct marketing. For instance, Flanagan (2009) refers to "direct voter contact" whereas Nesbitt-Larking (2001: 157) mentions the "direct recipient address." The common denominator is the word "direct," which refers to the ability of communicators to bypass editorial filters and communicate directly with recipients of the information.

2 Revelations that permanent campaigning by the BC Liberal government targeted allophones caused a controversy in early 2013 when its "multicultural strategy" was leaked. The episode further illustrates the prevalence of this emerging mindset in Canadian party politics.

3 On Election Day 2011 thousands of electors across 18 electoral districts received automated phone messages that purported to be from Elections Canada stating that their polling locations had been moved. It is widely alleged that political operatives within the Conservative Party attempted to suppress turnout among Liberal supporters in key ridings. At the time of writing an investigation by Elections Canada is ongoing.

References

Baines, Paul R., Robert M. Worcester, David Jarrett, and Roger Mortimore. 2003. "Market Segmentation and Product Differentiation in Political Campaigns: A Technical Feature Perspective." *Journal of Marketing Management* 19: 225–49.

Berkowitz, Dan, and Douglas B. Adams. 1990. "Information Subsidy and Agenda-Building in Local Television News." *Journalism Quarterly* 67 (4): 723–31. http://dx.doi.org/10.1177/107769909006700426.

Blanchfield, Mike, and Jim Bronskill. 2010. "Documents Expose Harper's Obsession with Control," *Toronto Star*, June 6. http://www.thestar.com/news/canada/2010/06/06/documents_expose_harpers_obsession_with_control.html

Blumenthal, Sidney. 1980. *The Permanent Campaign: Inside the World of Elite Political Operatives*. Boston: Beacon Press.

Boorstin, Daniel J. 1992. *The Image: A Guide to Pseudo-Events in America*. New York: Vintage Books.

Canada. 2012a. "Mother Tongue (Percentage Distribution), Canada, Provinces and Territories, 2011 Census." Statistics Canada. http://www12.statcan.gc.ca/census-recensement/lang-tab-eng.cfm.

Canada. 2012b. "2010–2011 Annual Report on Government of Canada Advertising Activities." Public Works and Government Services Canada. http://www.tpsgc-pwgsc.gc.ca/pub-adv/rapports-reports/2010-2011/tdm-toc-eng.html

Canada. 2013. "Description of the National Register of Electors." Elections Canada. http://www.elections.ca.

Canadian Association of Journalists. 2010. "An Open Letter to Canadian Journalists." June. http://www.caj.ca/?p=692.

Canadian Media Research Consortium. 2011. "Even in the Digital Era, Canadians Have Confidence in Mainstream News Media." http://journalism.ubc.ca/files/2011/05/CMRC_Trust_Report_11_May.pdf.

Cappella, Joseph N., and Kathleen Hall Jamieson. 1997. *Spiral of Cynicism: The Press and the Public Good*. Oxford: Oxford University Press.

CBC News. 2008. "Harper Lawsuit Smacks of Authoritarian State: Prof," August 7. http://www.cbc.ca/news/canada/harper-lawsuit-smacks-of-authoritarian-state-prof-1.707379/.

CBC News. 2013. "Attawapiskat Chief Slams Audit Leak as 'Distraction'." January 7. http://www.cbc.ca/news/politics/attawapiskat-chief-slams-audit-leak-as-distraction-1.1318113/.

Centre for Law and Democracy. 2013. "Global Right to Information Rating." http://www.rti-rating.org/index.php.

Druick, Zoë. 2007. *Projecting Canada: Government Policy and Documentary Film at the National Film Board*, vol. 1. Montreal, Kingston: McGill-Queens University Press.

Flanagan, Tom. 2009. *Harper's Team: Behind the Scenes in the Conservative Rise to Power*. 2nd ed. Montreal: McGill-Queen's University Press.

Fleras, Augie. 2011. *The Media Gaze: Representations of Diversities in Canada*. Vancouver: University of British Columbia Press.

Ivison, John. 2012. "Tory Database Likely Key to Cracking Robocall Mystery," *National Post*, March 5. http://fullcomment.nationalpost.com/2012/03/05/john-ivison-database-at-the-heart-of-conservatives-computer-system-likely-key-to-cracking-robocall-mystery/.

Karim, Karim H. 2012. "Are Ethnic Media Alternative?" In *Alternative Media in Canada*, eds. Kirstin Kozolanka, Patricia Mazepa, and David Skinner, 165–83. Vancouver: University of British Columbia Press.

Kozolanka, Kirsten. 2009. "Communication by Stealth: The New Common Sense in Government Communication." In *How Ottawa Spends, 2009–2010: Economic Upheaval and Political Dysfunction*, ed. M. Maslove, 222–40. Montreal: McGill-Queen's University Press.

Kozolanka, Kirsten. 2012. "'Buyer' Beware: Pushing the Boundaries of Marketing Communications in Government." In *Political Marketing in Canada*, eds. Alex Marland, Thierry Giasson, and Jennifer Lees-Marshment, 107–22. Vancouver: University of British Columbia Press.

Lees-Marshment, Jennifer. 2001. "The Product, Sales and Market-Oriented Party: How Labour Learnt to Market the Product, Not Just the Presentation." *European Journal of Marketing* 35 (9/10): 1074–84. http://dx.doi.org/10.1108/EUM0000000005959.

Levine, Allan. 1993. *Scrum Wars: The Prime Ministers and the Media.* Toronto: Dundurn Press.

Marland, Alex. 2011. "Constituency Campaigning in the 2011 Canadian Federal Election." In *The Canadian Federal Election of 2011*, eds. Jon H. Pammett and Christopher Dornan, 167–94. Toronto: Dundurn Press.

Marland, Alex. 2012. "Political Photography, Journalism and Framing in the Digital Age: The Management of Visual Media by the Prime Minister of Canada." *International Journal of Press/Politics* 17 (2): 214–33. http://dx.doi.org/10.1177/1940161211433838.

Masket, Seth E. 2009. "Did Obama's Ground Game Matter?: The Influence of Local Field Offices during the 2008 Presidential Election." *Public Opinion Quarterly* 73 (5): 1023–39. http://dx.doi.org/10.1093/poq/nfp077.

Mayer, Jeremy D. 2004. "The Presidency and Image Management: Discipline in Pursuit of Illusion." *Presidential Studies Quarterly* 34 (3): 620–31. http://dx.doi.org/10.1111/j.1741-5705.2004.00215.x.

Miljan, Lydia, and Barry Cooper. 2003. *Hidden Agendas: How Journalists Influence the News.* Vancouver: University of British Columbia Press.

Nesbitt-Larking, Paul. 2001. *Politics, Society and the Media.* Peterborough: Broadview Press.

Nolan, Michael. 1981. "Political Communication Methods in Canadian Federal Election Campaigns." *Canadian Journal of Communication* 7 (4): 28–46.

Ornstein, Norman, and Thomas Mann. 2000. *The Permanent Campaign and Its Future.* Washington: American Enterprise Institute.

Payton, Laura. 2012. "Permanent Campaign Means No Rest in Target Ridings." CBC News, October 25. http://www.cbc.ca/news/politics/permanent-campaign-means-no-rest-in-target-ridings-1.1142508/.

Québecor. 2013. "Quebecor at a Glance." http://www.quebecor.com/en/content/communications-giant.

Rose, Jonathan. 2012. "Are Negative Ads Positive? Political Advertising and the Permanent Campaign." In *How Canadians Communicate IV: Media and Politics*, eds. David Taras and Christopher Waddell, 149–68. Edmonton: Athabasca University Press.

Sauvageau, Florian. 2012. "The Uncertain Future of the News." In *How Canadians Communicate IV: Media and Politics*, eds. David Taras and Christopher Waddell, 29–44. Edmonton: Athabasca University Press.

Scheufele, Dietram A., and David Tewksbury. 2007. "Framing, Agenda Setting, and Priming: The Evolution of Three Media Effects Models." *Journal of Communication* 57 (1): 9–20.

Street, John. 2004. "Celebrity Politicians: Popular Culture and Political Representation." *British Journal of Politics and International Relations* 6 (4): 435–52. http://dx.doi.org/10.1111/j.1467-856X.2004.00149.x.

Taras, David. 1990. *The Newsmakers: The Media's Influence on Canadian Politics.* Scarborough: Nelson Canada.

Theckedath, Dillan, and Terrence J. Thomas. 2012. "Media Ownership and Convergence in Canada." Parliamentary Information and Research Service, Library of Parliament. April 10. http://www.parl.gc.ca/content/lop/researchpublications/2012-17-e.htm.

Trish, Barbara. 2012. "The Year of Big Data." *Campaigns & Elections* 33 (5): 10–13.

Whitehorn, A. 1994. "The NDP's Quest for Survival." In *The Canadian General Election of 1993*, ed. Alan Frizzell, Jon H. Pammett, and Anthony Westell, 43–58. Ottawa: Carleton University Press.

PART V

Groups, Movements, Gender, Diversity

fifteen
Are Interest Groups Useful
or Harmful? Take Two

ÉRIC MONTPETIT

Political discourses and media commentaries typically present interest groups as harmful to policy-making processes. In those discourses and commentaries, groups "hijack" policy-makers to better serve their "special interest." When groups spend large amounts of money on lobbying, they expect a return on their investment. As most of these groups' spending on lobbying would consist in buying favours for politicians who would have grown accustomed to these favours, policy would frequently contain lucrative payoffs for lobby groups. It goes without saying that such policy would come at a cost to society and the economy.[1] Interest groups would therefore be harmful to policy and would hurt their country. This perspective on interest groups is a cliché commonly found in the media, but the perspective is not deprived of scholarly support, especially in the United States (see Baumgartner and Leech, 1998).

This chapter is a substantial revision of the chapter on interest groups that I published in the fifth edition of *Canadian Politics*. Despite the revision, the argument remains similar: a brighter perspective on interest groups is possible than that presented by the cliché. The chapter explains how interest groups can contribute positively to policy-making. Putting their ideas, expertise, and knowledge at the service of problem-solving, interest groups can help improve policy and socio-economic conditions in their country. In contrast with the previously published version of this chapter, however, I raise several questions on the importance of policy networks, which feature prominently in the Canadian literature dealing with interest groups.

What Is an Interest Group?

Language rarely describes reality in a neutral fashion. The biases of language cannot be any more evident than with the concept of "interest group." For example, some analysts prefer the concept of "pressure group" (e.g., Pross, 1995). In this expression, the word *pressure* refers to the action of groups. Groups' actions would consist in exerting pressure to obtain decisions government would not otherwise be inclined to make. The image behind the expression "pressure group" is one of adversarialism between government and groups. Groups do not help government by providing advice or expertise, but press them to adopt policies against their will. Below, I will argue that this image of adversarialism is incorrect, as the relationship between government and groups is often one of cooperation.

Other analysts prefer the concept of "advocacy groups" (e.g., Young and Everitt, 2004; Seidle, 1993). From this perspective, instead of exerting pressure, the key action of groups would consist in advocating in favour of their ideas or beliefs. Here, the image of adversarialism disappears. The word *advocacy* projects an image of groups as primarily motivated by ideas, without a prior assumption about the hostility or acceptance of those ideas by government. In fact, those who use this concept often notice that groups are not exclusively turned toward government, but seek to convince just about everyone of the validity of their ideas. The expression does not always match reality, either. If groups are involved in advocacy, they also participate in political processes, where exerting power is the goal. In these latter processes, strategy is more important than ideas, and alliances, coalitions, and money are important assets.

Other analysts refrain from using a general expression to describe groups, preferring separate concepts for different types of groups. For example, some analysts use the expression "public interest groups" to distinguish groups that have a wide membership with weak material interests from groups with a narrower membership primarily motivated by their material interest (Young and Forsyth, 1991; Phillips, Pal, and Savas, 1992). A group advocating for women's rights would thus be considered a public interest group, while a group representing an industry would form a private interest group. In empirical research, the distinction between the two types of group is not always easy to establish (Stanbury, 1993). In addition, the dichotomy between public and private interest groups lends itself too easily to value judgements suggesting that the former are good and the latter are bad. Individuals whose political values make them prioritize the socio-economic advancement of society as a whole over individualism may in fact make such judgements. Yet even groups representing narrow material interests can make a valuable contribution to policy-making and to the interest of the general public.

In my own work, I prefer using the concept of interest group to encompass all civil society organizations that are involved in policy-making processes. I acknowledge the limitations associated with this analytical choice, which mostly stems from the common usage of the expression "interest group" in everyday language, as well as in analysis, in comparison to alternative concepts. When I speak of an interest group, however, it must be clear that I do not refer to actors in policy processes motivated strictly by narrow material interests, despite what the concept of interest group might suggest. In fact, some interest groups are motivated by their desire to contribute ideas and expertise in policy processes (Mansbridge, 1992). Researchers have not yet found a convincing method to separate the part of interest groups' motivations that is strictly self-interested from the part that is outward looking (that is, motivations stemming from groups' preoccupations for the socio-economic advancement of society as a whole). Without better knowledge on motivations, it would be a mistake to assume that groups always act selfishly, with only their self-interest in mind.

Inspired by Pross (1995, 1986), I define interest groups as follows: *organizations created to facilitate the collective action of members who share interests or ideas, with the objective of making a contribution to policy-making, without seeking public office.* It follows that interest groups are different from social movements, which are more spontaneous and not as organized. Interest groups, however, can be located at the centre of social movements and can act as social movement organizations (see Scala, Montpetit, and Fortier, 2005). Interest groups are also distinct from political parties, which, in contrast to groups, seek to have some of their members elected to public office.

Groups differ among themselves with regard to their organization. The literature often distinguishes between two ideal typical organizational forms: peak associations and specialized groups (Atkinson and Coleman, 1989). The members of peak associations are other groups, while specialized groups have individual members or simply do not have a well-defined membership structure. Peak associations have detailed rules and codified them into constitutions, whereby leaders are selected and exercise their authority. Specialized groups frequently function with a less formalized set of rules and may be led by charismatic leaders. The rules of peak associations enable an internalization of debates among members, while debates are frequently external to specialized groups. Lastly, peak associations deal with a wider range of issues than specialized groups. Most groups fall somewhere between these two ideal types, sometimes closer to peak associations, sometimes closer to specialized groups.

The Canadian Federation of Agriculture offers a good example of a peak association. Its membership is made of other farm groups, organized at the provincial level and frequently representing commodity sectors. Two vice-presidents, elected according to a formal set of rules, lead the Federation. Lastly, the Federation devotes important efforts to unite the Canadian farming community behind a single voice. The Federation has elaborate procedures to bridge differences among members in developing its policy positions on a wide range of issues. As most peak associations, the Federation is not always successful in this latter endeavour, with some competing groups making their dissonant voice heard effectively on several issues. However, the presence of a peak association in the Canadian agricultural sector organizes discussion and debate internally among farm interests over agricultural policy; that is, it seeks to contain discussion and debate within its structure, although with mixed success.

In several policy sectors, peak associations are much less successful than in agriculture. In fact, forming and sustaining a peak association over a long period is difficult, and as a result specialized groups prevail in several policy sectors. The environment provides a good example of such a sector. The environmental sector is characterized by the presence of a large number of small and specialized groups. Groups in this sector tend to speak on specific issues, be it the protection of specific geographical areas, of a river or of a given animal species; environmental groups rarely work on a wide range of issues at once. For example, Greenpeace, possibly one of the most encompassing environmental groups, focuses its efforts on a carefully selected set of campaigns, most notably climate change and genetically modified food. When environmental groups have actual members and not just financial donors, as with Greenpeace, the members are individuals. Lastly, debates among environmental interests are more important between groups than they are within groups, as in a sector in which a peak association prevails. Environmental groups will often challenge industry groups, but they also debate among themselves as they frequently promote competing policy ideas. Because peak associations are not as successful in the environmental sector as they are in the agricultural sector, policy-makers perceive the former sector as more fragmented than the latter.

Finally, interest groups carry out a range of activities, including the direct provision of services to their members. However, they are of interest to political scientists primarily because they are involved in policy-making. As discussed in the next section, involvement in policy-making can take several forms. Sometimes, groups contribute to policy in a simple manner, transmitting their preferences to policy-makers in hope of obtaining their incorporation into political decisions. Groups that feel insufficiently heard by policy-makers can decide to join in contentious politics as well. However, groups can also be genuinely motivated by the search for the best possible solution to collective problems (Montpetit, 2010). When this is the case, they are not as wedded to their own policy preferences and therefore are not as harmful to policy-making as is claimed by those who assume that groups only act selfishly.

What Does an Interest Group Do?

The forms of the involvement of interest groups in policy-making can be distinguished using a simple two-by-three table (Table 15.1). Columns 1, 2 and 3 correspond to the nature of the relationship between a group and government.

Table 15.1 Four Types of Policy Involvement by Interest Groups

		Group/Government interactions		
		1. Puzzling	2. Voice	3. Exit
Scope of issues	1. Wide	Participating	Advocating	Contesting
	2. Narrow	Self-Regulating	Lobbying	Retreating

Before explaining the columns further, I will focus on the lines that refer to the scope of the issues over which a group and government can interact.

Groups differ with regard to the ideas and interests they represent and therefore the scope of the policy issues over which they interact with government. Some groups address only a limited set of issues. As seen above, carefully selecting issues is common among specialized groups, whereas peak associations tend to have wider preoccupations. This logical pattern, however, has several exceptions in reality.[2] Circumstances can occasionally justify peak associations putting their important resources and capacity behind a narrow set of issues. Even more probable is the possibility that a divided membership will limit the capacity of a peak association to act simultaneously on several fronts. Members may even distrust the peak association, reducing their resources and therefore their capacity to adopt a comprehensive outlook on their policy sector. Likewise, not all specialized groups are poor in resources, and therefore they occasionally decide to take on big issues. In other words, peak associations, whose structure enables the mobilization of important resources, are likely to tackle a wide range of issues in their sector. However, when peak associations happen to have limited resources, they are likely to have a focus just as narrow as that of specialized groups. Likewise, specialized groups that happen to have access to important resources might decide to broaden their outlook on their sector.

It goes without saying that groups with a wide perspective interact differently with government than groups with a narrower one. Of course, the attitude government adopts toward groups does not entirely depend on the scope of issues taken on by groups. To better understand differences in group/government interactions, it is useful to briefly summarize political science knowledge on the behaviour of political actors, including interest groups and government.

At least three types of political behaviour have been catalogued by political scientists: *strategic action*, *contention*, and *puzzling*. In the case of *strategic action*, political actors interact with each other with the view of securing the incorporation of their preferences into public policy. The concepts of "voice" and "exit," developed by Albert Hirschman (1970), are used in several studies on interest groups to describe two distinct strategic actions (e.g., Coen,

1998). On the one hand, strategic interest groups will voice their preferences and expect government to act accordingly. Where groups have competing preferences, government simply cannot satisfy everyone and has to choose among groups' preferences. On the other hand, mobile businesses, that is, businesses whose assets and investments can be moved abroad, have a clear advantage in the competition among interest groups to influence government precisely because of their capacity to exit. Owing to the possibility that they might take their investments to countries with lower taxes and less stringent regulations, these businesses receive subsidies and tax advantages that other groups have more difficulty obtaining (Lindblom, 1977; Coleman, 1988). Whatever the case, this form of exit is available to only a narrow range of interests, even among businesses (only those that are mobile).

There is, however, a more common form of exit, which cannot be associated as clearly with strategic action, and this is the second type of political behaviour: *contention* (also known as *contentious politics*). The decision of groups to join in contentious politics stems from a profound sense of injustice and grievances toward those actors participating in the formulation of policy (Pinard, 2011). Contentious politics cannot be considered strategic action as readily as the threat from mobile businesses to exit; unlike businesses, the groups engaged in contentious politics are not motivated by a policy benefit, but by a felt moral obligation and a desire for a better world. In this sense their action is principled, as opposed to self-interested. The decision to engage in contentious politics can nonetheless be treated as a form of exit if only because it normally involves severing ties with government. The groups involved in contentious politics prefer action targeted at the media and public opinion. They can surely have an indirect effect on policy, notably when they influence public opinion to see things their way and recognize the rightfulness of their grievances, but they keep their distance from the actors who participate more directly in policy-making.

A third type of behaviour, *puzzling*, also defies characterization as strategic action. In fact, puzzling requires loyalty, an attitude that Hirschman (1970) himself distanced from voice and exit. Paraphrasing Hirschman, Walzer (2004: 76) writes that "loyalty has to be a central value of any decent associational life." Indeed, loyalty refers to actors' unwillingness to exit, even when their immediate preferences are not satisfied. Loyalty requires a sense of belonging to a community and in this sense is a prerequisite for "problem-solving," a common concept in the German literature (Scharpf, 1997; Risse, 2000). In the anglophone literature, the concepts of puzzling (the term preferred here) and deliberation largely overlap with the idea of problem-solving (Mansbridge, 1992; Freeman, 2006). In this alternative to strategic action, behaviours take the form of truth-seeking and argumentation, conditioned by the presence of actors loyal to their community. In fact, actors who puzzle are motivated by the search for arguments to support the best possible policies for their community and are therefore curious about alternative perspectives, even those coming from the "other side" (Mutz, 2006). When they adopt this behaviour, interest groups cooperate with government, as well as with other actors, in the development of policy for the betterment of their community (or their country). In fact, puzzling requires interactions with other actors that are more intensive than when they simply voice their preferences. Relatedly, interest groups that puzzle normally accept having preferences that are not as stable as those of groups that conduct themselves strategically.

Although tempting, one should avoid ranking these three types of behaviour from the most to the least desirable. Puzzling is not the preferred attitude of generous groups concerned for the well-being of their country, nor voicing preferences the strategy of selfish ones. Both voice and puzzling can make positive contributions to policy-making. If puzzling helps find efficient solutions, the concerns and preferences of actors who simply engage in voice can provide crucial information for policy-making. Even contentious politics has positive effects, keeping policy-makers aware that substantive and procedural legitimacy has to factor into policy decisions. It should also be said that puzzling is demanding on resources, which are not distributed equally among interest groups (Olson, 1965). To puzzle efficiently, groups need expensive expertise. In contrast, voicing preferences and contesting decisions come cheaper.

Table 15.1 thus suggests that interest groups can make six forms of contribution to policy-making: lobbying, advocating, participating in policy-making, self-regulating, contesting, and retreating. Lobbying typically involves voicing preferences or transmitting demands to government, exclusively on behalf of and for the benefit of members. Specialized groups, with a narrow membership, typically make this contribution to policy-making. Although the exact origin of the term lobbying is uncertain,[3] at the end of the nineteenth century it was used to refer to the private meetings between representatives of interest groups and government legislators in the lobby of the US Congress (Milbrath, 1968: 441–42; Boivin, 1987: 23–24). Given the lack of transparency at these meetings, all the activities included under the term lobbying are treated with suspicion. To make lobbying more transparent, many governments, including federal and provincial governments in Canada, have adopted constraining regulations (Chari, Murphy, and Hogan, 2007; Holtmann, 1993). Again, it bears reiterating that not all lobbying is detrimental. When citizens think about lobbying, they often have in mind large resourceful businesses seeking economic rents from government, that is, revenues without equivalent production in counterpart. In fact, a small association of street residents engages in lobbying when transmitting demands to city government through a simple letter—asking for an improvement of cleanliness on their street, for example. In turn, the information the demand carries about the lack of cleanliness can make a useful contribution to policy-making, helping the city administration to allocate resources where they are most needed, even though improving resource allocation is not the prime motivation of the group.

In fact, better resource allocation is a side benefit of the demand for a cleaner street. Rational-choice policy analysts would describe improvement in resource allocation as a positive externality. Unlike a cleaner street, a better allocation of resources is a benefit beyond that desired by the members of the group and for which they do not have the exclusive enjoyment. Goods for which exclusive enjoyment is impossible are known as *public goods.* Interestingly, rational-choice analysts would predict that public goods provide little motivation for group involvement in policy-making (Olson, 1965; Becker, 1983). The reality, however, is different; some groups demand the provision of more public goods by government and do not appear motivated by selective narrow incentives. A demand for cleaner streets provides a good example of a demand that cannot be motivated only by narrow interests. In other words, several groups seek policies that will improve the conditions of a large number of people, well beyond group membership. Their perspective is thus wide in scope. Groups advocating for a reduction in social inequalities, for a reduction in global-warming emissions, or for a deepening of democracy provide additional examples. Unlike groups that lobby, the prime motivation behind advocating (top middle cell in Table 15.1) is the improvement of conditions for all rather than the material interest of specific group members. Although the possibility that policies satisfying the demands of these groups will benefit members is real, group representatives who prefer advocating rather than lobbying insist on the positive externality of their preferences. In other words, they voice a broader perspective on their sector.

Several groups thus advocate for the provision of public goods. When these groups come to believe that their preference has no echo whatsoever among the participants in policy-making, they sometimes decide to join in contentious politics. They will express severe grievances toward the participants in policy-making, denounce the injustice that their decisions reinforce, and claim that a better world is possible (Pinard, 2011). Their hope will be to catch the attention of the media and to convince public opinion to over-throw policy-makers and the interest groups surrounding them. They also know that their chances of attracting media attention and thereby influencing public opinion will increase when their depiction of policy-makers is exag-geratedly negative.[4] Other groups, disappointed with policy-makers but with a narrower focus, may simply prefer to retreat, no longer voicing preferences but waiting for better circumstances (bottom right cell in Table 15.1).

Interest groups that advocate rather than participate in policy-making often do so because they lack the organizational capacity required for efficient participation.[5] Participating in policy-making involves puzzling, and puzzling is costly, requiring some level of professionalization (Klüver and Saurugger, 2013). In a perfect world, in which organizational capacities would be distributed equally, all groups that so desire would participate in policy-making. As I will argue in the next section, an interest group makes a particularly important contribution to policy-making when it puzzles with other actors who have wide perspectives on the sector. Before moving to the next section, however, I will say a few words on self-regulation (the bottom left cell in Table 15.1).

Some issues are so narrow and specialized that government cannot resort to only its own expertise to make good policies. In such cases, highly specialized interest groups play a prominent role in puzzling over policy solutions. Expert knowledge being a prime exigency in the medical field, for example, the regulation of medical practice is essentially performed by the Colleges of Doctors and Surgeons in collaboration with various associations of specialists. Wolfgang Streeck and Philippe Schmitter (1985) have explained well how certain interest groups set up "private interest governments" outside of governmental hierarchies. If only because they provide a needed expertise, groups engaged in self-regulation make a useful contribution to policy. However, just like group representatives who advocate rather than lobby, those involved in self-regulation frequently are suspected of being too motivated by the benefits self-regulation entails for their members and not enough by self-regulation's positive externalities.

In sum, interest groups' involvement with policy can take six forms: lobbying, advocating, self-regulating, contesting, retreating, and participating in policy-making. If some of these activities can harm democratic processes occasionally, all have the potential to make a helpful contribution to policy.[6] I have argued, however, that of all six forms of involvement, the contribution of participation in policy-making is unsurpassed. I now focus on this latter contribution to policy, represented by the top left cell of Table 15.1.

What Is It That Interest Groups Do That Is Most Useful to Policy-Making?

To highlight the usefulness of interest groups to policy-making, I focus on two of its key aspects: policy formulation and policy implementation. Policy formulation refers to discussions among actors and eventually decisions about policy objectives, the nature of related collective problems, their causes in particular, and the various instruments likely to correct those problems. Policy implementation refers to the administrative efforts required by the instruments to meet policy objectives. Figure 15.1 is a useful simplification of the challenges facing policy-makers in both policy formulation and policy implementation. Policy formulation can be characterized by low or high uncertainty. When certainty is high over a policy issue, actors agree on clear policy objectives, on the nature of the main problems, and on the best solutions to correct those problems. In contrast, when uncertainty prevails, policy actors do not have a clear understanding of objectives, problems, and solutions. To implement policies, policy-makers frequently resort to coercive policy instruments, including prohibitions and sanctions for violators. Indeed, coercion is a key governmental instrument, as the state possesses a monopoly over the legitimate use of force in modern societies (Weber, 1995). However, the use of coercion to deal with collective problems is inefficient sometimes because sanctions can be difficult to apply. In some cases, violators simply cannot be caught; in other cases, sanctions demobilize target populations and worsen problems (Schneider and Ingram, 1997). In short, from issue to issue, the degrees of uncertainty during policy formulation and the possibility of resorting to sanction vary. Depending on these variations, policy-makers will be faced with different challenges and interest groups are not of equal help in surmounting these challenges. The extent to which interest groups can be helpful in surmounting policy-making challenges is summarized in Figure 15.1.

Figure 15.1 Interest Groups' Usefulness to Policy-Making

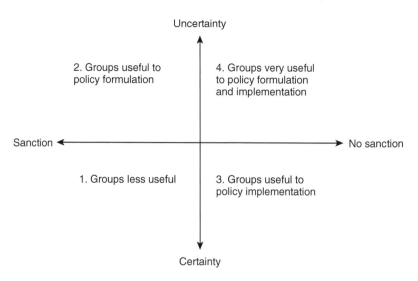

I begin with the easiest policy-making challenges, represented in quadrant 1 of Figure 15.1. Here, a great deal of certainty surrounds policy formulation. In such a case, the level of disagreement among actors on the objectives to aim for is relatively low. More importantly, actors know the causes behind the problems preventing goal attainment and know what instrument to apply to attain the goal. Here, sanction is an option that can improve policy implementation. Under such circumstances, government can make policy alone. Groups are of little use.

Water quality in a river along which several industrial plants operate provides a good example of a situation where government actors can be confident during policy formulation and resort to sanctions to correct problems. Industrial plants produce end-of-pipe or point-source pollution; that is, they release into the air or water the residues of their industrial processes. When the residues of industrial processes degrade water quality in a river, the source of the problem can be found with certainty. In fact, a simple comparison of the content of industrial run-offs with the various pollutants found in the river should make for easy identification of the polluters. Once polluters are identified, improvement in water quality can be achieved without too much difficulty. Government can adopt regulations imposing environmental release standards on polluters and sanction violators. It does not need the assistance of interest groups to improve water quality in a river polluted by industrial plants. Because the source of the problem and the instrument needed to correct it are known, puzzling with groups can improve policy formulation at the margin only. Moreover, given the small number of potential polluters, the application of sanctions can be handled efficiently by government inspectors. Government might have been alerted to the problem of water pollution by specialized interest groups, but groups' usefulness goes no farther than that in such a context.

Quadrant 2 shows that puzzling with groups can improve policy formulation because more uncertainty prevails than in the first quadrant. Improvement in road safety illustrates this situation. In most countries, the number of car accidents causing death or serious injuries is considered a serious problem. In the late 1960s, policy-makers believed that impaired driving was the main cause of the problem; therefore the road safety policies developed during this decade discouraged people from driving while under the influence of alcohol. At the outset, it was not entirely clear how the influence of alcohol could be measured. To develop regulations prohibiting drunk driving, policy-makers needed a precise standard to decide what drunk driving was and was not. Thus policy-makers had to puzzle over this issue with various experts, some belonging to interest groups. It was through such puzzling that a decision was made in most advanced countries to use the presence of alcohol in blood as a measuring method from which a standard could be devised.

Setting the standard was also the object of puzzling. Policy-makers had to decide whether the standard should be set at zero, thereby prohibiting drivers from having a glass of wine at dinner, or whether a reasonable limit should be set. What constituted a reasonable limit was itself subject to much uncertainty. Policy-makers welcomed group participation in collective puzzling, as they were uncertain about an appropriate course of action to increase road safety without losing sight of other important priorities, including economic prosperity and basic fairness. Puzzling and other forms of non-strategic group behaviour that enable a range of perspectives help policy-makers make up their mind, that is, decide which formulation offers the best solution. In this context, several groups, including health professionals, police associations, automobile clubs, and restaurant owners had something to contribute to policy formulation. They presented their distinct perspective and tested arguments against each other, helping policy-makers decide on an appropriate standard. And decisions are made easier when interest groups do not cling rigidly to their original preferences, but rather accept compromise with actors who initially had competing perspectives on the issue.

Interestingly, 20 years of policy efforts of this sort have contributed to the sharp decline of impaired driving in the developed world. This success can be attributed in part to severe sanctions for drunk drivers. However, the number of casualties on roads continues to be considered problematic in most countries. Consequently, the puzzling over this policy issue goes on. In fact, interest groups have contributed to expanding the issue beyond impaired driving, as government keeps puzzling conjointly with them on matters as diverse as youths' attitude toward driving, the use of cell phones while driving, and appropriate speed limits. In other words, the expansion of the issue of road safety beyond impaired driving has increased uncertainty, calling for continued puzzling and possibly justifying the participation of a wider range of interest groups in policy formulation.

In some policy issues, policy-makers value the participation of groups in policy-making primarily for their role during policy implementation rather than formulation. This is true when certainty prevails during policy formulation, thereby reducing the importance of puzzling, while sanction is not an option during implementation (quadrant 3 in Figure 15.1). Think, for example, of river wildlife endangered by the propagation of a non-native plant species unknowingly transported from another ecosystem by pleasure boaters. In this case, the cause of the problem is well known: non-native plants transported by pleasure boats. The solutions are also known: the removal of the invasive species and the prevention of future contamination by pleasure boats. The problem here is related not so much to the formulation of a policy as to its effective implementation. Indeed, removing invasive plants cannot be accomplished through sanction nor does sanction provide the best instrument to prevent future contamination. It is unlikely that government alone is capable of overcoming the challenges of policy implementation on such an issue. Interest groups, however, can help.

Interest groups representing the various users of the river can locate areas where the destructive plants are present and need to be removed. Government employees can certainly inspect the river, but their inspection will be all the more efficient if they can be alerted about problem areas by those who spend time on the river, including fishers, hunters, bird watchers, pleasure boaters, and members of various environmental groups. Concerned about the efficiency of their work, government employees responsible for the inspection of the river will be in contact with group representatives, who can sensitize their members to the problem and encourage the transmission of information. In any event, government employees are not sufficiently numerous to handle the problem by themselves. They need the help of concerned citizens in this task, and interest groups are naturally well placed to mobilize such citizens.

Sanctioning pleasure boaters might not be the best instrument to prevent future contamination, either. First, the inspection of boats to find violators would not be a simple task. It would require underwater inspection for plants trapped in keels and propellers. During peak boating season, such inspections would be expensive, requiring a large number of qualified government employees. Under these circumstances, sanction is unlikely to be the best instrument. It would probably be preferable to sensitize pleasure boaters about the importance of regularly carrying out their own inspections. Again, the representatives of the various associations of pleasure boaters are those who have the easiest access to pleasure boaters and are therefore well-placed to help government carry on information campaigns.

Quadrant 4 in Figure 15.1 represents issues for which groups are helpful for both policy formulation and implementation. Quadrant 4 includes issues such as the promotion of public health, the improvement of education, the reduction of non-point source environmental contamination, and so on. Uncertainty prevails about the causes of these problems, and therefore puzzling with interest groups might help improve policy formulation. For example, policy-makers used to believe that health problems could be effectively addressed through curative health care systems. This certainty no longer prevails among actors, as various interest groups argue that biological pathologies are often related to social or environmental conditions. The puzzling over the complex causes of health problems in advanced countries thus increasingly evolves toward improvements in the well-being of populations rather than just individuals. Moreover, the implementation of health-related policies frequently calls for the involvement of interest groups. Sanctions alone are not efficient solutions to resolve public health problems, as populations cannot be coerced into adopting healthy lifestyles. Groups that enjoy a high level of social trust, however, can help convince people to lead healthier lifestyles.

Reducing the proportion of the population without a high school diploma offers another example. Much uncertainty prevails on the best approach to this important problem. Some interest groups stress the importance of revising pedagogical approaches while other groups claim that the problem rests elsewhere, such as home life and the attitude of parents. Puzzling over this issue certainly has yet to reduce uncertainty about an appropriate policy formulation, and policy-makers are well advised to keep soliciting expertise and ideas from various groups. Whichever policy a country adopts, however, policy-makers cannot count on sanctions to implement it. Sanctioning high school dropouts to raise the level of education of a society, for example, can be grossly counterproductive. Sanctions might increase the number of students in classes and even graduation rates. However, forced school attendance might also cause alienation toward higher education, and even toward society as a whole. Clearly, persuading students that education not only has intrinsic value, but is also essential to future income, job, and career prospects is a better option than coercion. It is in this context that government policy-makers value the contribution of community and public education groups to the promotion of education, especially among socially disadvantaged youth.

Governments thus need the help of interest groups to formulate and implement policies. In fact, an increasing number of policy issues facing modern governments are located within the fourth quadrant of Figure 15.1. Policy-makers around the world realize the complexity of collective problems and therefore the uncertainty surrounding the selection of adequate policy approaches. Consequently, they value groups that puzzle over ways to address these complex problems. Long experience with the use of coercion and accompanying sanctions has also taught policy-makers that they have to consider a wider range of policy instruments, some of which the state cannot implement alone. Interest groups widen the choice of policy instruments policy-makers can rely on to meet policy objectives. In other words, government increasingly needs the involvement of interest groups in the policy-making process.

Does the Participation of Interest Groups in Policy-Making Depend on Policy Networks?

Government increasingly needs interest groups, but interest groups sometimes fail to make the expected contribution. I have already mentioned that groups have different organizational capacities, sometimes preventing effective participation in puzzling.[7] Peak associations in agriculture, for example, are likely to have more resources to gather expertise and contribute valuable ideas to policy formulation than are the small and specialized groups characterizing the environmental sector. Such an asymmetry in the distribution of organizational capacities biases the puzzling over issues that overlap agriculture and the environment (Montpetit, 2003).

Asymmetry in organizational capacity is surely a matter of whether members have an incentive to contribute to group resources (Olson, 1965). Farmers, the logic goes, gain more from contributing to farm groups than individuals do from contributing to environmental groups. Beyond this economic logic, history provides a useful explanation of differences in the degree and kind of contribution that groups make to policy. In every sector of every country, institutions, political parties, and organizational cultures have combined to create different historical circumstances that give shape to the relationship between interest groups and government (Martin and Swank, 2008). Sometimes, these relationships have developed into cooperation and sometimes into rivalry between interest groups and government. In the Canadian literature, these patterned relationships have been treated as social structures that Coleman and Skogstad (1990) have labelled *policy networks*. Following this literature, interest groups do not choose to participate in policy-making (or not); rather they find themselves in networks particularly conducive to such participation (or not). Interest groups might occasionally seek a change to the network within which they operate with a view to improving their contribution to policy. As networks are built over long periods, however, they evolve at the pace of change in historical circumstances, which are beyond the control of any single or small group of actors. In other words, the participation of interest groups in policy-making depends on the structure of the policy networks within which they happen to find themselves and not so much on choice.

In a prior version of this chapter, I distinguished between four network structures that would condition the participation of groups in policy-making: pluralist, corporatist, dirigist, and clientelist networks. To illustrate how networks might regulate the contribution of interest groups to policy-making, I argued that corporatist networks facilitate puzzling. Corporatist networks would limit participation to a small number of groups, enabling the development of loyalty and trust ties conducive to deliberation among groups (Öberg, 2002). The downside is that by limiting participation, corporatist networks also restrict the diversity of groups who puzzle over solutions to problems, therefore reducing the possibility of issue expansion in comparison to pluralist networks. The emergence of contentious actors with serious grievances about the representativeness of decision-makers would thus appear more likely in sectors governed by corporatist networks.

My recent research has convinced me that such reasoning overestimates the importance of network structures in the current political context (Montpetit, 2009). To be sure, I am persuaded that in countries where democracy is deficient, dirigist and clientelist networks are important. I doubt, however, that such networks can be sustained in advanced democracies. Though the evidence shows that corporatist networks have shaped some policy sectors in the past, I have come to believe that the actors in such networks, including government, are no longer able to select the exclusive sets of participants that characterized such networks in the past (Lundberg, 2013).

As a consequence, the contribution of groups to policy-making in advanced democracies occurs far more frequently in the context of pluralism, even in countries formerly well known for their corporatism (Streeck, 1992). Notwithstanding differences in organizational capacity, groups are free to choose the particular form of their contribution to policy-making. And far from what rational-choice analysts would suggest, interest groups frequently choose to puzzle with a view to helping policy-makers make better policies, even in the United States (see Holyoke, 2011). Due to resource limitations, some interest groups are only capable of voicing concerns, which can nonetheless be useful; they serve as alarm bells alerting policy-makers that important problems are not being attended to. Occasionally, when policy-makers ignore the alarm, interest groups can join in contentious politics. The point is that interest groups are not as chained to a particular form of contribution as was thought in the past; they are relatively free to decide how they want to contribute to policy-making.

Conclusion

Are interest groups useful or harmful? Do groups distort policy to their own advantage? Do groups prevent policy-makers from improving the socio-economic conditions of their country? Answers to these questions are more complex than the questions themselves. A simple yes or no would be unconvincing. Although no consensus exists among analysts on the effect of interest group action on policy (Baumgartner and Leech, 1998), the popular perspectives, consistent with rational choice theory, nevertheless answer that interest groups are generally harmful to policy-making, as well as to democracy itself. In reaction to this argument, I presented in this chapter an analysis that is intentionally focused on positive contributions by interest groups to policy.

To be sure, interest groups can occasionally harm policy, but the analyses supporting this conclusion do not need additional publicity. In light of these analyses, however, my own analysis might appear counterintuitive. I have explained how interest groups puzzle with government over policy solutions and assist civil servants in their implementation. In doing so, I have argued, interest groups help to make better policy and to improve socio-economic conditions. This chapter has highlighted some of the many ways whereby interest groups can be useful to policy-makers.

Unfortunately, few political scientists in Canada have made a career out of the study of interest groups. The Canadian thinking on interest groups has thus been influenced by the work of American colleagues, who perhaps have had a tendency to exaggerate the harm caused by interest groups (e.g., Stanbury 1993).[8] This is unfortunate, as the Canadian context might be particularly suited to observing interest groups playing more positive roles.[9]

Notes

1 A version of this argument can be found in Edsall (2013).

2 Some scholars even argue that group capacity does not vary significantly across group types. See Klüver and Saurugger (2013).

3 Sekwat (1998: 1293) in the *International Encyclopedia of Public Policy and Administration* attributes British origins to lobbying whereas Milbrath (1968: 441) in the *International Encyclopedia of the Social Sciences* places its origins in the United States.

4 I develop this argument in a forthcoming book titled *In Defence of Pluralism.*

5 In fact, some groups try to pursue both simultaneously, but they face serious difficulties (Montpetit, Scala, and Fortier, 2004).

6 The useful contribution of retreating is less obvious, although several retreats may send a signal to particularly alert policy-makers that something is wrong.

7 Although discrepancies in group capacity might be exaggerated in the literature. See Klüver and Saurugger (2013).

8 An excellent summary of this American literature is provided by Baumgartner and Leech (1998).

9 For instance, Canadian governments have adopted strict regulations governing the financing of political parties by interest groups, preventing some of the worst examples of the perverse contribution of groups to Washington politics.

References

Atkinson, Michael M., and William D. Coleman. 1989. "Strong States and Weak States: Sectoral Policy Networks in Advanced Capitalist Economies." *British Journal of Political Science* 19 (1): 47–67. http://dx.doi.org/10.1017/S0007123400005317.

Baumgartner, Frank R., and Beth L. Leech. 1998. *Basic Interest: The Importance of Groups in Politics and in Political Science.* Princeton: Princeton University Press.

Becker, Gary S. 1983. "A Theory of Competition Among Pressure Groups for Political Influence." *Quarterly Journal of Economics* 98 (3):371–400. http://dx.doi.org/10.2307/1886017.

Boivin, Dominique. 1987. *Le lobbying: ou le pouvoir des groupes de pression.* Montréal: Éditions du Méridien.

Chari, Raj, Gary Murphy, and John Hogan. 2007. "Regulating Lobbyists: A Comparative Analysis of the United States, Canada, Germany and the European Union." *Political Quarterly* 78 (3): 422–38. http://dx.doi.org/10.1111/j.1467-923X.2007.00870.x.

Coen, David. 1998. "The European Business Interest and the Nation State: Large-Firm Lobbying in the European Union and Member States." *Journal of Public Policy* 18 (1): 75–100. http://dx.doi.org/10.1017/S0143814X9800004X.

Coleman, William D. 1988. *Business and Politics: A Study of Collective Action.* Montreal: McGill-Queen's University Press.

Coleman, William D., and Grace Skogstad, eds. 1990. *Policy Communities and Public Policy in Canada: A Structural Approach.* Mississauga: Copp Clark Pitman.

Edsall, Thomas B. 2013. "Kill Bill," *New York Times,* May 22. http://opinionator.blogs.nytimes.com/2013/05/22/kill-bill/?hp&_r=0.

Freeman, Richard. 2006. "Learning in Public Policy." In *The Oxford Handbook of Public Policy,* eds. Martin Rein, Michael Moran, and Robert E. Goodin, 367–88. Oxford: Oxford University Press.

Hirschman, Albert O. 1970. *Exit, Voice and Loyalty: Responses to Decline in Firms, Organizations and States.* Cambridge: Harvard University Press.

Holtmann, Felix. 1993. *Sur la voie de la transparence: révision de la loi sur l'enregistrement des lobbyistes.* Ottawa: Rapport du Comité permanent de la consommation et des affaires commerciales et de l'administration gouvernementale.

Holyoke, Thomas T. 2011. *Competitive Interests: Competition and Compromise in American Interest Group Politics.* Washington, DC: Georgetown University Press.

Klüver, Heike, and Sabine Saurugger. 2013. "Opening the Black Box: The Professionalization of Interest Groups in the European Union." *Interest Groups & Advocacy* 2 (2): 185–205. http://dx.doi.org/10.1057/iga.2013.2.

Lindblom, Charles. 1977. *Politics and Markets.* New York: Basic Books.

Lundberg, Erik. 2013. "Does the Government Selection Process Promote or Hinder Pluralism? Exploring the Characteristics of Voluntary Organizations Invited to Public Consultations." *Journal of Civil Society* 9 (1): 58–77. http://dx.doi.org/10.1080/17448689.2013.771086.

Mansbridge, Jane J. 1992. "A Deliberative Theory of Interest Representation." In *The Politics of Interest: Interest Groups Transformed,* ed. M. Petracca, 32–57. Boulder: Westview Press.

Martin, Jo Cathie, and Duane Swank. 2008. "The Political Origins of Coordinated Capitalism: Business Organizations, Party Systems, and State Structure in the Age of Innocence." *American Political Science Review* 102 (02): 181–98. http://dx.doi.org/10.1017/S0003055408080155.

Milbrath, Lester W. 1968. "Lobbying." In *International Encyclopedia of the Social Sciences*, ed. D.L. Sills. New York: The Macmillan Company & the Free Press.

Montpetit, Éric. 2003. *Misplaced Distrust: Policy Networks and the Environment in France, the United States and Canada.* Vancouver: University of British Columbia Press.

Montpetit, Éric. 2009. "Governance and Policy Learning in the European Union: A Comparison with North America." *Journal of European Public Policy* 16 (8): 1185–203. http://dx.doi.org/10.1080/13501760903332720.

Montpetit, Éric. 2010. "The Deliberative and Adversarial Attitudes of Interest Groups." In *Oxford Handbook of Canadian Politics*, eds. John Courtney and David E. Smith, 244–62. Oxford: Oxford University Press. http://dx.doi.org/10.1093/oxfordhb/9780195335354.003.0014.

Montpetit, Éric, Francesca Scala, and Isabelle Fortier. 2004. "The Paradox of Deliberative Democracy: the National Action Committee on the Status of Women and Canada's Policy on Reproductive Technology." *Policy Sciences* 37 (2): 137–57. http://dx.doi.org/10.1023/B:OLIC.0000048531.47103.3a.

Mutz, Diana C. 2006. *Hearing the Other Side: Deliberative versus Participatory Democracy.* Cambridge: Cambridge University Press. http://dx.doi.org/10.1017/CBO9780511617201.

Öberg, Perola. 2002. "Does Administrative Corporatism Promote Trust and Deliberation?" *Governance: An International Journal of Policy, Administration and Institutions* 15 (4): 455–75. http://dx.doi.org/10.1111/0952-1895.00197.

Olson, Mancur. 1965. *The Logic of Collective Action: Public Goods and the Theory of Groups.* Cambridge: Harvard University Press.

Phillips, Susan D. 1993. "Of Public Interest Groups and Sceptics: A Realist's Reply to Professor Stanbury." *Canadian Public Administration* 36 (4): 606–16. http://dx.doi.org/10.1111/j.1754-7121.1993.tb00835.x.

Phillips, Susan D., Leslie A. Pal, and Daniel J. Savas. 1992. *Interest Groups in the Policy Process.* Ottawa: Working paper series, School of Public Administration, Carleton University.

Pinard, Maurice. 2011. *Motivational Dimensions in Social Movements and Contentious Collective Action.* Montreal: McGill-Queen's University Press.

Pross, Paul A. 1986. *Group Politics and Public Policy.* 2nd ed. Toronto: Oxford University Press.

Pross, Paul A. 1995. "Pressure Groups: Talking Chameleons." In *Canadian Politics in the 1990s*, eds. Michael S. Whittington and Glen Williams, 252–75. Toronto: Nelson Canada.

Risse, Thomas. 2000. "'Let's Argue!': Communicative Action in World Politics." *International Organization* 54 (1): 1–39. http://dx.doi.org/10.1162/002081800551109.

Scala, Francesca, Éric Montpetit, and Isabelle Fortier. 2005. "NAC's Organizational Practices and the Politics of Assisted Reproductive Technologies in Canada." *Canadian Journal of Political Science* 38: 581–604.

Scharpf, Fritz W. 1997. *Games Real Actors Play: Actor-Centered Institutionalism in Policy Research.* Boulder: Westview Press.

Schneider, Anne Larason, and Helen Ingram. 1997. *Policy Design for Democracy.* Lawrence: University Press of Kansas.

Seidle, F. Leslie. 1993. "Interest Advocacy through Parliamentary Channels: Representation and Accommodation." In *Equity & Community: The Charter, Interest Advocacy and Representation*, ed. F. Leslie Seidle, 189–225. Montreal: Institute for Research on Public Policy.

Sekwat, Alex. 1998. "Lobbying." In *International Encyclopedia of Public Policy and Administration*, vol. 3., ed. Jay M. Shafritz. Boulder: Westview Press.

Stanbury, William T. 1993. "A Sceptic's Guide to the Claims of So-Called Public Interest Groups." *Canadian Public Administration* 36 (4): 580–605. http://dx.doi.org/10.1111/j.1754-7121.1993.tb00834.x.

Streeck, Wolfgang. 1992. "From National Corporatism to Transnational Pluralism: European Interest Politics and the Single Market." In *Participation in Public Policy-Making: The Role of Trade Unions and Employers' Associations*, ed. Tiziano Treu, 97–126. Berlin: Walter de Gruyter. http://dx.doi.org/10.1515/9783110858709.97.

Streeck, Wolfgang, and Philippe C. Schmitter. 1985. "Community, Market, State—and Associations? The Prospective Contribution of Interest Governance to Social Order." In *Private Interest Government*, eds. Wolfgang Streeck and Philippe C. Schmitter, 1–29. London: Sage Publications.

Walzer, Michael. 2004. *Politics and Passion: Toward a More Egalitarian Liberalism*. New Haven: Yale University Press.

Weber, Max. 1995. *Économie et société*, vol. 1. Paris: Plon.

Young, Lisa, and Joanna Everitt. 2004. *Advocacy Groups*. Vancouver: University of British Columbia Press.

Young, R.A., and M. Shirley Forsyth. 1991. "Leaders' Communications in Public-Interest and Material-Interest Groups." *Canadian Journal of Political Science* 24 (03): 525. http://dx.doi.org/10.1017/S0008423900022678.

sixteen

Of Pots and Pans and Radical Handmaids: Social Movements and Civil Society[1]

MICHAEL ORSINI

If you're in costume, even 10 people is a visible demonstration.
—Ottawa-based activist Julie Lalonde of the Radical Handmaids

Knowing a lot of social movement theory does not make a good activist.
—J. Pickerill & J. Krinsky, *"Why Does Occupy Matter"*

Social movement activism comes in many shapes and sizes. From the tent communities inspired by the Occupy movement's efforts to expose corporate greed to the pot-clanging student protests in 2012 that paralyzed Quebec during the *printemps érable* to the theatrical antics of the Ottawa-based feminist collective the Radical Handmaids, it has been a busy time for social movement actors vying for public and media attention in Canada. How should we interpret these seemingly increasing episodes of protest activity, especially in the light of concerns that social movements are "past their apex" (Phillips, 1999)? Are these simply isolated pockets of protest activity that, like other movements, come and go with the ebb and flow of time? Is neoliberalism and the attendant retreat of the welfare state to blame for the emergence of many of these movements?

While critics are quick to point out that movements tend to attract an assortment of generally disgruntled people, there are also signs that citizens who might be less accustomed to protest are swelling the ranks of some movements, as was argued in a CBC *Fifth Estate* documentary, *You Should Have Stayed at Home*, which focused on the controversial arrests of several anti-G20 demonstrators in 2010 in Toronto (CBC, 2011). It is common—almost fashionable—to criticize movements for being unclear or confused regarding what they seek in terms of concrete goals. And while it is appropriate to ask what movements are demanding, it is equally critical to recognize that movements, by their very nature, reflect a range of competing and nascent demands, employ a "diversity of tactics" (Conway, 2003), and expend a great deal of their activist energy figuring out exactly what they want. Viewing movements in a narrow, instrumental sense as focused solely on scoring policy victories or on transforming, broad-scale value change, as political scientists often do, misses a crucial feature of social movement activism: movements are as concerned with *how* they do things as with *why* they engage in activism. The Occupy movement, which is discussed later in the chapter, is an excellent example.

This chapter introduces the reader to the changing landscape of social movement activism in Canada, and examines whether we need new tools and concepts to grapple with a rapidly evolving social movement field. Drawing on Staggenborg (2008), I discuss the Canadian social movement context by distinguishing three levels of analysis: macro (large-scale), meso (organizational), and micro (individual). While there are important connections between these three levels of analysis, each level asks specific questions that can help us to unpack the dynamic and evolving world of social movement activism. The macro level, which is of particular interest to political scientists, focuses on how large-scale structures influence movements. The meso (or organizational) level allows us to appreciate the role of internal factors in explaining movement strategies and outcomes, as well as interactions among and between social movement organizations, while the micro level informs, among other issues, the subjective experience of activism on individuals themselves. The goal here is not to privilege one level of analysis but to group some of the issues and challenges faced by social movements in terms of these levels of analysis.

Drawing on some contemporary examples, including feminist collectives such as the Radical Handmaids, Idle No More indigenous organizing, the Quebec student movement, and the G20 protests in Toronto, I explore whether we need to employ new theoretical and analytical tools to understand this dynamic social movement arena. Specifically, I suggest that the study of social movements can benefit from greater engagement with how emotions shape the field of collective action and movement actors themselves, which corresponds primarily with the micro level of analysis identified above. While there is general agreement that citizens and elected officials alike are "moved" by emotional appeals, there has been a general reluctance to bring emotions into our analytical toolkits. It is perhaps not surprising that scholars have been slow to integrate emotions, given that social movement theory itself emerged in response to approaches that sought to explain the rise of movements as little more than irrational outbursts of time and place (see Flam and King, 2005; Gould, 2009; Jasper, 2011, 1998; Orsini and Wiebe, forthcoming).

Political scientists have long lamented the "decline of deference" (Nevitte, 2000) and the ensuing drift from participation in traditional democratic institutions (e.g., voting and membership in political parties) toward increased engagement with social movements and organized interest groups. This explanation fails to appreciate, however, what exactly is going on in this crowded social movement field, not to mention the important links or disjunctures between and among social movements, and between social movements and democratic institutions. Many movement actors challenge state authority, but others seek to bypass the state altogether, which is itself a political act. Moreover, in addition to looking at the more familiar movements that provoke a strong police presence and media attention, I examine forms of protest that often escape the mass media glare, but provide equally dramatic expressions of new forms of solidarity and organizing that might be adopted later by other movements. One example is the feminist collective, the Radical Handmaids.

Before moving on to the three fields of analysis outlined above (macro, meso, and micro), I begin by identifying some key concepts discussed in the social movement literature.

Clarifying Terms

Pinning down a solid definition of a social movement is challenging, given the competing interpretations jockeying for position. For the purposes of this chapter, I use della Porta and Diani's definition as it best captures the dynamic nature of movements. Social movements, they note, are "informal networks, based on shared beliefs and solidarity, which mobilize about conflictual issues, through the frequent use of various forms of protest" (della Porta and Diani, 1999: 16).[2] Social movements include formal social movement organizations (SMOs) as well as loose networks of activists connected to a movement's broad goals but perhaps not linked to a formal organizational structure. Social movements often rely on these networks, which they can mobilize at a moment's notice. Empirically, however, we cannot isolate a social movement in the same way that we can study a social movement organization. Indeed, we must be careful not to view a social movement as *the* unit of analysis, treating action as though there are no actors: "Every empirical phenomenon offers us a cross section of a social structure, rather like a split in a rock reveals its inner composition and strata. Just as a photograph of a rock as a whole cannot be confused with the minerals and strata that compose it, so collective phenomena do not disclose their meaning to us if we only consider them in their totality" (Melucci, 1994: 106).[3] Therefore, the study of social movements should encompass a careful understanding of the organizations that populate the movement, the subjective interpretations of movement participants themselves, and the interactions among movement participants and between movement participants and authorities.

Another important distinction is between interest groups and social movements.[4] Sometimes, for instance, the two terms are folded into a broader notion of civil society and used interchangeably to emphasize their similarities

(Smith, 2005a; see Laforest, 2011, for a discussion of the "voluntary sector" in Canada). It is nonetheless useful to provide at least some conceptual clarity with respect to potential differences in the use of the two terms, recognizing that each represents a form of collective action outside of the formal political party system. Schwartz and Paul (1992: 221–222) identify two key factors that help to distinguish interest groups from movements:

> Interest groups always work with institutionally mandated authorities and follow prescribed institutional procedures for accomplishing their goal. Social movements may do this, but they may also break rules and disrupt normal processes in an effort to achieve this end.
>
> Interest groups may call upon their constituency for active support, but their predominant and perhaps exclusive *modus operandi* is interaction between group leaders and responsible officials. Social movements rely in some way on mass mobilization of their constituency to accomplish their goals, though membership action may be as moderate as petition signing.

Finally, there are various ways to classify movements. McCarthy and Wolfson distinguish *conflict* and *consensus* movements. Within the social movement literature, there is a bias for conflict-oriented movements, which are "typically supported by minorities or slim majorities of populations and confront fundamental, organized opposition in attempting to bring about social change" (McCarthy and Wolfson, 1992: 273). Examples include the feminist, civil rights, and labour movements. Consensus movements, on the other hand, are defined as "those organized movements for change that find widespread support for their goals and little or no organized opposition from the population of a geographic community" (McCarthy and Wolfson, 1992: 273).

A second distinction is between identity-oriented and strategy-oriented movements (see Cohen, 1985). Identity-oriented movements, often termed new social movements (NSMs), are described as relating "to other political actors and opponents not in terms of negotiations, compromise, reform, improvement or gradual progress to be brought about by organizational pressures and tactics, but, rather, in terms of sharp antinomies such as yes/no, them/us, the desirable and the tolerable, victory or defeat, now or never, etc." (Offe, 1985: 829). NSMs are presumed to be disinterested in the economy or the state, display post-material values and a concern with quality-of-life issues; strategy-oriented movements, on the other hand, have been associated with more instrumental action centred on the economy and the state. In reality, movements employ elements of both strategy and identity in their repertoires of contention, rather than being reducible to one or the other.

Macro Level: Seeing the Big Picture

A focus on a movement's external environment helped scholars to appreciate that it was insufficient to isolate the resources internal to a movement to explain its success or failure, as early proponents of resource mobilization theory had done (Eisinger, 1973; Tarrow, 1994, 1998; Orsini, 2002). The key term employed by advocates of a broader approach is "political opportunity structure." As Tarrow explains (1994: 18),

> the concept of political opportunity emphasizes resources external to the group—unlike money or power—that can be taken advantage of by weak or disorganized challengers. Social movements form when ordinary citizens, sometimes encouraged by leaders, respond to changes in opportunities that lower the cost of collective action, reveal potential allies and show where elites and authorities are vulnerable.

To speak of a structure of political opportunity is a misnomer, since opportunities are always "situational" or context-dependent. Nonetheless, the concept is useful because it helps us to understand how mobilization can move from actors with deep-seated grievances and an abundance of resources to those with fewer grievances and less than adequate resources.

Movements, of course, operate in a context not entirely of their own making. As Jenson correctly described, actors are "simultaneously *subjects of structures and acting subjects* carrying in their practices and meaning systems the possibilities of both social stability and change" (Jenson, 1989: 236). The structure of federalism in Canada, for instance, is a permanent feature of the institutional context in which movements must operate. But it is not static or fixed. While there are differing views on whether federal systems offer more institutional openings for movements, or in fact, muddy the waters for movement actors who must decide whether to focus on the provincial or federal scale or ignore this altogether in favour of transnational action (Jenson and Papillon, 2000), federalism is a structural feature of the political environment that is part of the furniture, so to speak. Movements might try to exploit opportunities afforded by the federal system, but they would be hard pressed to ignore it.

Meso Level: Finding the Middle Ground

A focus on the meso level brings sustained attention to the internal organizational dynamics at work in the social movement field. First, movement actors typically identify goals and desired outcomes. Gamson (1975), for instance, distinguishes two general types of movement goals: simple versus multiple, and displacing versus nondisplacing. The dilemma for many movements is choosing between a single issue or addressing a wide range of grievances (in the case of the Quebec student movement, seeking cancellation of a tuition hike or contesting the form of governance in the province). Each strategy has its strengths and weaknesses. Single-issue organizations that successfully achieve their goal may have greater difficulty in attracting a broad base of support than they would if they were addressing multiple issues. On the other hand, an organization pursuing a single issue can more successfully stave off dissension and factionalism within its ranks. A multiple-issue approach allows an organization that has achieved a particular goal to shift its energies to other goals, thus providing some degree of organizational longevity. Alternatively, multiple-issue organizations may spread their resources and energies too thin (Marx and McAdam, 1994: 109). Of the second type of goal, displacing versus non-displacing, Gamson is referring to a movement's attitude toward its opponents. Displacing goals seek to remove or replace the group's opponents.

Movement actors must also choose between three types of decisions: institutionalized versus non-institutionalized action, legal versus illegal, and nonviolent versus violent. According to Marx and McAdam (1994), if a social movement organization chooses to advance its interests through the "proper channels," it does not qualify as a social movement. Such an approach, however, freezes out the possibility that movements may blend the institutional with the non-institutional. In a study of activism by individuals infected with tainted blood in the 1980s, I found that movement actors were quite willing to use what they called "back room" and "front room" strategies: "My answer (to government negotiators) always was, 'you can deal with them (the demonstrators outside) or you can deal with me.' We can sit here and deal at the table and hopefully we will come up with a rational solution or you can go out and deal with them. And the more outrageous people became out there, the easier it was for us to say, 'deal with us.' It made a great deal of sense" (quoted in Orsini, 2002: 487).

The second choice, between legal and illegal means, is admittedly difficult. On the one hand, law-breaking may help the movement by eliminating normative and symbolic controls as an effective response to the movement. Law-breaking or rule-breaking, if used wisely, can be strategically advantageous, since it not only demonstrates to their opponents that fear of arrest will not faze protesters, but also limits the options available to their opponents to control the group, providing, of course, movement activists are careful enough not to cross over from rule-breaking into outright or wanton violence. On the other hand, such a tactic may hurt the movement in the court of public opinion, by reversing its previously favourable image in the media or solidifying previously held negative views. The third choice, violence versus nonviolence, is particularly tricky because any movement that opts for violence must recognize the possible repercussions of such action, both internally and externally. Internally, the use of violence poses the real threat of litigation, which may place undue financial strain on the movement and its resources. The issue of violence can be especially challenging when movements are seeking to broaden their support, while ensuring that some of the movement actors who join the fold do not discredit the movement, as was the case with Black Bloc anarchists, who were criticized for being "credibility-sapping parasites" who attach themselves to a range of protest movements, such as Occupy and the Quebec student movement (Hamilton, 2012).

A focus on the meso level also calls our attention to the role of framing, and how it interacts with the macro level of "political opportunity structures." Since an "opportunity unrecognized is no opportunity at all," it is crucial to determine "the shared meanings and definitions that people bring to their situation" (McAdam, McCarthy, and Zald, 1996: 5). Framing involves "the conscious strategic efforts by groups of people to fashion shared understandings of the world and of themselves that legitimate and motivate collective action" (cited in McAdam et al., 1996: 6). As Goffman wrote of framing, "There is a sense in which what is play for the golfer is work for the caddy" (Goffman cited in Gusfield, 1997: 202). Movement actors frame the problems/issues they seek to address, and the nature/substance of their claims. These "framing processes" constitute the critical work that movement actors perform to present issues and ideas to other actors in ways that motivate them to pursue collective action. It is insufficient, therefore, to chart solely the opportunities available to movement actors; rather, one must examine why, given the opportunity to do so, they choose to mobilize or not.

As noted, framing processes refer to the shared meanings and definitions that people bring to their situation. Collective action frames "underscore and embellish the seriousness and injustice of a particular social condition or redefine as unjust and immoral what was previously seen as unfortunate but perhaps tolerable" (Benford, 1997: 416). One of the main components of collective action frames is a sense of injustice. It "arises from moral indignation related to grievances," and may also refer to a feeling that authorities are not dealing adequately with a social problem. As Gamson notes: "When we see impersonal, abstract forces as responsible for our suffering, we are taught to accept what cannot be changed and make the best of it ... At the other extreme, if one attributes undeserved suffering to malicious or selfish acts by clearly identifiable groups, the emotional component of an injustice frame will almost certainly be there" (Gamson, in della Porta and Diani, 1999: 70).

Micro Level: Actors in Movement

As noted earlier, the micro level can often be the most volatile since it is shaped by individual interactions. As Staggenborg (2008) explains, this is the arena in which individuals come to decide that collective action is worth-while. This decision can be affected by a host of factors, including a sense that there is nothing to lose or a feeling that one has a personal responsibility to express a grievance in solidarity with others. Either way, what occurs at this micro level can provide us with important insights into movement success and outcomes, especially if we consider the underlying emotional features of movement activity. As noted earlier, scholars have begun to ex-plore how emotions figure in the individual decision-making of movement actors. Bringing emotions into the study of social movements represents an effort to destabilize the separation of emotion and reason in the study of social movements (Gould, 2009; Flam and King, 2005; Goodwin, Jasper, and Polletta, 2001). Once we accept/do not that emotions interfere with reason, we can begin to appreciate how emotions—hope, fear, rage, guilt, pride, shame, despair—are fundamental to politics, and necessitate a place in our analytical toolkits. Applying an emotions lens to the study of social move-ments helps us to think about how activists and policy discourses themselves contain emotional scripts that can normalize and legitimize certain modes of behaviour and belonging. While "rational" openings in political opportuni-ties matter, they do so "only to the extent that an emotional charge attaches to these openings" (Gould, 2009: 18). The turn to emotions challenges us to think about the ways in which seemingly rational behaviours and actions might operate within emotional scripts. It also connects with an interest in the macro level of analysis discussed earlier. Institutional opportunity struc-tures may present "openings" for movements, but they tell us little about the ways in which different groups and actors attach feelings and emotions to these vectors (Gould, 2009: 18). In this vein, the types of emotions that are privileged or discouraged in political discourse matter greatly. For instance, Mothers Against Drunk Driving, which was largely credited with helping to overturn prevailing views about the social acceptability of drinking and driv-ing, succeeded by shaping our individual and collective emotional responses to this emerging social problem (Jasper, 1998). While efforts to influence policy came later, the first line of attack was to appeal to our compassion for victims of drunk driving and to provoke our collective revulsion toward individuals who make the choice to drive while under the influence of alcohol.

A conventional focus on social movements as involving rational, strategic actors who are always "mobilizing resources," or fashioning collective identities, has provided little room to explore how feelings and emotions can be organizing sites of political agency in their own right. If we start from the assumption that institutions encompass formal and informal rules, the ways in which emotions are ordered and expressed in political environments, and the impact they have on social movement actors and their claims-making, could complement more conventional approaches. The concept of *feeling rules,* first used by Hochschild (1979) to talk about the emotional work performed by flight attendants, has begun to be applied to the social movement context (Gould, 2009; Broer and Duyvendak, 2009). Unlike other rules, feeling rules "do not apply to action but to what is often taken as a precursor to action" (Hochschild, 1979: 566). What might be appropriately felt in one context may not be in another. If one shifts this to the social movement context, one can imagine that activists might expect to feel something that is at odds with what they understand to be appropriate, given their understanding of the dominant feeling rules. Moreover, movement actors communicate with one another and with authorities, and might reproduce feelings that defy conventions because they deem it necessary to express themselves in ways that depart from what is expected of them. The feminist movement, for instance, expended significant effort over several decades to convince women that it was acceptable—and indeed vital—to express outrage about gender discrimination, just as the AIDS movement was able to channel anger over the reluctance of governments to take seriously the devastating toll of the virus into productive challenges to the scientific and medical establishment (see Gould, 2009). The slogan "Silence = Death," with its inverted pink triangle symbol, was adopted by the radical AIDS organization ACT UP to urge lesbians and gay men "to turn anger, fear, grief into action" (Gould, 2009: 129).

Situating Social Movements in Neoliberal Canada: Continuity or Rupture?

Movements operate in an increasingly neoliberal, globalized environment that can be enabling or constraining in direct and indirect ways. The ability of movement actors to connect with other like-minded individuals in faraway places can enable productive forms of organizing that might yield concrete results and allow supporters to become engaged without leaving the comfort of their computer keyboard. Directly, neoliberalism and the correspondingly shrinking role of the welfare state means some of the social movement organizations that previously might have been supported by the state find themselves struggling to survive, or defunded out of existence.[5] Indirectly, but perhaps more profoundly, the paradigm shift ushered in by neoliberalism and globalization places greater emphasis on values such as individualism, commodification, and marketization. These values can stand in direct opposition to the goals and tactics of social movements, which often emphasize solidarity, community, and opposition to the increasing "colonization" of the public sphere by market forces (Larner in Smith, 2005a: 15).

While movements may be influenced by a broader neoliberal discourse that has transformed the ways in which citizens interact with the state, movement actors also borrow from the scripts of their predecessors, adjust those messages, adapt forms of protest that have been successful in the past, or adopt new methods and strategies to reflect the given context in which they are operating.[6] In Canada, it is difficult to ignore the trailblazing efforts of equality-seeking movements, including the feminist, disability. and LGBT (lesbian, gay, bisexual, and transgender) movements, which have been influenced by key institutional features of our political system such as the advent of the Charter in 1982, as well as by a progressive "citizenship regime" (Jenson and Phillips, 1996) that supported the rights of marginalized people. This rights-based discourse, which was cemented by the arrival of the Charter, meant that movements that focused in their early years on collective identity building and consciousness-raising could now turn to legal strategies aimed at making rights-based claims against the state. But we should be careful about overstating institutional arguments to explain movement successes and failures in this regard. The Charter did not somehow magically transform these movements; a rich tradition of activism and contestation had preceded the arrival of the Charter, notwithstanding the criticisms of well-known critics such as Morton and Knopff, who lament the arrival of the so-called Charter-created "Court Party" (Morton and Knopff, 2000; also see Smith, 2005b).[7]

In addition to these equality-seeking movements, the Canadian social movement landscape has been characterized by a diverse range of movement activity, including an older labour movement, a strong environmental movement, and anti-poverty organizing, among others (see Smith, 2005a, for a good historical overview of key social movements). Tracing movements historically reveals that they are influenced by the resources they can mobilize internally as well as by a larger political environment over which they have little control. Normally, this environment can be daunting, forcing some to ask what compels individuals to opt for this type of activity in the first place when there are significant obstacles to participation, including the commitment of time in exchange for little or nothing in the way of tangible outcomes. One argument advanced to explain why individuals join movements has centred on issues of collective identity. Movements are said to provide a sense of "we-ness" to individuals, a sense of kinship or community. While some of these identities may be pre-existing, such as in the LGBT communities or the feminist movements, they can be transformed in the context of movement struggle. For groups with a history of being marginalized or stigmatized, this coming together can itself be a potent outcome if it means they are able to overcome an otherwise "spoiled identity" (Goffman, 1963). Building and constructing a narrative is a critical component of such collective identity formation: "In telling the story of our becoming—as an individual, a nation, a people—we establish who we are. Narratives may be employed strategically to strengthen a collective identity but they may also precede and make possible the development of a coherent community, or nation, or collective actor ... Stories thus explain what is going on in a way that makes an evolving identity part of the explanation" (Polletta, 1998: 141).

Economist Mancur Olson (1971), drawing on a rational choice approach, was less interested in subjective measures of collective identity building. Rather, he famously argued that the natural tendency is not to organize collectively. Groups must work hard to overcome the "free rider problem," which emerges because individuals can reap the rewards of collective action regardless of their involvement. Groups, therefore, must find ways in which to confer benefits (selective incentives or inducements) to discourage individuals from free-riding.

The tactics and strategies that movements employ may be familiar, such as marches or demonstrations or legal mobilization via courts, or they may be unconventional, in the way that the North American AIDS movement employed "die-ins" in the 1980s in which activists dropped to the ground and others drew police-like chalk outlines around their "dead" bodies to symbolize the deaths from the AIDS epidemic. Engaging in forms of protest that might stand outside the norms of conventional protest suggests that the "tried and true" might work in some environments, but not necessarily in others. Moreover, some critics suggest that demonstrations have become a more palatable form of protest that "succeeds," ironically, precisely because it sits well with moderates (see Samuel, 2012). The anti-G20 protests in Toronto and the Quebec student protests provoked a strong media backlash as well as internal infighting on whether to support violence and damage to property, which were linked to anarchists affiliated with the Black Bloc. In the G20 case, People First, a movement led by Ontario unions, clashed with other G20 activists such as the Black Bloc who supported more violent tactics. The focus on protester-led violence, however, tends to neglect the violence committed by the police against protesters, which is recounted in the powerful CBC documentary featuring interviews with activists who were injured in scuffles with police (CBC, 2011).

In addition to mobilizing others to join forces collectively on issues of common concern, social movements often challenge the very meaning of what is political. As Jenson has described, "the universe of political discourse" is constituted through interaction, when actors work to overturn or challenge problems that are not seen as "public" problems worthy of state or societal intervention (Jenson, 1989). In Ottawa, for instance, a feminist collective calling itself the Radical Handmaids (after the dystopian Margaret Atwood novel, *The Handmaid's Tale*) took to the streets in the fall of 2012 to repoliticize the issue of women's reproductive freedoms. They were protesting against attempts by federal Conservative MP Stephen Woodworth to reopen the debate on abortion and the legal definition of when a fetus becomes a human (Cruikshank, 2012).

Donning red robes and large white cardboard hats, the women blended humour and satirical performance to dramatize their concerns about attempts to introduce Motion 312, which would have supported the creation of a 12-member committee to study the legal definition of a fetus. The Handmaids also urged women to participate in the "Wall of Wombs," an activity in which supporters crocheted, knitted, or sewed uteruses and vaginas, mailing them to several MPs who were known to be anti-choice (Cruikshank, 2012). The action was notable for its effort to reposition reproductive justice in the public consciousness, to challenge the assumption that women no longer had to worry about access to a safe abortion, and that this was no longer a public problem worthy of political action. As one activist explained, "The idea that 'we shouldn't be protesting this anymore' is something that is felt among many feminists and many women across Canada."[8] The Radical Handmaids were "successful" in the sense that the bill to protect the rights of the fetus was eventually defeated. While it is difficult to discern whether the policy defeat could be attributed solely to their actions, the activist added: "We would like to say that our rallying and organizing—making people aware that these bills are being discussed in the House (of Commons)—had something to do with it. However, it was only defeated marginally. And there were still many people who wanted the Bill to pass."[9]

While some movement organizations such as the Radical Handmaids are roused to action in direct response to proposed policy change, others have a more complex genealogy. For instance, the contemporary indigenous movement, Idle No More, began, innocuously enough, with a tweet in November 2012 by movement co-founder Jessica Gordon. Here is the text of the tweet:

> @shawnatleo wuts being done w #billc45 evry1 wasting time talking about Gwen stefani wth!? #indianact #wheresthedemocracy #IdleNoMore

Idle No More supporters have targeted Indigenous leaders such as Shawn Atleo, the head of the Assembly of First Nations, claiming that they have "sold out" First Nations and have not done enough to protect existing treaty rights. Movement activists had expressed strong opposition to the omnibus legislation associated with Bill C-45, which they claimed tramples on these treaty rights, but it became clear that Bill C-45 was neither the sole nor primary target of their intervention. Instead, Idle No More might be more appropriately read as a form of Indigenous political resurgence, one that is connected to previous struggles, such as the "Oka Crisis" of 1990, which resulted in a 78-day standoff between Quebec provincial police and Mohawk protesters, including members of the Warrior Society. While perhaps less dramatic than the armed standoff during that summer more than two decades ago, Idle No More has surprised many by gaining steam quickly through a series of coordinated actions across the country in a range of venues, including a much-publicized hunger strike by Attawapiskat Chief Theresa Spence that attracted international media attention and became synonymous with the movement (Galloway, 2013; Simpson, 2013; Loewen and Matthews, 2013). As evidence of an interest in attracting and retaining the interest of Indigenous youth, activists have communicated their stories and perspectives using a variety of media—including film, video, song, spoken word, and visual art—broadcast primarily via social media. Moreover, they have taken direct aim at the media's portrayal of the movement through online commentary (see Divided No More, website) and blogs, as well as numerous teach-ins at colleges and universities across Canada.

New Movements, New Concerns, New Tools?

We now turn to one of the main issues raised at the start of the chapter. Do we need new theoretical tools that will enable us to capture emergent forms of protest that sometimes bypass the state, utilize a range of unconventional tactics that recall the importance of symbols, slogans, and emotions, and engage new actors using different forms of media, including do it yourself (DIY) media interventions?

If we accept Alberto Melucci's assertion that "movements no longer operate as characters but as signs" (1988: 249), then we need to train our analytical lens on examining how movements "translate their action into symbolic
challenges that upset the dominant cultural codes and reveal their irrational-
ity and partiality by acting at the levels (of information and communication)
at which the new forms of technocratic power also operate" (1988: 249).
This will require a more sophisticated treatment of the framing role media
actors play in articulating, countering, or reinforcing movement messages, not
to mention the increasingly common practice of movement actors to create
their own media that bypasses more conventional forms of engagement with
mainstream media. Of course, the media will continue to be an important
target for movements that lack resources. As Gusfield notes, "mass media
do more than monitor: they dramatize. They create vivid images, impute
leadership, and heighten the sense of conflict between movements and the
institutions of society" (Gusfield, 1994: 71).

Movements need the news media for three major purposes: mobilization, validation, and scope enlargement. While the media often rely on
social movements to provide "good copy," Gamson and Wolfsfeld argue
that movements need the media far more than the media need them.
As a result of this unequal power relationship, movements must "deal with a
potential contradiction between gaining standing (in the media) and getting their message across" (Gamson and Wolfsfeld, 1993: 121). Sometimes,
for instance, movement actors must resort to flashy or noisy tactics to attract
attention. Getting in, however, is only half of the battle, as this affects how the
movement actors are portrayed in the media: "(T)he framing of the group
may obscure any message it carries. Those who dress up in costume to be
admitted to the media's party will not be allowed to change before being
photographed" (Gamson and Wolfsfeld, 1993: 122). Interestingly, however,
the activists associated with Radical Handmaids sought precisely to draw attention to themselves as a result of what they were wearing, and categorically
reject the idea that "dressing up" necessarily implies that their interventions
are any less serious.

Returning to the Idle No More and the Quebec student movements,
both of which sustained intense (and sometimes negative) media attention,
what kinds of lessons can we learn from their forays into the social movement arena? First, as students of social movements, we need to pay closer
attention to the language and symbols that movements employ to communicate their messages, and the things or objects that sometimes become
synonymous with movements. In the case of the student movement, the red
square pinned to the lapels of many supporters of the student strike symbolizes "being squarely in the red" in terms of student debt (Messer, 2012).

As one activist explained: "I think most students don't know the history ... We chose a sign, a symbol for [the many] students in the chain. The chain of student debt. It's a very strong and powerful statement" (Messer, 2012). The red square also links the student struggle to the broader Quebec fight against poverty, which predates the student movement and is strongly associated with the province's progressive social policy. The *Collectif pour un Québec sans pauvreté* (Collective for a Poverty-Free Quebec) claims that it first used the red square in October 2004 when it appeared before the Committee on Social Affairs in the Quebec National Assembly to oppose Bill 57, a law to regulate social welfare and assistance.

For the Occupy movement, the slogan "We are the 99 per cent," whatever the critiques of the accuracy of that statement, was used successfully by the Occupy movement to communicate a sense of "we-ness" among potential supporters. Turning again to language, the use of the term *occupy* "turned politics on its head" and had a "stronger and more controversial implication than simply to set up a camp or hold a sit-in" (Pickerill and Krinsky, 2012: 281). Similarly, the use of the phrase "Idle No More" by First Nations protesters communicates as a call to action, as well as being a mobilizing expression for a range of political interventions aimed at bringing together generations of Indigenous people from all walks of life. While Chief Spence attracted some particularly negative media coverage as a result of her attachment to the movement, for better or worse, her plight became a potent symbol of the broader Indigenous struggle, and communicated a sense of urgency to the demands being made by leaders of the movement.

In addition to paying closer attention to the emotional components of language and symbols used by movement actors, we need to ask new questions about movements that do not target the state directly. What happens when a social movement seeks to bypass the state, partially or entirely? What does it mean to study social movements *without* the state? The Occupy movement, and to a lesser extent Idle No More, refuse to recognize the "legitimacy of the state as an agent capable of or willing to implement policy" (Pickerill and Krinsky, 2012: 283). In the case of Occupy, for instance: "By establishing temporary tent communities with kitchens, bathrooms, libraries, first-aid posts, information centres, sleeping areas and educational space, they recreated new spaces of provision: prefigurative alternative communities with very few resources" (Pickerill and Krinsky, 2012: 283). Thinking about the role of the state in the study of social movements does not mean assuming that the state has lost its relevance, however. Is it best, for instance, to "institutionally disaggregate the state into agencies with which movements are likely to make headway (at least at times) and ones they are not" (Pickerill and Krinsky, 2012: 283)?

Just as we need to challenge the ways in which we think about social movements, it might be wise to apply the same critical lens to the study of the state, recognizing that state power is diffuse, complex, and, at times, contradictory. In a different sense, Ladner's (2008) discussion of Indigenous social movement contention raises some similar issues with regard to the refusal of Indigenous activists to take the state as given, or at least to accept a particular vision of state power that fails to recognize a colonial history of subjugation. In other cases, however, state power is synonymous with more traditional Weberian notions of the state as retaining the monopoly over the legitimate use of physical force (violence). As Samuel argues (2012: 12) in an article on the G20 protests in Toronto, while many debate whether violent protesters tarnish otherwise legitimate forms of protest, "debates about the relationship among divergent protest tactics risk neglecting a central feature of domination: the impossibility of adopting a 'right' form of protest in a 'wrong' political field." A wrong political field is one wherein it is "impossible for dominated actors to gain sufficient position within that field to alter its basic structures and therefore the relations of domination that are structured by the field and ultimately to alter the social construction according to which the field is reproduced" (Samuel, 2012: 12).

Conclusion

This chapter has sought to chart the shifting terrain of social movement pro-test in Canada, with a focus on how these movements challenge or disrupt conventional ways of understanding the goals, outcomes, and meanings of protest. While some movements are only peripherally engaged in challenging particular policies and have difficulties articulating their specific demands, others, such as the Radical Handmaids, emerged directly in the wake of proposed legislation. While movements may "succeed" in the initial goal they set out for themselves—for instance, defeating a bill or reversing a policy stand—their actions do not end there. In other cases, movement actors might seek change, but they encounter difficulties in trying to organize the sources of their mobilization into easily digestible media sound bites. In still other cases, the purpose of the movement itself might be centred on wider cultural changes associated with creating alternative, self-sustaining communities that might be distinguished from the capitalist system against which the move-ment has railed. As the Occupy movement demonstrates, a critique of the capitalist system of accumulation does not always lend itself to a series of pithy, media-friendly demands.

While there are important questions to ask about why certain movements emerge or not during particular historical periods, it is equally critical to ask what difference social movements make. How should we assess what they do or achieve? Do they simply provide us with a glimpse into the growing well of discontent in society that has hardened or solidified into social movement protest? Do they remind us that the only way to initiate change is to refuse to play by the institutional rules of the game, to disrupt or challenge the boundaries of acceptable political expression or dissent?

The student movement in Quebec, which morphed into a broader movement of citizens displeased with the Liberal provincial government of then Premier Jean Charest, succeeded in gaining media attention, some of it especially negative in anglophone Quebec, because it chose to openly disrupt business as usual, shutting down many universities and colleges in the province and inciting others to communicate their anger through the simple gesture of making noise with pots and pans. Perhaps unbeknownst to the protesters, the Charest government's decision to impose Bill 78—which restricted the right to picket and protest on college and university campuses and throughout the province—gave a further boost to the movement, as supporters united in opposition to what they saw as an excessively draconian bill (National Assembly [Quebec], 2012). Characterized as one of the worst laws for civil liberties since the 1970 War Measures Act, the bill was later repealed by the newly elected Parti Québécois government.

Social movements are intriguing subjects of analysis precisely because they combine the unpredictable with the unconventional, because their actions are not always easy to interpret. While they may prove frustrating to journalists (and academics) who are eager to label them, movements' ability to disrupt what we understand as "politics as usual" is what makes them worthy of the interest of social scientists. Many of the issues and themes that have moved into the mainstream of Canadian politics—gay and lesbian issues, feminist concerns, Aboriginal grievances—owe much to the trailblazing efforts of social movement activists who struggled to position them when few people were paying any attention. The movements of today are not, however, simply a direct outgrowth of their forerunners. In the case of Aboriginal peoples, for instance, the Indigenous movement that mobilized in the early 1970s in the wake of opposition to the federal White Paper in the late 1960s that threatened to abolish the Indian Act (and with it the legal status of Indians) is qualitatively different from the media-savvy Idle No More movement that we have come to know, including the catalytic role played by Indigenous women in the founding of this movement. While Indigenous people have been resisting state authority and colonialism for several centuries (Simpson, 2013), they are using different methods and tactics today to confront colonial power and authority.

Collective actors in society will no doubt continue to interact with the state and with conventional institutions such as courts to make their demands heard and to transform their grievances into political issues, but we need to cast our net wider to think more closely about how groups and movements respond to and try to shape the political landscape itself, which contains and reflects shifting values and beliefs about the legitimate expression of dissent and collective action.

Notes

1 The author thanks the editors for helpful comments on this chapter. Some of the material presented here draws on ideas developed in Orsini (2008) and Orsini and Wiebe (under review).

2 In *The Power of Identity*, Castells (1997: 3) defines social movements as "purposive collective action whose outcome, in victory as in defeat, transforms the values and institutions of society." This definition can be problematic because the criteria used to judge a movement—actual effects on societal institutions and values—are difficult to satisfy, especially within such a limited time frame. Tarrow uses the term to describe "collective challenges by people with common purposes and solidarity in sustained interaction with elites, opponents, and authorities" (Tarrow, 1994: 4). In the second edition of *Power in Movement*, he revises this definition somewhat, referring to movements "as those sequences of contentious politics that are based on underlying social networks and resonant collective action frames, and which develop the capacity to maintain sustained challenges against powerful opponents" (Tarrow, 1998: 2).

3 Benford refers to this as the reification problem, or the tendency among social movement scholars to speak "about socially constructed ideas as though they are *real,* as though they exist independent of the collective interpretations and constructions of the actors involved" (Benford, 1997: 418) Benford has identified three problems related to reification. First, when we speak about movements, identities, ideologies, and frames, we tend to "anthropomorphize" them. That is, we speak of movements as if they are doing the "framing," "interpreting," and "acting," when in fact it is movement participants who engage in these activities. As he remarks: "Social movements do not frame issues; their activists or other participants do the framing" (Benford, 1997: 418). Second, there is a paradoxical tendency to neglect human agency. Social movements are not monolithic and rarely "speak" with one voice; rather, they comprise actors who interact, co-act, and react. Finally, the third problem relates to the neglect

of emotions, which is discussed in the chapter. Movement actors are not "Spock-like beings, devoid of passion and other human emotions" (Benford, 1997: 418).

4   Burstein suggests that the traditional distinction between interest groups and social movement organizations is deeply flawed. The key distinction—that SMOs are almost always operating at the margins with little or no direct link to the power holders in society, while interest groups enjoy relatively easy access—rests on a false dividing line. Instead, he counsels, the only useful distinction between non-governmental political organizations is a legal one. Political parties, which enjoy a special legal status as "political organizations that have a place on the ballot and a formal role in organizing legislatures" (Burstein, 1999: 9), occupy one end of the continuum, while "interest organizations," the term he uses to group interest groups and social movement organizations, occupy the other end.

5   On the recent cuts to key Aboriginal organizations, see Orsini and Papillon (2012).

6   See Meyer and Whittier's (1994) discussion of the concept of "social movement spillover."

7   In the case of the disability movement, despite some important advances in the recognition of their claims, there are persistent concerns about the invisibility of disabled people more generally in Canadian political life (see Prince, 2009; Vanhala, 2011).

8   Personal communication with activist Polly Leonard, Ottawa, March 2013.

9   Personal communication with activist Polly Leonard, Ottawa, March 2013.

References and Suggested Readings

Benford, Robert. 1997. "An Insider's Critique of the Social Movement Framing Perspective." *Sociological Inquiry* 67 (4): 409–30. http://dx.doi.org/10.1111/j.1475-682X.1997.tb00445.x.

Broer, Christian, and Jan Willem Duyvendak. 2009. "Discursive Opportunities, Feeling Rules, and the Rise of Protests Against Aircraft Noise." *Mobilization: An International Journal* 14 (3): 337–56.

Burstein, Paul. 1999. "Social Movements and Public Policy." In *How Social Movements Matter*, eds. Marco Giugni, Doug McAdam, and Charles Tilly, 3–21. Minneapolis: University of Minnesota Press.

Castells, Manuel. 1997. *The Power of Identity*. London: Blackwell Publishers.

CBC. 2011. *The Fifth Estate*, "You Should Have Stayed at Home." http://www.cbc.ca/fifth/episodes/2010-2011/youshouldhavestayedathome/.

Cohen, Jean L. 1985. "Strategy or Identity: New Theoretical Paradigms and Contemporary Social Movements." *Social Research* 52 (4): 663–716.

Conway, Janet. 2003. "Civil Resistance and the 'Diversity of Tactics' in the Anti-Globalization Movement: Problems of Violence, Silence, and Solidarity in Activist Politics." *Osgoode Hall Law Journal* 41 (2 & 3): 505–29.

Cruikshank, Julie. 2012. "Getting Radical: Handmaids Take Pro-choice Message to Parliament." *Xtra,* Oct. 12. http://www.xtra.ca/public/Ottawa/Getting_Radical-12648.aspx.

della Porta, Donatella, and Mario Diani. 1999. *Social Movements: An Introduction.* London: Blackwell Publishers.

Divided No More. n.d. Website. Accessed April 1, 2013. http://dividednomore.ca

Eisinger, Peter. 1973. "The Conditions of Protest Behavior in American Cities." *American Political Science Review* 67 (1): 11–28. http://dx.doi.org/10.2307/1958525.

Flam, Helen, and Debra King, eds. 2005. *Emotions and Social Movements.* New York: Routledge.

Galloway, Gloria. 2013. "With Hunger Strike Over, Chief Spence's Polarizing Legacy," *Globe and Mail,* January 24. http://www.theglobeandmail.com/news/politics/with-hunger-strike-over-chief-spences-polarizing-legacy/article7760372/.

Gamson, William. 1975. *The Strategy of Social Protest.* Homewood: The Dorsey Press.

Gamson, William, and David Meyer. 1996. "Framing Political Opportunity." In *Comparative Perspectives on Social Movements: Political Opportunities, Mobilizing Structures, and Cultural Framings,* eds. Doug McAdam, John D. McCarthy, and Mayer N. Zald, 275–90. Cambridge: Cambridge University Press. http://dx.doi.org/10.1017/CBO9780511803987.014.

Gamson, William, and Gadi Wolfsfeld. 1993. "Movements and Media as Interacting Systems." *Annals of the American Academy of Political and Social Science* 528 (1): 114–25. http://dx.doi.org/10.1177/0002716293528001009.

Goffman, Erving. 1963. *Stigma: Notes on the Management of Spoiled Identity.* Englewood Cliffs: Prentice Hall.

Goodwin, Jeff, James M. Jasper, and Francesca Polletta. 2001. *Passionate Politics: Emotions and Social Movements.* Chicago: Chicago University Press. http://dx.doi.org/10.7208/chicago/9780226304007.001.0001.

Goodwin, Jeff, James J. Jasper, and Francesca Polletta. 2004. "Emotional Dimensions of Social Movements." In *The Blackwell Companion to Social Movements,* eds. David A. Snow, Sarah A. Soule, and Hanspeter Kriesi, 413–32. Malden: Blackwell.

Gould, Deborah. 2009. *Moving Politics: Emotion and ACT UP's Fight Against AIDS.* Chicago: University of Chicago Press. http://dx.doi.org/10.7208/chicago/9780226305318.001.0001.

Gusfield, Joseph R. 1994. "The Reflexivity of Social Movements: Collective Behaviour and Mass Society Theory Revisited." In *New Social Movements: From Ideology to Identity,* eds. Enrique Laraña, Hank Johnston, and Joseph R. Gusfield, 58–78. Philadelphia: Temple University Press.

Gusfield, Joseph R. 1997. "The Culture of Public Problems: Drinking-Driving and the Symbolic Order." In *Morality and Health,* eds. Allan M. Brandt and Paul Rozin, 201–30. New York, London: Routledge.

Hamilton, Graeme. 2012. "Hard to Claim Montreal Violence Isn't Tied into Wider Protest Movement," *National Post,* May 4. http://fullcomment.nationalpost.com/2012/05/04/graeme-hamilton-hard-to-claim-montreal-violence-isnt-tied-into-wider-protest-movement/.

Hochschild, Arlie. 1979. "Emotion Work, *Feeling Rules,* and Social Structure." *American Journal of Sociology* 85 (3): 551–75. http://dx.doi.org/10.1086/227049.

Jasper, James M. 1998. "The Emotions of Protest: Affective and Reactive Emotions in and around Social Movements." *Sociological Forum* 13 (3): 397–424. http://dx.doi.org/10.1023/A:1022175308081.

Jasper, James M. 2011. "Emotions and Social Movements: Twenty Years of Theory and Research." *Annual Review of Sociology* 37 (1): 285–303. http://dx.doi.org/10.1146/annurev-soc-081309-150015.

Jenson, Jane. 1989. "Paradigms and Political Discourse: Protective Legislation in France and the United States Before 1914." *Canadian Journal of Political Science* 22 (02): 235–58. http://dx.doi.org/10.1017/S0008423900001293.

Jenson, Jane, and Martin Papillon. 2000. "Challenging the Citizenship Regime: The James Bay Cree and Transnational Action." *Politics & Society* 28 (2): 245–64. http://dx.doi.org/10.1177/0032329200028002005.

Jenson, Jane, and Susan D. Phillips. 1996. "Regime Shift: New Citizenship Practices in Canada." *International Journal of Canadian Studies* 14 (Fall): 111–36.

Ladner, Kiera. 2008. "*Aysaka'paykinit:* Contesting the Rope Around the Nations' Neck." In *Group Politics and Social Movements in Canada*, ed. Miriam Smith, 227–49. Peterborough: Broadview Press.

Laforest, Rachel. 2011. *Voluntary Sector Organizations and the State: Building New Relations.* Vancouver: University of British Columbia Press.

Loewen, Peter, and Scott Matthews. 2013. "Op-Ed: Aboriginal Issues Are on the Agenda," *Ottawa Citizen*, March 4. http://www2.canada.com/ottawacitizen/news/archives/story.html?id=83b93aa7-8777-4a22-ae08-5546c2e76d8e&p=2.

Marx, Gary T., and Douglas McAdam. 1994. *Collective Behaviour and Social Movements: Process and Structure.* New Jersey: Prentice Hall.

McAdam, Doug. 1985. *Political Process and the Development of Black Insurgency, 1930–1970.* Chicago: University of Chicago Press.

McAdam, Doug, John McCarthy, and Mayer N. Zald, eds. 1996. *Comparative Perspectives on Social Movements: Political Opportunities, Mobilizing Structures, and Cultural Framings.* Cambridge: Cambridge University Press. http://dx.doi.org/10.1017/CBO9780511803987.

McCarthy, John, and Mark Wolfson. 1992. "Consensus Movements, Conflict Movements, and the Cooptation of Civic and State Infrastructures." In *Frontiers in Social Movement Theory*, eds. Aldon Morris and Mueller McClurg, 273–97. New Haven: Yale University Press.

Melucci, Alberto. 1988. "Social Movements and the Democratization of Everyday Life." In *Civil Society and the State*, ed. John Keane, 245–60. London: Verso.

Melucci, Alberto. 1994. "A Strange Kind of Newness: What's 'New' in New Social Movements." In *New Social Movements: From Ideology to Identity*, eds. Enrique Laraña, Hank Johnston, and Joseph R. Gusfield, 101–30. Philadelphia: Temple University Press.

Messer, Olivia. 2012. "Squarely in the Red: The History Behind That Felt on Your Lapel," *McGill Daily*, March 31. http://www.mcgilldaily.com/2012/03/squarely-in-the-red/.

Meyer, David, and Nancy Whittier. 1994. "Social Movement Spillover." *Social Problems* 41 (2): 277–98. http://dx.doi.org/10.2307/3096934.

Morton, F.L., and Rainer Knopff. 2000. *The Charter Revolution and the Court Party.* Peterborough: Broadview Press.

Mueller, Carol. 1994. "Conflict Network and the Origins of Women's Liberation." In *New Social Movements: From Ideology to Identity*, eds. Enrique Laraña, Hank Johnston, and Joseph R. Gusfield, 234–63. Philadelphia: Temple University Press.

National Assembly (Quebec). 2012. Bill 78: An Act to enable students to receive instruction from the postsecondary institutions they attend. http://www2.publications duquebec.gouv.qc.ca/dynamicSearch/telecharge.php?type=5&file=2012C12A.PDF.

Nevitte, Neil. 2000. "Value Change and Reorientation in Citizen-State Relations." *Canadian Public Policy* 24: S74–94.

Offe, Claus. 1985. "New Social Movements: Challenging the Boundaries of Institutional Politics." *Social Research* 52 (4): 817–68.

Olson, Mancur. 1971. *The Logic of Collective Action: Public Goods and the Theory of Groups.* Rev. ed. Cambridge: Harvard University Press.

Orsini, Michael. 2002. "The Politics of Naming, Blaming and Claiming: HIV, Hepatitis C and the Emergence of Blood Activism in Canada." *Canadian Journal of Political Science* 35 (03): 475–98. http://dx.doi.org/10.1017/S0008423902778323.

Orsini, Michael. 2008. "Health Social Movements: The Next Wave in Contentious Politics?" In *Group Politics and Social Movements in Canada*, ed. Miriam Smith, 475–98. Peterborough: Broadview Press.

Orsini, Michael, and Martin Papillon. 2012. "Death by A Thousand Cuts," *The Mark News*, April 25. http://ca.news.yahoo.com/death-thousand-cuts-052241740.html.

Orsini, Michael, and Miriam Smith. 2010. "Social Movements, Knowledge and Public Policy: The Case of Autism Activism in Canada and the U.S." *Critical Policy Studies* 4 (1): 38–57. http://dx.doi.org/10.1080/19460171003714989.

Orsini, Michael, and Sarah Wiebe. Forthcoming. "Between Hope and Fear: Comparing the Emotional Landscapes of Autism Activism in Canada and the U.S." In *Canada Compared*, eds. Luc Turgeon, Jennifer Wallner, Martin Papillon, and Stephen White. Vancouver: University of British Columbia Press.

Phillips, Susan. 1999. "Social Movements in Canada: Past their Apex?" In *Canadian Politics*, 3rd ed., eds. James Bickerton and Alain-G. Gagnon 371–89. Peterborough: Broadview Press.

Phillips, Susan. 2004. "Social Movements, Interest Groups and the Voluntary Sector: En Route to Reducing the Democratic Deficit." In *Canadian Politics*, 4th ed., eds. James Bickerton and Alain-G. Gagnon, 323–47. Toronto: Broadview Press.

Pickerill, Jenny, and John Krinsky. 2012. "Why Does Occupy Matter?" *Social Movement Studies: Journal of Social, Cultural and Political Protest* 11 (3–4): 279–87. http://dx.doi.org/10.1080/14742837.2012.708923.

Pinard, Maurice. 2011. *Motivational Dimensions in Social Movements and Contentious Collective Action.* Montreal: McGill-Queen's University Press.

Pineault, Éric. 2012. "Quebec's Red Spring: An Essay on Ideology and Social Conflict at the End of Neoliberalism." *Studies in Political Economy* 90 (Autumn): 29–56.

Polletta, Francesca. 1998. "'It was like a fever ...' Narrative and Identity in Social Protest." *Social Problems* 45 (2): 137–59. http://dx.doi.org/10.2307/3097241.

Prince, Michael. 2009. *Absent Citizens: Disability Politics and Policy in Canada.* Toronto: University of Toronto Press.

Samuel, Chris. 2012. "Throwing Bricks at a Brick Wall: The G20 and the Antinomies of Protest." *Studies in Political Economy* 90 (Autumn): 7–27.

Schwartz, Michael, and Shuva Paul. 1992. "Resource Mobilization versus the Mobilization of People: Why Consensus Movements Cannot be Instruments of Social Change." In *Frontiers in Social Movement Theory*, eds. Aldon D. Morris and Carol Mc-Clurg Mueller, 205–23. New Haven and London: Yale University Press.

Simpson, Leanne. 2013. "Idle No More: Where the Mainstream Media Went Wrong." Feb. 27. http://dominion.mediacoop.ca/story/idle-no-more-and-mainstream-media/16023

Smith, Miriam. 2005a. *A Civil Society? Collective Actors in Canadian Political Life.* Peterborough: Broadview Press.

Smith, Miriam. 2005b. "Social Movements and Judicial Empowerment: Courts, Public Policy, and Lesbian and Gay Organizing in Canada." *Politics & Society* 33 (2): 327–53. http://dx.doi.org/10.1177/0032329205275193.

Smith, Miriam. 2008. *Group Politics and Social Movements in Canada*. Peterborough: Broadview Press.

Staggenborg, Suzanne. 2008. *Social Movements*. Don Mills: Oxford University Press.

Tarrow, Sidney. 1994. *Power in Movement: Social Movements, Collective Action and Politics*. Cambridge: Cambridge University Press.

Tarrow, Sidney. 1998. *Power in Movement: Social Movements, Collective Action and Mass Politics in the Modern State*. Cambridge: Cambridge University Press. http://dx.doi.org/10.1017/CBO9780511813245.

Vanhala, Lisa. 2011. *Making Disability Rights a Reality? Disability Rights Activists and Legal Mobilization in Canada and the United Kingdom*. Cambridge: Cambridge University Press.

Walia, Harsha. 2011. "2011: Reflecting on Social Movement Successes in Canada." http://canadiandimension.com/articles/3976/.

White, Deena. 2012. "Interest Representation and Organization in Civil Society: Ontario and Quebec Compared." *British Journal of Canadian Studies* 25 (2): 199–229. http://dx.doi.org/10.3828/bjcs.2012.11.

seventeen

Women (Not) in Politics: Women's Electoral Participation

MELANEE THOMAS AND LISA YOUNG

Compared to their counterparts elsewhere, Canadian women enjoy considerable political freedom, legal equality, and educational and economic opportunity. These are a result of decades of women's activism, both inside and outside the halls of power. Fundamental political freedoms like the right to vote, to run for office, and to be considered "persons" under the law were won by activists insisting that women were both qualified and entitled to participate in the democratic life of their country.

In many respects, these activists were successful: Canadian women now enjoy full equality under the law, and the *Canadian Charter of Rights and Freedoms* and various human rights acts explicitly ban discrimination based on gender. Women vote in Canadian elections in numbers similar to men and face no formal barriers to holding elected office. The current Chief Justice of the Supreme Court of Canada is a woman. There have been two female Governors General since 1999, and a woman has served briefly as prime minister. Women comprise the majority of undergraduate students on Canadian campuses and have made remarkable inroads into many previously male-dominated occupations. Canadian women have access to universal health care services and are largely able to control their reproductive functions. Although Canadian women still earn less, on average, than men (Statistics Canada, 2011), the gap is smaller than in many comparable countries (Hausmann, Tyson, and Zahidi, 2012).

In light of this, it would be reasonable to expect that Canada would be a world leader in terms of women's political representation. In fact, this is not the case. As of 2012, Canada ranked 47th internationally in a comparison of women's representation in national legislatures, lagging behind countries in Scandinavia and elsewhere in Western Europe, as well as behind emerging democracies like Afghanistan, Argentina, and Rwanda (Inter-Parliamentary Union, 2013). This chapter provides an overview of Canadian political scientists' efforts to understand the barriers to the representation of women in the formal political arena. The chapter does not address the studies that examine women's extensive participation in informal, but equally political, arenas such as activism through interest groups, social movements, and community organizations.[1] By focusing exclusively on the world of voting, parties, and elections, the chapter overlooks an important part of the story of Canadian women's political participation, but illuminates the extent to which the electoral arena remains foreign territory to many Canadian women.

A discussion of the patterns of women's involvement and non-involvement in the formal political arena must begin with some consideration of women's ambivalence toward electoral politics. Despite all the gains women have made in terms of education, participation in the workforce, and participation in public life, survey findings still report that women are less likely than men to be interested in politics and are less knowledgeable about the formal political arena. A recent study found that women are consistently less knowledgeable about political parties' policy stances and leaders than are men (Gidengil et al., 2004; Gidengil, Goodyear-Grant, et al., 2006). Even women's growing access to higher education does not diminish the gap: university-educated women score lower on measures of political knowledge than university-educated men. It is not clear why women are less interested in and knowledgeable about politics than are men. Perhaps the fact that men remain the majority of politicians and political leaders sends a subtle message to women that this world is closed to them. Perhaps the relative absence of women from political life means that the issues that matter to women are not constructed in a way that many women consider to be relevant to their lives. And, quite possibly, the social legacy of politics being "men's business" lives on, despite women's entry into all sorts of arenas that were just as exclusionary in the past. No matter what their source, these gender differences in political knowledge and interest are crucially important: knowledge is an essential resource for political activism of any kind, and if women lack it they will remain marginal to political life.

Other scholars have examined women's different political priorities and attitudes and concluded that women constitute a discernible subculture within the Canadian political culture (O'Neill, 2002). If we accept that this is the case, then an ambivalent relationship to formal politics is certainly a salient aspect of this subculture. This ambivalence provides the underpinnings for examining studies of women's participation in, and exclusion from, the formal political life of Canada; it provides at least a partial explanation for the title of this chapter, which notes that the examination of women's involvement in Canadian political life focuses as much on our absence as it does on our presence.

To organize this discussion of women's electoral participation, we divide the research into two broad categories: studies that ask "Where are the women in the political process?" and studies that ask "What do women do when they get there?" The former category encompasses studies of women as voters, women's participation in political parties, and women as candidates for election. The focus of these studies, for the most part, is on women's relative absence from the formal political process, and they probe the reasons for this. The latter category concentrates on what women do once they have entered the formal political arena, be it as political party members or legislators. A portion of these studies focus on women's experiences of discrimination within political institutions—as legislators who are subjected to abuse by their colleagues, or as party leaders who face extra scrutiny from the mass media. The larger body of literature addresses the question of whether women's participation in the formal political arena makes a difference in terms of their behaviour or policy outcomes.

Where Are the Women?

Although women's representation in political elites has increased steadily over the past three decades, it remains low when compared to many other countries and to the democratic ideal of representation proportionate to women's presence in the population. It is noteworthy that 35 years after Jill Vickers (1978) published an article in *Atlantis* asking "Where Are The Women in Canadian Politics?" we are still asking the same question. The consistent theme that emerges through these studies is: *where power is, women are not.* This applies equally to studies of women in municipal politics and analyses of the composition of the current federal Cabinet. The focus of much of this literature, then, has been to document this pattern and to explain it, usually with a view to suggesting some remedy.

Women as Voters

The most basic and fundamental form of participation in the formal political arena is voting. This fundamental democratic right was denied to most Canadian women until 1920, women in Quebec until 1940, and many Aboriginal women until the 1960s. Bewteen the 1920s and the 1960s, turnout tended to be lower among women than among men, but since the 1970s women have been as likely as, if not more likely than, men to cast a ballot.

Has the vote turned into a powerful political resource for women? Given that women constitute over half the electorate and are slightly more inclined to vote than their male counterparts, we have the theoretical potential as a numeric majority to exercise considerable control over the political process. For the most part, however, this theoretical possibility has not been realized. Like men, women do not vote as a bloc. They differ in their fundamental political perspectives and interests, and their voting behaviour varies accordingly. To the extent that there have been systematic patterns of difference between the voting behaviour of men and women—referred to as an electoral "gender gap"—political parties have shown some responsiveness to concerns specifically associated with women.

There are persistent gender gaps in party preferences in Canada at the federal level. Men are somewhat more likely to support parties on the right of the political spectrum (the Conservative Party), and women more likely to support parties on the centre and left (the Liberals and NDP). These gender gaps in party preference are reflective of consistent patterns of gender difference in policy attitudes, and should be understood as "cultural" in character, as they are rooted in men's greater support for free enterprise, closer ties to the United States, and social conservatism (Gidengil, Everitt, et al., 2006). By contrast, "women tend to be more sceptical than men of the workings of the market, they are less likely to favour close ties with the United States, and they are more open to diverse lifestyles and sexual mores" (Gidengil et al., 2012: 23; see also Gidengil et al., 2003, 154; Gidengil et al., 2005; Everitt, 1998; Gidengil, 1995).

These gender gaps in voting have, however, seldom been parlayed into a source of influence for women. Canadian feminist leaders have not followed the lead of their American counterparts in trying to construct a political meaning for gender differences in voting, thereby turning the gender gap into a political resource. This was due in part to the pattern of gender differences among Canadian voters, with the Liberal party rather than the more feminist NDP historically tending to benefit the most from gender gaps (Young 2000: 202). The ascendance of the NDP as the official opposition in 2011, however, may alter this calculus and yield a more politicized gender gap.

Women in Political Parties

Women were involved in Canadian political parties throughout most of the twentieth century, but until the 1970s their participation tended to be channelled into supportive roles. Women's involvement in the two major parties at the time (the Liberals and the Progressive Conservatives) took the form of activism in ladies' auxiliary organizations that supported the party but played no role in directing it. By the late 1960s, attitudes about women's roles in society were coming into question, and this led women inside the parties to challenge the character of their involvement in party affairs. In 1970, the Report of the *Royal Commission on the Status of Women* encouraged this, advocating that the parties should disband their ladies' auxiliaries and encourage women to participate in the mainstream of party life. Through the 1970s, women's organizations in the party were converted into feminist organizations that promoted women's participation in the parties on an equal footing.

Despite the activism of women in the three major federal political parties at the time, women remained underrepresented in most facets of party life through the 1980s. The most comprehensive study of women's underrepresentation in party politics in English Canada is Sylvia Bashevkin's *Toeing the Lines* (1993), which documented the systematic underrepresentation of women in the parties. Bashevkin found that the more electorally competitive the party, the greater the underrepresentation of women within it. She also found that women's participation in parties tended to be channelled into traditional roles such as secretary of the riding association, thereby creating "pink collar ghettoes" within the parties. Some parties, most notably the NDP at the federal level and in some provinces, have adopted internal affirmative action programs, and these have gone some distance toward improving women's representation within the party (Praud, 1998; Cross, 2004). In her analysis of the women's committee of the Parti Québécois, Jocelyne Praud (2003) found that the activism of that committee resulted in moderate numerical gains for women, generally exceeding that of the Liberal Party of Quebec.

A survey of members of the five major national political parties in 2000 (before the merger of the Canadian Alliance and Progressive Conservatives) found that women remained a minority among party members. Young and Cross (2003) report that only 38 per cent of party members in their survey were women. This proportion varied somewhat by party, with parties that maintained organizations focused on women's participation (the Liberals and New Democrats) exceeding those that eschewed them (the Progressive Conservatives and Canadian Alliance). In addition, this corresponds generally with the patterns of gender difference in electoral support for the parties. Examining patterns of recruitment into the parties, the study finds that women are more likely than men to have been asked to join the party, rather than taking the initiative themselves. Women were also more likely to have been recruited into the party to support a candidate for the party's nomination or leadership. According to these findings, once women were recruited into the party, their activities differed little from those of their male counterparts. Despite this, the study found that female party members saw themselves as insufficiently influential within their parties and were (with the exception of members of the Canadian Alliance) generally supportive of measures to increase their influence and the number of women holding elected office.

The underrepresentation of women in political parties reflects gender differences in evaluations of political parties versus interest groups. In a study of politically active young people on Canadian university campuses, Young and Cross (2007) found that young women were more likely to join interest groups than they were to join the youth wing of political parties, and that they were more negative in their evaluations of political parties than were young men.

Women as Candidates

The focus of much of the research on women in politics in Canada is on the issue of why women remain underrepresented in numeric terms in the House of Commons, provincial legislatures, and city councils. These institutions are at the heart of representative democracy in Canada; city councils act as decision-making bodies in their own right, and legislatures are the institutions from which Cabinets are drawn and to which Cabinets must answer. Exclusion of women from these representative institutions signifies exclusion from political decision-making. It is not surprising, then, that women's underrepresentation in these elected bodies has been the focus of much research.

Feminist political scientists began to study the barriers to women's election in the 1970s, roughly the time when the number of women elected gradually began to increase from few or no women to the roughly 20 per cent of provincial and federal elected representatives we now have. At first, studies examined the role political parties played as gatekeepers, consistently choosing men over women in electoral districts the party expected to win, but willing to nominate women in ridings where the party's prospects were poor. Other studies have emphasized the rules governing nomination campaigns, political culture, the party system, and women's unwillingness to run for office.

One would expect that the level of government for which the election is held makes some difference to the representation of women. Using longitudinal data, Tolley (2011: 573) concludes that women are present in "roughly equivalent proportions across all three levels of government." Although rates of women's representation vary from municipality to municipality and province to province, for all three levels of government women comprise between 20 and 25 per cent of the members; moreover, Tolley demonstrates that rates of representation at all three levels have tended to increase at roughly the same pace (see Tolley, 2011: 586, Fig. 2). Cross-provincial variations are explored in detail in Trimble, Arscott, and Tremblay (2013).

There is no evidence that the electorate is responsible for the underrepresentation of women. Studies at both the federal level (Denton, 1984; Goodyear-Grant and Croskill, 2011) and the municipal level (Kushner et al., 1997) show that voters do not discriminate against female candidates. How, then, has women's relative absence from the formal legislative sphere been explained?

- *Electoral Laws*: Like Great Britain and the United States, Canada uses a single member plurality electoral system. This is often cited as a potential barrier to women's election, as more proportional electoral systems and/or higher district magnitudes appear to be associated with a greater number of women in elected office. However, research shows that "electoral laws may not be the magic bullet for increasing women's representation," because countries that have changed their electoral system have not necessarily seen a commensurate increase in the proportion of women elected (Roberts, Seawright, and Cyr, 2012: 20). Generally speaking, the association between electoral laws and women's representation is smaller than initially anticipated, and it varies considerably across countries. Overall, the causes that underpin electoral system effects are, for the most part, poorly understood (ibid.).

  Where electoral law *can* have a significant effect is through the introduction of gender quotas for women's representation (Krook, 2009; Roberts, Seawright, and Cyr, 2012). In a single-member system such as Canada's, it is more difficult to design a quota system that ensures that a certain number of seats are set aside for women. In list-based proportional representation systems, it is possible to "zip" the lists so that the list alternates between the names of women and men. Women's representation tends to be much higher under these quota systems. There may be popular support for electoral gender quotas in Canada, as 64 per cent of Canadians agree that the best way to protect women's interests is to elect more women to Parliament. That said, gender quotas may not find fertile ground in the individualist political cultures of Anglo-American societies (Young, 2013).

- *Party gatekeepers*: Initial studies identified political parties as the "gatekeepers" preventing women from winning party nominations (Brodie, 1985). While there has been some debate in the literature around the question of whether parties' nomination processes have kept women from being nominated in "winnable" seats, Thomas and Bodet (2013) report that in the 2008 and 2011 federal elections, women were more likely than men to be nominated in a riding where their party's support was unstable, shrinking, or non-existent. Men, by contrast, were more likely than women to be nominated to run in party strongholds. This held for every party *except* the Bloc Québécois. Thomas and Bodet's findings are problematic for other federal parties. The NDP is notable because it has undertaken explicit affirmative action campaigns for women and members of minority groups. The Liberals use gender-equity arguments to appoint women candidates, circumventing the usual nomination process. Research shows, though, that most of the candidates appointed by the Liberals were "stars" destined for Cabinet posts (Koop and Bittner, 2011). And, in the lead-up to the 2008 and 2011 federal elections, all parties *except* the Conservative Party formally committed to Equal Voice—an advocacy group dedicated to electing more women to the House of Commons—that one-third to one-half of their candidates would be women. Though these nomination policies and promises have yielded promising results (Erickson, 1998), they do not go far enough, in part because parties continue to nominate more women candidates when they have little or no chance of winning. Thomas and Bodet (2013) contend that had the NDP followed their affirmative action nomination policy to the letter, seven additional women would have been nominated in NDP strongholds. Similarly, had the Conservative Party guaranteed real equality of opportunity in their nominations processes, the number of women nominated in safe Conservative seats would increase by about 9 or 10, potentially increasing the number of women in the Conservative caucus by up to 30 per cent (ibid.).

- *Political culture*: Political culture has been employed as an explanation for why the Atlantic provinces consistently lagged behind other provinces in the rate of increase in the number of women nominated and elected (see Arscott and Trimble, 1997). More recently, in a comparative analysis of rates of election to provincial and US state legislatures, Louise Carbert (2002) found evidence that higher rates of election of women are partially a consequence of a populist legacy, predominantly in Western states and provinces. More recently, however, there have been sharp increases in the representation of women in the Ontario, Quebec, Prince Edward Island, and Newfoundland and Labrador legislatures. Arguably, Quebec stands out as the province where women's representation is highlighted, with women making up nearly 40 per cent of the province's Cabinet.

- *Party systems*: Some analyses suggest that the constellation of parties present in the system affect the likelihood that women will be nominated in winnable ridings. Studlar and Matland (1996) found evidence that the NDP played a crucial role in accelerating the rate at which women's representation increased. Similarly, analyzing patterns of election of women at the provincial level, Arscott and Trimble (1997) found that election of NDP governments in three provinces in the 1990s was accompanied by sharp increases in the number of women elected. The province with the highest proportion of women in its legislature is Manitoba, which the NDP has governed for over a decade. In the case of Ontario, the defeat of the NDP Rae government by the Conservative Harris government also saw a decline in the proportion of women in the provincial legislature (Tolley, 2000).

- *Women's unwillingness to run for office*: In her analyses of patterns of women's candidacy, Erickson (1991, 1993) concludes that the major explanation for the relatively low number of women running for office is a question of supply: women are generally unwilling to come forward and run for office. There are two aspects to this. The first relates to women who might well be interested in running for office, but are not inclined to step forward, instead waiting to be invited. In cases such as these, Erickson's recommendation that party constituency associations employ search committees to encourage well-qualified candidates to run is relevant. Gender balance in local party associations is also important, as women riding association presidents are more likely than their male counterparts to recruit women candidates (Cheng and Tavits, 2011). The second and more intractable aspect of this is some degree of disinterest among women in pursuing political careers. It is difficult, if not impossible, to gauge the extent of this. Women's reasons for not wanting to enter the formal political arena are undoubtedly complex. Tolley's (2000) interviews with municipal politicians in Ontario suggest that role strain (the difficulty of combining family with a political career) is a significant factor at all three levels of government, but even more acutely at the provincial and federal levels, where extensive travel to a geographically distant capital is often a requirement of the job. Studying individuals in professions from which politicians are usually recruited in the United States, Fox and Lawless (2004) find that women are less likely to harbour political ambitions or to see themselves as qualified to run for political office. Similar factors are likely at play in the Canadian context, as Canadian women are significantly more likely than men to report that politics is "too complicated" for people like them to understand (Thomas, 2012). That said, some scholars argue that parties need to recruit so few women to achieve a gender-balanced candidate slate—approximately 155 at the federal level—that women's underrepresentation "can only be attributed" to demand-side gatekeeping, rather than to undersupply (Ashe and Stewart, 2012: 703).

One of the effects of women's underrepresentation in legislatures is a similar pattern of underrepresentation in Cabinets and among party leaders. With the exception of Quebec, where former Premier Jean Charest twice appointed a Cabinet with equal representation from the two genders, women comprise less than one-third of Cabinet ministers in all provinces and the federal Cabinet (Equal Voice, 2007). More encouragingly, at the time this chapter was being written, 10 women served as provincial party leaders. Of these, four— Christy Clark of British Columbia, Alison Redford of Alberta, Pauline Marois of Quebec, and Kathy Dunderdale of Newfoundland and Labrador—had been elected Premier. Kathleen Wynne serves as leader of the Liberal Party and premier of Ontario, but she has yet to be elected to that post. Of these, Redford, Wynne, Marois, and Dunderdale are the first women to serve as premier in their provinces. Another three women were leaders of the official opposition in provincial legislatures (Olive Crane of PEI, Elizabeth Hanson of the Yukon, and Danielle Smith of Alberta). Though this increase in women's leadership is encouraging, it must also be noted that several women leaders are in "glass cliff" situations. Research shows that women leaders are preferred to men when a party is on the decline. This glass cliff effect is heightened during times of crisis, when past leaders were men (Bruckmüller and Branscombe, 2010). Wynne appears to be in a glass cliff situation now; similarly, both Clark and Redford appeared to be in glass cliff situations in the past. As of the fall of 2013, if Wynne's Liberals in Ontario were to contest an election, they were expected, at best, to win by a slim margin. Though her party won a majority in April 2012, Redford's Alberta Progressive Conservatives were widely anticipated to lose government throughout the 2012 election campaign. Clark's position appeared to mimic that of Rita Johnson, a former premier of British Columbia who was soundly defeated in a general election after servings as premier through winning her party's leadership, and Kim Campbell, who held the post of prime minister briefly before her party lost the 1993 federal election. Though Clark's Liberals trailed in the polls throughout the BC election campaign, they secured a majority government in May 2013.

What Happens When They Get There?

Despite these barriers to the election of women, the number of women on city councils, in provincial legislatures, and in the House of Commons in Ottawa has increased over the past quarter-century. This raises the question of what happens when they get there. Have women transformed these representative institutions, bringing new perspectives and new issues into the political discourse? Or have they assimilated into the dominant political culture, and struggled to gain credibility in a sometimes hostile environment? Increasingly, research on women in politics really is on women who have entered the formal political arena.

Evidence of Discrimination

Studies of women who have been elected to serve in legislatures have found evidence that, once elected, they experience discrimination on the part of their male colleagues (e.g., see Trimble and Arscott, 2003: chap. 5, and O'Neill, 2002: 45). Clearly, these experiences are not universal, and like in many workplaces, are gradually improving over time. Nonetheless, these accounts are discouraging to those who might consider pursuing political careers.

Joanna Everitt and Elisabeth Gidengil (2003) examined media coverage and public perceptions of female party leaders. Analyzing the content of television coverage of leaders' debates in Canadian elections, they found journalists to be more inclined to describe female party leaders' behaviour as aggressive and, consequently, inappropriate for women. Compounding this, they found that female party leaders who avoided engaging in behaviours that might be considered aggressive were not rewarded for this by journalists; rather, they received very little media coverage at all. In short, the gendered character of media coverage created a catch-22 for women in politics: they can either engage fully and be mocked and criticized for their behaviour, or act in a conciliatory manner and be ignored. In another study, Gidengil and Everitt (2002) used the experimental method to determine whether students (standing in for the general public) rated the aggressiveness of fictitious political leaders differently when they used confrontational language. They found that female students, but not their male counterparts, were more likely to perceive the hypothetical female leader as aggressive when she used confrontational language. They conclude that this gendered mediation of speech makes it harder for female candidates to appeal to female voters. This had the potential to reverse any positive effect that identification with a candidate of the same sex might have for female candidates. In a similar vein, Sampert and Trimble (2003) found that in the 2000 federal election, the national news media provided less coverage of the female-led NDP than of the comparably placed, but male-led, Progressive Conservative party. According to their findings, what media coverage there was of Alexa McDonough and the NDP tended not to use the "aggressive action words" otherwise typical of political coverage.

Recent studies from the United States are more encouraging. In their analysis of the 2008 Democratic Party presidential primary, Miller, Peake, and Boulton (2010) conclude that Hillary Clinton was not ignored by the media, but instead garnered as much coverage as would be expected of the race's front-runner. However, the *tone* of Clinton's coverage was decidedly more negative and personal than the coverage of the male contender, Barack

Obama. Clinton had to beat Obama by at least 10 percentage points in a regional media market to receive comparably positive coverage in the press. This suggests that although women politicians may not necessarily be ignored, they are still mocked and criticized by the media in ways that men in politics are not.

Job Dissatisfaction

There is some evidence that women, once they are elected, find the constraints of political life more frustrating than do their male colleagues. In his study of members of Parliament, Docherty (1997: xxiii) notes that "women [in the House of Commons] are less likely to experience satisfying careers. Female MPs tend to enter elected life hoping to participate in policy changes and other substantive activities. As well, the House of Commons is best suited for an adversarial, combative type of debate and does not favour mechanisms of consensus. Many female MPs indicated that they would have preferred to engage in the latter type of debate and found the combative style inefficient and ineffective." This is in keeping with findings reported in studies of legislators in Alberta (Trimble, 1997) and Manitoba (Brock, 1997), which conclude that female legislators tend to focus more on substantive issues and to employ a distinctive, less combative style than their male colleagues.

Do Women Make a Difference?
The Substance-Numbers Connection

A key question in the women in politics research is the issue of whether the election of women makes a substantive difference. Put in other terms, the question asks whether there is a connection between the numeric representation of women (sometimes also referred to as "descriptive" or "symbolic" representation) and the substantive representation of women's interests. Some feminist scholars argue that pursuing the project of electing women may harm the substantive representation of women's interests because it allows right-wing parties to pursue neoconservative or neoliberal agendas that harm women, while legitimizing these actions by promoting the careers of like-minded women (Gotell and Brodie, 1991). In a similar vein, Maillé (1997) argues that, at least in Quebec, the women's movement has been more successful in representing women than have women holding political office, in large part because of the constraints placed upon women who hold formal political office. Indeed, women are a heterogeneous group; as more women are elected to public office, the diversity of views espoused by those women should also increase (Childs and Krook, 2008). This leads

Childs and Krook to critique the popular understanding of "critical mass" and instead focus on critical actors, or key women who speak on behalf of women's interests.

This question is itself a source of some controversy: is there such a thing as "women's interests" and if so, what precisely are these interests? This is an intractable problem in the literature. Efforts to define an objective set of common interests shared by all women have ultimately failed. While many women share objective interests stemming from their reproductive role or their shared experience of discrimination in the workplace, these interests are not universal among women. Moreover, even among women who share the same objective interests, there are differences in preference and belief that divide them. Political theorist Anne Phillips (1991: 90) argues "the representation of women *as women* potentially founders on both the difficulties of defining the shared interests of women and the difficulties of establishing mechanisms through which these interests are voiced." Consequently, efforts to define a set of common interests among women have failed. The most successful arguments hold not that women have a common set of interests, but rather that they share an interest in being represented, or in having access to the system (Jonasdottir, 1988; Skjeie, 1988). In her essay "Toward a Feminist Understanding of Representation," Jill Vickers (1997: 44) argues that the representation of women requires that the diverse needs, values, identities, and interests of women be articulated, that women representatives be held accountable to other women, and that women's participation be transformative, not reinforcing of existing hierarchies.

For the most part, scholars working in this field have acknowledged the difficulties inherent in discussing women's representation, and have opted to understand representing women's interests as furthering the policy agenda of the women's movement. The issues that are used as litmus tests, then, include support for women's equality, universal child care, and reproductive freedoms. In some studies, this list has been expanded to include women's health issues and measures designed to combat violence against women. This approach is, arguably, defensible, as it was the women's movement that prompted the influx of women into the formal political arena, and because this offers a benchmark of equality that is usable. That said, it must be noted that a substantial proportion of Canadian women do not support the policy agenda of the women's movement, and are consequently ignored by a literature that uses this definition. Moreover, as Ship (1998: 318) points out, these liberal feminist issues reflect the concerns of the predominant white and middle-class background of Canadian feminists in the 1970s and 1980s.

Studies of the attitudes and actions of women in political elites have generally found that gender does make some difference. Tremblay (1998) asked members of Parliament about what policy issues they were particularly interested in, and the priority that they thought should be given to women's issues. She found that the overall priority placed on women's issues was low, but was higher among female MPs than among men. In all five of the major parties, female MPs placed a higher priority on representing women than did men. Several studies of delegates to provincial and federal political party conventions and of candidates running in provincial and federal elections have found consistent patterns of gender difference between women and men in all the parties (Bashevkin, 1985; Brodie, 1988; Tremblay, 1995). Women in these political elites are more favourably inclined toward feminist policy stances, and place themselves further left on the political spectrum than do their male counterparts.

That said, in all these studies, differences *between* parties were more substantial than gender differences *within* each party. These findings are in keeping with Tremblay and Pelletier's (2000) conclusion based on their study of candidates in the 1997 federal election. They determine that feminist consciousness, rather than gender, is the strongest predictor of liberal positions on gender-related issues. Candidates who identified as feminists were more likely to be women than men, and were more likely to be found in the NDP, the Liberal Party, or the Bloc Québécois than in either of the two right-of-centre parties. Tremblay (1997) and Brock (1997) found similar partisan patterns in their studies of female legislators in Quebec and Manitoba. Based on these findings, they conclude that substantive and descriptive representation of women are not necessarily compatible. If one was interested in feminist policy outcomes, it was more reasonable to support an NDP man than a Reform woman. If, however, the descriptive representation of women was the utmost concern, then the reverse would be true.

Studies of what women do once they are elected are relatively few in number. The strict party discipline and caucus secrecy of the Canadian parliamentary tradition make it difficult to trace the extent to which female legislators intervene on behalf of women behind closed doors. To the extent that studies have focused on legislators, they have found some evidence supporting the numbers-substance connection. At the federal level, Manon Tremblay (1998) studied the interventions of MPs on women's issues in the form of private members' bills, private members' notices of motion, and statements by members. She concluded that female MPs are more likely than their male counterparts to use these opportunities to draw attention to women's issues. She does note, however, that "for both female and male MPs, the total proportion of each of these parliamentary activities devoted to women's issues remains marginal, even insignificant" (1998: 457). At the provincial level, Trimble studied all the interventions made in the Alberta legislature relating to women from 1972 to 1995. She found, first, than women's issues tended not to be mentioned frequently. Between 1972 and 1985, "the topic of irrigation ditches received more attention that women" (1997: 263). This increased somewhat between 1986 and 1993, a period when there was (by Alberta standards) a strong opposition presence in the legislature. Throughout the study, Trimble found that policy concerns of minority women—immigrant women, foreign domestic workers, Aboriginal women, or disabled women—were effectively invisible from discussion.

Arscott and Trimble (1997: 12), drawing on a series of studies of women's participation in provincial legislatures, conclude that the degree to which women holding political office makes a difference for women's representation is dependent on several factors, notably the province's political culture, the intensity of political party ideology as it affects women, the character of party competition in the legislature, the location of female representatives in the opposition or government party, Cabinet or backbenches, and the personal beliefs of the female representatives. Findings like this have caused feminist political scientists to fall back on arguments of justice and equality to support the ongoing effort to increase women's representation.

American research highlights the importance feminist organizations can have in holding female legislators to account on women's issues. Based on a survey of state legislators, Carroll concludes that ties to feminist organizations, especially feminist groups, "provide affirmation and sustenance for women legislators.... [They] also function as a conscience for women legislators ... providing ... reminders that women elected officials have a responsibility to represent women's interests within the institutions in which they serve" (Carroll, 2006: 375). The relative absence of membership-based feminist organizations in Canada means that this mechanism of accountability to women's organizations is missing for most female elected officials in Canada.

Conclusion

After more than three decades of women's efforts to enter the world of electoral politics, we can conclude that some progress has been made. The number of women holding elected office has increased from a mere handful of exceptions to almost a quarter of all legislators at the provincial and federal levels. Women have been elected party leaders, regularly serve in high-profile Cabinet posts, and have even been elected as premier and—for a fleeting moment in 1993—served as prime minister. But is this progress sufficient? A quarter of the legislature may be better than a handful, but it is far less than women's majority presence in the population. Women still remain substantially underrepresented in Cabinets, where crucial decisions are made. Several women serve as provincial and territorial premiers; this presence is especially important, because essential decisions about the character of the Canadian federation are made at meetings of the first ministers (premiers and the prime minister). However, as noted above, some of those women, such as Kathleen Wynne, are in precarious positions and are not expected to remain in the premier's office. This demonstrates that women's representation on the political executive in Canada is by no means guaranteed.

Does it matter that women remain excluded from the upper echelons of political power in Canada? On one hand, it is important to recall the extent of Canadian women's legal and economic equality and comparatively high standard of living. This speaks to the ability of women outside the formal arena to achieve outcomes favourable to women's equality. On the other hand, it is difficult to accept that in a country where women have entered and excelled in other highly demanding professions, the world of politics largely remains foreign territory. Politics matters to women. Governments decide whether women can have access to contraception, whether women can be paid less than men for doing similar jobs, whether abortions are legal and available, whether child care will be regulated or left to the forces of the market, whether women are entitled to have their job back after having a baby, whether health care is private or publicly funded, and how much university tuition will cost. All of these issues matter just as much—if not more—to women than to men. When women abdicate interest in politics, leaving it as a male preserve, they risk having decisions made on their behalf that make their lives more difficult. This does not mean that women must agree on how these kinds of issues are resolved. Women quite legitimately disagree among themselves on all these issues and others as well. But surely the diversity of women's views should be represented when public policy is made.

When feminist political scientists started to study women's involvement in electoral politics some 30 years ago, many of them imagined that women's involvement in politics would have a profound influence on how politics was conducted and what public policies were adopted. While we can certainly point to instances in which women have been able to influence the outcomes of political decisions, the larger story is still the relative absence of women—from legislatures, from political parties, and from that group of citizens who are strongly interested in and informed about politics. The task for the next generation of researchers is to come to terms with the underlying reasons why women remain ambivalent about something that affects them so personally and profoundly.

Note

1 See, for example, Young and Everitt (2004) and Stolle and Micheletti (2006).

References and Suggested Readings

Arscott, Jane, and Linda Trimble. 1997. "In the Presence of Women: Representation and Political Power." In *In the Presence of Women: Representation in Canadian Governments*, eds. Jane Arscott and Linda Trimble, 1–19. Toronto: Harcourt Brace.

Ashe, Jeanette, and Kennedy Stewart. 2012. "Legislative Recruitment: Using Diagnostic Testing to Explain Underrepresentation." *Party Politics* 18 (5): 687–707. http://dx.doi.org/10.1177/1354068810389635.

Bashevkin, Sylvia. 1985. "Political Participation, Ambition and Feminism: Women in the Ontario Party Elites." *American Review of Canadian Studies* 15 (4): 405–19. http://dx.doi.org/10.1080/02722018509480829.

Bashevkin, Sylvia. 1993. *Toeing the Lines: Women and Party Politics in English Canada*. Toronto: Oxford University Press.

Black, Jerome. 2003. "Differences That Matter: Minority Women MPs, 1993–2000." In *Women and Electoral Politics in Canada*, eds. Manon Tremblay and Linda Trimble, 59–75. Toronto: Oxford University Press.

Brock, Kathy. 1997. "Women and the Manitoba Legislature." In *In the Presence of Women: Representation in Canadian Governments*, eds. Jane Arscott and Linda Trimble, 180–200. Toronto: Harcourt Brace.

Brodie, Janine. 1985. *Women and Politics in Canada*. Toronto: McGraw-Hill Ryerson.

Brodie, Janine. 1988. "The Gender Factor and National Leadership Conventions in Canada." In *Party Democracy in Canada*, ed. George Perlin, 172–87. Scarborough: Prentice Hall.

Bruckmüller, Susanne, and Nyla E. Branscombe. 2010. "The Glass Cliff: When and Why Women Are Selected as Leaders in Crisis Contexts." *British Journal of Social Psychology* 49 (3): 433–51. http://dx.doi.org/10.1348/014466609X466594.

Carbert, Louise. 2002. "Historical Influences on Regional Patterns of Election of Women to Provincial Legislatures." In *Political Parties, Representation and Electoral Democracy in Canada*, ed. William Cross, 201–22. Toronto: Oxford University Press.

Carroll, Susan J. 2006. "Are Women Legislators Accountable to Women? The Complementary Roles of Feminist Identity and Women's Organizations." In *Gender and Social Capital*, eds. Brenda O'Neill and Elisabeth Gidengil, 357–78. New York: Routledge.

Cheng, Christine, and Margit Tavits. 2011. "Informal Influences in Selecting Female Political Candidates." *Political Research Quarterly* 64 (2): 460–71. http://dx.doi.org/10.1177/1065912909349631.

Childs, Sarah, and Mona Lena Krook. 2008. "Critical Mass Theory and Women's Political Representation." *Political Studies* 56 (3): 725–36. http://dx.doi.org/10.1111/j.1467-9248.2007.00712.x.

Cross, William. 2004. *Political Parties*. Vancouver: University of British Columbia Press.

Denton, Margaret A. 1984. "Do Female Candidates 'Lose Votes'? The Experience of Female Candidates in the 1979 and 1980 Canadian General Elections." *Canadian Review of Sociology and Anthropology. La Revue Canadienne de Sociologie et d'Anthropologie* 21: 395–406.

Docherty, David. 1997. *Mr. Smith Goes to Ottawa.* Vancouver: University of British Columbia Press.

Erickson, Lynda. 1991. "Women and Candidacies for the House of Commons." In *Women in Canadian Politics: Toward Equity in Representation*, ed. Kathy Megyery, 101–25. Toronto: Dundurn/Royal Commission on Electoral Reform and Party Finance.

Erickson, Lynda. 1993. "Making Her Way In: Women, Parties and Candidacies in Canada." In *Gender and Party Politics*, eds. Joni Lovenduski and Pippa Norris, 60–85. London: Sage.

Erickson, Lynda. 1998. "Entry to the Commons: Parties, Recruitment and the Election of Women in 1993." In *Women and Political Representation in Canada*, eds. Manon Tremblay and Caroline Andrew, 219–55. Ottawa: University of Ottawa Press.

Erickson, Lynda. 2003. "In the Eyes of the Beholders: Gender and Leader Popularity in a Canadian Context." In *Women and Electoral Politics in Canada*, eds. Manon Tremblay and Linda Trimble, 160–77. Toronto: Oxford University Press.

Everitt, Joanna. 1998. "Public Opinion and Social Movements: The Women's Movement and the Gender Gap in Canada." *Canadian Journal of Political Science* 35: 191–219.

Everitt, Joanna, and Elisabeth Gidengil. 2003. "Tough Talk: How Television News Covers Male and Female Leaders of Canadian Political Parties." In *Women and Electoral Politics in Canada*, eds. Manon Tremblay and Linda Trimble, 194–210. Toronto: Oxford University Press.

Equal Voice. 2007. *Fast Facts: Women in Provincial Politics.* www.equalvoice.ca.

Equal Voice. 2009. *Canada Challenge 2009: Building the Momentum to Elect More Women in Canada.* http://www.equalvoice.ca/challenge09.htm.

Federation of Canadian Municipalities. 2008. *Women in Local Government: Getting to 30% by 2026.* http://www.fcm.ca//Documents/reports/Women/Getting_to_30_percent_by_2026_EN.pdf.

Fournier, Patrick, Fred Cutler, Stuart Soroka, and Dietlind Stolle. 2011. The 2011 Canadian Election Study.

Fox, Richard L., and Jennifer L. Lawless. 2004. "Entering the Arena? Gender and the Decision to Run for Office." *American Journal of Political Science* 48 (2): 264–80. http://dx.doi.org/10.1111/j.0092-5853.2004.00069.x.

Gidengil, Elisabeth. 1995. "'Economic Man—Social Woman?' The Case of the Gender Gap in Support for the Canada-United States Free Trade Agreement." *Comparative Political Studies* 28 (3): 384–408. http://dx.doi.org/10.1177/0010414095028003003.

Gidengil, Elisabeth, André Blais, Richard Nadeau, and Neil Nevitte. 2003. "Women to the Left? Gender Differences in Political Beliefs and Policy Preferences." In *Women and Electoral Politics in Canada*, eds. Manon Tremblay and Linda Trimble, 140–59. Toronto: Oxford University Press.

Gidengil, Elisabeth, André Blais, Neil Nevitte, and Richard Nadeau. 2004. *Citizens.* Vancouver: University of British Columbia Press.

Gidengil, Elisabeth, and Joanna Everitt. 2002. "Damned if You Do, Damned if You Don't: Television News Coverage of Female Party Leaders in the 1993 Federal Election." In *Political Parties, Representation and Electoral Democracy in Canada*, ed. William Cross, 223–37. Toronto: Oxford University Press.

Gidengil, Elisabeth, Joanna Everitt, André Blais, Patrick Fournier, and Neil Nevitte. 2006. "Gender and Vote Choice in the 2006 Canadian Election." Paper presented at the annual meeting of the American Political Science Association.

Gidengil, Elisabeth, Elizabeth Goodyear-Grant, Neil Nevitte, and André Blais. 2006. "Gender, Knowledge and Social Capital." In *Gender and Social Capital*, eds. Brenda O'Neill and Elisabeth Gidengil, 241–72. New York: Routledge.

Gidengil, Elisabeth, Matthew Hennigar, André Blais, and Neil Nevitte. 2005. "Explaining the Gender Gap in Support for the New Right: The Case of Canada." *Comparative Political Studies* 38 (10): 1171–95. http://dx.doi.org/10.1177/0010414005279320.

Gidengil, Elisabeth, Neil Nevitte, André Blais, Joanna Everitt, and Patrick Fournier. 2012. *Dominance and Decline: Making Sense of Recent Canadian Elections.* Toronto: University of Toronto Press.

Gidengil, Elisabeth, and Richard Vengroff. 1997. "Representational Gains of Canadian Women or Token Growth? The Case of Quebec's Municipal Politics." *Canadian Journal of Political Science* 30 (03): 513–37. http://dx.doi.org/10.1017/S0008423 900015997.

Goodyear-Grant, Elizabeth, and Julie Croskill. 2011. "Gender Affinity Effects in Vote Choice in Westminster Systems: Assessing 'Flexible' Voters in Canada." *Politics & Gender* 7 (02): 223–50. http://dx.doi.org/10.1017/S1743923X11000079.

Gotell, Lise, and Janine Brodie. 1991. "Women and Parties: More Than an Issue of Numbers." In *Party Politics in Canada*, 6th ed., ed. Hugh G. Thorburn, 53–67. Scarborough: Prentice Hall.

Hausmann, Ricardo, Laura D. Tyson, and Saadia Zahidi. 2012. *The Global Gender Gap Report 2012*. World Economic Forum. http://www3.weforum.org/docs/WEF_GenderGap_Report_2012.pdf.

Inter-Parliamentary Union (IPU). 2013. *Women in National Parliaments*. http://www.ipu.org/wmn-e/classif.htm.

Jonasdottir, Anna. 1988. "On the Concept of Interests, Women's Interests and the Limitation of Interest Theory." In *The Political Interests of Gender*, eds. K.B. Jones and A.G. Jonasdottir, 47–63. London: Sage.

Koop, Royce, and Amanda Bittner. 2011. "Parachuted into Parliament: Candidate Nomination, Appointed Candidates, and Legislative Roles in Canada." *Journal of Elections, Public Opinion, & Parties* 21 (4): 431–52. http://dx.doi.org/10.1080/17457289.201 1.609297.

Krook, Mona Lena. 2009. *Quotas for Women in Politics: Gender and Candidate Selection Reform Worldwide*. Oxford: Oxford University Press. http://dx.doi.org/10.1093/acprof: oso/9780195375671.001.0001.

Kushner, Joseph, David Siegel, and Hannah Stanwick. 1997. "Ontario Municipal Elections: Voting Trends and Determinants of Electoral Success in a Canadian Province." *Canadian Journal of Political Science* 30 (03): 539–53. http://dx.doi.org/10.1017/ S0008423900016000.

Maillé, Chantal. 1997. "Challenges to Representation: Theory and the Women's Movement in Quebec." In *In the Presence of Women: Representation in Canadian Governments*, eds. Jane Arscott and Linda Trimble, 47–63. Toronto: Harcourt Brace.

Miller, Melissa K., Jeffrey S. Peake, and Brittany Anne Boulton. 2010. "Testing the Saturday Night Live Hypothesis: Fairness and Bias in Newspaper Coverage of Hillary Clinton's Presidential Campaign." *Politics & Gender* 6 (02): 169–98. http://dx.doi.org/10.1017/S1743923X10000036.

O'Neill, Brenda. 2002. "Sugar and Spice? Political Culture and the Political Behaviour of Canadian Women." In *Citizen Politics: Research and Theory in Canadian Political Behaviour*, eds. Joanna Everitt and Brenda O'Neill, 40–55. Toronto: Oxford University Press.

Phillips, Anne. 1991. *Engendering Democracy*. University Park: Pennsylvania State University Press.

Praud, Jocelyne. 1998. "Affirmative Action and Women's Representation in the Ontario New Democratic Party." In *Women and Political Representation in Canada*, eds. Manon Tremblay and Caroline Andrew, 171–93. Ottawa: University of Ottawa Press.

Praud, Jocelyne. 2003. "The Parti Québécois, Its Women's Committee, and the Feminization of the Quebec Electoral Arena." In *Women and Electoral Politics in Canada*,
eds. Manon Tremblay and Linda Trimble, 126–39. Toronto: Oxford University Press.

Roberts, Andrew, Jason Seawright, and Jennifer Cyr. 2012. "Do Electoral Laws Affect
Women's Representation?" *Comparative Political Studies* 46 (12): 1555–81. http://
dx.doi.org/10.1177/0010414012463906.

Sampert, Shannon, and Linda Trimble. 2003. "Wham, Bam, No Thank You Ma'am: Gender and the Game Frame in National Newspaper Coverage of Election 2000." In
Women and Electoral Politics in Canada, eds. Manon Tremblay and Linda Trimble,
211–26. Toronto: Oxford University Press.

Ship, Susan Judith. 1998. "Problematizing Ethnicity and 'Race' in Feminist Scholarship
on Women in Politics." In *Women and Political Representation in Canada*, eds. Manon
Tremblay and Caroline Andrew, 311–40. Ottawa: University of Ottawa Press.

Skjeie, Hege. 1988. *The Feminization of Power: Norway's Political Experiment*. Norway:
Institute for Social Research.

Statistics Canada. 2011. *Women in Canada: A Gender-based Statistical Report*. 6th ed.
Ottawa: Minister of Industry.

Stolle, Dietlind, and Michele Micheletti. 2006. "The Gender Gap Reversed: Political
Consumerism as a Woman-Friendly Form of Civic and Political Engagement." In
Gender and Social Capital, eds. Brenda O'Neill and Elisabeth Gidengil, 45–72. New
York: Routledge.

Studlar, Donley T., and Richard E. Matland. 1996. "The Dynamics of Women's Representation in the Canadian Provinces: 1975–1994." *Canadian Journal of Political Science*
29 (02): 269–94. http://dx.doi.org/10.1017/S000842390000771X.

Thomas, Melanee. 2012. "The Complexity Conundrum: Why Hasn't the Gender Gap
in Subjective Political Competence Closed?" *Canadian Journal of Political Science*
45 (02): 337–58. http://dx.doi.org/10.1017/S0008423912000352.

Thomas, Melanee, and Marc André Bodet. 2013. "Sacrificial Lambs, Women Candidates,
and District Competitiveness in Canada." *Electoral Studies* 32 (1): 153–66. http://
dx.doi.org/10.1016/j.electstud.2012.12.001.

Tolley, Erin. 2000. *The Higher the Fewer: Assessing the Presence of Women at Three Levels of
Government*. Unpublished MA Thesis, University of Western Ontario.

Tolley, Erin. 2011. "Do Women 'Do Better' in Municipal Politics? Electoral Representation across Three Levels of Government." *Canadian Journal of Political Science* 44 (03):
573–94. http://dx.doi.org/10.1017/S0008423911000503.

Tremblay, Manon. 1995. "Gender and Support for Feminism." In *Gender and Politics in
Contemporary Canada*, ed. François-Pierre Gingras, 31–55. Toronto: Oxford University Press.`

Tremblay, Manon. 1997. "Quebec Women in Politics: An Examination of the Research."
In *In the Presence of Women: Representation in Canadian Governments*, eds. Jane Arscott
and Linda Trimble, 228–51. Toronto: Harcourt Brace.

Tremblay, Manon. 1998. "Do Female MPs Substantively Represent Women? A Study of
Legislative Behaviour in Canada's 35th Parliament." *Canadian Journal of Political Science* 31 (03): 435–66. http://dx.doi.org/10.1017/S0008423900009082.

Tremblay, Manon, and Réjean Pelletier. 2000. "More Feminists or More Women? Descriptive and Substantive Representations of Women in the 1997 Canadian Federal Elections." *International Political Science Review* 21 (4): 381–405. http://dx.doi.
org/10.1177/0192512100214004.

Trimble, Linda. 1997. "Feminist Politics in the Alberta Legislature, 1972–1994." In *In
the Presence of Women: Representation in Canadian Governments*, eds. Jane Arscott and
Linda Trimble, 128–53. Toronto: Harcourt Brace.

Trimble, Linda, and Jane Arscott. 2003. *Still Counting: Women in Politics Across Canada.* Peterborough: Broadview Press.

Trimble, Linda, Jane Arscott, and Manon Tremblay, eds. 2013. *Stalled: The Representation of Women in Canadian Governments.* Vancouver: University of British Columbia Press.

Vickers, Jill. 1978. "Where Are the Women in Canadian Politics?" *Atlantis* 3 (2): 40–51.

Vickers, Jill. 1997. "Toward a Feminist Understanding of Representation." In *In the Presence of Women: Representation in Canadian Governments*, eds. Jane Arscott and Linda Trimble, 20–46. Toronto: Harcourt Brace.

Young, Lisa. 2000. *Feminists and Party Politics.* Vancouver: University of British Columbia Press.

Young, Lisa. 2013. "Slow to Change: Women in the House of Commons." In *Stalled: The Representation of Women in Canadian Governments*, eds. Linda Trimble, Jane Arscott and Manon Tremblay, 253–72. Vancouver: University of British Columbia Press.

Young, Lisa, and William Cross. 2003. "Women's Involvement in Canadian Political Parties." In *Women and Electoral Politics in Canada*, eds. Manon Tremblay and Linda Trimble, 92–109. Toronto: Oxford University Press.

Young, Lisa, and William Cross. 2007. "A Group Apart: Young Party Members in Canada." Canadian Policy Research Networks. http://www.cprn.org/doc.cfm?doc=1748&1.

Young, Lisa, and Joanna Everitt. 2004. *Advocacy Groups.* Vancouver: University of British Columbia Press.

eighteen

Diversity in Canadian Politics

YASMEEN ABU–LABAN

We call on the Canadian government to reverse its decision to eliminate the mandatory long form Canada census questionnaire. The information collected through this form is critical to understanding the character and diversity of Canada. The long form questionnaire is an essential tool to enable business and social planning, research, and development of programs for the well-being of Canadians. (online petition published by Marianne Levitsky, July 3, 2010)

Introduction

Conducting a population census is a major activity performed by modern states, and Canada is no different. In fact, stemming from constitutional requirements, Canada must undertake a "Census of Population" in decennial years (these are years ending in "1") and quinquennial years (these are years ending in "6"). However, Canada's most recent decennial census of 2011 generated unprecedented controversy as attested by an online bilingual petition, signed by more than 18,000 Canadians, calling on the Conservative government of Prime Minister Harper to reinstate the mandatory long-form questionnaire (Levitsky, 2010). Between 1971 and 2006 Statistics Canada, the government agency charged with overseeing the Census of Population conducted every five years, made use of two questionnaires that respondents were legally required to fill out: a long form with questions asking about ethnicity, language, household income, and the like given to a sample of households; and a short form with fewer questions given to the remaining households (Statistics Canada, 2012: 5). The Conservative government's decision to make 10 approved questions on the short form mandatory, but make the long form "National Household Survey" voluntary marks a major shift that was widely seen by many statisticians to introduce sample bias and carry negative implications for the quality and accuracy of data generated— in fact the head of Statistics Canada, Munir Sheikh, resigned his post for this very reason (CBC News, 2010; Tamburi, 2012). The stated rationale for the decision to disband the mandatory long-form questionnaire was privacy, although Canada's Privacy Commissioner received only one complaint about the 2001 Census, and two complaints about the 2006 Census (Chase, 2010), and Statistics Canada received less than 100 complaints in total about the 2006 Census, not all related to privacy (Brennan, 2011). By way of contrast, the premiers of the provinces of New Brunswick, Prince Edward Island, Quebec, Ontario, and Manitoba openly called on the federal government to retain the mandatory long form (Fekete, 2010) as did the City of Toronto, the Federation of Canadian Municipalities, and such diverse organizations as the Canadian Association of University Teachers, the Canadian Association for Business Economics, the Toronto-Dominion Bank, the Canadian Centre for Policy Alternatives, and the Canadian Council of Social Development (Siddiqui, 2010).

The controversy and debate generated by the 2011 Census changes alert us to the fact that governments, policy-makers, business and civil society groups, as well as many Canadians, have an interest in understanding Canada's demographic heterogeneity. As the results from the 2011 Census continue to be released, and the quality of these results is unknown and will take time to closely analyze (Statistics Canada, 2012: 7–8), it is the 2006 Census findings that are most helpful in portraying relevant characteristics about Canada's population. For example, the 2006 Census shows that 58 per cent claim English as their mother tongue, 22 per cent claim French as their mother tongue, and 20 per cent claim a language other than French or English (Statistics Canada, 2007a: 5). The 2006 Census also shows that close to 20 per cent of the population are foreign-born (Statistics Canada, 2007b) and Canadians are more ethnically diverse than they were historically. For instance, while the 1901 Canadian Census recorded membership in only 25 different ethnic groups, the 2006 Census recorded membership in over 200 (Statistics Canada, 2008: 6). In addition, there is increasing racial diversity, with just over 16 per cent of the population consisting of so-called visible minorities, who are defined by the Canadian government as "persons other than Aboriginal persons who are non-Caucasian in race or non-white in colour" (Statistics Canada, 2008: 11–12). Aboriginal peoples make up a further 5.4 per cent of the Canadian population (Statistics Canada, 2008: 11–12). Many Canadians regularly encounter "diversity" among friends, neighbours, colleagues, and even within their own families. Consider that over 60 per cent of those reporting Aboriginal ancestry also report other origins (Statistics Canada, 2008: 11) and that marriage and common-law relationships between visible minorities and non-visible minorities, as well as between visible minorities of different ethnic origins, are on the rise (Statistics Canada, 2008: 16). Such shifting demographic realities underscore why "diversity"—particularly when it comes to place of birth, language, ethnicity, or race—is a compelling consideration for so many in Canada.

This chapter focuses primarily on cultural, ethnic, and racial diversity and its relevance, both historically and currently, in Canadian politics. It examines how these forms of diversity have been addressed both by the Canadian state through its policies, and by Canadian political scientists in their research. It argues that diversity is significant for political analyses in both areas because it is relevant to power, a central disciplinary concern. Put differently, whether historic or contemporary, inequalities between identifiable groups are important to political scientists because such inequalities may impact the extent to which all groups feel their voices are heard and their interests are represented in Canadian institutions. This is closely related to what political scientists refer to as "legitimacy," or the popular acceptance of a governing authority or regime. More broadly, inequities can tell us about the character of Canadian liberal democracy.

To address this argument, this chapter takes a threefold approach. In the first section, major state policies and practices pertaining to diversity are reviewed in relation to Canada's history and evolution. In the second, three different emphases in Canadian political science approaches are highlighted: culture, race, and colonialism. To illustrate how each approach may inform us, the third section offers a close examination of religious diversity, especially as it pertains to both Aboriginal peoples historically and Muslim-Canadians today.

Diversity and the Evolving Canadian State

Canada's history as a settler colony, characterized by pre-existing and distinct Aboriginal societies, European settler colonization, and repeated waves of immigration, is a testimony to the fact that "diversity" is not new. Historically, both the British-origin and French-origin groups attempted to assert dominance over the Indigenous population, although the patterns of colonization of each were distinct (Dickason, 1992). It is, however, Canada's foundation as a so-called white settler colony of Britain that fostered a legacy of group-based inequalities that forms the basis of many grievances and ongoing political struggles. This is because the historic project of modelling Canada after Britain (in political, economic, cultural, and demographic terms) often led to assimilative and discriminatory measures.

The Royal Proclamation of 1763 established the framework by which British administration of the North American territories would take place and served to enforce British sovereignty while at the same time acknowledging Aboriginal tribes and land title rights. In particular, the Royal Proclamation outlawed the expropriation of Aboriginal lands by colonies or by settlers unless treaties with the Crown were completed. This was the beginning of the imperial government's contradictory policy of assimilation and recognition, which was later replicated by Canada (Stasiulis and Jhappan, 1995: 107).

Assimilation and recognition also characterized relations with the French, and these tensions were further woven into the development of liberal democracy and eventually federalism in Canada. The 1774 Quebec Act allowed freedom to practice the Catholic faith and restored French civil law and seigneurial landholding systems. While it did not say anything about the use of the French language, the appointed council (overseen by a colonial governor) allowed for Roman Catholics to hold office. The 1791 Constitutional Act created Upper Canada (the present-day province of Ontario) and Lower Canada (the southern part of present-day Quebec), governed by bicameral legislatures consisting of elected assemblies with limited powers and more powerful appointed legislative councils that worked on behalf of the colonial governors and the Crown. In both Upper and Lower Canada, reformers fought for responsible government. The response to these struggles, which took the form of armed uprisings in 1837–38, was the 1840 Act of Union that united Upper and Lower Canada into a single colony (Canada) with one Parliament and, notably, English as the only official government language. As well, in the 1840s and 1850s, thousands of immigrants, among them a significant number of Irish, were discriminated against by the British authorities (Cardin and Couture, 1996: 208).

In light of pre-Confederation practices, it is unsurprising that after 1867 the Canadian state also reflected linguistic, ethnic, and racial hierarchies in practices, policies, and laws (Stasiulis and Jhappan, 1995: 96), as exemplified, for instance, in the growing state security functions and intense surveillance directed at Irish Catholics for purported Fenian associations following the assassination of one of the Fathers of Confederation, Thomas D'Arcy McGee, in 1868 (Whitaker, Kealey, and Parnaby, 2012: 31). The founding of the modern Canadian state stemmed from several factors, not least of which were fears of an American invasion and the distinctly privileged position of "white settler colonies" to enjoy relative political autonomy within the British empire. With Confederation in 1867, the colonies of British North America—Canada, Nova Scotia, and New Brunswick—were united into a Dominion with British-style political institutions. Unlike Britain, however, and as outlined in the British North America Act/Constitution Act, 1867, Canada adopted a federal system of government. The province of Quebec gained control over education and culture (see Chapter 1 in this volume), and both French and English were to be the languages used in federal (and Quebec) legislative debates and records. The adoption of a federal system was the result of intense struggle by French Canadians, as many British-origin politicians (such as the first prime minister, Sir John A. Macdonald) would have preferred a unitary state (Abu-Laban and Nieguth, 2000: 478). Confederation ushered in a new discourse upholding the British and the French as Canada's "two founding peoples" or "two founding races" (Stasiulis and Jhappan, 1995: 110). This discourse held out the promise that the collective aspirations of two collectivities (the British and the French) could be simultaneously accommodated. Yet despite the discourse, and the stated provisions of the Constitution Act, 1867, the promise was never met. As summed succinctly by Richard Day (2000: 180), "the Canadian state ... lived, worked, and most importantly, *dreamed* in English."

As a by-product, the discourse on "two founding peoples" helped legitimize the federal government's assuming jurisdiction over Aboriginal affairs and lands reserved for Aboriginal peoples, paving the way for the seizure of Aboriginal lands by provinces both with and without the use of treaties (see Green, 1995; Green and Peach, 2007). Similarly, except in periods when the pool of labour was insufficient to fuel agricultural or industrial expansion, Canada's immigration policy favoured white, English-speaking, British-origin Protestants (Abu-Laban and Gabriel, 2002: 37–55). Even after World War II, Prime Minister Mackenzie King emphasized that Canada did not want immigration from "the orient" since this would negatively alter "the character" of the population (King, 1974). By "the orient" King meant to exclude all areas in the eastern hemisphere beyond Europe; this policy position guided Canada's immigration intake until 1967.

In 1967 a new immigration policy explicitly banned discrimination on the basis of race or ethnicity and introduced a "point system" of selection. The point system, still in effect today, ranks potential independent immigrants by assigning points on the basis of education and skills. (The point system is not formally used for family members of the principal applicant, nor is it used for refugees.) In addition to immigration, the decade of the 1960s marks an important turning point for policies in several areas. Combined, such changes may be related in part to the international level, where the saliency of the idea of human rights (emphasizing the equal worth and dignity of all persons) coincided with the growing success of many anti-colonial struggles and movements; the growth of the Keynesian-style welfare state, which opened new possibilities of social spending; and the remobilization of segments of the Canadian population into identity-based political movements and organizations demanding inclusion in the existing system and, in some cases, self-rule. This was clearly a period in which the inclusiveness of Canada's democracy, inequities in the distribution of power, and the legitimacy of its institutions were put into question.

In response, federal policies were shaped by the resurrection of older discourses and understandings in a new context. For example, in Quebec, the

Quiet Revolution was symbolized by the election of the provincial Liberal government of Jean Lesage in 1960. Commitment to a philosophy of *maîtres chez nous* (masters in our own house) led successive Quebec governments to assume greater jurisdictional and fiscal powers for the province as well as to seek federal recognition of the distinct constitutional status of Quebec because the French were a "founding people" at Confederation. Aboriginal people drew on the Royal Proclamation of 1763 that gave them status as "nations within" (or "first nations"); the Royal Proclamation also provided a legal basis for their contemporary and ongoing land and rights claims, including self-government.

In other cases, new federal discourses aiming to foster legitimacy also emerged. The rise of widespread contestation by francophones over their subordinate place across Canada, especially in Quebec and New Brunswick (where many young people identified with anti-colonial struggles in Algeria and South America), led the federal Liberals of Prime Minister Lester B. Pearson to form the Royal Commission on Bilingualism and Biculturalism. As a consequence of the findings of this commission, which demonstrated that the principle of equality between French and English had been systematically violated in the Canadian federation, the federal Liberal government of Prime Minister Pierre Elliott Trudeau passed the Official Languages Act in 1969. Emerging from its English dream, the Canadian state made clear through this act that English and French were the official languages of Canada, that public servants could use these languages at work (at least in many cases), and that most federal services were to be made available to Canadians in both languages. At the same time, the word "multiculturalism" was introduced as a way for the "third force" (i.e., non-French, non-British, and non-Aboriginal immigrants and their descendants) to be symbolically recognized by the Canadian state. Multiculturalism, too, was the outcome of a struggle by these groups, especially Ukrainian-origin Canadians in the Western provinces, for representation. By 1971 the Trudeau government announced a policy of multiculturalism within a bilingual framework.

Although the province of Quebec never received the constitutional recognition (or veto power) its leaders sought, the 1982 Canadian Charter of Rights and Freedoms did give recognition to English and French as the two official languages (Sections 16–22), official language minority education rights for French-speakers outside Quebec and for English-speakers in Quebec (Section 23), Aboriginal rights as recognized in the Royal Proclamation of 1763 (Section 25), and the multicultural heritage of Canada (Section 27).

The Charter, reflecting the value of human rights, also prohibited discrimination on the basis of race, ethnicity, gender, and mental or physical disability, among other grounds (Section 15). Nonetheless, Section 15 also allowed for the possibility of government programs designed to ameliorate disadvantage experienced by specific groups. This gave constitutional legitimacy to new programs, developed from the mid-1980s, dealing with employment equity for groups deemed to have been historically disadvantaged in the labour market. The specific focus of employment equity is on women, Aboriginal peoples, visible minorities, and persons with a disability. Employment equity seeks to increase the numeric representation of these four groups in federally regulated corporations (such as banks, broadcasting, and airlines). Similar employment equity policies were also adopted in the mid-1980s to increase the numerical representation of the same groups in the public service itself and in companies doing business with the government (so-called federal contractors).

The federal government's prioritizing of certain groups for employment was not entirely new—for instance, in 1918 the Canadian government favoured the recruitment of male veterans of World War I for jobs in the civil service. However, the consequences of employment equity for the four target groups have been uneven, depending on the group and the work sector. For example, in the federal public service visible minorities in particular have faced slow progress in achieving increased representation that corresponds to their numbers available for participation in the workforce (Abu-Laban, 2006: 72–73; Block and Galabuzi, 2011: 9–11). More broadly, the decade of the 1990s brought new challenges because of the rise of neoliberal ideology. Neoliberalism emphasizes balanced budgets through cuts to social spending, asserts the necessity for individual self-sufficiency, and assumes markets are fair and efficient allocators of public goods. In this context, many identity-based groups (women, minorities, Aboriginal people, etc.) were vilified for being "special interests" out of tune with "ordinary Canadians," and programs faced cuts and reworkings of their terms (Abu-Laban and Gabriel, 2002). As one example, under these new terms it has been impossible to get funding for certain kinds of activities previously funded through multiculturalism, and it has been cumbersome for community groups, many relying on underpaid workers or overworked volunteers, to apply for money. As such, the 1960s-style human rights and equality agenda for ethnic minorities has been weakened (Abu-Laban and Gabriel, 2002; Kobayashi, 2008; Abu-Laban, 2013).

However, the weakening of the human rights agenda does not mean that it has become less relevant because real inequality has disappeared. Consider the case of visible minorities. A 2011 study, published by the Canadian Centre for Policy Alternatives, makes use of 2006 Census data to show that visible minorities have slightly higher rates of labour force participation than others (suggesting both a need and a desire to work) but at the same time they also experience much higher rates of unemployment, earn less income, are more likely to be in insecure and poorly paid jobs, and are much more likely to experience poverty than non-racialized minorities (Block and Galabuzi, 2011: 3–5). These recent findings echo an earlier study that found that while visible minorities in Canada were more likely than others to have university degrees and other post-secondary training, they nonetheless experienced higher unemployment and poverty rates irrespective of whether they were foreign or Canadian-born (National Visible Minority Council on Labour Force Development [NVMCLFD], 2004). Such findings in different surveys raise profound questions about racism and discrimination (NVMCLFD, 2004) that are all the more pressing as the number of visible minorities is projected to more than double from that reported in the 2006 Census by the year 2031 (Whittington, 2012).

Notwithstanding the focus of employment equity on so-called visible minorities, or shifts in the federal multiculturalism policy away from "song and dance" toward fighting racism by the 1980s, for the most part it is ethnocultural and linguistic diversity that are central to how the modern Canadian state has conceptualized "diversity" in its policies (Bloemraad, 2006: 237–38). In other words, "race" (or "racism") is not a primary focus but is secondary to "culture." Just as critically, the two (race and culture) are not automatically linked in policies or policy-making processes. This creates a situation whereby certain groups who cross traditionally conceived divides may fall outside the policy radar—for example, French-speaking visible minorities outside Quebec face compounded disadvantages that have yet to be adequately addressed through policies at the federal level, as well as those of other levels of government (see M'pindou, 2002; Abu-Laban and Couture, 2010; Gallant, 2010/2011).

Likewise, redress for historic injustices and past policies has not been a central focus, though in recent years—and particularly under the Conservative government of Prime Minister Harper—the Canadian state has engaged with redress claims (James, 1999, 2004, 2013). This would include the 1988 federal apology and compensation for Japanese-Canadians who experienced internment during World War II; the 1996 apology on the part of the federal government for the physical and sexual abuse often suffered by Aboriginal children at residential schools that were run through a partnership of state and church; and the 2006 apology and compensation for Chinese-Canadians who experienced the "head tax." Moreover, in 2008 the federal government announced a "Truth and Reconciliation Commission" on residential schools. Its purpose is to offer a space to acknowledge individual experiences and to foster reconciliation between Aboriginal and non-Aboriginal Canadians, thus suggesting the potential value of South Africa's post-Apartheid "Truth and Reconciliation" model for Canada's settler-colonial legacies (Abu-Laban, 2000-01). Significant as the Truth and Reconciliation Commission may prove to be, thus far the federal government has not dealt with history in a way that views colonial oppression as an overarching system that persists even in the present (Henderson and Wakeham, 2009:2).

Despite these lingering challenges, in comparison with much of Canadian history, policies from the 1960s have a much less overt and blunt assimilative edge. "Angloconformity" as an ideal has given way to human rights and pluralism. In light of shifting federal policy historically and currently, it is clear that the politics of diversity are not static but dynamic and subject to change and ongoing contestation. This is also the case because the population of Canada itself is changing, as the 2006 Census reveals. Such complexities, along with the fact that even in its cultural emphasis federal policy has had to deal with racism and historical redress, may help attune us to how best to approach the study of diversity.

Diversity and the Evolution of Canadian Political Science

For much of the postwar period, Canadian political scientists paid uneven attention to issues of diversity, particularly when it came to racial minorities (or majorities), immigrants, and Aboriginal people. However, reflecting shifts since the late 1980s, in 2008 the Canadian Political Science Association (CPSA; the main national body representing political scientists across Canada) created a new conference section titled "Race, Ethnicity, Indigenous Peoples, and Politics/Race, Ethnicité, Peuples Autochtones et Politique" (CPSA, 2008). That this section symbolizes the growing interest and scholarship of political scientists in diversity studies may also be seen in the fact that in 2010 there was a special issue of the *Canadian Journal of Political Science/Revue canadienne de science politique* devoted to the theme of "diversity and democratic politics" (Harell and Stolle, 2010; see also Keith Banting's presidential address to the CPSA, 2010).

Indeed, since the late 1980s, Canadian political scientists (both political philosophers and empirical political scientists) have developed distinct approaches to understanding and studying diversity. Perhaps reflecting the dominant emphasis of the Canadian state on themes of culture, "culture" is undoubtedly the central lens through which diversity has been viewed. Less prominent, but equally worthy of consideration, are two other approaches, one emphasizing "race" and the other emphasizing "colonialism." Each approach alerts us to different dimensions of power inequalities experienced by different groups, and as such it may be useful, and indeed desirable, to use them in combination to better understand diversity in Canada.

Turning first to the *lens of culture,* it is notable that in addition to reflecting the dominant frame of the Canadian state's multiculturalism policy, the cultural approach is central to a larger international debate generated by a "Canadian" contribution to political philosophy. In his book *The Rights Revolution* (2000: 11), Michael Ignatieff talks about how Canadians have been at the forefront both politically and intellectually in dealing with the issue of group rights. This intellectual expression of rights philosophy Ignatieff attributes specifically to, among others, Will Kymlicka, Charles Taylor, and James Tully, who defend group-based recognition for cultural minorities.

This body of work is sensitive to existing power inequalities based on cultural difference—especially that of groups who fall outside the dominant culture and may utilize the language of nationalism (e.g., in Canada this would include French Canadians/Québécois as well as Aboriginal peoples). James Tully, for instance, has noted that demands for recognition by distinct cultural groups are based on a shared sense of longing for self-rule and a belief that the status quo is unjust (Tully, 1997: 4–5). At the heart of the defence of recognition given by philosophers such as Taylor and Kymlicka is the view that culture is centrally important to the quality of individual human existence. For example, Kymlicka argues that culture, stemming from a shared language and a shared way of life, "provides people with meaningful options, and with a sense of belonging and identity that helps them negotiate the modern world" (1998: 96). Taylor also suggests that "we become full human agents capable of understanding ourselves, and hence of defining our identity, through our acquisition of rich human languages of expression" (1992: 32). Because belonging to a culture is seen to be so central, it forms the justification for recognizing difference and providing differentiated rights and citizenship.

The emphasis on culture as the basis for rights and difference has generated a particular criticism for opponents of multiculturalism working within the liberal paradigm: the official recognition of group rights on the basis of cultural identity might allow grounds to violate the rights of the individual, and in this respect it is an affront to liberalism (Fierlbeck, 1996: 21). Others have added that the focus on cultural collectivities can strengthen the power of some members within the collectivity over others (e.g., men over women) and as such may be undemocratic. Canadian theorists like Avigail Eisenberg (2006) and Monique Deveaux (2006) have taken the lead in exploring and attempting to reconcile such potential tensions as those between gender justice and multiculturalism.

As a totality, the Canadian tradition since the 1980s has cracked open greater space for political science scholarship on diversity than was available earlier. For example, the Royal Commission on Bilingualism and

Biculturalism set the stage for what would eventually become Canada's bilingualism and multiculturalism policies, and through the 1960s and 1970s the multidisciplinary field of ethnic studies gained momentum. Yet in comparison with other disciplines, political scientists were not heavily involved (Palmer, 1977: 173). Even in 1989, Gilbert H. Scott observed that "thus far, the study of multiculturalism has been pursued mainly by sociologists, anthropologists and historians. Other social scientists such as political scientists have largely ignored the area" (Scott, 1989: 228).

Given this, the period since Scott's observation is somewhat remarkable, as multiculturalism and diversity moved onto the agenda of Canadian political science because of constitutional politics and the evident demands from ethnic minorities and Aboriginal peoples (Cairns, 1992; Abu-Laban and Nieguth, 2000). After the failure of the Charlottetown Accord in 1992, when constitutional politics was shifted to the back burner, issues surrounding diversity did not recede in the discipline's study of Canada. This may be seen to be related to the salience of these issues, as well as the ripple effects within the discipline of the intellectual contribution of the political theorists discussed above.

On a less positive note, however, there are ways in which the work represented by the Canadian political theory tradition has tended to conflate—under the rubric of culture—race, ethnicity, language, and religion. As such, this work has not directly challenged a larger tendency in the discipline to take "ethnic" or "racial" groups as somehow a natural given. Indeed, in Rupert Taylor's (1999) scathing assessment of political science as an international discipline whose epicentre lies in the United States, he critiques both the limited extent that ethnicity and race have been studied in the discipline overall, and also the manner in which race and ethnicity have been approached in that country. What concerns him are typical election studies that categorize in a very un-nuanced way "ethnic" or "racial" groups (e.g., the "Hispanic vote," the "ethnic vote," the "African-American vote"). For Rupert Taylor, political science cannot advance thinking without a different vision—similar to the vision that has inspired the sociological study of race and ethnicity.

The sociological tradition typically emphasizes the socially constructed character of ethnic groups, racial groups, and other identity groups, and their contextual and historical variability. In particular, British sociologist Robert Miles (2000) has advanced the argument that race should not be treated as a "thing." To this end, Miles favours abandoning the use of the term "race" in favour of looking at the experience of racism and processes of racialization. Racialization is understood as a socially created and historically specific process whereby members (or perceived members) of certain groups are viewed by the majority as inferior by reason of their supposed biology. More recently, culture (and cultural difference or cultural inferiority) has been seen by scholars of race as playing a prominent role in contemporary expressions of racism and processes of racialization. For example, the idea of a "clash of civilizations" between the West and the Rest—or more bluntly Christianity and Islam (Huntington, 1996)—has helped fuel some contemporary examples and discourses used by the far right (Betz, 2002). British political theorist Tariq Modood, who is specifically concerned with the experiences of British Muslims, usefully distinguishes "colour" and "cultural" forms of racism. As he puts it, "there are of course colour or phenotype racisms but there are also cultural racisms which build on 'colour' a set of antagonistic or demeaning stereotypes based on alleged or real cultural traits" (Modood, 2007: 44–45).

Drawing from these international currents, *the lens of "race"* and processes of racialization may be viewed as a second approach taken by Canadian political scientists. For many analysts concerned with racism and racialization, there is a sense that the Canadian policy emphasis on multiculturalism detracts from a focus on the reality of racism (Fernando, 2006; Smith, 2003). Moreover, an emphasis on cultural groups—insofar as this typically implies ethnicity, language, and nation—may be seen to detract from race or its intersection with other forms of diversity that generate inequality (Abu-Laban, 2007; Thompson, 2008; Dhamoon, 2009; Nath, 2011). For example, there are powerful ways in which "whiteness" has structured intellectual thought and power, as Bruce Baum shows in his genealogy of the meaning of "Caucasian" (2006), a classification still used by the Canadian state. As well, an uncritical emphasis on cultural difference may fuel forms of racialization and differential treatment, especially in the post-9/11 climate (Abu-Laban, 2002, 2004; Abu-Laban and Abu-Laban, 2007).

Political scientists working with race as a central concept have drawn attention to how race has played an important role in Canadian mythology, which ignores Canada's own history with slavery in favour of narratives stressing the role of Canadians in "rescuing" enslaved African-Americans (Bakan, 2008). Likewise, analysts working with the lens of race have underscored its significance in socio-economic differences both in Quebec (Salée, 2007) and in Canada as a whole—what Grace Edward Galabuzi refers to as economic apartheid (2006). A distinct aspect of the focus on race (as opposed to simply culture) is that analysts working in this tradition typically also are expressly concerned with identifying popular forms of combating racism (what is also referred to as anti-racism), rather than just taking existing power relations as a given (see, for example, Bakan and Kobayashi, 2007; Abu-Laban, 2007).

While "race" has emerged as an alternative lens to culture, yet another approach to consider would be one that uses the *lens of colonialism* and its legacies. The distinct characteristic of this approach is that it expressly draws attention to how inequalities emerged in the first place and links the past, and narratives of the past, to the present (Abu-Laban, 2000-01, 2007). Although the themes of colonialism and postcolonialism permeate the work of many scholars dealing with contemporary Quebec and French Canada (Lamoureux, Maillé, and de Sève, 1999; Maclure, 2003; Desroches, 2003; Gagnon, 2004; Labelle and Rocher, 2004), in recent years it has been Indigenous scholars in particular who have explicitly insisted on the salience of colonialism as the lens for understanding Aboriginal peoples and politics in Canada. Thus, for Taiaiake Alfred (1999, 2005) Canada remains a colonial state exerting power over the lives of Aboriginal peoples in ways that are obvious (the Indian Act) and less obvious (from extant self-government arrangements to how the consumption of food today differs from traditional practices). This emphasis on colonialism as a lens through which to view both history and the present is also to be found in the writings of Joyce Green (1995), Kiera Ladner (2008), and Glen Coulthard (2010). The value of this perspective is that it draws a clear connection between the history leading up to and emanating from the founding of Canada and the current relationships between settlers and the Aboriginal population.

Although anti-racist scholars have cautioned that the specific struggle of Indigenous peoples against colonialism is distinct from the struggle of racialized immigrants and their descendants against racism (Dua, 2008), it is arguably the case that the scholarly study of diversity needs to consider colonialism and racialization along with culture. Attending to the dominant foci of all three of these approaches can aid in understanding real and ongoing struggles reflective of power differentials. In the next section, religion will be used to illustrate how a multi-pronged approach considering culture, racialization, and colonialism may capture the complexity of power relations and policy-making when it comes to "diversity."

Religion, Power, and Complexity

Since September 11, 2001, "religion," especially Islam, has emerged as a political flashpoint in international relations because of the American-led "war on terror." Canadian politics has not been immune. Although the presence of Muslims in Canada dates back to the late nineteenth century, since 9/11 their presence has been "securitized" through the re-working of state border and security policies (Abu-Laban, 2004, 2005; Dobrowolsky, Rollings-Magnussen, and Doucet, 2009).

As this chapter has shown in the preceding historical discussion, religion has been one of many points of difference recognized through policies even before Confederation, and thus the twenty-first-century emphasis on religion (or religious difference) is not new. Religion, on the face of it, may seem to have everything to do with cultural difference rather than "racism" and how that difference structures material inequalities between groups, and rather than the impact of "colonialism" on historic relations between groups. However, a discussion framed primarily or only in relation to differences in values, beliefs, or culture may have limitations.

Consider, for example, the settler colony of Canada and Aboriginal spirituality. Aboriginal spirituality is tied to life-ways on the land and, as such, might be explored from the vantage point of culture and cultural difference in relation to Christianity or secularism. However, an exploration grounded only in relation to culture may miss some key realities. As religious studies professor David Seljak notes, in the Canadian context "no community has suffered more from Christian hegemony than Canada's Aboriginal peoples" (Seljak, 2007: 91). Residential schools epitomized the abuses of church and state, and were fuelled by both colonial practices and racism. The federal apology and compensation for residential schools, and even the unfolding Truth and Reconciliation Commission, may only go so far because the Canadian state has yet to deal with a deeper issue relating to the fact that any recognition of traditional Aboriginal spirituality (tied to the land) inevitably involves recognition of land claims. The failure to address land claims is complex, involving power, colonialism, and racism. As such, "[t]he conflict between Aboriginal peoples' definition of land, property and rights and that of mainstream Canadian society illustrates in the starkest terms the thorny issue of structural discrimination and the connection of the right to religious freedom to a host of broader public policy issues" (Seljak, 2007: 91).

The relevance of thinking about power and racism also pertains to the post-9/11 period since "what Muslims are up to" abroad and at home has become a national security concern. In this particular climate, debates that may at first glance seem to epitomize the demands for cultural recognition acknowledged by Canadian political theorists may in fact have peculiar features that do not neatly correspond to how analysts might envision group-based claims-making. To illustrate, consider more closely the federal debate over what (not) to wear to the ballot box.

It is extremely rare for the prime minister of Canada to publicly take exception to decisions made by Elections Canada (the independent and non-partisan body set up by Parliament to oversee federal elections and referenda). Yet on September 9, 2007, Prime Minister Stephen Harper did just that when he declared his profound disagreement with their decision to allow Muslim women who wear the *niqab* (a head and face cover) to vote without showing their faces (CBC News, 2007). In fact, Canada's Chief Electoral

Officer was subsequently called before the Procedure and House Affairs Committee of the House of Commons for an explanation. What is perhaps most notable in the question of the ballot box and the *niqab* is that Muslim Canadian organizations (and Muslim Canadians themselves) never asked or demanded that this issue be placed on the agenda for discussion (*Globe and Mail*, 2007). Rather, the exchange was given "urgency" because of three federal by-elections taking place in the province of Quebec on September 17, 2007—even though in the entire province it was estimated that a mere 50 Muslim Canadian women wear the *niqab* (Sara Elgazzar cited in CBC News, 2007). As such, it is hard to view this debate only through the lens of culture, at least as it concerns the idea of cohesive groups making demands for differentiated rights and citizenship in the way described by many Canadian political theorists.

In the particular discussion of "what not to wear," the way "culture" is important might be better understood by linking it with racialization and its possible fortification through colonial discourses. While the presence of Muslims in Canada spans three centuries, the most recent available figures show that approximately two-thirds of Canadian Muslims are immigrants (Bramadat and Seljak, 2005: Appendix 240), and the majority are visible minorities under the federal government's definition. Given Modood's (2007) idea of the linkage of colour and cultural racism, it is notable that Peter Beyer's 2005 study of religion, education, and income finds that Muslim Canadians who immigrated since the 1970s and their Canadian-born children have among the lowest income levels of all religious groups, even though they have the second-highest rate of educational attainment among all religious groups in Canada (Beyer, 2005). Muslim Canadians are also underrepresented in major Canadian institutions, such as the House of Commons (Abu-Laban and Trimble, 2006). However, the ballot box issue was not addressed by the Canadian government in relation to issues of power as reflected in political representation or socio-economic status (the immigrant status of many Muslim Canadians, their visible minority status, their employment earnings, and their high unemployment rates).

Nor was this debate ever framed in relation to real, everyday forms of racial and cultural prejudice or their linkage to older discourses of "orientalism." Orientalism is the term coined by the late Edward Said to explain the formation of Europe and its colonial expansion through stories, policies, and analyses that view the peoples and cultures of "the Orient" as different from and inferior to those of Europe (Said, 1979). Sherene Razack has drawn attention to the relevance of racism and these older discourses of colonialism and empire in her attempt to understand why "in the past, Canadians have had relatively little trouble" with schoolgirls wearing the *hijab* (a head covering), or by extension what women wear to vote, while after 9/11 "the apparently greater ease with different religions and cultures began to disappear" (2008: 174).

Given that the ballot box debate arose without Muslim Canadians making any demand, analysts would do well to consider the insights drawn from discussions of culture alongside race and colonialism/history and, in the case of Muslim Canadians, the possible lingering relevance of orientalism. Such a focus might also invite consideration into how, at the popular level, resistance to these developments is expressed by state and non-state actors (see, for example, Abu-Laban, 2002).

Conclusion

This chapter has addressed different policy responses of the Canadian state to diversity, as well as different approaches used by Canadian political scientists to understand diversity. As argued here, both the study of diversity and the responses to diversity say much about issues of power and the ongoing struggles to overturn (or in some cases to reinforce) group-based differences. The responses to such inequalities have much to do with the nature of Canadian democracy and the inclusivity of the practices, policies, and institutions that underpin liberal democracy.

As this chapter has noted, culture has been a dominant frame of reference both for the Canadian state and for Canadian analysts. While culture is important to help identify existing inequalities, the demands of some groups also draw attention to racism, processes of racialization, and anti-racism as a means of resistance. Other approaches draw attention to colonialism as a means for understanding the relationship between history and the present. This would suggest that, as political scientists continue to consider ways to best understand the politics of diversity in Canada, attention should be given to themes of culture along with race/racialization/anti-racism and colonialism. A multi-pronged approach will help deal with the constantly shifting terrain of state policies in this area, as well as understanding the ways in which people identify and make demands—some of which may have deep resonance in Canadian history. A multi-pronged approach could foster better and more inclusive dialogues across the field of Canadian politics and in the sphere of policy-making. It may help deal with new perspectives and demands, as well as new and hybrid forms of identity that Canadians may exhibit as their colleagues, friends, family, and acquaintances increasingly reflect both historic and new forms of diversity that characterize the changing demography of twenty-first-century Canada in a globalizing world. Finally, a multi-pronged approach can help us to distinguish between actual demands and attributed demands, as in the case of the ballot box and the *niqab*.

Returning to where this chapter began, the recent debate over the 2011 Census suggests that civil society and state actors in Canada have a great deal of interest in better understanding Canada's diversity in all its complexity. As such, we can expect that statisticians and researchers in many different disciplines will be working with policy-makers to find ways to ensure that the next Census of 2016 best represents Canada's diversity empirically (Tamburi, 2012). As this chapter has suggested, the study of diversity has grown in prominence within Canadian political science scholarship. As a result, political scientists now confront new questions that involve consideration of the impact of historic and contemporary state policies, as well as which analytical approach (or approaches) may best yield a greater understanding of group-based power inequities within Canada's increasingly diverse society.

References and Suggested Readings

Abu-Laban, Yasmeen. 2000–01. "The Future and the Legacy: Globalization and the Canadian Settler State." *Journal of Canadian Studies. Revue d'Etudes Canadiennes* 35 (4): 262–76.

Abu-Laban, Yasmeen. 2002. "Liberalism, Multiculturalism, and the Problem of Essentialism." *Citizenship Studies* 6 (4): 459–82. http://dx.doi.org/10.1080/1362102022000 041268.

Abu-Laban, Yasmeen. 2004. "The New North America and the Segmentation of Canadian Citizenship." *International Journal of Canadian Studies* 29: 17–40.

Abu-Laban, Yasmeen. 2005. "Regionalism, Migration, and Fortress North America." *Review of Constitutional Studies* 10 (1–2): 135–62.

Abu-Laban, Yasmeen. 2006. "Stalemate at Work: Visible Minorities and Employment Equity." In *New Citizens, New Policies: Developments in Diversity Policy in Canada and Flanders*, eds. Leen d'Haenenks, Marc Hooghe, Dirk Vanheule, and Hasibe Gezduci, 71–87. Ghent: Academia Press.

Abu-Laban, Yasmeen. 2007. "Political Science, Race, Ethnicity, and Public Policy." In *Critical Policy Studies*, eds. Michael Orsini and Miriam Smith, 137–57. Vancouver: University of British Columbia Press.

Abu-Laban, Yasmeen. 2013. "On the Borderlines of Human and Citizen: The Liminal State of Arab Canadians." In *Targeted Transnationals: The State, The Media and Arab Canadians*, eds. Bessma Momani and Jenna Hennebry, 68–88. Vancouver: University of British Columbia Press.

Abu-Laban, Yasmeen, and Baha Abu-Laban. 2007. "Reasonable Accommodation in a Global Village." *Policy Options* 28 (8): 28–33.

Abu-Laban, Yasmeen, and Claude Couture. 2010. "Multiple Minorities and Deceptive Dichotomies: The Theoretical and Political Implications of the Struggle for a Public French Education System in Alberta." *Canadian Journal of Political Science* 43 (02): 433–56. http://dx.doi.org/10.1017/S0008423910000119.

Abu-Laban, Yasmeen, and Christina Gabriel. 2002. *Selling Diversity: Immigration, Multiculturalism, Employment Equity, and Globalization*. Peterborough: Broadview Press.

Abu-Laban, Yasmeen, and Tim Nieguth. 2000. "Reconsidering the Constitution, Minorities and Politics in Canada." *Canadian Journal of Political Science* 33 (3): 465–97.

Abu-Laban, Yasmeen, and Linda Trimble. 2006. "Print Media Coverage of Muslim-Canadians at Recent Federal Elections." *Electoral Insight* 8 (2): 35–42.

Alfred, Taiaiake. 1999. *Peace, Power, Righteousness: An Indigenous Manifesto.* Don Mills: Oxford University Press.

Alfred, Taiaiake. 2005. *Wasasé: Indigenous Pathways of Action and Freedom.* Peterborough: Broadview Press.

Bakan, Abigail. 2008. "Reconsidering the Underground Railway: Slavery and Racialization in the Making of the Canadian State." *Social Studies* 4 (1): 3–29.

Bakan, Abigail B., and Audrey Kobayashi. 2007. "'The Sky Didn't Fall': Organizing to Combat Racism in the Workplace—The Case of the Alliance for Employment Equity." In *Race, Racialization, and Antiracism in Canada and Beyond,* eds. Genevieve Fuji Johnson and Randy Enomoto, 51–78. Toronto: University of Toronto Press.

Banting, Keith. 2010. "Is There a Progressive's Dilemma in Canada? Immigration, Multiculturalism and the Welfare State" (Presidential Address to the Canadian Political Science Association). *Canadian Journal of Political Science* 43 (04): 797–820. http://dx.doi.org/10.1017/S0008423910000983.

Baum, Bruce. 2006. *The Rise and Fall of the Caucasian Race.* New York: New York University Press.

Betz, Hans Georg. 2002. "Xenophobia, Identity Politics, and Exclusionary Populism in Western Europe." In *Fighting Identities: Race, Religion, and Ethno-Nationalism. Socialist Register 2003,* eds. Leo Panitch and Colin Leys, 193–210. London: Merlin Press.

Beyer, Peter. 2005. "Religious Identity and Educational Attainment Among Recent Immigrants to Canada: Gender, Age, and 2nd Generation." *Journal of International Migration and Integration* 6 (2): 177–99. http://dx.doi.org/10.1007/s12134-005-1009-2.

Block, Sheila, and Grace-Edward Galabuzi. 2011. *Canada's Color Coded Labour Market: The Gap for Racialized Workers.* Ottawa: Canadian Centre for Policy Alternatives.

Bloemraad, I. 2006. *Becoming a Citizen: Incorporating Immigrants and Refugees in the United States and Canada.* Berkeley: University of California Press.

Bramadat, Paul, and David Seljak, eds. 2005. *Religion and Ethnicity in Canada.* Toronto: Pearson Longman.

Brennan, Richard J. 2011. "Conservatives Relied on Few Complaints to Scrap the Census," *Toronto Star,* January 7. http://www.thestar.com/news/canada/2011/01/07/conservatives_relied_on_a_few_complaints_to_scrap_the_census.html

Cairns, Alan C. 1992. *Charter versus Federalism: The Dilemmas of Constitutional Reform.* Montreal: McGill-Queen's University Press.

Canadian Political Science Association. 2008. "CPSA 2009 Conference Section—Race, Ethnicity, Indigenous Peoples, and Politics." POLCAN email communiqué, April 16.

Cardin, Jean-François, and Claude Couture. 1996. *Histoire du Canada: Espace et différences.* Quebec: Les Presses de l'Université Laval.

CBC News. 2010. "Stats Can Head Quits Over Census Dispute," July 21. http://www.cbc.ca/news/canada/story/2010/07/21/statistics-canada-quits.html

CBC News. 2007. "Harper Slams Elections Canada Ruling on Veils," September 9. http://www.cbc.ca/news/canada/harper-slams-elections-canada-ruling-on-veils-1.648173

Chase, Steven. 2010. "Privacy Commissioner Not Consulted on Plan to Scrap Compulsory Census," July 14. http://www.theglobeandmail.com/news/politics/privacy-commissioner-not-consulted-on-plan-to-scrap-compulsory-census/article1212381/

Coulthard, Glen. 2010. "Place Against Empire: Understanding Indigenous Anti-Colonialism." *Affinities: A Journal of Radical Theory, Culture and Action* 2 (Fall): 79–83.

Day, Richard J.F. 2000. *Multiculturalism and the History of Canadian Diversity*. Toronto: University of Toronto Press.

Desroches, Vincent. 2003. "Présentation: En quoi la littérature québécoise est-elle postcoloniale?" *Québec Studies* 30 (Spring/Summer): 3–14.

Deveaux, Monique. 2006. *Gender and Justice in Multicultural Liberal States*. Oxford: Oxford University Press. http://dx.doi.org/10.1093/acprof:oso/9780199289790.001.0001.

Dhamoon, Rita. 2009. *Identity/Difference Politics: How Difference is Produced and Why It Matters*. Vancouver: University of British Columbia Press.

Dickason, Olive P. 1992. *Canada's First Nations: A History of Founding Peoples from Earliest Times*. Toronto: McClelland and Stewart.

Dobrowolsky, Alexandra, Sandra Rollings-Magnussen, and Marc G. Doucet. 2009. "Security, Insecurity and Human Rights: Contextualizing Post 9/11." In *Anti-Terrorism: Security and Insecurity After 9/11*, ed. Sandra Rollings-Magnussen, 13–31. Halifax: Fernwood Publishing.

Dua, Enakshi. 2008. "Thinking Through Anti-Racism and Indigeneity in Canada." *Ardent Review* 1 (1): 31–35.

Eisenberg, Avigail, ed. 2006. *Diversity and Equality: The Changing Framework of Freedom in Canada*. Vancouver: University of British Columbia Press.

Fekete, Jason. 2010. "Census Consensus Eludes Premiers: Several Scold Harper," *Montreal Gazette*, August 6. http://www.montrealgazette.com/news/Census+consensus+eludes+premiers+Several+scold+Harper/3369649/story.html.

Fernando, Shanti. 2006. *Race and the City: Chinese Canadian and Chinese American Political Mobilization*. Vancouver: University of British Columbia Press.

Fierlbeck, Katherine. 1996. "The Ambivalent Potential of Cultural Identity." *Canadian Journal of Political Science* 29 (01): 3–22. http://dx.doi.org/10.1017/S0008423900007228.

Gagnon, Alain-G., ed. 2004. *Québec: State and Society*. 3rd ed. Peterborough: Broadview Press.

Galabuzi, Grace-Edward. 2006. *Canada's Economic Apartheid: The Social Exclusion of Racialized Groups in the New Century*. Toronto: Canadian Scholars' Press.

Gallant, Nicole. 2010/2011. "Communautés francophones en milieu minoritaire et immigrants: entre ouverture et inclusion." *Revue du Nouvel-Ontario* 35–36: 69–105. http://dx.doi.org/10.7202/1005966ar.

Globe and Mail. 2007. "Editorial: Why Make Veils an Issue?" September 11: A20.

Green, Joyce A. 1995. "Towards a Détente with History: Confronting Canada's Colonial Legacy." *International Journal of Canadian Studies* 12 (Fall): 85–105.

Green, Joyce, and Ian Peach. 2007. "Beyond 'Us' and 'Them': Prescribing Postcolonial Politics and Policy in Saskatchewan." In *Belonging? Diversity, Recognition, and Shared Citizenship in Canada*, eds. Keith Banting, Thomas J. Courchene, and F. Leslie Seidle, 263–84. Montreal: Institute for Research on Public Policy.

Harell, Allison, and Dietlind Stolle. 2010. "Diversity and Democratic Politics: An Introduction." *Canadian Journal of Political Science* 43 (02): 235–56. http://dx.doi.org/10.1017/S000842391000003X.

Henderson, Jennifer, and Pauline Wakeham. 2009. "Colonial Reckoning, National Reconciliation?: Aboriginal Peoples and the Culture of Redress in Canada." *English Studies in Canada* 35 (1): 1–26.

Huntington, Samuel. 1996. *The Clash of Civilizations: Remaking of World Order*. New York: Simon and Schuster.

Ignatieff, Michael. 2000. *The Rights Revolution*. Toronto: Anansi.

James, Matt. 1999. "Redress Politics and Canadian Citizenship." In *The State of the Federation 1998/99: How Canadians Connect*, eds. Harvey Lazar and Tom McIntosh, 247–81. Montreal: McGill-Queen's University Press.

James, Matt. 2004. "Recognition, Redistribution, and Redress: The Case of the 'Chinese Head Tax'." *Canadian Journal of Political Science* 37 (04): 883–902. http://dx.doi.org/10.1017/S0008423904990130.

James, Matt. 2013. "Neoliberal Heritage Redress." In *Reconciling Canada: Critical Perspectives on the Culture of Redress*, eds. Jennifer Henderson and Pauline Wakeham, 31–46. Toronto: University of Toronto Press.

King, Mackenzie. 1947. "1947. *Hansard* (Thursday, 1 May)." In *Canada, Manpower and Immigration, A Report of the Canadian Immigration and Population Study, Volume Two: The Immigration Program*, 201–07. Ottawa: Information Canada.

Kobayashi, Audrey. 2008. "Ethnocultural Political Mobilization, Multiculturalism, and Human Rights in Canada." In *Group Politics and Social Movements in Canada*, ed. Miriam Smith, 131–57. Peterborough: Broadview.

Kymlicka, Will. 1998. *Finding Our Way: Rethinking Ethnocultural Relations in Canada*. Toronto: Oxford University Press.

Kymlicka, Will. 2007. "Ethnocultural Diversity in a Liberal State: Making Sense of the Canadian Models." In *Belonging? Diversity, Recognition, and Shared Citizenship in Canada*, eds. Keith Banting, Thomas J. Courchene, and F. Leslie Seidle, 39–104. Montreal: Institute for Research on Public Policy.

Labelle, Micheline, and François Rocher, eds. 2004. *Contestation transnationale, diversité et citoyenneté dans l'espace québécois*. Sainte-Foy: Presses de l'Université du Québec.

Ladner, Kiera. 2008. "*Aysaka'paykinit:* Contesting the Rope Around the Nations' Neck." In *Group Politics and Social Movements in Canada*, ed. Miriam Smith, 227–49. Peterborough: Broadview.

Lamoureux, Diane, Chantal Maillé, and Micheline de Sève. 1999. *Malaises identitaires: Échanges féministes autour d'un Québec incertain*. Montreal: Remue-Ménage.

Levitsky, Marianne. 2010. "Keep the Canadian Census Long Form; Gardons le formulaire long du recensement canadien," July 3. http://www.gopetition.com/petitions/keep-the-canadian-census-long-form.html.

Maclure, Jocelyn. 2003. *Quebec Identity*. Montreal: McGill-Queen's University Press.

Miles, Robert. 2000. "Apropos the Idea of 'Race' Again." In *Theories of Race and Racism: A Reader*, eds. Les Back and John Solomos, 125–43. London, New York: Routledge.

Modood, Tariq. 2007. *Multiculturalism: A Civic Idea*. Cambridge: Polity Press.

M'pindou, Jacques Luketa. 2002. "La Jeunesse congolaise dans la société canadienne." In *L'Alberta et le multiculturalisme francophone: témoignages et problématiques*, eds. Claude Couture and Josée Bergeron, 33–36. Edmonton: Canadian Studies Institute.

Nath, Nisha. 2011. "Defining Narratives of Identity in Canadian Political Science: Accounting for the Absence of Race." *Canadian Journal of Political Science* 44 (01): 161–93. http://dx.doi.org/10.1017/S0008423910001071.

National Visible Minority Council on Labour Force Development (NVMCLFD). 2004. *Building Our Future Workforce: A Background Paper on Visible Minority Labour Force Development*. Ottawa: NVMCLFD.

Palmer, Howard. 1977. "History and Present State of Ethnic Studies in Canada." In *Identities: The Impact of Ethnicity on Canadian Society. Canadian Ethnic Studies Association*, vol. 5, ed. Wsevolod Isajiw, 167–83. Toronto: Peter Martin.

Razack, Sherene. 2008. *Casting Out: The Eviction of Muslims from Western Law and Politics*. Toronto: University of Toronto Press.

Said, Edward. 1979. *Orientalism*. New York: Vintage Books.

Salée, Daniel. 2007. "The Quebec State and the Management of Ethnocultural Diversity: Perspectives on an Ambiguous Record." In *Belonging? Diversity, Recognition, and

Shared Citizenship in Canada, eds. Keith Banting, Thomas J. Courchene, and F. Leslie Seidle, 105–42. Montreal: Institute for Research on Public Policy.

Scott, Gilbert H. 1989. "Race Relations and Public Policy: Uncharted Course." In *Canada 2000: Race Relations and Public Policy*, eds. O.P. Dwivedi et al., 227–32. Guelph: Department of Political Studies, University of Guelph.

Seljak, David. 2007. "Religion and Multiculturalism in Canada: The Challenge of Religious Intolerance and Discrimination." *Report Prepared for the Department of Canadian Heritage. Strategic Policy, Research and Planning Directorate, Multiculturalism and Human Rights Program*. Ottawa: Department of Canadian Heritage.

Siddiqui, Haroon. 2010. "Gutting of Census Stirs Opposition to Stephen Harper," *Toronto Star*, July 10. http://www.thestar.com/news/canada/2010/07/10/siddiqui_gutting_of_census_stirs_opposition_to_stephen_harper.html

Smith, Malinda. 2003. "'Race Matters' and 'Race Manners'." In *Reinventing Canada*, eds. Janine Brodie and Linda Trimble, 108–29. Toronto: Prentice Hall.

Stasiulis, Daiva, and Radha Jhappan. 1995. "The Fractious Politics of a Settler Society: Canada." In *Unsettling Settler Societies: Articulations of Gender, Race, Ethnicity, and Class*, eds. Daiva Stasiulis and Nira Yuval-Davis, 95–131. London: Sage. http://dx.doi.org/10.4135/9781446222225.n4.

Statistics Canada. 2007a. *The Evolving Linguistic Portrait, 2006 Census*. Catalogue No. 97–555-XIE. Ottawa: Minister of Industry. http://www.statcan.gc.ca

Statistics Canada. 2007b. *Immigration in Canada: A Portrait of the Foreign-Born Population, 2006 Census*. Catalogue No. 97–557-XIE. December. Ottawa: Minister of Industry. http://www.statcan.gc.ca.

Statistics Canada. 2008. *Canada's Ethnocultural Mosaic, 2006 Census*. Catalogue No. 97–562-XIE. April. Ottawa: Minister of Industry. http://www.statcan.gc.ca.

Statistics Canada. 2012. *Final Report on 2016 Census Options: Proposed Content Determination and Methodology Options*. August 29. Ottawa: Census Management Office. http://www.statcan.gc.ca.

Tamburi, Rosanna. 2012. "Long-Form Census Remains Hot Topic for Canadian Researchers." *University Affairs* 4 (June). http://www.universityaffairs.ca.

Taylor, Charles. 1992. "The Politics of Recognition." In *Multiculturalism and the Politics of Recognition*, ed. Amy Gutmann, 25–73. Princeton: Princeton University Press.

Taylor, Rupert. 1999. "Political Science Encounters 'Race' and 'Ethnicity'." In *Ethnic and Racial Studies Today*, eds. Martin Bulmer and John Solomos, 115–23. London, New York: Routledge.

Thompson, Debra. 2008. "Is Race Political?" *Canadian Journal of Political Science* 41 (03): 525. http://dx.doi.org/10.1017/S0008423908080827.

Tully, James. 1997. *Strange Multiplicity: Constitutionalism in an Age of Diversity*. Cambridge: Cambridge University Press.

Whitaker, Reg, Gregory S. Kealey, and Andrew Parnaby. 2012. *Secret Service: Political Policing in Canada from the Fenians to Fortress America*. Toronto: University of Toronto Press.

Whittington, Les. 2012. "Visible Minorities Increasing in Canada." *Toronto Star*, May 17. http://www.thestar.com/news/canada/2012/05/17/visible_minorities_increasing_in_canada.html.

PART VI

Canada and the World

nineteen
Canada in the World

MARK R. BRAWLEY

The twenty-first century promises to be a time of change in international affairs. Economic activity and political power may be redistributed in fundamental ways. How well will Canada navigate this changing environment? Ten years ago, noted political scientist Jennifer Welsh wrote *At Home in the World* (2004), a reflection on Canadian foreign policy after the Cold War as well as a guide for redirecting and refocusing the country's efforts in the future. How does Welsh's vision stand up a decade later? What sort of international role are the country's citizens and their government establishing for Canada?

The answers vary in some important ways, depending on the specific issues one concentrates on. Therefore the discussion below separates the perspectives into a few different themes, flowing from traditional concerns about Canada's place in the global economy or in international alliances, to broader considerations regarding global governance structures and the informal ties linking Canadians to other societies. In the 1990s, debates concerning the direction of Canadian foreign policy were quite optimistic about the role Canada could play in international affairs—though the specific means and methods for promoting positive change were not always obvious or clear. The terrorist attacks of September 11th, 2001, changed much of our thinking about how the world was evolving, and Welsh laid out several reasons for Canadians to rethink the way their government represents their country in international affairs given the new challenges confronting key allies. Now we also need to think about how the international system is changing, as economic and military power will be redistributed in dramatic ways.

Economic Ties

Canada has deep and profound ties to the international economy. The country is relatively rich, and Canadians are generally well aware of how much of their wealth is tied up with the activities of others. They recognize this in the aggregate sense ("national" wealth depends on trading with and investing in other countries) as well as on a personal level (individuals see how their own incomes, or their own purchases, rest on direct links to other countries). As Welsh noted in 2004, domestic opinion regarding Canada's engagement with the international economy had shifted significantly from where it had been only some 20 years before. When free trade with the United States first came up for debate in the 1980s, many Canadians expressed fears that such an agreement would threaten cherished domestic social welfare policies (such as national health care). Those fears worsened when the free trade agreement was expanded to include Mexico. Economic performance over the last quarter-century demonstrated that those fears were largely ungrounded. That experience changed the nature of our discussions about international economic issues. As Welsh put it, Canadians have set aside their anxieties and embraced economic globalization (2004: 89).

Despite some of the fears associated with regional free trade in the 1980s and early 1990s—or perhaps because of those concerns—Canadian governments played a disproportionately large role in shaping the North American Free Trade Agreement. NAFTA currently represents the single largest free trade zone in the world (larger than the European Union). There's no question as to why—the United States remains the world's single largest national economy. While it may not hold on to that top position for much longer, the United States will be among the largest and richest states (judged on a per capita basis) well into the future. For Canada, being next door to the United States is both an economic blessing and an economic curse. Proximity (coupled with social similarities) makes it easy for Canadians to do business with the United States, a major reason that Canada's exports remain tightly focused on the American market. The Department of Foreign Affairs, Trade and Development (2013) reports over 70 per cent of exports (by value) went to the United States in 2012. Imports were slightly more diverse, with about 62 per cent coming from the United States. That link to the United States is a blessing, because the US market is very wealthy, quite open to Canadian exports, made up of consumers very similar to Canadians, and oh so near.

The curse, however, is that Canada comes to depend too heavily on this single market. That dependence could be turned against Canada in a conscious fashion. Sylvia Ostry, a former deputy trade minister, warned some time ago that the country could become too reliant on the American market, making itself vulnerable to heavy pressure should the US government choose to exercise political leverage over Canada (quoted in Welsh, 2004: 89). Less obvious, but just as important, the Canadian economy has become lashed to the American. During the 1990s, the American economy worked like a locomotive, moving along at a fast pace, and Canadians were happily pulled along. In recent years, the experience has been more like a roller coaster ride. The danger may be less that an American government would try to exploit Canada's dependence on the US market through politically motivated threats, but rather that the Canadian economy now automatically follows the performance of the American economy. When the latter rises, so too does the Canadian economy; when economic activity south of the border goes down,

the Canadian economy follows it down. Canada can do little to offset or avoid the cyclical gyrations of the American economy. Macroeconomic mismanagement originating in Washington, DC, necessarily means trouble here. This isn't good news, as the future will undoubtedly present Americans with some daunting economic challenges. The American government's debt will weigh heavily on future decisions made there. Canadians will have to endure the unpleasantness of having their economic fate determined by fights in the halls of power in Washington, rather than in Ottawa.

Canadian leaders have long recognized the need to diversify the country's economic connections. Liberal governments in the 1970s sought options for generating ties with other states, in what was then referred to as the "Third Option" (Muirhead, 2007: 137). The current government is exploring similar aims. At the Davos Economic Forum in January 2012, Prime Minister Stephen Harper laid out his government's ideas for managing Canada's foreign economic policies in the future. Harper referred to the need for Canada to diversify its trading relations away from its focus on the United States. In particular, Harper stressed the desire for Canadian exports of energy to reach markets outside North America. Gas and oil exports should be directed toward Asia, where economic growth continues to accelerate, he argued. He also described the goal of Canada concluding more free trade agreements in the future, to enhance opportunities to expand Canada's trade with a variety of other countries. Canada has therefore been pursuing a range of trade liberalization agreements over the past decade, successfully concluding one with the European Union in 2013, but pursuing others with India and several economically developing countries as well.

The energy sector has also been the specific focus of some debate. With the financial collapse of 2008, a series of policy decisions in Washington reshaped the economic calculations of investors and owners in a variety of settings. American policy-makers, worried about the health of their own financial institutions, pumped cash into their economy. The flood of dollars drove down interest rates in the United States, as designed; as an unintended consequence, however, the value of the US dollar slumped versus other currencies. Some foreigners decided it was better to spend cash now, either because their own currencies translated into more US dollars than before, or because the US dollars they held were losing value every month. Foreign investors went on spending sprees—especially those making decisions based on long-term calculations. These investors saw opportunities to buy up firms that were struggling during the economic slowdown that accompanied the financial meltdown of 2008.

To give a specific example, Chinese investors had accumulated substantial sums of US dollars, were calculating their needs for the decades to come, and had reasons to think it would now be wiser to spend dollars rather than hold on to them. Chinese investors began scanning potential sources around the globe and securing supplies of required imports. When the value of some Canadian firms slumped due to the broader economic slowdown, Chinese investors saw opportunities. China National Offshore Oil Corporation (CNOOC) bid to purchase Nexen, one of the key companies developing Alberta's oil sands. CNOOC offered slightly over $15 billion in December 2012. Nexen operates around the globe, but the tricky issues had to do with the resources it owns in Canada; the deal had to be approved by the federal government because all such purchases by foreign firms are reviewed, according to Canadian law. The more delicate matter, of course, concerns the true owners of CNOOC: the Chinese government. Should natural resources in Canada be owned by a foreign government? The Conservative government ruled that the assets could be sold, both in this agreement and in a similar purchase involving Petronas, an energy company owned by the government of Malaysia.

Diversifying trade ties would be one reason the Tory government would approve these sales. As already mentioned, the government would like to see more energy exports to Asia. Consistency in policy practice would be another. Canada has long supported the notion that its own firms should be allowed to set up shop in foreign lands; foreign direct investment often involves buying up an existing firm in the foreign market. Since Canadian governments have long adhered to this principle for Canadian businesses seeking to enter China, it must take up a similar position when Chinese firms come to Canada seeking to purchase local businesses. Nonetheless, the decision sparked public debate over the tensions between private and potentially national interests.

In general, Canadian governments have been strong supporters not only of freer flows of capital for international investment, but of a broadly open international economic order. This stance has been true for decades, and fluctuates little depending on the party in power. Canada was the first state to join the Organization for Economic Cooperation and Development (OECD), was a founding member of General Agreement on Trade and Tariffs (which later became the World Trade Organization), and helped shape the International Monetary Fund (IMF) at its inception. Canada remains heavily involved in all these international organizations, and in promoting the principles these institutions were built on. For example, Canadian diplomats have been negotiating several trade-liberalizing agreements for some time. After several years of negotiations, Canada and the EU concluded a major trade agreement in 2013, which should boost the volume of goods and services exchanged between the two. Negotiations dragged on, however, because of several sticking points—while not officially identified, one can assume there are a couple of areas where the two sides are unlikely to find common ground. (Opening up several Canadian service sectors, for instance, may be difficult for the government to accept. Canada's financial system remains fairly healthy because of the small number of banks allowed to offer the full range of services. This limitation on competition helps each of the banks earn profits through certain activities, offsetting losses elsewhere, which helps these banks weather economic crises. The government would not like to upset this arrangement, despite European desires to open up this sector for their firms to enter. Another contested area is agriculture, where both sides wish to liberalize trade in certain types of goods, but not others.)

In economic terms, Canada will probably remain most intimately linked to the United States for a long time. Yet, as the discussion above has illustrated, the country will surely develop stronger trade ties to China and other Asian countries. Canadian governments—under both Liberal and Conservative leadership—have pursued opportunities to expand trade with Europe and other countries in the western hemisphere over the past two decades. Canada has also consistently sought to bolster the organizations that govern the international economy, as a way to boost and maintain open economic flows between countries. These will undoubtedly remain the country's long-term policy objectives. The chief question is how well Canada diversifies its economic relations away from the United States.

Military Ties

In security affairs, too, Canada remains tightly bound to the United States. Relations with the United States in this area were once consistently smooth—but that changed in the past decade (Clarkson, 2008; Gotlieb, 2003). On September 11, 2001, Canadian and American military (and civil) authorities worked quite well together as they struggled to comprehend and then respond to the terrorist attacks. Canada participated (via the NATO alliance) in the combat operations launched against the Taliban regime in Afghanistan, first by deploying special operations units, then with large-scale ground and air forces. Yet when the Bush Administration chose to commit American forces against the government of Saddam Hussein in Iraq in 2003, Canada's Prime Minister Jean Chrétien declined to join the American-led "coalition of the willing." Canada's official position was that the United States and its allies needed new authorization from the UN Security Council before it would participate in a war against Iraq. Despite the Bush Administration's efforts in front of the UN diplomats, no authorization was forthcoming, so Chrétien had Canada stand aside. American officials took this as a rebuff, with some sharp words uttered by politicians on both sides of the border.

Canadian officials (whether speaking for Chrétien's government, his Liberal successor Paul Martin, or the Conservative governments led by Stephen Harper that followed) have taken pains to point out all the areas of increased cooperation between the United States and Canada on security matters during the past decade. Canadian Forces continued to support the American mission in Afghanistan even after the end of Canadian combat operations in 2011, through providing personnel to train Afghan military and police. This can be seen, at least in part, as a way to affirm Canada's commitment to future cooperation with the United States on security matters (a point heavily emphasized in an in-depth analysis by Janine Gross Stein and Eugene Lang (2007).

The two countries' law enforcement and border patrol and policing agencies have coordinated their efforts to an unprecedented degree. The terrorist attacks of September 11, 2001, could have triggered policy responses that would have severely restricted the flow of goods and people over the US-Canadian border; instead officials from Canada seized the initiative to develop several policies that would assuage American fears, yet maintain the relatively open border separating the two countries (Wark, 2008). These efforts have included the introduction of new identification systems for travellers to use, greater information sharing between the two governments regarding people crossing their borders, cooperative training to ensure law enforcement agencies work well together on border-related issues, and a host of other measures. Canada even went so far as to introduce a permanent resident card, to help ensure landed immigrants in Canada would be able to cross the border as freely as Canadian citizens. In all these ways, the Canadian government successfully found methods to prevent (or at least offset) side effects linked to the heightened security concerns of the United States in the wake of 9/11.

Canadian military forces did engage in combat alongside Americans, and participating in the war in Afghanistan took a toll on the Canadian military. Between early 2002 and 2011, 158 Canadian military personnel and 5 civilians died (via combat, accidents, or suicide), while more than 2,000 were injured. Canada deployed armored vehicles, artillery, and helicopters, and eventually sent tanks into the field. These deployment operations were costly in terms of military equipment, as well as exacting a heavy psychological and emotional cost on the troops. Moreover, the almost decade-long rotation of units in and out of Afghanistan meant fewer troops were available for use in other parts of the globe. The effort exposed both some positive aspects of Canada's military and some shortcomings. In the first decade after the Cold War, budget constraints led to difficult choices regarding equipment purchases. By and large, the more recent equipment served Canadian soldiers in the field well, though there were more than a few complaints about how the various pieces complemented each other in action. (And Canadian soldiers lacked one or two key elements—medium-lift helicopters, for example—which had to be resolved in the short term.)

The problems should not come as a surprise, since it was impossible to anticipate in the 1990s that Canadian soldiers would be sent on this kind of mission, or in this sort of terrain. Nor were the complaints heard from Canadian Forces in Afghanistan uncommon; most NATO members were no longer capable of fielding the entire range of combat and support units in an integrated fashion. To an extent, European members of the alliance had therefore committed to specializing their military contributions, so that they could pool together their smaller units into larger fighting formations. The disadvantage with that strategy, however, is that a government can then only operate when each of its allies agrees to contribute the specific units necessary. Without wide consensus among the partners, military deployments become impossible. (For a deeper discussion of these implications for Canada, see Jones and Lagassé, 2012.)

As several recent operations have shown—particularly with NATO members engaged in North Africa—even the larger countries in the alliance (such as France) have had difficulty gathering the entire package of combat and support units needed to pull off a small to moderate intervention. In comparison, Canadian units have done well in shouldering significant combat responsibilities in the past 10 years. They certainly carried heavy responsibilities in Afghanistan, taking on considerable burdens and contributing to the war and reconstruction efforts in the country. Canada was therefore able to make a greater contribution to the combat operations than several NATO members with larger populations.

On the downside, the smaller total size of the Canadian Forces—the number of regular personnel in the ground, naval, and air units had fallen to below 60,000 by the end of the 1990s—limited the ability to send troops abroad for a sustained period. Normal policy is for a unit to spend a set amount of time deployed (typically, this would be for six to nine months). Since the stresses associated with being in the field build up over time, troops are then rotated back to Canada for an extended period (a year or more) before being deployed overseas again. This means, however, that no more than a quarter of the ground forces should be sent on operations at the same time, if there is an expectation for the commitment to be sustained beyond six months. These same principles govern troops serving on peace-keeping missions, since these count as combat operations. As the total number of military personnel fell, the ability to deploy units overseas became increasingly constrained. This imposed constraints on when and where the government might be able to commit Canada to a military role.

To address these limitations and deal with the toll the Afghan mission took on equipment and general combat readiness, the Harper government developed an ambitious program for retooling and re-energizing the Canadian military. Recruitment targets were raised, in the hopes of increasing the number of regular personnel. Militia recruitment was also expanded. The government chose to purchase new transport aircraft (both medium- and long-range), to construct an array of new ships for the navy, to buy upgraded fighting vehicles for the army, and, most contentiously, to acquire a new fighter-bomber for the air force. (The air force bid is discussed in more detail below.) These purchases were justified in a planning document called *Canada First Defence Strategy*, released in 2008. As its title implies, the Conservative vision for the future identifies the priority for the Canadian Forces: the defence of Canada. Other goals follow. Of course, the purchasing programs indicate the desire to continue to project power beyond Canada's borders, hence the decisions to buy new C-130 Hercules and C-17 Globemaster transport planes.

Viewed overall, the coming challenges for the Canadian military remain quite similar to those confronted 20 years ago. It may be easy to recognize the need for forces capable of projecting power abroad, whether for peacekeeping, peace enforcement, or defeating a foreign threat; it is difficult to know the precise location or timing when the Canadian Forces will be called upon. It would have been difficult to anticipate the range of terrain and climate the forces have operated in, as well as the types of missions they have been asked to execute—from air patrols over the deserts of North Africa, to infantry slogging through the mountain valleys of Afghanistan, to search and rescue within the Arctic Circle. That makes choices about the form and equipment of the Forces difficult. Those challenges won't be any easier to resolve in the future, as we will undoubtedly ask the Forces to operate in a wide number of settings, some of which we haven't even thought of yet (see Cooper, Chapter 21 in this volume).

Global Governance/International Institutions

For most Canadians, the use of military force would be the last option for settling international disputes. Most Canadians would prefer problems between states be resolved through international mediation. Successful mediation requires having the appropriate international forums for states to deal with each other, as well as a full body of international law delineating rights and responsibilities. (States, either individually or through alliances, may still resort to the use of force as they interact, particularly when one state chooses to disregard international law.) Global governance is therefore central to Canada's future in international affairs, a point emphasized by Jennifer Welsh (2004).

Given the relative decline of the United States from its overwhelming position of dominance, and the increasing role of other nations on the global stage, some aspects of the current international order may well be questioned; thus it makes perfect sense to be concerned with how the international community handles changing demands or clashing interests. Canadian governments have, in the past, consistently followed the strategy that the institutions of global governance should be crafted or moulded to benefit Canada. The logic flows from the sense that Canada—as a country with a small population and a medium-sized, open economy—would suffer if international relations were to return to the power-politics of an earlier era, but also from the notion that Canada derives disproportionate gains from multilateral cooperation in international affairs. Cooperation serves as a "force multiplier" for Canadian efforts to influence events elsewhere, regardless of the means selected or the specific matter at hand. If well-designed international institutions help Canadians achieve their aims in international economic affairs, enhance the country's security, allow it to promote the values it cherishes, and so forth, the institutions themselves must be of concern to Canadian policy-makers. The more pressing problems looming in the future, such as responding to global warming or limiting the proliferation of weapons of mass destruction, will undoubtedly demand greater international cooperation. As Welsh (2004) underscored, Canadians—public and government officials alike—require little convincing when it comes to prioritizing the need for improvements in global governance.

The single most important body in global governance remains the United Nations. Canada played an important role in the establishment of the United Nations. Famously, the Canadian John Peter Humphrey penned the first draft of the Universal Declaration of Human Rights; he would go on to be an advocate for developing the UN High Commission for Human Rights (Stairs, 2005). However, Canada's relationship with the United Nations has not always been an easy or contented one. Over the decades, Canadian governments have largely tried to work within the United Nations on most issues.

The UN Security Council (UNSC) presents some of the challenges the international system will be dealing with in the future. When the United Nations was established, the Security Council had to be constructed to bring the world's most powerful states into a decision-making forum they would mutually accept. Accordingly, the United States, the Soviet Union, and the United Kingdom (as well as France and China) were granted permanent membership on the Security Council, as well as given the ability to veto UNSC decisions. This privileged position meant that key issues were determined by the UNSC before consideration by the General Assembly of the United Nations. These necessary political compromises in the way the United Nations conducts its business ensured the major powers' participation, but also seriously hampered how often the UNSC would allow the United Nations to take decisive action.

Canada could make no claim for a permanent seat on the UNSC then, nor could it now. Permanent membership is based on military power and/ or economic weight. Instead, Canada has routinely sought one of the rotating seats on the Council, which are chosen by the UN General Assembly. Canada has therefore been represented on the UNSC several times in the past—about once every decade or so beginning in the 1950s. To win broad approval, Canada traditionally promoted itself as a "good citizen" of the United Nations. Two of the rotating seats are currently reserved for Western advanced industrial countries; Canada ran for one of these seats in 2010, and for the first time lost to rivals. There will be other chances, but the voting was a clear indication Canada's standing in the international community has fallen (Stairs, 2011).

Of course, the other way to read the 2010 voting would be to recognize that other states seek representation, too. The broader issue confronting the Security Council is whether it can be reformed to make room for more diverse voices. Canada is seen as one more Western country that speaks for itself, rather than representing the views of several other states. The bigger challenge for the UNSC, however, has to do with the growing economic and military might of states such as Brazil and India—states representing large populations or regions of the world—that do not have a permanent seat at the Security Council table. Those enjoying permanent status remain the key states who emerged victorious from World War II—including two from Europe (Britain and France). Germany and Japan, as the defeated states in the last great war, have not held permanent seats, despite their economic or financial importance. With so many states jostling for a greater influence, it does not appear likely that Canada will achieve a greater role in the United Nations in the future.

Canada could be an important supporter of institutional change within the United Nations. As Welsh argued, "Canada's interests are best served if future superpowers are firmly embedded in international institutions and have been 'socialized' to co-operate with others in the management of common problems" (2004: 172). That statement may be even more true today, a decade later, given that India and China have continued to close the economic gap with the United States in the past 10 years. It is less clear how Canada can promote that change, however, if the current permanent members of the UNSC aren't willing to concede their power. This sort of challenge is duplicated in other institutional settings, such as the IMF, World Bank, and so on.

Canada has successfully promoted reforms in other affairs, which might prove a useful strategy across institutions. In response to charges that the G8 economic summits were failing to represent large swathes of the world's population, as well as omitting significant economic players from the discussions, Canadian Prime Minister Paul Martin proposed the creation of a larger grouping that could meet alongside the summits. The G8 meetings originated from efforts required to coordinate economic policy among the world's largest economies, beginning with ad hoc practices in the 1980s. These became regular affairs within a short amount of time, having proved their worth when resolving problems regarding exchange rate coordination. In 1999, then Finance Minister Paul Martin proposed a wider number of states meet—the G20. (Note that the G20 is not made up of the largest economies, but is meant to draw on a different sense of representation, so that members reflect different regions, populations, etc.)

Critically, Martin and Foreign Minister Lloyd Axworthy, did not advocate replacing the G8 with the G20, but encouraged the two to meet one after the other. In this way, the G8 could continue to function as it had, while the G20 meeting could then either bolster cooperation among those states along the same lines, or at least allow the other states to voice their own perspectives on the matters at hand. While there are advantages to having the G20 alongside the G8, there might also be drawbacks to this strategy. When more than one institution can claim purview over an issue-area, the possibility of "forum-shopping" arises. Forum-shopping describes the choice actors have in determining where a decision will be made. Each actor chooses the setting where it believes its perspective will prevail; it then pushes to have the decision made in its preferred arena. Forum-shopping can be problematic when a crisis that demands a rapid response occurs. (This could be a financial meltdown, a genocide erupting, or any other instance where events require a group of states to react with speed if they are to limit the damage.) If various actors each run to different venues to deal with the crisis, then surely the reaction time by the group is considerably slowed. Thus, building more institutions to serve alongside existing ones may not be the best fix.

While Welsh noted that Canadians recognize the utility of institutions for global governance, she thought it was important that Canadians think more consciously about why international institutions are important. "We need to explain to others, and to ourselves, why we seek to work through international institutions such as the WTO and the UN," she wrote (Welsh, 2004: 146). This was important, she said, in terms of appreciating what international institutions can—and cannot—do, so that Canada is prepared to work around such institutions, if need be.

Canadians in the World

Another important trend Welsh identified, which has accelerated in the last decade, is the level at which Canadians engage the rest of the world not through their government, but as individuals, or through a myriad of private organizations. Technological advances ensure that wealthier countries such as Canada have an ever wider array of means to connect with foreigners. Canadians have been quick to take advantage of those new opportunities. This may be producing some interesting interactions—Canadians engage the world, but in the process change their own sense of who they themselves are.

Beginning in the 1990s, both the government and Canadian society chose to invest in non-governmental organizations (NGOs). While the data on NGO activity remain somewhat vague (making it difficult to compare across countries, for instance), Canadian NGOs have established a presence on every continent. Typically Canadian NGOs were created to address specific problems outside the country. Some target environmental issues, some economic development, others poverty, some aim to improve children's rights in other lands, and so forth. Canadian NGOs continue to grow in number, size, and sophistication. Certainly we have anecdotal evidence suggesting a growing number of Canadian students are going abroad, either to attend school or to participate in volunteer work, which is probably changing the way the youngest generation of Canadians view the world (see Tiessen, 2007).

At the same time, government funding for NGOs has fluctuated, both in volume and direction. Every time governments alternate in power or budget situations change, public funding for NGOs shifts. Canadian NGOs have been particularly active in recent years in Iraq, Afghanistan, and Haiti, largely because the Conservative government redirected more of the development aid budget to these countries. NGOs respond to the money made available by designing programs to achieve targets set by donors. While the process works to keep Canadians involved, the ways in which NGOs have evolved in recent decades probably deserves more rigorous study and analysis. We know this is one of the many faces of Canada abroad, but we undoubtedly carry too many assumptions with us about how the actions of NGOs are viewed by others. NGOs come in many different shapes and sizes, with different levels of ambition, so they surely aren't all being perceived in the same way; nor are they all equally effective. Yet we can say little about these issues, because there has been too little analysis of NGO behaviour and its impact.

Many NGOs typically have a physical presence in other foreign countries, and improvements in communication and transportation have made it easier for them to execute their missions. Transportation costs have fluctuated over the past decade, but travel is in many ways easier than it has ever been. The number of Canadians making trips outside the country (defined as lasting more than 24 hours) hit some record highs in 2012 (CBC, 2012). The strength of the Canadian dollar versus both the euro and the US dollar undoubtedly contributed to this trend. Nonetheless, the statistics indicate Canadians enjoy a growing awareness of and exposure to other parts of the world.

The introduction of the option to hold dual or multiple citizenship has also created a trend toward Canadians not just visiting other countries, but being citizens of other states. This has prompted some interesting, if confusing, episodes for consideration. Canadian citizens have sat in foreign parliaments, while a Canadian with dual citizenship has served as the leader of the official opposition here. (Because his mother immigrated to Canada from France, Stéphane Dion held French and Canadian citizenship. For a more in-depth look at these issues, see Macklin and Crépeau, 2010.) In 2006, renewed civil conflict in Lebanon revealed that tens of thousands of resident Lebanese also held Canadian citizenship. These examples demonstrate how Canadian identity has evolved, but also illustrates the implications these links might have on Canadian foreign policy.

Canadians have virtual links to the rest of the world as well. Canadians are wired to the web as much as any people, anywhere. An estimated 80 per cent of the population has Internet access, and some 70 per cent have mobile phones. These figures are quite high when compared to most of the rest of the world. (Only Scandinavian countries and Iceland score higher.) Nearly two-thirds of Canadian adults have a social networking profile online. Canadians spend as much as 17 hours online each week (Statistics Canada, 2011). This presence on the Internet complements the prominent role of Canadians in international cultural media, where they rank among the top celebrities in film, popular music, and other arts. These individuals present a Canadian face to the rest of the world, as demonstrated so well by the opening and closing ceremonies of the Olympics in Vancouver in 2010. Of course, these same cultural channels also allow Canadians to consume a growing diet of foreign-produced media content. In future, the global exchange of cultural goods and identities may have some curious and unexpected political consequences (Goff and Dunn, 2004).

Canadian firms represent another dimension of the country's engagement with the rest of the world. The government has encouraged Canadian firms to find markets or other business opportunities abroad by investing in support for their outreach activities via the Global Opportunities for Associations program. This program is in addition to older forms of support, such as the Canadian Commercial Corporation, and Export Development Canada. There have been many good economic arguments that suggest Canadian firms need to have a growing presence in international markets if they are to remain vibrant and productive.

Sometimes Canadian international investments can be problematic. Canadian banks operating in the United States were caught up in the financial meltdown of 2008, and all were exposed to a certain extent. Our particular expertise in mining means that a growing number of Canadian firms have operations in developing countries, where their behaviour has often been more focused on profits than anything else. Canada places relatively few restrictions on how its firms do business abroad. As examples of environmental degradation or property rights disputes involving Canadian firms emerge, the demand may increase for more legal restraints on how firms engage in resource-extraction activities abroad.

Of course, on the flip side of this international engagement, Canada remains quite open for foreign producers to set up shop here. There are large numbers of foreign firms operating inside the country, and they include many of Canada's most prominent and popular employers. There continue to be issues raised about the extent of foreign penetration of the Canadian market, though protective legislation such as laws to defend the use of French, or to ensure Canadian content in print, radio, and other media, seems to be working. One has to wonder, however, how the increased use of the Internet will undercut the effectiveness of such laws. If anything, this is one more area where we might be looking at how Canada's engagement with the world may be changing Canadians' sense of themselves in new and unexpected ways.

Conceptualizing Canada in the World, Now and in the Years Ahead

Canadians have, for some time, tried to think about how Canada operates in the international arena, and struggled to come up with the appropriate labels to describe the country's aims and efforts. Since World War II, it has been popular to consider Canada a "middle power." The term "middle power" conveyed that Canada was not a great power, but one that could still carry influence in world affairs; "middle power" also implied modesty in the range and nature of the goals the country set for itself. The term quickly came to be tied to a particular set of means to be employed in international affairs as well, perhaps as a consequence of the scale and form of power that countries such as Canada could effectively employ internationally (James and Kasoff, 2008).

One of the acclaimed benefits of being a middle power was to be less threatening than a great power. Middle powers could not afford the ambitions of a great power, which affects how others perceive them. To paraphrase Welsh (2004: 133), middle powers are too weak to provoke suspicion or jealousy in the international system, but are still capable of wielding adequate hard power resources to contribute to the success of multilateral efforts in addressing shared problems. This is supposed to explain why Canada places so much faith in alliances, international organizations, and multilateralism more generally: when operating alone, its chances of success are diminished compared to when it cooperates with others.

Welsh noted, however, that the middle power label emphasized the means Canada was willing to employ in international affairs, rather than focusing on the country's goals (2004: 158). Middle powers build consensus, via coalitions and international institutions, as already noted. She suggested (citing the work of Denis Stairs) that the middle power tactics necessarily lend themselves to defence of the status quo; the example of the creation of the G20 suggests otherwise. The issue, however, comes down to how much the choice of means can constrain later choices about goals. In the case of Canadian foreign policy, discussion or debate often focuses on means rather than thinking through goals. (For a nice discussion of the utility of the middle power concept, and the ways in which it describes ends as well as means, see Hynek and Bosold, 2010.)

Of course, a deeper discussion about Canada's goals brings us back to a point raised earlier: the need for more serious debates in domestic politics to address key questions about what the country's aims should be. We are missing that level of debate in Parliament, but also in the media. Despite a widespread acknowledgement that Canada engages the world—indeed, a widespread agreement that Canada needs the rest of the world more than ever—we lack the tools and information to have meaningful exchanges over the formulation or elaboration of policy in this area. Hopefully, that situation will change in the near future.

Canada in the World As It Evolves

Writing a decade ago, Jennifer Welsh revealed several enduring insights regarding Canada and its place in the world. Despite the changes that have occurred over the past 10 years, despite the changes that will undoubtedly arise in the next decade, Canada can expect to face several vexing challenges in its relations with the rest of the world. Canada will always face certain difficulties in its interactions with the United States, because geography dictates such close and intense ties between the two, and we know Canada will never be the equal of its primary international partner. In terms of relations with the rest of the world, Canadians will need to identify the specific goals the country should seek to attain, as well as debate the proper means for pursuing those ends. Each of these areas has been a source of problems in the past, was difficult a decade ago, and promises to present obstacles for Canadians to deal with in the future.

As for relations between Canada and the United States, Welsh argued that Canada needed greater confidence in its dealings with America (2004: 19). The fates of the two countries are inextricably intertwined. That means Canadian governments must continually try to shape where the two are headed, even though it is incredibly difficult for the smaller, weaker partner to influence the direction or the speed of the trip! To its advantage, the Canadian government knows it must focus talent and attention on the United States; it must also continue to seize the initiative when opportunities to reconfigure the relationship present themselves.

The challenge in terms of establishing foreign policy goals rests most intently on the political processes that do not always appear to be working well. Ideally, the government would reflect on policy-making via public discussion and deliberation in Parliament. This would mean building domestic consensus behind important decisions, enabling the country's leaders to act more effectively in the international arena. This would require Canadian leaders to articulate policies to the public and to allies—which they have generally failed to do in the last quarter-century (Welsh, 2004: 19–20). The process is equally important for clarifying to Canada's international partners just what Canada is—or is not—willing to do. Unfortunately, Canadian governments tend to make decisions solely within Cabinet, or even more exclusively within the PMO; opposition parties have done a poor job of anticipating issues, and thus have failed to provoke the sort of debates within Parliament that would benefit the public. Ultimately, then, the public needs to demand a more open airing of foreign policy issues, though such issues rarely rank high in either voter awareness or its priorities.

Once goals have been established, then the appropriate means for achieving results have to be selected. Here, Welsh charged that Canada had too often failed to be strategic in its decisions (2004: 21). It had latched onto particular methods, and exploited certain openings to be sure; but it had also fallen back on the notion that being a middle power, or a niche player, dictated the policy instruments it should rely on. It made much more sense, Welsh argued, to let the goal define what would be required. For every task, there is undoubtedly a preferred set of tools. Yet, two sorts of problems

confront every state as it tries to establish its foreign policy strategies: match-
ing goals and means. The first comes whenever goals shift; in parliamentary
systems, foreign policy aims can vary widely, and change rapidly, since these
will reflect the party in power. With every election, new priorities can arise.
The second comes as budgetary constraints become more pressing. Lack of
funds demand that governments set priorities, but limited resources clearly
constrict the policies governments can implement. These are problems for all
governments. Canada cannot escape these restraints any more readily than
others. Projecting budgetary issues in the near future, we can assume the
formulation of foreign policy will be contentious, as the need to define clear
objectives will be more demanding, as will the selection of effective means
for attaining those goals.

Welsh's hope was that Canada can become a model citizen in the world
(2004: 189). Canada should set the example for others, meaning it must hold
itself to a higher standard. It must generate its soft power as well as the hard
power discussed earlier. It must not only bring resources to bear in a way
that is effective and meaningful (with or without allies), but also generate the
ideas and norms that others will appreciate and follow. These are demanding
goals, but ones that should be important to all Canadians.

References

CBC. 2012. "Canadian Travel Abroad Hits 40-Year High." http://www.cbc.ca/news/
business/canadian-travel-abroad-hits-40-year-high-1.1143487/.

Clarkson, Stephen. 2008. "The Inconsistent Neighbor." In *Big Picture Realities*, ed. Daniel
Drache, 107–22. Waterloo: Wilfrid Laurier University Press.

Foreign Affairs, Trade and Development Canada. 2013. "Canada's State of Trade: Trade
and Investment Update 2012." http://www.international.gc.ca/economist-econo
miste/performance/state-point/state_2012_point/2012_5.aspx?lang=eng.

Goff, Patricia, and Kevin C. Dunn, eds. 2004. *Identity and Global Politics, Empirical and
Theoretical Elaborations.* New York: Palgrave Macmillan. http://dx.doi.org/10.1057/
9781403980496.

Gotlieb, Allan. 2003. "Foremost Partner: The Conduct of Canada-U.S. Relations." In
Canada Among Nations 2003: Coping with the American Colossus, eds. Norman Hill-
mer, David Carment, and Fen O. Hampson, 19–31. Toronto: Oxford University
Press.

Hynek, Nik, and David Bosold, eds. 2010. *Canada's Foreign and Security Policy: Soft and
Hard Strategies of a Middle Power.* Toronto: Oxford University Press.

James, Patrick, and Mark J. Kasoff. 2008. *Canadian Studies in the New Millennium.* Toronto:
University of Toronto Press.

Jones, Peter, and Phillip Lagassé. 2012. "Rhetoric versus Reality: Canadian Defence Planning in a Time of Austerity." *Defense & Security Analysis* 28 (2): 140–51. http://
dx.doi.org/10.1080/14751798.2012.678160.

Macklin, Audrey, and François Crépeau. 2010. "Multiple Citizenship, Identity and Entitlement in Canada." IRPP Study No. 6. http://www.irpp.org/assets/research/

diversity-immigration-and-integration/multiple-citizenship-identity-and-entitle
ment-in-canada/IRPP-Study-no6.pdf.

Muirhead, Bruce. 2007. *Dancing Around the Elephant*. Toronto: University of Toronto Press.

Stairs, Denis. 2005. "Founding the United Nations: Canada at San Francisco, 1945." *Policy Options* 26 (7): 15–20.

Stairs, Denis. 2011. "Being Rejected in the United Nations: The Causes and Implications of Canada's Failure to Win a Seat in the UN Security Council." CDFAI Policy Update Paper. Accessed February 20, 2013. http://www.cdfai.org/PDF/Being%20 Rejected%20in%20the%20United%20Nations.pdf.

Statistics Canada. 2011. Accessed November 12, 2013. http://www.statcan.gc.ca/daily-quotidien/111012/dq111012a-eng.htm.

Stein, Janice Gross, and Eugene Lang. 2007. *The Unexpected War: Canada in Kandahar*. Toronto: Viking.

Tiessen, Rebecca. 2007. "Educating Global Citizens? Canadian Foreign Policy and Youth Study/Volunteer Abroad Programs." *Canadian Foreign Policy Journal* 14 (1): 77–84. http://dx.doi.org/10.1080/11926422.2007.9673453.

Wark, Wesley. 2008. "Smart Trumps Security: Canada's Border Security Policy Since 11 September." In *Big Picture Realities*, ed. Daniel Drache, 139–52. Waterloo: Wilfrid Laurier University Press.

Welsh, Jennifer. 2004. *At Home in the World*. Toronto: Harper Collins.

twenty

The Canada-United States Relationship

STEPHEN BROOKS

Introduction: Children of a Common Mother

The idea of Canada, one might argue, was born in 1776. The decision of the Thirteen Colonies to declare their independence from British rule drove a wedge between parts of what had been a continuous stretch of British North American territory extending from the colonies of Quebec, New Brunswick, and Nova Scotia in the north to Georgia in the south. Despite entreaties from no less a figure than George Washington, at the time the leader of the Continental Army, the northern colonies of British North America did not join in the revolution against British rule. They remained loyal and thus was born the idea of Canada as the place and the people who said no to the fledgling American republic.

"Americans do not know," writes Seymour Martin Lipset, "but Canadians cannot forget that two nations, not one, came out of the American Revolution" (1989: 1). The birth of the United States, Lipset argues, was in an important sense also the birth of Canada. The Revolution and its outcome launched these countries on different paths, Canada remaining a colony of Great Britain for nearly another century. When independence finally came in 1867 it was incomplete. The new Canadian government did not exercise all of the powers that generally are associated with a sovereign state. The formal political ties to Great Britain were not entirely severed, much less the psychological and emotional ones. Twenty years after Confederation Prime Minister John A. Macdonald could say, "A British subject I was born; a British subject I will die," and be both right and applauded by much of the country's English-speaking population. But even as Macdonald pronounced these words, the country he governed was steadily and inexorably passing from the gravitational field of Great Britain into that of the United States.

"Children of a Common Mother," proclaims the inscription on the Peace Arch at the border between Washington and British Columbia. This captures the intimacy of a relationship that predates Confederation and that, like most family relationships, has known some frictions at times. It is also a relationship between very unequal partners. No understanding of Canadian politics, identity, or economics is possible without an examination of the extensive web of economic, social, cultural, security, and political ties that join these two countries.

People and Culture

For much of their shared histories, the border between Canada and the United States was a very permeable affair. Indeed, it is not much of an exaggeration to describe it as almost inconsequential when it came to the movement of people until the twentieth century. An estimated 30,000 to 50,000 Loyalists left the newly independent United States for Canada during the Revolutionary War and the 1780s. They were followed by probably twice or even three times that number of non-Loyalist Americans in the years from about 1790 to the War of 1812 (Buckner, 1993). Most of these Americans settled in Ontario. According to historian Fred Landon (1967: 19–20), in 1812 people born in the United States accounted for about 80 per cent of Ontario's population of roughly 136,000. He estimated that only one in four of these immigrants from the United States were Loyalists. This post-Loyalist wave of immigration came in search of cheap land and economic prospects, not because they preferred to live under the British crown. Their numbers were so great and their allegiance to Britain so weak that the colonial authorities fretted openly about their loyalty and attempted to limit this source of immigration in the years following the War of 1812.

Increased immigration from the British Isles during the middle decades of the nineteenth century diminished the American character of what was then Canada's western frontier. Many fewer Americans than previously came north to Canada, not so much because of the colonial authorities' attempts to restrict their right to purchase land but because the American West was a far more powerful magnet for those in search of cheap arable land and other economic opportunities. Those born in Canada were not immune to the lure of America's expanding western frontier. Randall and Thompson (2002: 53) estimate that between 1840 and 1900 about 625,000 people emigrated from Ontario to the American Midwest, New England, and California, and another 427,000 from the Maritimes, mainly to the northeast of the United States. Writing at the end of the nineteenth century, historian Goldwin Smith observed that "if [Americans] do not annex Canada they are annexing the Canadians" (1891: 235).

French-speaking Canadians were not immune to this southerly pull. Between 1840 and 1930 an estimated 900,000 French-speaking Quebecers moved to the United States (Lavoie, 1979: Table 7). Most of them lived in the New England states where they worked in the mills and factories of what was the manufacturing hub of the industrializing American economy. To provide some perspective, the entire population of Quebec in 1901 was roughly 1.6 million.

Newcomers to Canada also were drawn in huge numbers to what they perceived to be superior opportunities on the American side of the border. One study concludes that about two of every three immigrants to Canada during the years 1901–21, a period during which total immigration to Canada was roughly three million, left for the United States (cited in Porter, 1965: 30–1). These were the years when federal policy included aggressive recruitment of Europeans to settle Canada's sparsely populated western territories. Many stayed, but at least as many crossed the 49th parallel into the United States at a time when this boundary was not much more than a surveyor's line. "In fact," observes demographer Yoland Lavoie, "until the second quarter of the 20th century the British part of North America and the United States presented no obstacle to the free movement of people within the continent" (Lavoie, 1979: chap. 1). These movements of people across what was an extremely porous border created intimate personal ties between the two countries that were very common until well into the twentieth century.

Canadians relocating to the United States for employment or crossing the border daily as commuters—the traffic in the other direction has been comparatively light—have reinforced these personal ties between the two countries. John Helliwell (1999) cites data indicating that the "brain drain" (the emigration of highly educated and skilled people) from Canada to the United States was quite significant at many points during the twentieth century. In his book *Star-Spangled Canadians*, Jeffrey Simpson (2000) focuses on Canadian professionals in the fields of business, entertainment, science and academe, and health care, whose reasons for relocating to the United States were varied and some of whom hoped or fully intended to return to Canada. One of the principal reasons for moving to and staying in the United States that Simpson heard repeatedly in nearly 250 interviews for his book was the perception of considerably greater professional opportunities and the resources needed to fulfill them on the American side of the border. These are, as Simpson calls them in the subtitle of his book, "Canadians living the American dream."

Silicon Valley, Madison Avenue, Wall Street, Hollywood, and all the other magnets for high-achieving professionals have long attracted talented and highly trained people from countries across the world. Canada is not alone in being on the contributing end of a brain drain that has benefited the American economy and helped to fuel innovation and creativity in that country. But the fact of having a common language and a broadly similar culture, to say nothing of geographic proximity, has surely contributed to this cross-border movement of people. Today, close to half a million Canadian citizens work in the United States (Dion and Vézina, 2010: Table 4). About one-tenth as many Americans work in Canada (Citizenship and Immigration Canada, 2011).

The citizens of one country working in the other represents only a tiny fraction of either country's labour force and population. More important numerically are the millions of people who cross the border to shop, vacation, or live in the other country for part of the year. Although no reliable numbers exist, thousands of Canadian "snowbirds" flee their country's harsher winter for such southern destinations as Florida and Arizona, spending several months of the year in the United States (Smith and House, 2006: S235–36). They are joined each year by millions of their fellow citizens who visit for shorter periods to vacation or shop. The fact that approximately 90 per cent of Canadians live within 200 kilometres of the Canada-US border, and that tens of millions of Americans live within a similar range of Canada, means that same-day trips for shopping or entertainment are both feasible and seen to be quite normal by many people. Vacationing in the country next door has also been a form of integration between the populations of Canada and the United States. For various reasons—principal among which may be the 9/11 terrorist attack in 2001 and the thickening of the border that occurred because of heightened security concerns on the American side—the number of these same-day trips and the volume of cross-border vacationing have declined significantly (Statistics Canada, 2012: 450).

For much of their shared history, then, Canada and the United States have been bound to one another by the close personal ties created as a result of people moving from one side of the border to the other. People crossing for employment, to visit family, to shop, to vacation, or to emigrate have contributed to integration between the two societies. In recent years, however, these personal ties appear to have weakened somewhat, although they remain an important and usually overlooked factor in discussions of Canada-US relations.

Culture

The most viewed and discussed Canadian television commercial of all time features a 20-something male named Joe who explains to an unseen audience what it means to be Canadian. In this ad, popularly known as "The Rant," Joe makes repeated and emphatic references to what he sees as American values, behaviours, and institutions. These are not, he insists, Canadian values, behaviours, and institutions. The story that he tells about what it means to be Canadian is also a story about how Canadians—many of them at least—perceive America and Americans. National identity is explained as a matter of difference from Canada's southern neighbour.[1]

The ad resonated powerfully with English-speaking Canadians. It did so because nationalism and identity in English Canada have always been linked to anti-Americanism. This anti-Americanism has ranged from rather mild forms—a vague sense of loss and unease over the effects that American cultural imports may have on Canadian values and culture—to full-blown disdain and calls for cultural protectionism. This sentiment has had important consequences for both Canadian public policy and politics more generally.

French-speaking Canadians have worried much less about the impact of American culture on their values, beliefs, and institutions. Language has served as a bulwark that makes American popular culture less seductive (and therefore less threatening) than it is in English-speaking Canada. This may be seen in the television viewing habits of French- and English-speaking Canadians. During a typical week, almost all of the most viewed non-news programs in the English-Canadian market will be American. Broadcasts of Hockey Night in Canada and the occasional Canadian Football League match are usually the only exceptions. In other words, English Canadians are watching what Americans are watching. This is not the case in the French Canadian communities. French-language programs, most of them produced in Quebec, are always among the most viewed programs. American programs such as The Voice (*La Voix*) and The Biggest Loser (*Qui perd gagne*), dubbed into French, are also popular. But their presence is not as dominant as it is in the English-Canadian market (Bureau of Broadcast Measurement, 2013).

When it comes to culture and its protection, French Canadians have been far more likely to worry about the threat posed by the English language than by American ideas and values. Whereas cultural protectionism in English Canada is part of Canada-US relations, policies intended to protect the French language and culture in Quebec are not directly inspired by or targeted at American culture. In other ways, however, what are perceived to be American values and ideas influence the political conversation in Quebec.

This has been apparent on two important occasions in recent years. When it was clear that the US administration of George W. Bush was intent on invading Iraq and removing Saddam Hussein from power, Canadian public opinion was divided. But it was not divided in Quebec. Quebecers were massively opposed to the invasion of Iraq. The fact that the Liberal government of Jean Chrétien resisted American pressure to be even a passive participant in the coalition that invaded Iraq and, moreover, that the government appeared publicly unsupportive and some of its members openly critical of the United States was chiefly due to public opinion in Quebec.

This imminent invasion was perceived by most Quebecers and their opinion leaders as an act of unwarranted aggression, outside of international law, that reflected American militarism and unilateralism. Prime Minister Chrétien's Quebec caucus was solidly and vociferously opposed to Canadian support in any form. Chrétien knew that appearing to be close to the Bush administration on this issue, much less participating militarily in some form, would have rebounded to the advantage of the Bloc Québécois in a federal election that was expected to be held within the next year.

The other recent case of Quebec politics being strongly influenced by perceptions of American culture involved the 2012 student strike in that province. The strike's ostensible and immediate trigger was the Quebec government's plan to increase university tuition fees by 82 per cent over a seven-year period. But it soon became apparent that this protest was seen by many, and certainly by its leaders and those who supported them, as a moment of *contestation*—of challenge—to what was seen as a neoliberal, corporate agenda of globalization and a diminished role for the state. Montreal journalist Patrick Lagacé (2012) described it as "our Seattle moment," a reference to the 1999 clashes between anti-globalization activists and the police at a meeting of the World Trade Organization. Journalist Chantal Hébert (2012) observed that protesters saw themselves as "foot soldiers in a more global battle." There were frequent critical references made to what was argued to be the American model of a smaller state and a society willing to tolerate greater inequalities.

Quebecers are certainly the most collectivist and secular of Canadians (Adams, 2004; Wiseman, 2007). So it comes as no surprise that they are even more likely than other Canadians to dislike what they see as the unprogressive values held by many Americans. American ideas about the state, religion, guns, and the use of military force are particularly likely to elicit their rejection.

Many in English Canada share this negative opinion about certain aspects of American culture. They too tend to see America as a place where religion plays too great a role in public life; where there is an atavistic mistrust of the state; where there is a largely unfounded belief that opportunities are equally open to all and economic success is simply a matter of talent and hard work; and where there is a tolerance for levels of inequality that are unacceptable in a wealthy, modern democracy. In fact, there is nothing particularly Canadian or Québécois about these perceptions of the USA. They are widely held by intellectuals and by national populations across most of the western world.

What is special about English Canada's relationship to American culture is the degree to which American ideas and stories dominate much of Canada's cultural space and the long-standing perception that this represents not merely a cultural threat—which would be bad enough in the eyes of Canadian nationalists—but also a threat to Canadian political sovereignty. The issue was expressed succinctly by Graham Spry, one of the founders of Canada's broadcasting system. "In Canada," he observed before a House of Commons hearing, "it must be either the state or the United States" (Canada, 1932). The immediate circumstances that gave rise to Spry's dictum involved whether the Canadian broadcasting system should emulate the British model of state ownership or the private ownership/public regulation model that was already operating in the United States and whose radio programming reached most Canadian homes. Spry was almost certainly correct that a private ownership model would have seen American broadcasters dominate the English-Canadian market. The creation in 1932 of the publicly owned Canadian Broadcasting Corporation (originally the Canadian Radio Broadcasting Commission) was the Canadian government's response to this fear.

The sentiment expressed in the dictum "the state or the United States" predated the issue of what sort of broadcasting system Canada should adopt. Moreover, it has not been restricted to cultural matters. Canada's National Policy of 1879 was inspired by similar fears of American dominance. High tariffs were needed to protect small domestic manufacturers from giant American competitors. A trans-Canada railroad was needed to provide the infrastructure for a national market based on east-west trade in the face of the relentless north-south pull of market forces. And an aggressive policy of attracting immigrants and populating the vast western expanse of Canada was needed not only to provide consumers for the products of Canadian industries but also to assert Canadian sovereignty over territories that lay on the doorstep of an aggressively expanding United States, at a time when sentiments of American Manifest Destiny ran high.

It was not until the technology of broadcasting developed, however, that Canadian governments felt compelled to legislate in ways intended to protect Canadian values (and the industries, jobs, and status of those who directly benefited from this protection) from the world's unrivalled exporter of popular culture. The creation of the CBC was followed in 1939 by the National Film Board, whose mandate has been to produce feature films, documentaries, and animation by and about Canadians: production that would, in most instances, not see the light of day if left to the private sector. This general concern with the status and future of Canadian culture was further reflected in the appointment of a Royal Commission on the Arts, Letters and Sciences (the Massey Commission, 1949–51), which recommended wide-ranging state support for Canadian artists, musicians, writers, researchers, and the organizations in which they worked. These recommendations led to the establishment of the Canada Council and extensive state support for Canadian artists, writers, and researchers. Telefilm Canada, whose purpose has been to subsidize Canadian-made feature films and television programming, was created in 1967. Soon after, in 1971, the Canadian Radio and Telecommunications Commission (CRTC), the regulatory body for Canadian broadcasting, established Canadian content quotas for all radio and television broadcasters. Several years earlier the Canadian and American governments had become embroiled in a conflict over Canadian requirements that *Reader's Digest*, *Time*, and *Sports Illustrated*, among the most popular magazines in English Canada, include several pages of Canadian content to qualify for advertising deductions available to Canadian-owned magazines. Canadian-owned book publishers began receiving special subsidies, some of them provided by provincial governments. Further evidence of this wave of cultural nationalism was the introduction in the 1970s of preferential hiring policies for Canadian scholars, mandated for all Canadian universities.

All these measures have aimed to protect Canadian culture and the industries and jobs that are associated with its creation and distribution. They do this mainly by encouraging the production of Canadian culture, or at least culture created by Canadians, that would either not be produced or not to the same degree. Some of these nationalist measures also appear to have the goal of restraining the flood of American cultural imports, as in the case of the Canadian content regulations enforced by the CRTC.

But if nationalist critics are to be believed, these moderate measures to stem the tide of American culture in Canada have little hope of succeeding. George Grant, whose writings had a powerful influence on English-Canadian nationalism in the 1960s and 1970s, lamented what he saw as the irreversible loss of a sense of independent nationhood in Canada. It was not simply that American capital had come to dominate so much of the Canadian economy, but that the values and beliefs that made Canadian society distinct and, in Grant's eyes, morally superior to the United States had been undermined by the juggernaut of American popular culture and the modern technology of communications through which this culture spread. In such circumstances, the notion that Canada could remain politically independent of the USA, except in the most symbolic of terms, was impossible (Grant, 1965).

The core premise of Grant's argument, if not all of its details and reasoning, continues to be influential on the Canadian nationalist left. In 2010, nationalist voices, including that of celebrated writer Margaret Atwood, were raised in opposition to the possibility that media group Quebecor might receive a broadcast license for Sun TV News, whose news model is based on that of Fox News in the United States. This was, they charged, tantamount to accepting the Trojan horse of "American-style hate media" into Canadian television programming (Avaaz, 2010). The policy platforms of both the New

Democratic and Liberal Parties continue to endorse the spirit of cultural protectionism that insists on the need for significant state regulation and support for Canadian values, attitudes, and beliefs in the cultural sector, without which the American cultural behemoth could be expected to wash away any semblance of Canadian distinctiveness and independence in this realm (New Democratic Party, 2012; Liberal Party of Canada, 2011).

On the whole, however, the tide of cultural protectionism that crested in the 1960s and 1970s has abated in recent years. Part of the reason is doubtless that the Conservative government, in power since 2006, does not share the fears of American cultural domination harboured by English Canada's centre-left parties and cultural organizations. But even before the Conservatives came to power, it was clear that the influence of cultural nationalism was already on the wane. Globalization and the technology of the Internet and social media are fundamentally at odds with restrictions on the free movement of and access to information, whatever their sources. Of course, this does not stop some interests from trying! In 2012 the CRTC held hearings concerning the possible extension of Canadian content guidelines to websites accessed through Canadian service providers, deciding that "this is not necessary at this time." Since then the Supreme Court of Canada has ruled (2012) that service providers are not broadcasters and thus do not fall under the authority of the CRTC.

Economics

For almost half a century the Canada-US trade relationship has been the largest in the world. This may change very soon. The value of US-China trade in 2011 ($512 billion) is now just marginally less and seems certain to surpass Canada-US trade ($534 billion) in the near future. But even if and when China replaces Canada as the United States' leading trade partner, the breadth and depth of Canada-US economic integration will remain remarkable.

Consider the following facts:

- Canada has been for many years the largest source of energy imports for the United States, including 24 per cent of petroleum imports, 90 per cent of natural gas imports, 20 per cent of the uranium used at American nuclear power plants, and virtually all of the electrical power that is imported by the United States.
- Canada is the single largest trading partner for 35 of the 50 states.
- The United States is the leading foreign trade partner for every Canadian province. Moreover, the value of trade with the United

States is greater than the value of interprovincial trade for all but a couple of Canada's provinces. In the case of Ontario, Canada's industrial and manufacturing powerhouse, roughly one-quarter of provincial Gross Domestic Product (GDP) is tied to trade with the United States.

- In 2011 the United States was the destination for 73.7 per cent of the total value of Canadian merchandise exports. This was over 17 times greater than the value of the second leading market for Canadian merchandise exports, the United Kingdom (4.2 per cent).
- In 2011 the United States accounted for about half the total value of all merchandise exports to Canada (49.5 per cent), a figure almost five times greater than China, the second leading source of imports to Canada.
- The value of American direct investment in Canada ($326 billion in 2011) represents about 54 per cent of all foreign direct investment. The value of Canadian direct investment in the United States is almost as great at $276 billion (2011), but this represents only a small fraction of foreign investment in the much larger American economy.
- Sales by the foreign affiliates of Canadian companies have been of growing importance in recent years. About 50 per cent of these sales are in the United States. (All data from Foreign Affairs and International Trade Canada, 2012)

As is true of other aspects of Canada-US relations, the economic relationship is very asymmetrical. We are each other's major trading partner, but this matters much more to Canada than it does to the United States. Foreign trade accounts for about 12 per cent of American GDP but twice that in the case of Canada. Moreover, American trade is more diversified across a range of important partners, including China, Mexico, Japan, and the economies of the European Union. Although Canada's trade dependence on the United States is less today than it was a decade ago, leading some to talk about Canada's growing trade diversification, the fact remains that the dominant characteristic of Canadian trade is dependence on the United States.

The extraordinary level of economic integration between the Canadian and American economies has been formalized through several treaties and agreements. The Canada-US Free Trade Agreement (1989) and the North American Free Trade Agreement (1994) are the best known of these. In fact, however, the history of Canada-US free trade goes back to the mid-nineteenth century and the Reciprocity Treaty that was signed between the United States and the colony of Upper Canada in 1854, allowing free trade in natural resources. Free trade with the United States remained an important issue in Canadian politics after Confederation and throughout the twentieth century, occasionally erupting in flashpoints of conflict as during the 1911 federal election. The pro-free trade Liberal Party was defeated by the protectionist Conservative Party after a campaign that divided the country on the basis of this issue. Economic protectionism remained the general tendency of Canadian policy for much of the century, a policy that, as many economic historians have observed, encouraged American companies to invest directly in Canada (Bliss, 1990).

The global trend toward trade liberalization after World War II contributed to a lowering of trade barriers between Canada and the United States. So too did the signing of sectoral free trade agreements, notably in military production through the Defence Production Sharing Agreement (1956) and the Auto Pact (1965). The decision of Canada's new Progressive Conservative government to approach the Reagan Administration in 1985 with an offer to negotiate a comprehensive free trade agreement ignited a firestorm of political tensions in Canada. Long-simmering fears about the extent and consequences of Canada's economic dependence on the United States were met by arguments about the economic security and prosperity that would be guaranteed by such an agreement. This culminated in the dramatic "free trade election" of 1988, which was, in fact, triggered by the refusal of the Liberal-controlled Senate to pass the legislation to implement the treaty. With the re-election of a majority Progressive Conservative government, the Canada-US Free Trade Agreement came into force a couple of months later.

The political division in Canada over free trade did not, however, subside. The 1993 election campaign included opposition criticisms of various provisions of the NAFTA treaty that had replaced the Canada-US Agreement. Liberal Party leader Jean Chrétien went so far as to claim that he would withhold approval pending renegotiation of the labour standards and environmental regulation provisions of the treaty. This did not happen. The treaty came into effect on January 1, 1994, further deepening formal trade integration between Canada and United States and widening it to include Mexico.

The integration of the Canadian and American economies is far from complete. Proposals for a common currency (realistically this could only mean Canada adopting the American dollar and accepting the authority of the Federal Reserve Board in matters of monetary policy) surface occasionally on the edge of the policy conversation, but the political obstacles are very high. Nor does free trade under NAFTA include the free movement of workers, except for certain classes of professionals. Even the movement of goods across the Canada-US border continues to be subject to inspections and delays that seem contrary to the spirit and letter of the free trade agreement and that have long since been abolished in the European Union (which also features a common currency and the free movement of workers).

Still, Canada-US economic relations have never been as intimate as they are today. The automotive sector, which accounts for roughly 15 per cent of bilateral trade, is a major case in point. A single component in an automobile may cross the border as many as eight times before the vehicle in which it is installed finally comes off the assembly line. The energy sector, which accounts for roughly one-third of total Canadian exports to the United States, provides another example. It is, for most purposes, a single integrated market, with a web of oil and gas pipelines crossing the Canada-US border at 31 different points. The electrical grid that supplies power to homes and businesses in both countries is, in fact, a unified distribution network that sometimes sees the United States importing Canadian energy and at other times Canadian consumers using power generated in the United States. Vast and enormously important hydro-electric projects in Canada, including James Bay in Quebec, Churchill Falls in Labrador, and the Keeyask and Conawapa generating stations currently being built in Manitoba would not exist, or at least not on their existing scale, without the long-term contracts that these electricity producers have with American customers.

These energy mega-projects in Canada have always depended on markets in the United States and have never failed to generate considerable political opposition, especially in their early stages. In recent years the proposal to build the Keystone XL pipeline that would carry oil from Alberta to refineries on the Gulf of Mexico, crossing five American states on the way, has been at the centre of political controversy on both sides of the border. Canadian and American environmentalists have condemned it on the grounds that the process of extracting oil from the sandy bitumen of northern Alberta makes a significant contribution to CO_2 emissions and, moreover, that the excavation necessary to exploit this resource has other damaging consequences for the local ecosystem. Nebraskans expressed fears over the pipeline's projected route, which was to pass over a huge aquifer that supplies much of the state's water needs, while native groups on both sides of the border voiced their opposition to the project (Financial Post, 2013).

Of course, the project was not without powerful supporters in both countries. They included the federal and Alberta governments, petroleum industry associations, unions, and some state governments. Supporters argue that it represents an important step toward North American self-sufficiency in energy (although at least some of the oil would be exported to foreign buyers), while being crucial to the economy of Alberta and future prosperity of Canada. The proposal was put on hold by the US State Department in 2012, a decision that was widely seen as a concession to elements of the Democratic Party's voter base during a presidential election year. One year later the State Department issued a preliminary assessment indicating that the

environmental effects of the pipeline were likely to be small. This was followed by bipartisan support for the pipeline in the US Senate (United Press
International, 2013). Prime Minister Harper and President Obama discussed
the Keystone XL project in June of 2013, but no decision emerged from
these talks.

The Keystone XL case demonstrates the complexity and scale of Canada-
US economic integration. If approved, the pipeline would represent the
further integration of an already consolidated continental energy market.
In addition to the economics of oil sands development and exports to the
United States, environmental and aboriginal issues are part of the complicated political mix associated with this project. Finally, the case demonstrates
just how interdependent are the political systems of Canada and the United
States. The State Department's decision to withhold necessary approval for
the pipeline led to intense lobbying of key US political actors by both the
Canadian and Alberta governments. It also led to a search for other options,
specifically the export of oil sands petroleum to China. As it happened, however, the political obstacles in the path of constructing a "Northern Gateway"
pipeline to carry oil from Alberta to the west coast of British Columbia (and
thence to world markets) proved to be at least as challenging as navigating
the shoals of the American political system.

Security

The year 2012 marked the bicentennial of the start of the War of 1812.
Canadian government television ads created to commemorate the occasion
declared, "200 years ago the United States invaded our territory ... but we
defended our land and won the fight for Canada." The conflict was, in fact, a
war between Britain and the United States in which British soldiers and sail-
ors engaged American forces. It did, however, contribute to the emergence
of a separate English-Canadian identity at a point in time when most of
the population of Ontario had been born in the United States and felt little
loyalty to the British crown (notwithstanding the mythology of Loyalism that
runs so powerfully through the usual narrative of Canadian history).

One fact is quite certain. American troops did invade British North
American territory that eventually would be part of a sovereign Canada. This
was the first and only time that such an invasion or any other militarized
cross-border conflict would occur. The Fenian raids into Canada in the late
1860s, involving Irish-Americans who supported Irish independence from
Britain, were not carried out or authorized by the American government. By
the early twentieth century, it became common to refer to the line separating
Canada and the United States as "the world's longest undefended border."

Occasional fears that the United States might annex Canadian territory were replaced by an affinity of security interests and increasing bilateral cooperation and even harmonization in matters of defence.

"[N]ecessity has made us allies," said President John F. Kennedy in his 1961 speech before the Canadian Parliament. He continued, "Those whom nature hath so joined together, let no man put asunder." It was not until World War II, however, that defence cooperation between Canada and the United States assumed forms that went beyond good neighbourliness. As allies in the war effort in Europe and the Pacific, military cooperation between the two countries became frequent and formalized. The Permanent Joint Board on Defence, an advisory body with both civilian and military representation from the two countries, was created in 1940. Canada and the United States also cooperated at the level of defence production. The two governments agreed to permit the free movement of military products between their economies. This was the beginning of sectoral free trade between Canada and the United States, formalized through the 1956 Defence Production Sharing Agreement (Granatstein, 2002).

The Cold War that followed the end of World War II generated even greater levels of security cooperation between the two countries. American fears of Soviet bomber planes crossing the Arctic and travelling through Canadian airspace on their way to targets in the United States led to the creation in 1955 of the North American Aerospace Defence Command (NORAD) with a structure of shared command. Early-warning radar stations were established across the Canadian North to detect incoming bombers. NORAD also created a web of obligations with respect to missiles that would be used to intercept incoming planes and, as the technology of the Cold War became more sophisticated, intercontinental ballistic missiles. The North Atlantic Treaty Organization, created in 1949 under the leadership of the United States, also imposed certain continental military obligations on Canada.

These obligations under NORAD and NATO became a cause of serious conflict between the Canadian government of John Diefenbaker and the Kennedy administration when the Diefenbaker government refused to allow anti-ballistic missiles with nuclear warheads on Canadian territory. This became a major issue in the 1963 Canadian election. Despite having the support of Canadian nationalists, Diefenbaker was defeated in that election (although the reasons for his defeat were more numerous and complicated than this single issue). The Liberal government that was elected in 1963 immediately allowed the nuclear warheads on Canadian soil (Richter, 2002).

This conflict would prove to be just one among several that would roil what are, most of the time and in most respects, calm waters in the

Canada–US security relationship. Public criticism of the Vietnam War by Prime Minister Lester Pearson in a 1967 speech given in Philadelphia created frostiness with President Lyndon Johnson. Pearson's successor, Pierre Trudeau, mused about Canadian withdrawal from NATO early in his first term as prime minster and, under his watch, began cuts to defence spending that would continue for 30 years, leading American officials to occasionally castigate Canada for not pulling its weight in the western defence alliance. The American embargo of Cuba, which began in 1958, became a source of constant, albeit usually low-level irritation between the governments of Canada and the United States. From the beginning of the embargo Canada refused to support the American attempt to isolate the Castro regime, allowing Canadians to travel to Cuba and Canadian companies to trade with that country.

Another source of disagreement involved Canada's claims to full sovereignty over the waters of the Arctic Ocean. In 1969 the S.S. Manhattan, an American icebreaker, travelled through the Northwest Passage from the Atlantic on its way to Alaska. It did so without Canadian authorization. The Canadian government protested what it called a violation of Canadian territorial sovereignty, but the American position (one that is supported today by Russia, China, Denmark, and several other states) is that these are international waters over which Canada has no exclusive claim (World Affairs Council, 2011).

The terrorist attacks of September 11, 2001, raised the security relationship to a level of importance that had not been seen in many years. The border between the two countries became "thicker." Crossing times into the United States became longer and more frustrating for individuals and businesses, no small matter given the level of economic integration between the two economies. American demands for greater sharing of information about air passengers between the two countries were met with Canadian protests about privacy and Canadian sovereignty, although these flight lists are now shared between Canadian and American authorities. Indeed the border has been transformed in many important ways by heightened security concerns in the wake of 9/11. American officials now perform some screening at airports on Canadian soil. Cooperation on the Great Lakes between the coast guards of the two countries, including joint patrols, now takes place. Drones patrol some of the isolated stretches of what is the longest border between any two countries. And special pre-clearances are permitted for businesses and individuals who cross the border on a frequent basis (Anderson, 2012).

The attacks of 9/11 led directly to the invasion of Afghanistan. Canadian forces played a significant role in the NATO mission that ousted the Taliban regime and then fought Taliban and other forces for more than a decade.

These attacks also led indirectly to the 2003 invasion of Iraq. The Canadian government, however, rejected the Bush Administration's attempts to persuade Canada to join the American-led "Coalition of the Willing" against Iraq. Moreover, it even seemed that the Canadian government—or at least some of its members—were critical of the decision to depose Iraqi dictator Saddam Hussein by force of arms. The US Ambassador to Canada, Paul Cellucci, in a speech approved by the State Department, went so far as to accuse the Canadian government of turning its back on family in an hour of need (Cellucci, 2005: 139).

No sooner had this rift opened than it was widened by the Liberal government's refusal to join with the United States in a system of Continental Missile Defence (CMD). This was an updated version of NORAD cooperation, including a joint command structure, adapted to the newer realities of satellite surveillance and highly sophisticated missile technology. Canadian nationalists, including influential voices in the Liberal Party, portrayed CMD as the militarization of space and a development likely to fuel a new arms race. The main defence consequence of Canada's refusal to cooperate in CMD was that Americans would take all of the decisions, including those affecting missiles in Canadian airspace, without any Canadian voice at the table.

At the same time as these differences were causing some turbulence in the usually smooth security relationship between Canada and the United States, Canadian defence spending was increasing. This began under the Chrétien and Martin Liberal governments and continued under the Harper Conservatives, doubling the defence budget from about $12.3 billion in 2000 to $24.5 billion in 2010 (NATO, 2011). Since then the level of spending in terms of percentage of GDP has remained about the same. This ramping up of Canada's defence capabilities was not lost on Washington. While American administrations dating as far back as the Reagan years had made known their unhappiness with Canada's level of defence spending (as exemplified by the American reaction to Pierre Trudeau's "peace initiative" in the early 1980s), by 2011, when US Defence Secretary Robert Gates warned NATO allies about inadequate spending levels by NATO countries, he lauded Canada for carrying their weight in the alliance (Gates, 2011).

The Environment

The world's longest undefended border is crossed by 15 transboundary water basins (International Joint Commission, 2010). The waters that move through the rivers, lakes, and water tables that are shared by Canada and the United States are influenced by private actions and policy decisions on both sides of the border. So too are the air, migratory animal species, biodiversity, and virtually every other aspect of the environment. This interconnectedness does not stop at the ocean's edge. Fisheries and coastlines on the Atlantic, Pacific, and Arctic sides of the continent are affected by the actions of Canadian and American governments.

Ecological interdependence has been recognized for more than a century, long before environmental policy made its way onto the political radar screen in Canada and the United States. As population moved westward across the continent, the need for water for agriculture and then for urban and industrial purposes led to conflict. The damming and diversion of rivers in one country often had consequences in the other. The building of the Chicago Diversion, which carries water from Lake Michigan to the Mississippi basin, began in the late 1800s and was protested from the beginning by the Canadian government. In other cases the two countries managed to reach agreement on sharing water resources and managing diversions, as was true of the 1909 Boundary Waters Treaty concerning the diversion of the Niagara River.

This treaty also created the International Joint Commission (IJC), consisting of three commissioners from each country and with headquarters in Ottawa and Washington, DC. The IJC involved an innovative model of shared sovereignty and consensus decision-making, a model that may well seem appropriate in view of the indivisible nature of the cross-border resources that concern the Commission. But this structure has often proved to be a weakness. Finding consensus when governments and private interests on opposing sides of the border disagree has been elusive. When it comes to major issues that might appear to be precisely the sort where the IJC would be expected to play a decisive role—Great Lakes water quality agreements, invasive species, hydro-electric dams, and their effects on transnational watersheds—the Commission has often been sidelined. Especially in the United States, there has been a reluctance to see the IJC play a role that would limit or compete with the authority of other federal agencies and Congress, as well as state governments (Brooks, 2012).

The IJC is only a part of an extensive network of cross-border consultation, cooperation, and even decision-making when it comes to environmental matters. Debora VanNijnatten (2008) has mapped this network, which includes dozens of organizations that bring together provincial and state governments, municipal governments, private stakeholders from both countries, and aboriginal groups affected by transnational environmental regulation. The particular configuration of participants from each country depends on the issue and where its effects are experienced. Alongside this level of formal consultation and cooperation there is a vast web of informal information-sharing and lobbying that operates through meetings of academics and other policy experts and environmental groups (VanNijnatten, 2008).

This vast, multilevelled, and complex web of cross-border activity sometimes produces agreement and common policies. This was the case in 1991 when the Canadian and American governments negotiated the Air Quality Agreement that set limits on pollutants contributing to acid rain and smog. Other times cooperation has proved elusive, as continues to be the case with the Chicago Canal linking the Mississippi river basin to Lake Michigan. This canal is viewed by many, including the governments of Canada, Ontario, Michigan, and Ohio, as an entry point for the Asian carp, an invasive species that already has caused the decline of native freshwater fish in the Mississippi and its tributaries.

The lesson from these and other cases appears to be that agreement at the top is usually needed to resolve major transnational environmental issues. This agreement existed in the case of the acid rain issue, leading to the Air Quality Agreement of 1991, but it does not exist in the case of Asian carp. State, provincial, and local governments all are significant actors when it comes to environmental policy. Indeed, it is hardly deniable that the constitutional authority of provincial governments exceeds that of Ottawa in many matters relating to the environment. But when an environmental issue assumes transboundary dimensions, the federal governments of both countries become a key part of the picture and necessary components of any solution.

Conclusion: "Close, but Not Too Close"

Canadians have often felt a certain degree of unease in the face of their country's obvious and extensive dependence on the United States. They have been aware that the relationship between the two countries is not one of equals and that Canada will usually, though not always,[2] have less leverage than its superpower neighbour. "Close, but not too close" captures the ambivalence that many Canadians feel when they contemplate a long-term relationship that has known many moments of friction. However, these moments have been vastly overshadowed by the dense and complex web of cooperation and shared values and interests that ensure, once again in President Kennedy's words, that "what unites us is far greater than what divides us." Since these words were spoken over 50 years ago, Canada-US relations have deepened in virtually every respect except the cross-border movement of people. Pulling in the other direction, however, are three developments that are viewed by some as having the potential to loosen the ties between Canada and the United States.

One of these developments is globalization. Canada is less dependent today on trade with the United States than at any time in the last half-century. A significant part of this apparent diversification in Canada's trade, on the import side at least, involves the rise of China as a manufacturing powerhouse and source of merchandise imports. China has also become a significant source of investment capital, in Canada as elsewhere in the world. On the export side, although it is true that the share of total Canadian exports accounted for by the American market has declined since the all-time high reached in 2001 (83 per cent), the current level of about 70 per cent is more or less the average over the past four decades. Moreover, although Canadian investment abroad has increased significantly since the 1980s, most of it has been in the United States. Globalization has meant some loosening in Canada's economic dependence on the United States, but with the exception of significantly increased imports of merchandise and capital from China, it has not produced the level of diversification that is oftentimes claimed.

A second related development involves what many believe to be gradual but inexorable American decline. This is, it needs to be said, a highly contested characterization of the role and influence of the United States in the world. The safest observation is that a relative decline of American power, certainly economically, has occurred over the last decade, due principally to the rise of China. If, indeed, American economic power is on the wane and growth prospects seem brighter in emerging economies, perhaps a policy of trade diversification makes sense for Canada. This appears to be the logic behind a series of initiatives undertaken by the Canadian government in recent years, such as free trade negotiations and agreements with South Korea, the European Union, and several countries of South America, as well as the expressed willingness to look to China as a market for Canadian oil in the event that the Keystone XL pipeline is not approved.

A final potential source of loosening in the Canada-US relationship involves border security. It is simply a fact that crossing the border is a more time-consuming and frustrating affair since 9/11 than it was previously. Almost all of this thickening of the border has been due to security concerns on the American side. This has created some amount of pressure for the Canadian government to harmonize certain aspects of its immigration screening policy with that of the United States, most notably through the 2011 Canada-US Perimeter Security Agreement. This agreement was a step toward an anticipated Immigration Information Sharing Treaty that, by 2014, will see the beginning of much greater sharing of biographic and biometric information on all travellers entering the two countries and crossing the border between them. There are, however, political limits on how far any Canadian government can move toward this sort of policy harmonization without paying a price with voters who see this as an unacceptable sacrifice of Canadian sovereignty. Despite the extensive cooperation that has taken place between the two governments and their agencies since 9/11, and even though the Immigration Sharing Treaty has become law, security is likely to remain a factor that makes the border somewhat less rather than more permeable.

The world's longest undefended border, as it has long been described, is a metaphor for the profound trust characterizing the Canada-US relationship. As metaphors go, it may not be as apt today as it was during the twentieth century. Nevertheless, the depth and intimacy of this relationship continues to be remarkable. The ties of culture, economics, security, and geography that spurred Kennedy's remarks during his visit to Ottawa in 1961 ensure that the United States will continue to be Canada's most important bilateral relationship, far overshadowing all others.

Notes

1 The commercial was for Molson beer which, ironically, was purchased by Colorado-based Coors a short time later.
2 In their book *Power and Interdependence*, Joseph Nye and Robert Keohane (2011) use case studies from the Canada-US relationship to demonstrate their argument that the smaller and weaker partner in a bilateral relationship is not without influence, depending on the issue and the circumstances of the conflict.

References

Adams, Michael. 2004. *Fire and Ice: The United States, Canada and the Myth of Converging Values*. Toronto: Penguin.

Anderson, Bill. 2012. *The Border and the Ontario Economy*. Windsor: University of Windsor Cross-Border Transportation Centre.

Avaaz. 2010. "Canada: Stop 'Fox News North'." http://www.avaaz.org/en/no_fox_news_canada/.

Bliss, Michael. 1990. *Northern Enterprise: Five Centuries of Canadian Business*. Toronto: Mc-Clelland and Stewart.

Brooks, Stephen. 2012. "La Commission mixte internationale: convergence, divergence ou submersion?" In *Politique étrangère comparée: Canada-États-Unis*, eds. Jean-Michel Lacroix and Gordon Mace, 125–43. Brussels: Peter Lang.

Buckner, Phillip. 1993. "The Peopling of Canada." *History Today* 43 (11): 48–54. http://www.historytoday.com/phillip-buckner/peopling-canada.

Bureau of Broadcast Measurement. 2013. http://www.bbm.ca/.

Canada, House of Commons. 1932. *Special Committee on Radio Broadcasting: Minutes and Proceedings of Evidence*. Ottawa: F. A. Acland.

Cellucci, Paul. 2005. *Unquiet Diplomacy: The Memoir of Ambassador Paul A. Cellucci.* Toronto: Key Porter.

Citizenship and Immigration Canada. 2011. "Facts and Figures 2011 – Immigration Overview: Permanent and Temporary Residents." http://www.cic.gc.ca/english/resources/statistics/facts2011/temporary/08.asp.

Dion, Patrice, and Mireille Vézina. 2010. "Emigration from Canada to the United States from 2000 to 2006." *Canadian Social Trends.* July 13. http://www.statcan.gc.ca/pub/11-008-x/2010002/article/11287-eng.pdf

Financial Post. 2013. "'We, As a Nation, Have to Wake Up': First Nations Leaders Vow to Do What It Takes to Block Oil Pipelines," March 20. http://business.financialpost.com/2013/03/20/first-nations-oil-sands/.

Foreign Affairs and International Trade Canada. 2012. *Canada's State of Trade: Trade and Investment Update 2012.* http://www.international.gc.ca/economist-economiste/assets/pdfs/performance/SoT_2012/SoT_2012_Eng.pdf.

Gates, Robert. 2011. "The Security and Defense Agenda (Future of NATO)." June 10. http://www.defense.gov/speeches/speech.aspx?speechid=1581.

Granatstein, J.L. 2002. *A Friendly Agreement in Advance: Canada-US Defence Relations, Past, Present and Future.* Toronto: C.D. Howe Institute. http://www.cdhowe.org/pdf/commentary_166.pdf

Grant, George. 1965. *Lament for a Nation: The Defeat of Canadian Nationalism.* Toronto: McClelland and Stewart.

Hébert, Chantal. 2012. "Quebec's Streets Not Unique in Staging Discontent," *Toronto Star,* May 16.

Helliwell, John. 1999. "Checking the Brain Drain: Evidence and Implications." *Policy Options* (September): 6–17.

International Joint Commission. 2010. "Canada-US Transboundary Hydrographic Data Harmonization Effects Gain Momentum." http://nhd.usgs.gov/Canada-US_Hydro_Harmonization.pdf.

Kennedy, John F. 1961. *Speech to the Canadian Parliament.* May 17. http://www.presidency.ucsb.edu/ws/index.php?pid=8136.

Lagacé, Patrick. 2012. "Quebec Is No Egypt: Why the Student Protests Are Not a Revolution," *Globe and Mail,* April 27.

Landon, Fred. 1967. *Western Ontario and the American Frontier.* Toronto: McClelland and Stewart.

Lavoie, Yolande. 1979. *L'émigration des Québécois aux États-Unis de 1840 à 1930.* Québec: Éditeur officiel.

Liberal Party of Canada. 2011. *Your Family, Your Future, Your Canada.* Party platform for the 2011 election. http://www.liberal.ca/files/2011/04/liberal_platform.pdf

Lipset, Seymour Martin. 1989. *Continental Divide: The Values and Institutions of the United States and Canada.* Toronto: C.D. Howe Institute.

NATO. 2011. *Information on Defence Expenditures.* http://www.nato.int/nato_static/assets/pdf/pdf_2011_03/20110309_PR_CP_2011_027.pdf.

New Democratic Party. 2012. "Policy Book." http://xfer.ndp.ca/2012/2012-12-17-Email-Convention/Mtl2013_PolicyBook_E.pdf.

Nye, Joseph, and Robert Keohane. 2011. *Power and Interdependence.* 4th ed. Toronto: Pearson.

Porter, John. 1965. *The Vertical Mosaic.* Toronto: University of Toronto Press.

Randall, Stephen J., and John Herd Thompson. 2002. *Canada and the United States: Ambivalent Allies.* 3rd ed. Montreal: McGill-Queen's University Press.

Richter, Andrew. 2002. *Avoiding Armageddon: Canadian Military Strategy and Nuclear Weapons, 1950–63.* Vancouver: University of British Columbia Press.

Simpson, Jeffrey. 2000. *Star-Spangled Canadians: Canadians Living the American Dream.* Toronto: Harper Collins.

Smith, Goldwin. 1891. *Canada and the Canadian Question.* London: Macmillan.

Smith, Stanley K., and Mark House. 2006. "Snowbirds, Sunbirds, and Stayers: Seasonal Migration of Elderly Adults in Florida." *Journal of Gerontology* 61B (5): S232–39.

Statistics Canada. 2012. *Canada Yearbook 2012.* http://www.statcan.gc.ca/pub/11-402-x/2012000/chap/tt-ut/tt-ut-eng.htm.

Supreme Court of Canada. 2012. "*Reference re Broadcasting Act*, 2012 SCC 4, [2012] 1 SCR 142." http://scc.lexum.org/decisia-scc-csc/scc-csc/scc-csc/en/item/7989/index.do.

United Press International. 2013. "Support Growing for Keystone XL," March 25. http://www.upi.com/Business_News/Energy-Resources/2013/03/25/Support-growing-for-Keystone-XL/UPI-91391364212873/.

VanNijnatten, Debora. 2008. "Environmental Cross-Border Regions and the Canada-U.S. Relationship: Building from the Bottom Up in the Second Century?" Wilfrid Laurier University (PowerPoint). http://www.wilsoncenter.org/sites/default/files/CI_090415_Occasional%20Paper3.pdf.

Wiseman, Nelson. 2007. *In Search of Canadian Political Culture.* Vancouver: University of British Columbia Press.

World Affairs Council. 2011. *The Arctic: Who Owns It and How Long Will It Be There?* San Francisco. http://www.world-affairs.org/wp-content/uploads/2012/03/the_arctic_2-16-11.pdf.

twenty-one

The Changing Nature of Like-Mindedness in Canadian Diplomacy

ANDREW F. COOPER

The search for partners persists as a central theme in Canadian diplomacy. Throughout the post-1945 era, the ingrained Canadian impulse has been to want not only to belong, but also to play an active part in as many international organizations as possible (Cooper, 1997). A constant principle of Canadian statecraft remains that Canada can do little by standing alone on the sidelines. The only way that Canada can influence the international agenda is through constructive involvement with other actors at the heart of the action. At one level, therefore, Canadian diplomacy has a considerable degree of continuity built into it. Yet, while it exhibits a solid core of recognizable features, Canadian diplomacy, as conceptualized and put into practice under the government of Prime Minister Stephen Harper (2006 to present), has undergone great changes. Although a comprehensive review of the overall shift in Canadian foreign policy is beyond the purview of this chapter, the theme of "like-mindedness" captures some key ingredients about this process of continuity and evolution.

The area of continuity in Canada's choice of diplomatic partners is expressed through association and joint activity with the United States and the other pivotal members within the Western alliance/industrial world. The institutional ties established above all through the North Atlantic Treaty Organization (NATO) have traditionally positioned Canada as a loyal (if junior) partner. This set of strategically oriented ties is embellished further by Canada's membership in a variety of mainstream economic forums, such as the General Agreement on Tariffs and Trade/World Trade Organization (GATT/WTO), the Organisation for Economic Co-operation and Development (OECD), the International Monetary Fund (IMF) and the World Bank, and the Group of Seven/Eight most industrialized countries (G7/G8).

The motivation for this well-entrenched side of the search for partners is easily understood. By establishing a primary identification toward and running in tandem with this set of influential partners, Canada has gained a number of benefits. The image of Canada as a solid team player paid off in several ways throughout the post-1945 period. Canada's membership in the strategically oriented Western alliance helped take care of Canada's own security needs. The wider set of arrangements, built up in the economic as well as the security domain, allowed Canada to sit at the high table of decision makers. Canada's close association with the Western alliance or the Atlantic community also helped to alleviate the risks of estrangement from the United States, Canada's central bilateral relationship and much larger neighbour in North America.

Before the Harper years, this interpretation of partnership, however, left out another important side of Canadian diplomacy. This alternative side highlighted the tendency of Canada to cluster together with a very different group of countries, not the pivotal countries of the Western alliance/G-7 but a loose network of so-called like-minded countries—the traditional candidates being Australia, New Zealand, and the Nordic countries—exhibiting a degree of common attitudes and common modes of diplomatic operation. From this less dominant perspective, Canada shared a sense of identity or belonging that is based not on close geographic proximity or the structure of power, but on an adherence to values and sentiments concerning the rules of the game within the international system.

Significantly, the hallmark feature of this like-minded group was a bias toward institutionalism generally and multilateralism more specifically. Unquestionably, much of the impulse toward this alternative role for Canada derived from fear about entrapment by the United States. All of the countries Canada tended to work with in this like-minded fashion were not those that were firmly attached to a single regional home, but rather those that straddled regions (Australia and New Zealand in Asia-Pacific, the Nordic countries in Europe). In addition to this attraction based on a shared situational dilemma, these countries were available because of their strong inclination toward good international citizenship. All of these countries were firmly attached to the ideals and operations of the United Nations and other international institutions.

The extent and impact of this alternative side of Canadian diplomacy should not be exaggerated. Structurally, the space available for these like-minded countries to make a difference was tightly constrained by the context of the Cold War and the system of bi-polarism. What influence these countries had in international affairs tended to be located at the margins of the global agendas. Situationally, the degree to which these like-minded countries opposed the great powers, especially the United States, was limited. While willing to take on the United States on selected issues, these countries remained supporters or even followers of the United States. Even in disagreement, these countries could be considered the US's loyal opposition in the international system (Andrew, 1993: 166).

Equally, though, the value of this like-minded diplomatic activity should not be underestimated. The explicit privileging of diplomacy is important here. Diplomacy and foreign policy are usually discussed as though they were synonymous, and there is some truth in this interpretation. The ends of diplomacy should be consistent with the ends of foreign policy. These ends, however, need to be separated from the means by which they are pursued. Diplomacy, from this more nuanced perspective, is about the set of instruments used in the conduct of international affairs; its techniques operate in the sphere of representation, information, communication, and negotiation. This refinement of emphasis highlights not only the institutional component (the work of the actual diplomats) but also the wider machinery of diplomacy.[1]

In terms of diplomatic practice, the like-minded countries could compensate in a collective fashion for their lack of structural capabilities and power resources by agility and a concentration of effort on specific issues. Their adoption of special functional roles such as bridge-building, mediation, and peacekeeping reinforced the notion that there is considerable value in the ability to play margins. Individually, an identification with this loose cluster of like-minded countries provided Canada with an extension of its sense of belonging.

Although quite intangible in nature, this sense of belonging brings to the surface a larger and significant debate about the artificial or even the invented nature of this group identity. Certainly, an emphasis on belonging or shared identity in the relationship introduces serious questions about how much this alternative source of partnership has been based on the construct of an imaginary community not easily translated into diplomatic outcomes. At a more tangible level, conversely, this identification with the like-minded grouping may be interpreted as providing a key operational guide for more autonomous diplomatic activity. Determining who Canada "is with" in the world, when examined through this different sort of lens, has significant behavioural implications. If Canada had another identity beyond that of being "a safely predictable ally" (Andrew, 1993: 166), this more diffuse sense of belonging adds a greater element of nonconformity and spark to Canadian statecraft. As Arthur Andrew noted in his retrospective look at Canadian diplomacy after a long career in the Department of External Affairs, "No Great power is going to encourage any country to play the role of gadfly, but the role is a necessary one and it can be played with an effect out of all proportion to the importance of the country doing it. ... [This was a role Canada played] very effectively in co-operation with like-minded countries—the Scandinavians, Australia, New Zealand and others" (Andrew, 1993: 178–79).

Like-Mindedness across the Pearson and Axworthy Eras

In many ways this dualism is in the process of becoming a spent force in Canadian diplomacy. As highlighted in snapshots on Canadian approaches to the Afghanistan and Libya interventions, the dominant side of Canadian diplomacy has been tightened. At the same time there has been a corresponding closing of alternative design for diplomatic partners. That is to say, as the dominant assumption about the personality of Canada in international affairs has become more firmly solidified, many of the fundamental tenets about the subsidiary side of Canadian diplomacy have become less visible. If the concept of like-mindedness is still evoked as an animator for Canadian diplomacy, its application reinforces the dominant side in that the like-minded partners are the United States along with other core allies.

The contrast between the Harper government's approach and the Canadian diplomatic activities through the 1990s is especially striking. With the shattering of the structural disciplines of the Cold War era, Canada was provided with additional space for the creative use of statecraft across a fuller range of expanding global agendas. The greater salience accorded to multilateralism and institutions in this earlier era can be interpreted as contributing to the fuller expression of Canadian talents and outlooks.

This evolutionary process can be nuanced by highlighting the manner in which like-mindedness shifted in two earlier eras, mutating significantly while hanging on to some of its older meaning. In the era of tight bipolarity, like-mindedness was conceived and applied in a fixed or *table d'hôte* manner in terms of fund, the range of actors involved, and intensity. In the looser post–Cold War period that followed the break-up of the Soviet Union in 1991–92, this side of Canadian diplomacy has taken on a more ad hoc character, with the concept of like-mindedness being transformed from a fixed to a more diffuse or *à la carte* activity. Although an array of like-minded countries remains at the core of selective "coalitions of the willing," civil society generally and non-governmental organizations (NGOs) more specifically have become like-minded actors as well. Just as importantly, the intensity of this form of activity increased greatly. From a cautious low-key style, like-mindedness has taken on a fast-moving quality. The role of gadfly long built into the concept of like-mindedness has become far more accentuated.

With an engagement right across the spectrum of international affairs, the best known of these coalitions of the willing was directed toward nudging and tweaking the great powers, especially the United States, on selected issues in a determined and time-sensitive manner. This pronounced (and unanticipated) component of the larger shape shift has arisen out of a combination of circumstances. In large part, the process became interconnected with the larger elements of transformation within global affairs. Many of these elements, it must be cautioned, did not come about just because of the end of the Soviet Union and bi-polarity. The number of both state and societal actors with a stake in international relations had expanded considerably through the 1960s and 1970s. During the same period, the agenda of international politics had opened up to a considerable extent, with the traditional dominance of the so-called "high" security agenda relating to questions of war and peace being challenged by the ascendancy of the economic and social agendas. Without question, however, the pace and impact of these changes in the late 1980s and 1990s went well beyond those of the 1960s and 1970s. The scope of the international relations agenda became far more complex. Not only did the question concerning what the security agenda encompasses increasingly become the source of debate, but also the economic and social agendas both widened and deepened. At the same time, the space for a wider group of actors to operate expanded considerably. The relaxation of the disciplines imposed by the Cold War provided greater opportunities for innovative action by secondary states, and made more room available for a variety of subnational/non-central actors as well as a host of non-state actors.[2]

The intensity of these changing features of the international system was reinforced by the spillover into diplomatic practice of new forms of technology and methods of communication. At the cutting edge of this shift was the highly publicized CNN effect, a media phenomenon that introduced a mixture of heightened focus and volatility into the public's perception of specific issues. Governments were pushed to "do something" (or alternatively to pull away from doing something) because of the images presented by the media. In parallel fashion, NGOs could present their own alternative images and interpretations of issues and events.[3]

Finally, the role of personality must also be factored into this evolutionary process of shape shifting. The rise of like-mindedness in the late 1940s and early 1950s was closely associated with the Pearsonian era of Canadian diplomacy. In substance, this reference point for Canadian diplomacy corresponded to former Prime Minister Lester B. Pearson's own concerns about entrapment vis-à-vis the United States. As he put it his *Memoirs*, "In one form or another, for Canada, there was always security in numbers. We do not want to be left alone with our close friend and neighbor" (Munro and Inglis, 1973: 80).

The low-key style in which Pearson applied this principle went hand-in-hand with his preference for quiet diplomacy and behind-the-scenes problem-solving. In his bid to launch a more active form of like-mindedness in the 1990s, Lloyd Axworthy as Minister of Foreign Affairs adopted an approach that was firmly embedded in this older architecture. Axworthy frequently declared that Canadian diplomatic practice must be founded upon the notion of like-mindedness. Addressing the question of how best to adapt Canada's international contribution to a fast-changing global environment, Axworthy highlighted the centrality of this concept. As he suggested, "In a global-ized world ... cooperation with like-minded countries will be de rigueur" (Axworthy, 1997b: 193).

Nonetheless, Axworthy's interpretation of how this notion could and should be carried out was very different from Pearson's. Indeed, Axworthy's role as change agent included a strange mix of the old and the new. Consistent with the older notion of diplomatic functionalism, Axworthy placed great weight on issue-specific activity, or a logic of "niche" selec-tion vis-à-vis the process of coalition building. But Axworthy extended the boundaries of this focused activity and the speed with which it was applied. Functionalism, as practised in the Pearson era, legitimized the application of issue-specific strengths and skills. On the basis of this criterion, Canada should marshal its time and energy in a compartmentalized way. Instead of pointing Canada in a direction where it tried to "do everything" and "be everywhere," functionalism underscored the logic of defining priorities and calculating how Canada's limited resources could be applied to maximum advantage.

Where Axworthy departed from the established tenets of the past was in his impatience with the static quality of the traditional form of like-mindedness. Explicitly, he wanted to liberate the like-mindedness concept from its iden-tification with the fixed world view of the Pearson era to a more fluid focus on ad hoc, issue-specific coalitions of the willing. This impatience was a long-standing condition, which may be traced back to Axworthy's younger days as a critical observer of Pearson's "worth[y]" but "grey and oh so solid" diplomacy. As neatly captured, for instance, in a series of newspaper articles that Axworthy wrote for the *Winnipeg Free Press* in September 1965, this sense of impatience pointed toward diplomatic activity that was more noisy and public-oriented (Axworthy, 1965).

In terms of operation, it is valuable to examine three case studies as snap-shots of like-mindedness in the Axworthy era. The first of these cases is the Canadian-led initiative in the African Great Lakes region at the end of 1996. This case featured an attempt to put together a multinational force (MNF) to aid Rwandan refugees threatened by the escalating ethnic fighting/civil war centred in Zaire. Although highly controversial in both its motivation and its consequences, this initiative was portrayed by Axworthy as a good illustration of the ability of like-minded countries "to get things done by building coalitions ... rather than by coercion" (Axworthy, 1997a).

A second case features the coalition of the like-minded at the core of the campaign to ban anti-personnel land mines. As early as 1995, a core group of pro-ban nations was identified. Subsequently, these countries were "brought together to plan further collaboration, and it was those nations that remained in the lead" through to the takeoff point associated with a conference held in Ottawa October 3–5, 1996, at which moment Axworthy challenged other countries to return to the Canadian capital in 14 months (December 1997) to sign an international treaty (Goose, 1998).

The third case highlights the efforts of some 44 like-minded countries in pushing for progress on a charter for a strong and permanent International Criminal Court (ICC) in the run-up to and during the 1998 UN Rome conference on the issue. Dubbed by some as "the Group of Lifeline Nations," this coalition sought an independent court with an independent prosecutor, as opposed to a body under Security Council control. This coalition held together from 1995 to 1998, a period during which the emphasis was on the development of a detailed draft treaty (Mortimer, 1998: 12).

At first glance, a sense of the traditional attributes of Canadian like-mindedness still lingered in all of these episodes. All three cases focused on some form of shared activity directed toward the multilateral arena. Bilateral solutions, especially in respect to deals cut between the great powers, were uniformly treated with suspicion. The organizational mechanisms continued to be loose and flexible, with no formal structure such as a secretariat. At the heart of this sort of activity remained the traditional grouping of like-minded countries, featuring the Nordic nations, Australia, New Zealand, and some of the other smaller or medium-sized European countries. Canada kept in close contact with Australia, Norway, Sweden, Denmark, and the Netherlands as well as Spain and Belgium in developing the Zaire MNF. Australia, New Zealand, and the Nordic states were out in front with Canada on the ICC. On the land mines case, Canada, Belgium, the Netherlands, Austria, Norway, Denmark, Ireland, Australia, New Zealand, Germany, and Switzerland became part of the "core group" (Greenaway, 1997: B2).

Indeed, the comfort level was enhanced by a rough division of labour that developed between some of these core countries. Australia, for example, drafted the treaty text. Germany took on the compliance issues. Norway hosted the final treaty negotiations in September 1997. When these episodes are looked at more closely, however, it can be seen that these ingrained components of like-mindedness had become overshadowed by the push for new forms of coalitions of the willing. The fixed method of diplomatic activity was replaced by an ad hoc menu. As for their intensity, all of these campaigns featured a good deal of speed and energy. Instead of the reactive quality so firmly entrenched in traditional like-mindedness, the emergent coalitions of the willing of the 1990s were activist and mission-oriented. Put another way, these episodes showcased a form of "just in time" diplomatic practice. For example, one of the strongest images with respect to the Zaire/Great Lakes intervention is the extensive use of telephone diplomacy by Prime Minister Chrétien. Another image is the use of a form of "virtual diplomacy." An upgrading of the technological capacities of the Department of Foreign Affairs and International Trade (DFAIT) was seen as vital to enabling the "mobility of our operations [to allow] rapid responses to emergencies and to situations which require temporary communications hookups ... during such crises as Zaire where Canada formed a virtual team with members in Africa, Ottawa, New York and Washington" (Smith, 1997).

With respect to the trigger for action, all of these cases were influenced by the structural change found within the international system. The erosion of the discipline of the bi-polar system in the post-Cold War era facilitated the mobilization of the coalitions of the willing. Autonomy of action was extended as the common enemy disappeared and the concept of security became extended to include non-military issues. In some cases, such as the Zaire/Great Lakes intervention, this autonomy allowed clear demonstrations of like-minded leadership behaviour. Frustrated by the lack of action on the part of the United States and Britain, smaller and medium-sized countries tried to fill the gap. In other cases, such as those of the land mines and the International Criminal Court, this autonomy allowed more space for disagreement between the coalitions of the willing and the permanent members of the Security Council (and especially the United States, France, Russia, and China).

The range of actors involved in these coalitions of the willing also expanded considerably. One aspect of the change from a fixed to a more ad hoc expression is a reinforcement of the notion of cross-cutting coalitions, involving a greater array of countries from not only the developed but also the developing world. If the traditional core of like-minded countries remains necessary, they are no longer sufficient for the application of this mode of diplomacy. Although he framed the question more in the context of a coalition of the willing/big power differentiation, Axworthy picked up on this theme at the country level in his *International Journal* article on human security: "The concept of a 'like-minded country' is assuming a whole new meaning. Though Canada will continue to work with established allies in many fields, it will increasingly work with new partners. ... Issue-based coalitions will become as important to the management of Canadian foreign policy as the alliance structure once was" (Axworthy, 1997b: 193).

This greater inclusiveness in the concept of the coalition of the willing provided both symbolic and tangible benefits. Working with several non-traditional countries helped increase the credibility and efficiency of these coalitions. At times, this activity also compensated for a decline in the support offered by the traditional like-minded countries, or for that matter any discomfort in that relationship (a discomfort brought to the fore by Axworthy's land-mine challenge in December 1997, to which countries such as Australia and Belgium responded negatively). One good example of this mixed pattern of coalition activity is South Africa's role on the International Criminal Court. The increased targeting of these non-traditional countries as potential partners is a significant example of the expansion of the range of alternative diplomatic partnerships. Getting Mexico and many Central American countries on side was important for both the credentials and the operation of the land-mines coalition. The support of Mexico, Argentina, and Costa Rica buttressed the ICC campaign.

In cases where it proved difficult to get non-traditional countries firmly on board, initiative diplomacy foundered. The prime case in point here is the Zaire/Great Lakes mission. Partially as a result of Prime Minister Chrétien's campaign of personal telephone diplomacy, which targeted President Nelson Mandela for special attention, South Africa had originally offered to provide support (possibly even including troops) for the operation (Sallot, 1996: A1, A14). Sensitive to charges that it was subordinating a comprehensive "made in Africa" solution to an "outside" (and inadequate) form of international intervention, however, South Africa soon pulled back from this initial burst of enthusiasm.

The other face of this change from a set to an ad hoc menu involves the increased scope of engagement taking place between governments and NGOs. At one end of the range of interactive behaviour, NGOs acted as catalysts for action, a pattern by which the activity of NGOs stimulates corresponding or complementary activities by governments. At the core of this dynamic is a triggering effect, in which out-in-front behaviour on the part of NGOs helps frame the agenda for action by government. It was the call for help from societal groups loosely clustered around the Rwanda NGO Executive Committee that did much to prepare the way for the Zaire/Great Lakes initiative. Organizations such as the Red Cross, Oxfam, Care Canada, and Médecins sans frontières all sent out early warnings that the refugee situation in Central Africa was deteriorating because of the changes on the ground in October and early November 1996.

Several NGOs, most notably Amnesty International, Human Rights Watch, and the Lawyers Committee for Human Rights, performed a similar triggering role on the ICC. For its part, the anti-land mines campaign provides a classic episode of this triggering effect. Beginning in the early 1990s, the International Committee of the Red Cross was mobilized into action against the "scourge" of land mines by its field workers. Going beyond the organization's traditional low-key, technical mode of operation, the Red Cross took the lead in gathering a broad-based NGO coalition calling for a total ban on the production, export, and use of anti-personnel mines. Eventually united under the auspices of the International Campaign to Ban Land Mines, this NGO coalition included the Vietnam Veterans of America, the German group Medico International, and the French group Handicap International, together with Human Rights Watch and Physicians for Human Rights.

Critiques of Canada's Traditional Pattern of Diplomacy

Several critiques were offered up about the traditional pattern of Canadian diplomacy as it played out in the Axworthy era. The first critique turns on the issue of what this variable pattern of diplomacy means in terms of influence. As previously noted, the advocates of an extended form of like-minded diplomacy cast this activity in a positive light as the best way of breaking through inertia and top-down domination. The mutation toward an ad hoc approach is said to generate immediate benefits in terms of mobilization of support on specific issues as well as progress toward longer-term systemic reform. The key is to take risks through the activation and focused targeting of a centrifugally oriented diplomacy.

Dissenting voices assess Canada's performance in a very different manner. Rather than raising Canada's position on the world stage, ad hoc coalitions of the willing are said to threaten Canada's status in international affairs. By identifying itself with a multifaceted group of high-minded but not pivotal like-minded actors, it is argued, Canada has moved away from a more appropriate centripetal approach to the margins of diplomacy. This sense that Canada's coalition behaviour is reducing its status comes out most forcefully in Conrad Black's stinging critique of this diplomatic pattern: "Canadians tend to feel keenly that Canada is on the verge of becoming a country of the first rank but it is not widely perceived to be so. To be at the forefront of a large group of secondary powers such as the Scandinavians and the Dutch and even the Australians is something of an underachievement for a wealthy nation of some 30 million people" (Black, 1997–8: 1).

Looking at the issue of influence from an instrumental perspective, the importance of this question can be exaggerated. Particular coalitions of the willing, such as that in the land-mines case, may be viewed as providing opportunities for Canada and other non-big powers to make a difference on specific issues. Yet, even as this sort of issue took on a higher profile, its long-term impact remains contested. For some observers, the key issue was the legitimacy of the public diplomacy used by the coalitions of the willing. For others, it is an issue of whether diplomacy had become democratized through the participation of transnational NGOs, or, conversely, whether these actors had become co-opted by a concept and practice that is closely identified with the state and with patterns of intergovernmental relations.

A second question about coalitions of the willing rested on the issue of resources. Critics looked at the ad hoc trend in Canadian diplomacy in a far more pessimistic fashion. Rather than viewing these initiatives as a means to secure adequate funding, they cast this form of mobilization and focused activity as a drain, in budgetary terms. Kim Nossal, in one of his typical evocative phrases, sums up the trend as "penny-pinching diplomacy" (Nossal, 1998–99).

These critics, identifying this form of ad hoc diplomacy as a component of a "soft power" agenda, contrast the emphasis that had been placed on it with the lack of emphasis given to "hard power" in the form of defence and intelligence assets. In principle, this connection makes sense. Few would disagree that the Zaire/Great Lakes crisis could be used to indicate, not the expanded definition of the security agenda, but the ingrained significance of the military component of the security agenda. While Canadian strengths centred on diplomatic bargaining could be appreciated (and prove useful), these same strengths could be quickly sapped when placed in situations where military capabilities were vital. Yet, in practice, it was far more difficult to make the case that the absence of this initiative-oriented diplomacy would enable the defence budget to be strengthened. The problem of a lack of military capability is grounded in fundamental choices already made by the Canadian public. As Nastro and Nossal contend, "'defence lite' [remains] pleasing to most Canadians (and their pocketbooks)" (Nastro and Nossal, 1997: 21–22).

A third and final question is whether or not there is a solid logic built into this alternative side of Canadian diplomacy. Critical commentators focused not on its rationality but on its emotional and volatile flavour. From this critical standpoint, rather than providing a framework for structuring Canadian diplomacy on a rational basis, this approach imposed a sense of awkwardness and even ill discipline.

Moving Canada Back to the Main Game in Afghanistan

One significant snapshot of the transition in Canadian like-mindedness in the Harper years centres on Afghanistan. Whereas the Axworthy approach focused on niche diplomacy with diffuse partners, the Harper government has chosen to concentrate on core concerns with key allies. Such a view also merges the rebranding efforts by analysts with those of key practitioners to dispel the image of Canada as an UN-centric peacekeeper and replacing it with, or returning it to, a more militaristic reputation. The motor for this rebranding approach was national pride, as Canada moved in its deployment in Afghanistan to become part of NATO's inner circle, as the International Security Assistance Force (ISAF) gradually spread its coverage beyond Kabul.

In his paper "Mr. Harper Goes to War: Canada, Afghanistan and the Return of 'High Politics' in Canadian Foreign Policy" (2007), Duane Bratt explored the question of how and why Prime Minister Harper was prepared to ramp up the Canadian mission, as much symbolically as instrumentally, to the point where it is often called "Mr. Harper's War." The "how" is connected with Prime Minister Harper's willingness to go to the front lines in Afghanistan, complete with his statements that "we don't make a commitment and then run away at the first sign of trouble" (CBC News, 2006). Moreover, he kept to this approach by his determination to both extend and expand the mission. For one thing, he took the initiative to have Parliament lengthen Canada's commitment to ISAF around Kandahar from 2007 to 2009 and then to 2011. For another thing, he deepened the commitment with an increase in the scale and nature of the Canadian Force's commitment, including the addition of a tank squadron in September 2006.

With this shift to a new main game, however, come big risks. At the forefront of these risks is the physical danger faced by the Canadian military and Canadian state officials more generally, of which the death of Glyn Berry of DFAIT in Kandahar is stark testimony (Pardy, 2006: 20–1). It has been well publicized that the Canadian military engagement in Afghanistan—as showcased both by the decision in August 2005 to send 2,300 military personnel to Kandahar as part of Task Force Afghanistan and the onset of Operation Archer—was its largest since the Korean War.

To these external risks were joined the internal political and societal risks, as Canada becomes increasingly divided over the costs and benefits of the Afghanistan mission. Afghanistan loomed as the main, if increasingly contested, game in Canadian foreign policy. This prospect is indelibly linked to the more controversial aspects of the conflict. An image through this lens is the association of Canada with an increasingly unpopular war. A September 2008 Environics poll confirmed that a declining number of Canadians supported the mission in Afghanistan, with only 41 per cent of respondents approving of the mission (CBC News, 2008). This growing unpopularity was related to the high risks of the mission, but it was also connected to other negative images—reliance on warlords, corruption by the Karzai government, and the contamination with what many saw as a narco-state. Faced with what could become an even more precarious situation, Canada inevitably found itself faced with problematic choices.

Another more positive scenario is that Canada will be able to take some glory (albeit with some considerable blood and sacrifice) from its robust support of the mission, while gradually disengaging from Afghanistan and beginning to focus again on other core foreign policy issues. Potentially at least, it reversed the criticism by Denis Stairs of the Axworthy approach: "speak loudly and carry a bent twig" (Stairs, 2001). Through this perspective, Afghanistan shifted the focus from alternative allies back to the robust and reliable, above all Canada's traditional like-minded partners of the United States and Great Britain.

Libya and the Centrality of NATO

Canadian involvement in Libya reinforced the emphasis on reassurance to key allies while holding a comparatively stronger economic position, particularly with the unfolding of the Eurozone crisis and the impact of this on the defence spending of European NATO allies (Rasmussen, 2011). Canada experienced significantly less of a budgetary impact than did other of the G8/NATO countries in the wake of the financial crisis and was thus strategically positioned to bolster the confidence of its allies by playing a more visible role in collective defence missions.

Canada's enhanced efforts were spelled out in the decision to participate in the Libyan Contact group. Although in some ways running parallel with the normative orientation of Responsibility to Protect (R2P) under the Axworthy approach, the key divergence with R2P was that the NATO-led mission sought not only to protect the security of Libyan citizens, but also to carry out a full-scale elimination of the Gaddafi regime, on which both NATO and rebel forces converged (Boreham, 2011). This difference also reflects a key component of the Libyan conflict—how NATO played a supporting role, facilitating the rebel advance.

The escalating attacks on the civilian population by the Gaddafi forces elicited a quick initial response from the Harper government. On February 19, 2011, Canada's Minister of Foreign Affairs, Lawrence Cannon, raised concerns about the atrocious events unfolding in Libya. Cannon called on the Libyan government to exercise restraint and immediately cease attacking peaceful demonstrators. He also reiterated the importance of the right to exercise freedom of association and freedom of assembly and called on the Libyan government to engage in peaceful, open dialogue to answer legitimate concerns of civil society (Cannon, 2011a). Cannon noted, "Canada is monitoring events in Libya very closely. We are deeply concerned about reports of extremely violent attacks on and arrests of peaceful protesters. We regret the loss of life in Libya and call on all parties to refrain from violence"

(2011a). Canada's response to the first day of serious clashes between protestors and the Libyan government and police were the first of its kind among the NATO allies surveyed.

Cannon issued a statement on February 21 in response to the reported violence, warning against non-essential travel to Libya for all Canadians. While the majority of this statement had emphasized evacuation measures available to Canadians in Libya, Cannon made the following remark at the outset of the statement:

> Canada strongly condemns the violent crackdowns on innocent protesters that have resulted in many injured and killed. We call on the Libyan security forces to respect the human rights of demonstrators and uphold their commitment to freedom of speech and the right to assembly. The Libyan authorities must show restraint and stop the use of lethal force against protesters. (Cannon, 2011b)

That same day in Wakefield, Quebec, Cannon stated, "We support the rule of law; we support freedom" and "We also put forward our considerations in terms of promoting democracy" (Carmen, 2011). The foreign minister had made the first public references from a NATO power about a desired end game. Normative references to "freedom" and "democracy" were distinctive. These moral references were further reinforced, that same day, by Prime Minister Stephen Harper's sharper tone in a Vancouver meeting with the press: "We find the actions of the government firing upon its own citizens to be outrageous and unacceptable" and "We call on the government to cease these actions immediately" (Harper, 2011a).

On February 24, Prime Minister Harper spoke in depth with UK Prime Minister David Cameron regarding the situation in Libya. The two raised concerns regarding the "grave and disturbing situation unfolding in Libya" and the "deeply disturbing actions of the Gaddafi regime in suppressing and attacking its own citizens" (Harper, 2011b). They vowed to stay in touch to form a diplomatic response to the atrocities.

Through the rest of the Libya intervention, Canada's focus concentrated on NATO as opposed to the UN, illustrating the comparative privileging of the two international organizations (Granatstein, 2012). Indeed, in overall terms during the Harper years, Canada has made a point of channelling concrete efforts into organizations it deems to be more significant, rather than posturing in organizations with decidedly less significance. The efforts channelled into the NATO-led mission on Libya stood in stark contrast to the comparative disengagement with the UN, a point reinforced by the unprecedented failure by Canada in its bid to win a temporary seat on the UN Security Council in 2010.

Conclusion

The aim of this chapter has been to provide an overview of the shift in Canadian diplomacy from the earlier Pearson and Axworthy eras to the Harper years. Although providing only a couple of snapshots of the evolution, these key cases confirm some basic themes: that Canada has made a turn away from the ad hoc approach undertaken in the 1990s to a concentration on core issues and key like-minded allies. In making this turn, moreover, the Harper government has endeavoured to make itself a key ally to the United States and NATO. Such an emphasis is markedly different from the diffuse approach deployed most robustly by Axworthy in the 1990s, and risks isolation from wider like-minded coalitions. Yet, from the perspective of the Harper government, this is very much a worthwhile risk, in that it shifts attention away from style to substance with Canadian diplomacy pointed more effectively toward delivery in a few central domains with partners that make a difference. Well after the end of the Libyan intervention, for example, Prime Minister Harper highlighted this approach. "So let no one ever question whether Canada is prepared to stay the course in defence of what is right," he said. "For we believe that in a world where people look for hope and cry out for freedom, those who talk the talk of human rights must from time to time be prepared to likewise walk the walk" (Harper, 2011c).

Notes

1 For a full analysis of these trends see Cooper, Heine, and Thakur (2013).
2 For one innovative account of these trends see Rosenau (1990).
3 On the effect of the media in cases involving humanitarian intervention see Gowing (1997).

References and Suggested Readings

Andrew, Arthur. 1993. *The Rise and Fall of a Middle Power: Canadian Diplomacy from King to Mulroney.* Toronto: James Lorimer.
Axworthy, Lloyd. 1965. "Canada's Role as a Middle Power." *Winnipeg Free Press*, September 8–9.
Axworthy, Lloyd. 1997a. Minister of Foreign Affairs. "Canadian Foreign Policy in a Changing World." Speech to the National Forum on Foreign Policy, Winnipeg,

December 13, 1996. *Canadian Speeches*, (January/February). http://dx.doi.org/10.1 080/11926422.1997.9673100.

Axworthy, Lloyd. 1997b. "Canada and Human Security: The Need for Leadership." *International Journal* 52 (2): 183. http://dx.doi.org/10.2307/40203196.

Black, Conrad. 1997–8. "Taking Canada Seriously." *International Journal* 53 (1): 1.

Boreham, Kevin. 2011. "Libya and R2P: The Limits of Responsibility." *East Asia Forum*, March 31. http://www.eastasiaforum.org/2011/03/31/libya-and-r2p-the-limits-of-responsibility/.

Bratt, Duane. 2007. "Mr. Harper Goes to War: Canada, Afghanistan and the Return of 'High Politics' in Canadian Foreign Policy." Paper presented at the 79th annual conference of the Canadian Political Science Association, May 30–June 1, 2007. http://www.cpsa-acsp.ca/papers-2007/Bratt.pdf.

Cannon, Lawrence. 2011a. "Statement by Minister Cannon on Situation in Libya." February 19. http://www.international.gc.ca/media/aff/news-communiques/2011/72. aspx.

Cannon, Lawrence. 2011b. "Statement by Minister Cannon on Situation of Civil Unrest in Libya." February 21. http://news.gc.ca/web/article-eng.do?crtr.sj1D=&crtr. mnthndVl=3&mthd=advSrch&crtr.dpt1D=&nid=590039&crtr.lc1D=&crtr. tp1D=&crtr.yrStrtVl=2011&crtr.kw=Libya&crtr.dyStrtVl=11&crtr.aud1D=&crtr. mnthStrtVl=2&crtr.page=3&crtr.yrndVl=2011&crtr.dyndVl=1.

Carmen, Chal. 2011. "Harper Vigorously Condemns Violence in Libya." *Postmedia*, February 21. http://www2.canada.com/story.html?id=4319868.

CBC News. 2006. "Canada Committed to Afghan Mission, Harper Tells Troops." March 13. http://www.cbc.ca/news/world/canada-committed-to-afghan-mission-harper-tells-troops-1.573722.

CBC News. 2008. "Public Support for Afghan Mission Lowest Ever: Poll." *CBCNews.ca*, September 5. http://www.cbc.ca/news/canada/public-support-for-afghan-mission-lowest-ever-poll-1.707644.

Cooper, Andrew F. 1997. *Canadian Foreign Policy: Old Habits and New Directions*. Scarborough: Prentice Hall Allyn and Bacon.

Cooper, Andrew F., Jorge Heine, and Ramesh Thakur, eds. 2013. *Oxford Handbook of Modern Diplomacy*. Oxford: Oxford University Press.

Goose, Steven. 1998. *Minutes*. The Ottawa Process Forum, December 5, 1997. Ottawa.

Gowing, Nik. 1997. *Media Coverage: Help or Hindrance for Conflict Prevention?* Washington, DC: Carnegie Commission.

Granatstein, Jack L. 2012. "Harper's Foreign Policies Have Made Canada a World Player." *National Post*. January 30. http://fullcomment.nationalpost.com/2012/01/30/jack-granatstein-harpers-foreign-policies-have-made-canada-a-world-player/.

Greenaway, Norma. 1997. "Stopping a Scourge." *Ottawa Citizen*, November 29, B2.

Harper, Stephen. 2011a. "Libyan Crackdowns 'Outrageous': PM." CBC. February 21. http://www.cbc.ca/news/canada/libyan-crackdowns-outrageous-pm-1.1034072.

Harper, Stephen. 2011b. "Prime Minister Harper Speaks with Prime Minister Cameron." Office of the Prime Minister. February 24.

Harper, Stephen. 2011c. "Harper Hails Libya Mission as 'Great Military Success'." *Globe and Mail*, November 24. http://www.theglobeandmail.com/news/politics/harper-hails-libya-mission-as-great-military-success/article4106634/.

Mortimer, Edward. 1998. "An End to Impunity." *The Financial Times* [London], April 8: 12.

Munro, John A., and Alex I. Inglis, eds. 1973. *Mike: The Memoirs of the Right Honourable Lester B. Pearson*, vol. 2: 1948–1957. Toronto: University of Toronto Press.

Nastro, Louis, and Nossal, Kim Richard. 1997. "The Commitment-Capability Gap: Implications for Canadian Foreign Policy in the Post-Cold War Era." *Canadian Defence Quarterly* (Autumn): 19–22.

Nossal, Kim Richard. 1998–99. "Pennypinching Diplomacy: The Decline of 'Good International Citizenship' in Canadian Foreign Policy." *International Journal* 54 (1, Winter 1998–99): 88–105.

Pardy, Gar. 2006. "When Diplomacy Turns Deadly." *Diplomat & International Canada* (May–June): 20–21.

Rasmussen, Anders Fogh. 2011. "Nato After Libya." *Foreign Affairs* (July/August).

Rosenau, J.N. 1990. *Turbulence in World Politics: A Theory of Change and Continuity*. Hemel Hempstead: Harvester.

Sallot, Jeff. 1996. "Canada Offers to Lead Aid Force." *Globe and Mail*, November 12: A1, A14.

Smith, Gordon. 1997. *The Challenge of Virtual Diplomacy*. http://www.usip.org/events/virtual-diplomacy-the-global-communications-revolution-and-international-conflict-management

Stairs, Denis. 2001. "Canada in the 1990s: Speak Loudly and Carry a Bent Twig." http://www.irpp.org/en/po/2001-our-space-odyssey/canada-in-the-1990s-speak-loudly-and-carry-a-bent-twig/

appendix

The Constitution Act, 1982

Enacted as Schedule B to the Canada Constitution
Act 1982, (UK) 1982, c. II.

PART I

Canadian Charter of Rights and Freedoms

Whereas Canada is founded upon principles that recognize the
supremacy of God and the rule of law:

GUARANTEE OF RIGHTS AND FREEDOMS

1 The *Canadian Charter of Rights and Freedoms* guarantees the
rights and freedoms set out in it subject only to such reasonable
limits prescribed by law as can be demonstrably justified in a free
and democratic society.

Rights and freedoms in Canada

FUNDAMENTAL FREEDOMS

2 Everyone has the following fundamental freedoms:

Fundamental freedoms

- (a) freedom of conscience and religion;
- (b) freedom of thought, belief, opinion and expression,
  including freedom of the press and other media of
  communication;
- (c) freedom of peaceful assembly; and
- (d) freedom of association.

DEMOCRATIC RIGHTS

3 Every citizen of Canada has the right to vote in an election of
members of the House of Commons or of a legislative assembly
and to be qualified for membership therein.

Democratic rights of citizens

4 (1) No House of Commons and no legislative assembly shall
continue for longer than five years from the date fixed for the
return of the writs of a general election of its members.

Maximum duration of legislative bodies

Continuation
in special
circumstances

(2) In time of real or apprehended war, invasion or insurrection, a House of Commons may be continued by Parliament and a legislative assembly may be continued by the legislature beyond five years if such continuation is not opposed by the votes of more than one-third of the members of the House of Commons or the legislative assembly, as the case may be.

Annual sitting
of legislative
bodies

5 There shall be a sitting of Parliament and of each legislature at least once every twelve months.

MOBILITY RIGHTS

Mobility of
citizens

6 (1) Every citizen of Canada has the right to enter, remain in and leave Canada.

Rights to move
and gain
livelihood

(2) Every citizen of Canada and every person who has the status of a permanent resident of Canada has the right

(a) to move to and take up residence in any province; and
(b) to pursue the gaining of a livelihood in any province.

Limitation

(3) The rights specified in subsection (2) are subject to

(a) any laws or practices of general application in force in a province other than those that discriminate among persons primarily on the basis of province of present or previous residence; and
(b) any laws providing for reasonable residency requirements as a qualification for the receipt of publicly provided social services.

Affirmative
action
programs

(4) Subsections (2) and (3) do not preclude any law, program or activity that has as its object the amelioration in a province of conditions of individuals in that province who are socially or economically disadvantaged if the rate of employment in that province is below the rate of employment in Canada.

LEGAL RIGHTS

7 Everyone has the right to life, liberty and security of the person and the right not to be deprived thereof except in accordance with the principles of fundamental justice.

Life, liberty and security of person

8 Everyone has the right to be secure against unreasonable search or seizure.

Search or seizure

9 Everyone has the right not to be arbitrarily detained or imprisoned.

Detention or imprisonment

10 Everyone has the right on arrest or detention

Arrest or detention

    (a) to be informed promptly of the reasons therefor;

    (b) to retain and instruct counsel without delay and to be informed of that right; and

    (c) to have the validity of the detention determined by way of *habeas corpus* and to be released if the detention is not lawful.

11 Any person charged with an offence has the right

Proceedings in criminal and penal matters

    (a) to be informed without unreasonable delay of the specific offence;

    (b) to be tried within a reasonable time;

    (c) not to be compelled to be a witness in proceedings against that person in respect of the offence;

    (d) to be presumed innocent until proven guilty according to law in a fair and public hearing by an independent and impartial tribunal;

    (e) not to be denied reasonable bail without just cause;

    (f) except in the case of an offence under military law tried before a military tribunal, to the benefit of trial by jury where the maximum punishment for the offence is imprisonment for five years or a more severe punishment;

    (g) not to be found guilty on account of any act or omission unless, at the time of the act or omission, it constituted an offence under Canadian or international law or was criminal according to the general principles of law recognized by the community of nations;

(h) if finally acquitted of the offence, not to be tried for it again and, if finally found guilty and punished for the offence, not to be tried or punished for it again; and

(i) if found guilty of the offence and if the punishment for the offence has been varied between the time of commission and the time of sentencing, to the benefit of the lesser punishment.

Treatment or punishment

12 Everyone has the right not to be subjected to any cruel and unusual treatment or punishment.

Self-crimination

13 A witness who testifies in any proceedings has the right not to have any incriminating evidence so given used to incriminate that witness in any other proceedings, except in a prosecution for perjury or for the giving of contradictory evidence.

Interpreter

14 A party or witness in any proceedings who does not understand or speak the language in which the proceedings are conducted or who is deaf has the right to the assistance of an interpreter.

EQUALITY RIGHTS

Equality before and under law and equal protection and benefit of law

15 (1) Every individual is equal before and under the law and has the right to the equal protection and equal benefit of the law without discrimination and, in particular, without discrimination based on race, national or ethnic origin, colour, religion, sex, age or mental or physical disability.

Affirmative action programs

(2) Subsection (1) does not preclude any law, program or activity that has as its object the amelioration of conditions of disadvantaged individuals or groups including those that are disadvantaged because of race, national or ethnic origin, colour, religion, sex, age or mental or physical disability.

OFFICIAL LANGUAGES OF CANADA

Official languages of Canada

16 (1) English and French are the official languages of Canada and have equality of status and equal rights and privileges as to their use in all institutions of the Parliament and government of Canada.

Official languages of New Brunswick

(2) English and French are the official languages of New Brunswick and have equality of status and equal rights and privileges as to their use in all institutions of the legislature and government of New Brunswick.

(3) Nothing in this Charter limits the authority of Parliament or a legislature to advance the equality of status or use of English and French.

Advancement of status and use

16 (1) The English linguistic community and the French linguistic community in New Brunswick have equality of status and equal rights and privileges, including the right to distinct educational institutions and such distinct cultural institutions as are necessary for the preservation and promotion of those communities.

English and French communities in New Brunswick

(2) The role of the legislature and government of New Brunswick to preserve and promote the status, rights and privileges referred to in subsection (1) is affirmed.

Role of the legislature and government of New Brunswick

17 (1) Everyone has the right to use English or French in any debates and other proceedings of Parliament.

Proceedings of Parliament

(2) Everyone has the right to use English or French in any debates and other proceedings of the legislature of New Brunswick.

Proceedings of New Brunswick legislature

18 (1) The statutes, records and journals of Parliament shall be printed and published in English and French and both language versions are equally authoritative.

Parliamentary statutes and records

(2) The statutes, records and journals of the legislature of New Brunswick shall be printed and published in English and French and both language versions are equally authoritative.

New Brunswick statutes and records

19 (1) Either English or French may be used by any person in, or in any pleading in or process issuing from, any court established by Parliament.

Proceedings in courts established by Parliament

(2) Either English or French may be used by any person in, or in any pleading in or process issuing from, any court of New Brunswick.

Proceedings in New Brunswick courts

20 (1) Any member of the public in Canada has the right to communicate with, and to receive available services from, any head or central office of an institution of the Parliament or government of Canada in English or French, and has the same right with respect to any other office of any such institution where

Communications by public with federal institutions

(a) there is a significant demand for communications with and services from that office in such language; or

(b) due to the nature of the office, it is reasonable that communications with and services from that office be available in both English and French.

Communications by public with New Brunswick institutions

(2) Any member of the public in New Brunswick has the right to communicate with, and to receive available services from, any office of an institution of the legislature or government of New Brunswick in English or French.

Continuation of existing constitutional provisions

21 Nothing in sections 16 to 20 abrogates or derogates from any right, privilege or obligation with respect to the English and French languages, or either of them, that exists or is continued by virtue of any other provision of the Constitution of Canada.

Rights and privileges preserved

22 Nothing in sections 16 to 20 abrogates or derogates from any legal or customary right or privilege acquired or enjoyed either before or after the coming into force of this Charter with respect to any language that is not English or French.

MINORITY LANGUAGE EDUCATIONAL RIGHTS

Language of instruction

23 (1) Citizens of Canada

(a) whose first language learned and still understood is that of the English or French linguistic minority population of the province in which they reside, or

(b) who have received their primary school instruction in Canada in English or French and reside in a province where the language in which they received that instruction is the language of the English or French linguistic minority population of the province,

have the right to have their children receive primary and secondary school instruction in that language in that province.

(2) Citizens of Canada of whom any child has received or is receiving primary or secondary school instruction in English or French in Canada, have the right to have all their children receive primary and secondary school instruction in the same language.

(3) The right of citizens of Canada under subsections (1) and (2) to have their children receive primary and secondary school instruction inthe language of the English or French linguistic minority population of a province

    (a) applies wherever in the province the number of children of citizens who have such a right is sufficient to warrant the provision to them out of public funds of minority language instruction; and

    (b) includes, where the number of those children so warrants, the right to have them receive that instruction in minority language educational facilities provided out of public funds

ENFORCEMENT

24 (1) Anyone whose rights or freedoms, as guaranteed by this Charter, have been infringed or denied may apply to a court of competent jurisdiction to obtain such remedy as the court considers appropriate and just in the circumstances.

(2) Where, in proceedings under subsection (1), a court concludes that evidence was obtained in a manner that infringed or denied any rights or freedoms guaranteed by this Charter, the evidence shall be excluded if it is established that, having regard to all the circumstances, the admission of it in the proceedings would bring the administration of justice into disrepute.

GENERAL

25 The guarantee in this Charter of certain rights and freedoms shall not be construed so as to abrogate or derogate from any aboriginal, treaty or other rights or freedoms that pertain to the aboriginal peoples of Canada including

    (a) any rights or freedoms that have been recognized by the Royal Proclamation of October 7, 1763; and

    (b) any rights or freedoms that now exist by way of land claims agreements or may be so acquired.

26 The guarantee in this Charter of certain rights and freedoms shall not be construed as denying the existence of any other rights or freedoms that exist in Canada.

Multicultural
heritage

27 This Charter shall be interpreted in a manner consistent with the preservation and enhancement of the multicultural heritage of Canadians.

Rights
guaranteed
equally to both
sexes

28 Notwithstanding anything in this Charter, the rights and freedoms referred to in it are guaranteed equally to male and female persons.

Rights
respecting
certain schools
preserved

29 Nothing in this Charter abrogates or derogates from any rights or privileges guaranteed by or under the Constitution of Canada in respect of denominational, separate or dissentient schools.

Application
to territories
and territorial
authorities

30 A reference in this Charter to a Province or to the legislative assembly or legislature of a province shall be deemed to include a reference to the Yukon Territory and the Northwest Territories, or to the appropriate legislative authority thereof, as the case may be.

Legislative powers
not extended

31 Nothing in this Charter extends the legislative powers of any body or authority.

APPLICATION OF CHARTER

Application of
Charter

32 (1) This Charter applies

(a) to the Parliament and government of Canada in respect of all matters within the authority of Parliament including all matters relating to the Yukon Territory and Northwest Territories; and

(b) to the legislature and government of each province in respect of all matters within the authority of the legislature of each province.

Exception

(2) Notwithstanding subsection (1), section 15 shall not have effect until three years after this section comes into force.

Exception
where express
declaration

33 (1) Parliament or the legislature of a province may expressly declare in an Act of Parliament or of the legislature, as the case may be, that the Act or a provision thereof shall operate notwithstanding a provision included in section 2 or sections 7 to 15 of this Charter.

Operation of
exception

(2) An Act or a provision of an Act in respect of which a declaration made under this section is in effect shall have such operation

as it would have but for the provision of this Charter referred to in the declaration.

(3) A declaration made under subsection (1) shall cease to have effect five years after it comes into force or on such earlier date as may be specified in the declaration.

Five year limitation

(4) Parliament or the legislature of a province may re-enact a declaration made under subsection (1).

Re-enactment

(5) Subsection (3) applies in respect of a re-enactment made under subsection (4).

Five year limitation

CITATION

34 This Part may be cited as the Canadian Charter of Rights and Freedoms.

Citation

PART II
Rights of the Aboriginal Peoples of Canada

35 (1) The existing aboriginal and treaty rights of the aboriginal peoples of Canada are hereby recognized and affirmed.

Recognition of existing aboriginal and treaty rights

(2) In this Act, "aboriginal peoples of Canada" includes the Indian, Inuit and Métis peoples of Canada.

Definition of "aboriginal peoples of Canada"

(3) For greater certainty, in subsection (1) "treaty rights" includes rights that now exist by way of land claims agreements or may be so acquired.

Land claims agreements

(4) Notwithstanding any other provision of this Act, the aboriginal and treaty rights referred to in subsection (1) are guaranteed equally to male and female persons.

Aboriginal and treaty rights are guaranteed equally to both sexes

35.1 The government of Canada and the provincial governments are committed to the principle that, before any amendment is made to Class 24 of section 91 of the "*Constitution Act, 1867,*" to section 25 of this Act or to this Part,

Commitment to participation in constitutional conference

(a) a constitutional conference that includes in its agenda an item relating to the proposed amendment, composed of the Prime Minister of Canada and the first ministers of the provinces, will be convened by the Prime Minister of Canada; and

(b) the Prime Minister of Canada will invite representatives of the aboriginal peoples of Canada to participate in the discussions on that item.

PART III
Equalization and Regional Disparities

Commitment to promote equal opportunities

36 (1) Without altering the legislative authority of Parliament or of the provincial legislatures, or the rights of any of them with respect to the exercise of their legislative authority, Parliament and the legislatures, together with the government of Canada and the provincial governments, are committed to

(a) promoting equal opportunities for the well-being of Canadians;

(b) furthering economic development to reduce disparity in opportunities; and

(c) providing essential public services of reasonable quality to all Canadians.

Commitment respecting public services

(2) Parliament and the government of Canada are committed to the principle of making equalization payments to ensure that provincial governments have sufficient revenues to provide reasonably comparable levels of public services at reasonably comparable levels of taxation.

PART IV
Constitutional Conference

37 [Repealed. See section 54]

PART IV.I
Constitutional Conference

37.1 [Repealed. See section 54.1]

PART V

Procedure for Amending Constitution of Canada

38 (1) An amendment to the Constitution of Canada may be made by proclamation issued by the Governor General under the Great Seal of Canada where so authorized by

General procedure for amending Constitution of Canada

   (a) resolutions of the Senate and House of Commons; and

   (b) resolutions of the legislative assemblies of at least two-thirds of the provinces that have, in the aggregate, according to the then latest general census, at least fifty per cent of the population of all the provinces.

(2) An amendment made under subsection (1) that derogates from the legislative powers, the proprietary rights or any other rights or privileges of the legislature or government of a province shall require a resolution supported by a majority of the members of each of the Senate, the House of Commons and the legislative assemblies required under subsection (1).

Majority of members

(3) An amendment referred to in subsection (2) shall not have effect in a province the legislative assembly of which has expressed its dissent thereto by resolution supported by a majority of its members prior to the issue of the proclamation to which the amendment relates unless that legislative assembly, subsequently, by resolution supported by a majority of its members, revokes its dissent and authorizes the amendment.

Expression of dissent

(4) A resolution of dissent made for the purposes of subsection (3) may be revoked at any time before or after the issue of the proclamation to which it relates.

Revocation of dissent

39 (1) A proclamation shall not be issued under subsection 38(1) before the expiration of one year from the adoption of the resolution initiating the amendment procedure thereunder, unless the legislative assembly of each province has previously adopted a resolution of assent or dissent.

Restriction on proclamation

(2) A proclamation shall not be issued under subsection 38(1) after the expiration of three years from the adoption of the resolution initiating the amendment procedure thereunder.

Idem

Compensation **40** Where an amendment is made under subsection 38(1) that transfers provincial legislative powers relating to education or other cultural matters from provincial legislatures to Parliament, Canada shall provide reasonable compensation to any province to which the amendment does not apply.

Amendment by unanimous consent **41** An amendment to the Constitution of Canada in relation to the following matters may be made by proclamation issued by the Governor General under the Great Seal of Canada only where authorized by resolutions of the Senate and House of Commons and of the legislative assembly of each province:

(a) the office of the Queen, the Governor General and the Lieutenant Governor of a province;

(b) the right of a province to a number of members in the House of Commons not less than the number of Senators by which the province is entitled to be represented at the time this Part comes into force;

(c) subject to section 43, the use of the English or the French language;

(d) the composition of the Supreme Court of Canada; and

(e) an amendment to this Part.

Amendment by general procedure **42** (1) An amendment to the Constitution of Canada in relation to the following matters may be made only in accordance with subsection 38(1):

(a) the principle of proportionate representation of the provinces in the House of Commons prescribed by the Constitution of Canada;

(b) the powers of the Senate and the method of selecting Senators;

(c) the number of members by which a province is entitled to be represented in the Senate and the residence qualifications of Senators;

(d) subject to paragraph 41(*d*), the Supreme Court of Canada;

(e) the extension of existing provinces into the territories; and

(f) notwithstanding any other law or practice, the establishment of new provinces.

(2) Subsections 38(2) and (4) do not apply in respect of amendments in relation to matters referred to in subsection (1).

Exception

43 An amendment to the Constitution of Canada in relation to any provision that applies to one or more, but not all, provinces, including

Amendment of provisions relating to some by not all provinces

   (a) any alteration to boundaries between provinces, and

   (b) any amendment to any provision that relates to the use of the English or the French language within a province, may be made by proclamation issued by the Governor General under the Great Seal of Canada only where so authorized by resolutions of the Senate and House of Commons and of the legislative assembly of each province to which the amendment applies.

44 Subject to sections 41 and 42, Parliament may exclusively make laws amending the Constitution of Canada in relation to the executive government of Canada or the Senate and House of Commons.

Amendments by parliament

45 Subject to section 41, the legislature of each province may exclusively make laws amending the constitution of the province.

Amendments by provincial legislatures

46 (1) The procedures for amendment under sections 38, 41, 42 and 43 may be initiated either by the Senate or the House of Commons or by the legislative assembly of a province.

Initiation of amendment procedures

(2) A resolution of assent made for the purposes of this Part may be revoked at any time before the issue of a proclamation authorized by it.

Revocation of authorization

47 (1) An amendment to the Constitution of Canada made by proclamation under section 38, 41, 42 or 43 may be made without a resolution of the Senate authorizing the issue of the proclamation if, within one hundred and eighty days after the adoption by the House of Commons of a resolution authorizing its issue, the Senate has not adopted such a resolution and if, at any time after the expiration of that period, the House of Commons again adopts the resolution.

Amendments without Senate resolution

Computation of period

(2) Any period when Parliament is prorogued or dissolved shall not be counted in computing the one hundred and eighty day period referred to in subsection (1).

Advice to issue proclamation

48 The Queen's Privy Council for Canada shall advise the Governor General to issue a proclamation under this Part forthwith on the adoption of the resolutions required for an amendment made by proclamation under this Part.

Constitutional conference

49 A constitutional conference composed of the Prime Minister of Canada and the first ministers of the provinces shall be convened by the Prime Minister of Canada within fifteen years after this Part comes into force to review the provisions of this Part.

PART VI
Amendment to the Constitution Act, 1867

50 [The amendment is set out in the Consolidation of the Constitution Act, 1867, as section 92A thereof.]

51 [The amendment is set out in the Consolidation of the Constitution Act, 1867, as the Sixth Schedule thereof.]

PART VII
General

Primacy of Constitution of Canada

52 (1) The Constitution of Canada is the supreme law of Canada, and any law that is inconsistent with the provisions of the Constitution is, to the extent of the inconsistency, of no force or effect.

Constitution of Canada

(2) The Constitution of Canada includes

(a) the *Canada Act 1982,* including this Act;
(b) the Acts and orders referred to in the schedule; and
(c) any amendment to any Act or order referred to in paragraph (a) or (b).

Amendments to Constitution of Canada

(3) Amendments to the Constitution of Canada shall be made only in accordance with the authority contained in the Constitution of Canada.

53 (1) The enactments referred to in Column I of the schedule are hereby repealed or amended to the extent indicated in Column II thereof and, unless repealed, shall continue as law in Canada under the names set out in Column III thereof.

Repeals and new names

(2) Every enactment, except the *Canada Act 1982,* that refers to an enactment referred to in the schedule by the name in Column I thereof is hereby amended by substituting for that name the corresponding name in Column III thereof, and any British North America Act not referred to in the schedule may be cited as the *Constitution Act* followed by the year and number, if any, of its enactment.

Consequential amendments

54 Part IV is repealed on the day that is one year after this Part comes into force and this section may be repealed and this Act renumbered, consequentially upon the repeal of Part IV and this section, by proclamation issued by the Governor General under the Great Seal of Canada.

Repeal and consequential amendments

54.1 Part VI.1 and this section are repealed on April 18, 1987.

55 A French version of the portions of the Constitution of Canada referred to in the schedule shall be prepared by the Minister of Justice of Canada as expeditiously as possible and, when any portion thereof sufficient to warrant action being taken has been so prepared, it shall be put forward for enactment by proclamation issued by the Governor General under the Great Seal of Canada pursuant to the procedure then applicable to an amendment of the same provisions of the Constitution of Canada.

French version of Constitution of Canada

56 Where any portion of the Constitution of Canada has been or is enacted in English and French or where a French version of any portion of the Constitution is enacted pursuant to section 55, the English and French versions of that portion of the Constitution are equally authoritative.

English and French versions of certain constitutional texts

57 The English and French versions of this Act are equally authoritative.

English and French versions of this Act

58 Subject to section 59, this Act shall come into force on a day to be fixed by proclamation issued by the Queen or the Governor General under the Great Seal of Canada.

Commencement

Commencement of paragraph 23(1)(a) in respect of Quebec

59 (1) Paragraph 23(1)(*a*) shall come into force in respect of Quebec on a day to be fixed by proclamation issued by the Queen or the Governor General under the Great Seal of Canada.

Authorization of Quebec

(2) A proclamation under subsection (1) shall be issued only where authorized by the legislative assembly or government of Quebec.

Repeal of this section

(3) This section may be repealed on the day paragraph 23(1)(*a*) comes into force in respect of Quebec and this Act amended and renumbered, consequentially upon the repeal of this section, by proclamation issued by the Queen or the Governor General under the Great Seal of Canada.

Short title and citations

60 This Act may be cited as the *Constitution Act, 1982,* and the Constitution Acts 1867 to 1975 (No. 2) and this Act may be cited together as the *Constitution Acts, 1867 to 1982.*

References

61 A reference to the "*Constitution Acts, 1867 to 1982*" shall be deemed to include a reference to the "*Constitution Amendment Proclamation, 1983.*"

Index

Abella, Rosalie, 211
Aboriginal Affairs and Northern Development,
      114, 125
Aboriginal governance, 114, 127
   Aboriginal, federal, and provincial partner-
      ships, 125–26
   entrepreneurial view of, 125
   traditional Aboriginal governing structures,
      115, 119
Aboriginal governments as third order of gov-
      ernment. *See* third order of government
Aboriginal land rights, 34–35, 399–400, 408
Aboriginal nationalism, 3, 17, 28, 404
Aboriginal peoples, 22, 57, 61, 66, 107–8, 243,
      396. *See also* First Nations; Indigenous
      activists
   assimilation of, 128, 397–98
   Constitution Act (1867) and, 49
   define themselves as nations, 24, 38, 232
   differentiated citizenship, 33
   diplomatic relationships (French and British),
      115, 119
   duty to consult on resource development, 60
   employment equity, 401
   federal government responsibility, 71, 399
   increased political power, 60
   invited to participate in the market economy,
      125
   living conditions, 124
   radicalization, 53
   rejection of 1969 *Statement on Indian Policy*,
      13, 116, 127
   religious diversity and, 397
   right to vote, 52, 375
   self-government (*see* Aboriginal self-
      government)
   Senate representation, 31
   settler society pressure on (*see* settler societies)
   "special interests" label, 401
   underrepresentation in government, 291
   in urban centres, 115
   victories in the courts, 61–62, 88, 114

Aboriginal resistance, 116
Aboriginal rights, 16, 61
   constitutional recognition, 54
   neoliberal governance and, 114
Aboriginal self-government, 14, 18, 28, 32–33,
      35, 52, 57, 80, 101, 113–28, 400. *See also*
      band councils
   change from rights-based to "good gover-
      nance" focus, 114, 125
   as coexisting sovereignties, 119–20
   court decisions on, 88
   gap between principle and practice,
      114
   as inherent right, 118–19, 122
   integral part of Canada's institutional
      landscape, 113
   in neoliberal times, 124–27
   second generation agreements, 121–22
   Alfred on, 113
Aboriginal spirituality, 408
Aboriginal-state relations in Canada,
      114, 128. *See also* nation-to-nation
      governance
Aboriginal Truth and Reconciliation
      Commission, 18
Aboriginal women, 34, 387
   voting rights, 375
abortion, 360, 388
Access to Information Act (ATIA), 192,
      311–12
accommodation rights, 21, 24, 28–30, 33–35,
      87
   reflect desire to participate in
      mainstream, 37
acid rain, 454
Act of Union (1840), 398
ACT UP, 357
advocacy groups, 330, 335–37
Afghan detainees affair, 282
Afghanistan, 141, 423, 451
   Canadian equipment and combat readiness,
      425–26